PSYCHOLOGY RESEARCH PROGRESS

PSYCHOLOGY RESEARCH BIOGRAPHICAL SKETCHES AND RESEARCH SUMMARIES

PSYCHOLOGY RESEARCH PROGRESS

Additional books in this series can be found on Nova's website under the Series tab.

Additional e-books in this series can be found on Nova's website under the E-book tab.

PSYCHOLOGY RESEARCH PROGRESS

PSYCHOLOGY RESEARCH BIOGRAPHICAL SKETCHES AND RESEARCH SUMMARIES

NANCY E. WODARTH
AND
ALEXIS P. FERGUSON
EDITORS

Nova Science Publishers, Inc.
New York

Copyright © 2012 by Nova Science Publishers, Inc.

All rights reserved. No part of this book may be reproduced, stored in a retrieval system or transmitted in any form or by any means: electronic, electrostatic, magnetic, tape, mechanical photocopying, recording or otherwise without the written permission of the Publisher.

For permission to use material from this book please contact us:
Telephone 631-231-7269; Fax 631-231-8175
Web Site: http://www.novapublishers.com

NOTICE TO THE READER

The Publisher has taken reasonable care in the preparation of this book, but makes no expressed or implied warranty of any kind and assumes no responsibility for any errors or omissions. No liability is assumed for incidental or consequential damages in connection with or arising out of information contained in this book. The Publisher shall not be liable for any special, consequential, or exemplary damages resulting, in whole or in part, from the readers' use of, or reliance upon, this material. Any parts of this book based on government reports are so indicated and copyright is claimed for those parts to the extent applicable to compilations of such works.

Independent verification should be sought for any data, advice or recommendations contained in this book. In addition, no responsibility is assumed by the publisher for any injury and/or damage to persons or property arising from any methods, products, instructions, ideas or otherwise contained in this publication.

This publication is designed to provide accurate and authoritative information with regard to the subject matter covered herein. It is sold with the clear understanding that the Publisher is not engaged in rendering legal or any other professional services. If legal or any other expert assistance is required, the services of a competent person should be sought. FROM A DECLARATION OF PARTICIPANTS JOINTLY ADOPTED BY A COMMITTEE OF THE AMERICAN BAR ASSOCIATION AND A COMMITTEE OF PUBLISHERS.

Additional color graphics may be available in the e-book version of this book.

Library of Congress Cataloging-in-Publication Data

ISBN: 978-1-61470-491-1

Published by Nova Science Publishers, Inc. † New York

CONTENTS

Preface		xlv
Part 1 - Research Biographies		1
Chapter 1	Lise Abrams	3
Chapter 2	Xenia Anastassiou-Hadjicharalambous	7
Chapter 3	Debra Anderson	13
Chapter 4	Tamás Bödecs	17
Chapter 5	Shari L. Britner	21
Chapter 6	Amy Brogan	23
Chapter 7	John O. Brooks, III	25
Chapter 8	Jane Bybee	29
Chapter 9	Gianluca Campana	31
Chapter 10	Kathleen A. Carroll	33
Chapter 11	Kimberley A. Clow	35
Chapter 12	Lindsey Cohen	37
Chapter 13	Robert J. Cramer	41
Chapter 14	James Danckert	43
Chapter 15	James A. Danowski	47
Chapter 16	María Luisa Sanz de Acedo Lizarraga	49
Chapter 17	Laurie Elit	53
Chapter 18	Stephen Erdle	59
Chapter 19	Nicolas Fieulaine	61
Chapter 20	Trude Furunes	63
Chapter 21	Janet M. Gibson	65

Chapter 22	Yigal Goldshtrom	67
Chapter 23	Lidan Gu	69
Chapter 24	Sylvia Maria Gustin	71
Chapter 25	Sara Konrath	73
Chapter 26	Kallipe Kounenou	75
Chapter 27	Gary D. Laver	77
Chapter 28	Pauwels Lieven	79
Chapter 29	Angus W. MacDonald, III	81
Chapter 30	Brent R. MacNab	85
Chapter 31	Robert Marcus	93
Chapter 32	Rosario J. Marrero Quevedo	95
Chapter 33	Keita Masui	97
Chapter 34	Dennis M. McInerney	101
Chapter 35	Yukinori Nagakura	107
Chapter 36	Simona Nicolosi	109
Chapter 37	Pantelis Nikolaidis	113
Chapter 38	Toru Sato	115
Chapter 39	James Schuurmans-Stekhoven	117
Chapter 40	Bruce W. Smith	119
Chapter 41	David Trafimow	123
Chapter 42	Matthew J. Traxler	127
Chapter 43	Ruud van den Bos	131
Chapter 44	Christopher Was	133
Chapter 45	Philip M. Wilson	135
Chapter 46	Joseph Wu	139
Part 2 - Research Summaries in Psychology from Selected Book Chapters and Journal Articles		141
Chapter 47	A Competitive Anxiety Review: Recent Directions in Sport Psychology Research *Stephen D. Mellalieu, Sheldon Hanton and David Fletcher*	143
Chapter 48	A Multiple Self Theory of Personality *David Lester*	145

Chapter 49	An Evolutionary Psychology of Leader-Follower Relations *Patrick McNamara and David Trumbull*	**147**
Chapter 50	Anorexia Nervosa: A Multi-Disciplinary Approach: From Biology to Philosophy *Antonio Mancini, Silvia Daini and S. J. Louis Caruana*	**149**
Chapter 51	Attention Deficit Hyperactivity Disorder: Creativity, Novelty Seeking, and Risk *Michael Fitzgerald*	**151**
Chapter 52	Behavioral Pediatrics, 3rd Edition *Donald E. Greydanus, Dilip R. Patel, Helen D. Pratt and Joseph L. Calles Jr.*	**153**
Chapter 53	Behavioral Theories and Interventions for Autism *Phil Reed*	**155**
Chapter 54	Beyond the Words: Communication and Suggestion in Medical Practice *Katalin Varga*	**157**
Chapter 55	Bio-Psycho-Social Perspectives on Interpersonal Violence *Martha Frias-Armenta and Victor Corral-Verdugo*	**159**
Chapter 56	Bullying among Youth: Issues, Interventions and Theory *Stavros Kiriakidis*	**161**
Chapter 57	Career Counseling and Constructivism: Elaboration of Constructs *Mary McMahon and Mark Watson*	**163**
Chapter 58	Category-Specificity: Evidence for Modularity of Mind *Keith R. Laws, Rebecca L. Adlington, F. Javier Moreno-Martinez and Tim M. Gale*	**165**
Chapter 59	Children's Dreams *Barbara Szmigielska*	**167**
Chapter 60	Children's Social Competence: Theory and Intervention *Melissa L. Greene, Jo R. Hariton, Andrew L. Robins and Barbara L. Flye*	**169**
Chapter 61	Cognitive and Neuroscientific Aspects of Human Love: A Guide for Marriage and Couples Counseling *William A. Lambos and William G. Emener*	**171**
Chapter 62	Cognitive Therapy of Eating Disorders on Control and Worry *Sandra Sassaroli and Giovanni Maria Ruggiero*	**173**
Chapter 63	Cognitive-Behavioral and Neuropsychological Models of Obsessive-Compulsive Disorder *Claudio Sica, Luigi Rocco Chiri, Dean McKay and Marta Ghisi*	**175**

Chapter 64	Cognitive-Behavioural Indicators of Substance Abuse *Samuel Pombo, Filipe Barbosa,* *Marco Torrado and Nuno Félix da Costa*	177
Chapter 65	Consciousness, Attention and Meaning *Giorgio Marchetti*	179
Chapter 66	Contemporary Sport Psychology *Robert Schinke*	181
Chapter 67	Depression, Subjective Well-Being and Individual Aspirations of College Students *Ferenc Margitics and Zsuzsa Pauwlik*	183
Chapter 68	Emotional Intelligence: Theoretical and Cultural Perspectives *Robert J. Emmerling, Vinod K. Shanwal* *and Manas K. Mandal*	185
Chapter 69	Managing Interpersonal Sensitivity: Knowing When — and When Not — To Understand Others *Jessi L. Smith, William Ickes,* *Judith A. Hall and Sara Hodges*	187
Chapter 70	Maternal Sensitivity: A Scientific Foundation for Practice *Deborah Winders Davis and M. Cynthia Logsdon*	189
Chapter 71	Mental Health and Some Sociocultural Issues in Deaf People *Benito Daniel Estrada Aranda*	191
Chapter 72	Multiple Facets of Anger: Getting Mad or Restoring Justice? *Farzaneh Pahlavan*	193
Chapter 73	My Loving Relationships *William G. Emener and William A. Lambos*	195
Chapter 74	New Hope for Mental Disturbances *Vladimir Lerner and Chanoch Miodownik*	197
Chapter 75	Our Loving Relationship *William G. Emener and William A. Lambos*	199
Chapter 76	Perchance to Dream: The Frontiers of Dream Psychology *Stanley Krippner and Debbie Joffe Ellis*	201
Chapter 77	Personality and Individual Differences: Theory, Assessment, and Application *Simon Boag and Niko Tiliopoulos*	203
Chapter 78	Perspectives on Cognition and Action in Sport *Duarte Araujo, Hubert Ripoll and Markus Raab*	205
Chapter 79	Problems of Developmental Instruction: A Theoretical and Experimental Psychological Study *V. V. Davydov*	207

Chapter 80	Psychological Approaches to Sustainability: Current Trends in Theory, Research and Applications *Victor Corral-Verdugo, Cirilo H. Garcia-Cadena and Martha Frias-Armenta*	**209**
Chapter 81	Psychology and the Church *Mark. R. McMinn and Amy W. Dominguez*	**211**
Chapter 82	Traffic Psychology: An International Perspective *Dwight Hennessy*	**213**
Chapter 83	War and Suicide *Leo Sher and Alexander Vilens*	**215**
Chapter 84	War: An Introduction to Theories and Research on Collective Violence *Tor G. Jakobsen*	**217**
Chapter 85	Rumination and Avoidance in Depression: The Relationship Between Rumination, Avoidance and Depression in Depressed Inpatients *Filip Raes, Heleen Vandromme and Dirk Hermans*	**219**
Chapter 86	The Spectrum of Self-Harm In Adolescence and Young Adulthood: Moving Toward an Integrative Model of Pathogenic Mechanisms *Christa D. Labouliere and Marc S. Karverh*	**221**
Chapter 87	Modeling of Dyslexia: Is a Unitary Model of Dyslexia Possible? *Timothy C. Papadopoulos, George K. Georgiou and Sotirios Douklias*	**223**
Chapter 88	Overgeneral Attachment Memory: Overgeneral Attachment-Related Autobiographical Memory in Children *Jessica L. Borelli, Daryn H. David, Michael J. Crowley and Linda C. Mayes*	**225**
Chapter 89	Depression and a Parenting Intervention: Can Caregiver Depression Bring a Good Parenting Intervention Down? The Case of Parent-Child Interaction Therapy *Mark Scholes, Melanie J. Zimmer-Gembeck and Rae Thomas*	**227**
Chapter 90	The Role of Negative Affective Valence in Return of Fear *Inneke Kerkhof, Debora Vansteenwegen, Tom Beckers, Trinette Dirikx, Frank Baeyens, Rudi D'Hooge and Dirk Hermans*	**229**
Chapter 91	The Neuropsychology of Alcoholism *J. Uekermann and I. Daum*	**231**

Chapter 92	Perception Without Awareness: The Qualitative Differences Approach *Juan J. Ortells, María T. Daza, Carmen Noguera, Encarna Carmona, Elaine Fox and María J. F. Abad*	233
Chapter 93	Intrapsychic Factors Contributing to Adolescent Depression *Lisa C. Milne and Philip Greenway*	235
Chapter 94	A Hermeneutic Approach to Culture and Psychotherapy *John Chambers Christopher, Gary Foster and Susan James*	237
Chapter 95	Adolescent Brain Development, Behavior, Premorbid Psychosis and Risk for Schizophrenia: A Review of Structural and Functional MRI Studies *Ozgur Oner, Haluk Ozbay and Kerim M. Munir*	239
Chapter 96	The Association of Visuospatial Memory and Working Memory with Adolescent Onset Schizophrenia *Alasdair Vance*	241
Chapter 97	Psychotic Symptoms in Children and Adolescents *Michelle Harley, Aileen Murtagh, Ian Kelleher and Mary Cannon*	243
Chapter 98	Psychoanalytical Teamwork on Schizophrenic Young Patients in a Day-hospital (Revisiting Some Developmental Pre-conditions for Patient's Subjective Appropriation) *Bernard Penot*	245
Chapter 99	Treatment Approaches to Aggressive Behavior in Schizophrenia *Jan Volavka*	247
Chapter 100	Body Image Deviation in Chronic Schizophrenia: A New Research *Reiko Koide and Akira Tamaoka*	249
Chapter 101	Sex Differences in Aggressive and Delinquent Behavior in Schizotypal Adolescents *Amanda McMillan and Elaine Walker*	251
Chapter 102	Fetal Origins of Antisocial Personality Disorder and Schizophrenia: Evidence from the Dutch Hunger Winter *Richard Neugebauer and Ezra Susser*	255
Chapter 103	Self-Concept Disturbances in Eating-Disordered Female Students Compared to Normal Controls *Laurence Claes, Joke Simons and Walter Vandereycken*	257
Chapter 104	Linking Student Behaviours and Attitudes Towards Information and Communication Technology with Learning Processes, Teacher Instruction and Classroom Environment *Robert F. Cavanagh and Joseph T. Romanoski*	259

Chapter 105	Social Anxiety in the College Student Population: The Role of Anxiety Sensitivity *Angela Sailer and Holly Hazlett-Stevens*	**261**
Chapter 106	Test Anxiety and Its Consequences on Academic Performance among University Students *Mohd Ariff Bin Kassim, Siti Rosmaini Bt Mohd Hanafi and Dawson R. Hancock*	**263**
Chapter 107	Writing your Way to Health? The Effects of Disclosure of Past Stressful Events in German Students *Lisette Morris, Annedore Linkemann and Birgit Kröner-Herwig*	**265**
Chapter 108	Stress Among Students in Developing Countries - An Overview *Shashidhar Acharya*	**267**
Chapter 109	Coping, Mental Health Status, and Current Life Regret in College Women Who Differ in their Lifetime Pregnancy Status: A Resilience Perspective *Jennifer Langhinrichsen-Rohling, Theresa Rehm, Michelle Breland and Alexis Inabinet*	**269**
Chapter 110	Gender Differences in Proneness to Depression among Hungarian College Students *Ferenc Margitics and Zsuzsa Pauwlik*	**271**
Chapter 111	An Intervention Programme for the Improvement of Students' Academic Goals *Antonio Valle, Ramón G. Cabanach, Susana Rodríguez, Isabel Piñeiro, María García and Ingrid Mosquera*	**273**
Chapter 112	The Impact of a Lecture Series on Alcohol and Tobacco Use in Pharmacy Students *Arjun P. Dutta, Bisrat Hailemeskel, Monika N. Daftary and Anthony Wutoh*	**275**
Chapter 113	Burden of Syndromal Antisocial Behavior in Adulthood *Risë B. Goldstein and Bridget F. Grant*	**277**
Chapter 114	Antisocial Behavior in Children with ADHD: Causes and Treatment *Efrosini Kalyva*	**279**
Chapter 115	Vicious Dog Ownership: Is it a Thin Slice of Antisocial Personality? *Laurie L. Ragatz, Allison M. Schenk and William J. Fremouw*	**281**
Chapter 116	Adolescent Substance Use Disorder and Attention Deficit Hyperactivity Disorder: A Literature Review *Robert Eme*	**283**

Chapter 117	Perverted Justice: A Content Analysis of the Language Used by Offenders Detected Attempting to Solicit Children for Sex *Vincent Egan, James Hoskinson and David Shewan*	285
Chapter 118	Is Developmentally Informed Therapy for Persons with ID and Criminal Personality/Offenses Relevant? *Lino Faccini*	287
Chapter 119	Cocaine-Dependent Patients with Antisocial Personality Disorder, Cocaine-Dependence and Treatment Outcomes *Nena Messina, David Farabee and Richard Rawson*	289
Chapter 120	Delinquency and Antisocial Behaviour among High Risk Young People in Adolescence *Patrick McCrystal and Kareena McAloney*	291
Chapter 121	Genetic Epidemiology of Borderline Personality Disorder *Marijn A. Distel, Timothy J. Trull and Dorret I. Boomsma*	293
Chapter 122	Correlates and Course of Recovery in Patients with Borderline Personality Disorder – A Review *Willem H. J. Martens*	295
Chapter 123	Neuropsychobiology, Comorbidity and Dimensional Models in Borderline Personality Disorder: Critical Issues for Treatment *Bernardo Dell'Osso, Heather Berlin, Marta Serati and Alfredo Carlo Altamura*	297
Chapter 124	Neurobiology of Borderline Personality Disorder: Present State and Future Directions *Thomas Zetzsche, Thomas Frodl, Ulrich W. Preuss, Doerthe Seifert, Hans-Jürgen Möller and Eva Maria Meisenzahl*	299
Chapter 125	Proving the Efficiency of Music Psychotherapy with Borderline Adolescents By Means of a Quasi-Experimental Design *Lony Schiltz*	301
Chapter 126	A Dissociative Model of Borderline Personality Disorder *Colin A. Ross*	303
Chapter 127	Borderline Symptomatology and Empathic Accuracy *William Schweinle, Judith M. Flury and William Ickes*	305
Chapter 128	Patterns of Interpersonal Behaviors and Borderline Personality Characteristics *Glenn Shean and Kimberly Ryan*	307
Chapter 129	Borderline Personality and Somatic Symptomatology *Randy A. Sansone and Lori A. Sansone*	309
Chapter 130	Borderline Personality and Sexual Impulsivity *Randy A. Sansone and Lori A. Sansone*	311

Chapter 131	An Historical Perspective of Body Image and Body Image Concerns among Male and Female Adolescents in Japan *Naomi Chisuwa and Jennifer A. O'Dea*	313
Chapter 132	Body Image Among Aboriginal Children and Adolescents in Australia *Renata L. Cinelli and Jennifer A. O'Dea*	315
Chapter 133	The Psychology of Body Image: Understanding Body Image Instability and Distortion *Jennifer S. Mills, Kaley Roosen and Rachel Vella-Zarb*	319
Chapter 134	Measurement of the Perceptual Aspects of Body Image *Rick M. Gardner and Dana L. Brown*	321
Chapter 135	Body Image and Cancer *Özen Önen Sertöz*	323
Chapter 136	Beyond the Media: A Look at Other Socialisation Processes that Contribute to Body Image Problems and Dysfunctional Eating *Marion Kostanski*	325
Chapter 137	Alexithymia, Body Image and Eating Disorders *Domenico De Berardis, Viviana Marasco, Daniela Campanella, Nicola Serroni, Mario Caltabiano, Luigi Olivieri, Carla Ranalli, Alessandro Carano, Tiziano Acciavatti, Giuseppe Di Iorio, Marilde Cavuto, Francesco Saverio Moschetta and Massimo Di Giannantonio*	327
Chapter 138	A Meta-Analytic Review of Sociocultural Influences on Male Body Image *Bryan T. Karazsia and Kathryn Pieper*	329
Chapter 139	Touch and Body: A Role for the Somatosensory Cortex in Establishing an Early Form of Identity (Review Article) *Michael Schaefer*	331
Chapter 140	Nothing Compares to You: The Influence of Body Size of Models in Print Advertising and Body Comparison Processes on Women's Body Image *Doeschka J. Anschutz, Tatjana Van Strien, Eni S. Becker and Rutger C. M. E. Engels*	333
Chapter 141	Body Image in People of African Descent: A Systematic Review *D. Catherine Walker*	335
Chapter 142	Low SES Children's BMI Scores and their Perceived and Ideal Body Images: Intervention Implications *Simone Pettigrew, Melanie Pescud and Robert J. Donovan*	337

Chapter 143	Theoretical and Methodological Considerations in Assessing Body Image among Children and Adolescents *Margaret Lawler and Elizabeth Nixon*	339
Chapter 144	Issues Pertaining to Body Image Measurement in Exercise Research *Rebecca L. Bassett and Kathleen A. Martin Ginis*	341
Chapter 145	Negative Body Image Perception and Associated Attitudes in Females *Tamara Y. Mousa and Rima H. Mashal*	343
Chapter 146	Body Image in Young and Adult Women with Physical Disabilities *Nancy Xenakis and Judith Goldberg*	345
Chapter 147	The Non Satisfied Patient in Aesthetic Surgery – Medical Attitude *Alberto Rancati, Maurizio Nava, Marcelo Irigo and Braulio Peralta*	347
Chapter 148	Motivated Behaviors: The Interaction of Attention, Habituation and Memory *John W. Wright and Roberta V. Wiediger*	349
Chapter 149	Attention and Motivation Interdependence in Self-regulation. A Neurocognitive Approach *M. Rosario Rueda, Alberto Acosta and Milagros Santonja*	351
Chapter 150	The Motivational Function of Emotions: A "Feeling is for Doing" Perspective *Rob M. A. Nelissen and Marcel Zeelenberg*	353
Chapter 151	Social Psychological Motivations and Foundations of Dietary Preference *Marc Stewart Wilson and Michael W. Allen*	355
Chapter 152	Self-Determination Theory and the Theory of Planned Behavior: An Integrative Approach toward A More Complete Model of Motivation *Martin S. Hagger and Nikos L. D. Chatzisarantis*	357
Chapter 153	Motivation and Risk Behaviors: A Self-Determination Perspective *Clayton Neighbors, Melissa A. Lewis, Nicole Fossos and Joel R. Grossbard*	359
Chapter 154	A Motivational-Cognitive Model of Prospective Memory: The Influence of Goal Relevance *Suzanna L. Penningroth and Walter D. Scott*	361
Chapter 155	The Role of Goal Facilitation and Goal Conflict in Motivation *Winifred A. Gebhardt*	363
Chapter 156	The Implicit Nature of Goal-Directed Motivational Pursuits *Jay L. Wenger*	365

Chapter 157	Procrastination and Motivations for Household Safety Behaviors: An Expectancy-Value Theory Perspective *Fuschia M. Sirois*	367
Chapter 158	Stimulus and Information Seeking Behavior – A Comparative and Evolutionary Perspective *Wojciech Pisula*	369
Chapter 159	Psychosocial Correlates of Personal Norms *K. P. H. Lemmens, R. A. C. Ruiter, I. J. T. Veldhuizen and H. P. Schaalma*	371
Chapter 160	Strategies Involved in the Motivation of Individuals to Pursue Testing to Determine the Presence of HIV *Brad Donohue, Courtney Irwin, John Fordham and Daniel N. Allen*	373
Chapter 161	Motivational Incontinence: Philosophical Views across the Gap between Normative Beliefs and Actions *Suzie Ferrie*	375
Chapter 162	Community Psychoanalysis: Developing a Model of Psychoanalytically-Informed Community Crisis Intervention *Mark B. Borg, Jr.*	377
Chapter 163	Social Representations: The Heart of Community Psychology *Inari Sakki, Raul Kassea, Teemu Vauhkonen and Anna-Maija Pirttilä-Backman*	379
Chapter 164	Health, Social and Educational Impacts of Two Flood Disasters in England: Psychological Processes, Community Responses and Strategies *Bob Carroll, Ian Convery, Ruth Balogh, Hazel Morbey and Gonzalo Araoz*	381
Chapter 165	How do we Teach them? Using Self-Help Support Groups to Promote Knowledge Translation *Ann Dadich*	383
Chapter 166	The Promise and Challenge of Applying Community Psychology's Praxis of Empowerment to the Burgeoning Field of Community-Based Conservation *Daniel A. DeCaro*	385
Chapter 167	Family Psycho-Social Factors Impacting Parent's Own Current Life Perception in Families of Children with Leukemia during their First Hospitalization *Marta Tremolada, Sabrina Bonichini, Marta Pillon and Modesto Carli*	387

Chapter 168	The Quality of Participation in the Perception of Citizens: Findings from a Qualitative Study *Terri Mannarini and Angela Fedi*	389
Chapter 169	School as a Resilient Context for Resilient African American Youth *Anne Gregory and Robert Jagers*	391
Chapter 170	Meeting the Mental Health and Community Care Needs of Asylum Seekers and Refugees in Switzerland: Integrating Social and Political Concerns in Clinical Practice *Betty Goguikian Ratcliff*	393
Chapter 171	Aggressive Behavior of Drivers: A New Questionnaire Defining the difference between Hostile and Instrumental Behavior while Driving *Lipaz Shamoa-Nir and Meni Koslowsky*	395
Chapter 172	The Rhizomatic Potential in/for/of Community Psychology *Mark B. Borg, Jr.*	397
Chapter 173	Limits to General Expertise: A Study of in- and out-of-Field Graph Interpretation *Wolff-Michael Roth*	399
Chapter 174	Conceptual Combination: Models, Theories, and Controversies *Bing Ran and P. Robert Duimering*	401
Chapter 175	A Test of the Cognitive Theory of Obsessions: Study of Internal Structure and Validity of the Obsessive Beliefs Questionnaire in Italian Individuals *Stella Dorz, Caterina Novara, Massimiliano Pastore, Ezio Sanavio, Luigi Rocco Chiri and Claudio Sica*	403
Chapter 176	Haptic Abilities in Infancy and Their Relation to Vision: A Review *Arlette Streri*	405
Chapter 177	Emotional Modulation of Selective Attention: Experimental Evidence in Specific Phobia *Marlen Figueroa, Sonia Rodríguez-Ruiz, José L. Mata, Walter Machado-Pinheiro and Jaime Vila*	407
Chapter 178	The Moderating Effect of Switching Costs in Consumers' Relationship Dissolution: A Cross-Cultural Analysis *Carmen Antón Martín and Carmen Camarero Izquierdo*	409
Chapter 179	Tripartite Concepts of Mind and Brain, with Special Emphasis on the Neuroevolutionary Postulates of Christfried Jakob and Paul MacLean *Lazaros C. Triarhou*	411

Chapter 180	Category-Specific Semantics in Alzheimer's Dementia and Normal Aging? *Keith R. Laws, Tim M. Gale, F. Javier Moreno-Martínez, Rebecca L. Adlington, Karen Irvine and Sunil Sthanakiya*	413
Chapter 181	Preverbal Category Formation The Role of Real-World Experience *Birgit Träuble, Lysett Babocsai and Sabina Pauen*	415
Chapter 182	Peripheral Responses Elicited By Motor Imagery: A Window on Central and Peripheral Nervous System Relationships through Motor Commands Inhibition. *C. Collet and A. Guillot*	417
Chapter 183	Rationality: The Desire for an Absolute without a Cause *Todd McElroy, Jacob Conrad and Dominic Mascari*	419
Chapter 184	The Cognitive Effects of Anxiety on Sexual Arousal *Philippe Kempeneers, Romain Pallincourt and Sylvie Blairy*	423
Chapter 185	Experiencing Loneliness in Childhood: Consequences for Psychosocial Adjustment, School Adjustment, and Academic Performance *Lucy R. Betts and Anna S. A. Bicknell*	427
Chapter 186	Ageing and Psychological Well-Being *Juan Carlos Meléndez-Moral*	429
Chapter 187	Loneliness in Sexual Offenders *Emily Blake and Theresa A. Gannon*	431
Chapter 188	Loneliness and Life: From Beginning to End *Ami Rokach*	433
Chapter 189	The Experience of Loneliness while Studying Abroad *Holly A. Hunley*	435
Chapter 190	Denying the Need to Belong: How Social Exclusion Impairs Human Functioning and How People Can Protect against It *Richard S. Pond, Jr., Joseph Brey and C. Nathan DeWall*	437
Chapter 191	Sexual Alienation: A Review of Factors Influencing the Loneliness of Gay, Lesbian, and Bisexual Adolescents *Bradley J. Bond*	439
Chapter 191	Being Lonely in a Crowd: Population Density Contributes to Perceived Loneliness in China *Zhenzhu Yue, Cong Feng, Xinyue Zhou and Ding-Guo Gao*	441
Chapter 193	Coping with Genetic Risk: Imposing Control on the Uncertainty of Risk *Holly Etchegary*	443

Chapter 194	Self-Handicapping as an Anticipatory Self-Protection Strategy *Sean M. McCrea, Andrea L. Myers and Edward R. Hirt*	445
Chapter 195	Automatic Optimism The Role of Desire in Judgments About the Likelihood of Future Events *Heather C. Lench, Shane W. Bench, Sarah A. Flores and Peter H. Ditto*	447
Chapter 196	Social Identities, Prejudices and Symbolic Boundaries: Contributions from Sociocultural Psychology *Ana Flávia do Amaral Madureira*	449
Chapter 197	Who Is Supporting East European Immigrants in Portugal? An Exploratory Study of Their Social Networks *Liliana Sousa and Madalena Alarcã*	451
Chapter 198	Where Fantasy Meets Reality: Media Exposure, Relationship Beliefs and Standards, and the Moderating Effect of a Current Relationship *Bjarne M. Holmes and Kimberly R. Johnson*	453
Chapter 199	The Relationship between Gender and Depression, Self-Esteem, Hopelessness, Submissive Acts, Guilt, Shame and Anger in Adolescents *Erol Özmen, Dilek Özmen, Aynur Çakmakçı Çetinkaya, E. Oryal Taşkın and Pınar Erbay Dündar*	455
Chapter 200	Effects of Gender-Related Images on Beverages Intake for Young Japanese Men and Women *Kumi Hirokawaaand Kazuko Yamazawa*	457
Chapter 201	Outside the Laboratory: The Linguistic Intergroup Bias in a Natural Multiple-Comparison Setting *Monica Rubini, Anna Rita Graziani and Silvia Moscatelli*	459
Chapter 202	Alienation, Inaction, and Engagement in Political Decision-Making: Passive War Opponents Actively Avoid News of the War and Are Motivated to Derogate Protestors *Winnifred R. Louis, Fiona Kate Barlow and Deborah J. Terry*	461
Chapter 203	The Social Psychology of Urban Legends *David Main and Sandy Hobbs*	463
Chapter 204	Socio-Cultural Factors that Affect the Traditional Edirne House *Nevnihal Erdoğan and Damla Atik*	465

Chapter 205	Social Representations of Religion of Maltese University Students *Mary Anne Lauri, Josef Lauri and Bart Duriez*	**467**
Chapter 206	Self-Stereotyping and Sun Sign: Further Evidence that Astrology-Related Beliefs Influence the Self-Concept *Michael Riketta*	**469**
Chapter 207	Values and Fear of Crime *Silvia Russo and Michele Roccato*	**471**
Chapter 208	Social Physique Anxiety, Body Image, Disability, and Physical Activity *Jeffrey J. Martin*	**473**
Chapter 209	Social Anxiety and Psychosis *Erguvan Tugba Ozel-Kizil and Bora Baskak*	**475**
Chapter 210	The Relationship between Social Anxiety and Drinking Behaviour: A Review of the Literature *Annette Raber and Penelope A. Hasking*	**477**
Chapter 211	Social Anxiety is Contagious *Anna Park, Nicole Sharp and William Ickes*	**479**
Chapter 212	The Relationship between Social Physique Anxiety and Exercise Behavior: Does the Fulfillment of Basic Psychological Needs Matter? *Diane E. Mack, Philip M. Wilson, Benjamin D. Sylvester, J. Paige Gregson, Susanna Cheung and Samuel Rimmer*	**481**
Chapter 213	Social Anxiety and Cardiovascular Reactivity: An Interpretation in Terms of Differential Effort Mobilization *Margit Gramer*	**483**
Chapter 214	Why Is the Anxiety Level of Japanese People High? A Cross-Cultural Study on Anxiety and System Trust among Japan, China, and The United States *Yumiko Nara*	**485**
Chapter 215	The Cognitive Etiology of Social Anxiety Disorder *Iulian Iancu and Damian Barenboim*	**487**
Chapter 217	Social Anxiety in the College Student Population: The Role of Anxiety Sensitivity *Angela Sailer and Holly Hazlett-Stevens*	**489**
Chapter 217	Fluent Speakers' Advice for Communicating with People who Stutter: The Concept of Mutual Help and its Effects on Successful Stuttering Management *Stephanie Hughes, Rodney Gabel and Farzan Irani*	**491**

Chapter 218	Stereotypes as Attributions *Mark J. Brandt and Christine Reyna*	493
Chapter 219	Public Attitudes toward Cluttering and Stuttering in Four Countries *Kenneth O. St. Louis, Yulia Filatova, Mehmet Coşkun, Seyhun Topbaş, Sertan Özdemir, Dobrinka Georgieva, Elise McCaffrey and Reshella D. George*	495
Chapter 220	The Formation of Stereotypes in Children: Evidence from age and Race Studies *Denise Davidson, Vanessa R. Raschke and Sandra B. Vanegas*	497
Chapter 221	Bayesian Racism: A Modern Expression of Contemporary Prejudice *Eric Luis Uhlmann and Victoria L. Brescoll*	499
Chapter 222	Stereotypes on the Brain: Using Event-Related Brain Potentials to Investigate Stereotyping *Silvia Tomelleri and Luigi Castelli*	501
Chapter 223	Do Managers' Perceptions Coincide with Established Stereotyping of Older Workers' Capabilities *Trude Furunes and Reidar J. Mykletun*	503
Chapter 224	Ads and Sports: Stereotypical Scenes *Stephane Heas, D. Bodin, L. Robene and J. Blumrodt*	505
Chapter 225	Psychological Implications of Stereotyping American Indiansthrough the use of Native-Themed Mascots, Nicknames, and Logos *Jesse A. Steinfeldt, Paul Hagan and M. Clint Steinfeldt*	507
Chapter 226	The Complex Role of Motivation in Stereotyping and Stereotype Threat Effects *Lisa R. Grimm and Julie Milligan Hughes*	509
Chapter 227	Ambivalence in Stereotypes and Attitudes: The Implications of Possessing Positive and Negative Perceptions *Kimberley A. Clow and Rosemary Ricciardelli*	511
Chapter 228	Epilepsy: Myths, Stereotypes and Stigma *Jane McCagh*	513
Chapter 229	Stereotypes Toward Food and Eating Behavior *Atsushi Kimura, Yuji Wada and Takashi Oka*	515

Chapter 230	Gender Stereotypes and Mental Rotation: The Role of Self-Belief *Angelica Moè*	517
Chapter 231	When Stereotypes become Life Threatening: Knowledge and Attitudes about HIV/AIDS among Older Women and the Health Care Providers who Treat Them *Jennifer Hillman and Molly Beiler*	519
Chapter 232	An Analysis of Response Time Characteristics with Strength and Reversibility of Stereotypes for Determining Optimum Control Position on a Horizontal Display *Alan H. S. Chan*	521
Chapter 233	A Frenchman, An Englishman, and A German... Stereotypes in Humorous Texts *Arthur Asa Berger*	523
Chapter 234	A Stochastic Model of Prospective Memory *Jack D. Arnal and James M. Lampinen*	525
Chapter 235	Predicting Where Fly Balls Will Land: Lack of Conscious Awareness of How We Navigate to Catch Baseballs *Dennis M. Shaffer, Andrew B. Maynor, April Utt and Bethany A. Briley*	527
Chapter 236	Cognitive Processes in Communication between Pilots and Air Traffic Control *Alice F. Healy, Vivian I. Schneider and Immanuel Barshi*	529
Chapter 237	The Effect of Visuo-Spatial Attention on Long-Term Memory Encoding *Stephan Josef Stegt and Cristina Massen*	531
Chapter 238	Exposure to Ambiguous Tone Sequences Induces Short-Term Plasticity of Pitch Perception *Annemarie Seither-Preisler, Linda Johnson, Erich Preisler, Stefan Seither and Bernd Lütkenhöner*	533
Chapter 239	The Interaction of Automatic Processes and Cognitive Resources in Reading: A Compensatory Framework *Jeffrey J. Walczyk, Min Wei, Peijia Zha and Diana A. Griffith-Ross*	535
Chapter 240	A Motivational-Cognitive Approach to Prospective Memory *Suzanna L. Penningroth and Walter D. Scott*	537

Chapter 241	Laboratory Memory Tasks and Autobiographical Recollection: Cognitive and Neurofunctional Evidence for Differential Forms of Episodic Memory *Martina Piefke*	539
Chapter 242	A Comparative Neuropsychological Approach to Cognitive Assessment in Clinical Populations *Isabelle Boutet, Cary Kogan and Norton W. Milgram*	541
Chapter 243	The Mechanisms of Masked Semantic Priming: A State of the Art *Eva Van den Bussche and Bert Reynvoet*	543
Chapter 244	The Role of Alleles 4 and 2 of the APOE Gene and Cognitive Tests in the Early Conversion of Mild Cognitive Impairment to Alzheimer Dementia *Ana Barabash, Alberto Marcos, Inés Ancin, Blanca M. Vazquez, Pedro Gil, Cristina Fernández, Juan José López-Ibor and José Antonio Cabranes*	545
Chapter 245	How Dyslexic Teenagers Cope at School: Could a New Measure Be Helpful in Screening those in Difficulty? *Neil Alexander-Passe*	547
Chapter 246	Interest and Motivation: A Cultural-Historical and Discursive Psychological Approach *Wolff-Michael Roth and Pei-Ling Hsu*	549
Chapter 247	Reading Fluency and Dyslexia: Innovative Developments in the Role of Associative Learning and Repetitive Exposure in Skill Acquisition *Sebastián Aravena and Jurgen Tijms*	551
Chapter 248	Cultural Influences on the Learning of Science: An African Perspective *Fred N. Keraro and Mark I.O. Okere*	553
Chapter 249	Non-Linear Dynamic Modeling of Microdevelopmental Processes of Students' Conceptual Change in Science *Li Sha and Xiufeng Liu*	555
Chapter 250	Phonology, Discrepancy, Instruction and Dyslexia: Adversaries or Allies? *Peter Brooks and John Everatt*	557
Chapter 251	Dyslexia and Loss of the Learning Dialogue *Neil Alexander-Passe and Bob Zimmer*	559
Chapter 252	Cognitive Load Theory and Instructional Design: An Outline of the Theory and Reflections on a Need for New Directions to Cater for Individual Differences and Motivation *Wayne Michael Leahy*	561

Chapter 253	Attitude towards School, Motivation, Emotions and Academic Achievement *Angelica Moè, Francesca Pazzaglia, Patrizio Tressoldi and Cristina Toso*	**563**
Chapter 254	Individual Differences in Attitude to School and Social Reputation among Peers: Implications for Behavioural Adjustment in Educational Settings *Estefanía Estévez and Nicholas Emler*	**565**
Chapter 255	Dyslexia as a Syndrome: Don't Let 'Reading Disability' Steal the Show *Tim Miles*	**567**
Chapter 256	Gender-Motivated Bias Crimes: Examining Why Situational Variables are Important in the Labeling of Hate Crimes *H. Colleen Sinclair and Jordan T. Hertl*	**569**
Chapter 257	Toward a Psychological Construct of Enmity *Christopher R. Jones and Chris Loersch*	**571**
Chapter 258	Hate, Revenge and Forgiveness: A Healthy, Ego-Strengthening Alternative to the Experience of Offense *Patrick F. Cioni*	**573**
Chapter 259	Do You Hate Me? Have I Hurt You?: Defenses against Growth, Separation, and Individuation That Create Interpretive Enactments Part One: Fender Benders and the Shared Defensive Systems of Less Difficult Patients *Robert Waska*	**575**
Chapter 260	Do You Hate Me? Have I Hurt You?: Defenses against Growth, Separation, and Individuation That Create Interpretive Enactments Part Two: Pit Stops and the Shared Defensive Systems of More Difficult Patients *Robert Waska*	**577**
Chapter 261	Hate and Love Scripts – Common Elements *Barbara Gawda*	**579**
Chapter 262	Hate: No Choice Agent Simulations *Krzysztof Kulakowski, Malgorzata J. Krawczyk and Przemyslaw Gawroński*	**581**
Chapter 263	The Influence of Prenatal Mother-Child Attachment on the Attachment at the Age of 6 Months and Its Objectivation by the Intrauterine Fetal Activity *Helmut Niederhofer and Alfons Reiter*	**583**

Chapter 264	Mother-Infant Interaction in Cultural Context: A Study of Nicaraguan and Italian Families Ughetta Moscardino, Sabrina Bonichini and Cristina Valduga	**585**
Chapter 265	Fussy Mothers and Fuzzy Boundaries – Relationships in Families with Overweight Children Laurel D. Edmunds	**587**
Chapter 266	Maternal Sensitivity and the Characteristics of Child-Directed Speech Leila Paavola, Kaarina Kemppinen and Sari Kunnari	**589**
Chapter 267	Recruitment and Relationships: Research with Stigmatized and Socially Isolated Mothers Nicole L. Letourneau, Linda A. Duffett-Leger and Catherine S. Young	**591**
Chapter 268	Shifting Patterns of Parenting Styles between Dyadic and Family Settings: The Role of Marital Distress Allison F. Lauretti and James P. McHale	**593**
Chapter 269	The Interrelations of Perceptions of Family Adaptability and Cohesion, Self-Esteem and Anxiety/Depression in Late Adolescence Rapson Gomez and Suzanne McLaren	**595**
Chapter 270	Communicative Functions of Emotions in Sibling Relationships Nazan Aksan, H.H. Goldsmith, Marilyn J. Essex and Deborah Lowe Vandell	**597**
Chapter 271	Childhood Sibling Relationship Quality and Achievement Outcomes in University Students: Mediation by Psychological Distress and Personal Mastery Amy Kraft, Charles Stayton, Arthi Satyanarayan and Linda J. Luecken	**599**
Chapter 272	Linking Children's Personal Characteristics, Externalizing Behavior and Relationships in Family and Social Environments: Some Developmental Cascades I. Roskam, J.C. Meunier, M. Stievenart and G. Van De Moortele	**601**
Chapter 273	Prevention of the Negative Effects of Marital Conflict: A Child-Oriented Program Patricia M. Mitchell, Kathleen P. McCoy, E. Mark Cummings, W. Brad Faircloth and Jennifer S. Cummings	**603**

Chapter 274	Psychological Processes Affecting Post-Divorce Paternal Functioning *Nehami Baum*	**605**
Chapter 275	Big, Buff and Dependent: Exercise Dependence, Muscle Dysmorphia and Anabolic Steroid Use in Bodybuilders *Dave Smith, Bruce Hale, Deborah Rhea, Tracy Olrich and Kevan Collier*	**607**
Chapter 276	*Seeking Safety* Therapy for Men: Clinical and Research Experiences *Lisa M. Najavits, Martha Schmitz, Kay M. Johnson, Cary Smith, Terry North, Nancy Hamilton, Robyn Walser, Kevin Reeder, Sonya Norman and Kendall Wilkins*	**609**
Chapter 277	Relationship between Personality Scales of Impulsiveness and Discounting of Monetary Gains and Losses in Smokers and Never Smokers *Taiki Takahashi, Hidemi Oono, Yu Ohmura, Nozomi Kitamura and Mark Radford*	**611**
Chapter 278	Sexual Abuse in Men with Substance Use Problems: Assessment and Treatment Issues *Christine M. Courbasson, Jim Cullen and Karolina Konieczna*	**613**
Chapter 279	Explaining Type 2 Diabetes: Comparing Patients' and Physicians' Models in Mexico *Raminta Daniulaityte, Javier E. García de Alba García and Ana L. Salcedo Rocha*	**615**
Chapter 280	Cognitive Dysfunction in Cocaine Abuse: Evidence for Impairments in Impulse Control and Decision-Making *Laurie M. Rilling and Bryon Adinoff*	**617**
Chapter 281	Current Controversies in the Assessment and Treatment of Heroin Addiction *Robert J. Craig*	**619**
Chapter 282	New Research on Methamphetamine Abuse (Gender Differences in Methamphetamine Effects: Review of Animal and Human Studies) *Bin Liu and Dean E. Dluzen*	**621**
Chapter 283	Social Norms and Areca Quid Chewing in Taiwanese Adolescents - A Preliminary Study *Shih-Ming Li and Jehn-Shyun Huang*	**623**

Chapter 284	For the Health of It: A Brief Version of the Situational Humor Response Questionnaire (Martin & Lefcourt, 1984) *Dave Korotkov, Ian Fraser, Mihailo Perunovic and Marvin Claybourn*	625
Chapter 285	Developments in Cultural Competency Research *Georgia Michalopoulou, Pamela Falzarano, Cynthia Arfken and David Rosenberg*	627
Chapter 286	The Dynamics of Pain and Affect: Toward a Salient Phenotype for Chronic Pain *Patrick H. Finan and Howard Tennen*	629
Chapter 287	Hypnosis as an Adjunct to Cognitive-Behavioural Therapy Intervention for the Treatment of Fibromyalgia *Antoni Castel Rosalía Cascón and Maria Rull*	631
Chapter 288	Can Technology Improve the Treatment of Chronic Insomnia? A Review of Best Practices *Norah Vincent*	633
Chapter 289	Benefit Finding Predicts Improved Emotional Health Following Cardiac Rehabilitation *Bruce W. Smith, Paulette J. Christopher, Laura E. Bouldin, Erin M. Tooley, Jennifer F. Bernard and J. Alexis Ortiz*	635
Chapter 290	Negotiating Blame as a Fat Child's Parent: A Case Study *Riina Kokkonen*	637
Chapter 291	Trust in Health Care: Conceptual Issues and Empirical Research *Rocio Garcia-Retamero and Yasmina Okan*	639
Chapter 292	Improving the Public Health Impact of Internet-Delivered Interventions *Rik Crutzen*	641
Chapter 293	Leisure and Depression in Midlife: A Taiwanese National Survey of Middle-Aged Adults *Luo Lu*	643
Chapter 294	Following the Life-Course of an Expectation: A Case Study Examining the Exchange of Expectations in a Homeless Shelter in New York City *Mark B. Borg, Jr. and Leroy Porter*	645
Chapter 295	Exploring the Black Box of Trust on Outcomes: The Case of Patient-Physician Encounters *Yin-Yang Lee and Julia L. Lin*	647

Chapter 296	Expectations in a Time of Self-Doubt *A. Ralph Barlow and Pastor Emeritus*	**649**
Chapter 297	Coping with the Expectation of Social Acceptance *C. Nathan DeWall, Richard S. Pond, Jr. and Ian Bonser*	**651**
Chapter 298	Group Hardiness: A Response to the Stresses of Complex Adaptive Systems *Joshua L. Ray and Donde Ashmos Plowman*	**653**
Chapter 299	The Influence of Expectations on Recovery, Quality of Life, and Treatment Satisfaction in Surgical Patients *Maren Weiss, Michael Siassi, Werner Hohenberger and Friedrich Lösel*	**655**
Chapter 300	Future from the Past: The Mistakes of Futurology *A. V. Yurevich*	**657**
Chapter 301	A Christian Perspective on Hope, Expectancies and Therapy *Thomas V. Frederick*	**659**
Chapter 302	Human Antidepressants and the Old Song-and-Dance Routines: Zeroing in on the Life-Course (and Lack Thereof) of Expectations in Clinical Practice *Mark B. Borg, Jr.*	**661**
Chapter 303	The Psychology of Denial in the Political Context: The Case of Torture *Daryn Reicherter, Alexandra Aylward, Ami Student and Cheryl Koopman*	**663**
Chapter 304	Repression: Finding Our Way in the Maze of Questionnaires *Bert Garssen*	**665**
Chapter 305	Hidden Curriculum in Education and the Social Psychology of Denial: Global Multicultural Education for Social Transformation *Beth Salyers and Greg Wiggan*	**667**
Chapter 306	Repression Questionnaires Compared *Bert Garssen, Margot Remie and Marije van der Lee*	**669**
Chapter 307	Where Are All the Black Male Students? African Americans' School Achievement, the Social Psychology of Denial, and Arts Education as a Mediating Influence *Calvin W. Walton and Greg Wiggan*	**671**
Chapter 308	High Denial and Moderate Acceptance Led to Success and Reduced Guilt *Marilyn Lanza and Scott Prunier*	**673**

Chapter 309	The Conditional Adjustment Hypothesis: Two Ways of Dealing with Dissonance Tor G. Jakobsen	675
Chapter 310	Exploring the Usefulness of "Denial" as a Concept for Understanding Chronic Illness and Disability Sally Lindsay	677
Chapter 311	Child and Adolescent Personality Development and Assessment: A Developmental Psychopathology Approach Tina D. Du Rocher Schudlich, Ryan C. Erps, Britnee Davenport and Alyssa Hertel	679
Chapter 312	Integrating Evidence-Based Treatment into an Attachment Guided Curriculum in a Therapeutic Preschool: Initial Findings Karen Stubenbort, Veronica Trybalski and Krista Zaccagni	681
Chapter 313	Assessing Individuals for Team Worthiness": Investigating the Intersection of the Big Five Personality Factors, Organizational Citizenship Behavior and Teamwork Aptitude Janet L. Kottke and Shinko Kimura	683
Chapter 314	Personality Traits and Daily Moods Cristina Ottaviani, David Shapiro, Iris Goldstein and Valerie Gofman	685
Chapter 315	Weight? Wait! Importance Weighting of Satisfaction Scores in Quality of Life Assessment Chia-huei Wu	687
Chapter 316	A Psycho-Social Approach to Meanings and Functions of Trait Labels Astrid Mignon and Patrick Mollaret	689
Chapter 317	Comparing the Psychometric Properties of the Common Items in the Short and Abbreviated Versions of the Junior Eysenck Personality Questionnaires: A Mean and Covariance Structures Analysis Approach Rapson Gomez and Andre Gomez	691
Chapter 318	Successful Psychopathy: Unresolved Issues and Future Directions Kristin Landfield, Meredith Jones and Scott Lilienfeld	693
Chapter 319	Score Reliability in Personality Research Matt Vassar, Denna L. Wheeler and Jody A. Worley	695
Chapter 320	Restyling Personality Assessments Willem K. B. Hofstee	697
Chapter 321	Theory and Practice in the Use and Interpretation of Likert-Type Scales within a Cross-Cultural Context Boaz Shulruf	699

Chapter 321	Construct and Response Bias Correlates in Summated Scale Definitions of Personality Traits *John T. Kulas and Alicia A. Stachowski*	701
Chapter 323	Academic and Everyday Procrastination and their Relation to the Five-Factor Model *Gidi Rubenstein*	703
Chapter 324	Personality and Attitude Toward Dreams *Barbara Szmigielska and Małgorzata Hołda*	705
Chapter 325	Social Dominance Orientation, Ambivalent Sexism, and Abortion: Explaining Pro-choice and Pro-life Attitudes *Danny Osborne and Paul G. Davies*	707
Chapter 326	Factor Structure, Sex Effects and Differential Item Functioning of the Junior Eysenck Personality Questionnaire Revised - Abbreviated: A Multiple-Indicators Multiple-Causes Approach *Rapson Gomez and Andre Gomez*	709
Chapter 327	Online Collaborative Learning: The Challenge of Change *Baruch Offir, Ingrid Barth and Orit Zeichner*	711
Chapter 328	The Influence of Personality and Symptoms Severity on Functioning in Patients with Schizophrenia *Ana Fresan, María García-Anaya, Rogelio Apiquian and Humberto Nicolini*	713
Chapter 329	Circumventing Self-Reflection When Measuring Emotions: The Implicit Positive and Negative Affect Test (IPANAT) *Markus Quirin, Miguel Kazén and Julius Kuhl*	715
Chapter 330	Structured MMPI-2 Client Feedback in the Identification of Potential Supplemental Targets of Change *Alan R. King and Joseph C. Miller*	717
Chapter 331	Beyond the Traits of the Five Factor Model: Using Deviant Personality Traits to Predict Deviant Behavior in Organizations *James M. LeBreton and Jane Wu*	719
Chapter 332	On the Test-Retest Reliability of the Autobiographical Memory Test *Filip Raes, J. Mark G. Williams and Dirk Hermans*	721
Chapter 333	Trait Anger, Anger Expression, and Themes of Anger Incidents in Contemporary Undergraduate Students *Sandra P. Thomas*	723
Chapter 334	Social Anxiety in the College Student Population: The Role of Anxiety Sensitivity *Angela Sailer and Holly Hazlett-Stevens*	725

Chapter 335	Coping, Mental Health Status, and Current Life Regret in College Women Who Differ in their Lifetime Pregnancy Status: A Resilience Perspective *Jennifer Langhinrichsen-Rohling, Theresa Rehm, Michelle Breland and Alexis Inabinet*	727
Chapter 336	Sexual Behavioral Determinants and Risk Perception Related to HIV among College Students *Su-I Hou and Joseph M. Wisenbaker*	729
Chapter 337	The Impact of a Lecture Series on Alcohol and Tobacco Use in Pharmacy Students *Arjun P. Dutta, Bisrat Hailemeskel, Monika N. Daftary and Anthony Wutoh*	731
Chapter 338	The Gould versus Heckhausen and Schulz Debate in the Light of Control Processes among Chinese Students *Wan-chi Wong, Yin Li and Ji-liang Shen*	733
Chapter 339	Writing your Way to Health? The Effects of Disclosure of Past Stressful Events in German Students *Lisette Morris, Annedore Linkemann and Birgit Kröner-Herwig*	735
Chapter 340	Test Anxiety and Its Consequences on Academic Performance among University Students *Mohd Ariff Bin Kassim, Siti Rosmaini Bt. Mohd Hanafi and Dawson R. Hancock*	737
Chapter 341	The Prevalence of Depression among Female University Students and Related Factors *Fernando L. Vázquez, Ángela Torres, María López, Vanessa Blanco and Patricia Otero*	739
Chapter 342	Relationships between Mood, Coping and Stress Symptoms among Students who Work in Schools *Dafna Kariv and Tali Heiman*	741
Chapter 343	Examining Anger Expression Reactions and Anger Control Behaviors of Turkish Students *Ibrahim Kisac*	743
Chapter 344	Coronary Pressure Measurement in Decision Making for Equivocal Left Main Coronary Artery Disease *Kohichiro Iwasaki*	745
Chapter 345	Antiterrorist Emergency Ventilation: System, Strategy and Decision-making *Xianting Li, Hao Cai and Lina Zhao*	747

Chapter 346	Decision-Making in a Structured Connectionist Agent Architecture *Carter Wendelken and Lokendra Shastri*	**749**
Chapter 347	Cognitive Dysfunction in Cocaine Abuse: Evidence for Impairments in Impulse Control and Decision-Making *Laurie M. Rilling and Bryon Adinoff*	**751**
Chapter 348	Expert Systems, GIS, and Spatial Decision Making: Current Practices and New Trends *Khalid Eldrandaly*	**753**
Chapter 349	Development of Response Inhibition and Decision-Making across Childhood: A Cognitive Neuroscience Perspective *Wery P. M. van den Wildenberg and Eveline A. Crone*	**755**
Chapter 350	Enabling Pregnant Women to Participate in Informed Decision-Making Regarding their Labour Analgesia *Camille Raynes-Greenow, Christine Roberts and Natasha Nassar*	**757**
Chapter 351	Adolescent Decision-Making about Substance Use: A Video-Based Assessment *Kristen G. Anderson and Sara J. Parent*	**759**
Chapter 352	Interprofessional Decision Making in Elderly Care: Morality, Criteria and Help Allocation *Pirjo Nikander*	**761**
Chapter 353	Analysing the Effects of Mortality Salience on Prejudice and Decision-Taking *Agustin Echebarria- Echabe and Francisco J. Valencia Gárate*	**763**
Chapter 354	Burnout and Compassion Fatigue: The Case of Professional Nurses in Primary Health Care Facilities in the Free State Province, South Africa *Michelle Engelbrecht, Henriëtte van den Berg and Coen Bester*	**765**
Chapter 355	Burnout and the Antithesis of Burnout: Developing Positive Interventions for the Well-Being of Chinese Teachers in Hong Kong *David W. Chan*	**767**
Chapter 356	Reducing Burnout through Support in the Workplace and the Family Domain *Lieke L. ten Brummelhuis*	**769**

Chapter 357	The Role of Personality and Coping Style in Burnout Development: A Study on Need for Recovery from Work *Marc van Veldhoven and Geertje van Daalen*	771
Chapter 358	Whose Exhaustion is Greater than Whose? Burnout in Colorectal Surgeons, Vascular Surgeons and Colorectal Nurse Specialists Working in the National Health Service *A. Sharma, L. G. Walker and J. R. T. Monson*	773
Chapter 359	The Role of Achievement and Social Strategies and of Work-Life Areas in Job Burnout *Hely Innanen, Aino Juvakka and Katariina Salmela-Aro*	775
Chapter 360	Secondary Traumatization - Just Another Form of Burnout? *Judith Daniels*	777
Chapter 361	Emotional Openness as a Protective Factor Against Burnout *Philippe A. Genoud and Michaël Reicherts*	779
Chapter 362	Influence of Emotional Labor in Demanding Classroom Situations on Health and Well-Being of Teachers *Anja Philipp and Heinz Schüpbach*	781
Chapter 363	The Influence of Social Competence on Occupational Stress of Nursing Home Staff Caring for Dementia Patients *J. Haberstroh, J. Franzmann, K. Krause and J. Pantel*	783
Chapter 364	Family Violence Therapists: Personal and Social Resources, Role Competence, Secondary Traumatization, and Burnout *Anat Ben-Porat and Haya Itzhaky*	785
Chapter 365	Relationship Between Desire for Control and Job Control and their Effects on Job Burnout in Health-Care Personnel *Marcel Lourel, Farida Mouda, Maude Paltrier and Sandra Chevaleyre*	787
Chapter 366	Dimensions of Teacher Burnout and Relations with Perceived School Context *Einar M. Skaalvik and Sidsel Skaalvik*	789
Chapter 367	Hospital Pharmacists' Job Stresses: Managerial Recommendation for Professional Work Health *Blossom Yen-Ju Lin, Ying-Chen Yeh and Wen-Hung Lin*	791
Chapter 368	`Male Depression' in Male Adolescents: A German Community Study *A. M. Möller-Leimküher, J. Heller and N. C. Paulus*	793

Chapter 369	Psychological Aspects of Burnout among Staffs in Long-Term Care Homes *Jin Narumoto*	795
Chapter 370	Burnout Among French High-School Students *Sandra Zakari, Vera Walburg and Henri Chabrol*	797
Chapter 371	The Contribution of Personality to Positive Psychology *Ashley B. Love and Mark D. Holder*	799
Chapter 372	Study of Male Body Image and Factors in the Development of Eating Disorders in Fraternity and Non-Fraternity Males *Kylee K. Ferris and F. Richard Ferraro*	801
Chapter 373	Efficacy at Fulfilling the Need for Closure: The Construct and Its Measurement *Yoram Bar-Tal and Małgorzata Kossowska*	803
Chapter 374	Narcissistic and Borderline Personality Traits: Their Relationship with Childhood Abuse Experiences in a Student Population in Japan *Hiromi Igarashi, Chieko Hasui, Masayo Uji, Masahiro Shono, Toshiaki Nagata, Zi Chen and Toshinori Kitamura*	805
Chapter 375	The Imaginary Companion Experience in Adults: Asset, Disorder or Personality Feature? *Lino Faccini*	807
Chapter 376	How "To Be or Not To Be": The Answer is in Identity *Lino Faccini*	809
Chapter 377	Is Developmentally Informed Therapy for Persons with ID and Criminal Personality/Offenses Relevant? *Lino Faccini*	811
Chapter 378	Aggregating Personality Constructs to Second-Order Categories for Acquiring Insights to a Field of Fragmentation: The Case of Entrepreneurship Research *Joakim Wincent and Daniel Örtqvist*	813
Chapter 379	Personality Traits and Lay Conceptions of Intelligence *Tomas Chamorro-Premuzic, Georgia Dissou, Adrian Furnham and Amber Bales*	815
Chapter 380	Personality Traits and Daily Moods *Cristina Ottaviani, David Shapiro, Iris Goldstein and Valerie Gofman*	817

Chapter 381	Addiction: Frontal Personality Change but Not Personality Disorder Comorbidity Implications for Treatment of Addictive Disorders *Eduardo J. Pedrero-Pérez, Ana López-Durán and Alvaro Olivar-Arroyo*	819
Chapter 382	Circadian Preference and Personality: A Minireview *Lorenzo Tonetti*	821
Chapter 383	The Imaginary Companion Experience in Adults: Asset, Disorder or Personality Feature? *Lino Faccini*	823
Chapter 384	Schizotypal Personality Traits: Auditory Hallucination-like Experiences and Atypical Hemispheric Lateralization *Tomohisa Asai, Eriko Sugimori and YoshihikoTanno*	825
Chapter 385	Genetics of Personalitity Disorders *Gonzalo Haro, Ernesto Tarragón, César Mateu, Ana Benito and Cecilio Álamo*	827
Chapter 386	Structural and Functional Neuroimaging Studies of the Anxiety-Related Personality Trait: Implications for the Neurobiological Basis of Human Anxious Personality *Yuko Hakamata and Toshiya Inada*	829
Chapter 387	Too Much of a Good Thing?: Optimistic or Pessimistic Personality Traits *Francine Conway and Laura Kelly*	833
Chapter 388	Illness Recognition and Beliefs about Treatment for Schizophrenia in a Community Sample of Mexico City: Differences According to Personality Traits *Ana Fresán and Rebeca Robles-García*	835
Chapter 389	Personality Traits: Reflections in the Brain *Feryal Cam Celikel*	837
Chapter 390	The Caregivers of Persons with Alzheimer's Disease: The Impact of Personality Traits on Own Stress Perception and in Evaluating Cognitive and Functional Impairment of Their Relatives *Marco Vista, Lucia Picchi and Monica Mazzoni*	839
Chapter 391	Communicating Empathies in Interpersonal Relationships *Grace Anderson and Howard Giles*	841
Chapter 392	Interpersonal Representations: Their Structure, Content, and Nature *Shanhong Luo*	843

Chapter 393	Generalized Anxiety Disorder and Interpersonal Relationships: The Case For a Systemic Intervention *Danielle Black, Amanda Uliaszek, Alison Lewis and Richard Zinbarg*	845
Chapter 394	Another Kind of "Interpersonal" Relationship: Humans, Companion Animals, and Attachment Theory *Jeffrey D. Green, Maureen A. Mathews and Craig A. Foster*	847
Chapter 395	The Role of Oxytocin in the Pathophysiology of Attachment *Marazziti Donatella, Catena Dell'Osso Mari, Consoli Giorgio and Baroni Stefano*	849
Chapter 396	Identity Exploration and Commitment Associations with Gender Differences in Emerging Adults' Romantic Relationship Intimacy *H. Durell Johnson, Kristen A. Loff, George Bell, Evelyn Brady, Erin A. Grogan, Elizabeth Yale, Robert J. Foley and Trishia A. Pilosi*	851
Chapter 397	Development of an Interview for Assessing Relationship Quality: Preliminary Support for Reliability, Convergent and Divergent Validity, and Incremental Utility *Erika Lawrence, Robin A. Barry, Rebecca L. Brock, Amie Langer, Eunyoe Ro, Mali Bunde, Emily Fazio, Lorin Mulryan, Sara Hunt, Lisa Madsen and Sandra Dzankovic*	853
Chapter 398	Assessing Relationship Quality: Development of an Interview and Implications for Couple Assessment and Intervention *Erika Lawrence, Rebecca L. Brock, Robin A. Barry, Amie Langer and Mali Bunde*	855
Chapter 399	The Tendency to Forgive in Premarital Couples: Reciprocating the Partner or Reproducing Parental Dispositions? *F. Giorgia Paleari, Silvia Donato, Raffaella Iafrate and Camillo Regalia*	857
Chapter 400	Is the Serotonergic System Altered in Romantic Love? A Literature Review and Research Suggestions *Sandra J. E. Langeslag*	859
Chapter 401	Update on Pheromone Research *Donatella Marazziti, Irene Masala, Stefano Baroni, Michela Picchetti, Antonello Veltri and Mario Catena Dell'Osso*	861

Chapter 402	Normal and Obsessional Jealousy: An Italian Study *Donatella Marazziti, Marina Carlini, Francesca Golia,* *Stefano Baroni, Giorgio Consoli* *and Mario Catena Dell'Osso*	863
Chapter 403	Jealousy, Serotonin and Subthreshold Psychopathology *Donatella Marazziti, Francesca Golia, Marina Carlini,* *Stefano Baroni, Irene Masala, Mario Catena Dell'Osso* *and Giorgio Consoli*	865
Chapter 404	Advances in Dyadic and Social Network Analyses for Longitudinal Data: Developmental Implications and Applications *William J. Burk, Danielle Popp and Brett Laursen*	867
Chapter 405	Mother-Infant Interaction in Cultural Context: A Study of Nicaraguan and Italian Families *Ughetta Moscardino, Sabrina Bonichini* *and Cristina Valduga*	869
Chapter 406	"It's Saturday…I'm Going out with My Friends": Spending Time Together in Adolescent Stories *Emanuela Rabaglietti and Silvia Ciairano*	871
Chapter 407	Prevention of the Negative Effects of Marital Conflict: A Child-Oriented Program *Patricia M. Mitchell, Kathleen P. McCoy,* *E. Mark Cummings, W. Brad Faircloth* *and Jennifer S. Cummings*	873
Chapter 408	Mother-Infant Bonds: The Effects of Maternal Depression on the Maternal-Child Relationship *Deana B. Davalos, Alana M. Campbell* *and Amanda L. Pala*	875
Chapter 409	Social Networks and Psychosocial Functioning among Children and Adolescents Coping with Sickle Cell Disease: An Overview of Barriers, Considerations, and Best Practices *Rebecca H. Foster, HaNa Kim, Robbie Casper,* *Alma Morgan, Wanda Brice and Marilyn Stern*	877
Chapter 410	Parenting and Children's Involvement in Bullying at School *Ken Rigby*	879
Chapter 411	Neurobiology of Social Bonding *Donatella Marazziti, Alessandro Del Debbio,* *Isabella Roncaglia, Carolina Bianchi* *and Liliana Dell'Osso*	881

Chapter 412	Cooperative and Non-cooperative Behavior in Pairs of Children: The Reciprocal Effects of Social Interaction in the Ongoing Construction of a Play Sequence *Emanuela Rabaglietti, Fabrizia Giannotta and Silvia Ciairano*	883
Chapter 413	Social Relationships and Physical Health: Are We Better or Worse off because of Our Relationships? *Julianne Holt-Lunstad and Briahna Bushman*	885
Chapter 414	Living in Discrepant Worlds: Exploring the Cultural Context of Sexuality among Turkish and Moroccan Male Adolescents *Barbara C. Schouten and Chana van der Velden*	887
Chapter 415	HIV/AIDS Prevention on Mexican Adolescents: The Synthesis of two Theories Considering the Interpersonal, Individual, and Psychological Influences *Raquel A. Benavides-Torres, Georgina M. Núñez Rocha, Esther C. Gallegos Cabriales, Claude Bonazzo, Yolanda Flores-Peña, Francisco R. Guzmán Facudo and Karla Selene López García*	889
Chapter 416	Adolescents with Cancer: Adjustment and Supportive Care Needs *Luisa M. Massimo*	891
Chapter 417	The Quality of Caring Relationships *Tineke A. Abma, Barth Oeseburg, Guy A. M. Widdershoven and Marian Verkerk*	893
Chapter 418	An Attachment-Based Pathways Model Depicting the Psychology of Therapeutic Relationships *Geoff Goodman*	895
Chapter 419	A Study of the Relationship between Self-conscious Affects, Coping Styles, and Depressive Reaction after a Negative Life Event *Masayo Uji, Toshinori Kitamura and Toshiaki Nagata*	897
Chapter 420	The Neuropsychology of Passionate Love *Elaine Hatfield and Richard L. Rapson*	899
Chapter 421	Women, Substance Use and Post-Traumatic Stress Disorder *Christine M. Courbasson and Irina Schelkanova*	901
Chapter 422	Self-Narrative and the Construction of Identity in Asian American Young Adults *Qi Wang, Jessie Bee Kim Koh, Yan-Xiang Amber Liang, Yexin Jessica Li and Sean Lindsey*	903

Chapter 423	Sexual Abuse in Men with Substance Use Problems: Assessment and Treatment Issues *Christine M. Courbasson, Jim Cullen and Karolina Konieczna*	905
Chapter 424	Construct and Criterion Validity of an Objective Measure of Respondents' Subjectively Accepted Level of Risk in Road Traffic *Andreas Hergovich, Martin E. Arendasy, Markus Sommer and Bettina Bognar*	907
Chapter 425	The Psychological Disturbances of War-Traumatized Adolescents in Rural and Urban Areas of Bosnia and Herzegovina and it's Correlation with Poverty and Hopelessness *Mevludin Hasanović, Edin Haračić, Šemsa Ahmetspahić, Sanja Kurtović and Hajrudin Haračić*	909
Chapter 426	What the Spiritual and Religious Traditions Offer Psychologists *Thomas G. Plante*	911
Chapter 427	An Attachment-Based Pathways Model Depicting the Psychology of Therapeutic Relationships *Geoff Goodman*	913
Chapter 428	Modalities of Emotion Regulation Following Negative Life Events in Adulthood and Old Age *Olimpia Matarazzo*	915
Chapter 429	An Assessment of an Instrument with Which to Conduct Internal Audits *Mohd Ariff Bin Kasim, Siti Rosmaini Bt Mohd Hanafi, Asmah Abdul Aziz and Dawson R. Hancock*	917
Chapter 430	Recruitment and Relationships: Research with Stigmatized and Socially Isolated Mothers *Nicole L. Letourneau, Linda A. Duffett-Leger and Katherine Young*	919
Chapter 431	A Study of the Relationship between Self-Conscious Affects, Coping Styles, and Depressive Reaction after a Negative Life Event *Masayo Uji, Toshinori Kitamura and Toshiaki Nagata*	921
Chapter 432	The Workplace Affective Commitment Multidimensional Questionnaire: Factor Structure and Measurement Invariance *Alexandre J. S. Morin, Isabelle Madore, Julien Morizot, Jean-Sébastien Boudrias and Michel Tremblay*	923

Chapter 433	Is Caring for the Elderly a Health Risk? A Qualitative Study on Work Experience, Coping and Health Behaviours of Nurses *Brigitte Jenull, Ingrid Salem and Eva Brunner*	925
Chapter 434	Psycholinguistic Challenges in Processing Arabic Language *Raphiq Ibrahim*	927
Chapter 435	The Context of Domestic Violence: Social and Contextual Factors Associated with Partner Violence against Women *Enrique Gracia*	929
Chapter 436	Extraversion and Suicidal Behavior *David Lester*	933
Chapter 437	Alcohol Related Experiences – The Good, the Bad and the Ugly *Karin Helmersson Bergmark*	935
Chapter 438	Physiological Assessment of Forgiveness, Grudges, and Revenge: Theories, Research Methods, and Implications *Everett L. Worthington and Goli Sotoohi*	937
Chapter 439	Application of LCA to a Comparison of the Global Warming Potential of Industrial and Artisanal Fishing in the State of Rio De Janeiro (Brazil) *D. P. Souza, K. R. A. Nunes, R. Valle, A. M. Carneiro and F. M. Mendonça*	939
Chapter 440	The Effect of Sexually Explicit Rap Music on Sexual Attitudes, Norms, and Behaviors *Lucrezia M. Alcorn and Anthony F. Lemieux*	941
Chapter 441	Treatments for Cystic Fibrosis: The Role of Adherence, Importance and Burden *Lynn B. Myers*	943
Chapter 442	The Relationship between Adolescents' Music Video Viewing and Risky Driving: A Two Wave Panel Survey *Kathleen Beullens, Keith Roe and Jan Van den Bulck*	945
Chapter 443	Individuals with Eating Disorders and Stress *Christine Courbasson and Jenany Jeyarajan*	947
Chapter 444	Extraversion and the Autonomic Nervous System: An Alternative to Eysenck's Theory *David Lester*	949
Chapter 445	Extraversion and Interviewing for Employment *Joshua Fogel and Mayer Schneider*	951
Chapter 446	The Influence of Gender Stereotypes on Causal Attributions about Successful Leadership *R. Garcia-Retamero, S. M. Müller and E. López-Zafra*	953

Chapter 447	Athlete Performance, Coping and Anxiety: Clinical Issues for the Consultant *Thomas W. Miller*	955
Chapter 448	Cultural Factors Influencing Olive Oil Purchase Behaviour: Empirical Analysis Using Scanner Data *Juan Carlos Gázquez-Abad, Francisco J. Martínez-López and Juan Antonio Mondéjar-Jiménez*	957
Chapter 449	Family Stress and Psychological Adjustment among Welfare and Non Welfare Immigrants *Gila Markovizky, Doron Hadas and Miri Sarid*	959
Chapter 450	The Effects of Postpartum Depression on the Mother-Infant Relationship and Child Development *Deana B. Davalos, Alana M. Campbell and Amanda L. Pala*	961
Chapter 451	Treating a Clinical Sample of Highly Gifted Underachievers with Music Therapy an Exploratory Study *Lony Schiltz-Ludwig*	963
Chapter 452	Marital Patterns and Psychological Adjustment among Immigrants from Ethiopia and FSU *Gila Markovitzky and Hadas Doron*	965
Chapter 453	Family Stress and Psychological Adjustment among Welfare and Non Welfare Immigrants *Gila Markovizky, Hadas Doron and Miri Sarid*	967
Chapter 454	Memory for Object Location: Encoding Strategies in Children *Annalisa Lucidi, Clelia Rossi-Arnaud, Laura Pieroni and Vincenzo Cestari*	969
Chapter 455	Prevalence of Post Traumatic Stress and Emotional and Behavioral Problems among Israeli Adolescents Exposed to Ongoing Terrorism *Orna Braun-Lewensohn, Smadar Celestin-Westreich, Leon-Patrice Celestin, Dominique Verté and Ingrid Ponjaert-Kristoffersen*	971
Chapter 456	Extending the Stressor-Strain Perspective: A Review and Elaboration of the Possibility to Reverse Causality in Role Stress Models *Daniel Örtqvist and Joakim Wincent*	973
Chapter 457	Role Stress in Flexible and Creative Roles: Some Suggestions on How to Identify Positive Consequences *Joakim Wincent and Daniel Örtqvist*	975

Chapter 458	The Role of Contextual Cues and Logical Training in Differentiating Conditional from Biconditional Statements in Inference Task *Olimpia Matarazzo and Ivana Baldassarre*	977
Chapter 459	A Theoritical Review of Psychosocial Stress and Health *Yin Paradies*	979
Chapter 460	Empathy: Reflexions on a Concept *C. Boulanger and C. Lançon*	981
Chapter 461	Organizational Safety Climate: Impact of Gender on Perception of Workplace Safety *Seth Ayim Gyekye and Simo Salminen*	983
Chapter 462	His, Her and Their Perceptions of Family Life: A Comparative Analysis of Fathers, Mothers, and Adolescents *Liat Kulik*	985
Chapter 463	Case-Based Reasoning: A Theory for Learning through Problem-Solving *Michael Gr. Voskoglou*	987
Chapter 464	Extraversion and Perceived Energy: Direct and Indirect Impacts on Stress and Health *Dave Korotkov*	989
Chapter 465	Job Satisfaction and Organisational Commitment: The Effect of Gender *Norazah Mohd Suki and Norbayah Mohd Suki*	991
Chapter 466	The Impact of Emotional Intelligence on Nursing: An Overview *José María Augusto Landa and Esther López-Zafra*	993
Chapter 467	The Role of Dispositional Optimism in Health Related Quality of Life among Health Care Professionals with Musculoskeletal Pain *George N. Lyrakos and Georgia Kostopanagiotou*	995
Chapter 468	Method for Developing a Scale to Evaluate Maternal Psychological Status with Regard to Children's Oral Care *Naoki Kakudate*	997
Chapter 469	Moderating Effect of Concern for Face on Help Seeking Intention Who Experienced Intimate Partner Violence during Pregnancy: A Retrospective Cross-sectional Study *Ying Lau*	999

Chapter 470	Correlates of Antenatal Depressive Symptomatology among Chinese Women: A Longitudinal Study *Ying Lau*	1001
Chapter 471	New Model for Bilingual Minds in Sociolinguistic Variation Situations: Interacting Social and Linguistic Constraints *Rania Habib*	1003
Chapter 472	I Wouldn't Really Call it News: Audience Consumption of Physical Activity Research in the News Media *Guy Faulkner, Vanessa Richichi, Stephannie C. Roy and Sara-Jane Finlay*	1005
Chapter 473	An Ecological Interpretation of Teacher and Teaching Schemas as Cognitively Constructed by Candidates in Training *Calliope Haritos*	1007
Chapter 474	Analysis of the Genetics of Behaviour Using Animal Models *M. Murphy, Y. M. Wilson, A. J. Lawrence, T. C. Brodnicki and M. C. Jawahar*	1009
Chapter 475	Symbolic Persuasion and the Social Politics of Everyday Life *Hugh M. Lewis*	1011
Chapter 476	Reflections on the Past and Explorations of the Future: Understanding Food Consumption in Romantic Relationships *Jennifer Bonds-Raacke*	1013
Chapter 477	Aggressive Behavior of Drivers: A New Questionnaire Defining the Difference between Hostile and Instrumental Behavior While Driving *Lipaz Shamoa-Nir and Meni Koslowsky*	1015
Chapter 478	Religiosity and Youth Destructive Behaviors: A Meta-Analysis *Jerf W. K. Yeung, Howard Chi-ho Cheng, Freeman K. H. Chan and Yuk-chung Chan*	1017
Chapter 479	MMPI-2 Correlates of PTSD among Gulf War Combat Veterans *Shenell D. Evans, Samuel T. Gontkovsky and William R. Leber*	1019
Chapter 480	Cognitive Issues in Idiopathic Epilepsy *Sherifa A. Hamed*	1021
Chapter 481	Cultural Variation in Nightmare: A Content Analysis *Kuang-ming Wu and Ruth Chu-lien Chao*	1023
Chapter 482	Health-Related Internet Discussion Groups as a Source of Social Support *Craig D. Murray, Rachel van Schaick and Jezz Fox*	1025

Chapter 483	Metaphorical Sentence Processing and Topic Abstractness *Xu Xu and Lisa Paulson*	**1027**
Chapter 484	Structuring Thought: Four Unique Methods and the Challenge of Synthesis *Michael J. Hogan and Zachary Stein*	**1029**

PREFACE

This new book compiles biographical sketches of top professionals in the field of psychology, as well as research summaries from a number of different focuses in this important field.

PART 1 - RESEARCH BIOGRAPHIES

In: Psychology Research Biographies and Summaries
Editors: Nancy E. Wodarth and Alexis P. Ferguson
ISBN: 978-1-61470-491-1
© 2012 Nova Science Publishers, Inc.

Chapter 1

BIOGRAPHICAL SKETCH – PSYCHOLOGY RESEARCH

Lise Abrams

Affiliation: University of Florida

Address:
Department of Psychology, University of Florida, Gainesville, FL 32611-2250

Date of Birth: 2-2-70

Education:

University of California Los Angeles, Ph.D. in Cognitive Psychology, 1997, with a minor in Measurement and Psychometrics
University of California Los Angeles, M.A. in Cognitive Psychology, 1992
Pomona College, B.A. *cum laude* in double major Psychology and Mathematics, 1991

Research and Professional Experience:

Memory and language processes in young and older adults, specifically the processes involved in comprehending and retrieving words and the changes in these processes that occur with normal aging. Specific areas of interest include: (1) memory retrieval failures such as the tip-of-the-tongue states, which are naturally-occurring retrieval failures that are characterized by a temporary inability to recall a known word; and (2) language errors such as the production of spelling errors and homophone substitution errors.

Professional Appointments:

Undergraduate Coordinator, University of Florida, Department of Psychology, July 2008-Present

Associate Professor, University of Florida, Department of Psychology, August 2006-Present

Affiliate Professor, University of Florida, Department of Educational Psychology, 2007-2009

Director, Cognitive and Sensory Processes Doctoral Program, University of Florida, Department of Psychology, 2006-2008

Assistant Professor, University of Florida, Department of Psychology, December 1997-August 2006

Faculty Associate, University of Florida Center for Gerontological Studies, 1998-2006

Core Faculty, University of Florida Institute on Aging, 1999-2003 Visiting Lecturer, Pomona College, 1995

Honors:

Florida Blue Key Distinguished Mentor of Undergraduate Research Award, 2010

HHMI Science for Life Distinguished Mentor Award, 2010

Psi Chi / Psychology Club Professor of the Year Award, University of Florida, 2006-2007, 2008-2009

Anderson Scholar Faculty Honoree, 1999-2002, 2008, 2009

Who's Who of Emerging Leaders, 2007-2008

Sigma Xi Young Investigator Award, 2007

APA Division 20 and the Retirement Research Foundation Mentor Award in Adult Development and Aging, 2007

Who's Who of American Women, 2006-2007

Who's Who in American Education, 2006-2007

Women in Cognitive Science Mentorship Award, 2004

College of Liberal Arts and Sciences Teaching Award, University of Florida, 2001-2002

Who's Who in Science and Engineering, 1998-1999

Psychology Department Supplemental Dissertation Award, University of California Los Angeles, 1996-1997

National Science Foundation Graduate Fellowship, University of California Los Angeles, 1991-1995

William Lincoln Honnold Fellowship, Pomona College, 1991

Pew Foundation Undergraduate Summer Research Fellowship, Stanford University, June 1990-August 1990

Senior Prize in Psychology, Pomona College, 1991

Pomona College Scholar, 1989-1991

Publications Last 3 Years:

Abrams, L., & Farrell, M. T. (2011). Language processing in normal aging. In J. Guendouzi, F. Loncke, & M. J. Williams (Eds.), *The handbook of psycholinguistic and cognitive processes: Perspectives in communication disorders* (pp. 49-73). New York, NY: Psychology Press.

Bahrick, H. P., Baker, M. K., Hall, L. K., & Abrams, L. (2011). How should we define and differentiate metacognitions? In A. S. Benjamin (Ed.), *Successful remembering and successful forgetting: A Festschrift in honor of Robert A. Bjork* (pp. 329-346). New York, NY: Psychology Press.

Farrell, M. T., & Abrams, L. (2011). Tip-of-the-tongue states reveal age differences in the syllable frequency effect. *Journal of Experimental Psychology: Learning, Memory, and Cognition, 37,* 277-285.

Abrams, L., Farrell, M. T., & Margolin, S. J. (2010). Older adults' detection of misspellings during reading. *Journal of Gerontology: Psychological Sciences, 65B,* 680-683.

Abrams, L., & White, K. K. (2010). Influences of word frequency, context and age on spelling. In B. C. Fabini (Ed.), *Spelling skills: Acquisition, abilities and reading connection* (pp. 51-76). Hauppauge, NY: Nova Science Publishers, Inc.

White, K. K., Abrams, L, McWhite, C. B., & Hagler, H. L. (2010). Syntactic constraints in the retrieval of homophone orthography. *Journal of Experimental Psychology: Learning, Memory, and Cognition, 36,* 160-169.

Abrams, L. (2009). Exploring the generality of retest effects: Commentary on "When does age-related cognitive decline begin?" *Neurobiology of Aging, 30,* 525-527.

Margolin, S. J., & Abrams, L. (2009). Not may not be too difficult: The effects of negation on older adults' sentence comprehension. *Educational Gerontology, 35,* 306-320.

Trunk, D. L., & Abrams, L. (2009). Do younger and older adults' communicative goals influence off-topic speech in autobiographical narratives? *Psychology and Aging, 24,* 324-337.

White, K. K., Abrams, L., & Byrd, A. L. (2009). Generation, intentionality of processing at encoding and retrieval, and age-related associative deficits. *Memory, 17,* 481-492.

Abrams, L. (2008). Tip-of-the-tongue states yield language insights. *American Scientist, 96,* 234-239.

Abrams, L., Trunk, D. L., & White, K. K. (2008). Visual and auditory priming influences the production of low-frequency spellings. *Reading and Writing: An Interdisciplinary Journal, 21,* 745-762.

White, K. K., Abrams, L., & Zoller, S. M., & Gibson, S. M. (2008).Why did I right that? Factors that influence the production of homophone substitution errors. *The Quarterly Journal of Experimental Psychology, 61,* 977-985.

In: Psychology Research Biographies and Summaries
Editors: Nancy E. Wodarth and Alexis P. Ferguson
ISBN: 978-1-61470-491-1
© 2012 Nova Science Publishers, Inc.

Chapter 2

BIOGRAPHICAL SKETCH – PSYCHOLOGY RESEARCH

Dr. Xenia Anastassiou-Hadjicharalambous

Affiliation: Assistant Professor of Child Psychopathology, University of Nicosia

Address:
Dr. Xenia Anastassiou-Hadjicharalambous, CPsychol
Assistant Professor of Child Psychopathology
Department of Psychology
University of Nicosia
46 Makedonitissas Ave., P.O.Box 24005, 1700 NICOSIA CYPRUS
Tel: + 357 (0) 22 351274, Ext 112
Fax: + 357 (0) 22 353682
Email: hadjicharalambous.x@unic.ac.cy

Date of Birth: 15/2/71

Education: BSc, MSc, PhD

Research and Professional Experience:

Area of Concentration / Research Interests: Child Development and Psychopathology

Over 20 scholarly publications; over 30 conference presentations; Panel's Chair for over 4 conferences; Supervisor or external examiner for over 10 MSc/PhD dissertations/theses.

Professional Appointments:

Assistant Professor of Child Psychopathology, University of Nicosia, Cyprus

Honors:

Chartered Psychologist (C.Psychol.), The British Psychological society (BPS), UK.
Member, Division of Teachers and Researchers, BPS
Member, Society of Paediatric Psychology
Member, The Cyprus Psychological Association
Member, The Cyprus Association of Family Therapy
Editorial Board Member, Encyclopedia of Child Behavior and Development
Ad Hoc Editorial Consultant, Child Psychiatry and Human Development.

Publications Last 3 Years:

Chapters in Books

Anastassiou-Hadjicharalambous, X. (under preparation) Pediatric Psychoses: Causes, Diagnosis, Differential Diagnoses, Pathophysiology, Cognitive Aspects, Developmental Considerations, & Treatment. In Psychosis: Causes, Diagnosis and Treatment. Nova Science Publisher, Inc.

Anastassiou-Hadjicharalambous, X. & Essau, C., & (in press). Violence and abuse in Cyprus. To appear in A. Browne Miller (Ed.), Violence and abuse in society: Across time and nations. New York: Praeger-Greenwood Publishing Group.

Anastassiou-Hadjicharalambous, X. (in press) Childhood Psychosis. In S. Goldstein and J. Naglieri (Eds.), *Encyclopedia of Child Behavior and Development*. New York: Springer-Verlag.

Anastassiou-Hadjicharalambous, X. & Stylianou, M. (in press) Developmental Coordination Disorder. In S. Goldstein and J. Naglieri (Eds.), *Encyclopedia of Child Behavior and Development*. New York: Springer-Verlag

Anastassiou-Hadjicharalambous, X. & Stylianou, M. (in press) Double-blind Design. In S. Goldstein and J. Naglieri (Eds.), *Encyclopedia of Child Behavior and Development*. New York: Springer-Verlag

Anastassiou-Hadjicharalambous, X. & Georgiou, N. (in press) Emotional Disturbance. In S. Goldstein and J. Naglieri (Eds.), *Encyclopedia of Child Behavior and Development*. New York: Springer-Verlag

Anastassiou-Hadjicharalambous, X. & Stylianou M.,(in press) Longitudinal Methods. In S. Goldstein and J. Naglieri (Eds.), *Encyclopedia of Child Behavior and Development*. New York: Springer-Verlag.

Essau, C., & **Anastassiou-Hadjicharalambous, X.** (in press) Conduct Disorder and Oppositional Defiant Disorder. To appear in A.S. Davis (ed.), *The Handbook of Pediatric Neuropsychology*, Springer Publishing.

Christodoulou L., & **Anastassiou-Hadjicharalambous, X.** (in press) Maternal Smoking. In S. Goldstein and J. Naglieri (Eds.), *Encyclopedia of Child Behavior and Development*. New York: Springer-Verlag.

Hadjicosta, R., & **Anastassiou-Hadjicharalambous, X.** (in press) Maternal Alcohol Consumption. In S. Goldstein and J. Naglieri (Eds.), *Encyclopedia of Child Behavior and Development*. New York: Springer-Verlag.

Hadjicosta, R., & **Anastassiou-Hadjicharalambous, X.** (in press) Post-natal Depression. In S. Goldstein and J. Naglieri (Eds.), *Encyclopedia of Child Behavior and Development*. New York: Springer-Verlag.

Hadjicosta, R., & **Anastassiou-Hadjicharalambous, X.** (in press) Rett Syndrome. In S. Goldstein and J. Naglieri (Eds.), *Encyclopedia of Child Behavior and Development*. New York: Springer-Verlag.

Hadjicosta, R., & **Anastassiou-Hadjicharalambous, X.** (in press) Sociopathy. In S. Goldstein and J. Naglieri (Eds.), *Encyclopedia of Child Behavior and Development*. New York: Springer-Verlag.

Koulenti, T. & **Anastassiou-Hadjicharalambous, X.** (in press) Development of Guilt in the Child. Nova Science Publisher, Inc.

Koulenti, T., & **Anastassiou-Hadjicharalambous, X.** (in press) Emotional Connection, Parent-Child. In S. Goldstein and J. Naglieri (Eds.), *Encyclopedia of Child Behavior and Development*. New York: Springer-Verlag.

Koulenti, T., & **Anastassiou-Hadjicharalambous, X.** (in press) Non-normative Life Events. In S. Goldstein and J. Naglieri (Eds.), *Encyclopedia of Child Behavior and Development*. New York: Springer-Verlag.

Koulenti, T., & **Anastassiou-Hadjicharalambous, X.** (in press) Temper Tantrum. In S. Goldstein and J. Naglieri (Eds.), *Encyclopedia of Child Behavior and Development*. New York: Springer-Verlag.

Koulenti, T., & **Anastassiou-Hadjicharalambous, X.** (in press) Uninvolved Parents. In S. Goldstein and J. Naglieri (Eds.), *Encyclopedia of Child Behavior and Development*. New York: Springer-Verlag.

Papayiannis, S. & **Anastassiou-Hadjicharalambous, X.** (in press) Cross-cultural Studies. In S. Goldstein and J. Naglieri (Eds.), *Encyclopedia of Child Behavior and Development*. New York: Springer-Verlag.

Perdikogianni, M. & **Anastassiou-Hadjicharalambous, X.** (in press) Child Rearing Practices. In S. Goldstein and J. Naglieri (Eds.), *Encyclopedia of Child Behavior and Development*. New York: Springer-Verlag.

Perdikogianni, M. & **Anastassiou-Hadjicharalambous, X.** (in press) Childhood Amnesia. In S. Goldstein and J. Naglieri (Eds.), *Encyclopedia of Child Behavior and Development*. New York: Springer-Verlag.

Perdikogianni, M. & **Anastassiou-Hadjicharalambous, X.** (in press) Infantile Amnesia. In S. Goldstein and J. Naglieri (Eds.), *Encyclopedia of Child Behavior and Development*. New York: Springer-Verlag.

Phaedonos, P., & **Anastassiou-Hadjicharalambous, X.** (in press) Self-judgment. In S. Goldstein and J. Naglieri (Eds.), *Encyclopedia of Child Behavior and Development*. New York: Springer-Verlag.

Spirrison, C., & **Anastassiou-Hadjicharalambous, X.** (in press) Developmental Disabilities. In S. Goldstein and J. Naglieri (Eds.), *Encyclopedia of Child Behavior and Development*. New York: Springer-Verlag.

Stavrou, A., & **Anastassiou-Hadjicharalambous, X.** (in press) Infant Mortality. In S. Goldstein and J. Naglieri (Eds.), *Encyclopedia of Child Behavior and Development*. New York: Springer-Verlag.

Stylianou M., & **Anastassiou-Hadjicharalambous, X.** (in press) HELLP Syndrome. In S. Goldstein and J. Naglieri (Eds.), *Encyclopedia of Child Behavior and Development*. New York: Springer-Verlag.

Stylianou M., & **Anastassiou-Hadjicharalambous, X.** (in press) Unipolar Major Depression. In S. Goldstein and J. Naglieri (Eds.), *Encyclopedia of Child Behavior and Development*. New York: Springer-Verlag.

Stylianou M., & **Anastassiou-Hadjicharalambous, X.** (in press) Werner Syndrome. In S. Goldstein and J. Naglieri (Eds.), *Encyclopedia of Child Behavior and Development*. New York: Springer-Verlag.

Tsola, M.E., & **Anastassiou-Hadjicharalambous, X.** (in press) Indifferent Parenting Style. In S. Goldstein and J. Naglieri (Eds.), *Encyclopedia of Child Behavior and Development*. New York: Springer-Verlag.

Tsola, M.E., & **Anastassiou-Hadjicharalambous, X.** (in press) Psychosomatic. In S. Goldstein and J. Naglieri (Eds.), *Encyclopedia of Child Behavior and Development*. New York: Springer-Verlag.

Tsola, M.E., & **Anastassiou-Hadjicharalambous, X.** (in press) Self Identity, Sexual Abuse of Adolescents. In S. Goldstein and J. Naglieri (Eds.), *Encyclopedia of Child Behavior and Development*. New York: Springer-Verlag.

Tsola, M.E., & **Anastassiou-Hadjicharalambous, X.** (in press) Stranger Anxiety. In S. Goldstein and J. Naglieri (Eds.), *Encyclopedia of Child Behavior and Development*. New York: Springer-Verlag.

Thierbach, A, Misho C., & **Anastassiou-Hadjicharalambous, X.** (2010) Happiness in the Developing Child. In A. Makinen and P. Hájek (Eds.), *Psychology of Happiness* (pp95-107). Nova Science Publisher, Inc.

Anastassiou-Hadjicharalambous, X. & Stavrou, A. (2009) Marital Conflict and Child Maladjustment. In K.S. Pearlman (Ed.), *Marriage: Roles, Stability and Conflict*. Nova Science Publisher, Inc.

Anastassiou-Hadjicharalambous, X. (2009) Social Phobia in Children and Adolescents. In C.P. Axelby (Ed.), *Social Phobia: Etiology, Diagnosis and Treatment* (pp159-174). Nova Science Publisher, Inc.

Journal Articles – in print or submitted for publication (Accepted)

*	Journals (refereed)
**	Invited papers
***	Electronic Journal
****	Non-refereed Journals

* Essau, C, Guzmán, B. **Anastassiou-Hadjicharalambous, X.**, Pauli, G., Gilvarry, C. Bray, D. & Ollendick, H. (Manuscript under Review) Psychometric Properties of the Strength and Difficulties Questionnaire from Five European Countries.

* Essau, C, Sasagawa, S., **Anastassiou-Hadjicharalambous, X.**, Guzmán, B. Ollendick, H. (*2011*). Psychometric Properties of the Spence Child Anxiety Scale with Adolescents from Five European Countries. *Journal of Anxiety Disorders 25 (1):19-27.*

*Munoz, L. **Anastassiou-Hadjicharalambous, X.,** (In Press) Disinhibited Behaviors in Young Children: Relations with Impulsivity and Autonomic Psychophysiology. *Biological Psychology.*

* Essau, C., **Anastassiou-Hadjicharalambous, X.,** & Munoz, L. (revise & resubmit) Psychometric Properties of the Spence Children's Anxiety Scale (SCAS) in Cypriot children and adolescents.

* Essau, C., **Anastassiou-Hadjicharalambous, X,** & Munoz, L. (Manuscript under review) Psychometric Properties for the Screen for Child Anxiety Related Emotional Disorders (SCARED) in Cypriot children and adolescents.

**Anastassiou-Hadjicharalambous, X., Essau, C., Georgiou, G. (2009). Alcohol use and binge drinking in Cyprus. In A. Browne (Ed.), *The Praeger International Collection on Addictions, vol 1* (pp.157-171). Westport, CT: Praeger-Greenwood.

* **Anastassiou-Hadjicharalambous, X,** Warden, D. (2008). Physiologically-Indexed and Self -Perceived Affective Empathy in Conduct-Disordered Children High and Low on Callous-Unemotional Traits. (2008) *Child Psychiatry and Human Development, 39*(4), 503-517.

*** **Anastassiou-Hadjicharalambous, X,** Warden, D. (2008). Cognitive and Affective Perspective-taking in Conduct-disordered Children High and Low on Unemotional Traits. *Child and Adolescent Psychiatry and Mental Health, 2: 16.*

*** **Anastassiou-Hadjicharalambous, X,** Warden, D. (2008). Children's Hearth Rate and Vicariously Aroused Affect in Response to Others' Differing Emotional Experience. *The Open Psychology Journal 1,* 78-83.

*****Anastassiou-Hadjicharalambous, X.,** Warden, D. (2007). Convergence Between Physiological, Facial and Verbal Self-report Indices of Affective Empathy in Children. *Infant and Child Development*, 16, 237-254.

In: Psychology Research Biographies and Summaries
Editors: Nancy E. Wodarth and Alexis P. Ferguson
ISBN: 978-1-61470-491-1
© 2012 Nova Science Publishers, Inc.

Chapter 3

BIOGRAPHICAL SKETCH – PSYCHOLOGY RESEARCH

Professor Debra Anderson

Affiliation: Professor and Director of Research, Nursing and Midwifery, Queensland University of Technology

Academic Qualifications:

1999	**Doctor of Philosophy** in the field of Social and Preventive Medicine (University of Queensland)
1993	**Master of Nursing** (The Flinders University of South Australia)
1988	**Graduate Diploma of Nursing Studies (Education)** (Armidale College of Advanced Education)
1986	**Bachelor of Arts** (University of Queensland)
1982	**General Nursing Certificate** (Princess Alexandra Hospital)

Employment (University Sector):

2006 – 2010	**Associate Professor**
	School of Nursing and Midwifery
	Director of Academic Programs (Postgraduate)
	Nurse Practitioner Subject Area Coordinator
1995 - 2005	**Lecturer and Senior Lecturer positions,** QUT, Deakin University

Fellowships/Awards:

2009	**Nurse Scholar**, Nursing and Midwifery, Department of Human Resources for Heath, World Health Organisation Headquarters, Geneva, Switzerland
2007	**Vice-Chancellor's Performance Award**
2005	**Invitational Research Fellow**, Australian Academy of Science, Japanese Society for the Promotion of Science (JSPS) (Faculty of Medicine, Tohoku University, Japan)
2004	**Postdoctoral Summer Nursing Research Institute** (University of Pennsylvania, United States of America)
2003	**Visiting Fellow**, School of Nursing (University of Washington, United States of America)

Relevant Current Professional Leadership *(International)*:

Editorial Board: **Journal of Nursing Scholarship**

Board Member: **International Council of Women's Health Issues**

President: **STTI Phi Delta Nursing Honor Society Chapter-at-large chapter**

World Health Organization Team: **Strategic Directions for Nursing and Midwifery 2010-2015**

Selected Recent Research Grants: Competitive External Funding
1. 2011, *Indigenous Woman's health and diabetes*, Diabetes Australia (Qld), $20,000
2. 2009/2010, *A Behavioral Intervention for Managing Menopausal Symptoms in Women with Breast Cancer*, The Cancer Council Queensland, $130,825
3. 2009, *Development of cancer survivorship self management plans,* Australian Government Department of Health and Ageing Chronic Disease self-management lifestyle and risk modification grant project, $200,000
4. 2008, *A novel method for delivering a non pharmacological intervention for managing risk factors in women with a chronic disease: a randomized controlled trial*, ARC Linkage projects with APAI components, $162,395
5. 2008, *The neglected dimension of community livability: Impact on Social connectedness and active ageing*, ARC Linkage projects with APAI components, $391,123

Selected Recent Refereed Publications
1. World Health Organisation, WHO writing team, Yan, J., Chan, E., Phiri, M., Malvares, S., Aldarazi, F., Sivertesen, B., Suchaxaya, P., Fritsch, K., Nkowane, A., Largado, V., Land, S., <u>Anderson, D.</u>, *Nursing and Midwifery Services Strategic Directions, 2011-2015*, Health Professions Networks, Nursing and Midwifery Office, Department of Human Resources for Health, World Health Organization, 2010

2. Footitt, J, <u>Anderson, D.</u>, Associations between perception of wellness and health related quality of life, co-morbidities, modifiable life style factors and demographics in older Australians. Australasian Journal of Ageing (in press accepted 10 Jan, 2011)
3. Yang, U, Wang, H.H., <u>Anderson, D</u>. Immigration distress and associated factors among Vietnamese women in transnational marriages in Taiwan, Kaohsiung Journal of Medical Sciences, 2010
4. Anderson, R., <u>Anderson ,D.</u>, Hurst, C., "Modeling exercise and dietary changes among a sample of midlife Australian women", Maturitas ,2010, 67(2), pp.966-976
5. Xu, Q., <u>Anderson, D.</u>, "A Longitudinal Study of the Relationship between Lifestyle and Mental Health among Midlife and Older Women in Australia: findings from the Healthy Ageing of Women Study", Health Care for Women International, 2010, 31(12),pp.1082-1096
6. Smith-DiJulio, K., Windsor, C., <u>Anderson, D.</u>, "The Shaping of Midlife Women's Views of Health and Health Behaviors", Qualitative Health Research, 2010, 20(7), pp.966-976
7. Smith-DiJulio, K., <u>Anderson, D.</u>, Sustainability of a Multimodal Intervention to Promote Lifestyle Factors Associated with the Prevention of Cardiovascular Disease in Midlife Australian Women: A 5-year follow-up, Health Care for Women International, vol 30, No 12, 2009
8. <u>Anderson, D.</u>, Gardner, G., Ramsbotham, J., Tones, M., "E-Portfolios: towards a new innovation in nurse practitioner education", Australian Journal of Advanced Nursing, June 2009 Vol 26, Issue, 4 , 74-75Available: *http://www.ajan.com.au/Vol26/26-4_Anderson.pdf*
9. Gollschewski, S., Kitto, S., <u>Anderson, D.</u>, Lyons-Wall, P., "Women's perceptions and beliefs about the use of complementary and alternative medicines during menopause:, Complementary Therapies in Medicine (2008), 16, 163-168
10. Shiu-Yun, K.F., <u>Anderson, D.</u>, Courtney, M., & Wenbiao, H. (2007). The relationship between culture, attitude, social networks and quality of life in midlife Australian and Taiwanese citizens. Maturitas, 58, 285-295.
11. <u>Anderson, D.</u>, Yoshizawa, T., "Cross Cultural Comparisons of Health Related Quality of Life in Australian and Japanese Midlife Women: The Australian and Japanese Midlife Women's Health Study", Menopause – The Journal of the North American Menopause Society, Vol 14(4), July/August 2007; 697-707.
12. <u>Anderson, D.</u>, Mizzarri, K., Kain, V., Webster, J., "The effects of a multi-modal intervention trial to promote lifestyle factors associated with the prevention of cardio-vascular disease in menopausal and post menopausal Australian women", *Health Care for Women International*, 2006, , 27(3), p: 238-253
13. Mizzarri, K., <u>Anderson D.</u>, Barnes, M., The Relationship between Exercise, Body Mass Index and Menopausal Symptoms in Midlife Australian Women, The International Journal of Nursing Practice, Vol 12 No1, 2006, p: 28-34
14. Fu, K., <u>Anderson, D.</u>, Courtney, M., The relationship between country of residence, gender and the quality of life in Australian and Taiwanese midlife residents", Social Indicators Research, Springer, 2006, on-line DOI 10.1007/s11205-005-3002-8

In: Psychology Research Biographies and Summaries
Editors: Nancy E. Wodarth and Alexis P. Ferguson
ISBN: 978-1-61470-491-1
© 2012 Nova Science Publishers, Inc.

Chapter 4

BIOGRAPHICAL SKETCH - PSYCHOLOGY RESEARCH

Tamás Bödecs MD, PhD

Affiliation: Department of Midwifery, Institute of Nursing and Patient Care, Faculty of Health Sciences, University of Pécs

Address:
14 Jókai Road, Szombathely, 9700 HU
btamas@etk.pte.hu
Tel: 0036-94/311-170
Fax: 0036-94/316-820

Date of Birth: 08/08/1963

Education:

PhD degree	2006-2010
Pediatrician	1991
Medical University	1981-1987

Research and Professional Experience:

perinatal depression and anxiety, self-esteem, folate-intake, health-behavior in pregnancy

Publications Last 3 Years:

Tamás Bödecs, EnikÅ' Szilágyi, Péter Cholnoky, János Sándor, Xénia Gonda, Zoltán Rihmer, Boldizsár Horváth: Prevalence and psycho-social background factors of antenatal depression and anxiety in a population based Hungarian sample in the first trimester of pregnancy. Depression Research and Treatment (under submission)

Tamás Bödecs, Orsolya Máté, Boldizsár Horváth, Lajos Kovács, Zoltán Rihmer, Beata Sebestyén, Xénia Gonda, János Sándor: Barriers of antenatal folate-supplementation: The role of depression and trait-anxiety on periconceptional folate intake. Int J Psychiatr Clin Pract, **2010**; 14(2) 102-108

Tamás Bödecs, Boldizsár Horváth, EnikÅ' Szilágyi, Xénia Gonda Zoltán Rihmer, János Sándor: The effects of depression, anxiety, self-esteem, and health behavior on neonatal outcomes in a population based Hungarian sample. Eu J Obstet Gynecol Reprod Biol, **2010**; 154(1) 45-50. (DOI: 10.1016/j.ejogrb.2010.08021)

Tamás Bödecs M.D., Boldizsár Horváth M.D., Ph.D., EnikÅ' SzilágyiM.D., Marietta Diffellné Németh, János Sándor M.D., Ph.D.: Association between Health Beliefs and Health Behavior in Early Pregnancy. Matern Child Health J. 2010 Oct 19. [Epub ahead of print];

Beáta Sebestyén, Zoltán Rihmer, Lajos Bálint, Nóra Szókontor, Xénia Gonda, Béla Gyarmati, **Tamas Bödecs**, János Sándor: Gender differences in antidepressant use-related seasonality change in suicide mortality in Hungary, 1998-2006. The World Journal of Biological Psychiatry; **2010**; 11: 579-585

János Sándor, Éva Brantmüller, **Tamás Bödecs**, Lajos Bálint, Mária Szücs, Eszter Péntek: The introduction of call-recall method into national cancer screening program organization and the social gradient of participation. Studia Sociologia, **2008**; 2: 39-62.

Bödecs T, Horváth B. Associations between health-knowledge about pregnancy, openness towards sources of health-knowledge and peri-concepcional health-behavior in a Hungarian sample. (A várandóssággal kapcsolatos ismeretek, az ismeretek forrásai iránti nyitottság, és a periconcepcionális egészségmagatartás összefüggéseinek vizsgálata hazai mintán.) Egészségakadémia **2010**; 1(2): 89-98.

Bödecs Tamás, Horváth Boldizsár, Szilágyi EnikÅ', Diffelné Németh Marietta, Sándor János: Effects of anxiety, depression, self-esteem and social capital on health-beliefs and openness towards health-improving interventions among pregnant Hungarian women. (A szorongás, a depresszió, az önértékelés és a társadalmi tÅ'ke hatása várandósok egészség-képére és az egészségjavító intervenciók iránti nyitottságára.) Egészségfejlesztés, **2010**; 5-6 (30-38)

Bödecs Tamás, Horváth Boldizsár, Szilágyi EnikÅ', Diffelné Németh Marietta, Sándor János: Effects of anxiety, depression, self-esteem and social capital on the health-behavior in pregnancy. (A szorongás, a depresszió, az önértékelés és a társadalmi tÅ'ke hatása várandósok egészségmagatartására.) Mentálhigiéné és Pszichoszomatika, **2010**; 11(2): 17-30

Bödecs Tamás, Horváth Boldizsár, Szilágyi EnikÅ', Sándor János: Effect of demographic factors on folate-supplementation and health-behavior of pregnant women. (Demográfiai tényezÅ'k hatása a várandósok folsav-bevitelére és egészségmagatartására.) Orvosi Hetilap, **2010**; 151(12): 494-500

Bödecs T, Horváth B, Kovács L, Diffellné Németh M, Sándor J: *Prevalence of depression* (A várandósság alatti depresszió és szorongás gyakorisága az elsÅ' trimeszterben hazai mintán.) Orvosi Hetilap, **2009**; 150: 1888-1893.

Bödecs Tamás, Horváth Boldizsár, Kovács Lajos, Diffellné Németh Marietta, Sándor János: Effects of health-beliefs on the openness towards health-improving interventions in a sample of pregnant Hungarian women. Az egészségkép hatása az egészségjavító intervenciók iránti nyitottságra magyar várandósok körében. Egészségfejlesztés, **2009**. 5-6: 33-40

Bödecs T, Horváth B. Prevalence of antenatal depression in market economic countries. (review article) (Várandósság alatti depresszió elÅ'fordulási gyakorisága a fejlett országokban.) Magyar Epidemiológia, **2008**, 5: 15-22.

Bödecs T, Horváth B. Effects of antenatal depression on the prevalence of preterm birth and birth-weight. **(**Várandósság alatti depresszió hatása a koraszülési gyakoriságra és a születési súlyra.) (Review article) Magyar Epidemiológia, **2008**; 5: 23-29.

Bödecs Tamás, Cser Krisztina, Sándor János, Horváth Boldizsár: Effects of stress and coping strategies on the prevalence of depressive-somatoform symptoms in a Hungarian adolescent population. (A stressz és a coping stratégiák hatása a kevert depresszív - szomatoform tünetek gyakoriságára hazai serdülÅ' populációban.) Mentálhigiéné és Pszichoszomatika, **2009**; 10(1): 63-76.

Kirchfeld Á. - Schaffer É. - Puskás T. - Lórántfy M. - **Bödecs T**. Effects of hypothermia on the success of reanimation. (Reanimáció közben alkalmazott terápiás hipotermiával szerzett tapasztalataink.) *Aneszteziológia és intenzív terápia*, **2010**. (40. évf.) 2. sz. 77-80. Old

Csákváry V, Puskás T, **Bödecs T**, LÅ'csei Z, Oroszlán G, Kovács L G, Salamonné Toldy E: Investigation of adolescents' bone metabolism in the western part of Transdanubia. (SerdülÅ'k csontanyagcsere-markereinek vizsgálata a nyugat-dunántúli régióban.) Orvosi Hetilap, **2009**. 150: 1963-71.

Horváth B, Kovács L, Riba M, Farkas G, **Bödecs T**, Bódis J: *The metabolic syndrome* (Metabolikus tünet-együttes és egyes szülészeti szövÅ'dmények kapcsolata.) Orvosi Hetilap, **2009**; 150: 1361-5.

In: Psychology Research Biographies and Summaries
Editors: Nancy E. Wodarth and Alexis P. Ferguson

ISBN: 978-1-61470-491-1
© 2012 Nova Science Publishers, Inc.

Chapter 5

BIOGRAPHICAL SKETCH - PSYCHOLOGY RESEARCH

Shari L. Britner, Ph.D.

Affiliation: Bradley University

Address:
  4934 N. Woodview Ave., Peoria, IL 61614
  Research and Professional Experience:

Date of Birth: 8/10/54

Education: Ph.D. Emory University

Professional Appointments:

  2002 Present Department of Teacher Education, Bradley University, Peoria, IL.
  Tenured and promoted to Associate Professor Fall, 2008

Honors:

  Caterpillar Inc. Faculty Award for Scholarship, 2007, Bradley University
  Outstanding Faculty Researcher Award, College of Education and Health Sciences, Bradley University, 2007

Publications Last 3 Years:

Britner, S. L. (2010). Science anxiety: Relationship to achievement, self-efficacy, and pedagogical factors. In J. C. Cassady (Ed.) Anxiety in Schools (pp 80-94). New York: Peter Lang.

Britner, S. L. & Pajares, F. (2009). Science anxiety, self-efficacy, and self-concept of undergraduate biology students. In A. Selkirk & M. Tichenor (Eds.) Teacher education: Policy, practice and research (pp. 251-264). Hauppauge, NY: Nova Science Publishers.

Wolffe, R. J., Finson, K. D., Edgcomb, M. R., McConnaughay, K. D., & Britner, S. L. (2009). Developing inquiry skills along a teacher professional continuum. In Robert E. Yager (Ed.) Inquiry: The key to exemplary science (pp.83-94). Arlington, VA: National Science Teachers Association.

Zeldin, A. L., Britner, S. L., & Pajares, F. (2008). A comparative study of the self-efficacy beliefs of successful men and women in mathematics, science, and technology careers. Journal of Research in Science Teaching, 45, 1036-1058.

Britner, S. L. (2008). Motivation in high school science students: A comparison of life, physical, and Earth science classes. Journal of Research in Science Teaching, 45, 955-970.

Edgecomb, M., Britner, S. L., McConnaughay, K., & Wolffe, R. (2008). Science 101: An integrated, inquiry-oriented science course for education majors. Journal of College Science Teaching, 38(1), 22-27.

Wolffe, R. J., & Britner, S. L. (2008). Bradley University student teaching assessment specific to science programs. In A. E. Wise, P. Ehrenberg, & J. Leibbrand (Eds.) It's all about student learning: Assessing teacher candidates' ability to impact P-12 students. Washington, DC: National Council for the Accreditation of Teacher Education.

Previous self-efficacy related articles beyond the 3-years specified above:

Britner, S. L., & Pajares, F. (2006). Sources of science self-efficacy in middle school students. Journal of Research in Science Teaching, 43, 485-499.

Britner, S. L., & Pajares, F. (2001). Self-efficacy beliefs, race, gender, and gender orientation in middle school science. Journal of Women and Minorities in Science and Engineering, 7, 271-285.

Chapter 6

BIOGRAPHICAL SKETCH - PSYCHOLOGY RESEARCH

Dr. Amy Brogan

Affiliation: The University of Dublin, Trinity College, Dublin 2, Ireland.

Address: 40 Castleknock Drive, Castleknock, Dublin 15, Ireland.

Date of Birth: 12-08-1984

Education:

Amy Brogan was a foundation scholar of Trinity College Dublin where she completed her undergraduate degree in psychology in 2007, graduating with a gold medal. Since then, she was a scholar of the Irish Research Council for the Humanities and Social Sciences completing her PhD in 'Affective and Cognitive Influences on Decision Making in Obesity' in 2010.

Research and Professional Experience:

In completing her PhD, Amy has published in national and international peer-reviewed journals and has presented her research at numerous conferences at home and abroad. She is a graduate member of the Psychological Society of Ireland (PSI) and of the Division of Health Psychology.

Professional Appointments: None.

Honors:

Foundation Scholarship Trinity College Dublin, 2005 The Graduate's Prize in Psychology 2006, 2007, Psychological Society of Ireland Student Award 2007, Gold Medal in Psychology 2007, George White Memorial Award 2008. Government Scholarship from the Irish Research Council for the Humanities and Social Sciences 2008 - 2010,

Publications Last 3 Years:

-Brogan, A., Hevey, D., O'Callaghan, G. Yoder, R., O'Shea, D. (2011). Impaired decision making in morbidly obese adults. *The journal of Psychosomatic Research. 70 (2),* 189 – 196.

-Brogan, A., & Hevery, D. (2010). Network Analysis. In N. J. Salkind (Ed.), *Encyclopedia of Research Design* (pp. 1776). Kansas: Sage Publications Inc.

-Brogan, A., Hevey, D., & Pignatti, R. (2010). Anorexia, Bulimia, and obesity: Shared decision making deficits on the Iowa Gambling Task (IGT). *Journal of the International Neuropsychological Society, 16,* 1 – 5.

-Brogan, A., & Hevey, D. (2009). The Structure of the Causal Attribution Belief Network of Patients with Obesity. *British Journal of Health Psychology, 14,* 35 – 48.

-Mohan, A., Hevey, D., & Brogan, A. (2009). Community placement planning for a long stay in-hospital population. *Irish Journal of Psychological Medicine, 26*(1), 43 – 46.

In: Psychology Research Biographies and Summaries
Editors: Nancy E. Wodarth and Alexis P. Ferguson
ISBN: 978-1-61470-491-1
© 2012 Nova Science Publishers, Inc.

Chapter 7

BIOGRAPHICAL SKETCH – PSYCHOLOGY RESEARCH

John O. Brooks, III, Ph.D., M.D.

Affiliation: UCLA Medical School

Address: 760 Westwood Plaza, B-267, Los Angeles, CA. 90024

Date of Birth: 5/9/64

Education:

   Ph.D. Rice University
   M.D. Stanford University

Research and Professional Experience:

   I have been actively engaged in research in cognition with a focus on special psychiatric populations for almost 25 years. My research hasher includes investigations of implicit memory and other memory abilities in a variety of patient populations. Over the past six years my work has focused on advancing our understanding the neurophysiological substrates of bipolar disorder and their relation to cognitive deficits through the use of neuroimaging techniques.

Professional Appointments:

   Associate Professor, Dept of Psychiatry, UCLA Semel Institute

Honors:

American Psychological Assn. (APA) Dissertation Research Award, 1988
National Science Foundation (NSF) Graduate Fellowship, 1986-89

Publications Last 3 Years:

Brooks, J. O. III, Karnik, N. S., & Hoblyn, J. C. (2008). High initial dosing of olanzapine for stabilization of acute agitation: A retrospective case series. journal of Pharmacy Technology, 24, 7-11.

Ketter, T. A., Brooks, J. O. III, Hoblyn, J. C., Champion, L. M., Nam, J. Y., Culver, J. L., Marsh, W. K., & Bonner, J. C. (2008). Effectiveness of lamotrigine in a clinical setting. Journal of Psychiatric Research, 43, 13-23.

Brooks, J. O. III, Hoblyn, J. C., Woodward, S. A., Rosen, A. C., & Ketter, T. A. (2009). Corticolimbic metabolic dysregulation in euthymic older adults with bipolar disorder. Journal of Psychiatric Research, 43, 497-502.

Hoblyn, J.C., Balt, S.L., Woodard, S. A., & Brooks, J.O. III. (2009). Substance use disorders as risk factors for psychiatric hospitalization in bipolar disorder. Psychiatric Services, 60, 50-55.

Brooks, J. O. III, Wang, P. W., Bonner, J. C., Rosen, A. C., Hoblyn, J. C., Hill, S. J., & Ketter, T. K. (2009). Decreased prefrontal, anterior cingulate, insula, and ventral striatal metabolism in medication-free depressed outpatients with bipolar disorder. Journal of Psychiatric Research, 43, 181-188.

Brooks, J. O. III, Chang, H-S., & Kraznykh, O. (2009). Metabolic risks in older adults receiving second-generation antipsychotics. Current Psychiatry Reports, 11, 33-40.

Law, C. W. Y., Soczynska, J. K., Woldeyohannes, H. O., Miranda, A., Brooks, J. O. III, McIntyre, R. S. (2009). Relation between cigarette smoking and cognitive function in euthymic individuals with bipolar disorder. Pharmacology, Biochemistry and Behavior, 92, 12-16.

Gruber, J., Harvey, A. G., Wang, P. W., Brooks, J. O. III, Thase, M. E., Sachs, G. S., & Ketter, T. A. (2009). Sleep functioning in relation to mood, function, and quality of life at entry to the Systematic Treatment Enhancement Program for Bipolar Disorder (STEP-BD). Journal of Affective Disorders, 114, 41-49.

Goldberg, J. F., Brooks, J. O. III, Kurita, K., Hoblyn, J. C., Ketter, T. A., Ghaemi, N., Perlis, R. H., Miklowitz, D. J., Ketter, T. A., Sachs, G. S., & Thase, M. E. (2009). Depressive illness burden associated with complex polypharmacy in patients with bipolar disorder: Findings from the STEP-BD. Journal of Clinical Psychiatry, 70, 155-162.

Brooks, J. O. III, Bonner, J. C., Rosen, A. C., Wang, P. W., Hoblyn, J. C., Hill, S. J., & Ketter, T. K. (2009). Dorsolateral and dorsomedial prefrontal gray matter density changes associated with bipolar depression. Psychiatry Research: Neuroimaging, 172, 200-204.

Brooks, J. O. III, Hoblyn, J. C., Woodard, S. A., Rosen, A. C., Krasnykh, O., & Ketter, T. A. (2009). Resting prefrontal hypometabolism and paralimbic hypermetabolism related to verbal recall deficits in euthymic older adults with bipolar disorder. American Journal of Geriatric Psychiatry, 17, 1022-1029.

Rasgon, N., Kenna, H., Wroolie, T., Kelley, R., Silverman, D., Brooks, J. O. III, Williams, K., Powers, B., & Reiss, A. (2009). Insulin resistance and hippocampal volume in women at risk for Alzheimer's disease. Neurobiology of Aging.

Brooks, J. O. III, Hoblyn, J. C., & Ketter, T. A. (2010). Cerebral metabolic evidence of corticolimbic dysregulation in bipolar mania. Psychiatry Research: Neuroimaging, 181, 136-140.

Ketter, T. A., Brooks, J. O. III, Hoblyn, J. C., Holland, A. A., Nam, J. Y., Culver, J. L., Marsh, W. K., Bonner, J. C. (2010). Long-term effectiveness of quetiapine in bipolar disorder in a clinic setting. Journal of Psychiatric Research, 44, 921-929.

Brooks, J. O. III, , Bearden, C. E., Hoblyn, J. C., Woodard, S. A., & Ketter, T. A. (2010). Resting cerebral metabolism and sustained attention deficits in euthymic older adults with bipolar disorder. Bipolar Disorders, 12, 866-874.

Brooks, J. O. III, Goldberg, J. F., Ketter, T. A., Miklowitz, D. J., Calabrese, J. R., Bowden, C. L., & Thase, M. E. (2010). Safety and tolerability associated with second generation antipsychotic polytherapy in bipolar disorder: Findings from STEP-BD. Journal of Clinical Psychiatry, 72, 240-247.

Silverman, D. H. S., Geist, C. L., Kenna, H. A., Williams, K., Wroolie, T. Powers, B., Brooks, J., Rasgon, N. L. (2010). Differences in regional brain metabolism associated with specific formulations of hormone therapy in postmenopausal women at risk for AD. Psychoneuroendocrinology.

Brooks, J. O. III, Foland-Ross, L. C., Thompson, P. M., & Altshuler, L. L. (in press). Within-subject changes in gray matter density associated with remission of bipolar depression. Psychiatry Research: Neuroimaging.

In: Psychology Research Biographies and Summaries
Editors: Nancy E. Wodarth and Alexis P. Ferguson
ISBN: 978-1-61470-491-1
© 2012 Nova Science Publishers, Inc.

Chapter 8

BIOGRAPHICAL SKETCH – PSYCHOLOGY RESEARCH

Jane Bybee

Affiliation: Boston Leadership Institute

Address: JBybee@aya.yale.edu

Date of Birth: 12/19/59

Education:

Yale University, Department of Psychology, Ph.D. 1986, M.S. 1983
University of Virginia, Bachelor of Arts with High Honors, 1981

Research and Professional Experience:

Departmental Statistical Consultant; Chair, Departmental Research Committee; Chair, Departmental Child Clinical Committee; ad hoc reviewer for various professional journals

Professional Appointments:

Boston Leadership Institute (current) Founding Partner
Suffolk University (1998-2008)
    Associate Professor of Psychology
    Assistant Professor of Psychology
    Visiting Assistant Professor of Psychology
Northeastern University (1989-1998)

Assistant Professor of Psychology;
Yale School of Medicine, Yale Child Study Center (1986-1989)
NIMH Post-Doctoral Fellow

Honors:

Outstanding Faculty Nomination (2001-2002) Suffolk University
Excellence-in-Teaching Award (1994-1995) Northeastern University
Excellence-in-Teaching Nomination (1992-1993) Northeastern University
NIMH Post-Doctoral Fellow (1986-1989) Yale University
Fellow, Bush Center in Child Development and Social Policy (1983-1989) Yale University
NIMH Fellow (1981-1986) Yale University
Dean's List University of Virginia
Psi Chi Honor Society University of Virginia
Intermediate Honors Award University of Virginia

Publications Last 3 Years:

Bybee, J., & Wells, Y. (2006). Possible selves: Diverse perspectives across the life span. Journal of Adult Development, 13, 95-101.

Landa, C. E. & Bybee, J. A. (2007). Adaptive elements of aging: Self-image discrepancy, perfectionism, and eating problems. Developmental Psychology, 43, 83-93.

Donatelli, J. L., Bybee J. A., & Buka. S. L. (2007). What do mothers make adolescents feel guilty about? Incidents, reactions, and relation to depression. Journal of Child and Family Studies, 16, 859-875.

Bybee, J., Sullivan, E., Zielonka, E., & Moes, E. (2009). Are gay men in worse mental health than heterosexual men? The role of age, shame and guilt, and coming-out. Journal of Adult Development, 16, 144-154.

Chapter 9

BIOGRAPHICAL SKETCH – PSYCHOLOGY RESEARCH

Gianluca Campana

Affiliation: Department of General Psychology, University of Padova

Address: Via Venezia, 8 – 35131 Padova – ITALY

Date of Birth: 08th of April 1971

Education: PhD

Research and Professional Experience:

Mechanisms and levels of processing of visual and attentional processing. Visual motion. Visual awareness. Visual neurosciences. The role of past experience in visual perception, short- and long-term plasticity of the visual system (e.g.: visual priming, perceptual learning, visual motion aftereffects). Visual memory. Improvement of visual functions in patients with low vision via perceptual learning.

Professional Appointments: Assistant Professor

Publications Last 3 Years (2008-2011):

Pavan, A., Cuturi, F.L., Maniglia, M., Casco, C., & Campana, G. (2011). Implied motion from static photographs influences the perceived position of stationary objects. Vision Research, 51, 187-194.

Kristjansson, A, & Campana, G. (2010). Where perception meets memory: A review of repetition priming in visual search tasks. Attention, Perception & Psychophysics, 72, 5-18.

Alberti, C.F, Pavan, A., Campana, G., & Casco, C. (2010). Segmentation by single and combined features involves different contextual influences. Vision Research, 50, 1065, 1073.

Pavan, A., Campana, G., Maniglia, M., & Casco, C. (2010). The role of high-level visual areas in short- and longer-lasting forms of neural plasticity. Neuropsychologia, 48, 3069-3079.

Pavan, A., Campana, G., Guerreschi, M., Manassi, M., & Casco, C. (2009). Separate motion-detecting mechanisms for first- and second-order patterns revealed by rapid forms of visual motion priming and motion aftereffect. Journal of Vision, 9(11), 1-16.

Casco, C., Campana, G., Han, S. & Guzzon, D. (2009). Psychophysical and electrophysiological evidence of independent facilitation by collinearity and similarity in texture grouping and segmentation. Vision Research, 49(6), 583-593.

Cipolli, C., Campana, G., Campi, C., Mattarozzi, K., Mazzetti, M., Tuozzi, G., Vandi, S., Vignatelli, L., & Plazzi, G. (2009). Sleep and time course of consolidation of visual discrimination skills in patients with narcolepsy-cataplexy. Journal of Sleep Research, 18, 209-220.

Fuggetta, G., Lanfranchi, S., & Campana, G. (2009). Attention has memory: Priming for the size of attentional focus. Spatial Vision, 22, 147-159.

Campana, G. & Casco, C. (2009). Repetition effects of features and spatial position: evidence for dissociable mechanisms. Spatial Vision, 22, 325-338.

Campana, G. (2009). Visual Memory. In Goldstein, B. Encyclopedia of Perception (pp. 1093-1094), Sage Publications Inc., Thousand Oaks, CA.

Chapter 10

BIOGRAPHICAL SKETCH – PSYCHOLOGY RESEARCH

Kathleen A. Carroll

Affiliation: University of Maryland, Baltimore County (UMBC)

Address:
   Department of Economics, University of Maryland, Baltimore County, 1000 Hilltop Circle, Baltimore, MD 21250

Date of Birth: n/a

Education:

   Ph.D. Economics and Environmental Engineering, Johns Hopkins University; B.A. Economics, Cleveland State University

Research and Professional Experience:

   Kathleen Carroll does research in the areas of organization theory, decision analysis, and regulation. Her research focuses on the effects of institutional arrangements on decision processes; the way that multiple decision makers affect decision outcomes; and the impact of these conditions on predicted responses to regulations. She compares the outcomes due to institutional variations and multiple decision makers to predictions made under single decision maker, single objective, for-profit environments. Professional Appointments: Associate Professor, UMBC; Visiting Assistant Professor, Johns Hopkins University; Senior Economist, Hittman Associates Honors: University of Maryland Baltimore County, $5000 Economics Department Research Support awarded 2007 (Principal investigator)

Publications Last 3 Years:

"Modeling Internal Decision Process: An Explanation of Conflicting Empirical Results on Nonprofit and For-Profit Hospitals," Contemporary Economic Policy, (forthcoming) doi:10.1111/j.1465-7287.2010.00245.x (with Jane E. Ruseski); Book Review: Equal Play: Title IX and Social Change (2007: Philadelphia, PA: Temple University Press), edited by Nancy Hogshead-Makar and Andrew Zimbalist in J. Sports Econ 10, June 2009: 326-30.

Chapter 11

BIOGRAPHICAL SKETCH – PSYCHOLOGY RESEARCH

Kimberley A. Clow

Affiliation: University of Ontario Institute of Technology

Address: 2000 Simcoe Street North, Oshawa, ON, L1H 7K4

Date of Birth: September 28, 1974

Education: University of Western Ontario (PhD)

Research and Professional Experience:

Publications Last 3 Years:

Referenced Journal Articles (* Indicates a student author)
Bartfay, W.J., Bartfay, E., & Clow, K.A. (in press). Challenges faced by men in nursing. Nursing Management.
Ricciardelli, R., & Clow, K.A. (in press). The impact of an exonoree's guest lecture on students' attitudes toward wrongly convicted persons. Journal of Criminal Justice Education.
Clow, K.A., & Esses, V.M. (2010). Mental representation of familiar others: The impact of occupation, sex, and race. Basic and Applied Social Psychology, 32(2), 144-154.
Clow, K.A., & Olson, J.M. (2010). Conceptual-motor compatibility and homonegativity: Approaching and avoiding words associated with homosexuality. Canadian Journal of Behavioural Science, 42(4), 222-233.
*Ricciardelli, R., Clow, K.A., & White, P. (2010). Investigating hegemonic masculinity: Portrayals of masculinity in men's lifestyle magazines. Sex Roles, 63(1-2), 64-78.

Bartfay, W.J., Bartfay, E., Clow, K.A., & Wu, T. (2010). Attitudes and perceptions towards men in nursing education. Internet Journal of Allied Health Sciences and Practice, 8(2), 1-7.

*Ricciardelli, R., *Bell, J.G., & Clow, K.A. (2009). Student attitudes toward wrongful conviction. Canadian Journal of Criminology and Criminal Justice, 51(3), 411-430.

*Ricciardelli, R., & Clow, K.A. (2009). Men, appearance, and cosmetic surgery: The role of self-esteem and comfort with the body. Canadian Journal of Sociology, 34, 105-134.

Book Chapters:

Clow, K.A., Leach, A-M, & Ricciardelli, R. (in press). Consequences of wrongful conviction. In B.L. Cutler's (Ed.) Conviction of the Innocent: Lessons from Psychological Research. APA Books.

Clow, K.A., & Ricciardelli, R. (2011). Ambivalence in stereotypes and attitudes: The implications of possessing positive and negative perceptions. In E.L. Simon's (Ed.), Psychology of Stereotypes (pp. 243-264). New York: Nova Science Publishers, Inc.

In: Psychology Research Biographies and Summaries
Editors: Nancy E. Wodarth and Alexis P. Ferguson
ISBN: 978-1-61470-491-1
© 2012 Nova Science Publishers, Inc.

Chapter 12

BIOGRAPHICAL SKETCH – PSYCHOLOGY RESEARCH

Lindsey Cohen, PhD.

Affiliation: Georgia State University

Address: Dept of Psychology, Georgia State University, Atlanta, GA 30302-5010

Date of Birth: 6/24/68

Education: PhD

Research and Professional Experience:

Earned PhD in 1998; held tenure-track or tenured professor positions from 1998 – current

Professional Appointments: Associate Professor with Tenure; Director of Graduate Studies

Honors:

- Fellow, APA, Division 54 (Society of Pediatric Psychology) (8/10 – present) Awarded the Georgia State University Outstanding Faculty Achievement Award for Excellence in Research, Teaching, and Service (08-09)
- APA, Division 54 (Society of Pediatric Psychology) International Travel Award recipient (08)
- Awarded the David Parkin Visiting Professorship, University of Bath, England, United Kingdom (8/08 - 8/09)

Invited outside expert regarding pain management and participant retention for the National Institutes of Health project, The Environmental Determinants of Diabetes in the Young (TEDDY) (9/07)

Collaborated/mentored a medical colleague on a project, which was awarded "Young Investigator Award" from the Society of Pediatric Anesthesia/American Academy of Pediatric Anesthesiology (3/07)

APA, Division 54 (Society of Pediatric Psychology) Donald Routh Early Career Award Nominee (03)

Association for Advancement of Behavior Therapy (AABT) President's New Researcher Award (00)

Manuscript entitled 'Comparative study of distraction versus topical anesthesia for pediatric pain management during immunizations' selected by the Continuing Education Committee of APA Division 38 (Health Psychology) for outstanding scientific merit and clinical application (99)

Publications Last 3 Years:

Peer-Reviewed Journal Articles (student advisees indicated by asterisks)*

Baxter, A. L., Cohen, L. L., Lawson, M. L., von Baeyer, C. L. (in press). An integration of vibration and cold relieves venipuncture pain in a pediatric emergency department. *Pediatric Emergency Care.*

Masuda, A., Cohen, L. L., Wicksell, R., Kemani, M. K., & Johnson, A. (2011). Acceptance and Commitment Therapy for pediatric sickle cell disease: A case study. *Journal of Pediatric Psychology, 36,* 398-408.

Cohen, L. L., Vowles, K. E., & Eccleston, C. (2010). Parenting an adolescent with chronic pain: An investigation of how a taxonomy of adolescent functioning relates to parent distress. *Journal of Pediatric Psychology, 35,* 748-757.

Cohen, L. L., Vowles, K. E., & Eccleston, C. (2010). The impact of adolescent chronic pain on functioning: Disentangling the complex role of anxiety. *Journal of Pain, 11,* 1039-1046.

Cohen, L. L., Vowles, K. E., & Eccleston, C. (2010). Adolescent chronic pain-related functioning: Concordance and discordance of mother-proxy and self-report ratings. *The European Journal of Pain, 14,* 882-886.

Vowles, K. E., Cohen, L. L., McCracken, L. M., & Eccleston, C. (2010). Disentangling the complex relations among caregivers and adolescent responses to adolescent chronic pain. *Pain, 151,* 680-686.

Sadhasivam, S., Cohen, L. L., Hosu, L., Gorman, G., Wang, Y., Nick, T. G., Fang Jou, J., Samol, N., Szabova, A., Hagerman, N., Hein, E., Boat, A., Varughese, A., Kurth, C. D., Willging, P., & Gunter, J. (2010). Real-time assessment of perioperative behaviors in children and parents: Development and validation of the perioperative adult child behavioral interaction scale. *Anesthesia and Analgesia, 110,* 1109-1115.

*Cobb, J. E., & Cohen, L. L. (2009). A randomized controlled trial the ShotBlocker® for children's immunization distress. *Clinical Journal of Pain, 25,* 790-796.

Cohen, L. L., *MacLaren, J. E., *DeMore, M., *Fortson, B., *Friedman, A., *Lim, C. L., & Gangaram, B. (2009). A randomized controlled trial of vapocoolant for pediatric immunization distress relief. *Clinical Journal of Pain, 25,* 490-494.

Mularoni, P. P., Cohen, L. L., DeGuzman, M., *Mennuti-Washburn, J., Greenwald, M., & Simon, H. K. (2009). A randomized clinical trial of lidocaine gel for reducing infant distress during urethral catheterization. *Pediatric Emergency Care, 25,* 439-443.

McClellan, C. B., Cohen, L. L., & Moffett, K. (2009). Time-out based discipline strategy for children's noncompliance with cystic fibrosis treatment. *Disability and Rehabilitation, 31,* 327-336.

*Bernard, R. S., Cohen, L. L., & Moffett, K. (2009). A token economy for exercise adherence in pediatric cystic fibrosis: A single-subject analysis. *Journal of Pediatric Psychology, 34,* 354-365.

Sadhasivam, S., Cohen, L. L., Szabova, A., Varughese, A., Kurth, C. D., Willging, P., Wang, Y, Nick, T. G., & Gunter, J. (2009). Real-time assessment of perioperative behaviors and prediction of perioperative outcomes. *Anesthesia and Analgesia, 108,* 822-826.

*Vlahou, C. V., Cohen, L. L., *Woods, A., Gold, B., & Lewis, J. (2008). Age and Body Satisfaction Predict Diet Adherence in Adolescents with Inflammatory Bowel Disease. *Journal of Clinical Psychology in Medical Settings, 15,* 278-286.

Cohen, L. L. (2008). Behavioral approaches to anxiety and pain management for pediatric venous access. *Pediatrics, 122,* s1134-s139.

*Jones, T., *DeMore, M., Cohen, L. L., O'Connell, C., & Jones, D. J. (2008). Childhood healthcare experience, healthcare attitudes, and optimism as predictors of adolescents' healthcare behavior. *Journal of Clinical Psychology in Medical Settings, 15,* 234-240.

Blount, R. L., Simons, L. E., Devine, K. A., Jaaniste, T., Cohen, L. L., Chambers, C. T., & Hayutin, L. G. (2008). Evidence-Based Assessment of Coping and Stress in Pediatric Psychology. *Journal of Pediatric Psychology, 33,* 1021-1045.

Cohen, L. L., Lemanek, K., Blount, R. L., Dahlquist, L. M., *Lim, C. S., Palermo, T. M., McKenna, K. D., Weiss, K. E. (2008). Evidence-Based assessment of pediatric pain. *Journal of Pediatric Psychology, 33,* 939-955.

Cohen, L. L., La Greca, A. M., Blount, R. L., Kazak, A. E., Holmbeck, G. N., & Lemanek, K. L. (2008). Introduction to special issue: Evidence-based assessment in pediatric psychology. *Journal of Pediatric Psychology, 33,* 911-915.

*MacLaren, J. E., Cohen, L. L., Larkin, K. T., & Shelton, E. (2008). Training nursing students in evidence-based behavioral pediatric pain management techniques. *Journal of Nursing Education, 47,* 351-358.

Pillai Riddell, R. R., Stevens, B. J., Cohen, L. L., Flora, D. B., & Greenberg, S. (2007). Predicting maternal and behavioural measures of infant pain: The relative contribution of maternal factors. *Pain, 133,* 138-149.

Cohen, L. L., & MacLaren, J. E. (2007). Breaking Down the Barriers to Pediatric Procedural Preparation. *Clinical Psychology: Science and Practice, 14,* 144-148.

*McClellan, C. B., & Cohen, L. L. (2007). Family functioning in children with chronic illness compared with healthy controls: A critical review. *The Journal of Pediatrics, 150,* 221-223.

Schechter, N. L., Zempsky, W. T., Cohen, L. L., McGrath, P. J., McMurtry, M., & Bright, N. S. (2007). Pain reduction during pediatric immunizations: Evidence-based review and recommendations. *Pediatrics, 19,* e1184-1198.

MacLaren, J. E., & Cohen, L. L. (2007). Interventions for paediatric procedure-related pain in primary care. *Paediatrics and Child Health, 12,* 111-116.

Cohen, L. L. (2007). Introduction to the special series on pediatric pain: Contextual issues in children's pain management. *Children's Health Care, 36* (3), 197-202.

*MacLaren, J. E.., Cohen, L. L., & Cohen, S. (2007). Children's behavior during immunization injections: A principle components analysis. *Children's Health Care, 36* (3), 237-248.

Book Chapters and Other Publications (student advisees indicated by asterisks*)

Cohen, L. L., Joffe, N., & Welkom, J. (2011). Infusing diversity training in pediatric psychology training. *Progress Notes, 35,* 10.

Cohen, L. L. (2010). A multifaceted distraction intervention may reduce pain and discomfort in children 4-6 years of age receiving immunisation. *Evidence-based Nursing, 13,* 15-16.

Baxter, A., & Cohen, L. L. (2009). Pain management. In G. R. Strange, W. R. Ahrens, R. W. Schaftermeyer, & R. A. Wiebe (Eds.). *Pediatric emergency medicine, 3rd edition.* New York: McGraw Hill.

*Joffe, N. E., Cohen, L. L., *Bearden, D. J., & *Welkom, J. S. (2009). Behavioral approaches for infant pain relief. In. S. D'Alonso & K. L. Grasso (Eds.). *Acute pain: Causes, Effects and Treatment.* New York: Nova Science Publishers.

Bearden, D. J., Cohen, L. L., *Welkom, J. S., & *Joffe, J. E. (2009). Assessment of acute pediatric pain. In. S. D'Alonso & K. L. Grasso (Eds.). *Acute pain: Causes, Effects and Treatment.* New York: Nova Science Publishers.

Welkom, J. S., Cohen, L. L., *Joffe, N. E., & *Bearden, D. J. (2009). Psychological approaches to acute pediatric pain management. In. S. D'Alonso & K. L. Grasso (Eds.). *Acute pain: Causes, Effects and Treatment.* New York: Nova Science Publishers.

Blount, R. L., Zempsky, W. T., Jaaniste, T., Evans, S., Cohen, L. L., Devine, K. A., & Zeltzer, L. K. (2009). Management of pain and distress due to medical procedures. In M. C. Roberts & R. Steele (Eds.). *Handbook of pediatric psychology* (4th ed., pp. 171-188). New York: Guilford Press.

Cohen, L. L. (2009). Pediatric psychology across the pond. *Progress Notes, 33,* 12.

Cohen, L. L., & Baxter, A. (2008). Distraction techniques for procedural pain in children. *Medscape Pediatrics.* http://www.medscape.com/viewprogram/17791. Published November 25, 2008.

Cohen, L. L., & *Lim, C. S. (2008). The transition from supervisee to supervisor. In A. K. Hess, K. K. Hess, & T. H. Hess (Eds.). *Psychotherapy supervision: Theory, research, and practice, 2nd edition* (pp. 82-96). New York: Wiley.

Cohen, L. L., *MacLaren, J. E., & *Lim, C. S. (2008). Pain and pain management. In R. G. Steele, T. D. Elkin, & M. C. Roberts (Eds.). *Handbook of evidence based therapies for children and adolescents: Bridging science and practice* (pp. 283-296). New York: Springer Publishers.

Feinstein, A. B., Forman, E. M., Masuda, A., Cohen, L. L., Herbert, J. D., Moorthy, L. N., & Goldsmith, D. (in press). Pain intensity, psychological inflexibility, and acceptance of pain as predictor of functioning in adolescents with juvenile idiopathic arthritis: A preliminary investigation. *Journal of Clinical Psychology in Medical Settings.*

Chapter 13

BIOGRAPHICAL SKETCH – PSYCHOLOGY RESEARCH

Robert J. Cramer

Affiliation: Sam Houston State University

Address:
Department of Psychology, Sam Houston State University, Box 2447, Huntsville, TX 77341

Date of Birth: 1981

Education: Ph.D. Psychology (Clinical/Psychology-Law) University of Alabama

Research and Professional Experience:

Witness Research Lab (University of Alabama), and Department of Psychiatry at University of California San Francisco.

Professional Appointments: Assistant Professor at SHSU.

Honors:

Witness Self-Efficacy: Development and Validation of the Construct. (Primary Investigator). American Academy of Forensic Psychology Dissertation Grant: Spring, 2008 (Funded: $300)

The Five-Factor Model of Personality in Australian Criminal Defendants.(Primary Investigator).National Science Foundation/Australian Academy of Science East Asian and Pacific Summer Institute (EAPSI; Award no. OISE-0714111): Spring, 2007 (Funded: $7,500) (Co-PI Jack White, Ph.D.)

Factors Affecting Juror Perceptions of Hate Crimes.(Primary Investigator). American Psychology-Law Society Diversity Research Grant: Spring, 2006 (Funded: $1,000)

Predictors of Expert Witness Credibility: Juror Personality and Expert Witness Confidence. (Primary Investigator).American Psychology-Law Society Grant-in-aide: Spring, 2005 (Funded: $250)

Predictors of Expert Witness Believability: Juror Personality and Expert Witness Confidence. (Primary Investigator) American Society of Trial Consultants Research Grant: Spring, 2005 (Funded: $350)

Publications Last 3 Years:

Cramer, R.J., McNiel, D.E., Holley, S.R., Shumway, M., &Bocelarri.A. (In Press). Mental health outcomes and violent crime victimization: Does sexual orientation matter? *Law and Human Behavior.*

Lerner, U., Brooks, K., McNiel, D.E., **Cramer, R.J.**, & Haller, E. (In Press). Coping with patient suicide: A curriculum for psychiatry residency training programs.*Academic Psychiatry.*

McNiel, D.E., Hung, E.K., **Cramer, R.J.**, Hall, S.E., & Binder, R.L. (2011) An approach to evaluating competency in assessment and management of violence risk. *Psychiatric Services, 62,* 90-92.

Brodsky, S.L., Griffin, M.P., &**Cramer, R.J**. (2010). The Witness Credibility Scale: An outcome measure for expert witness research. *Behavioral Science & the Law, 28,* 892-907.

Cramer, R.J., Neal, T.M.S. DeCoster, J., & Brodsky, S.L. (2010).Witness Self-Efficacy: Development and validation of the construct.*Behavioral Sciences & the Law, 28,* 784-800.

Cramer, R.J., Chandler, J.F., &Wakeman, E.E. (2010). Attribution of blame as a moderator of assigning the death penalty in sexual-orientation based crimes. *Journal of Interpersonal Violence, 25,* 848-862.

Brodsky, S.L., Neal, T.M.S., **Cramer, R.J.**, &Ziemke, M.H. (2009). Credibility in the courtroom: How likeable should an expert witness be? *Journal of the American Academy of Psychiatry and Law, 37,* 525-532.

Cramer, R.J., Adams, D.D., & Brodsky, S.L. (2009). Jury selection in a child sex abuse trials: A case analysis. *Journal of Child Sexual Abuse, 18,* 190-205.

Cramer, R.J., Brodsky, S.L., &DeCoster, J. (2009). Expert witness confidence and juror personality: Their impact on credibility and persuasion in the Courtroom. *Journal of the AmericanAcademy of Psychiatry and the Law, 37,* 63-74.

Cramer, R.J., Neal, T.M.S., & Brodsky, S.L. (2009). Self-efficacy and confidence: Theoretical distinctions and implications for trial consultation. *Consulting Psychology Journal: Practice and Research, 61,* 319-334.

Prentice-Dunn, S., McMath, B.F., &**Cramer, R.J.** (2009).Protection motivation theory and stages of change in sun protective behavior.*Journal of Health Psychology, 14,* 297-305.

Shealy, R.C., **Cramer, R.J.**, & Pirelli, G. (2009). Third party presence during criminal forensic evaluations: Psychologists' opinions, attitudes and practices. *Professional Psychology: Research and Practice, 39(6),* 561-569.

In: Psychology Research Biographies and Summaries
Editors: Nancy E. Wodarth and Alexis P. Ferguson

ISBN: 978-1-61470-491-1
© 2012 Nova Science Publishers, Inc.

Chapter 14

BIOGRAPHICAL SKETCH – PSYCHOLOGY RESEARCH

James Danckert

Affiliation: Department of Psychology
University of Waterloo
200 University Avenue West
Waterloo, Ontario, N2L 3G1 CANADA

Address: Department of Psychology
University of Waterloo
200 University Avenue West
Waterloo, Ontario, N2L 3G1 CANADA

Date of Birth: 01 September 1972

Education:

BA (University of Melbourne); Masters in Clinical Neuropsyhology (La Trobe University);
PhD (La Trobe University)

Research and Professional Experience:

Completed my PhD in 2000. Completed a Postdoctoral Fellowship under Dr. Melvyn Goodale at the University of Western Ontario, with a smaller PDF stay in Lyon France under Dr. Yves Rossetti, all completed in 2002. Awarded a Canada Research Chair in 2002 in Cognitive Neuroscience. Have published 50 journal articles and 6 book chapters with an h index of 19 and a total citation count of more than 700.

Professional Appointments:

Assistant Professor in 2002; Associate Professor in 2007. Tier II Canada Research Chair in 2002 - present.

Honors:

Canada Research Chair (2002); Early Researcher Award (2007); Waterloo Region Record's Top 40 Under 40 (2009); several Postdoctoral Awards (Lyon Bourse, 2001; La Trobe and Howard Florey PDFs declined in 2002). External grants totalling more than $2 million dollars to date.

Publications Last 3 Years: (students supervised are underlined).

1. Goldberg, Y., Eastwood, J., LaGuardia, J., & **Danckert, J.** (in press). Boredom: an emotional experience distinct from apathy, anhedonia or depression. *Journal of Social and Clinical Psychology.*
2. Cavezian, C., Michel, C., Rossetti, Y., **Danckert, J.**, d'Amato, T., & Saoud, M. (in press). Visuospatial processing in schizophrenia : Does it share common mechanisms with pseudoneglect ? *Laterality.*
3. Hurwitz, M., Valadao, D., & **Danckert, J.** (2011) Dynamic judgments of spatial extent: dissociating hand-centered and gaze-centered reference frames. *Experimental Brain Research, 209,* 271-286.
4. **Valadao, D., Hurwitz, M.,** & Danckert, J. **(2010).** Examining the influence of 'noise' on judgments of spatial extent. *Experimental Brain Research, 207,* 157-164.
5. Merrifield, C., Hurwitz, M., & **Danckert, J.** (2010) Multimodal temporal perception deficits in a patient with left spatial neglect. *Cognitive Neuroscience, 1(4),* 244-253.
6. Striemer, C., & **Danckert, J.** (2010). Through a prism darkly: re-evaluating prisms and neglect. *Trends in Cognitive Sciences, 14,* 308-316.
7. **Danckert, J.**, & Culham, J.C. (2010). Reflections on blindsight: Neuroimaging and behavioural explorations clarify a case of reversed localisation in the blind field of a patient with hemianopia. *Canadian Journal of Experimental Psychology, 64,* 86-101.
8. Striemer, C., & **Danckert, J.** (2010). Dissociating perceptual and motor effects of prism adaptation in spatial neglect. *NeuroReport, 21,* 436-441.
9. **Locklin, J., Bunn, L.,** Roy, E.A., & **Danckert, J. (2010). Measuring Deficits in Visually Guided Action Post-Concussion. Sports Medicine, 40,** *183-187.*
10. Danckert, J., **Goldberg, L.,** & **Broderick, C. (2009). Damage to superior parietal cortex impairs pointing in the sagittal plane.** *Experimental Brain Research, 195, 183-191.*
11. Striemer, C., Locklin, J., Blangero, A., Rossetti, Y., Pisella, L., & **Danckert, J.** (2009). Attention for action? Examining the link between attention and visuomotor control deficits in a patient with optic ataxia. *Neuropsychologia, 47,* 1491-1499.
12. Striemer, C., Blangero, A., Rossetti, Y., Boisson, D., Rode, G., Salemme, R., Vighetto, A., Pisella, L., **Danckert, J.** (2008). Bilateral parietal lesions disrupt the

beneficial effects of prism adaptation: Evidence from a patient with optic ataxia. *Experimental Brain Research, 187,* 295-302.
13. **Danckert, J.,** Ferber, S., & Goodale, M.A. (2008) Direct effects of prismatic lenses on visuomotor control: an event-related functional MRI study. *European Journal of Neuroscience, 28,* 1696-1704.
14. Vasquez, B., & **Danckert, J.** (2008). Direction specific costs to spatial working memory from saccadic and spatial remapping. *Neuropsychologia, 46,* 2344-2354.

Chapter contribution for the proposed book entitled "The Psychology of Neglect" to be published by Nova Publishers.

Title: Neglect as a disorder of representational updating.

In: Psychology Research Biographies and Summaries
Editors: Nancy E. Wodarth and Alexis P. Ferguson
ISBN: 978-1-61470-491-1
© 2012 Nova Science Publishers, Inc.

Chapter 15

BIOGRAPHICAL SKETCH – PSYCHOLOGY RESEARCH

James A. Danowski

Affiliation: University of Illinois at Chicago

Address: Department of Communication, MC 132, Chicago, 60607

Date of Birth: August 2, 1949

Education: Ph.D., Communication, Michigan State University, 1975

Research and Professional Experience:

Publications Last 3 Years:

Danowski, J. A., Riopelle, K., & Gluesing, J. (2011). The revolution indiffusion models caused by new media: The shift from s-shaped to convexcurves. In G.A. Barnett & A. Vishwanath (Eds.) Advances in the study of the diffusion of innovations: Theory, methods, and applications. New York:Peter Lang Publishing.

Danowski, J. A. (2011). Counterterrorism mining for individuals semantically-similar to watch list members. U. K. Wiil (Ed.). Counterterrorism and open-source intelligence. Berlin: Springer.

Danowski, J. A. (2011). Mining social networks at the organizational level. In I-Hsien Ting, Tzung-Pei Hong and Leon S.L. Wang (Eds.) Socialnetwork mining, Analysis and research trends: Techniques and applications. Hershey, PA: IGI-Global.

Danowski, J. A., & Cepela, N. (2010). Automatic mapping of social networks of actors from text corpora: Time series analysis, in Memon, N., Jie Xu, J., Hicks, D. L., & Chen, H. (Eds.) Data mining for social network data. Annals of information science, 12, (pps. 31-46). New York: Springer Science+Business Media.

Barnett, G.A., Danowski, J. A., Feeley, T., & Stalker, J. (2010). Measuring the quality of doctoral programs in communication. Journal of Communication, 60(2), 388-411.

Danowski, J. A. (2010). Inferences from word networks in messages. In K. Krippendorff & M. Bock (Eds.) The content analysis reader (pp. 421-430). Sage Publications.

Danowski, J. A. & Park, D.W. (2009). Networks dead or alive: Public intellectuals in the mass and internet media. New Media and Society,11(3), 337-356.

Danowski, J. A. (2008). Short-term and long-term effects of a public relations campaign on semantic networks of newspaper content: Priming or framing? Public Relations Review, 34(3), 288-290.

Zywica, J. & Danowski, J. (2008). The faces of facebookers: Investigating social enhancement and social compensation hypotheses; predicting Facebook™ and offline popularity from sociability and self-esteem, and mapping the meanings of popularity with semantic networks. Journal of Computer-Mediated Communication, 14(1), 1-34.

Danowski, J. A. (2008). Evaluative word locations in semantic networks from news stories about Al Qaeda and implications for optimal communication messages in anti-terrorism campaigns. In Ortiz-Arroyo, D. et al (Eds.) Intelligence and Security Informatics: EuroISI 2008, LNCS 5376 (pp. 271-273). Berlin Heidelberg: Springer-Verlag.

In: Psychology Research Biographies and Summaries
Editors: Nancy E. Wodarth and Alexis P. Ferguson
ISBN: 978-1-61470-491-1
© 2012 Nova Science Publishers, Inc.

Chapter 16

BIOGRAPHICAL SKETCH – PSYCHOLOGY RESEARCH

María Luisa Sanz de Acedo Lizarraga

Titles: Self-regulation and Executive functions

Date of Birth: 09-10-1944

Contact Points: Public University of Navarre

Education: Phd of thinking skills and creativity

Research and Professional Experience: Interventions in Thinking Skills and Creativity.

Publications last 3 Years:

Books
1. Sanz de Acedo Lizarraga, M. L., y Sanz de Acedo Baquedano, M. T. (2007). **Creatividad individual y grupal en la educación**. Madrid: Ediciones Internacionales Universitarias, EIUNSA (pp. 182). ISBN: 978-84-8469-198-3.
2. Sanz de Acedo Lizarraga, M. L. (2010). **Competencias cognitivas en el Espacio Europeo de Educación Superior**. Madrid: Ediciones Narcea (pp. 160). ISBN: 978-84-1690-2.

Charters in books:
1. Sanz de Acedo Lizarraga, M. L., Sanz de Acedo Baquedano, M. T., y Ardaiz O. (2010). Self-regulation of learning supported by Web 2.0 tools: An example of the

competence of creativity and innovation. G. Dettori & D. Persico (Eds.). *Fostering self-regulated learning through ICTs* (pp. 295-314). Hershey, PA: IGI Global.
2. Cardelle-Elawar, M., y <u>Sanz de Acedo Lizarraga, M. L</u>. (2010). Self-regulation and WebQuest. A model to transform learning to teach. In J. De la Juente (Ed.). *Handbook on applying self-regulated learning in different settings* (pp. 425-442). Almeria: Education & Psychology.

Articles

1. <u>Sanz de Acedo Lizarraga, M. L</u>., y Sanz de Acedo Baquedano, M. T. (2008). Instrucciones explícitas para la ejecución creativa según dos tests de creatividad teniendo en cuenta la inteligencia. *Anales de Psicología, 24(1),* 129-137. ISSN: 1695-2294.
2. <u>Sanz de Acedo Lizarraga, M. L</u>., Sanz de Acedo Baquedano, M. T., Soria Oliver, M., y Closas, A. (2009). Dvelopment and validation of a decisión-making questionnaire. *British Journal of Guidance & Counselling, 37(3)*, 357-373. ISSN 0306-9885.
3. <u>Sanz de Acedo Lizarraga, M. L</u>., Sanz de Acedo Baquedano, M. T., Goicoa, T., y Cardelle-Elawar, M. (2009). Enhancement of thinking skills: Effects of two intervention methods. *Thinking Skills and Creativity 4(1)*, 30-43. ISSN: 1871-1871.
4. <u>Sanz de Acedo Lizarraga, M. L</u>., Sanz de Acedo Baquedano, M. T., Soria Oliver. M. (2010). Stimulation of Thinking Skills in High School Students. *Educational Studies, 36*(3), 329-340. ISSN: 1465-3400.
5. <u>Sanz de Acedo Lizarraga, M. L</u>., Sanz de Acedo Baquedano, M. T., Soria Oliver, M. (2010). Psychological Intervention in Thinking Skills with Primary Education Students. *School Psychologial International. 31*(2), 131-145. ISSN: 0967-0734.
6. <u>Sanz de Acedo Lizarraga, M. L</u>., Sanz de Acedo Baquedano, M. T., y Pollán Rufo, M. (2010). Effects of an instruction method in thinking with students from compulsory secondary education. *The Spanish Journal of Psychology, 13*(1), 126-136. ISSN: 1138-7416.
7. Cardelle-Elawar, M., y <u>Sanz de Acedo Lizarraga, M. L</u>. (2010). Looking at teacher identity through self-regulation. *Psicothema, Vol. 22*(2), 293-298. ISSN: 0214-9915.
8. <u>Sanz de Acedo Lizarraga, M. L</u>., y Sanz de Acedo Baquedano, M. T. (2010). Cognitive and emocional variables in university students. *Studia Psicologica. 52*(1), 41-51. ISSN: 1138-7416.
9. Humberto Closas, A., <u>Sanz de Acedo Lizarraga. M. L</u>., y Ugarte, M. D. (2011). Explanatory Model of the Relations Between Cognitive and Motivational Variables and Academic Goals. *Revista de Psicodidáctica, 16*(1). ISSN: 1136-1034. Impress.
10. <u>Sanz de Acedo Lizarraga, M. L</u>., y Sanz de Acedo Baquedano, M. T. (2011). Effects of analogical reasoning on open problem solving. *School Psychology International.* IImpress.
11. <u>Sanz de Acedo Lizarraga, M. L</u>., y Sanz de Acedo Baquedano, M. T., Closas, A. (2011). Development and Validation of a Questionnaire to Assess Analogy and Creativity in Open Problem-Solving. *Studia Psychology.* Impress.
12. Sanz de Acedo Baquedano, M. T., <u>Sanz de Acedo Lizarraga, M. L</u>., y Ardaiz, O. (2011). Efectos de variables tecnológicas y de la titulación universitaria en la creatividad ideacional. *Anales de Psicología.* Impress.

13. Sanz de Acedo Lizarraga, M. L., Ardaiz O., y Sanz de Acedo Baquedano, M. T. (2011). Evaluation of Computer Tools for the Idea Generation and Project Group Formation. *Computers and Education.* Impress.
14. Sanz de Acedo Baquedano, M. T., y Sanz de Acedo Lizarraga, M. L. (2011). Un estudio correlativo y predictivo entre creatividad y personalidad con alumnos universitarios. *Spanish Journal of Psychology*. Impress.

In: Psychology Research Biographies and Summaries
Editors: Nancy E. Wodarth and Alexis P. Ferguson
ISBN: 978-1-61470-491-1
© 2012 Nova Science Publishers, Inc.

Chapter 17

BIOGRAPHICAL SKETCH – PSYCHOLOGY RESEARCH

Laurie Elit

Affiliation: McMaster University, Hamilton, Canada

Address: 699 Concession Street, Hamilton, Ontario, Canada, L8V 5C2

Date of Birth: 24 Jun 1960

Education:

Doctor of Medicine 1984 Western University, London Canada. MSc in the Dept of Epidemiology and Biostatistics at McMaster University 1995

Research and professional experience:

Clinical trials and Health services research in gynecologic malignancies and preinvasive disease of the gynecologic tract. Qualitative research in treatment decision making in ovarian cancer and ethics of international work in low resource countries.

Professional Appointments: Professor in the Dept of Ob Gyn, McMaster University

Honors: -none

Publications:

Howard, M., Koteles, J., Lytwyn, A., **Elit, L.**, Kaczorowski,J., Randazzo,J. Giving patients information on abnormal cytology and human papillomavirus: survey of health providers. Eur J Gyn Onc 2007;28(1):15-17

Elit, L., Ziztelsberger L, Fung Kee Fung M, Brouwers M, Graham ID, Browman G, Hoskins P, Lau S. and the Society of Gynecologic Oncology Canada. Use of Systemic Therapy in Women with Recurrent Ovarian Cancer – Development of a National Clinical Practice Guideline. Gyn Onc 106(1):2007, 181-192 IF 2.919

Hirte HW, Strychowsky JE, Oliver T, Fung-Kee-Fung M, **Elit L**, Oza AM. Chemotherapy for Recurrent, Metastatic, or Persistent Cervical Cancer: A Systematic Review. Int J Gynecol Cancer. 17:1194-1204;2007 IF=1.932

Elit, L., Julian, J., Sellors, J., Levine, M. Colposcopist agreement study on worst site to biopsy on the cervix. Clinical and Experimental Obstetrics and Gynecology 34(2):2007, 88-90

Elit, L., Fung-Kee-Fung M, Oliver T, Jolicoeur L, Le T. Intraperitoneal chemotherapy for women with stage 3 epithelial ovarian cancer: Improving survival outcomes for patient. The American Journal of Hematology/Oncology 2007 Aug 6(8):459-464 IF 2.126

Fung-Kee-Fung M, Oliver T, **Elit L**, Oza A, Hirte HW, Bryson P. The optimal chemotherapy treatment for women with recurrent ovarian cancer: a clinical practice guideline. Curr Oncol. 2007 Aug;14(5):195-208.

Lytwyn A, **Elit L,** Sellors J. Letter to the editor re: Franco article of 18Oct2007 Human Papillomavirus DNA versus papanicolaou screening tests for cervical cancer. New England Journal of Medicine. 2008 Feb 7;358(6):641; author reply 643 IF 50.017

Barbera L, Thomas G, **Elit L**, Covens A, Fyles A, Osborne R, Yn L. Treating Vulvar Cancer in the New Millennium: Are Patients receiving optimal care? Gynecologic Oncology 109(1);71-75,2008 IF 2.919

Ceballos KM, Chapman W, Daya D, Julian J, Lytwyn A, McLachlin CM, **Elit L.** Reproducibility of the histological diagnosis of cervical dysplasia among pathologists from four continents. Int J Gyne Path 27(1);101-107, 2008 IF 1.766

Oza AM, Eisenhauer EA, **Elit L**, Cutz J, Sakurada A, Tsao MS, Hoskins PJ, Biagi J, Ghatage P, Mazurka J, Provencher D, Dore N, Dancy J, Fyles A. Phase 2 study of Erlotinib (Tarceva, OSI 774) in Women with recurrent or metastatic endometrial cancer. A trial of the National Cancer Institute of Canada Clinical Trials Group (NCIC IND 148) JCO 2008 Sep 10:26(26):4319-25 IF=17.157

Elit,L., Bondy, S., Paszat, L., Chen, Z., Hollowaty, E., Thomas, G., Levine, M. Outcomes in Surgery for Ovarian Cancer. Canadian Journal of Surgery 2008;51(5)346-354 IF 0.961

Elit L, Schultz S, Prysbysz R, Saskin R, Gunraj N, Wilton A, Urbach D. Patterns of Care for the Initial Management of Ovary Cancer in Ontario. EJGO 30(4):2009, 261-264

Elit L, Schultz S, Prysbysz R, Kwon J., Saskin R, Gunraj N, Wilton A, Urbach D. Patterns of Surgical Care for Uterine Cancer in Ontario. EJGO 30(3):255-8,2009

Elit L, Charles C, Dimitry S, Tedford-Gold S, Gafni A, Gold I, Whelan T. It's a choice to move forward: women's perceptions about treatment decision making in recurrent ovarian cancer. accepted PsychOncol 2010;19(3)318-325 IF 3.150,

Foster WG, Elias R, Faghih M, Dominguez M, **Elit L**, Boutross-Tadross O. Immunohistochemical localization of tyrosine receptor kinases A and B (Trk A and Trk

B) in endometriosis associated ovarian cancer (EAOC). Histopathology 54(7):907-12, 2009 Jun IF 4.131

Elit L, Schultz S, Prysbysz R, Barbera L., Saskin R, Gunraj N, Wilton A, Urbach D. Patterns of Care for the Initial Management of Cervical Cancer in Ontario. EJGO 30(5):2009, 493-496

Elit L, Schultz S, Prysbysz R, Barbera L., Saskin R, Gunraj N, Wilton A, Urbach D. Patterns of Surgical Care for the Initial Management of Vulva Cancer in Ontario. EJGO30(5):2009, 503-505

Finch A, Metcalfe K, Lui J, Springate C, Demsky R, Armel S, Rosen B, Murphy J, **Elit L**, Sun P, Narod S. Breast and ovarian cancer risk perception after prophylactic salpingo-oophorectomy due to an inherited mutation in the BRCA1 or BRCA2 gene. Social and Behavioural Research in Clinical Genetics 2009;75:220-224

Kwon J, **Elit L**, Saskin R, Hodgson D, Grunfeld E. Opportunities for secondard cancer prevention after endometrial cancer. Obstet Gynecol. 2009 Apr;113(4):790-795. IF=3.81

M. Fung-Kee-Fung, R.I. Howlett, T. Oliver, J. Murphy, **L. Elit**, J. Strychowsky, N. Roth, P. Bryson, C.M. McLachlin, M. Bertrand MD, M. Shier M, E. McMahon, S. McFaul, B. McAuley, R. Cosby The Optimum Organization for the Delivery of Colposcopy Service in Ontario: A Systematic Review JLTGD 2010; 14(1)

Elit L, Schultz S, Simunovic M, Urbach D,. Who are the providers of gynecologic oncology surgery in Ontario? JOGC 31(8): 721-729, 2009

Elit L, Fyles A, Fung-Kee-Fung M, Oliver T, and the Gynecology Cancer Disease Site Group. Follow-up for women after treatment for cervical cancer: A systematic review. Gynecol Oncol. 2009 Sep;114(3):528-35 IF=17.157

Elit L. Role of Professional Societies in the global battle against Gynecologic Cancers. Distinguished Expert Series. EJGC 30(6):605-608, 2009

MC Gainford, A Tinker, J Carter, E Petru, J Nicklin, M Quinn, I Hammond, **L Elit**, M Lenhard, M Friedlander. Malignant Transformation within Ovarian Dermoid Cysts. An Audit of Treatment Received and Patient Outcomes. A Gynaecologic Cancer Intergroup (GCIG) Study. Internation Journal of Gynecologic Cancer 2010;20(1):75-81

Elit L, Fyles A, Fung-Kee-Fung M, Oliver T, and the Gynecology Cancer Disease Site Group. Follow-up for women after treatment for cervical cancer: A systematic review. Current Oncology 2010;17(3):65-9

Halla S. Nimeiri, Amit M. Oza, Robert J. Morgan, Dezheng Huo, **Laurie Elit,** James A. Knost, James L.Wade III, Edem Agamah, Everett E. Vokes, Gini F. Fleming. A Phase II Study of Sorafenib in Advanced Uterine Carcinoma / Carcinosarcoma: A Trial of the Chicago, PMH, and California Phase II Consortia. Gyn Onc 2010;117:37-40

Bentley J, Diener T, **Elit L***. Cervical Cancer: Worldwide Health Priority. Canadian Journal of Diagnosis. Feb 2010, 51-56

Elit L, Trim K, Mohan R, Harnish D, Nastos S. Knowledge, Attitudes and Behaviour of Health Sciences University Students concerning HPV. Clinical Medicine: Reproductive Update. 2009;3:1-8

Mittmann N, Au HJ, Tu D, O'Callaghan CJ, Isogai PK, Karapetis CS, Zalcberg JR, Evans WK, Moore MJ, Siddiqui J, Findlay B, Colwell B, Simes J, Gibbs P, Links M, Tebbutt NC, Jonker DJ; Working Group on Economic Analysis of National Cancer Institute of Canada Clinical Trials Group; Australasian Gastrointestinal Interest Group. Prospective cost-effectiveness analysis of cetuximab in metastatic colorectal cancer: evaluation of

National Cancer Institute of Canada Clinical Trials Group CO.17 trial. J Natl Cancer Inst. 2009 Sep 2;101(17):1182-92. Epub 2009 Aug 7.

Barbera L, **Elit L**, Krzyzanowska M, Saskin R, Bierman A. End of life care for women with Gynecologic Cancer. Results from the Project for an Ontario Women's Health Evidence-based Report Card (POWER) Study. Gynecologic Oncology 118(2) (2010), pp. 196-201

L.Schwartz, C.Sinding, M.Hunt, **L.Elit**, L.Redwood-Campbell, N.Adelson, L.Luther, J.Ranford, S.DeLaat. Ethics in humanitarian aid work: Learning from the narratives of humanitarian aid health workers. The American Journal of Bioethics. *AJOB Primary Research*, 2150-7724, Volume 1, Issue 3, 01 July 2010, Pages 45 – 54

Christina Sinding, Lisa Schwartz, Matthew Hunt, Lynda Redwood-Campbell, **Laurie Elit**, Jennifer Ranford. "Playing God because you have to": Canadian health professionals' experiences of rationing care in humanitarian and development work Public Health Ethics 2010;1-11 doi: 10.1093/phe/phq015

Elit L, Rosen B, Jimenez W, Giede C, Cybulska P, Dodge J, Erdenejargal A, Omenge E, Bernardini M, Finlayson S, McAlpine J, Miller D for the International Community of Practice Committee of the Society of Gynecologic Oncology of Canada. Teaching Cervical Cancer Surgery in Low or Middle Resource Countries IJGC 2010:20(9);

Elit L, Levine M, Julian J, Sellors H, Lytwyn A, Gu C, Finch T, Zeferino L, Bentley J, Chong S, Mahony J. Expectant management versus immediate treatment for low-grade cervical intraepithelial neoplasia: A randomized trial in Canada and Brazil. Accepted Cancer 2010Nov8

Welch S, Hirte H, **Elit L**, Schilder RJ, Wang L, Kovacs J, Wright J, Oza AM. Sorafenib in combination with gemcitabine in recurrent epithelial ovarian cancer – a study of the Princess Margaret Hospital Phase II Consortium. IJGC 2010;20(5):787-793

Hoskins P, Vergote I, Cervantes A, Tu D, Stuart G, Zola P, Poveda A, Provencher D, Katsaros D, Ojeda B, Ghatage P, Grimshaw R, Casado A, **Elit L**, Mendiola C, Sugimoto A, D'Hondt V, Oza A, Germa JR, Roy M, Brotto L, Chen D, Eisenhauer EA. Advanced Ovarian Cancer: Randomized Study of Sequential

Cisplatin –Topotecan/Carboplatin-Paclitaxel versus Carboplatin-Paclitaxel. A Gynecologic Cancer Intergroup Study of the NCIC Clinical Trials Group (NCIC CTG), the European Organization for Research and Treatment of Cancer) - Gynecologic Cancer Group (EORTC-GCG) and the Grupo de Investigación de Cáncer de Ovario (GEICO). JNCI 102;20;1547-56

Elit, L., Krzyzanowski M, Saskin R, Barbera L, Razzaq A, Yertsinia A, Beirman A. Sociodemographic factors associated with cervical cancer screening and followup of abnormal results in a population-based cohort. Canadian Family Physician Accepted Oct2010

J.E. Kurtz, M.C. Kaminsky, A. Floquet, A.S. Veillard, R. Kimmig, A. Dorum, **L. Elit**, M. Buck, E. Petru, N. Reed, G. Scambia, N. Varsellona, C. Brown, E. Pujade-Lauraine, on behalf of Gynecologic Cancer Intergroup (GCIG) Ovarian Cancer in Elderly Patients: Carboplatin and Pegylated Liposomal Doxorubicin versus Carboplatin and Paclitaxel in Late Relapse: A GCIG CALYPSO Sub-study. Accepted in Annals of Oncology Dec2010

Finch A, Metcalfe KA, Chiang JK, **Elit L**, McLaughlin J, Springate C, Demsky R, Murphy J, Rosen B and Narod SA The impact of prophylactic salpingo-oophorectomy on menopausal symptoms and sexual function in women who carry a BRCA mutation. Gyn Onc 2011 Jan 7

Elit, L., Charles C, Gafni A. Treatment decision making in Ovarian Cancer. Psicooncologia 2010;7(2-3):269-286

Elit L, Hunt M, Redwood-Campbell L, Ranford J, Luther L, Adelson N, Schwartz L.Ethical issues experienced by medical students during international health electives (IHE). Medical Education Accepted Dec 2010

Kollmannsberger C, Hirte H , Siu LL, Mazurka J, Chi K, **Elit L,** Walsh W, Sederias J, Chen H, Eisenhauer EA, Oza AM. Temsirolimus in combination with carboplatin and paclitaxel in patients with advanced solid tumors: A NCIC-CTG phase I, open-label, dose escalation study (IND 179)Accepted Annals of Oncology Feb2011

In: Psychology Research Biographies and Summaries
Editors: Nancy E. Wodarth and Alexis P. Ferguson
ISBN: 978-1-61470-491-1
© 2012 Nova Science Publishers, Inc.

Chapter 18

BIOGRAPHICAL SKETCH – PSYCHOLOGY RESEARCH

Stephen Erdle, PhD

Affiliation: Huron University College at the University of Western Ontario, London, Ontario, Canada

Address: Huron University College, 1349 Western Road, London, Ontario, Canada, N6G 1H3

Date of Birth: 22/05/1958

Education: PhD in Psychology from the University of Western Ontario, 1986.

Research and Professional Experience:

25 years as researcher and instructor of Psychology at Huron University College Professional Appointments: Associate Professor in the Department of Psychology at Huron University College

Publications Last 3 Years:

Erdle, S., Gosling, S. D. & Potter, J. (2009). Does self-esteem account for the higher-order factors of the Big Five? Journal of Research in Personality, 43, 921-922.

Erdle, S., Irwing, P., Rushton, J. P., & Park, J. (2010). The General Factor of Personality and its relation to self-esteem in 628,640 internet respondents. Personality and Individual Differences, 48, 343-346.

Erdle, S. & Rushton, J. P. (2010). The General Factor of Personality, BIS-BAS, expectancies of reward and punishment, self-esteem, and positive and negative affect. Personality and Individual Differences, 48, 762-766.

Rushton, J. P. & Erdle, S. (2010). No evidence that social desirability reponse set explains the General Factor of Personality and its affective correlates. Twin Research and Human Genetics, 13, 131-134.

Erdle, S. & Rushton, J. P. (2011). Does self-esteem or social desirability account for a general factor of personality (GFP) in the Big Five? Personality and Individual Differences, 50, 1152-1154.

In: Psychology Research Biographies and Summaries ISBN: 978-1-61470-491-1
Editors: Nancy E. Wodarth and Alexis P. Ferguson © 2012 Nova Science Publishers, Inc.

Chapter 19

BIOGRAPHICAL SKETCH – PSYCHOLOGY RESEARCH

Nicolas Fieulaine

Titles: Dr, Associate Professor

Date of Birth: 04/24/1976

Contact Points:

Institute of Psychology
Social Psychology Research Group (GRePS, EA 4163)
University of Lyon – FRANCE
5, avenue Pierre Mendès-France - 69676 Bron cedex - FRANCE
Tel. : (+33) 478 772 619
Fax : (+ 33) 478 742 217
Mail : Nicolas.Fieulaine@univ-lyon2.fr
Web : http://fieulaine.socialpsychology.org/
http://recherche.univ-lyon2.fr/greps

Education:

Master degree in social psychology from Toulouse Le-Mirail University in 2000; Doctoral degree for the University of Provence in 2006.

Research and Professional Experience:

Lecturer at University of Lyon, from 2004 to 2006
Research Fellow, Lyon town council, from 2006 to 2007
Associate Professor, University of Lyon, from 2007 to date

Professional Appointments:

Dean for International Exchanges, Institute of Psychology, University of Lyon
Vice-Dean of undergraduates studies, Institute of Psychology, University of Lyon
Executive director of the "Applied Social Psychology" Professional Master degree

Honors:

Since 2006, I was awarded by Research Grants form Minister of Justice, National Health Institute, Town Council of Lyon, Regional Council for Universities and Research. I was elected for the best poster presentation at the European Health Psychology Society conference in 2005

Publications Last 3 Years:

- Fieulaine, N. & Martinez, F. (2010). Time under control : Time perspective and Desire for Control in Substance Use.Addictive Behaviors, 35/8, 799-802.
- Kalampalikis, N., Haas, V., Fieulaine, N., Doumergue, M.,Deschamps, G. & Chiron, H. (2010). Enjeux psychosociaux du don de sperme : le point de vue des couples [Psychosocial aspects of sperm donation : the couples point of view]. Andrologie, 20, 37-44.
- Sircova, A., Zimbardo, P.G., Boyd, J.N., Fieulaine, N., & al. (2007). The Phenomenon of Time Perspective across Different Cultures : Review of Researches Using ZTPI Scale. Journal of Cultural-Historical Psychology, 4, 18-35.
- Fieulaine, N. & Apostolidis, T. (2007). Time perspective in socially deprived contexts and psychological health. Health Psychology Review, 1-1, 62.
- Fieulaine, N., Apostolidis, T., & Olivetto, F. (2006). Précarité et troubles psychologiques : l'effet médiateur de la perspective temporelle. Les Cahiers Internationaux de Psychologie Sociale, 72, 51-64.
- Apostolidis, T., Fieulaine, N., & Soulé, F. (2006). Future time perspective as predictor of cannabis use : Exploring the role of substance perception among French adolescents. Addictive Behaviors, 31 (12), 2339-2343.
- Apostolidis, T., Fieulaine, N., Rolland, G., & Simonin, L. (2006). Cannabis use, Time Perspective and risk perceptions : Evidence of a moderating effect. Psychology & Health, 21, 571-592.
- Apostolidis, T., & Fieulaine, N. (2004). Validation française de l'échelle de temporalité : The Zimbardo Time Perspective Inventory. Revue Européenne de Psychologie Appliquée, 54 (3), 207-217.

In: Psychology Research Biographies and Summaries ISBN: 978-1-61470-491-1
Editors: Nancy E. Wodarth and Alexis P. Ferguson © 2012 Nova Science Publishers, Inc.

Chapter 20

BIOGRAPHICAL SKETCH – PSYCHOLOGY RESEARCH

Trude Furunes [First Author]

Affiliation: University of Stavanger, Norway

Address: UiS, 4036 Stavanger, Norway

Date of Birth: 14th June 1975

Education: PhD in Leadership

Publications Last 3 Years:

Furunes, T., Mykletun, R. J., & Solem, P. E. (2011). Age Management in the Public Sector: Managers' Decision Latitude, *International Journal of Human Resource Management*, forthcoming.

Furunes, T. & Mykletun, R.J. (2011). Managers' Decision Latitude for Age Management: Do managers and employees have the same (implicit) understanding? In Ennals & Salomon (Eds.), *Older Workers in a sustainable society*, Oslo, forthcoming.

Mykletun, R. J., & Furunes, T. (2011). The Ageing Workforce Management Program in Vattenfall AB Nordic, Sweden: Concluding report. In Ennals & Salomon (Eds.), *Older Workers in a sustainable society*, Oslo, forthcoming.

Mykletun, R. J., & Furunes, T. (2011). The Vattenfall 80-90-100 working schedule as an age management tool: A four year follow-up study. In Nygård et al. (Eds.), Age management during the life course, Tampere, forthcoming.

Furunes, T., & Mykletun, R.J. (2010). Do managers' perceptions coincide with established stereotyping of older workers' capabilities, In Simon, E.L. (ed.) *Psychology of Stereotypes,* Nova Science Publishers.

Furunes, T., & Mykletun, R.J. (2010). Age Discrimination in the Workplace: validation of the Nordic Age Discrimination Scale (NADS). *Scandinavian Journal of Psychology,* 51, 23-30.

Furunes, T., & Mykletun, R. J. (2009). Managers' decision making latitudes in relation to managing ageing workers. In M. Kumashiro (Ed.), *Promotion of Work Ability: Towards Productive Aging*. Hanoi, Vietnam: Taylor & Francis, 177-181.

Mykletun, R. J., & Furunes, T. (2009). Promoting health and workability in Vattenfall AB Nordic, Sweden. In M. Kumashiro (Ed.), *Promotion of Work Ability: Towards Productive Aging*. Hanoi: Taylor & Francis, 169-175.

Chapter 21

BIOGRAPHICAL SKETCH – PSYCHOLOGY RESEARCH

Janet M. Gibson, Ph.D.

Affiliation: Grinnell College

Address: Dept. of Psychology, Grinnell College Grinnell IA 50112

Date of Birth: July, 1959

Education: Ph.D., Rice University

Research and Professional Experience: Professor of Psychology

Professional Appointments: Grinnell College faculty since 1989

Honors: cum laude, Temple University B.A.

Publications Last 3 Years:

Macan, T. H., Gibson, J. M., & Cunningham, J. (2010). Will you remember to read this article later when you have time? The relationship between prospective memory and time management. Journal of Personality and Individual Differences, 48, 725-730.

Gibson, J. M., Dhuse, S., Hrachovec, L., & Grimm, L. R. (2010). Priming insight in groups: Facilitating and inhibiting solving an ambiguously-worded insight problem. Memory & Cognition. 39, 128-146. http://dx.doi.org/10.3758/s13421-010-0014-7

Gibson, J. M., Macan, T., Potter, K., & Cunningham, J. . (2011). In an ideal world self-report scales predict memory experimental data. Cognitive Technology, 15, 44-60.

In: Psychology Research Biographies and Summaries
Editors: Nancy E. Wodarth and Alexis P. Ferguson
ISBN: 978-1-61470-491-1
© 2012 Nova Science Publishers, Inc.

Chapter 22

BIOGRAPHICAL SKETCH – PSYCHOLOGY RESEARCH

Yigal Goldshtrom

Affiliation: Pillar of Light

Address: 37-03 Berdan Ave, Fair Lawn, NJ

Date of Birth: 9/14/51

Education: Health Psychology, PhD

Research and Professional Experience: Rhythmic exercises, Rehabilitation of Neurological patients

Publications Last 3 Years:

1. Goldshtrom, Y., Knorr, G., & Goldshtrom, I. (2010). Rhythmic Exercises in Rehabilitation of TBI Patients: A case report. Journal of Bodywork and Movement Therapies, 14(4). doi: 10.1016/j.jbmt.2009.06.002
2. Goldshtrom, Y., Korman, D., Goldshtrom, I., & Bendavid, J. (2011). The effect of rhythmic exercises on cognition and behaviour of maltreated children: A pilot study. Journal of Bodywork and Movement Therapies, In Press, Corrected Proof. doi: 10.1016/j.jbmt.2010.06.006

In: Psychology Research Biographies and Summaries
Editors: Nancy E. Wodarth and Alexis P. Ferguson
ISBN: 978-1-61470-491-1
© 2012 Nova Science Publishers, Inc.

Chapter 23

BIOGRAPHICAL SKETCH – PSYCHOLOGY RESEARCH

Lidan Gu

Affiliation: Department of Educational Psychology, University of Minnesota

Address: 250 Education Sciences Bldg
56 East River Road
Minneapolis, MN
55455-0364 USA

Date of Birth: 05/14/1979

Education:

Doctoral Student, Department of Educational Psychology, University of Minnesota, 2007 – Present
Master of Education, Department of Psychology, South China Normal University (China), 2001 – 2004
Bachelor of Science, Department of Psychology, South China Normal University (China), 1997 – 2001

Research and Professional Experience:

Dissertation Research. Project: Delay Discounting as a Measure of Impulsivity. Mentor: Angus W. MacDonald, III, PhD. Spring 2010 — Current.
Lab research. Project: Persecutory Ideation and the Medial Prefrontal Cortex, Mentor: Angus W. MacDonald, III, PhD, Fall 2009 – Spring 2010.
Pre-dissertation research. Project: Boundary Issues and Multiple Relationships in Genetic Counseling Supervision. Mentor: Pat McCarthy Veach, PhD. 2007 – 2009.

Publications Last 3 Years:

Gu, L., McCarthy Veach, P., Callanan, N., Eubanks, S., & LeRoy, B.S. (2011). Boundary Issues and Multiple Relationships in Genetic Counseling Supervision: Supervisor, Non-supervisor, and Student Perspectives. *Journal of Genetic Counseling. 20(1),* 35-48.

Huang, G., Gu, L. (2009). Risk Perception in Health Service. *Psychological Science (China),* 32, 688-690.

In: Psychology Research Biographies and Summaries ISBN: 978-1-61470-491-1
Editors: Nancy E. Wodarth and Alexis P. Ferguson © 2012 Nova Science Publishers, Inc.

Chapter 24

BIOGRAPHICAL SKETCH – PSYCHOLOGY RESEARCH

Dr. Sylvia Maria Gustin

Affiliation: Department of Anatomy and Histology, School of MedicalSciences, University of Sydney, Australia

Address: University of Sydney, Dep. of Anatomy & Histology, School of Medical Sciences, NSW 2006 Australia

Date of Birth: 26.09.1974

Education: PhD in Natural Sciences, Masters of Psychology, Bachelor of Psychology

Research and Professional Experience:

I have two streams of interest and expertise. My primary clinical interest is the application of clinical psychological approaches to the treatment of chronic pain. I have had extensive clinical training and possess vast experience inclinical psychology from leading German research institutes and much of this work has involved pain management. My primary scientific interest is to explore the brain mechanisms that underlie chronic pain using new and innovative imaging techniques such as spectroscopy, functional or structural magnetic resonance imaging. I have received extensive training in Germany and Australia in magnetic resonance imaging, yielding in a strong history of publications in the field of functional and structural magnetic resonance imaging.

Professional Appointments: Clinical Research Fellow, Clinical Psychologist

Honors:

Recipient of a clinical research fellowship from the NSW Spinal Cord Injury and Related Neurological Conditions Research Grant Program, Australia; recipient of an early career researcher grant from the University of Sydney, Australia

Publications Last 3 Years:

1. Gustin S.M., Peck, C.C., Wilcox S.L., Nash, P.G, Murray, G.M. and Henderson, L.A. Different pain, different brain: thalamic anatomy in neuropathic and non-neuropathic chronic pain syndromes. Journal of Neuroscience, 2011, 1(16): 5956 - 64.
2. Gustin S.M., Wilcox, S.L. Peck C.C. Murray G.M. and Henderson L.A. Similarity of suffering: equivalence of psychological and psychosocial factors in neuropathic and non-neuropathic orofacial pain patients. Pain, 2011, 152 (4): 825 - 832.
3. Henderson L.A., Gustin S.M., Macey, P.M., Wrigley, P.J and Siddall P.J. Functional reorganization of the brain in humans following spinal cord injury: Evidence for underlying changes in cortical anatomy. Journal of Neuroscience, 2011,31 (7): 2630 - 2637.
4. Gustin S.M., Schwarz A., Birbaumer N., Sines N., Schmidt A.C., Veit R., Larbig W., Flor H., Lotze M. NMDA-receptor antagonist and morphine decrease CRPS-pain and cerebral pain representation. Pain, 2010, 148 (3): 438 - 445.
5. Nash P.G., Macefield V.G., Klineberg I.J., Gustin S.M., Murray G.M., Henderson L.A. Changes in Human Primary Motor Cortex Activity During Acute Cutaneous and Muscle Orofacial Pain. Journal ofOrofacial Pain, 2010, 24 (3): 379 - 390.
6. Gustin S.M., Wrigley P.J., Henderson L.A., Siddall P.J. Braincircuitry underlying pain in response to imagined movement in people with spinal cord injury. Pain, 2010, 148 (3): 438 ? 445.
7. Gustin, S.M., Wrigley, P.J., Siddall, P.J. and Henderson, LA. Brain anatomy changes associated with persistent neuropathic pain following spinal cord injury Cerebral Cortex, 2010, 20 (6): 1409 - 1419.
8. Nash P.G., Macefield V.G., Klineberg I.J., Gustin S.M., Murray G.M., Henderson L.A. Bilateral activation of the trigeminothalamic tract by acute orofacial cutaneous and muscle pain in humans. Pain, 2010, 151 (2): 384 ? 393.
9. Wrigley, P.J., Press, S.R., Gustin, S.M., Macefield, V.G., Gandevia, S.C., Cousins, M.J., Middleton, J.W., Henderson, L.A., Siddall, P.J. Neuropathic pain and primary somatosensory cortex reorganization following spinal cord injury. Pain, 2009, 141 (1-2): 52 ? 59.
10. Wrigley, P., Gustin, S.M., Macey, P.M, Macefield, V.G., Gandevia, S.C., Siddall, P.J. and Henderson, LA. Anatomical changes in human motor cortex and motor pathways following complete thoracic spinal cord injury. Cerebral Cortex, 2009, 19 (1): 224 ? 232.
11. Gustin, S.M., Wrigley, P.J., Gandevia, S.C., Middleton, J.W., Henderson, L.A., Siddall, P.J. Movement imagery evokes pain in people with neuropathic pain following complete thoracic spinal cord injury.Pain, 2008, 137 (2): 237 ? 244.

Chapter 25

BIOGRAPHICAL SKETCH – PSYCHOLOGY RESEARCH

Sara Konrath

Affiliation: Research Center for Group Dynamics, Institute for Social Research, University of Michigan

Address: 426 Thompson Street, Ann Arbor, MI 48104

Date of Birth: N/A

Education: MS, Ph.D. in Social Psychology

Research and Professional Experience:

Professional Appointments:

    2010- Adjunct Assistant Professor & Lecturer, Department of Psychology, University of Michigan
    2009- Research Assistant Professor, Institute for Social Research, University of Michigan
    2009- Adjunct Assistant Professor, Department of Psychiatry, University of Rochester Medical Center
    2009-2010 American Association for University Women Fellow
    2008-2009 Postdoctoral Research Investigator, Institute for Social Research, University of Michigan
    2008-2009 Research Supervisor, Early Steps Early Intervention Autism Study, University of Michigan Autism and Communication Disorders Center (UMACC)

Honors:

2010: Outstanding Research Mentor Award, Undergraduate Research Opportunity Program

2008: Top three finalist, Tenth Martin E.P. Seligman Award for Outstanding Dissertation Research in Positive Psychology

2007: Nominated for Rackham Distinguished Dissertation Award: *Each university department selects one student nominee for a competitive university wide award. Only 51 dissertations were selected from over 780 in the Graduate School in 2007.*

2007: Marquis Outstanding Dissertation Award, University of Michigan: *Awarded annually to the student judged to have submitted the best doctoral dissertation in Psychology*

2007: Philip Brickman Award, University of Michigan: *Awarded to the outstanding graduate student paper in social psychology for overall scholarly excellence, originality, & significance of the research. (The paper was published in Psychological Science.)*

Selected topically relevant publications in past 5 years:

Konrath, S., Bushman, B. & Campbell, W. K. (2006). Attenuating the link between threatened egotism and aggression. *Psychological Science, 17,* 995-1001.

Twenge, J., Konrath, S., Campbell, W. K., Foster, J., & Bushman, B. J. (2008a). Egos inflating over time. A cross-temporal meta-analysis of the Narcissistic Personality Inventory. *Journal of Personality, 76,* 875-901.

Konrath, S., Bushman, B., & *Grove, T. (2009). Seeing my world in a million little pieces: Narcissism, self-construal, and cognitive-perceptual style. *Journal of Personality, 77,* 1197-1228.

Chandler, J., Konrath, S., & Schwarz, N. (2009). Online and on my mind: Temporary and chronic accessibility influence the assimilation of online characters. *Media Psychology, 12,* 210–226.

Konrath, S., *Grynberg, D., Corneille, O., *Hammig, S., & Luminet, O. (2011) On the social cost of interdependence: Alexithymia is enhanced among socially interdependent people. *Personality and Individual Differences, 50,* 135-141.

Sripada, C. & Konrath, S. (in press) *Telling more than we can know about intentional action.* Mind & Language.

Konrath, S., *O'Brien, E., & *Hsing, C. (in press). *Changes in dispositional empathy in American college students over time: A meta-analysis.* Personality and Social Psychology Review.

In: Psychology Research Biographies and Summaries   ISBN: 978-1-61470-491-1
Editors: Nancy E. Wodarth and Alexis P. Ferguson   © 2012 Nova Science Publishers, Inc.

Chapter 26

BIOGRAPHICAL SKETCH – PSYCHOLOGY RESEARCH

Kallipe Kounenou

Affiliation: Assist. Prof. of Counseling & Guidance

Address: School of Pedagogical & Technological Education, Athens, Greece
141 21, N. Herakleion, Attica, Greece, +30 210 2896932
kkounen@aspete.gr

Education: BSc., MSc., Ph.D. in Psychology

Research and Professional Experience: "The role of family and personality constructs in a person's personal, social and career development"

Publications Last 3 Years:

Koumoundourou, G., Kounenou, K., Siavara, E. (accepted for publication). Core Self-Evaluations, Career Decision Self-Efficacy, and Vocational Identity among Greek Adolescents. Journal of Career Development.

Kounenou, K., Koutra, Aik., Katsiadrami, A., & Diakogianis, G. (in press/2011). An epidemiological study of university students' mental health. Journal of College Student Development

Koumoundourou, G., Tsaousis, I., & Kounenou, K. (2011). Parental influences on Greek adolescents career decision making difficulties: The mediating role of Core-Self Evaluations. Journal of Career Assessment.

Kounenou, Ê. & Koutra Aik. (2008). Exploration of emotional expression in university students: gender differences. Tetradia Psychiatrikis, Psychology Issue, 101, 114-123.

Koutra, Aik, Kounenou, Ê., Katsiadrami, Á., & Diakogianis, G. (2010). Group counselling intervention: comparison and assessment. Clinical Psychology-Health Psychology: Research & Practice. Athens: Papazissi Publications

Kounenou, Ê. (2008). Diabetes type 1 regulation under the impact of family relationship: literature review. In F. Anagnostopoulos & E.Karademas (Eds.) Contemporary Issues of Health Pyschology. Athens: Livani Publications

Kounenou, K. (in press). Drug use by university students and preventive actions. Procedia. Social & Behavioral Sciences Journal. Elsevier, WCES-2011

Pappas, T. S., & Kounenou, K. (in press). Career decision making of Greek post secondary vocational students and career decision making self-efficacy. Procedia. Social & Behavioral Sciences Journal. Elsevier, WCES-2011

Kounenou, K. (2010). Children's and adolescents' career development: the family and parental impact. Proceedings of the Conference Kultura Pedagogiczna Wspolczesnej Rodjny (The pedagogical Culture in contemporary family), PWSZ, Glogow 2010, p. 99-104, Poland.

Kounenou, K., Koumoundourou, G., & Makri-Botsari, E. (2010).The Greek school career counselors competencies and burnout syndrome. Procedia. Social & Behavioral Sciences Journal 2(2), 1890-1895.. Elsevier, WCES-2010.

Kounenou, K. (2010).Exploration of the relationship among drug use & alcohol drinking, entertainment activities, and self-esteem in Greek university students. Procedia. Social & Behavioral Sciences Journal, 2(2), 1906-1910.. Elsevier, WCES-2010.

Athansoula Reppa, A., Makri Botsari, E., Kounenou, K., & Psycharis, S. (2010). School leadership innovations and creativity: The case of communication between school and parents. Procedia- Social & Behavioral Sciences, 2(2), 2207-2211, Elsevier WCES 2010.

Êounenou, K., Koutra, K., (2008). Self-esteem & academic achievement in university students. Electronic Proceedings of the 2007 Fedora-Psyche Conference in Crete, Rethymnon.

In: Psychology Research Biographies and Summaries ISBN: 978-1-61470-491-1
Editors: Nancy E. Wodarth and Alexis P. Ferguson © 2012 Nova Science Publishers, Inc.

Chapter 27

BIOGRAPHICAL SKETCH – PSYCHOLOGY RESEARCH

Gary D. Laver

Affiliation: Psychology & Child Development Department, Cal Poly, San Luis Obispo, CA 93407

Date of Birth: 9-29-61

Education:

1983 B.A. Psychology, UC Santa Cruz (with honors)
1987 M.A. Cognitive Psychology, Claremont Graduate University
1992 Ph.D. Cognitive Psychology, Claremont Graduate University
1999-2000 Participant, Research Training Program in Psychology of Aging, sponsored by the National Institute of Aging at TheCollege of St. Scholastica

Research and Professional Experience:

Gary Laver received his B.A. with honors in psychology from UC Santa Cruz, and his M.A. and Ph.D. from the Claremont Graduate University. His doctoral dissertation, supported by a fellowship from The John Randolph Haynes and Dora Haynes Foundation, investigated differences in the time course of semantic priming processes in young and older adults using a speed-accuracy analysis of word recognition processes. He is currently a professor of psychology and chair of the Psychology and Child Development Department at Cal Poly, San Luis Obispo, where he has taught since 1991. During this time his research in cognitivepsychology, supported by the National Institutes of Health, has included a meta-analysis of studies on aging differences in semantic priming as well as other studies of changes in word recognition and other automatic memory processes through adulthood. He is a member of the American Psychological Association, the Western Psychological

Association, and American Association of University Professors and has reviewed for the journals Psychology and Aging and Aging and Cognition. In addition to his work in semantic memory and aging, he also has a strong interest in statistical analysis and methodology. His teaching includes courses in introductory psychology, quantitative research methods, psychological testing, and cognitive psychology. Beyond teaching and research, Dr. Laver provides consultation in research design and analysis, and he has received grants to develop methodological curriculum. He is also a statistical consultant for the California Department of Mental Health.

Professional Appointments:

2008-present Professor and Chair, Department of Psychology & Child Development, Cal Poly, San Luis Obispo, CA
2002-2008 Associate Professor, Cal Poly, San Luis Obispo, CA
1998-2002 Assistant Professor, Cal Poly, San Luis Obispo, CA

Publications Last 3 Years:

Laver, G. D. (2009). Adult aging effects on semantic and episodic priming in word recognition. Psychology and Aging, 24, 2839.

In: Psychology Research Biographies and Summaries
Editors: Nancy E. Wodarth and Alexis P. Ferguson
ISBN: 978-1-61470-491-1
© 2012 Nova Science Publishers, Inc.

Chapter 28

BIOGRAPHICAL SKETCH – PSYCHOLOGY RESEARCH

Pauwels Lieven

Affiliation: Ghent University

Address: Universiteitstraat 4 B-9000 Ghent

Date of Birth: March 29th 1974

Education: Ph.D. in criminology, M.A. in criminology, B.A. in criminology

Research and Professional Experience: Professor of criminology, interest in the study of causes of offending, neighbourhood differences in crime and fear of crime

Professional Appointments:

December 1st 2000- September 30th 2001: Researcher (100%) Department of Criminal Law and Criminology, Faculty of Law, University of Ghent

October 1st 2001 May 31st 2007 : Academic Assistant (100%) Department of Criminal Law and Criminology, Faculty of Law, University of Ghent

June 1st 2007-September 30th 2008: Assistant Professor (100%) in Quantitative Methodology and Crime Causation Theory

October, 1st 2008– December 31t 2008h: Associate Professor of Criminology, Ghent University (70%) and Post-Doctoral Research Fellow (30%- IWT Social Cohesion Project for the Region of Flanders)

January 1st2009 – January 31st 2010: Associate Professor of Criminology, Ghent University (80%) and Post-Doctoral Research Fellow (20%- IWT Social Cohesion Project for the Region of Flanders)

February 1st 2010-now: Associate Professor of Criminology (100%) responsible for courses on quantitative analysis, statistics, criminological theories
September 2008- now: President of the Flemish Society of Criminology

Honors:

Winner of the Dutch Willem Nagem Award 2006-2008 for the best PhD written in Dutch during that period Publications Last 3 Years: see my publication list at http://www.sva.ugent.be/biblio.php?pid=5

In: Psychology Research Biographies and Summaries
Editors: Nancy E. Wodarth and Alexis P. Ferguson
ISBN: 978-1-61470-491-1
© 2012 Nova Science Publishers, Inc.

Chapter 29

BIOGRAPHICAL SKETCH – PSYCHOLOGY RESEARCH

Angus W. MacDonald, III

Affiliation: Department of Psychology, University of Minnesota

Address: N218 Elliot Hall, 75 E. River Rd
Minneapolis, Minnesota, 55455

Primary Appointment:
Assistant Director for Practicum and Internship Placement, Clinical Science and Psychopathology Research Program, Dept. of Psychology

Secondary Appointments:
Area Director, Biological Psychopathology Program, Dept. Psychology Cognitive and Biological Sciences Program, Dept. Psychology; Personality, Individual Differences & Behavior Genetics Program, Dept. Psychology; Center for Cognitive Sciences; Graduate Program in Neuroscience; University of Minnesota School of Medicine, Department of Psychiatry

Date of Birth: 4/10/68

Education:

Post-Doctoral Fellowship 2001-2002
Clinical Cognitive Neuroscience Laboratory
Western Psychiatric Institute & Clinic, Department of Psychiatry University of Pittsburgh Medical Center

Mentor: Cameron Carter, M.D.
Ph.D. University of Pittsburgh **Graduation Date:** August 2001

Clinical Psychology Program, Department of Psychology & Center for the Neural Basis of Cognition;
Clinical Internship: Western Psychiatric Institute & Clinic
Co-advisors: Michael F. Pogue-Geile, Ph.D. & Cameron Carter, M.D.
Dissertation Title: A differential deficit in context processing associated with the genetic liability to schizophrenia: a sibling study.
B.A. Amherst College, Amherst, MA **Graduation Date:** December 1990
Psychology & Philosophy Majors

Research and Professional Experience:

Professional Appointments:

Associate Professor, University of Minnesota 2008 – present
Assistant Professor, University of Minnesota 2003 – 2008

Honors:

NARSAD Sidney R. Baer, Jr. Prize for Schizophrenia Research (2008, National Alliance for Research on Schizophrenia and Depression & Sidney R. Baer, Jr. Foundation)
Francoeur Investigator Award (2009-2010, NARSAD)
Chronicle of Higher Education Neuroscience in Psychology: Scholars to Watch (10 December 2008)
McKnight Land-Grant Professorship (2006-2008, University of Minnesota)
Young Investigator Award (2005 & 2008, National Alliance for Research on Schizophrenia and Depression)
Smadar Levine Award Runner Up (2001, Society for Research in Psychopathology)
Bassell Award for Excellence in Psychological Research (2000, University of Pittsburgh)
Travel Fellowship, Organization for Human Brain Mapping (2000)
Center for the Neural Basis of Cognition Training Fellowship (1998-1999, National Science Foundation)

Publications Last 3 Years:

1. Goghari, V.M.* & **MacDonald, A.W., III** (2008). Effects of varying the experimental design of a cognitive control paradigm on behavioral and functional imaging outcome measures. *Journal of Cognitive Neuroscience, 20*, 20-35.
2. Becker, T.M.*, Kerns, J.G., **MacDonald, A.W., III**, Carter, C.S. (2008). Prefrontal dysfunction in first-degree relatives of schizophrenia patients during a Stroop task. *Neuropsychopharmacology, 33*, 2619 – 2625.
3. **MacDonald, A.W., III** (2008). Building a clinically-relevant cognitive task: Case study of the AX paradigm. *Schizophrenia Bulletin, 34*, 619-628.

4. **MacDonald, A.W., III**, Thermenos, H.W., Barch, D.M., & Seidman, L.J. (2009). Imaging genetic liability to schizophrenia: A systematic review of fMRI studies of patients' non-psychotic relatives. *Schizophrenia Bulletin, 35,* 1142-1162.
5. Barch, D.M., Berman, M.G., Engle R., Jones, J.H., Jonides, J., **MacDonald, A.W., III**, Nee, D.E., Redick, T.S., Sponheim, S.R. (2009). CNTRICS final task selection: working memory. *Schizophrenia Bulletin*, 35, 136-152.
6. **MacDonald, A.W., III** & Kang, S.S. (2009). Misinterpreting schizophrenia relatives' impairments. *American Journal of Medical Genetics B: Neuropsychiatric Genetics*, 150B, 443-444.
7. Johnson, M.K.*, Rustichini, A., **MacDonald, A.W., III** (2009). Suspicious personality predicts behavior on a social decision-making task. *Personality and Individual Differences, 47,* 30-35.
8. **MacDonald, A.W., III** & Schulz, S.C. (2009). What we know: findings that every theory of schizophrenia should explain. *Schizophrenia Bulletin, 3,* 493–508. Translated into Spanish in *Schizophrenia Bulletin, Spanish excerpted Edition*.
9. Goghari, V.*, **MacDonald, A.W., III** (2009). The neural basis of cognitive control: response selection and inhibition. *Brain & Cognition, 71,* 72-83.
10. Camchong, J.*, Lim, K.O., Sponheim, S.R., **MacDonald, A.W., III** (2009). Frontal white matter integrity as an endophenotype for schizophrenia: Diffusion tensor imaging in monozygotic twins and patients' nonpsychotic relatives. *Frontiers in Human Neuroscience, 3,* 1-6.
11. Goghari, V.*, Sponheim, S.R., **MacDonald, A.W., III** (2010). The functional neuroanatomy of symptom dimensions in schizophrenia: A qualitative and quantitative review of a persistent question. *Neuroscience & Biobehavioral Reviews, 34,* 468-486.
12. Jones, J.A.H.*, Sponheim, S.R., **MacDonald, A.W., III** (2010). The dot pattern expectancy (DPX) task: reliability and replication of deficits in schizophrenia. *Psychological Assessment, 22,* 131-141.
13. Camchong, J.*, **MacDonald, A.W., III**, Bell, C., Mueller, B.A., Lim, K.O. (2010). Altered functional and anatomical connectivity in schizophrenia. *Schizophrenia Bulletin.*
14. Kang, S.S.* & **MacDonald, A.W., III** (2010). Limitations of true score variance to measure discriminating power: Psychometric simulation study. *Journal of Abnormal Psychology, 119,* 300-306.
15. Haut, K.M.*, Lim, K.O., **MacDonald, A.W., III** (2010). Prefrontal cortical changes following cognitive training in patients with chronic schizophrenia: effects of practice, generalization and specificity. *Neuropsychopharmacology, 35,* 1850-1859. Featured on MDLinx.com; *NPP* "Top Ten" download list.
16. Haut, K.M.*, **MacDonald, A.W., III** (2010). Persecutory delusions and the perception of trustworthiness in unfamiliar faces in schizophrenia. *Psychiatry Research, 178,* 456-60.
17. Goghari, V., **MacDonald, A.W., III**, Sponheim, S.R. (in press). Temporal lobe structures and facial emotion recognition in schizophrenia patients and non-psychotic relatives. *Schizophrenia Bulletin.*

18. Camchong, J.*, **MacDonald, A.W., III,** Nelson, B., Bell, C., Mueller, B.A., Specker, S., Lim, K.O. (in press). Frontal hyperconnectivity related to delayed discounting and reversal learning task performance in cocaine subjects. *Biological Psychiatry.*
19. Yzer, M.C., Vohs, K.D., Luciana, M., Cuthbert, B.N., & **MacDonald, A.W., III** (in press). Affective antecedents of the perceived effectiveness of antidrug advertisements: an analysis of adolescents' momentary and retrospective evaluations. *Prevention Science.*

Chapter 30

BIOGRAPHICAL SKETCH – PSYCHOLOGY RESEARCH

Brent R. MacNab, Ph.D.

Affiliation: Discipline of International Business, University of Sydney

Address: University of Sydney
Building H03, #306
Sydney, NSW 2006
Phone: 61-2-9036-6411
Email: *brent*
Website: http://sydney.edu.au/business/staff/brentm

Education:

Ph.D.	University of Hawai'i at Manoa
	Ph.D. in International Management
	Major Field: Organizational Behavior
	Thesis: "Effective ethics management and culture: Examination of internal reporting and whistle-blowing within a NAFTA member context"
	Supervisor: Dr. Richard Brislin
	GPA: 4.0
Fulbright Scholar	Simon Fraser University, Canada
	Sponsor: Dr. David C. Thomas
M.B.A.	University of Hawai'i at Manoa
	Major Field: International Management
	Thesis: "Practicum Project – Development of a Functioning Business"
	GPA: 4.0
B.A.	Portland State University
	Major Field: Business Administration

Minor Field: Economics
Certificate: International Business (German language emphasis)
GPA: 3.84

Certificate	Karls-Eberhard Universität, Tübingen, Germany
German Studies

Research Interests and Projects:

Research Interests

I am interested in the influence of culture, systems and individual traits on management of organizations. My research emphasizes: a) experiential cultural intelligence development; b) cross-cultural settings; c) regional and sub-cultural realities; d) the appropriateness of adjusting management tools to effectively fit context; e) cross-cultural training; f) other experiential education. A variety of management related topics are relevant within this framework and my recent work focuses on ethics management, workplace motivation, crossvergence and teaching cultural intelligence.

Current Research Projects

I currently manage a research team that has been supported by funding from the University of Sydney. The team involves collaborators in the US and Australia. The focus is developing and quantitatively examining experiential approaches to cultural intelligence training. Additionally, I continue an examination of ethics management within a NAFTA context. In the past I have successfully managed an extensive network of collaborators examining Fulbright-supported research on ethics management in the NAFTA area.

Publications and Research Activity:

Refereed Journal Articles

1. MacNab, B. & Worthley, R. (2011 forthcoming) Individual characteristics as predictors of cultural intelligence development: The relevance of self-efficacy. International Journal of Intercultural Relations.
2. MacNab, B., Jenner, S. & Worthley, R. (2010) Patterns of Self-Efficacy within NAFTA: United States, Canada and Mexico. Latin America Business Review. 11(3): 249-265.
3. MacNab, B., Worthley, R. & Jenner, S. (2010) Regional Cultural Differences and Ethical Perspectives within the U.S.: Avoid pseudo-emic ethics research. Business and Society Review. 115(1): 27-55.
4. Worthley, R., MacNab, B., Brislin, R., Ito, K. & Rose, B. (2009) Workforce motivation in Japan: An examination of gender influences and management perceptions. International Journal of Human Resource Management. 20(7): 1503-1520.
5. MacNab, B. & Worthley, R. (2008) Self-efficacy as an intrapersonal predictor for internal whistle-blowing: A U.S. and Canada examination. Journal of Business Ethics. 79(4): 407-422.

6. Jenner, S., MacNab, B., Briley, D., Brislin, R. and Worthley, R. (2008) Cultural change and marketing. The Journal of Global Marketing. 21(2): 161-172.
7. MacNab, B., Worthley, R., Brislin, R., Galperin, B., Jenner, S., Lituchi, T., Munoz, G., T., Ravlin, E., Tiessen, J., Turcotte, M. & Bess, D. (2007) Culture and ethics management: External whistle-blowing and internal reporting within a NAFTA member context. International Journal of Cross-Cultural Management. 7(1): 5-28.
8. MacNab, B. & Worthley, R. (2007) Culture typing versus sample specific accuracy: An examination of uncertainty avoidance, power distance and individualism for business professionals in the U.S. and Canada. Multinational Business Review. 15(3): 1-23.
9. MacNab, B., Brislin, R., Galperin, B., Lituchy, T., & Worthley, R. (2007) National homogeneity v. regional specificity: An examination of the Canadian cultural mosaic and whistle-blowing. Canadian Journal of Regional Studies. 30(2): 293-312.
10. Jenner, S., MacNab, B., Brislin, R. & Worthley, R. (2006) Cultural change in the United States, Canada and Mexico. Journal of International Business and Economy. 7(1): 67-86.
11. Brislin, R., Worthley, R. & MacNab, B. (2006) Cultural intelligence: Understanding behaviors that serve people's goals. Group and Organization Management. 31(1): 40-55.
12. Kelley, L., MacNab, B. & Worthley, R. (2006) Crossvergence and cultural tendencies: A longitudinal test of the Hong Kong, Taiwan and United States banking sectors. Journal of International Management. 12(1): 67-84.
13. Brislin, R., MacNab, B. & Worthley, R. (2005) Evolving perceptions of Japanese workplace motivation: an employee - manager comparison. International Journal of Cross-Cultural Management. 5(1): 87-104.
14. Kelley, L., MacNab, B., Worthley, R., Huff, L., & Pagano, I. (2004) Adaptability and change in Japanese management practice: A longitudinal inquiry into the banking industry through the bubble economy and beyond. Advances in International Management. 17: 3-30.

Chapters in Books :
1. Brislin, R., MacNab, B., & Nayani, F. (2008) Cross-cultural training: Applications and research (pp. 397-410). In P. Smith, M. Peterson, & D. Thomas (Eds.), Handbook of Cross-Cultural Management Research. Thousand Oaks, CA: Sage.
2. MacNab, B. (2004). China – The middle kingdom takes center stage, in I. Chow, N. Holbert, L. Kelley & J. Yu (Eds.) Business Strategy: An Asia-Pacific Focus. New York: Prentice-Hall.
3. MacNab B. (2004) Korea – managing the invisible hand, in I. Chow, N. Holbert, L. Kelley & J. Yu (Eds.) Business Strategy: An Asia-Pacific Focus. New York: Prentice-Hall. (Note: There was an error in publishing this chapter and another person was incorrectly listed as the chapter's author within the text.)
4. Brislin, R. & MacNab, B. (2004). Inter-cultural communication and effective decision making: Contributions to successful international business ventures, in K. Leung & S. White (Eds.) Handbook of Asian Management. New York: Kluwar.
5. Brislin, R., MacNab, B. & Bechtold, D. (2004) Translation. In C. Spielberger (Ed.) Encyclopedia of Applied Psychology. San Diego: Academic Press.

Refereed Conference Proceedings
1. MacNab, B., Worthley, R. & Rosenblatt, V. Developing cultural intelligence: The role of optimal contact, disconfirmed expectations, stereotype awareness and

stereotype alteration. Association of Applied Business and Entrepreneurship International (ABEAI) Conference. Hawaii, USA. November, 2010.
2. MacNab, B. & Worthley, R. An Experiential Education Approach to Teaching cultural intelligence: Individual and Contextual Influences. Invited paper for presentation at the AOM symposium on cultural intelligence – OB and HR divisions. Academy of Management (AOM) Conference. Montreal, Quebec. August, 2010.
3. MacNab, B. Experiential stereotype awareness training: The relevance of context and self-efficacy. Presented at the Academy of Management (AOM) Conference. Chicago, IL. August 2009.
4. MacNab, B. Regional Cultural Differences and Ethical Perspectives within the U.S.: Avoiding pseudo-emic ethics research. Presented at the Applied Business and Entrepreneurial Association International (ABEAI) Conference. Kauai, USA. November 2008.
5. MacNab, B., Worthley, R. & Brislin, R. An experiential approach to teaching cultural intelligence: The relevance of context and intra-personal characteristics within the learning process. Presented at the Applied Business and Entrepreneurial Association International (ABEAI) Conference. Maui, USA. November 2007. *Conference Section Best Paper Award.*
6. MacNab, B. & Worthley, R. Self-efficacy as an intrapersonal predictor for internal reporting: A US and Canada examination. Presented at the Australia and New Zealand International Business Academy (ANZIBA) Conference. Wellington, New Zealand. November 2006.
7. MacNab, B., Brislin, R., Ito, K., Rose, E. & Worthley, R. Workforce motivation in Japan: An examination of gender differences and management perceptions. Presented at the joint Academy of International Business (AIB) and Association of Japanese Business Studies (AJBS) conferences. Beijing, June 2006.
8. Jenner, S., MacNab, B. & Worthley, R. Cultural change in the U.S., Canada and Mexico. Presented at the International Business and Economics conference. Honolulu, Hawaii, January 2006.
9. MacNab, B., Brislin, R., Galperin, B., Lituchy, T., & Worthley, R. The Canadian cultural mosaic and whistle-blowing. Presented at the Australia and New Zealand International Business Academy (ANZIBA) Conference. Melbourne, Australia, November 2005.
10. MacNab, B., Brislin, R., Worthley, R., Galperin, B., Jenner, S., Lituchi, T., Munoz, G., Ravlin, E., Tiessen, J., Turcotte, M. & Bess, D. Effective ethics management and culture: Examination of internal reporting and whistle-blowing within a NAFTA context. Presented at the 9th annual International Society for the Study of Work and Organizational Values (ISSWOV) Conference. New Orleans, LA. August 2004.
11. Kelley, L., Mac Nab, B., Worthley, R., Huff, L. & Pagano, I. Adaptability and change in Japanese management practice: A longitudinal inquiry into the banking industry through the bubble economy and beyond. Presented at the Association of Japanese Business Studies (AJBS) Conference and Advances in International Management Special Issue Conference. St. Louis, MO, June 2002. Conference Best Paper Award.

Newspaper and Other Published Media
Note: Website hardcopy versions of all published media available upon request.

1. MacNab, B. (2010) Move beyond diversity training for diversity effectiveness. Forbes.com Newsletter. April 06.
2. MacNab, B. (2009) Developing stereotype awareness through education. Reuters. August 03.
3. MacNab, B. (2008) International travel experience to help improve global effectiveness. Forbes.com Newsletter. July 10.
4. MacNab, B. (2007) How businesses can help curb ethical abuse and whistle-blowing. NBC, Channel 26 News. Green Bay, Wisconsin. April 20.
5. MacNab, B. (2007) Specific guidance for improving your business' internal reporting system to help curb ethical abuses and whistle-blowing. Investor's Business Daily (Investors.com.). April 19.
6. MacNab, B. (2006) Ethics in the U.S., Canada and Mexico. Who would you want to do business with? Forbes.com Newsletter. June 06.
7. MacNab, B. (2006) Ethics in the U.S., Canada and Mexico. Who would you want to do business with? Fox, Channel 5 News. Las Vegas, Nevada. April 20.
8. MacNab, B. (2004) Ethics: Local vs. Mainland. The Honolulu Star-Bulletin. May 29.

Submitted Work (currently in review)
1. MacNab, B. An experiential approach to cultural intelligence education. Journal of Management Education. (Second revise and resubmit).
2. MacNab, B. Stereotype awareness development and effective cross-cultural management: An experiential approach. International Journal of Cross-Cultural Management.
3. MacNab, B. Brislin, R. & Worthley, R. Experiential cultural intelligence training and development: The relevance of self-efficacy and context. International Journal of Human Resource Management. (Conditional acceptance, second revise and resubmit).

Work in Progress
1. MacNab, B., Rosenblatt, V. & Worthley, R. Embrace the unexpected: A road to cultural intelligence via contact, disconfirmation and awareness.
2. MacNab, B. & Worthley, R. Social affiliation-efficacy: Concept and scale development with individual and cultural examination.
3. Jenner, S., MacNab, B., & Worthley, R. Individual traits as predictors of cultural intelligence self perception.
4. MacNab, B. & Worthley, R. Cultural intelligence self perception bias: A beta-change effect examination.
5. MacNab, B. & Worthley, R. Context in Experiential Cultural Intelligence (CQ) Education.

Teaching Experience and Interests

Courses Taught at the University of Sydney   Current-2005   Head instructor
IBUS2102: Cross-cultural Management, undergraduate   and course designer
IBUS6002: Cross-cultural Management, postgraduate

Courses Taught at the University of Hawai'i at Manoa

HRM 353: Leadership and Group Processes	Fall (sabbatical)	2008	Head instructor
BUS 315: Mgmt. & Organizational Behavior	Spring	2004	Head instructor
	Spring	2001	Lab instructor
	Fall	2000	Lab instructor
MGMT 650: Asia Pacific Strategy, MBA	Summer	2003	Team taught
	Summer	2002	Assistant instructor

Teaching Interests

Cross-Cultural Management, O.B., Leadership, Strategy, International Marketing, Introduction to Management, Ethics Management, Negotiation.

Statement of Teaching Philosophy

Students tend to perform best when learning is enjoyable. In line with Social and Experiential Learning Theory, experiential, communicative and interactive environments tend to be highly effective in teaching certain subjects like cross-cultural management and organizational behavior. A reasonable work load is often better for solidifying key themes, and focusing on quality, as opposed to stressfully high work loads.

Associations

Alumnus, Canada-US Fulbright (2002 and 2003)
Member, Friends of Fulbright
Member, American Psychological Association (APA)
Member, International Association of Applied Psychology (IAAP)
Member, International Academy of Intercultural Research (IAIR)
Member, Academy of Management (AOM)
Member, Academy of International Business (AIB)
Member, Organizational Behavior Teaching Society (OBTS)
Reviewer, Journal of International Management
Reviewer, Journal of Business Ethics
Reviewer, International Journal of Cross-Cultural Management
Reviewer, International Journal of Intercultural Relations
Reviewer, Academy of Management Learning and Education
Reviewer, Human Resource Management Journal

Fellowships, Grants, Scholastic Awards, Honors

Doctoral and Post Doctoral Level

1. Faculty Research Grant award 2008. A pedagogy for cultural intelligence.
2. Wayne Lonergan Outstanding Teaching Award nominee, 2006. University of Sydney.
3. SBUS Research Grant. 2006. University of Sydney.

4. International Academy of Intercultural Research (IAIR) Outstanding Dissertation Award. 2005.
5. Chancellor's Research Achievement Award (Doctoral Level), 2004. University of Hawai'i.
6. Fulbright Research Fellow, Canada, 2002 – 2003.
7. Fulbright Travel Grant, Mexico, 2003.
8. CIBER (Center for International Business Education and Research) grant, 2002, research development of NAFTA ethics management project.

Graduate and Undergraduate Level
1. Oscar Fish Scholarship for Excellence, University of Hawai'i MBA program, 1997-1998.
2. Graduate, Magna cum Laude Portland State University 1990.
3. Dean's List, Portland State University, 1988 and 1989.

University Community Service
1. Director for Master in International Business Program, University of Sydney (2005-2009).
2. University of Sydney, Office of Learning and Teaching Committee Member and International Business Representative (2006-current.)
3. University of Sydney, Postgraduate Studies Board Committee Member (2006-2009).

Employment History

Academic

Current:	Sr. Lecturer (Associate Professor) Faculty of Economics and Business. International Business Discipline. University of Sydney.
2006-2009:	Director, Master of International Business program. University of Sydney.
2005 – 2008:	Lecturer (Assistant Professor). Faculty of Economics and Business. International Business Discipline. University of Sydney.
2004 – Fall:	Postdoctoral Researcher, University of Hawai'i.
2004 – Spring:	Instructor, University of Hawai'i, Business 315 (Organizational Behavior).
2003 – Fall:	Travel research grant for data collection, Fulbright Program, Mexico.
2003 – Summer:	Team Instructor, University of Hawai'i, Business 650 (Asia Pacific Management).
2002 – 2003:	Research Fellow, Canada-U.S. Fulbright Program, SFU, Vancouver, Canada.
2002 – Summer:	Assistant Instructor, University of Hawai'i, Business 650 (Asia Pacific Management).
2002 – Fall/Spring:	Research Assistant to Professor Richard Brislin, University of Hawai'i.
2000 – 2001:	Lab Instructor, University of Hawai'i, Business 315 (Organizational Behavior).

Corporate and Private Sector

1997 – 2000:	Product Manager, AT&T Wireless, Hawai'i.
1996:	Interim Marketing Director & Consultant, Stan Wiley Realtors, Inc., Oregon.
1994 – 1995:	Product Manager, BankAmerica Corp., California (promotion).
1994:	Sr. Advertising Officer, BankAmerica Corp., California (promotion).
1993 – 1994:	Advertising Officer, BankAmerica Corp., California.
1992 – 1993:	Manufacturer Representative, Volkswagen of America, Inc., California.
1990 – 1992:	Merchandising Specialist, Volkswagen of America, Inc., Oregon & California.

References

1. Dr. Donnel Briley, Professor. Faculty of Economics and Business, University of Sydney, Australia. (61-2) 9036-6449. *d.briley@econ.usyd.edu.au*
2. Dr. Richard Brislin, Chair. Shidler College of Business, University of Hawai'i at Manoa, USA. (808) 956-8720. *rbrislin@hawaii.edu*
3. Dr. Reg Worthley, Professor. Shidler College of Business, University of Hawai'i at Manoa, USA. (808) 956-8150. *worthley@hawaii.edu*
4. Dr. Bahran Adrangi, Professor. Pamplim School of Business, Univerity of Portland, USA. *adrangi@up.edu*
5. Dr. Amy Kenworthy, Associate Professor / Director "LEAP". Bond University, Australia. (61-7) 5595-2241. *akenwort@bond.edu.au*

In: Psychology Research Biographies and Summaries
Editors: Nancy E. Wodarth and Alexis P. Ferguson
ISBN: 978-1-61470-491-1
© 2012 Nova Science Publishers, Inc.

Chapter 31

BIOGRAPHICAL SKETCH – PSYCHOLOGY RESEARCH

Robert Marcus

Affiliation: Department of Human Development

Address: Department of Human Development, 3304 Benjamin, Univ. of Md., College Park, Md. 20742

Date of Birth: August 3, 1943

Education: Ph.D. Pennsylvania State University, 1973

Research and Professional Experience: Associate Professor, 38 years; Licensed Psychologist in Md.

Professional Appointments: Associate Professor, 1978 to present

Publications Last 3 Years:

Marcus, R.F., & Jamison, E. (in press). Violence in emerging adulthood: A developmental perspective. In The Psychology of Teen Violence. Paludi, M. (Ed) Praeger

Marcus, R.F. (2009). Cross-sectional study of violence in emerging adulthood. Aggressive Behavior. 35, 188-202.

Chapter 32

BIOGRAPHICAL SKETCH – PSYCHOLOGY RESEARCH

Rosario J. Marrero Quevedo

Titles: PhD in Psychology

Contact Points: University of La Laguna.

Date of Birth: March 9, 1966

Education: Ph.D. in Psychology in the University of La Laguna. Spain

Research and Professional Experience:

Lecturer in the University of La Laguna. Research in several topics: stress and gender, cancer, family violence and positive psychology.

Publications Last 3 Years:

De Miguel, A., Carballeira, M., & Marrero, R.J. (2008). IX Jornada SEIDI. Sociedad Española para la Investigación de las Diferencias Individuales. Documentos Congresuales. Servicio de Publicaciones: Universidad de La Laguna. España

Carballeira, M. & Marrero, R.J. (2008). Subjective well-being: The role of humour and coping. *International Journal of Psychology. Abstracts of the XXIX international Congress of Psychology, 43*, 591.

Marrero, R.J. & Carballeira, M. (2008). The impact of attachment style on subjective well-being. *International Journal of Psychology. Abstracts of the XXIX international Congress of Psychology, 43*, 287.

Marrero, R.J. & Carballeira, M. (2010). El papel del optimismo y del apoyo social en el bienestar subjetivo. *Salud Mental, 33*, 39-46.

Marrero, R.J. & Carballeira, M. (2010). Contacto con la naturaleza y bienestar personal, *Psyecology,* 1, 309-320.

Marrero, R.J. & Carballeira, M. (2011). Well-being and personality: facet-level analyses. *Personality and Individual Differences, 50,* 206-211.

In: Psychology Research Biographies and Summaries
Editors: Nancy E. Wodarth and Alexis P. Ferguson
ISBN: 978-1-61470-491-1
© 2012 Nova Science Publishers, Inc.

Chapter 33

BIOGRAPHICAL SKETCH – PSYCHOLOGY RESEARCH

Keita Masui

Affiliation: Hiroshima University, Research Fellow of the Japan Society for the Promotion of Science

Address: 1-7-1, Kagamiyama, Higashi-Hiroshima, Hiroshima, 739-8521, Japan

Date of Birth: Jun 18, 1984

Education:

M. A. Hiroshima University in Integrated Arts and Science, 2008-2010
B. A. Shinshu University in Faculty of Arts, 2004-2008

Research and Professional Experience:

2010-present Research Fellow of the Japan Society for the Promotion of Science
2010-present Adjunct Instructor, Exercise of Document and Design, Hijiyama

Professional Appointments:

2010-present Adjunct Instructor, Exercise of Document and Design, Hijiyama
2009-2010 Teaching Assistant, Elementary Experiment of Behavioral Science, Hiroshima
2008-2009 Teaching Assistant, Laboratory Teaching of Behavioral Science, Hiroshima

Honors:

2009 OKAMOTO Award, Hiroshima
2009 Excellent Student Scholarship, Hiroshima

Publications Last 3 Years:

Journal Articles
[First author]

Masui, K., & Nomura, M. (2011). The effect of reward and punishment on response inhibition in non-clinical psychopathy. Personality and Individual Differences, 50, 69-73.

Masui, K., & Nomura, M. (2010). A review of impulsivity from structure concept, brain function, and genetic phenotype: The perspectives from stop-signal paradigm. The Japanese Journal of Research on Emotions, 18, 15-24.

Masui, K., Kashino, M., & Nomura, M. (2009). Ventrolateral prefrontal cortex activity during reward-punishment go/nogo task: A near-infrared spectroscopy study. Psychologia: An International Journal of Psychological Sciences, 52, 137-146.

[Coauthor]

Yanagisawa, K., Masui, K., Furutani, K., Nomura, M., Ura, M., & Yoshida, H. (in press). Does higher general trust serve as a psychosocial buffer against social pain? : A NIRS study of social exclusion. Social Neuroscience.

Yanagisawa, K., Masui, K., Furutani, K., Nomura, M., Yoshida, H., & Ura, M. (in press). Imagining the distant future insulates against immediate social pain. Social Neuroscience.

Yanagisawa, K., Masui, K., Onoda, K., Furutani, K., Nomura, M., Yoshida, H., & Ura, M. (2011). The effects of the behavioral inhibition and activation systems on social inclusion and exclusion. Journal of Experimental Social Psychology, 47, 502-505.

Poster Presentation

Masui, K., & Sugiura, Y. (2011). The effect of impulsivity, compulsivity, and psychopathy on self-injurious behavior in nonclinical adolescents. At the 12th Annual Meeting of the Society for Personality and Social Psychology, San Antonio, Texas.

Masui, K., & Nomura, M. (2010). The relationship between response disinhibition and rVLPFC deactivation in psychopathic participants: A near-infrared spectroscopy study. At the 50th Annual Meeting of Society for Psychophysiological Research, Portland, Oregon.

Masui, K., & Nomura, M. (2010). The influence of psychopathic trait, reward sensitivity, and punishment sensitivity on impulsivity. At the 74th Annual Meeting of the Japanese Psychological Association, Osaka, Japan.

Yanagisawa, K., Masui, K., Onoda, K., Furutani, K., Nomura, M., Ura, M., & Yoshida, H. (2010). The effects of BIS/BAS and EC on estimation and regulation processes of social pain: A NIRS study. At the 74th Annual Meeting of the Japanese Psychological Association, Osaka, Japan.

Masui, K., & Nomura, M. (2009). The influence of conflict evoked by reward and punishment on impulsivity. At the 73th Annual Meeting of the Japanese Psychological Association, Kyoto, Japan.

Masui, K., & Sugiura, Y. (2008). The factor structure of Obsessive-Compulsive Spectrum Disorder: The perspectives from internalizing and externalizing model. At the 34th Annual Meeting of Japanese Association of Behavior Therapy, Tokyo, Japan.

Verbal presentation

Yanagisawa, K., Masui, K., Furutani, K., Nomura, M., Ura, M., & Yoshida, H. (2010). Examination of the function of psychological resource in adaptive process after social exclusion: A NIRS study. At the 51st Annual Meeting of the Japanese Society of Social Psychology, Hiroshima, Japan.

Masui, K. (2010). The emotion of criminals: psychopathy and impulsivity. In workshop $B!H(BCriminal and Emotion$B!I(B. At the 18th Annual Meeting of Japan Society for Research on Emotions, Hiroshima, Japan.

In: Psychology Research Biographies and Summaries
Editors: Nancy E. Wodarth and Alexis P. Ferguson

ISBN: 978-1-61470-491-1
© 2012 Nova Science Publishers, Inc.

Chapter 34

BIOGRAPHICAL SKETCH – PSYCHOLOGY RESEARCH

Dennis M. McInerney

Affiliation: The Hong Kong Institute of Education

Address: Psychological Studies Department, The Hong Kong Institute of Education, 10 Lo Ping Road, Tai Po, New Territories, Hong Kong

Date of Birth: 12th May, 1948

Education: Ph.D. Sydney University

Research and Professional Experience: See brief bio below

Professional Appointments: Chair Professor Educational Psychology, Associate Vice President (Research and Development

Publications Last 3 Years:

Books
1. Information Age Publishing (McInerney, D. M., Cheng, R. W. Y., & Lai, P. Y. (2010). *Utilize motivation to fulfil potentials: Tips for teaching and learning*. Charlotte, NC: Information Age Publishing. (in Chinese).
2. McInerney, D. M., & McInerney, V. (2010). *Educational Psychology: Constructing learning. 5th ed*. Sydney: Pearson.
3. McInerney, D. M. (2006). *Developmental Psychology for Teachers: An Applied Approach*. Sydney: Allen & Unwin.
4. McInerney, D. M., & McInerney, V. (2006). *Educational Psychology: Constructing learning. 4th ed*. Sydney: Pearson.
5. McInerney, D. M. (2005). *Helping Kids Achieve Their Best. Understanding and Using Motivation in the Classroom (Revised)*. Greenwich, CT: Information Age Publishing.

Books (Edited)

1. McInerney, D. M., Brown, T. L., & Liem, G. A. D. (2009). Student Perspectives on Assessment: What Students Can Tell Us about Assessment for Learning. In D. M. McInerney (Ed.), *Research on Sociocultural Influences on Motivation and Learning. Vol. 9.* Charlotte, NC: Information Age.
2. Tan, O S., McInerney, D. M., Liem, A. D., & Tan, A-G. (2008). *What the West can Learn from the East. Asian Perspectives on the Psychology of Learning and Motivation. Vol. 7 in Research in Multicultural Education and International Perspectives* (Series Editors F. Salili and R. Hoosain). Charlotte, NC: Information Age.
3. McInerney, D. M., & Liem, A. D. (2008). *Teaching and Learning: International Best Practice.* In D. M. McInerney & S. Van Etten (Ed.,) *Research on Sociocultural Influences on Motivation and Learning. Vol. 8.* Charlotte, NC: Information Age.
4. Marsh, H. W., Craven, R., & McInerney, D. M. (2008). *Advances in Self Research. Vol. 3. Self-Processes, Learning, and Enabling Human Potential: Dynamic New Approaches.* Charlotte, NC: Information Age.

Chapters in books

1. McInerney, D. M., Fasoli, L/. & Stephenson, P (under review). Building the future for remote students in Australia: An examination of future goals, motivation, learning and achievement in cultural context. Chapter prepared for publication in *International Advances in Education: Global initiatives for equity and social justice.* Charlotte, NC: Information Age
2. McInerney, D. M. & Liem, A. D. (2009). Achievement motivation in cross-cultural context: Application of Personal Investment Theory in educational settings. In A. Kaplan., S.A. Karabenick, & E. V. De Groot (Eds.), *Culture, self and motivation: Essays in honor of Martin L. Maehr.* Charlotte, NC: Information Age Publishing.
3. McInerney, D. M. (2009). Educational psychology ¨C Theory, research, and teaching: A 25-year retrospective. 2nd Ed. In K. Wheldall (Ed.), *Developments in educational psychology.* London: Routledge.
4. Liem, A. D., & McInerney, D. M. (2009). Indonesian students and their citizenship-related attributes: Motivational perspective of the attainment of civic education desirable outcomes. In K. J. Kennedy, W. O. Lee, & D. L. Grossman (Eds.), *Citizenship Education Pedagogies in Asia and the Pacific.* Springer.
5. McInerney, D.M., & Liem, A. D. (2008). Motivation theory and engaged learning. In P. A. Towndrow, C. Koh, & H. C. Tan (Eds.), *Motivation and practice for the classroom.* The Netherlands; Sense Publishers.
6. McInerney, D. M., & Liem, A. D. (2008). Individualism/collectivism ¨C fact or fiction? In D. Westen, L. Burton & R. Kowalski (Eds.), *Psychology: Australian and New Zealand Edition* (2nd ed.). Sydney: John Wiley & Sons.
7. McInerney, D. M. (2007) Personal investment, culture, and learning. Insights into the most salient influences on school achievement across cultural groups. In F. Salili & R. Hoosain (Eds.), *Culture, Motivation and Learning: A multicultural perspective. Vol 6 in Research in Multicultural Education and International Perspectives.* Greenwich, CT: Information Age Publishing.
8. McInerney, D. M. (2007) The motivational roles of cultural differences and cultural identity in self-regulated learning. (Invited) In D. Schunk & B. Zimmerman (Eds.), *Motivation and Self-Regulated Learning: Theory, Research, and Applications.* New York: Lawrence Erlbaum.

9. Green, J., Martin, A.J., Marsh, H.W., & McInerney, D. M. (2006). Academic motivation and engagement: Examining relations with key educational outcomes. In R.G. Craven., J. S. Eccles, & T. M. Ha (Eds.), *Self-concept, Motivation, Social and Personal Identity for the 21st Century*. Proceedings of the Fourth International Biennial SELF Research Conference, Ann Arbor, University of Michigan (ISBN 1 74108 148 3).
10. Green, J., Martin, A.J., Marsh, H.W., & McInerney, D. M. (2006). Gender and grade effects in the structure of academic motivation and engagement: A higher order confirmatory factor analysis approach. In R.G. Craven., J. S. Eccles, & T. M. Ha (Eds.), *Self-concept, Motivation, Social and Personal Identity for the 21st Century*. Proceedings of the Fourth International Biennial SELF Research Conference, Ann Arbor, University of Michigan (ISBN 1 74108 148 3).
11. McInerney, D. M. (2006). Educational psychology "C Theory, research, and teaching: A 25-year retrospective. In K. Wheldall (Ed.), *Developments in Educational Psychology. How far have we come in 25 years?* London: Routledge.

Chapters in books (self edited)

1. Brown, G., McInerney, D. M, & Liem, G. A. D. (2009). Student perspectives of assessment: Considering what assessment means to learners. In D. M. McInerney, G. Brown, & G. A. Liem, G. A. D. (Eds.), *Research on Sociocultural Influences on Motivation and Learning. Vol. 9 Student Perspectives on Assessment: What Students Can Tell Us about Assessment for Learning*.Charlotte, NC: Information Age.
2. Liem, A. D., & McInerney, D. M. (2008). Best International Practice in Teaching and Learning. In D. M. McInerney & S. Van Etten (Eds.), *Teaching and learning: International best practice. Vol. 8 in Research on sociocultural influences on motivation and learning*. Charlotte, NC: Information Age.
3. Da Silva, D., & McInerney, D. M. (2008). Motivational and self-goals of female students in contemporary Japan. In O. S. Tan, D. M. McInerney, A. D. Liem, & A-G. Tan (Eds.), *What the West can learn from the East: Asian perspectives on the psychology of learning and motivation, Research on Multicultural Education and International Perspectives Series (Vol. 7)*. Charlotte, NC.: Information Age Publishing.
4. McInerney, D.M., Liem, A. D., Ortiga, Y. P. Y., Lee, J. Q., & Manzano, A. S. (2008). Future goals and self-regulated learning among Singaporean Chinese students: The mediating role of utility values of schooling, perceived competence, academic self-concept and academic motivation. In O. S. Tan, D. M. McInerney, A. D. Liem, & A-G. Tan (Eds.), *What the West can learn from the East: Asian perspectives on the psychology of learning and motivation, Research on Multicultural Education and International Perspectives Series (Vol. 7)*. Charlotte, NC: Information Age Publishing.
5. Tan, O. S., McInerney, D. M., Liem, A. D., & Tan, A. G. (2008). West-East and East-West learning: Some psychological and cultural Insights. In O. S. Tan, D. M. McInerney, A. D. Liem & A.-G. Tan (Eds.), *What the West Can Learn from the East: Asian Perspectives on the Psychology of Learning and Motivation. Vol. 7 in Research on Multicultural Education and International Perspectives Series*. Charlotte, NC: Information Age Publishing
6. McInerney, D. M., Marsh, H. W., & Craven, R. G. (2008). Self-processes, learning, and enabling human potential. In H. W. Marsh, R. G. Craven, & D. M. McInerney (Eds.), *Advances in Self Research. Vol. 3. Self-Processes, Learning, and Enabling Human Potential: Dynamic New Approaches*. Charlotte, NC: Information Age Publishing.

Journal articles

1. King, R.B., McInerney, D.M., & Watkins, D.A. (in press). Can social goals enrich our understanding of students' motivational goals? *Journal of Psychology in Chinese Societies*.
2. Lee, J. Q., McInerney, D.M., Liem, G. A. D., & Ortiga, Y. Y. (2010). The relationship between future goals and achievement goal orientations: An intrinsic-extrinsic motivation perspective. *Contemporary Educational Psychology, 35,* 264-279.
3. Brickman, S., McInerney, D. M., & Martin, A. (2009). Examining the valuing of schooling as a motivational indicator of American Indian students: Perspectives based on a model of future oriented motivation and self-regulation. *Journal of American Indian Education, 48,* 33-54.
4. Martin, A.J., Marsh, H.W., McInerney, D.M., & Green, J. (2009). Young people¡¯s interpersonal relationships and academic and non-academic outcomes: The relative salience of teachers, parents, same-sex peers, and opposite-sex peers. *Teachers College Record*. Published March 23, 2009 http://www.tcrec.org/Home.asp ID Number: 15593.
5. Van Etten, S., Pressley, M., McInerney, D. M., & Liem, A. D. (2008). College seniors¡¯ theory of their academic motivation. *Journal of Educational Psychology,* 100, 812-828.
6. McInerney, D. M. (2008). Personal investment, culture and learning: Insights into school achievement across Anglo, Indigenous, Asian and Lebanese students in Australia. *International Journal of Psychology, 43,* 870-879.
7. McInerney, D. M., Dowson, M., & Yeung, A. S. (2008). Impact of support from significant others on adolescents¡¯ academic performance, self-esteem and interest in academic work. *Australian Educational and Developmental Psychologist, 25,* 48-67.
8. Martin, A.J., Marsh, H.W., McInerney, D.M., Green, J., & Dowson, M. (2007). Getting along with teachers and parents: The yields of good relationships for students¡¯ achievement motivation and self-esteem. *Australian Journal of Guidance and Counselling, 17,* 109-125.
9. Yeung, A. S., Yuk Hun Hon, R., & McInerney, D. M. (2007). Learning to learn: How 4th and 5th Grade boys and girls differ. *Australian Educational and Developmental Psychologist, 24,* 69-89.
10. McInerney, D. M. (2006). The motivational profiles and perceptions of schooling of Asian students in Australia. *Malaysian Journal of Learning and Instruction. 3,* 1-31.
11. Dowson, M., McInerney, D. M., & Nelson, G. (2006). An investigation of the effects of school context and sex differences on students¡¯ motivational goal orientations. *Educational Psychology, 26,* 781-811.
12. Nelson, G. F., O¡¯Mara, A. J., McInerney, D. M., & Dowson, M. (2006). Motivation in cross-cultural settings: A Papua New Guinea Psychometric Study. *International Education Journal, 7,* 400-409 (http://iej.cjb.net).
13. Suliman, R., & McInerney, D. M (2006). Motivational goals and school achievement: Lebanese-background students in south western Sydney. *Australian Journal of Education, 50,* 242-264.
14. McInerney, D. M. & Ali, J. (2006) Multidimensional and hierarchical assessment of school motivation: Cross-cultural validation. *Educational Psychology: An International Journal of Experimental Educational Psychology, 26,* 717-734.
15. Sinclair, C., Dowson, M., & McInerney, D. M. (2006). Motivations to teach: Psychometric perspectives across the first semester of teacher education. *Teachers College Record, 108,* 1132-1154.

Brief Bio

Dennis McInerney joined the Institute as Chair Professor of Educational Psychology, Department of Educational Psychology, Counselling and Learning Needs. He has a concurrent appointment as Associate Vice President (Research and Development). Prior to this he was Research Professor and Associate Dean (Education Research) at the National Institute of Education, Nanyang Technological University, Singapore having served for a period as Vice-Dean (Research and Methodology) within the Centre for Research in Pedagogy and Practice. Previous to this Professor McInerney was Research Professor and Associate Director of the Self Research Centre at the University of Western Sydney.

Professor McInerney has a BA from Macquarie University, a B. Ed and M. Ed (Hons) from the University of New England, and a PhD from the University of Sydney. He is a registered psychologist and a member of the Australian Psychological Association and the American Psychological Association.

Professor McInerney has published over 200 research articles in refereed international journals, books and conferences. He edits two international research series, *Research on Sociocultural Influences on Motivation and Learning* (Vols 1-10) and *International Advances in Self Research* (Vols 1-3). He has received many research grants including seven Australian Research Council grants. He was awarded the University of Western Sydney¡s Senior Researcher Award and was the first Professor to receive a Personal Chair at the University of Western Sydney, Macarthur.

Professor McInerney has written a number of textbooks including *Educational Psychology: Constructing Learning* (Pearson 5th Edition, 2010) which is the best selling educational psychology text in Australia; *Developmental Psychology for Teachers* (Allen & Unwin, 2006); *Helping Kids Achieve Their Best: Understanding and Using Motivation in the Classroom* (published by Allen & Unwin, 2000 and republished by Information Age Publishing, 2005), and *Publishing Your Psychology Research* (Sage and Allen & Unwin, 2001). Professor McInerney is on the Editorial Boards of *Educational Psychology, Contemporary Educational Psychology, Educational Psychologist, Educational and Developmental Psychology and Malaysian Journal of Learning & Instruction* and reviews for over a dozen international research journals including *British Journal of Educational Psychology, Educational and Psychological Measurement, Educational Psychologist, Journal of Educational Psychology, Review of Educational Research, American Educational Research Journal, Australian Journal of Education,* and *Journal of Cross-cultural Psychology*.

In: Psychology Research Biographies and Summaries
Editors: Nancy E. Wodarth and Alexis P. Ferguson

ISBN: 978-1-61470-491-1
© 2012 Nova Science Publishers, Inc.

Chapter 35

BIOGRAPHICAL SKETCH – PSYCHOLOGY RESEARCH

Yukinori Nagakura

Affiliation: Drug Discovery Research, Astellas Pharma Inc.

Address: 21 Miyukigaoka, Tsukuba, Ibaraki 305-8585, Japan

Date of Birth: April 28, 1965

Education:

Ph.D., February 1998: Faculty of Pharmaceutical Sciences, Chiba University, Japan
M.Sc., March 1991: Faculty of Pharmaceutical Sciences, Chiba University, Japan
B.Sc., March 1989: Faculty of Pharmaceutical Sciences, Tokyo University of Science, Japan

Research and Professional Experience:

2007-present
Pharmacologist, Research Fellow,
Research on pain mechanisms and analgesics
Pharmacology Research Labs., Drug Discovery Research, Astellas Pharma Inc., Japan

2006-2007
Visiting scholar
Research on pain mechanisms
Department of Anesthesiology, University of California San Diego, USA

2005-2006
Pharmacologist, Research Fellow,
Research on pain mechanisms and analgesics
Neuroscience, Pharmacology Research Labs., Drug Discovery Research,

Astellas Pharma Inc., Japan

1996-2005
Pharmacologist, Assistant Research Officer,
Research on pain mechanisms and analgesics
Neuroscience Research, Pharmacology Labs., Institute for Drug Discovery Research, Yamanouchi Pharmaceutical Co. Ltd., Japan

1991-1996
Pharmacologist,
Research on gastrointestinal functions
Institute for Drug Discovery Research, Yamanouchi Pharmaceutical Co. Ltd., Japan

Professional Appointments: Research Fellow

Publications Last 3 Years:

:Corresponding author

1. Watabiki T, Nagakura Y*, Wegner K, Kakimoto S, Tozier NA, Malkmus SA, Yaksh TL. Assessment of canine sensory function by using sine-wave electrical stimuli paradigm. Physiol Behav 101:327-330, 2010.
2. Oe T, Tsukamoto M, Nagakura Y*. Reserpine causes biphasic nociceptive sensitivity alteration in conjunction with brain biogenic amine tones in rats. Neuroscience 169:1860-1871, 2010.
3. Nagakura Y*, Oe T, Aoki T, Matsuoka N. Biogenic amine depletion causes chronic muscular pain and tactile allodynia accompanied by depression: A putative animal model of fibromyalgia. Pain 146:26-33, 2009.
4. Nagakura Y, Jones TL, Malkmus SA, Sorkin L, Yaksh TL*. The sensitization of a broad spectrum of sensory nerve fibers in a rat model of acute postoperative pain and its response to intrathecal pharmacotherapy. Pain 139 569-577, 2008.
5. Kakimoto S*, Nagakura Y, Tamura S, Watabiki T, Shibasaki K, Tanaka S, Mori M, Sasamata M, Okada M. Minodronic acid, a third generation bisphosphonate, antagonizes purinergic P2X2/3 receptor function and exerts an analgesic effect in pain models. Eur J Pharmacol 589:98-101, 2008.
6. Nagakura Y, Malkmus S, Yaksh TL*. Determination of current threshold for paw withdrawal with sine-wave electrical stimulation in rats: Effect of drugs and alteration in acute inflammation. Pain 134:293-301, 2008.

In: Psychology Research Biographies and Summaries
Editors: Nancy E. Wodarth and Alexis P. Ferguson

ISBN: 978-1-61470-491-1
© 2012 Nova Science Publishers, Inc.

Chapter 36

BIOGRAPHICAL SKETCH – PSYCHOLOGY RESEARCH

Simona Nicolosi

Affiliation: Kore University of Enna

Address: Via Degli Oleandri n.19, 94100 Enna (Sicily, Italy)

Date of Birth: July 23th 1974

Education: Degree in Philosophy; Master degree in Evaluation of educational systems; High training course on Performance Analysis

Research and Professional Experience:

Researcher at Kore University of Enna from 2006. From 2009 to present, lecturer of "General and Sport Psychology" in I level course degree of Physical Activities and Sport Sciences at Kore University of Enna; From 2011, lecturer of "Cognitive and emotional functions in sport activities" in II level course degree of Physical Activities and Sport Sciences for the Health Care. From 2006 to 2010 lecturer of General Psychology in I level course degree in Psychological Sciences and Techniques.

From 2010, member of the Scientific Commission of PhD Course in "Physical activities and sport sciences in education and high performance".

From 2006 to 2009, member of Didactic Commission of I level course degree in Psychological Sciences and Techniques at Kore University of Enna. From 2010, member of Didactic Commission of I level course degree in Physical Activities and Sport Sciences at Kore University of Enna. In 2008, held a seminar on "Researches in Vocational Guidance Pshychology" in University of Cordoba, Faculty of Educational Sciences (in EU Erasmus Programme).

In 2007, coordinator of Master degree course in Methodology of Vocational Guidance (Kore University of Enna).

In 2006, lecturer of General Psychology in Master degree course Psychobiology of physical activities (Kore University of Enna).

Currently, she is involved in a longitudinal study in a project with over 200 early adolescents from 11 to 14 years old. The aim of the research is to investigate the effects of a specific physical activities programme and educational itineraries on Self perception, physical and social self-esteem, self-efficacy and interpersonal psychological adjustment. She is also working to an experimental design about attentional styles, coping and problem solving in handball players.

The main topics of Nicolosi's research are:

Physical activity and Self development, physical activities and meta-cognitive processes in problem solving in early adolescence;
Personality, self-esteem, self-efficacy, risk taking in adolescence and sport;
Interpersonal Psychological Adjustment and Physical Activities.

Professional Appointments: --

Honors: --

Main Publications Last 3 Years (2009-2011):

- Nicolosi S., Schembri R., Sgrò F., Mango P., & Lipoma M. (2011). Physical activities in early adolescence: implications for self-description and interpersonal perception. In: *Research in Sports Science 5*, in press.
- Schembri R., Mango P., Arpino M., Tangusso R., & Nicolosi S. (2011) Empowerment, locus of control and professional interests: an action research with Kore University students. In: *Research in Sports Science 5*, in press.
- Nicolosi S., Schembri R., & Lipoma M. (2011) Identità e interessi professionali nei processi di scelta. Un'esperienza professionale e di ricerca post lauream nelle scuole medie secondarie di Enna. In Petruccelli F., D'Amario B., & Giordano V. (Eds) *La scelta formativa: attitudini, competenze e motivazioni*. Franco Angeli, Milano.
- Nicolosi S., Schembri R., Pignato S., Lo Piccolo A., Mango P., Sgrò F., & Lipoma M. (2010) Self and physical activities in early adolescence: an action research with middle-school students. *Procedia. Social and Behavioral Sciences*. 9, 239–243.
- Nicolosi S., Schembri R., Tangusso R., & Mango P., & Lipoma M., Sé corporeo e attività motorie nella preadolescenza: dalla ricerca all'intervento didattico integrato. In *Atti delle Giornate di studio "Il corpo e il movimento nella ricerca didattica"*, Salerno, 28-29 maggio 2010, in press.
- Nicolosi S. & M.Lipoma (2009) Inhabilidad y actividad motriz en la escuela de la infancia: desde la idea de integraciòn hasta la realizaciòn de acciones educativas. In Lipoma M., *Itinerarios didàctico-pedagogicos en la labor educativa de la actividad motora y deportiva*. UCO. Universidad de Cordoba. Dipartamento de educatciòn artistica y corporal. Cordoba.

- S.Pignato, P.Mango, Nicolosi S. & M.Lipoma (2009) Social integration and sport practice of students with intellective disability. In Hughes M., Dancs H. & Nagyvaradi K. (Eds) *Research in Sport Science*. West of Hungary University (Savaria), Szombathely, Hungary.
- S.Nicolosi (2009) Correlati psicologici della partecipazione delle persone con disabilità ad attività motorie e sportive: spunti applicativi della Performance Analysis. In Hughes M., Lipoma M. & Sibilio M. (a cura di) *La Performance Analysis: elementi di base ed aspetti applicativi in campo educativo ed integrativo*. Franco Angeli, Milano.

Chapter 37

BIOGRAPHICAL SKETCH – PSYCHOLOGY RESEARCH

Pantelis Nikolaidis

Affiliation: Laboratory of Human Performance and Rehabilitation, Hellenic Army Academy, Greece

Address: Thermopylon 7, Nikaia 18450, Greece

Date of Birth: 20/4/1979

Education: Ph.D. in Exercise Physiology, MSc in Exercise Physiology, BSc in Physical Education

Research and Professional Experience:

2008-2011, Laboratory of Human Performance and Rehabilitation, Hellenic Army Academy, Greece;
2004-2008, Biomedical Laboratory, Charles University in Prague, Czech Republic

Professional Appointments:

Lecturer, Laboratory of Human Performance and Rehabilitation, Hellenic Army Academy, Greece

Honors:

Scholarship (State Foundation of Scholarships of Greece, 2004-2008), Scholarship (Marie Curie Foundation, 2007)

Publications Last 3 Years:

Nikolaidis, P.T. and Papadopoulos, V.E. (2011): Cardiorespiratory power and force-velocity characteristics in road cycling: the effect of aging and underlying physiological mechanisms. Medicina Sportiva (in print).

Nikolaidis, P.T. and Karydis, N.V. (2011): Physique and body composition in soccer players across adolescence. Asian Journal of Sports Medicine, 2(2): 75-82.

Nikolaidis, P.T. (2010): Familial aggregation and maximal heritability of exercise participation: A cross-sectional study in schoolchildren and their nuclear families. Science & Sports (DOI 10.1016/j.scispo.2010.09.010).

Nikolaidis, P. (2010): Physiological characteristics of elite Greek female soccer players. Medicina dello Sport, 63(3): 343-351.

Nikolaidis, P. (2010): Obesity and sport in childhood - a case of a track and field club. Acta Facultatis Educationis Physicae Universitatis Comenianae, 50(1): 49-54.

Nikolaidis, P. (2010): Core stability of male and female football players. Biomedical Human Kinetics, 2: 30-33.

Nikolaidis, P. (2009): Inactivity, nutritional and lifestyle habits: a cross-sectional study in Czech schoolchildren and their nuclear families. Facta Universitatis Series Physical Education and Sport, 7(2): 141-151.

Nikolaidis, P. (2009): Gender differences in anaerobic power in Physical Education and Sport students. Citius Altius Fortius Journal of Physical Education and Sport 24(3): 140-145.

In: Psychology Research Biographies and Summaries
Editors: Nancy E. Wodarth and Alexis P. Ferguson
ISBN: 978-1-61470-491-1
© 2012 Nova Science Publishers, Inc.

Chapter 38

BIOGRAPHICAL SKETCH – PSYCHOLOGY RESEARCH

Toru Sato

Affiliation: Shippensburg University

Address:
Dept. of Psychology
Shippensburg University
1871 Old Main Drive
Shippensburg, PA, 17257-2299

Date of Birth: 1967

Education: Ph.D. Psychology

Research and Professional Experience: Researcher and Teaching Faculty at Shippensburg University, Dept. of Psychology

Professional Appointments:

2005- present: Associate Professor of Psychology, Shippensburg University,
1997-2010: Consulting Editor of The Journal of Psychology

Honors: none

Publications Last 3 Years:

Sato, T., Harman, B. A., Donohoe, W. M., Weaver, A., & Hall, W. A. (2010). Individual differences in ego-depletion: The role of sociotropy-autonomy. Motivation and Emotion, 34, 205-213.

Sato, T., & Gonzalez, M. A. (2009). Interpersonal patterns in close relationships: The role of sociotropy-autonomy. British Journal of Psychology, 100, 327-345.

Sato, T., Feight, K., Goshorn, J., Materek, A., Scott, V. L., Spohn, K., & Gonzalez, M. A. (2009). Interaction patterns of sociotropic and autonomous individuals. In A. T. Heatherton & V. A.

Walcott (Eds.), Handbook of Social Interactions in the 21st Century (pp. 265-289). Hauppage, New York: Nova Science.

Chapter 39

BIOGRAPHICAL SKETCH – PSYCHOLOGY RESEARCH

Dr. James Schuurmans-Stekhoven

Affiliation: Charles Sturt University

Address: CSU LPO Box 8049, Bathurst, NSW, 2795

Date of Birth: Not applicable

Education: B.Ec. (hon), Grad Dip. Ag. Ec., B.Sc. (hon), PhD (clin. psych.)

Research and Professional Experience: NA

Professional Appointments: NA

Honors: NA

Publications Last 3 Years:

Schuurmans-Stekhoven, J. B. (2009). Cutting your losses: Could best-practice pedagogy involve acknowledging that even robust hope may be vain? *Asia-Pacific Journal of Teacher Education, 37(3),* 333-345. DOI: 10.1080/13598660903056523

Schuurmans-Stekhoven, J. B. (2010). "Moved by the spirit". Does spirituality moderate the inter-relationships between Subjective Well-Being (SWB) subscales? *Journal of Clinical Psychology, 66(7),* 709-725. DOI: 10.1002/jclp.20694

Schuurmans-Stekhoven, J. B. (2011). Is it God or just the data that moves in mysterious ways? How well-being research might be mistaking faith for virtue? *Social Indicators Research, 100(2),* 313-330. DOI: 10.1007/s11205-010-9630-7

Schuurmans-Stekhoven, J. B. & Buckingham M. J. (2010). Ratio or length? A proposed methodology for understanding digit ratio and personality using a female sample *Journal of Individual Differences*, *31(3)*, 150-157. DOI: 10.1027/1614-0001/a000023

In: Psychology Research Biographies and Summaries ISBN: 978-1-61470-491-1
Editors: Nancy E. Wodarth and Alexis P. Ferguson © 2012 Nova Science Publishers, Inc.

Chapter 40

BIOGRAPHICAL SKETCH – PSYCHOLOGY RESEARCH

Bruce W. Smith

Affiliation: University of New Mexico

Address: Department of Psychology, University of New Mexico, Albuquerque, NM 87131

Date of Birth: 5/13/58

Education: Ph.D.

Research and Professional Experience: Associate Professor (see attached CV for additional detail)

Professional Appointments: Clinical Psychology at the University of New Mexico

Honors:

> Honor: Senior Fellow of the Robert Wood Johnson Foundation
> Description: The fellowship includes funds for research, travel, course buyouts, and support for graduate students.
> Date: December 2009
> Organization: Robert Wood Johnson Foundation
>
> Honor: Nominated for inclusion in Who's Who in America.
> Description: I was independently nominated and invited to submit my biography for inclusion in the 2010 version of Who's Who in America.
> Date: November 2009
> Organization: Marquis Who's Who, New Providence, New Jersey

Honor: Invited to submit a feature article for "The Pain Practitioner" which is the official journal of the American Academy of Pain Management.

Description: This invitation was based on my research published in the journal "Pain" (Smith, Tooley, Montague, Robinson, Cosper, & Mullins, 2008). The Pain Practitioner is circulated to 10,000 pain practitioners (e.g., physicians, physical therapists, psychologists) and is a primary source of treatment-related information for pain clinicians. The purpose of the article was to apply my research findings to the care and treatment of people with fibromyalgia (Smith, 2009).

Date: January 2009

Organization: The American Academy of Pain Management, Sonora, California

Honor: Best submission to the 2005 annual meeting of the American Psychological Association.

Description: My submission titled "Neural Bases of Reappraisal of Pleasant and Unpleasant Pictures" was selected as a best submission to the Division of Clinical Neuropsychology for the annual meeting of the American Psychological Association in Washington, D.C.

Date: August 2005

Organization: Division of Clinical Neuropsychology of the American Psychological Association, Washington, DC.

Honor: Meeting highlight of the 2003 annual meeting of the American Psychiatric Association.

Description: My paper titled "Anxiety and Depression as Predictors of Pain in Women with Arthritis" was selected as a meeting highlight of the annual meeting of the American Psychiatric Association in San Francisco, California.

Date: May 2003

Organization: CNS News, McMahon Publishing, New York, New York.

Honor: Doctoral Dissertation Award

Description: My dissertation proposal titled "The Role of Resilience in Adaptation to Rheumatoid Arthritis and Osteoarthritis" was awarded first place in a national competition.

Date: August 2000

Organization: Arthritis Foundation, Atlanta, Georgia.

Honor: Ellin Bloch and Pierre Ritchie Honorary Scholarship

Description: I was awarded first place in this national competition based on a proposal articulating my goals, my research, and how the scholarship would enable me to reach my goals.

Date: August 1999

Organization: American Psychological Association, Washington, DC.

Publications Last 3 Years:

Dalen, J., Smith, B.W., Shelley, B.M., Sloan, A.L., Leahigh, L, & Begay, D. (2010). Mindful Eating and Living (MEAL): Eating behaviors and psychological outcomes associated with a mindfulness-based intervention for people with obesity. *Complementary Therapies in Medicine, 18,* 260-264.

Hoyt, T., Pasupathi, M., Smith, B.W., Yeater, E.A., Kay, V.S., & Tooley, E. (2010). Disclosure of emotional events in groups at risk for PTSD. *International Journal of Stress Management, 17,* 78-95.

Smith, B.W., Papp, Z., Tooley, E.M., Montague, E.Q., Robinson, A.E., & Cosper, C.J. (2010). Traumatic events, perceived stress, and health in women with fibromyalgia and healthy controls. *Stress and Health, 26,* 83-93.

Smith, B.W., Tooley, E.M., Christopher, P.J., & Kay, V.S. (2010). Resilience as the ability to bounce back from stress: A neglected personal resource? *Journal of Positive Psychology, 5,* 166-176.

Delaney, H.D., Forcehimes, A.A., Campbell, W.P., & Smith, B.W. (2009). Integrating spirituality into alcohol treatment. *Journal of Clinical Psychology, 65,* 185-198.

Smith, B.W., Kay, V.S., Hoyt, T.V., & Bernard, M.L. (2009). Predicting the anticipated emotional and behavioral responses to an avian flu outbreak. *American Journal of Infection Control, 37,* 371-380.

Smith, B. W., Mitchell, D. G. V., Hardin, M. G., Jazbec, S., Fridberg, D., Pine, D. S., Blair, R. J. R., Ernst, M. (2009). Neural substrates of reward magnitude, probability, and risk during a wheel of fortune decision-making task. *Neuroimage, 44,* 600-609.

Smith, B.W., & Tonigan, J.S. (2009). AA benefit and social attachment. *Alcoholism Treatment Quarterly, 27,* 164-173.

Smith, B.W., Tooley, E.M., Montague, E.Q., Robinson, A.E., Cosper, C.J, & Mullins, P.G.M. (2009). The role of resilience and purpose in life in habituation to heat and cold pain. *The Journal of Pain, 10,* 493-500.

Alim, T. N, Feder, A., Graves, E., Wang, Y., Weaver, J., Alonso, A., Aibogun, N., Smith, B. W., Doucette, J. T., Mellman, T. A., Lawson, W. B., Charney, D. S. (2008). Trauma, resilience, and recovery in a high-risk population. *The American Journal of Psychiatry, 165,* 1566-1575.

Blair, K.S., Shaywitz, J., Smith, B.W., Rhodes, R., Geraci, M., Jones, M., McCaffrey, D., Vythilingam, M., Finger, E., Mondillo, K., Jacobs, M., Charney, D.S., Blair, R.J.R., Drevets, W.C., & Pine, D.S. (2008). Response to emotional expressions in Generalized Social Phobia (GSP) and Generalized Anxiety Disorder (GAD): Evidence for separate disorders. *The American Journal of Psychiatry, 165,* 1193-1202.

Feder, A., Southwick, S.M., Goetz, R.R., Wang, Y., Alonso, A., Smith, B.W., Buchholz, K.R., Waldeck, T., Ameli, R., Moore, J., Hain, R., Charney, D.S., & Vythilingham, M. (2008). Posttraumatic growth in former Vietnam prisoners of war. *Psychiatry-Interpersonal and Biological Processes, 71,* 359-370.

Smith, B.W., Dalen, J., Bernard, J.F., & Baumgartner, K.B. (2008). Posttraumatic growth in non-Hispanic white and Hispanic women with cervical cancer. *Journal of Psychosocial Oncology, 26,* 91-109.

Smith, B.W., Dalen, J., Wiggins, K., Christopher, P., Bernard, J., & Shelley, B.M. (2008). Who is willing to use complementary and alternative medicine? *Explore, 4,* 359-367.

Smith, B.W., Dalen, J., Wiggins, K., Tooley, E., Christopher, P., & Bernard, J. (2008). The Brief Resilience Scale: Assessing the ability to bounce back. *International Journal of Behavioral Medicine, 15,* 194-200.

Smith, B.W., Shelley, B.M., Dalen, J., Wiggins, K., Tooley, E., & Bernard, J. (2008). A pilot study comparing the effects of Mindfulness-Based and Cognitive-Behavioral Stress Reduction. *Journal of Alternative and Complementary Medicine, 14,* 251-258.

Smith, B.W., Tooley, E.M., Montague, E.Q., Robinson, A.E., Cosper, C.J, & Mullins, P.G.M. (2008). Habituation and sensitization to heat and cold pain in women with fibromyalgia and healthy controls. *Pain, 140,* 420-428.

Smith, B.W., & Zautra, A.J. (2008). The effects of anxiety and depression on weekly pain in women with arthritis. *Pain, 138,* 354-361.

Smith, B.W., & Zautra, A.J. (2008). Vulnerability and resilience in women with arthritis: Test of a two-factor model. *Journal of Consulting and Clinical Psychology, 76,* 799-810.

In: Psychology Research Biographies and Summaries
Editors: Nancy E. Wodarth and Alexis P. Ferguson
ISBN: 978-1-61470-491-1
© 2012 Nova Science Publishers, Inc.

Chapter 41

BIOGRAPHICAL SKETCH – PSYCHOLOGY RESEARCH

David Trafimow

Affiliation: New Mexico State University

Address: Department of Psychology, MSC 3452/P.O. Box 30001/New Mexico State University/Las Cruces, NM 88003-8001

Date of Birth: May 12, 1962

Education: Ph.D.

Research and Professional Experience: Professor of Psychology

Professional Appointments: Executive Editor of Journal of General Psychology

Honors: Fellow, Association for Psychological Science

Publications Last 3 Years:

Rice, S. & Trafimow, D. (in press). It's a just world no matter which way you look at it. *Journal of General Psychology*.

Trafimow, D. & Rice, S. (in press). Using a sharp instrument to parse apart strategy and consistency: An evaluation of PPT and its assumptions. *Journal of General Psychology*.

Hughes, J. S., & Trafimow, D. (in press). Inferences about character and motive influence intentionality attribution about side effects. *British Journal of Social Psychology*.

Hughes, J. S., Sandry, J., & Trafimow, D. (in press). Intentional inferences are not more likely than unintentional ones: Some evidence against the intentionality bias hypothesis. *Journal of Social Psychology*.

Trafimow, D. (in press). Specific Mechanisms versus General Theories in the Classification of Disorders. *Dialogues in Philosophy, Mental and Neuro Sciences*.

Trafimow, D. (in press). The role of auxiliary assumptions for the validity of manipulations and measures. *Theory and Psychology*.

Rice, S., Trafimow, D., Hughes, J. & Hunt, G. (in press). Extending a courtesy stigma to a computer programmer, his work product, and his associates. *International Journal of Technology, Knowledge and Society*.

Rice, S., & Trafimow, D. (2011). Known Versus Unknown Threats to Internal Validity: A Response to Edwards. *American Journal of Bioethics*, *11*, 20-21.

Trafimow, D. & Rice, S. (2011). Korn and Freidlin's misunderstanding of the null hypothesis significance testing procedure. *American Journal of Bioethics*, *11*, 15-16.

Trafimow, D., Hunt, G. Rice, S. & Geels, K. (in press). Using potential performance theory to test five hypotheses about meta-attribution. *Journal of General Psychology*.

Trafimow, D. (in press). Using Pictures to Enhance Students' Understanding of Bayes' Theorem. *Teaching Statistics*.

Rice, S., Trafimow, D., Keller, D. & Bean, N. (in press). Confluence Theory: Uniting two houses divided. *Theoretical Issues in Ergonomics Science*.

Sandry, J., Hunt, G., Rice, S., Trafimow, D., & Geels, K. (in press). Can priming yourself lead to punishing others? *The Journal of Social Psychology*.

Rice, S., Trafimow, D., Keller, D., Hunt, G. & Geels, K. (2011). Using PPT to Correct for Inconsistency in a Speeded Task. *The Journal of General Psychology, 138*, pp. 12-34.

Trafimow, D. (2010). On Making Assumptions about Auxiliary Assumptions: Reply to Wallach and Wallach. *Theory and Psychology*, *20*, 707-711.

Rice, S., Trafimow, D., Rahmania, A., Keller, D., Hunt, G., Taruc, K., Dirhamsyah, M., & Ridha, M. (2010). Sound the alarmdeath Approaches (*Suarakan GenderangMaut Menyerang*): The tsunami early warning system in Indonesia. *The International Journal of Technology, Knowledge & Society*, *6*, 13-26.

Trafimow, D. (2010). The Implications of Meaning for the Validity of Diagnostic Categories: Comment on Rodriguez and Banzato. *Dialogues in Philosophy, Mental and Neuro Sciences*, *3*, 23-24.

Trafimow, D., Clayton, K. D., Sheeran, P., Darwish, A-F. E, & Brown, J. (2010). How do people form behavioral intentions when others have the power to determine social consequences? *Journal of General Psychology, 137,* 287-309.

Rice, S., Keller, D., Trafimow, D. & Sandry, J. (2010). Retention of a Time Pressure Heuristic in a Target Identification Task. *Journal of General Psychology*, *137*, 239-255.

Trafimow, D., MacDonald, J., Rice, S., & Clason, D. L. (2010). How often is prep close to the true replication probability? Psychological Methods, 15, 300-307.

Rice, S., Trafimow, D., Keller, D., & Hunt, G. (2010). We don't dislike the alarm; we dislike complying with the alarm. The International Journal of Technology, Knowledge, and Society, 6, 93-105.

Rice, S., Trafimow, D., Keller, D., & Hunt, G. (2010). Should I stay or should I run? The International Journal of Technology, Knowledge, and Society, 6, 81-91.

Rice, S. & Trafimow, D., & Hunt, G. (2010). Using PPT to analyze sub-optimal human-automation performance. Journal of General Psychology, 137, 310-329.

Rice, S., & Trafimow, D. (2010). How many people have to die for a Type II error? *Theoretical Issues in Ergonomics Science*, *11*, 387-401.

Hughes, J. S., & Trafimow, D. (2010). Intentionality attributions about perfect and imperfect duty violations. *Journal of Social Psychology*, *150*, 198-210.

Rice, S., Trafimow, D., Hunt, G. & Sandry, J. (2010). Generalizing Kant's distinction between perfect and imperfect duties to trust in different situations. *Journal of General Psychology, 137*, 20-36

Trafimow, D., & Rice, S. (2010). The Role of Auxiliary Assumptions in the Falsification of Ergonomics Theories. *Theoretical Issues in Ergonomics Science, 11*, 220-229.

Elliot, L, Rice, S., Trafimow, D., Hipshur, M., Madson, L. & Vigil, H. (2010). Students' perceptions of their learning due to summarizing articles, attending class, and participating in research. *Teaching of Psychology, 37*, 1-3.

Verplanken, B., Trafimow, D., Khusid, I. K., Holland, R. W., & Steentjes, G. (2009). Different selves, different values: Effects of self-construals on value activation and use. *European Journal of Social Psychology, 39*, 909-919.

Hughes, J. S., Rice, S., Trafimow, D., & Clayton, K. (2009). The automated cockpit: A comparison of attitudes toward human and automated pilots. Transportation Research Part F: Traffic Psychology and Behavior, 12, 428-439.

Rice, S., Clayton, K. D., Trafimow, D., Keller, D., & Hughes, J. (2009). Effects of private or collective self-priming on visual search: Taking advantage of organized contextual stimuli. *British Journal of Social Psychology, 48*, 467-486.

Trafimow, D., & Rice, S. (2009). A Test of the NHSTP Correlation Argument. *Journal of General Psychology, 136*, 261-269.

Trafimow, D. (2009). The Theory of Reasoned Action: A Case Study of Falsification in Psychology. *Theory & Psychology, 19*, 501-518.

Trafimow, D. (2009). Reeder's MIM as a special case of confluence theory. *Psychological Inquiry, 20*, 48-52.

Trafimow, D., & Rice (2009). Potential performance theory (PPT): Describing a methodology for analyzing task performance. Behavior Research Methods, 41, 359-371.

Trafimow, D., & Rice, S. (2009). What If Social Scientists Had Reviewed Great Scientific Works of the Past? *Perspectives in Psychological Science, 4*, 65-78.

Rice, S., Trafimow, D., Clayton, K. & Hunt, G. (2008). Impact of the contrast effect on trust ratings and behavior with automated systems. *Cognitive Technology Journal, 13*, 30-41.

Trafimow, D., & Rice, S. (2008). Potential performance theory (PPT): A general theory of task performance applied to morality. *Psychological Review, 115*, 447-462.

Chapter 42

BIOGRAPHICAL SKETCH – PSYCHOLOGY RESEARCH

Matthew J. Traxler

Affiliation: University of California, Davis

Address: UC Davis Department of Psychology
1 Shields Avenue
Davis, CA 95616

Date of Birth: 10.25.1965

Education: BA, MS, Ph.D.

Research and Professional Experience:

Postdoctoral Research Fellow, University of Glasgow 1993-1996
Visiting Assistant in Cognitive Science, The Florida State University 1996-1999
Director, Eye-Movement Lab, University of South Carolina, 1999-2002
Director, Eye-Movement Lab, University of California, Davis, 2002-Present

Professional Experience

2008-Present	Professor (Tenured)
	Department of Psychology and Center for Mind and Brain
	University of California at Davis
	Davis, California
2004-2008	Associate Professor (Tenured)
	Department of Psychology and Center for Mind and Brain
	University of California at Davis
	Davis, California

2002-2004	Assistant Professor (Tenure Track) Department of Psychology and Center for Mind and Brain University of California at Davis Davis, California
1999 - 2002	Assistant Professor (Tenure Track) Department of Psychology University of South Carolina Columbia, South Carolina
1996 - 1999	Visiting Assistant in Cognitive Science Department of Psychology The Florida State University Tallahassee, Florida
1996 - 1999	Honorary Research Fellow Human Communication Research Centre Department of Psychology University of Glasgow Glasgow, Scotland
1993 - 1996	Postdoctoral Research Assistant Human Communication Research Centre Department of Psychology University of Glasgow

Professional Appointments:

2008-Present	Professor (Tenured) Department of Psychology and Center for Mind and Brain University of California at Davis Davis, California
2004-2008	Associate Professor (Tenured) Department of Psychology and Center for Mind and Brain University of California at Davis Davis, California
2002-2004	Assistant Professor (Tenure Track) Department of Psychology and Center for Mind and Brain University of California at Davis Davis, California
1999 - 2002	Assistant Professor (Tenure Track) Department of Psychology University of South Carolina Columbia, South Carolina
1996 - 1999	Visiting Assistant in Cognitive Science Department of Psychology The Florida State University Tallahassee, Florida
1996 - 1999	Honorary Research Fellow

	Human Communication Research Centre
	Department of Psychology
	University of Glasgow
	Glasgow, Scotland
1993 - 1996	Postdoctoral Research Assistant
	Human Communication Research Centre
	Department of Psychology
	University of Glasgow
1992 - 1993	Lecturer
	Department of Psychology
	University of Wisconsin
	Madison, Wisconsin
1990, 1991	Instructor
	Department of Psychology
	University of Oregon
	Eugene, Oregon
1989-1992	Research Assistant
	Department of Psychology
	University of Oregon

Honors:

2001	Outstanding Achievement Award, University of South Carolina Department of Psychology
1988	Research Fellowship, National Science Foundation, University of Minnesota Undergraduate Research Opportunities Program
1988	Phi Kappa Alpha - National Scholastic Honor Society
1984	National Merit Finalist

Publications Last 3 Years:

1. Johns, C.L., Tooley, K.M., & Traxler, M.J. (2008). Right hemisphere language disorders. *Language and Linguistics Compass*, 2, 1038-1062.
2. Traxler, M.J. (2008a). Lexically independent priming in online sentence comprehension. *Psychonomic Bulletin and* Review, 15, 149-155.
3. Traxler, M.J., (2008b). Structural priming among prepositional phrases: Evidence from eye-movements. *Memory & Cognition*, 36, 659-674.
4. Traxler, M.J., & Tooley, K.M. (2008). Priming in sentence comprehension: Strategic or syntactic? *Language and Cognitive Processes*, 23, 609-645.
5. Traxler, M.J., & Frazier, L. (2008). The role of pragmatic principles in resolving attachment ambiguities: Evidence from eye-movements. *Memory & Cognition*, 36, 314-328.

6. Tooley, K.M., Traxler, M.J., & Swaab, T.Y. (2009). Electrophysiological and Behavioral Evidence of Syntactic Priming in Sentence Comprehension. *Journal of Experimental Psychology: Learning, Memory, & Cognition*, **35**, 19-45.
7. Traxler, M.J. (2010). A hierarchical linear modeling analysis of working memory and implicit prosody in the resolution of adjunct attachment ambiguity. *Journal of Psycholinguistic Research*, **38**, 491-509.
8. Traxler, M.J., & Long, D.L. (in press). Working memory in language comprehension. *The Encyclopdia of the Mind*. San Diego, CA: Sage.
9. Traxler, M.J. (in press a). Parsing. *Wiley Interdisciplinary Reviews: Cognitive Science.*
10. Traxler, M.J. (in press b). *Language Science*. Boston, MA: Wiley-Blackwell.
11. Traxler, M.J., Long, D.L., Johns, C.L., Tooley, K.M., Zirnstein, M., & Jonathan, E. (in press). Individual differences in eye-movements during reading: Working memory and speed-of-processing effects. *Journal of Eye Movement Research.*
12. Tooley, K.M., & Traxler, M.J. (in press a). Syntactic priming in comprehension: A dual mechanism account. In R. Mishra (Ed.), *The Relationship between Language and Thought.*
13. Frazier, L., & Traxler, M.J. (in press). The syntax-pragmatic interface: Attachment preferences revisited. In R. Di Matteo & L. Tommasi (Eds.), *Cross-Linguistic Perspectives on Language Processing*. New York, NY: John Benjamins.
14. Tooley, K.M., & Traxler, M.J. (in press b). Syntactic priming effects in comprehension: A critical review. *Linguistics and Language Compass.*
15. Traxler, M.J., Caplan, D., Long, D.L., & Waters, G.S. (in press). Working memory in sentence comprehension and production. In F. Columbus (Ed.), *Working Memory: Capacity, Developments, and Improvement Techniques*. Hauppage, NY: Nova Science Publishers.

In: Psychology Research Biographies and Summaries
Editors: Nancy E. Wodarth and Alexis P. Ferguson
ISBN: 978-1-61470-491-1
© 2012 Nova Science Publishers, Inc.

Chapter 43

BIOGRAPHICAL SKETCH – PSYCHOLOGY RESEARCH

Ruud van den Bos PhD

Affiliation: Department of Animals in Science and Society, Division of Behavioural Neuroscience, Faculty of Veterinary Medicine, Yalelaan 2, 3584 CM, Utrecht University, Utrecht, the Netherlands; Rudolf Magnus Institute of Neuroscience, Utrecht University, Utrecht, the Netherlands

Address: Yalelaan 2, 3584 CM Utrecht, the Netherlands

Date of Birth: 20th December 1960

Education: Radboud University Nijmegen, Nijmegen, the Netherlands (MSc: 1986; PhD: 1991)

Research and Professional Experience:

Translational studies on decision-making related to sex, stress and anxiety; extensive experience in teaching (BSc-, MSc-, PhD-students).

Professional Appointments: Assistant professor at the above address.

Publications Last 3 Years (relevant to the topic):

1. Visser, de L, Baars, AM, Lavrijsen, M, Weerd, van der CMM & **Bos, van den R** (2011) Decision-making performance is related to levels of anxiety and differential recruitment of frontostriatal areas in male rats. Neurosci. (in press);
2. Visser, de L, Knaap van der, LJ, Loo van de AJAE., Weerd, van der CMM, Ohl, F & **Bos, van den R** (2010) Trait anxiety affects decision-making differently in healthy men and

women: towards gender-specific endophenotypes of anxiety. Neuropsychologia 48:1598-1606;
3. **Bos, van den R,** Harteveld M & Stoop H (2009) Stress and decision-making in humans: performance is related to cortisol-reactivity, albeit differently in men and women. Psychoneuroendocrinol. 34: 1449-1458;
4. Koot, S., **Bos, van den R.**, Adriani, W. & Laviola, G. (2009). Gender differences in delay-discounting under mild food restriction. Behav. Brain Res. 200: 134-143;
5. **Bos, van den R.**, Homberg, J., Gijsbers, E., den Heijer, E. den & Cuppen, E. (2009). The effect of COMT Val158 Met genotype on decision-making and preliminary findings on its interaction with the 5-HTTLPR in healthy females. Neuropharmacol. 56: 493-498;
6. Homberg, JR, **Bos, van den R**, Heijer, den E, Suer, R & Cuppen, E (2008) Serotonin transporter dosages modulates long-term decision-making in rat and human. Neuropharmacol. 55:80-84;

In: Psychology Research Biographies and Summaries
Editors: Nancy E. Wodarth and Alexis P. Ferguson

ISBN: 978-1-61470-491-1
© 2012 Nova Science Publishers, Inc.

Chapter 44

BIOGRAPHICAL SKETCH – PSYCHOLOGY RESEARCH

Christopher Was

Affiliation: Kent State University

Address: 405 White Hall, Kent State University, Kent, OH 44242

Date of Birth: 06/01/1967

Education: Ph.D. University of Utah; Learning, Memory and Cognition

Research and Professional Experience:

Professional Appointments: Assistant Professor of Educational Psychology Kent State University

Publications Last 3 Years:

Isaacson, R. M., & Was, C. A. (2010). Believing You're Correct vs. Knowing You're Correct: A Significant difference? *The Researcher* <http://faculty.kent.edu/cwas/Isaacson_and_Was_in_press.pdf> ,*23*(1), 1-12.

Was, C. A., (2010). Individual differences in reading are more than just working memory: The case for available long-term memory. *Individual Differences Research, 8*(3), 132-139.

Was, C. A. (2010). The persistence of content-specific memory operations: Priming effects following a 24-hour delay. *Psychonomic Bulletin & Review, 17(3), 362-368.* <http://faculty.kent.edu/cwas/Was_2010.pdf>

*Al-Harthy, I., Was, C. A., & Isaacson, R. M. (2010). Efficacy and Metacognitive Self-Regulation: A Path Analysis. *International Journal of Education, 2(1), 1-20.* <

http://faculty.kent.edu/cwas/Al-Harthy%20Was%20and%20Isaacson%202010.pdf >

Was, C. A., *Al-Harthy, I., *Stack-Oden, M., & Isaacson, R. M. (2009). Academic Identity Status and the Relationship to Achievement Goal Orientation. *Electronic Journal of Research in Educational Psychology, 7*(2), 627-652.
<http://www.investigacion-psicopedagogica.org/revista/new/english/ContadorArticulo.php?323 >

Was, C. A., & Isaacson, R. M. (2008). The Development of a Measure of Academic Identity Status. *Journal of Research in Education, 18, 94-105.*
< **http://faculty.kent.edu/cwas/Was%20and%20Isaacson%202008.pdf**>

Cook, A. E., Gueraud, S., Was, C. A., & O'Brien, E. J (2007). Foregrounding Effects During Reading, Revisited. *Discourse Processes, 44(2), 91–111*
< **http://faculty.kent.edu/cwas/reappointment/Cook_etal_2007.pdf**>.

Was, C. A. (2007). Further Evidence that Not All Executive Functions are Equal. *Advances in Cognitive Psychology, 3* < **http://faculty.kent.edu/cwas/Was_ACP.pdf**> (3), 399-407.

Was, C. A., & Woltz, D. J. (2007) Reexamining the relationship between working memory and comprehension: The role of available long-term memory. *Journal of Memory and Language, 56* < **http://faculty.kent.edu/cwas/Was_and_Woltz_2007.pdf**> (1), 86-102.

Woltz, D. J., & Was, C. A. (2007). Available but Unattended Conceptual Information in Working Memory: Temporarily Active Semantic Knowledge or Persistent Memory for Prior Operations? *Journal of Experimental Psychology: Learning, Memory, and Cognition, 33* < **http://faculty.kent.edu/cwas/Woltz_and_Was_2007.pdf**> (1), 158-168.

In: Psychology Research Biographies and Summaries
Editors: Nancy E. Wodarth and Alexis P. Ferguson
ISBN: 978-1-61470-491-1
© 2012 Nova Science Publishers, Inc.

Chapter 45

BIOGRAPHICAL SKETCH – PSYCHOLOGY RESEARCH

Philip M. Wilson, PhD

Affiliation: Brock University

Address: Behavioural Health Sciences Research Lab, Department of Physical Education & Kinesiology, Faculty of Applied Health Sciences, Brock University, St Catharines, Ontario, L2S3A1, Canada

Date of Birth: February 5th, 1972

Education: BSc (University of North Carolina Greensboro, 1994); MSc (University of North Dakota, 1996); PhD (University of Alberta, 2003)

Research and Professional Experience:

My research interests concern understanding the determinants and consequences of participation behaviour (e.g., physical activity, food intake, substance use) using motivational concepts, and applied measurement issues with an emphasis on instrument development and evaluation. I am particularly interested in applications of Self-Determination Theory to the study of motivational and psychological well-being issues in various contexts. More about my research activities can be found on our lab's webite at the following link: http://bhsrl.weebly.com

Professional Appointments: I am currently appointed in the following areas:

- Associate Professor (Faculty of Applied Health Science, Brock University, Canada)
- Adjunct Professor (Faculty of Science, McMaster University, Canada)
- Member-Faculty of Self-Determination Theory (University of Rochester, USA)

- International Faculty Member-Motivation in Educational Research Lab (National Institute of Education, Singapore)

Honors: Select honours earned over the course of my career include:

- Research funding from the Social Sciences and Humanities Research Council of Canada (2005-present), the Canadian Foundation for Innovation (2003-2004), and the Ontario Innovation Trust (2003-2004)
- Franklin M. Henry Young Scientist Award (2004, Canadian Society for Sport Psychology & Psychomotor Learning)
- Killam Scholar (2002-2003, University of Alberta)
- George Christenberry Award (1994, Big South Conference)

Publications Last 3 Years:

Articles in Peer-Reviewed Journals
1. Mack, D. E., **Wilson, P. M.**, Gunnell, K. E., & Gilmour, J. (in press). Leisure-time physical activity in Canadians living with Crohn's Disease and Ulcerative Colitis: Population-based estimates. *Gastroenterology Nursing*, Accepted December 13th 2010.
2. Duncan, L., Rodgers, W. M., Hall, C. R., & **Wilson, P. M.** (in press). Using imagery to enhances three types of exercise self-efficacy among sedentary women. *Applied Psychology: Health & Well-Being*. Accepted November, 11th 2010.
3. **Wilson, P. M.**, & Bengoechea, E. G. (2010). The Relatedness to Others in Phsyscal Activity Scale: Evidence for structural and criterion validity. *Journal of Applied Biobehavioral Research, 15*, 61-87.
4. Gunnell, K. E., Mack, D. E., **Wilson, P. M.**, Adachi, J. (in press). Psychological needs as mediators? The relationship between leisure time physical activity and well being in people diagnosed with osteoporosis. *Research Quarterly for Exercise & Sport*. Accepted May 6th, 2010.
5. Sabiston, C. M., Brunet, J., Kowalski, K. C., Wilson, P., Mack, D. E. & Crocker, P. R. E. (2010). The role of body-related self-conscious emotions in motivating women's physical activity. *Journal of Sport & Exercise Psychology, 32*, 417-437.
6. Duncan, L. R., Hall, C. R., **Wilson, P. M.**, & O, J. (2010). Exercise motivation: A cross-sectional analysis examining its relationships with frequency, intensity, and duration of exercise. *International Journal of Behavioural Nutrition & Physical Activity*, 7:7.
7. Arbour Nicitopoulos, K., P., Martin Ginis, K. A., **Wilson, P.M.**, & the SHAPE SCI Research Group (2010). Examining individual and neighbourhood environmental associations of leisure-time activity behaviours in persons with spinal cord injury. *Annals of Behavioral Medicine, 39*, 192-197.
8. Hall, C. R., Rodgers, W. M., **Wilson, P. M.**, & Norman, P. (2010). Imagery use and self-determined motivations in a community sample of exercisers and non-exercisers. *Journal of Applied Social Psychology, 40*, 135-152.
9. Mack. D. E., **Wilson, P. M.**, Lightheart, V., Oster, K., Gunnell, K. (2009). Healthy campus 2010: Physical activity trends and the role of information provision. *Journal of Physical Activity & Health, 6*, 435-443.

10. Rodgers, W. M., Hall, C. R., **Wilson, P. M.**, Berry, T. R. (2009). Do non-exercisers also share the positive exercise stereotype? An elicitation and comparison of beliefs about exercisers. *Journal of Sport & Exercise Psychology*, 31, 3-17.
11. **Wilson, P. M.**, Mack, D. E., Blanchard, C. M., & Gray, C. E (2009). The role of perceived psychological need satisfaction in exercise-related affect. *Hellenic Journal of Psychology*, 6, 183-206.
12. Mack, D. E., **Wilson, P. M.**, Oster, K. G., & Gunnell, K. E. (2008). Identity foreclosure? A preliminary investigation of the self-complexity model in sport. *Journal of Contemporary Athletics*, 3, 53-64.
13. **Wilson, P. M.** & Rogers, W. T. (2008). Examining relationships between psychological need satisfaction and behavioural regulations in exercise. *Journal of Applied Biobehavioral Research, 13,* 119-142.
14. **Wilson, P. M.**, Mack. D. E., & Grattan, K. P. (2008). Understanding motivation for exercise: A self-determination theory perspective. *Canadian Psychology, 49, 250-256.*
15. **Wilson, P. M.**, & Muon, S. (2008). Psychometric properties of the Exercise Identity Scale in a university sample. *International Journal of Sport & Exercise Psychology*, 6, 115-131.
16. Milne, M. I., Rodgers, W. M., Hall, C. R., & **Wilson, P. M.** (2008). Starting up or starting over: The role of intentions to increase or to maintain exercise behaviour. *Journal of Sport & Exercise Psychology, 30*, 285-301.
17. Rodgers, W. M., **Wilson, P. M.**, Hall, C. R., Fraser, S. N., & Murray, T. C. (2008). Evidence for a multidimensional self-efficacy for exercise scale. *Research Quarterly for Exercise & Sport, 79*, 222-234
18. Gray, C. E., & **Wilson, P. M.** (2008). The relationship between organizational commitment, perceived relatedness and intentions to continue in Canadian track and field officials. *Journal of Sport Behavior, 30*, 44-63.

Book Chapters/Monographs in Edited Volumes

1. **Wilson, P. M.**, Mack, D. E., & Sabiston, C. M. (in press). Measurement of physical self-confidence/competence. In T. Cash (Ed.), *Encyclopaedia of body image and human appearance (pp.* <TBA>). Oxford, UK: Elsevier. (Acceptance Date: January 30th, 2011).
2. Mack, D. E., **Wilson, P. M.**, Sylvester, B. D. & Gilchrest, J. (in press). Psychological well-being and health behaviours in college females with eating disorders: Comparisons with a non-eating disorder cohort. In F. Columbus (Ed.), <TBA>, NY: Nova Science. (Acceptance Date: November 24th, 2010).
3. **Wilson, P. M.**, Mack, D. E., & Sylvester, B. D. (in press). When a little myth goes a long way: The use (or misuse) or cut-points, discourse, and interpretations with coefficient alpha in exercise psychology research. In A. L. Columbus (Ed.), *Advances in Psychology* (pp. <TBA>). Hauppauge, NY: Nova Science. (Acceptance Date: July 8th, 2010).
4. **Wilson, P. M.** (in press). Exercise Motivation. In G. Tenenbaum, R. C. Eklund, & Kamata, A. (Eds.), *Handbook of measurement in sport and exercise psychology (pp. <TBA>).* Champaign, IL: Human Kinetics.
5. Mack, D. E., Sabiston, C. M., McDonough, M. H., **Wilson, P. M.**, & Paskevich, D. (2011). Motivation and behavioural change. In P. R. E. Crocker (Ed.), *Introduction to sport and exercise psychology: A Canadian perspective (2nd Edition; pp. 79-110).* Toronto, ON: Pearson.
6. **Wilson, P. M.** & Bengoechea, E. G. (2011). Research perspectives in sport and exercise psychology (pp. 22-46). In P. R. E. Crocker (Ed.), *Introduction to sport and exercise psychology: A Canadian perspective (2nd Edition; pp.26-52).* Toronto, ON: Pearson.

7. Mack, D. E., **Wilson, P. M.**, Sylvester, B. D., Gregson, J. G., Cheung, S., & Rimmer, S. (2010). The relationship between social physique anxiety and exercise behaviour: Does the fulfillment of basic psychological needs matter?. In T. M. Robinson (Ed.), *Social anxiety: Symptoms, causes, and techniques (pp. 93-105)*. Hauppauge, NY: Nova Science.
8. **Wilson, P. M.**, Mack, D. E., Bengoechea, E. G., Bin, X., Rimmer, S., Cheung, S., & Sylvester, B. D. (2010). *Understanding sport friendships in adapted sport athletes: Does fulfilling basic psychological needs matter?* In B. Geranto (Ed.), *Sport Psychology* (pp. 113-130). Hauppauge, NY: Nova Science.
9. Lightheart, V., Oster, K., & **Wilson, P. M.** (2010). Strength versus balance: The contributions of two different models of psychological need satisfaction to well-being in adapted sport athletes. In I. E. Wells (Ed.), *Psychological Well-Being (pp. 157-170)*. Hauppauge, NY: Nova Science.
10. **Wilson, P. M.**, Gregson, J. P., & Mack, D. E. (2009). The importance of interpersonal style in competitive sport: A Self-Determination Theory approach. In C. H. Chang (Ed.), *Handbook of Sport Psychology* (pp. 259-276). Hauppauge, NY: Nova Science.
11. Mack, D. E., **Wilson, P. M.**, Waddell, L., & Gasparotto, J. (2008). Social physique anxiety across physical activity settings: A meta-analytic review. In J. N. Fuchs (Ed.), *Eating Disorders in Adult Women (pp.149-166)*. Hauppauge, NY: Nova Science.
12. Fox, K. R., & **Wilson, P. M.** (2008). Self-perceptual systems and physical activity. In T. Horn's (Ed.), *Advances in sport psychology*-3rd edition (pp.49-64). Champaign, IL: Human Kinetics.
13. **Wilson, P. M.**, Mack, D. E., Gunnell, K., Oster, K., & Gregson, J. P. (2008). Analyzing the measurement of psychological need satisfaction in exercise contexts: Evidence, issues, and future directions. In M. P. Simmons & L. A. Foster (Eds.), *Sport and exercise psychology research advances* (pp.361-391). Hauppauge, NY.
14. **Wilson, P. M.**, Mack, D. E., & Lightheart, V. (2008). How important are basic psychological needs to women's well-being? In J. P Coulter (Ed.), *Progress in Exercise and women's health research* (pp.139-158). Hauppauge, NY: Nova Science.

Chapter 46

BIOGRAPHICAL SKETCH – PSYCHOLOGY RESEARCH

Joseph Wu

Affiliation: City University of Hong Kong, Hong Kong, China

Address: Room 7409, Academic Building, Department of Applied Social Studies, City University of Hong Kong, Tat Chee Avenue, Kowloon, Hong Kong, China.

Date of Birth: 24th March 1962

Education: Ph.D in Educational Psychology, Master of Statistics, Master of Education

Research and Professional Experience:

Research on Self-esteem and self-concept clarity, coping with stress, scale development and scale validation in cross-cultural studies.
Graduate member of British Psychological Society (MBPsS)

Professional Appointments: External Examiner of Associate Degree programme at Lingnan University, Hong Kong, China.

Honors: Not Applicable

Publications Last 3 Years:

Wu, J., Siu, A., & Ho, W.C. (in press). A factor analytical study of the COPE questionnaire by sex of respondents. *Psychological Reports*.
Li, J., Lo, T.W., Cheng, C.H.K. & Wu, J. (in press). Measuring the subjective perceptions of risk and reward of Chinese juvenile thieves. *Psychology, Crime & Law*.

Wu, J., Lo, W., Au, E., & Rochelle, T. (in press). Motives behind volunteerism: A study of Hong Kong university students and influence of gender. *Advances in Sociology research, vol. 9*. NY: Nova.

Au, E., Wu, J., & Lo, T.W. (in press). Conceptualizing and implementing volunteerism to a group of Chinese university students: Enhancing volunteer participation through service matching and organizational support. In B. Eng (Ed.), *A Chinese perspective on teaching and learning*. London: Routledge.

Wu, J., Watkins, D., & Hattie, J. (2010). Self-concept clarity: A longitudinal study of Hong Kong adolescents. *Personality and Individual Differences, 48,* 277-282.

Wu, J., Lo, W., & Liu, E. (2009). Psychometric properties of Volunteer Functions Inventory with Chinese students. *Journal of Community Psychology, 37,* 769-780.

Wu, J., & Watkins, D. (2009). Development and validation of a Chinese version of the Self-Concept Clarity Scale. *Psychologia, 52(1),* 67-79.

Ho, W.C., Lee, W.C., Chan, C.M., Rochelle, T., & Wu, J. (2009). Controlling Hong Kong from afar: The Chinese Politics of Elite Absorption after the 2003 Crisis. *Issues & Studies, 45,* 121-164.

Part 2 - Research Summaries in Psychology from Selected Book Chapters and Journal Articles

In: Psychology Research Biographies and Summaries ISBN: 978-1-61470-491-1
Editors: Nancy E. Wodarth and Alexis P. Ferguson © 2012 Nova Science Publishers, Inc.

Chapter 47

A COMPETITIVE ANXIETY REVIEW: RECENT DIRECTIONS IN SPORT PSYCHOLOGY RESEARCH

Stephen D. Mellalieu[1] and Sheldon Hanton and David Fletcher[2]
[1]Swansea University, United Kingdom
[2]University of Wales Institute, Cardiff, United Kingdom

RESEARCH SUMMARY

This book provides a review and discussion of the recent move towards the positive aspects and consequences of competitive anxiety. Following a description of competitive stress-related terminologies, conceptual and psychometric developments are considered including the notion of directional anxiety interpretations. The commentary then focuses on the theories and models that outline the potential positive aspects of anxiety in relation to athletic performance. Applied implications and future research directions are also discussed together with a number of explicatory statements regarding the nature of the precompetitive stress experience in sport.

In: Psychology Research Biographies and Summaries
Editors: Nancy E. Wodarth and Alexis P. Ferguson

ISBN: 978-1-61470-491-1
© 2012 Nova Science Publishers, Inc.

Chapter 48

A MULTIPLE SELF THEORY OF PERSONALITY

David Lester
The Richard Stockton College of New Jersey, Pomona, NJ, US

RESEARCH SUMMARY

This book presents a new theory of personality. The use of the term "personality" by psychologists is odd since it does not coincide with the dictionary definition of personality. "The state or quality of being a person".

Chapter 49

AN EVOLUTIONARY PSYCHOLOGY OF LEADER-FOLLOWER RELATIONS

Patrick McNamara and David Trumbull
Boston Univ. School of Medicine, US

RESEARCH SUMMARY

The purpose of the book is to summarize recent advances in our understanding of leader-follower interactions and to illustrate these principles with the lives of ancient political and military leaders from Greece and Rome. The authors review psychologic, cognitive neuroscientific and evolutionary approaches to leader-follower dynamics and illustrate these dynamics as they played out in the lives of the most eminent of the military and political leaders of the classical world. The authors summarize what is known about leader-follower relations by reviewing all extant papers on the topic in the psychology, neuroscientific and evolutionary psychology literature. The raw material for the book came from Plutarch's compendium of 46 biographies of Greek and Roman leaders.

Chapter 50

ANOREXIA NERVOSA: A MULTI-DISCIPLINARY APPROACH: FROM BIOLOGY TO PHILOSOPHY

Antonio Mancini[1], Silvia Daini[1] and S.J. Louis Caruana[2]
[1]Catholic University of Sacred Heart, Rome, Italy
[2]Heythrop College University of London, UK

RESEARCH SUMMARY

This is a book that attempts to propose itself as a new trigger in the wide world of anorexia nervosa. The originality of its proposal consists in approaching anorexia nervosa, not only by endocrinological and psychological perspectives, but also by anthropological, philosophical and ethical point of view. In this way it's not only an update of specific literature, but also an integration with a new method to study this condition. The purpose of the book is to approach anorexia nervosa from different points of view, to reach a new interpretation which involves notions from biological and human sciences interpreted in a unique model and which could allow a new method of treatment.

In: Psychology Research Biographies and Summaries
Editors: Nancy E. Wodarth and Alexis P. Ferguson
ISBN: 978-1-61470-491-1
© 2012 Nova Science Publishers, Inc.

Chapter 51

ATTENTION DEFICIT HYPERACTIVITY DISORDER: CREATIVITY, NOVELTY SEEKING, AND RISK

Michael Fitzgerald
Dept. of Psychiatry, Trinity College, Dublin, Ireland

RESEARCH SUMMARY

There is a great deal of information on the negative aspects of Attention Deficit Hyperactivity Disorder but very little on the positive aspects or the potentially creative aspects of this disorder. This is of enormous importance to, not alone academics, but parents and families of persons with this disorder. This book offers intelligent information about both the positive and negative aspects as well as a possible link to creativity.

In: Psychology Research Biographies and Summaries
Editors: Nancy E. Wodarth and Alexis P. Ferguson
ISBN: 978-1-61470-491-1
© 2012 Nova Science Publishers, Inc.

Chapter 52

BEHAVIORAL PEDIATRICS, 3RD EDITION

Donald E. Greydanus, Dilip R. Patel, Helen D. Pratt and Joseph L. Calles Jr.

Michigan State University College/Kalamazoo Center for Medical Studies, Kalamazoo;
Michigan State University College of Human Medicine, East Lansing, Michigan, US

RESEARCH SUMMARY

Children, adolescents and their families are presented with prodigious difficulties as they face the challenges of the 21st century. Our children pass through intricate developmental phases as they traverse through childhood and adolescence on their inevitable journey into adulthood. Since many parents face considerable challenges in their endeavors to help their children, many families turn to their primary care professionals for counsel in this regard. There are a limited number of books summarizing current concepts of behavioral pediatrics as defined by the first edition of this book: "what the clinician does to diagnose, to treat, and most importantly, to prevent mental illness in children and adolescents." The authors have compiled this updated information for various health care professionals who are seeking to provide comprehensive health care for our children and adolescents—pediatricians, family medicine physicians, internists, physician assistants, nurse practitioners, psychologists, social workers, health educators and others involved in the care of children and adolescents.

Much has evolved in this field since the publication of the first edition in 1992. Research in child and adolescent psychiatry, psychology, behavioral sciences, pediatrics, family therapy, individual therapy and related fields have led to new and exciting information. Advancements in psychopharmacology have lead to an explosion of medications used to treat a wide variety of mental health disorders, including depression, anxiety, schizophrenia, disruptive behavioral disorders, eating disorders, attention-deficit/hyperactivity disorder (ADHD), and others.

'Behavioral Pediatrics, 3rd edition' is designed to provide the primary-care clinician with a practical guide to early recognition and intervention in the significant problems increasingly affecting the emotional health of children and adolescents. It is the hope of the editors of this edition that this updated information will be of considerable help to clinicians in helping to meet the complex needs of the children, adolescents, and families that they serve. Today, our families expect us to look at both the medical and mental health aspects which affect our children and teenagers.

In: Psychology Research Biographies and Summaries
Editors: Nancy E. Wodarth and Alexis P. Ferguson
ISBN: 978-1-61470-491-1
© 2012 Nova Science Publishers, Inc.

Chapter 53

BEHAVIORAL THEORIES AND INTERVENTIONS FOR AUTISM

Phil Reed
Swansea University, Swansea, UK

RESEARCH SUMMARY

"Behavioral interventions for Autistic Spectrum Disorders (ASD) are among the most widely used approaches, and have proved both extremely popular with parents, and controversial with professionals. These behavioral techniques are some of the few practical applications of psychology in this area to be scientifically evaluated and validated, and this availability of evidence allows both their strengths and weaknesses to be debated. Much of this debate has focused on the initial claims made about these behavioral approaches two decades ago, and the scientific evidence following these initial claims often does not enter into the debate. However, there have been enormous developments and diversifications in the approaches offered by behavioral psychologists to the treatment of ASD, and this text now brings together new evidence regarding these contemporary developments in one place, offering an essential handbook of contemporary behavioral practice for ASD, provided by the key researchers in the field. This book provides detailed empirically-based reviews of many of the behavioral interventions that are used to help children and adults with ASD, and these chapters are organized into three sections for easy reference.

Chapter 54

BEYOND THE WORDS: COMMUNICATION AND SUGGESTION IN MEDICAL PRACTICE

Katalin Varga
Eötvös Loránd University, Budapest, Hungary

RESEARCH SUMMARY

This book provides a guide for health professionals concerned about communicating more effectively with patients as well as their families and colleagues. People in many life situations, either waiting for a diagnosis, during delivering a child, being hospitalized due to some life threatening medical condition, are almost always highly susceptible to suggestions. These people seem like as if they were hypnotized without any formal hypnosis. The very same suggestive techniques can be applied to them that are used in hypnosis, utilizing their highly susceptible state. This new book demonstrates the power of our words and to improve the readers' skills in minimizing harmful effects and maximizing beneficial effects of communication with people in medical settings.

Chapter 55

BIO-PSYCHO-SOCIAL PERSPECTIVES ON INTERPERSONAL VIOLENCE

Martha Frias-Armenta and Victor Corral-Verdugo
Universidad de Sonora, Mexico

RESEARCH SUMMARY

The purpose of the book is to analyze interpersonal violence from an international, multi-thematic and theoretically-diverse perspective. An international team of scholars offers theoretical explanations and research results related to this insidious manifestation of aggressive behavior. They also discuss the effectiveness of interventional programs and their evaluations. The text includes a wide range of topics on interpersonal violence, unveiling its multi-factorial nature. The resulting models involve situational and personal explanations of this instance of violence, including the analysis of complex relations among those factors. Neuropsychological variables, for instance, are studied as risk factors for antisocial behavior; authors in this book show that neuropsychological delay makes juveniles vulnerable and prone to criminal acts.

Chapter 56

BULLYING AMONG YOUTH: ISSUES, INTERVENTIONS AND THEORY

Stavros Kiriakidis
ATEI of Athens, Greece

RESEARCH SUMMARY

This book presents an overview of the main parameters of school bullying. Emphasis is put on the definition of bullying, the extent of bullying, the stability of the bully and victim roles, ways of coping with bullying, the forms bullying can take, the characteristics of bullies, the characteristics of victims, age differences, as well as other measurements.

Chapter 57

CAREER COUNSELING AND CONSTRUCTIVISM: ELABORATION OF CONSTRUCTS

Mary McMahon[1] and Mark Watson[2]
[1]The University of Queensland, Australia
[2]Nelson Mandela Metropolitan University, South Africa

RESEARCH SUMMARY

Vocational guidance fits industrial societies and career counseling suits corporate cultures. However, neither guidance nor counseling seems to be the best practice for career intervention in the global economy of the information era. Thus, the emergence of career construction theory for comprehending vocational behavior and life-design interventions to assist people in choosing an adapting to work roles. This book examines and elaborates the structural elements assembled into models of self-making, career constructing, and life designing.

Chapter 58

CATEGORY-SPECIFICITY: EVIDENCE FOR MODULARITY OF MIND

Keith R. Laws[1], Rebecca L. Adlington[1], F. Javier Moreno-Martinez[2] and Tim M. Gale[3]

[1]University of Hertfordshire, Hatfield, UK
[2]Departamento de Psicología Básica I, Madrid, Spain
[3]Department of Psychiatry, QEII Hospital, UK

RESEARCH SUMMARY

From a neuropsychological perspective, our understanding about how knowledge is organized in the human brain has emerged largely from the study of so-called 'category-specific' deficits in neurological patients. Category-specificity is, in very broad terms, the relative loss of cognitive performance in one domain of knowledge over another. The most frequently reported and discussed pattern concerns a dissociation between knowledge about nonliving things (e.g. tools) and living things (e.g. animals). Most reports of categorical impairment have emerged from case studies of patients with pathologies such as herpes simplex encephalitis, strokes or head injuries and the dementias (especially Alzheimer's disease). These category specific effects have been fundamental in forming theories and models about the organization and modular structure of semantic knowledge in the brain. The different chapters of this book illustrate a broad range of interesting and strongly debated issues arising from the category-specific literature, all of them fundamental to cognitive neuropsychology. This book, written by researchers who during the last decade have intensively researched this intriguing field, present an up-to-date exploration of major neuropsychological issues that have general implications beyond the field of category knowledge e.g. issues such as modularity, computational modeling of cognitive processing, gender-related asymmetries and functional imaging.

Chapter 59

CHILDREN'S DREAMS

Barbara Szmigielska
Jagiellonian Univ., Inst. of Psychology, Poland

RESEARCH SUMMARY

The present book is one of very few monographs in the world literature devoted to various aspects of children's dreams. It reviews the extant literature on the topic, as well as provides the results of the author's own research concerning children's understanding of the sleep process and dream phenomenon. The book presents data from the literature and compares them with the results of the author's own research. The findings obtained by the present author constitute a substantial contribution to modern psychological knowledge on the development of children's thinking and their dreams. They demonstrate, for example, that it is possible to find out what children dream about without asking them directly, merely by talking about sleep in general. This approach can be useful when direct conversation with the child about their dreams is not possible. Apart from data on children's knowledge about the process of sleep, the book also presents the basic facts on this process that are indispensable for understanding the relations between sleep and dreams. The book presents results of research on how children understand two related concepts: sleep and dream. The monograph presents not only analysis of dream reports but also colour drawings made by children to illustrate their dreams. Since this approach is not discussed in the literature, the author offers several suggestions on how to use drawings in the analysis of children's dreams. The book discusses findings concerning the relations between children's daytime experiences and their nocturnal dreams. Presented are, among others, relations between dreams and such traumatic events as illness, war or parental divorce. The analysis of children's reports provided an answer to the question of development of knowledge concerning the nature and function of sleep during childhood.

In: Psychology Research Biographies and Summaries
Editors: Nancy E. Wodarth and Alexis P. Ferguson

ISBN: 978-1-61470-491-1
© 2012 Nova Science Publishers, Inc.

Chapter 60

CHILDREN'S SOCIAL COMPETENCE: THEORY AND INTERVENTION

Melissa L. Greene, Jo R. Hariton,
Andrew L. Robins and Barbara L. Flye
Weill Cornell Medical College, White Plains, NY, US

RESEARCH SUMMARY

This new book discusses peer relationships and social skills in school-age children. The historical and current understanding of the importance of peer relationships and effective social skills for development and well-being are discussed herein. In addition, this book reviews and discusses the concepts of social skills and social competence, as well as current understanding of the social difficulties of children with ADHD, autistic spectrum disorders, and Social Anxiety Disorder. Recent research on the effectiveness of social skills training are presented and four commonly utilized training programs are discussed in order to assist children with peer relationships.

In: Psychology Research Biographies and Summaries
Editors: Nancy E. Wodarth and Alexis P. Ferguson
ISBN: 978-1-61470-491-1
© 2012 Nova Science Publishers, Inc.

Chapter 61

COGNITIVE AND NEUROSCIENTIFIC ASPECTS OF HUMAN LOVE: A GUIDE FOR MARRIAGE AND COUPLES COUNSELING

William A. Lambos[1] and William G. Emener[2]
[1]Cognitive Neuro Sciences, Inc. Wellness, FL, US
[2]Department of Rehabilitation and Mental Health Counseling,
Univ. of South Florida, US

RESEARCH SUMMARY

This book is about the science of human love, and the authors do a thorough and illuminating job discussing it. But to many people, wise and important as well as ordinary and work-a-day, love encompasses much more than any scientific treatment of it could offer. Having taught many courses over the years on love, marriage and family psychology, Dr. Emener and Dr. Lambos often have asked their students, both young and old, many newly graduated with their bachelor's degree and some who held doctorates in other subjects, what the term love meant to them.

Chapter 62

COGNITIVE THERAPY OF EATING DISORDERS ON CONTROL AND WORRY

Sandra Sassaroli[1] *and Giovanni Maria Ruggiero*[2]
[1]Studi Cognitivi, Milano Italia, Italy
[2]"Psicoterapia Cognitiva e Ricerca" Post-Graduate Cognitive Psychotherapy School and Research Center, Milano and Bolzano, Italy

RESEARCH SUMMARY

The aim of this book is to illustrate a variant of the standard cognitive treatment for eating disorders. This therapy is based on the principle that assessing and treating the patient's process of worry and sense of control fosters greater understanding of the psychopathology of the eating disorder and increases the efficacy of cognitive treatment. The book is an edited collection of chapters that discuss the psychopathological roles played by control and worry in eating disorders, and provide a detailed description of the therapeutic protocol, which primarily focuses on the treatment of the cognitive factors of control and worry as core factor of a psychotherapy of eating disorders. In addition, the book shows contributions from other theorists in the field who have investigated the role of worry, preoccupation, and control, or who explore the connections between worry, control, and other emotional factors underlying eating disorders, such as perfectionism, self-esteem, and impulsivity.

Chapter 63

COGNITIVE-BEHAVIORAL AND NEUROPSYCHOLOGICAL MODELS OF OBSESSIVE-COMPULSIVE DISORDER

Claudio Sica, Luigi Rocco Chiri[1], Dean McKay[2] and Marta Ghisi[3]

[1]University of Firenze, Italy
[2]Fordham University, NY, US
[3]University of Padova, Italy

RESEARCH SUMMARY

Obsessive compulsive disorder (OCD) is characterized by persistent, intrusive, and distressing obsessions (unwanted thoughts, impulses, or images) that may or may not be accompanied by compulsions (repetitive behaviors or mental acts). It is a severe and persistent psychological problem with significant negative effects on the individuals' social, family, and occupational functioning. This book reports on recent research examining phenomenology, neurobiology, psychological models, and computational modeling of obsessive-compulsive disorder. This book offers a general view of the most recent psychological and neurobiological research on OCD to researchers, psychologists, psychiatrists, mental-health professionals and students.

Chapter 64

COGNITIVE-BEHAVIOURAL INDICATORS OF SUBSTANCE ABUSE

Samuel Pombo, Filipe Barbosa, Marco Torrado and Nuno Félix da Costa
University of Lisbon, Portugal

RESEARCH SUMMARY

Problems related to substance use, abuse and dependence are a major concern on societies today, persisting to require considerable attention from the community. For decades studies have been showing that drug consumption represents a main risk factor for physical, social and mental health problems. Unfortunately, reality shows that in many cultures and fractions of population, heavy substance use is the norm. This new book examines the cognitive-behavioral indicators of substance abuse and various corresponding treatment techniques.

In: Psychology Research Biographies and Summaries
Editors: Nancy E. Wodarth and Alexis P. Ferguson
ISBN: 978-1-61470-491-1
© 2012 Nova Science Publishers, Inc.

Chapter 65

CONSCIOUSNESS, ATTENTION AND MEANING

Giorgio Marchetti
University of Urbino, Italy

RESEARCH SUMMARY

This book presents a comprehensive theoretical framework that explains both human consciousness and meanings through the working of attention.

By arguing for a first-person approach to consciousness, this book offers a critical overview of the major theories and empirical findings on consciousness and attention, and exemplifies how one of the most difficult and fundamental conscious experiences to account for, that is, time, can be analyzed by adopting the kind of semantics developed within the presented theoretical framework: Attentional Semantics.

Chapter 66

CONTEMPORARY SPORT PSYCHOLOGY

Robert Schinke
Laurentain University, Ontario, Canada

RESEARCH SUMMARY

'Contemporary Sport Psychology' captures the contributions of world-wide experts, based upon earlier special editions of a peer reviewed sport psychology journal titled Athletic Insight. Most often sport psychology books either contain similar chapters across books pertaining to theoretical concepts or applied practices. On occasion, textbooks also contain a special topics section placed at the very end of the compendium with a few contributions regarded as a special topics issue. The present compilation is built entirely of special topics, where the focus is to forefront diverse perspectives through three distinct sections, each with contributions pertaining to research and practice. Section One is comprised of practical application, Within Section One the reader will find contributions pertaining to applied practice with Olympic and professional athletes based upon the first hand experiences of elite practitioners from several continents. The intent through section one is to propose strategies, reflecting several national perspectives that applied practitioners might employ as they enter the field or seek positions with elite sport organizations in the global sport community.

Section Two reflects contributions about Cultural Sport Psychology (CSP). CSP is a burgeoning research and practice trajectory within sport and exercise psychology, launched formally through a special installment of Athletic Insight. Most recently the International Journal of Sport and Exercise Psychology, the peer reviewed journal for the International Society of Sport Psychology has also featured a devoted installment to the topic (Autumn, 2009). Section Two provides the reader with the most current work on CSP written by several highly creditable researchers a the forefront of the trajectory. Section Three is devoted to the intersection of sport psychology and ethics. Within Section Three the authors provide their respective views on the topic, carrying from the role of student practitioners struggling with matters of ethic to consultants of high-risk Olympic and professional sport teams faced with the ethical implications they encounter when working in the field.

Chapter 67

DEPRESSION, SUBJECTIVE WELL-BEING AND INDIVIDUAL ASPIRATIONS OF COLLEGE STUDENTS

Ferenc Margitics and Zsuzsa Pauwlik
Department of Psychology, College of Nyíregyháza, Hungary

RESEARCH SUMMARY

The subclinical depression syndrome refers to an emotionally negative state which significantly influences level of achievement and quality of life, but which cannot be yet classified as an illness. Based on the seriousness of the symptoms, it can be measured on different scales of depression as mild or moderate.

One of the aims of the research was to find out what characterizes the state of mind of college students, whether the hopelessness, despondency and subclinical depressive mood are also typical of them. The other aim of the research was to examine and discover in their complexity those factors which have a role in the development of subclinical syndrome. The authors approach the factors responsible for the development of the subclinical syndrome in their complexity, taking into account the biological, psychic, and social relations, as well. Beyond revealing the background factors of sub-clinical depressive syndromes the authors were also interested in what the subjective well-being of college students was like and what individual aspirations were typical of them.

Chapter 68

EMOTIONAL INTELLIGENCE: THEORETICAL AND CULTURAL PERSPECTIVES

Robert J. Emmerling[1], Vinod K. Shanwal[2] and Manas K. Mandal[3]

[1]Competency International, Walnut Creek, CA, US
[2]Inst. of Human Behaviour & Allied Sciences, Delhi, India
[3]Defense Inst. of Psychological Research, Delhi, India

RESEARCH SUMMARY

This book is designed to meet the growing need among researchers, graduate students, and professionals to look into the existing theoretical models as well as developing theories related to emotional intelligence. The primary aim of the book is to help readers get a view of current conceptualizations of emotional intelligence, while providing an opportunity to see how emotional intelligence has been interpreted and applied throughout the world. Psychological processes are expected to vary according to cultural meaning and practices.

Recent studies indicate that emotional intelligence influences behavior in a wide range of domains including school, community, and the workplace. At the individual level, it has been said to relate to academic achievement, work performance, our ability to communicate effectively, solve everyday problems, build meaningful interpersonal relationships, and even our ability to make moral decisions. Given that emotional intelligence has the potential to increase our understanding of how individuals behave and adapt to their social environment, it is an important topic for study.

In: Psychology Research Biographies and Summaries
Editors: Nancy E. Wodarth and Alexis P. Ferguson
ISBN: 978-1-61470-491-1
© 2012 Nova Science Publishers, Inc.

Chapter 69

MANAGING INTERPERSONAL SENSITIVITY: KNOWING WHEN — AND WHEN NOT — TO UNDERSTAND OTHERS

Jessi L. Smith[1], William Ickes[2], Judith A. Hall[3] and Sara Hodges[4]

[1]Montana State University, MT, US
[2]University of Texas at Arlington, TX, US
[3]Northeastern University, MA, US
[4]University of Oregon. OR, US

RESEARCH SUMMARY

Findings from the past two decades of interpersonal sensitivity research presented a big surprise to the researchers who were working in this area. These findings, at first suggestive and then unmistakably clear, showed that scores on various interpersonal sensitivity measures were not as stable as scores on other measures of cognitive ability (for example, IQ scores) seemed to be. The accumulating data further suggested that differences in situationally-evoked motivational states were the most probable cause of these variations in interpersonal sensitivity. This book examines this discovery and how it has completely changed the research agenda for those working in this field of study.

Chapter 70

MATERNAL SENSITIVITY: A SCIENTIFIC FOUNDATION FOR PRACTICE

Deborah Winders Davis and M. Cynthia Logsdon
University of Louisville, Louisville, KY, US

RESEARCH SUMMARY

Globally and across the lifespan, children spend more time with their mothers than any other person and they have optimal cognitive and social development and appropriate behavior if their mothers are sensitive. Thus, promoting maternal sensitivity is a public health concern. A sensitive mother is a good communicator and is able to quickly read nonverbal cues, "be in the moment" in her focus on interactions with the child, respect the child's desire for more or less space between them, react positively and consistently, and speak in a way that is appealing to the child. This book brings together the work of the most highly respected scholars in the field of maternal sensitivity in order to provide a firm foundation for clinical practice.

Chapter 71

MENTAL HEALTH AND SOME SOCIOCULTURAL ISSUES IN DEAF PEOPLE

Benito Daniel Estrada Aranda
Universidad Autonoma De Nuevo Leon, Mexico

RESEARCH SUMMARY

This book brings together a number of important issues within the area of mental health and deafness. The book is aimed at mental health professionals interested in learning more about the psychological reality of deaf people, and in particular, the course that takes two mental health disorders including, depression and stress. The psychological reality presented in this book also refers to other issues, firstly the issue of cultural identity and sexuality in other Deaf people and the abuse and violence against Deaf women and how this affects their social interactions.

In: Psychology Research Biographies and Summaries ISBN: 978-1-61470-491-1
Editors: Nancy E. Wodarth and Alexis P. Ferguson © 2012 Nova Science Publishers, Inc.

Chapter 72

MULTIPLE FACETS OF ANGER: GETTING MAD OR RESTORING JUSTICE?

Farzaneh Pahlavan
Université René Descartes, Cedex, France

RESEARCH SUMMARY

This book examines the current state of research on anger and reflects the expanding understanding of how anger as an emotion interfaces with other aspects of psychological functioning, including behavior. It takes into account work by pioneers in this field as well as efforts by new investigators, all of which have to deal with the ambiguity and subjectivity of the construct by being clear about how they conceptualize it. This book provides a representative sampling of cutting-edge research and theory on anger.

Chapter 73

MY LOVING RELATIONSHIPS

William G. Emener[1] *and William A. Lambos*[2]
[1]Department of Rehabilitation and Mental Health Counseling,
Univ. of South Florida, Tampa, US
[2]Cognitive Neuro Sciences, Inc., (CNS), Tampa, FL, US

RESEARCH SUMMARY

A number of avenues of research indicate that neurobiological abnormalities may be involved in eating disorders. An important component of this may be some form of dysfunction in cognitive processing. The aim of this book is to review the results and implications of previous research into neuropsychological function in Eating Disorders (ED), focusing on the diagnoses of Anorexia Nervosa (AN) and Bulimia Nervosa (BN). Published articles on this topic, uncovered in a recent systematic literature search, are summarised here in a table format, allowing the straightforward comparison of materials, methods and results across studies. Whilst providing insight into potential areas of cognitive dysfunction in this clinical group, the neuropsychological data that exists for eating disorders is somewhat unclear. A number of methodological limitations are inherent in this literature; with issues ranging from sample characteristics to study design and the variety of tests employed, thus restricting the conclusions that may be derived. Suggestions as to how these limitations may be overcome and potential directions for future research are discussed accordingly. We advocate the adoption of a hypothesis driven approach to explore neuropsychological processing in Eating Disorders, the utility of which has been confirmed in the ongoing work of our department. Based on clinical observation and personality research, our hypotheses with regards to reduced cognitive flexibility in individuals with AN have consistently been endorsed. Neuropsychological research has both important theoretical and clinical implications, advancing understanding with regards to aetiology and phenotypes of disorder. The knowledge derived from hypothesis driven neuropsychological studies may be applied practically in research and treatment settings, with the potential to initiate the development of innovative treatment interventions, as has been seen with other psychiatric disorders.

Chapter 74

NEW HOPE FOR MENTAL DISTURBANCES

Vladimir Lerner and Chanoch Miodownik
Ben Gurion Univ. of the Negev, Be'er Sheva Mental Health Center,
Be'er Sheva, Israel

RESEARCH SUMMARY

The purpose of this book is to introduce the importance of vitamins and its use in the treatment of schizophrenia, mood and movement disorders. This subject has been already known for many years. In the last years this issue has become "hot" again. To date there is new modern data based on controlled studies leading to a new attitude in consumption of these preparations. The present experience is related to higher doses in contrast to those which were used previously in addition to the scientific base data consisting of new knowledge about the mechanism of action and the influence on different dimensions. The chapters will include theoretical and scientific background as well as practical data based conclusions which might be useful for the clinician in everyday practice.

In: Psychology Research Biographies and Summaries
Editors: Nancy E. Wodarth and Alexis P. Ferguson

ISBN: 978-1-61470-491-1
© 2012 Nova Science Publishers, Inc.

Chapter 75

OUR LOVING RELATIONSHIP

William G. Emener[1] and William A. Lambos[2]
[1]Department of Rehabilitation and Mental Health Counseling,
Univ. of South Florida, Tampa, US
[2]Cognitive Neuro Sciences, Inc., (CNS), Tampa, FL, US

RESEARCH SUMMARY

For any healthy individual or couple experiencing a difficult, problematic or less than enjoyable loving relationship in today's crazy world (and who hasn't?) – this book is perfect for you. The primary focus is on mutual ("us", "we", and "me and you") issues pertinent to loving relationships – the couple and their relationship. Using case vignettes from the authors' clinical experiences as psychologists, the first 14 chapters address the loving relationship topics of Love, Loving, Our Pasts, Relationship Analysis, Congruence and Balance, Outside Factors and Features, Other People, Needs and Wants, Expectations and Dependence, Boundaries and Control, Lifestyles, Monetary and Equity Issues, and Problems, and Relationship Skills. The last three address where to look for more help when serious situations arise: Seeing a Professional Counselor, Therapist or Family Mediator, How a Professional Counselor or Therapist Can be Helpful to You, and Some Suggestions About Getting Help from a Professional. The book is very reader-friendly, simplistic, solution-focused and down to earth, and also includes 39 Figures from their case files that graphically display the issues and helpful recommendations.

The book's authors, with many years of experience as psychologists, professors and scholars, conceptualize loving relationships and improving them as representing developmental processes that are best seen as a kind of ongoing and ever-evolving "dance" between two individuals – relationships are not events! Reading this book will contribute to, enrich and enhance any individual's or couple's developmental processes- and especially themselves and their relationship.

In: Psychology Research Biographies and Summaries
Editors: Nancy E. Wodarth and Alexis P. Ferguson
ISBN: 978-1-61470-491-1
© 2012 Nova Science Publishers, Inc.

Chapter 76

PERCHANCE TO DREAM: THE FRONTIERS OF DREAM PSYCHOLOGY

Stanley Krippner[1] *and Debbie Joffe Ellis*[2]
[1]Saybrook Graduate School, San Francisco, CA, US
[2]New York, NY, US

RESEARCH SUMMARY

This book, 'Perchance to Dream: New Frontiers in Dreams and Dreaming', presents valuable research-based information, which encourages us to explore the powerful potential of dreams to contribute to growth, self-actualization, and stability in our waking lives. Recognizing and utilizing the insights and lessons that may be found in our dreams may be one of the most enriching and life-enhancing actions we can take for ourselves.

Chapter 77

PERSONALITY AND INDIVIDUAL DIFFERENCES: THEORY, ASSESSMENT, AND APPLICATION

Simon Boag[1] and Niko Tiliopoulos[2]
[1]Macquarie University, Sydney, NSW, Australia
[2]University of Sydney, Sydney, NSW, Australia

RESEARCH SUMMARY

Personality and individual differences research is relevant to practically every facet of human existence. For instance, since theories of persons either explicitly or implicitly guide clinical work, the field contributes to discussions of understanding abnormal psychology and provides a guide for conceptualising best treatment. Additionally, the field is relevant to understanding human development across the lifespan, and our understanding of personality and individual differences impacts upon our views of socialisation and interpersonal relations. This book presents research which draws attention to the rich scientific literature that continues to emerge with respect to personality and individual differences psychology.

In: Psychology Research Biographies and Summaries
Editors: Nancy E. Wodarth and Alexis P. Ferguson
ISBN: 978-1-61470-491-1
© 2012 Nova Science Publishers, Inc.

Chapter 78

PERSPECTIVES ON COGNITION AND ACTION IN SPORT

Duarte Araujo[1], Hubert Ripoll[2] and Markus Raab[3]

1Faculty of Human Kinetics, Technical University of Lisbon, Portugal
[2]Universite de la Mediterrance, Marseille Cedex, France
[3]German Sport University Cologne, Germany

RESEARCH SUMMARY

There has been considerable debate on sport psychology about the status and the function of cognition and action in sport. This debate is very relevant since there was a refinement of the different positions, and there were several attempts to integrate apparently contrasting perspectives.

A main goal of this book is to put the links between cognition, perception and action into the discussion both oriented towards theory and practice, and thus, cast a new look on cognition and action in sport. The book is organized in three sections. Section I discusses the organization of action attending to its dynamics and complexity. It shows how multiple levels of complexity are involved in performance and learning. Section II discusses not only what is knowledge, but also how athletes use it during performance. Section III presents different perspectives about judgment and decision-making as well as applications to training.

In: Psychology Research Biographies and Summaries
Editors: Nancy E. Wodarth and Alexis P. Ferguson
ISBN: 978-1-61470-491-1
© 2012 Nova Science Publishers, Inc.

Chapter 79

PROBLEMS OF DEVELOPMENTAL INSTRUCTION: A THEORETICAL AND EXPERIMENTAL PSYCHOLOGICAL STUDY

V. V. Davydov
Translated by Peter Moxhay, Peaks Island, Maine, US

RESEARCH SUMMARY

"...the theory of developmental instruction is a sensation in world psychological science..."

Professor Kunio Kumbayashi

Based on the results of many years of experimental and theoretical research, it is impossible not to conclude that the problems of developmental instruction and upbringing are among the most significant problems of contemporary psychology, especially in the fields of developmental and pedagogical psychology. The overall orientation of pedagogical thought and practice will in large part depend on their successful elaboration. The essence of these problems can be expressed concisely as follows: Do a person's instruction and upbringing determine the processes of his psychical development, and if they do determine them then is it possible to understand the nature of the link between psychical development and instruction and upbringing? In other words, can we assert that developmental instruction and upbringing exist, and, if they exist, then what laws do they obey? In everyday life, these problems sometimes take the form of the question: Can we, by means of instruction and upbringing, develop in a person certain psychical capacities or qualities that previously did not exist?

In the history of psychology, several theories have been created with respect to these problems, each of the theories being based on data from a given pedagogical practice, on materials derived from experience. These theories may provisionally be divided into two groups. The adherents of the first group of theories deny that instruction and upbringing can have any significant effect on a person's psychical development, i.e. they deny the very existence of developmental instruction and upbringing. Adherents of the second group of theories acknowledge the determining role of instruction and upbringing in a person's psychical development and try to study the laws of developmental instruction and upbringing. Each of these two basic groups of theories has many different variants. The authors notes that the accepted techniques of instruction and upbringing in different educational institutions are in some way connected with these theories. Therefore, the pedagogical practitioners who are guided by such techniques realize, consciously or unconsciously, fully or partially, the principles of one or the other of these groups of theories.

In: Psychology Research Biographies and Summaries
Editors: Nancy E. Wodarth and Alexis P. Ferguson
ISBN: 978-1-61470-491-1
© 2012 Nova Science Publishers, Inc.

Chapter 80

PSYCHOLOGICAL APPROACHES TO SUSTAINABILITY: CURRENT TRENDS IN THEORY, RESEARCH AND APPLICATIONS

Victor Corral-Verdugo[1], Cirilo H. Garcia-Cadena[2] and Martha Frias-Armenta[3]

[1]Universidad de Senora, Mexico
[2]Universidad Autonoma de Neuvo Leon, Mexico
[3]Universidad de Sonora, Hermosillo, Mexico

RESEARCH SUMMARY

An international team of leading scholars and young researchers in environmental psychology offers a relatively new perspective on the origin and solutions of the current environmental crisis. They explain how human nature has played a prominent role in the emergence of ecological problems such as global warming, threats to biodiversity, resources scarcity and pollution. But also, they demonstrate that such problems are interlinked with social problems such as poverty, famine, social and economical inequities and violence. According to this book's authors, psychological theories and empirical evidence show that the solutions for those socio-ecological problems are to be found in human nature and its psychological predispositions. These include personal motives, world-visions, future perspective, environmental emotions, altruistic tendencies and behavioral capacities among other psychological predispositions that could allow the adoption of sustainable lifestyles. Meeting the ideals of sustainability requires the participation of the natural and social sciences, including psychology, in order to guarantee the fulfillment of its purposes. Behavioral sciences study the psychological characteristics and the contextual factors that lead people to adopt more sustainable lifestyles. In addition, these sciences investigate how sustainable behaviors promote happiness, psychological well being and restoration, which are considered among the aims of sustainable development by governments throughout the world. The authors, who are recognized experts in these areas, offer a state-of-the-art review and data on what it is known regarding the psychological dimensions of the environmental crisis, its behavioral solutions and the repercussions of sustainable behavior on human well being.

Chapter 81

PSYCHOLOGY AND THE CHURCH

Mark. R. McMinn and Amy W. Dominguez
Wheaton College, US

RESEARCH SUMMARY

Today's psychology with increasing openness to spirituality, multiple ways of knowing, cultural diversity, and community emphases and provides a promising context for studying Christian communities. And today's church with increasing reliance on technology and science, growing engagement with contemporary culture, and a willingness to elevate various Christian psychologists to a near-prophetic role may be more open to the influence of psychology than ever before. This book highlights exemplars who are blending the strengths of the church with the skills of psychology in applied settings to promote psychology and spiritual health.

The volume is divided into five sections. The first section includes three survey and interview studies assessing psychologists' and clergy perspectives on collaboration. Each of remaining sections is comprised of three to six vignettes demonstrating how psychologists are working with the church, organized by congregation-based collaboration, clinically-focused collaboration, research-focused collaboration, and community-focused collaboration.

Chapter 82

TRAFFIC PSYCHOLOGY: AN INTERNATIONAL PERSPECTIVE

Dwight Hennessy
State University of New York, College at Buffalo, NY, US

RESEARCH SUMMARY

Traffic Psychology involves the scientific study of thoughts, feelings, and actions surrounding road user behavior, which includes the dynamic transaction between drivers, vehicles, physical surroundings, and social environment. Despite the fact that it is a relatively young sub-discipline of psychology, traffic psychology has begun to make a significant impact in academic, political policy, and public arenas. Driving is no longer seen as simply a means of transporting from point A to point B. Rather it is a dynamic, and constantly changing, life event that can impact immediate and long term physical, social, emotional and psychological well-being. This book discusses research from a broad spectrum of traffic psychology professionals from around the globe, with particular emphasis placed on topics with international impact.

Chapter 83

WAR AND SUICIDE

Leo Sher[1] and Alexander Vilens[2]
[1]Columbia University, New York, US
[2]Relational Architects International, Hoboken, NJ, US

RESEARCH SUMMARY

Suicidal behavior is a critical problem in the military, among civilians during a war and among returning war veterans. Millions of people around the world were involved in many wars and military conflicts during the past 100 years. Nowadays, suicidal behavior is a critical problem among soldiers and marines deployed to Operation Iraqi Freedom (OIF), Operation Enduring Freedom (OEF) and returning war veterans. The U.S. Army's top Medical Officer has been reported as saying that commanders are seeking ways to address the alarming increase in suicides, including looking to their counterparts in the Air Force and in civilian agencies. This book is dedicated to the relationship between war and suicidal behavior. The relationship between war and suicide is perplex. Understanding the impact of war on suicidal behavior in the military, among civilians and war veterans is an important challenge for future research. This book is of interest to physicians, psychologists, other clinicians, experts in public health management, military people and war veterans.

In: Psychology Research Biographies and Summaries
Editors: Nancy E. Wodarth and Alexis P. Ferguson

ISBN: 978-1-61470-491-1
© 2012 Nova Science Publishers, Inc.

Chapter 84

WAR: AN INTRODUCTION TO THEORIES AND RESEARCH ON COLLECTIVE VIOLENCE

Tor G. Jakobsen
Trondheim Business School, Trondheim, Norway

RESEARCH SUMMARY

Many students have come to the study of war and peace from a background heavily influenced by media exposure and political commitment. Some tend to see rebellion against autocratic rule mainly in terms of political ideals and the struggle for justice. The academic study of civil war, on the other hand, in recent years has focused more on the opportunity factors, even claiming that the greed of rebel leaders can play an important role in driving an insurrection. Discovering this, some students have become disillusioned, but many have taken up the challenge to show that wars in general and civil wars in particular are also fought for more than material gain. This book offers a balanced assessment of grievance and opportunity theories, and will serve as food for thought as the readers attempt to hammer out their own projects and move the field forward.

In: Psychology Research Biographies and Summaries
Editors: Nancy E. Wodarth and Alexis P. Ferguson

ISBN: 978-1-61470-491-1
© 2012 Nova Science Publishers, Inc.

Chapter 85

RUMINATION AND AVOIDANCE IN DEPRESSION: THE RELATIONSHIP BETWEEN RUMINATION, AVOIDANCE AND DEPRESSION IN DEPRESSED INPATIENTS

Filip Raes[1], Heleen Vandromme and Dirk Hermans
Department of Psychology
University of Leuven, Belgium

RESEARCH SUMMARY

Currently, there is a renewed interest for the concept of avoidance in the field of depression research (e.g., Moulds, Kandris, Starr, & Wong, 2007; Ottenbreit & Dobson, 2004). A recent hypothesis is that rumination, which refers to constant dwelling on negative mood and its causes, functions as an avoidance strategy in depression (see Moulds et al., 2007). Hitherto, this idea remained untested in a clinically depressed group. The present study examined the relationship between rumination and avoidance. A clinical sample of depressed inpatients ($n = 37$) completed self-report measures of avoidance, rumination, depression, and anxiety. Results showed that rumination is significantly associated with cognitive forms of avoidance, even when controlled for anxiety levels. These findings are consistent with the hypothesis that rumination functions as a (cognitive) avoidance strategy, and extend prior observations of such association to a clinical group. As a whole, the results further underscore the potential value of the construct of avoidance in the conceptualization of depression.

---

[1] Department of Psychology, University of Leuven, Tiensestraat 102, 3000 Leuven, Belgium; Tel : ++ 32 - (0)16 - 32.58.92; Fax : ++ 32 - (0)16 - 32.60.99; E-mail: filip.raes@psy.kuleuven.be.

Chapter 86

THE SPECTRUM OF SELF-HARM IN ADOLESCENCE AND YOUNG ADULTHOOD: MOVING TOWARD AN INTEGRATIVE MODEL OF PATHOGENIC MECHANISMS

Christa D. Labouliere and Marc S. Karverh
University of South Florida, Tampa, Florida, US

RESEARCH SUMMARY

The "spectrum of self-harm" is commonly used to describe a wide range of behaviors of different levels of severity, all with overlapping risk factors, spanning health-risk behavior (such as reckless driving or sexual activity), deliberate non-suicidal self-injury (in the form of cutting, burning, or other superficial tissue damage without conscious suicidal intent), suicide attempts, and actual death by suicide. Extensive research in self-harm so far has focused on predisposing factors, including demographic (i.e., gender, age), biological (i.e., neurotransmitter abnormalities, hypersensitivity to emotional response, slow return-to-baseline), temperamental (i.e., shy/withdrawn, emotionally-reactive, or impulsive), environmental (i.e., childhood abuse, family conflict), and intrapersonal (i.e., psychopathology, low self-esteem) diatheses. However, although predisposing factors identify those at increased risk, not much is known about how these factors are connected with self-harm outcomes. Considering that the central goal of clinical intervention with those who self-harm is to replace maladaptive patterns of thinking and behavior with more adaptive ones, a more practical focus of research and theory would be potential pathogenic mechanisms that link risk factors to self-harm outcomes.

In this chapter, we proposed a theoretical model that linked Joiner's (2005) theory of suicide to our own model of affect regulation as a critical mechanism in the development, escalation, and maintenance of self-harm behaviors. This proposed model draws upon the existing research, existing theories, and unstated theories that appear to underlie self-harm research. By integrating models of self-harm into one comprehensive theory that considers predisposing, precipitating, and maintenance factors in light of the mechanisms of emotion dysregulation and maladaptive coping, researchers and clinicians alike can lay the groundwork for further study informed by the literature.

Chapter 87

MODELING OF DYSLEXIA: IS A UNITARY MODEL OF DYSLEXIA POSSIBLE?

Timothy C. Papadopoulos[*,1], *George K. Georgiou*[2] *and Sotirios Douklias*[3]

[1]Department of Psychology, University of Cyprus, Greek
[2]Department of Educational Psychology, University of Alberta, Canada
[3]Department of Psychology, University of Cyprus, Greek

RESEARCH SUMMARY

For many years, the study of dyslexia relied heavily on exclusionary definitions. In turn, dyslexics were defined simply in terms of a reading score that was far below a specific reading age when IQ, socio-educational, emotional, neurological, and psychiatric reasons had also been excluded. Two problems emerged from such an approach, one being conceptual and one being related to the assessment of dyslexia. This chapter advocates that dyslexia concept is better understood only if attention is drawn to the wide range of problems and the constitutional nature of the difficulties encountered by individuals with dyslexia. Therefore, four major stands in current dyslexia research are discussed: (a) the nature of the phonological impairment that is mainly associated with a pervasive problem at the level of underlying phonological representations, (b) the nature of naming speed and automaticity impairments that are seen either as a consequence of an impairment of a timing mechanism or are attributed to abnormal cerebellar functioning, providing a more neuropsychological explanation for dyslexia, (c) the nature of the cognitive deficits that are more general and modality unspecific, such as deficits at information processing level, and (d) the nature of language based problems attributed to impaired semantic, syntactic and/or orthographic awareness. The ultimate aim is to understand the biological basis of the disorder and how this

---

[*] Timothy C. Papadopoulos, PhD Department of Psychology, University of Cyprus, P.O. Box 20537, 1678, Nicosia, Cyprus, TEL: +357 22 892079; FAX: +357 22 892071; E-mail: tpapadop@ucy.ac.cy. This work was supported by EU-UCY Grants for Applied Research Projects for Cyprus to the first author (Grant No. 8037-16013).

brain-based disposition can lead to subtle impairments at the cognitive and behavioral levels. It is concluded that with the advent of cognitive neuroscience which revolutionizes the medical approach we can build unitary definitions and models of dyslexia, making it possible to study links between brain and behavior in this specific developmental disorder.

In: Psychology Research Biographies and Summaries
Editors: Nancy E. Wodarth and Alexis P. Ferguson
ISBN: 978-1-61470-491-1
© 2012 Nova Science Publishers, Inc.

Chapter 88

OVERGENERAL ATTACHMENT MEMORY: OVERGENERAL ATTACHMENT-RELATED AUTOBIOGRAPHICAL MEMORY IN CHILDREN

Jessica L. Borelli[*,1], *Daryn H. David,*[1]
Michael J. Crowley[2] *and Linda C. Mayes*[2]

[1]Yale University, US
[2]Yale University Child Study Center.
New Haven, Connecticut, US

This research was supported by grants from National Science Foundation and the Center for Mental Health Promotion awarded to the first author. Special thanks are due to Nicki Hunter, Eric Langlois, Donald F. Nathanson, and Erika McCarty for their assistance with data processing, to Susan Nolen-Hoeksema, Kelly Brownell, Doug Mennin, and Nancy Suchman for their comments on an earlier draft, and to all of the children and families who participated in this project

RESEARCH SUMMARY

Overgeneral memory, or the tendency to report general rather than specific autobiographical memories, has been explored from different theoretical perspectives and has been linked to depressive and anxiety symptoms. Another perspective, attachment theory, suggests that individuals with a history of difficult parenting may show a bias toward remembering more general rather than specific autobiographical memories. At present, however, empirical work that may disentangle the important role of early relationships on autobiographical memory function is lacking. This study examined the associations among depressive symptoms, dismissing attachment, and the specificity of attachment-related

---

[*] jessica.borelli@yale.edu; Yale University, Department of Psychology, Box 208205, New Haven, CT, 06520; phone: (203) 432-1557; Fax: (203)-432-7172.

memory in a sample of school-aged children. A total of 97 children between the ages of 8 and 12 completed the Child Attachment Interview and the Children's Depression Inventory. Results indicated that children with a dismissing attachment organization are not more likely to report clinically-significant levels of depressive symptoms as compared to other children. In addition, dismissing attachment moderates the association between depressive symptoms and memory specificity, such that for dismissing children, there are no group differences in memory specificity across clinical and non-clinical depression groups, whereas non-dismissing children with clinically-significant symptoms have lower specificity as compared to non-dismissing children with non-clinical levels of symptoms. Results are discussed in terms of their contribution to the literature on overgeneral memory.

Chapter 89

DEPRESSION AND A PARENTING INTERVENTION: CAN CAREGIVER DEPRESSION BRING A GOOD PARENTING INTERVENTION DOWN? THE CASE OF PARENT-CHILD INTERACTION THERAPY

Mark Scholes, Melanie J. Zimmer-Gembeck and Rae Thomas
School of Psychology, Griffith University, Queensland, Australia

RESEARCH SUMMARY

Depressed caregivers who present for parenting assistance often display excess difficulties with maintaining positive parent-child interactions and report that they cannot manage their children's problem behaviours. In addition to this, they often report other life stressors such as marital distress, lack of social support and/or socioeconomic disadvantage. This confluence of problems means that engaging depressed caregivers in parenting services can be challenging and depression is believed to impede successful intervention outcomes. For example, research has shown that depressed participants are at increased risk of intervention dropout and that they more often fail to maintain positive parenting behaviours (Assemany & McIntosh, 2002; Forehand, Furey & McMahon, 1984). However, others have suggested that engagement in parenting interventions in order to improve parent-child relationships may provide additional benefits such as reducing caregiver stress and depressive symptoms (Sameroff, 2004). In this randomised controlled trial of Parent-Child Interaction Therapy (PCIT), we assessed depression using three methods -- an interview, a self-report questionnaire and observation. We anticipated that nonattendance and attrition would be higher in depressed compared to nondepressed caregivers. In addition, those who attended 12 weeks of treatment ($n = 68$) were compared to those on a supported waitlist (n = 27); we expected that caregivers receiving PCIT would have greater declines in depressive symptoms than those on the waitlist. Participants were female caregivers (age $M = 34$, $SD = 8.9$) and their young children (ages 3 to 7). Caregivers were at risk of child maltreatment based on a child maltreatment inventory and reported that their children had clinical levels of externalising symptoms. Survival analysis showed that attrition was similar to previous studies of PCIT and there was no significant difference in attrition rate when depressed and nondepressed caregivers were compared. Measures of attendance such as the number of missed appointments also did not differ between groups. Regarding parenting outcomes, treatment participants showed greater improvements in observed interactions with their children than those on waitlist. Yet, the anticipated difference between depressed and nondepressed caregivers was not found; groups did not differ when we compared observed interactions with children prior to treatment and during treatment, with the exceptions of reflections/descriptions and negative talk. When depression was compared, it declined similarly and rapidly for caregivers regardless of whether they were receiving PCIT or were on the waitlist. Caregiver depression does not correlate with attendance and length of PCIT or observed parent-child interactions when participants are female caregivers with high risk of maltreatment and children with behaviour problems. In summary, study findings suggest that PCIT is an effective intervention for improving the observed parenting skills of both depressed and nondepressed caregivers with young children, but PCIT is not directly implicated in reducing caregivers' depressive symptoms.

Chapter 90

THE ROLE OF NEGATIVE AFFECTIVE VALENCE IN RETURN OF FEAR

Inneke Kerkhof[1], Debora Vansteenwegen, Tom Beckers, Trinette Dirikx, Frank Baeyens, Rudi D'Hooge and Dirk Hermans
University of Leuven, Belgium

RESEARCH SUMMARY

Epidemiological research shows that about 30 percent of the general population will develop an anxiety disorder at some point in life (Kessler, Koretz, Merikangas, & Wang, 2004). Unsurprisingly, much research is invested in unveiling the processes that are responsible for the origin and maintenance of anxiety disorders, as well as in the principles that constitute the core of successful treatment. The general efficacy of exposure-based treatments for these disorders is irrefutable. Nevertheless, return of fear after successful exposure is a common finding and constitutes a challenge for clinical practice and fear research.

According to contemporary learning theories, fear can be acquired through an associative learning process. In a fear conditioning procedure a neutral stimulus (the Conditioned Stimulus or CS) comes to evoke fear after it was repeatedly paired with an aversive stimulus (the Unconditioned Stimulus or US). From this perspective extinction – a decrease in conditioned responding to the CS due to repeated presentations of the CS alone – can be viewed as an experimental model for exposure therapy. Return of conditioned responses after extinction then can be seen as a model for relapse after treatment. Experimental research suggests that during a fear acquisition procedure the reinforced CS (CS+) does not only become a valid predictor for the US but also acquires a negative connotation that is resistant to extinction. This is in line with the clinical observation that even after avoidance behavior has been drastically reduced through exposure, spider fearful individuals continue to consider spiders as negative animals (Baeyens, Eelen, Van den Berg, & Crombez, 1989). This

---

[1] Department of Psychology, University of Leuven, Tiensestraat 102, 3000 Leuven, Belgium; Tel : ++32 - (0)16 - 32.58.67; Fax : ++32 - (0)16 - 32.60.99; Email : Inneke.Kerkhof@psy.kuleuven.be.

remaining negative valence after extinction/exposure might function as an affective-motivational source for return of fear. Procedures that alter the valence of the fear eliciting stimulus after extinction/exposure (e.g., counterconditioning procedures) might then be effective in diminishing return of fear.

In this chapter, we will give an overview of the research literature on the role of affective valence in (return of) fear. In addition, we discuss results of an animal (mice) study that was designed to investigate the impact of a counterconditioning procedure after extinction on return of conditioned responding.

Chapter 91

THE NEUROPSYCHOLOGY OF ALCOHOLISM

J. Uekermann and I. Daum
Institute of Cognitive Neuroscience, Department of Neuropsychology,
Ruhr-University of Bochum, Germany

RESEARCH SUMMARY

Studies on neuropsychological functions in alcoholism have reported a range of impairments including visuo-spatial abilities, attention, memory, executive functions and social cognition. On the basis of neuropsychological studies as well as imaging data different models have been proposed for the interpretation of these deficits. The present chapter aims to give an overview of findings concerning the neuropsychology of alcoholism by reviewing investigations on cognitive functions as well as imaging and electrophysiological data. In addition, the potential contribution of drinking variables, family history of alcoholism, gender and affective variables as well as the presumable relevance of cognitive deficits for the treatment of alcoholism will be discussed.

In: Psychology Research Biographies and Summaries
Editors: Nancy E. Wodarth and Alexis P. Ferguson
ISBN: 978-1-61470-491-1
© 2012 Nova Science Publishers, Inc.

Chapter 92

PERCEPTION WITHOUT AWARENESS: THE QUALITATIVE DIFFERENCES APPROACH

Juan J. Ortells[1], María T. Daza[1], Carmen Noguera[1], Encarna Carmona[1], Elaine Fox[2] and María J. F. Abad[3]

[1] University of Almería, Spain
[2] University of Essex, England
[3] University of Jaén, Spain

RESEARCH SUMMARY

Is it possible to perceive stimulus information even when there is no awareness of perceiving? This question has been the focus of considerable research and discussion for more than 100 years (see Adams, 1957, for a review of earlier studies). However, despite the numerous experimental reports suggesting that our behavior and thoughts may be influenced by unconscious processes, research on perception without awareness has usually been plagued by continual controversy (Merikle, 1992). Much of this controversy stems directly from the logic underlying the task-*dissociation paradigm*, which has traditionally been the most widely followed approach to address that issue.

Although various versions of this paradigm have been used, the basic assumption underlying all versions is that unconscious perception can be demonstrated via a dissociation between two different indices or measures of perception. One *direct* measure (e. g., stimulus recognition) would reflect the effect of a perceived stimulus on the instructed responses to that stimulus (which is typically assessed by a measure of accuracy at the instructed task). Such a direct effect is assumed to indicate whether any relevant stimulus information is consciously perceived. A second *indirect* measure of stimulus perception would be an uninstructed effect of the task stimulus on behavior, which is assumed to be also sensitive to unconsciously perceived information. As an illustration, a well-known indirect effect is semantic priming (see also the Stroop's (1935) interference effect), which consists of a facilitation of responses (in terms of speed and/or accuracy) to a target stimulus (e.g., CAT) when it is preceded by a semantically related (prime) word (e.g., DOG), than when the preceding prime word is unrelated to the target (e.g., ARM). A dissociation is demonstrated whenever there is a reliable indirect effect by a stimulus that is unaccompanied by any direct effect of that stimulus. In other words, perception without awareness would be demonstrated whenever the indirect measure of perception (e.g., semantic priming) shows some sensitivity to stimuli under conditions on which the direct measure shows null sensitivity.

In spite of this relatively straightforward logic underlying the dissociation paradigm, it has proven difficult to design experiments that provide compelling, uncontroversial evidence for perception without awareness. On the one hand, there usually has been a lack of agreement about what constitutes an adequate direct measure of conscious perception. On the other hand, the means of using dissociation data to draw conclusions about unconscious perception have remained controversial. As noted by some authors (e.g., Holender, 1986; Reingold & Merikle, 1988), this is because the interpretation of a dissociation pattern mainly depends on assumptions being made about the relation of conscious and unconscious perception to performance on direct and indirect tasks. In an influential review, Holender (1986) suggested that in order that the occurrence of an indirect effect in the absence of a direct effect (i.e., an *indirect-without-direct-effect pattern*) provides compelling evidence for unconscious perception, the direct measure must be assumed to be sensitive to all relevant conscious effects of stimuli, and such a measure must exhibits null sensitivity. If this *exhaustiveness assumption* (as labelled by Reingold & Merikle, 1988) cannot be justified, then any dissociation between measures may simply indicate that the direct and indirect indices are sensitive to different aspects of consciously perceived stimuli. In addition, the direct measure should *exclusively* be influenced by conscious processes (i.e., an *exclusiveness assumption*). If a direct effect is sensitive to both consciously and unconsciously perceived information, then the attempt to establish null sensitivity for the direct measure could eliminate or underestimate any evidence for unconscious perception.

Chapter 93

INTRAPSYCHIC FACTORS CONTRIBUTING TO ADOLESCENT DEPRESSION

Lisa C. Milne[1] and Philip Greenway[2]
[1]Australian Catholic University, Fitzroy, Victoria, Australia
[2]Monash University, Clayton, Victoria, Australia

RESEARCH SUMMARY

Depression during adolescence is both a normal phenomena and cause for concern, with the sequelae sometimes including poorer academic and occupational outcomes, social withdrawal, and suicide. The etiology of depression, especially during adolescence has been associated with a number of factors, including biological factors (Riddle and Cho, 1989), early physiological and psychological trauma (Toolan, 1981), psychological and psychosocial factors (National Institute of Mental Health, 1981). There have also been attempts to understand depression as a result of intrapsychic factors, such as a failure to individuate (Blos, 1968), insecure attachments (Armsden, McCauley, Greenberg, Burke and Mitchell, 1990) negative parental representations, and object relations that lack self-other differentiation (Blatt, Wein, Chevron, and Quinlan, 1979).

The separation-individuation process, where adolescents attempt to let go of their dependence on their parents, in a process similar to that which occurs in infancy, is central to adolescent development. The quality of attachment to the primary caregiver also impacts upon the ability of adolescents to re-negotiate the changes in these attachments. Parental representations both conscious and unconscious are also related to adjustment in adolescence. Self-report measures of perceptions of maternal care as being either over-protective or uncaring; have also been related to depression, suicidal thoughts and disrupted interpersonal relationships (Blatt, Wein, Chevron, and Quinlan, 1979).

During childhood the estimates of rates of depression do not tend to show gender differences, yet by adolescence females are diagnosed with depression at twice the rate that

---

[1] Correspondence: Dr. Lisa Milne, 266 Middleborough Rd Blackburn South, Victoria, Australia, 3168. EMAIL: lcmilne@netspace.net.au.

males are – and this gender difference in epidemiology remains throughout adulthood (Angold and Worthman, 1993). This would suggest that the causal and maintaining factors are in some way related to gender. The present study examines from a psychoanalytic perspective, the intrapsychic factors associated with symptoms of depression in adolescents, and in particular gender differences are examined.

A non-clinical sample of 81 adolescents was assessed on a number of theoretically related measures: separation-individuation; anaclitic depression; introjective depression; attachment style; parental representations, and symptoms of depression. The aim of this study was to analyse the factors that mediate the relationship between parenting variables and symptoms of depression in adolescent males and females.

Chapter 94

A HERMENEUTIC APPROACH TO CULTURE AND PSYCHOTHERAPY

John Chambers Christopher[1], Gary Foster[2] and Susan James[3]

[1] Health and Human Development
Montana State University; Bozeman, Montana, US
[2] Department of Philosophy; Wilfrid Laurier University;
Waterloo, Ontario, Canada
[3] Educational and Counselling Psychology and Special Education;
University of British Columbia;
Vancouver, Canada

RESEARCH SUMMARY

Despite the growing awareness of culture within psychology, critics contend that understandings of culture remain largely superficial. Hermeneutics is a way of thinking interpretively about cultural meanings and discerning their specific manifestations that helps to remedy this situation. Hermeneutics offers a comprehensive theory of culture that (a) details how the self is embedded in culture, (b) highlights culture's inherently moral nature, and (c) provides conceptual tools for approaching culture in specific encounters. It can be utilized by psychotherapists not only to help understand clients from different cultural backgrounds but also to better recognize how the dominant Western cultural outlook, individualism, influences psychotherapy theory, research, and practice. These concepts are applied to cross-cultural cases.

In: Psychology Research Biographies and Summaries
Editors: Nancy E. Wodarth and Alexis P. Ferguson
ISBN: 978-1-61470-491-1
© 2012 Nova Science Publishers, Inc.

Chapter 95

ADOLESCENT BRAIN DEVELOPMENT, BEHAVIOR, PREMORBID PSYCHOSIS AND RISK FOR SCHIZOPHRENIA: A REVIEW OF STRUCTURAL AND FUNCTIONAL MRI STUDIES

Ozgur Oner[*,1], *Haluk Ozbay*[2] *and Kerim M. Munir*[†,3]

[1]Ankara Diskapi Children's Hospital, Child Psychiatry Department, Ankara, Turkey
NIMH Fogarty International Center Mental Health and Developmental Disabilities (MHDD) Program, Children's Hospital, Boston, US
[2]Yildirim Bayazit Hospital Psychiatry Department, Ankara, Turkey
[3]Children's Hospital Boston, Harvard Medical School, Division of General Pediatrics and Department of Psychiatry, Boston, US

RESEARCH SUMMARY

During adolescence, important changes take place in the brain development. These changes make adolescence a period of both vulnerability and opportunity. Emergence of psychosis and schizophrenia may be associated with abnormal brain development during adolescence. In this chapter, first, we describe findings of structural and functional MRI studies related to some of the deviant behaviors during adolescence, in the context of risks and opportunities associated with brain development in this period. Second, we focus on findings of studies of abnormal brain development during the premorbid period of psychosis in general, and of szhizophrenia, in particular.

---

[*] Correspondence concerning this article should be addressed to: Ozgur Oner, M.D., Child Psychiatry Service, Ankara Diskapi Children's Hospital, Advanced in Country Fellow, NIMH Fogarty International Center Mental Health and Developmental Disabilities (MHDD) Program, Children's Hospital, Boston, USA. E-mail: ozz_oner@yahoo.com.
[†] Kerim M Munir, M.D., M.P.H., D.Sc., Children's Hospital Boston, Harvard Medical School, Division of General Pediatrics and Department of Psychiatry, Boston, USA. Tel: 617-818-1853; Fax: 617 730-0049; E-mail: kerim.munir@childrens.harvard.edu.

In: Psychology Research Biographies and Summaries
Editors: Nancy E. Wodarth and Alexis P. Ferguson
ISBN: 978-1-61470-491-1
© 2012 Nova Science Publishers, Inc.

Chapter 96

THE ASSOCIATION OF VISUOSPATIAL MEMORY AND WORKING MEMORY WITH ADOLESCENT ONSET SCHIZOPHRENIA

Alasdair Vance[*]

Head Academic Child Psychiatry, Department of Paediatrics, University of Melbourne
Murdoch Childrens Research Institute, Royal Children's Hospital, Parkville, Melbourne
VIC 3052, Australia

RESEARCH SUMMARY

This chapter investigates the nature of and association between visuospatial memory, and, separately, visuospatial working memory in adolescent onset schizophrenia. The data presented suggest that both the visuospatial memory and working memory performance of the adolescent-onset schizophrenia group are impaired compared to the healthy control group. Further, the type and magnitude of the deficits are similar to those reported in the adult-onset schizophrenia patients suggesting these deficits are developmental stage independent. The import of these findings is examined within the context of emerging neurobiological models of progressive parietal-temporal-frontal linked neural network dysfunction in schizophrenia, whether of adolescent- or adult-onset. Also, the implications of these findings for the current aetiological understanding of schizophrenia and the current assessment and treatment approaches are discussed.

---

[*] Phone: 61 3 9345-4666; Fax: 61 3 9345-6002; email: avance@unimelb.edu.au.

In: Psychology Research Biographies and Summaries
Editors: Nancy E. Wodarth and Alexis P. Ferguson
ISBN: 978-1-61470-491-1
© 2012 Nova Science Publishers, Inc.

Chapter 97

PSYCHOTIC SYMPTOMS IN CHILDREN AND ADOLESCENTS

Michelle Harley[1,2], Aileen Murtagh[2], Ian Kelleher[1] and Mary Cannon[1]

[1]Department of Psychiatry, Royal College of Surgeons in Ireland, Dublin, Ireland
[2]Department of Child and Adolescent Psychiatry,
Mater Misericordiae Hospital, Dublin, Ireland
[2]Department of Child and Adolescent Psychiatry,
National Children's Hospital, Tallaght, Dublin, Ireland

RESEARCH SUMMARY

Recent studies suggest that psychosis exists along a continuum in the general population, rather than as an all-or-none phenomenon. This is supported by the finding that the prevalence of psychotic symptoms in the general population far exceeds the prevalence of psychotic disorders. Only 1% of the overall population will develop schizophrenia during their lifetime whereas international epidemiological research suggests that between 5% and 38% of the adult general population may experience at least one psychotic symptom in their lives, with rates of 2.1% to 58.9 % reported for child and adolescent populations. The significance of psychotic symptoms in children and adolescents is not as yet fully established: they have been found to be associated with a variety of psychiatric disorders in this age group, in particular depression and anxiety, and social factors including childhood abuse. There is emerging evidence that psychotic symptoms in childhood and adolescence may be risk markers for psychotic illness in adulthood. Poulton et al. (1999) [1] found that self-reported psychotic symptoms at age 11 years predicted a very high risk of a schizophrenia spectrum disorder at age 26 years. Therefore, adolescents who report psychotic symptoms could be conceptualised as a 'high risk' group for schizophrenia. This paradigm may prove valuable in exploring early risk factors for psychosis-vulnerability and in predicting psychotic outcomes.

Chapter 98

PSYCHOANALYTICAL TEAMWORK ON SCHIZOPHRENIC YOUNG PATIENTS IN A DAY-HOSPITAL (REVISITING SOME DEVELOPMENTAL PRE-CONDITIONS FOR PATIENT'S SUBJECTIVE APPROPRIATION)

Bernard Penot
Paris Psychoanalytical Institute, Paris, France

RESEARCH SUMMARY

Psychoanalytical psychotherapeutic "teamwork" may be recommended for dealing with this particular kind of mental pathology characterized by schizophrenic symptoms in young patients. In such cases, the degree of alienation is such that repetition is usually induced in other people (the therapists), filling in for fantasy construction that seems then to be lacking in the patient's psyche. A case like that of "Angel" can give some idea of this phenomenon, wherein several caregivers have to harbor fragmented and incompatible elements of the case's particular history, which are in need of more mental representation. Any subjective restitution and appropriation of these elements by the patient would require a sort of detour (often a trying one!) by way of the psychical space of caregivers whose initial task will be to "work it through" among themselves.

Chapter 99

TREATMENT APPROACHES TO AGGRESSIVE BEHAVIOR IN SCHIZOPHRENIA

*Jan Volavka**
Nathan Kline Institute and New York University, NY, US

RESEARCH SUMMARY

Treatment of psychiatric disorders is hampered by the fact that their causes are poorly understood. Our ignorance is even deeper when it comes to aggressive behavior in psychiatric patients. Clearly, without better understanding of underlying neuropsychobiology of aggression we cannot improve the existing treatments. This chapter therefore first reviews neurobiological and psychosocial factors affecting aggression in schizophrenia, and then proceeds to discuss their implications for treatment. Finally, the current state of the psychopharmacology of aggression in schizophrenia is briefly reviewed.

---

* Email: janvolavka@gmail.com. Phone 406 995 2776. Mailing address: 55 Blue Spruce Road #E3, P.O. Box 160663, Big Sky, MT 59716-0663.

Chapter 100

BODY IMAGE DEVIATION IN CHRONIC SCHIZOPHRENIA: A NEW RESEARCH

Reiko Koide and Akira Tamaoka
University of Tsukuba, Japan

RESEARCH SUMMARY

Since the time of Kraepelin (1919) and Bleuler (1911/1950), schizophrenics' deviant perceptions, feelings, and beliefs concerning their bodies have been described. In this section, the symptoms relevant to body image aberration that have been discussed for over the past half century, as well as psychological measures that were developed to understand these aberrations, are reviewed, to lead to the current status and future prospects for the study of the body image aberration in schizophrenia.

In: Psychology Research Biographies and Summaries
Editors: Nancy E. Wodarth and Alexis P. Ferguson
ISBN: 978-1-61470-491-1
© 2012 Nova Science Publishers, Inc.

Chapter 101

SEX DIFFERENCES IN AGGRESSIVE AND DELINQUENT BEHAVIOR IN SCHIZOTYPAL ADOLESCENTS[1]

Amanda McMillan and Elaine Walker
Department of Psychology, Emory University, Atlanta, Georgia

RESEARCH SUMMARY

There is a well-documented link between schizophrenia and antisocial behavior. For example, studies of violent offenders worldwide find a significantly elevated prevalence of schizophrenia and spectrum disorder diagnoses (Gosden, Kramp, Gabrielsen, and Sestoft, 2003; Arseneault, Moffitt, Caspi, Taylor, and Silva, 2000). Conversely, studies of patient populations reveal higher rates of antisocial behavior. In an investigation of a large Danish birth cohort in their forties, proportionately more of the men and women who developed schizophrenia were convicted of non-violent and violent crimes (Brennan, Mednick, and Hodgins, 2000). Similar results were obtained in investigations of population cohorts in Australia (Mullen, Burgess, Wallace, Palmer, and Ruschena, 2000), Israel (Stueve and Link, 1997), and New Zealand (Arseneault et al., 2000).

Investigations into the specific links between symptoms and antisocial behavior suggest that the severity of positive symptoms is the strongest predictor of aggressive and violent behavior. Further, some findings indicate that individuals at risk for developing schizophrenia and spectrum disorders are more likely to manifest antisocial behaviors. The link between premorbid antisocial behavior and psychosis has been examined in both retrospective and prospective longitudinal studies. In a retrospective study of childhood-onset schizophrenia, Schaeffer and Ross (2002) found a high proportion of parents reporting oppositional behavior, violence, aggression, temper tantrums, and rages as premorbid signs in their children. Similarly, Arsenault et al. (2000) found that individuals with schizophrenia-spectrum disorders were more likely to have a childhood history of conduct disorder.

---

[1] This research was supported by Grant # RO1 MH62066-01 awarded to Dr. Walker from the National Institute of Mental Health.

The rate of premorbid antisocial behaviors appears to increase with age as the individual approaches late adolescence/early adulthood, the peak risk period for the onset of psychosis. In examining the premorbid developmental course through childhood, Neumann, Grimes, Walker and Baum (1995), used the Child Behavior Checklist (CBCL) and found a significant increase in aggressive behaviors in preschizophrenic children between 8 and 12 years of age. Two empirically-derived clusters were observed; Cluster I manifested early onset and escalating behavioral abnormalities, whereas Cluster II did not begin to differ from controls until adolescence. By 8 to 12 years, Cluster I was not only exhibiting more aggressive behavior than control subjects but Cluster II individuals as well. Using a similar retrospective design, Rossi, Pollice, Daneluzzo, Marinangeli and Stratta (2000) collected maternal reports of behavioral abnormalities for five age periods from birth through adolescence and found that all behavioral abnormality dimensions, including delinquent and aggressive behavior, were higher in the patient group when compared to the normal controls, and increased consistently with age.

Prospective studies of children at high risk for psychotic disorders yield similar findings. Bearden et al. (2000) followed a population cohort from childhood into adulthood to identify behavioral problems that preceded schizophrenia. They assessed a range of behaviors, including emotional reactivity and hostility, when the subjects were aged 4 and 7 years. Their findings indicate that a progression from initial social deficits to more severe behavioral deviance precedes adult-onset schizophrenia. Bergman, Wolfson and Walker (1997) examined behavioral problems in the offspring (mean age 9.75 years) of parents with a diagnosis of schizophrenia. Compared to those whose parents had no mental illness, the high-risk children exhibited elevated levels of externalizing behaviors (aggression and delinquency) on the CBCL. Further, the rate of behavior problems increased from the initial assessment to the follow-up, one year later. In a subsequent report from the Edinburgh High Risk Study, Miller, Byrne, Hodges, Lawrie and Johnstone (2002) obtained reports on the CBCL at two time periods, prior to age 13 and from ages 13-16. The high-risk individuals who later developed schizophrenia displayed significantly more externalizing behaviors when compared to those who did not go on to develop the illness. Specifically, prior to age 13, high risk children who later developed schizophrenia were more aggressive, and the difference became stronger in the 13-16 age period, with a much higher incidence of aggressive and delinquent behaviors in those individuals who later developed schizophrenia.

There is evidence that premorbid externalizing behaviors are linked with more pronounced cognitive impairment and clinical symptoms in patients. Baum and Walker (1995) used retrospective CBCL data, and found that patients who showed more childhood aggression and delinquency between ages 8 and16 years also manifested greater cognitive disorganization in adulthood. Neumann, Baum, Walker and Lewine (1996) found that escalating childhood delinquency predicted deficits in adult motor functioning, whereas both childhood delinquency and aggression predicted cognitive impairment. Replicating this pattern of findings, in a study of adult-onset schizophrenia patients, the presence of premorbid disciplinary problems was associated with more pronounced adult neuropsychological deficits (Silverstein, Mavrolefteros, and Turnbull, 2003). Among the various disciplinary problems, physical violence showed the strongest relation with adult neuropsychological deficits. Additionally, there is evidence to suggest that the association between childhood behavior and adult cognitive function may reflect underlying brain dysfunction. Walker, Lewine and Neumann (1996) found that premorbid externalizing problems in childhood were related with greater brain abnormalities in adult schizophrenia patients. Specifically, increases in delinquent behaviors were associated with ventricular enlargement and smaller whole brain volume.

In: Psychology Research Biographies and Summaries
Editors: Nancy E. Wodarth and Alexis P. Ferguson
ISBN: 978-1-61470-491-1
© 2012 Nova Science Publishers, Inc.

Chapter 102

FETAL ORIGINS OF ANTISOCIAL PERSONALITY DISORDER AND SCHIZOPHRENIA: EVIDENCE FROM THE DUTCH HUNGER WINTER

Richard Neugebauer[1,2,3,4] *and Ezra Susser*[1,5]

[1] Epidemiology of Developmental Brain Disorders Department,
New York State Psychiatric Institute, New York, NY, US
[2] G.H. Sergievsky Center,
Columbia University, New York, NY, US
[3] International Program on Refugee Trauma, New York, N.Y., US
[4] The Department of International Health and Development,
School of Public Health and Tropical Medicine, Tulane University, US
[5] Department of Epidemiology, Mailman School of Public Health,
Columbia University, New York, N.Y., US

RESEARCH SUMMARY

Risk factors for mortality and morbidity are divisible into three categories: those present before conception, others occurring postpartum and finally, those that operate in the interval between conception and birth. Until comparatively recently, this last period received limited attention in epidemiological research on psychiatric and (to a lesser degree) other disorders first emerging beyond the childhood years. One notable exception is the early and sustained interest in possible prenatal viral etiology of schizophrenia. Nonetheless, the operation of genetic factors, present at conception, and of macro and micro-level environmental factors, in the postnatal period were the primary focus of attention.

The past two decades have witnessed a growing interest in the prenatal and perinatal origins of adolescent and adult onset somatic and psychiatric diseases. Early, ground breaking work by Ravelli in the 1970s on prenatal nutrition and adult onset obesity (Ravelli et al., 1976) was followed two decades later by studies on low birth weight and raised risk for cardiovascular disease (Barker, 2003a; Barker, 2003b; Roseboom et al., 2001; Leon, 2001; Harding, 2001) A separate vein of research, emerging in the 1980s, examined prenatal and perinatal factors in risk for psychiatric disorders, initially motivated by an interest in a 'neurodevelopmental hypothesis' of schizophrenaia (Cannon, Kendell, Susser and Jones, 2003), now broadened to include a life course approach to neuropsychiatric disorders (Terry and Susser, 2001). These two research initiatives link the knowledge of established perinatal risk factors for diseases of early life, acquired through several decades of pediatric and perinatal epidemiologic research, with an equally extensive literature on the distribution and determinants of adult onset disorders, thereby creating conditions for a greatly enhanced understanding of both the proximal and distal etiologies of disease and dysfunction across the life span. Some initial scientific insights yielded by this approach in the area of psychiatric disorders, specifically, of ASPD (ASPD) and schizophrenia, are the subject of the present chapter.

In: Psychology Research Biographies and Summaries
Editors: Nancy E. Wodarth and Alexis P. Ferguson
ISBN: 978-1-61470-491-1
© 2012 Nova Science Publishers, Inc.

Chapter 103

SELF-CONCEPT DISTURBANCES IN EATING-DISORDERED FEMALE STUDENTS COMPARED TO NORMAL CONTROLS

Laurence Claes, Joke Simons and Walter Vandereycken
Catholic University of Leuven, Department of Psychology, Leuven, Belgium

RESEARCH SUMMARY

Self-concept disturbances have been considered to play a determining role in the development of eating disorders. However, questions remain unanswered about the aspects of self-concept that distinguish eating-disordered women from other populations, and about the mechanisms that link the self-concept to the disordered behaviors. Referring to Markus' self-schema model (1977), a limited collection of positive self-schema available in memory, in combination with a chronically and inflexibly accessible schema about body weight, may contribute to the development of an eating disorder. To test this model, two multidimensional self-concept questionnaires, the Self Description Questionnaire III and the Physical Self Description Questionnaire, were administered to two groups of female high school students: 125 eating-disordered (both anorexic-like and bulimic-like) students and 103 normal controls. No significant differences emerged in the academic-related aspects of the self-concept. However, nonacademic-related dimensions, particularly body-weight/appearance aspects, revealed significantly differences between the eating-disordered students and their normal peers. Less differences appeared between the anorexic-like and bulimic-like subgroups. Disturbances in body-weight/appearance aspects of the self-concept may be useful as early signals in the detection of students at risk for developing an eating disorder.

In: Psychology Research Biographies and Summaries
Editors: Nancy E. Wodarth and Alexis P. Ferguson
ISBN: 978-1-61470-491-1
© 2012 Nova Science Publishers, Inc.

Chapter 104

LINKING STUDENT BEHAVIOURS AND ATTITUDES TOWARDS INFORMATION AND COMMUNICATION TECHNOLOGY WITH LEARNING PROCESSES, TEACHER INSTRUCTION AND CLASSROOM ENVIRONMENT

Robert F. Cavanagh and Joseph T. Romanoski
Curtin University of Technology, Perth, Australia

RESEARCH SUMMARY

This chapter describes how the Rasch model was applied to construct an interval-level scale measuring student use and disposition towards information and communication technology (ICT). Scale development was based upon an hypothesised model of classroom ICT learning culture comprising self and collective values, attitudes and behaviours. Specifically, the study aimed to produce a scale that: Measured student self-reported learning behaviours and attitudes towards use of ICT; had calibrated item difficulties and self-reported learning behaviours and attitudes towards ICT measures on the same scale; and elicited data to fit the theoretical model. A 126 item Likert scale type instrument was developed, administered to 439 primary and secondary school students, and then refined and validated by Rasch analysis. The validated data comprised 62 items on five aspects of ICT learning culture. These five aspects were: Student reported learning attitudes and behaviours; student reported teacher attitudes and behaviours; student reported attitudes and behaviours towards ICT networks; student reported home ICT attitudes and behaviours; and student reported values towards ICT use at school. Examination of the psychometric properties of the data identified common and uncommon attitudes and behaviours. This illustrated how students viewed their classroom ICT learning culture.

In: Psychology Research Biographies and Summaries
Editors: Nancy E. Wodarth and Alexis P. Ferguson

ISBN: 978-1-61470-491-1
© 2012 Nova Science Publishers, Inc.

Chapter 105

SOCIAL ANXIETY IN THE COLLEGE STUDENT POPULATION: THE ROLE OF ANXIETY SENSITIVITY

Angela Sailer and Holly Hazlett-Stevens[*]
University of Nevada,
Reno Nevada, US

RESEARCH SUMMARY

Most college students experience some degree of social anxiety on occasion. However, many suffer chronic anxiety across social situations coupled with a strong fear of negative evaluation. In addition to impaired occupational and social functioning, severe social anxiety or social phobia can carry profound consequences for college students. Social anxiety is a prominent motivation for college student drinking (Burke and Stephens, 1999). In addition to social isolation, social anxiety is associated with depressogenic cognitions, both of which leave socially anxious students at an increased risk for depression (Johnson et al., 1992). Anxiety sensitivity – fear of anxiety-related sensations due to perceived consequences of physical, mental, or social harm – might play an important role in the development of social anxiety (Hazen et al., 1995). Unlike panic disorder, in which individuals typically fear anxiety symptoms out of fear of physical harm or loss of mental control, socially anxious individuals fear perceived social consequences of others noticing their anxiety. Socially anxious college students also judge others who appear anxious more negatively than do college students without social anxiety (Purdon et al., 2001). Although panic disorder treatments target anxiety sensitivity directly with interoceptive exposure strategies, this approach is just beginning to receive attention for the treatment of social anxiety. After a brief review of the literature describing the nature of social anxiety among college students, this chapter will examine the specific role of anxiety sensitivity in its development and maintenance. Finally, results from a preliminary investigation comparing the effects of interoceptive exposure delivered in a social context to social context exposure without the interoceptive component will be presented and discussed.

---

[*] Correspondence concerning this article should be addressed to Holly Hazlett-Stevens, University of Nevada, Department of Psychology/298 Reno, NV 89557, or the author can be reached via email at: hhazlett@unr.edu.

Chapter 106

TEST ANXIETY AND ITS CONSEQUENCES ON ACADEMIC PERFORMANCE AMONG UNIVERSITY STUDENTS

Mohd Ariff Bin Kassim[1,*], *Siti Rosmaini Bt Mohd Hanafi*[1,†] *and Dawson R. Hancock*[2,‡]

[1]Universiti Tenaga Nasional, 26700 Muadzam Shah, Pahang, Malaysia
[2]University of North Carolina at Charlotte, 9201 University City Boulevard, Charlotte, North Carolina, US

RESEARCH SUMMARY

Some educators have failed to acknowledge the prevalence of test anxiety and its effect on academic performance among university students. This study addresses this issue at the university level using data collected through the Revised Test Anxiety (RTA) instrument and Sarason's four-factor model as a basis for measuring test anxiety. The study also investigates the effect of demographic factors on test anxiety. Findings reveal that test anxiety is significantly and negatively related to academic performance. Reasons for these findings are addressed.

Although testing is an important and widely used means for evaluating ability and achievement of individuals, many motivated and talented college students suffer from test anxiety (Austin & Patridge, 1995). Students often experience increased testing as they progress from primary school to post-secondary levels. Although most students experience normal nervousness during tests, others experience severe anxiety.

Obviously, test anxiety can be considered an important factor in relation to academic performance. It has been proposed that test anxiety is one of the most disruptive factors

---

[*] E-mail address: ariff@kms.uniten.edu.my. Telephone: 012-6097503.
[†] E-mail address: rosmaini@kms.uniten.edu.my. Telephone: 09-4552043.
[‡] E-mail address: DHancock@email.uncc.edu. Telephone: (704)687-8863. Corresponding author: Dawson R. Hancock, Ph.D. Address for Correspondence: University of North Carolina at Charlotte, 9201 University City Boulevard, Charlotte, North Carolina, U.S.A. 28223.

associated with underachievement of students. Sarason (1984) stated that test anxiety is a debilitating factor at all academic levels. Because of its strong influence on academic achievement, test anxiety has been identified as one of the variables in the motivation and learning strategies model proposed by Pintrich (Paulsen & Gentry, 1995).

Chapter 107

WRITING YOUR WAY TO HEALTH? THE EFFECTS OF DISCLOSURE OF PAST STRESSFUL EVENTS IN GERMAN STUDENTS

Lisette Morris, Annedore Linkemann and Birgit Kröner-Herwig*
Clinical Psychology and Psychotherapy
University of Göttingen, Germany

RESEARCH SUMMARY

In 1986 Pennebaker and Beall published their renowned study on the long-term beneficial health effects of disclosing traumatic events in 4 brief sequential writing sessions. Their results have been confirmed in various studies, but conflicting results have also been reported. The intent of our study was to replicate the experiments from Pennebaker and Beall (1986), Pennebaker et al. (1988), and Greenberg and Stone (1992) using a German student sample. Additionally, essay variables that point to the emotional processing of events (e.g., depth of self-exploration, number of negative/positive emotions, intensity of emotional expression) were examined as potential mechanisms of action. Trait measures of personality which could moderate the personal consequences of disclosure (alexithymia, self-concealment, worrying, social support) were also assessed. In a second study the experimental condition (disclosure) was varied by implementing "coping" vs. "helping" instructions as variations of the original condition. Under the coping condition participants were asked to elaborate on what they used to do, continue to do, or could do in the future to better cope with the event. Under the helping condition participants were asked to imagine themselves in the role of a adviser and elaborate on what they would recommend to persons also dealing with the trauma in order to better cope with the event. The expected beneficial effects of disclosure on long-term health

---

* Prof. Dr. B. Kroener-Herwig; Georg-Elias-Mueller-Institut für Psychologie; Dep. Clinical Psychology and Psychotherapy; Gosslerstr. 14; D - 37073 Goettingen; Email: bkroene@uni-goettingen.de.

(e.g., physician visits, physical symptoms, affectivity) could not be corroborated in either the first or the second study. None of the examined essay variables of emotional processing and only a single personality variable was able to explain significant variance in the health-related outcome variables influence. Nevertheless, substantial reductions in posttraumatic stress symptoms (e.g., intrusions, avoidance, arousal), were found in both experiments. These improvements were significantly related to essay variables of emotional expression and self-exploration and were particularly pronounced under the activation of a prosocial motivation (helping condition).

Repeated, albeit brief, expressive writing about personally upsetting or traumatic events resulted in an immediate increase in negative mood but did not lead to long-term positive health consequences in a German student sample. It did, however, promote better processing of stressful or traumatic events, as evidenced by reductions in posttraumatic stress symptoms. The instruction to formulate recommendations for persons dealing with the same trauma seems more helpful than standard disclosure or focusing on one's own past, present, and future coping endeavours. Overall, expressive writing seems to be a successful method of improving trauma processing. Determining the appropriate setting (e.g., self-help vs. therapeutic context) for disclore can be seen as an objective of future research.

In: Psychology Research Biographies and Summaries
Editors: Nancy E. Wodarth and Alexis P. Ferguson
ISBN: 978-1-61470-491-1
© 2012 Nova Science Publishers, Inc.

Chapter 108

STRESS AMONG STUDENTS IN DEVELOPING COUNTRIES - AN OVERVIEW

Shashidhar Acharya
Manipal College of Dental Sciences, Manipal, India

RESEARCH SUMMARY

Mankind since the dawn of history has been afflicted with various forms of diseases. Communicable diseases that took a heavy toll of human life in medieval and prehistoric times, have been replaced by non- communicable diseases and conditions in the recent times. Among the six factors which are responsible for the major share of these diseases, Stress occupies an important place (Rose, G.A. and Blackburn H. 1968). The Oxford English dictionary defines stress as pressure, tension or worry resulting from the problems in one's life. It is thus a condition of the mind, in which a person loses his calm tranquility and equanimity and experiences extreme discomfiture.

Chapter 109

COPING, MENTAL HEALTH STATUS, AND CURRENT LIFE REGRET IN COLLEGE WOMEN WHO DIFFER IN THEIR LIFETIME PREGNANCY STATUS: A RESILIENCE PERSPECTIVE*

Jennifer Langhinrichsen-Rohling[†], Theresa Rehm, Michelle Breland and Alexis Inabinet
University of South Alabama, Mobile, Alabama US

RESEARCH SUMMARY

This study examined the current mental health status, coping strategies, and perceived life regret of three types of female college students ($n = 277$): those who had never been pregnant (67.9%, $n = 188$); those who became pregnant at or before age 18 who were a priori considered to be resilient (14.8%, $n = 41$); and those who had experienced a pregnancy after age 18 (17.3%, $n = 48$). Data were collected at a diverse urban public university in the Southeast. This university has a significant number of commuter and non-traditional students. Results indicated that college women who had experienced an adult pregnancy reported significantly fewer maladaptive coping strategies than never-pregnant college women and those who had experienced a teenage pregnancy. Surprisingly, both groups of ever pregnant college women expressed significantly more life regret than never pregnant college women. Among the college women who had experienced a teenage pregnancy, two groups were delineated: those who were "thriving" versus those who were "at-risk" with regards to their

---
* This project was supported by Grant No. 2001-SI-FX-0006 awarded by the Office of Juvenile Justice and Delinquency Prevention, Office of Justice Programs, U.S. Department of Justice. Points of view or opinions in this document are those of the author and do not necessarily represent the official position or policies of the U.S. Department of Justice.
[†] Correspondence concerning this article should be addressed to Jennifer Langhinrichsen-Rohling, 385 Life Sciences Building, Psychology Department, University of South Alabama, Mobile, AL, 36688-0002, or the author can be reached via email at jlr@usouthal.edu.

current symptoms of depression, hostility, and hopelessness. Women in the "at-risk" group were significantly *less* likely to be simultaneously parenting and attending college than those in the "thriving" group. One potential implication is that identifying and intervening with these potentially at-risk college women may help improve retention rates and student morale at universities with a diverse student body.

Chapter 110

GENDER DIFFERENCES IN PRONENESS TO DEPRESSION AMONG HUNGARIAN COLLEGE STUDENTS

Ferenc Margitics and Zsuzsa Pauwlik
Department of Psychology at College of Nyíregyháza, Hungary

RESEARCH SUMMARY

Aims: Our research aimed to find out what role the risk mechanisms, as described in Goodman and Gotlib's (1999) model (genetic-biological, interpersonal, social learning related cognitive and stress related factors), play in the development of increased risk for depression in the case of men and women.

Methods: The genetic-biological factors were examined with certain temperament characteristics, the interpersonal factors with parental educational purpose, educational attitudes, educational style and parental treatment. In the case of factors related to social learning we looked at the dysfunctional attitudes and the attributional style. As far as the stressors are concerned, we observed the quality of family atmosphere, and the number of the positive and negative life events of the preceding six months and their subjective evaluation. Six hundred and eighty-one students took part in the research (465 female and 216 male).

Results: Our research results show that all of the increased risk mechanisms, namely the genetic-biological, interpersonal, social learning related cognitive, and stress related factors are connected with the development of vulnerability to depression, explaining 41.4% of the depression symptoms' variance in the case of women, and 36.5% in the case of men. Harm avoidance, a genetic-biological factor, proved to be the most significant risk mechanism, irrespective of the sexes. From among the environmental factors – irrespective of the sexes – one stress-related factor, the subjective evaluation of negative life experiences, which implies an increased sensitivity to stress, proved to be the strongest risk mechanism. While the above factors played an important role in the development of vulnerability to depression in both sexes, the social learning related cognitive and interpersonal risk mechanisms differed in their degree in women and men. In the case of women, the social learning-related mechanisms proved to be stronger and higher impact risk factors than in the case of men. The effect of interpersonal factors seemed to be relatively the weakest in the development of increased risk for depression.

Limitations: The results of our research cannot be generalised to represent present day 18- to 23-year-old Hungarian youth due to the limitations of our sample.

Conclusion: The mental hygienic interpretation of our research findings is that in the future there should be more emphasis put on the personality development of college and university students, especially on the development of such competencies which aid them in effectively coping in their struggle with the depressive mood.

Chapter 111

AN INTERVENTION PROGRAMME FOR THE IMPROVEMENT OF STUDENTS' ACADEMIC GOALS

Antonio Valle, Ramón G. Cabanach, Susana Rodríguez, Isabel Piñeiro, María García and Ingrid Mosquera
University of A Coruña, Spain

RESEARCH SUMMARY

The question of what lies behind students' motivated behaviour has given rise to a complex network of models and constructs in an attempt to clarify this important issue. A fundamental component of motivation, regardless of the theoretical perspective adopted, is that of value, which includes the goals adopted by students in order to ensure involvement in their tasks, as well as their beliefs regarding the importance, usefulness or interest of the latter (Pintrich, 2003; Pintrich and DeGroot, 1990).

Essentially, the value component of motivation responds to the following question: *"Why am I doing this task?"*, alluding, therefore, to the motives, purposes or reasons for becoming involved in the performance of an activity, these all being aspects closely related to both cognitive and self-regulating activities and choice, effort or persistence (Pintrich, 1999). Despite the existence of a wide range of value conceptualisations, two elements appear as being particularly relevant: academic goals and the value assigned to tasks.

Higgins and Kruglanski (2000) point out that a significant issue in motivational research is to discover how people really manage to achieve what they set out to do. If basic needs give rise to interests, values and goals, how then do people translate these needs, goals and beliefs into action? A fundamental approach to this question implies the use of self-regulation models to describe the planning, supervision and regulation of cognition, motivation and behaviour at the service of a person's goals. The popularity and usefulness of this approach is reflected in the proliferation of self-regulation models that attempt to explain behaviour in different domains that go beyond the field of education (see Boekaerts, Pintrich and Zeidner, 2000).

Models of self-regulated learning currently occupy a central position in educational research, demonstrating that students who set goals and then attempt to control and regulate their own cognition, motivation and behaviour accordingly tend to make adequate progress in academic contexts (Pintrich, 2000a; Zimmerman, 2000).

However, as Rodríguez has pointed out (2000, p.154): *"All too often we restrict use of the term self-regulation of learning to the regulation by students of their cognition and effort through the use of certain strategies. Nevertheless, students should also regulate their beliefs, emotions and attitudes, for which the possession of cognitive and behavioural strategies alone does not suffice, motivational strategies also being needed".*

In fact, research into self-regulated learning has basically looked at the links between a student's conceptual knowledge, his or her use of cognitive and metacognitive strategies and the quality of the learning that has taken place. On the other hand, the relation between students' motivation and self-regulation has generally been limited to exploring how certain motivational variables (self-efficiency, goal orientation, interest, etc.) may explain students' efforts to commit themselves to their learning and their use of cognitive and metacognitive strategies.

This, notwithstanding, an increasing number of studies look at the need to recognise the active role played by students in managing the affective/motivational bases of their learning process. The analysis of self-motivation or motivation-regulating strategies is thus a key factor in obtaining a deeper understanding of self-regulated learning, and has now become one of the most promising domains of motivational research (Dörney, 2000; Pintrich, 2003; Schunk and Zimmerman, 2003; Wolters, 2003; Winne, 2004).

Motivational strategies, unlike cognitive ones, are not directly linked to the codification and processing of the content being studied and learned. They are, instead, procedures adopted by students to seek favourable states of mind and positive results, or at the very least, attempts to avoid undesired events and unfavourable results (Rodríguez, Cabanach and Piñeiro, 2002).

As is the case with cognitive strategies, strategies for managing motivation may be consciously adopted or may come into play in a more automatic way. Thus, for example, some authors (see Bargh, Gollwitzer, Lee-Chai, Brandollar and Trotschel, 2001) have shown that goal achievement can be the result of an nonconscious process, so that the actions taken are of an automated nature and outside a student's conscious control. This implies that motivation and learning models should take into account, in addition to conscious, intentional and self-regulated processes, others of an implicit or unconscious nature (Epstein, 1994). However, students can always actively modify their motivational strategies, in accordance with both personal and contextual factors, and can learn new and/or more adaptive ones.

It is precisely this possibility for students to learn, and therefore to be taught, to manage their motivational resources, in the expectation that this learning will have a positive effect on their academic performance, that has led us to design an intervention programme intended, basically, to enable students to understand and adopt the reasons and motives that lie behind their personal commitment to studying as well as to acquire a repertory of strategies that will allow them to maintain this involvement in an adaptive manner.

The aim of our proposal, in line with the approach adopted by Beltrán (1998) to student motivation, is to ensure that students readily adopt an enthusiastic attitude to the performance of academic learning tasks, persist in their effort to bring them to fruition and, furthermore, direct their actions along the right path towards achieving this goal.

In: Psychology Research Biographies and Summaries
Editors: Nancy E. Wodarth and Alexis P. Ferguson
ISBN: 978-1-61470-491-1
© 2012 Nova Science Publishers, Inc.

Chapter 112

THE IMPACT OF A LECTURE SERIES ON ALCOHOL AND TOBACCO USE IN PHARMACY STUDENTS

Arjun P. Dutta,[*] *Bisrat Hailemeskel,*[†] *Monika N. Daftary*[‡] *and Anthony Wutoh*[Π]

Howard University, College of Pharmacy, Nursing and Allied Health Sciences, School of Pharmacy, Washington, DC US

RESEARCH SUMMARY

Studies related to alcohol and drug use in healthcare students, namely nursing, pharmacy, and medicine suggest that drug and alcohol abuse continues to be a growing problem among health profession students. A review of the more recent literature involving pharmacy students, has noted higher levels of alcohol and drug use when compared to the undergraduate student population. Interestingly, the use and/or abuse of tobacco have largely been overlooked in studies involving substance abuse in pharmacy students. This study documented the current alcohol and tobacco use in pharmacy students and conducted a lecture series on the use and abuse of alcohol and tobacco. The lecture series was successful in increasing the awareness of the use and potential abuse of alcohol in the students. Attitudinal changes in students following the lecture series were also assessed.

---

[*] Office: 503-352-7281; Fax: 202-806-4478; Email: adutta@pacificu.edu; The author is currently the Assistant Dean for Academic Affairs at Pacific University, School of Pharamcy, Forest Grove, OR.
[†] Office: 202-806-4210; Email: bhailemeskel@howard.edu.
[‡] Office: 202-806-4206; Email: mdaftary@howard.edu.
[Π] Office: 202-806-4209; Email: awutoh@howard.edu.

Chapter 113

BURDEN OF SYNDROMAL ANTISOCIAL BEHAVIOR IN ADULTHOOD

Risë B. Goldstein[*] and Bridget F. Grant

Laboratory of Epidemiology and Biometry, Division of Intramural Clinical and Biological Research, National Institute on Alcohol Abuse and Alcoholism, National Institutes of Health, Department of Health and Human Services, Bethesda, MD, US

RESEARCH SUMMARY

Antisocial personality disorder (ASPD) affects 3% to 5% of adults in the general population of the United States and Canada. It is associated with substantial burden on affected individuals, their families, and society, both in its own right and because of its high comorbidity with medical illnesses and injuries as well as a broad range of other psychiatric disorders, notably including substance use disorders. Diagnostic criteria for ASPD under the *Diagnostic and Statistical Manual of Mental Disorders, Third Edition* (DSM-III), the *Diagnostic and Statistical Manual of Mental Disorders, Third Edition - Revised* (DSM-III-R), and the *Diagnostic and Statistical Manual of Mental Disorders, Fourth Edition* (DSM-IV) require both conduct disorder (CD) with onset before age 15 years, and a persistent pattern of aggressive, irresponsible, impulsive, and remorseless behaviors thereafter. However, many individuals with syndromal antisocial behavior in adulthood do not report enough symptoms to meet criteria for CD before age 15 (adult antisocial behavioral syndrome, or AABS). AABS is not a codable DSM-IV diagnosis. Nevertheless, while individuals with AABS display fewer antisocial symptoms, and in particular fewer violent symptoms, in adulthood than those with ASPD, these 2 groups differ little on antisocial symptom profiles in adulthood, many forms of psychiatric and general medical comorbidity, and, among addiction treatment clients, substance use histories. This chapter reviews what is known about the comorbidity of antisocial behavioral syndromes in adulthood with other psychiatric disorders

---

[*] Corresponding author: Risë B. Goldstein, Ph.D., M.P.H., Staff Scientist; Laboratory of Epidemiology and Biometry, Room 3068; Division of Intramural Clinical and Biological Research; National Institute on Alcohol Abuse and Alcoholism; National Institutes of Health, M.S. 9304; 5635 Fishers Ln. Bethesda, MD 20892-9304; Tel. 301-443-3528; Fax 301-443-1400; E-mail: goldster@mail.nih.gov.

and general medical conditions, including similarities and differences between individuals with ASPD and those with AABS and the relationships of comorbid antisociality to the clinical presentation of co-occurring conditions. Gaps in current knowledge, including mechanisms underlying comorbidity and its associations with clinical presentation, implications for clinical care of comorbid individuals, and burdens on persons besides antisocial adults that are specifically attributable to antisocial syndromes, will be highlighted and directions for future research will be suggested. Implications for the development and prioritization of preventive and therapeutic interventions targeting antisociality across the lifespan will be discussed.

Chapter 114

ANTISOCIAL BEHAVIOR IN CHILDREN WITH ADHD: CAUSES AND TREATMENT

Efrosini Kalyva
Senior Lecturer, City College, Thessaloniki, Greece

RESEARCH SUMMARY

Attention Deficit/Hyperactivity Disorder (ADHD) is a prevalent disorder among school aged children and adolescents worldwide. Many children and adolescents with ADHD exhibit antisocial behavior that usually takes the form of aggression or conduct disorder. This chapter starts with definitions of ADHD and antisocial behaviors, while it reviews recent studies on the aetiology of this behavior. Since genes and physiology alone do not determine behavior, emphasis will be placed also on the role that the environment plays in creating and shaping certain antisocial behaviors. There will be reference to academic and social underachievement that may trigger antisocial behavior in children and young adults with ADHD, as well as other family factors. The last part of the chapter will focus on interventions that can effectively address the antisocial behavior of children and adolescents with ADHD and involve not only individuals, but also their families and their communities.

In: Psychology Research Biographies and Summaries
Editors: Nancy E. Wodarth and Alexis P. Ferguson

ISBN: 978-1-61470-491-1
© 2012 Nova Science Publishers, Inc.

Chapter 115

VICIOUS DOG OWNERSHIP: IS IT A THIN SLICE OF ANTISOCIAL PERSONALITY?

Laurie L. Ragatz*, Allison M. Schenk and William J. Fremouw
West Virginia University, US

RESEARCH SUMMARY

The concept of "thin slice" suggests that a person's personality can be predicted from just observing a fragment of his or her behavior. For instance, Fowler, Lilienfeld, and Patrick (2009) had 40 graduate and undergraduate students rate the degree to which individuals exhibited traits of psychopathy and other personality disorders in 5, 10, and 20 second video clips. Hare (2003) described psychopathy as having two key components: Factor 1 (e.g., superficial charm, callousness, remorselessness, grandiosity) and Factor 2 (e.g., parasitic lifestyle, lack of responsibility, impulsiveness, versatility in criminal acts). The construct of psychopathy has been found to be predictive of committing violent crimes upon release from prison (Porter, Birt, & Boer, 2001; Serin & Amos, 1995), committing disciplinary infractions in prison (Edens, Poythress, Lilienfeld, & Patrick, 2008), and a greater likelihood of recidivism (Hare, Clark, Grann, & Thornton, 2000). All the respondents for the Fowler et al. study used a Likert scale to provide "thin slice" ratings on the individual in the video. The researchers demonstrated that the "thin slice" ratings provided for the psychopathy items were significantly correlated with several measures of psychopathy (Psychopathy Checklist-Revised [PCL-R; Hare, 1991; 2003], Interpersonal Measure of Psychopathy [Kossen, Steuerwald, Forth, & Kirkhart, 1997]). Moreover, "thin slice" psychopathy ratings were significantly correlated with scores on the PCL-R when raters watched a five second video, but not when raters watched a 10 or 20 second video. Also, ratings provided by individuals that viewed videos without audio were more highly correlated with PCL-R scores than were

---

* Correspondence concerning this article should be addressed to Laurie L. Ragatz, West Virginia University, Department of Psychology, 53 Campus Drive, 1124 Life Sciences Building, PO Box 6040, Morgantown, WV 26506-6040; Laurie.Ragatz@mail.wvu.edu.

audio only clips or clips that included both audio and picture video. In addition to predictions of psychopathy, thin slice behavior has been found to be predictive of intelligence scale scores (Borkenam, Mauer, Riemann, Spinath, & Angleitner, 2004), personality test scores (Borkenam et al., 2004), job performance evaluation ratings (Hecht & LaFrance, 1995), and teacher evaluation ratings (Babad, Avni-Babad, & Rosenthal, 2004). Could a "thin slice" of behavior, such as dog ownership, give us some clue about an individual's broader personality? Do certain individuals select to own dogs that are more likely to be aggressive?

The first dogs were wild wolves tamed by humans in southeastern Asia, approximately 16,300 years ago. The development of the dog occurred around the same time that cultural groups within Asia became less nomadic and more sedentary. From southeastern Asia, the culture of having a dog spread throughout Asia, Europe, and worldwide (Pang et al., 2009). Presently, in the United States (U.S.), there are over 72 million dogs (American Veterinary Medical Association, 2010). Nearly 160 breeds of dogs have been recognized by the American Kennel Club (AKC). The five most popular dog breeds in 2009 among U.S. dog owners were Labrador Retrievers, German Shepherds, Yorkshire Terriers, Golden Retrievers, and Beagles, respectively (AKC, 2010).

Many people assume that dogs and their owners share personality and physical characteristics. In fact, Roy (2004) found that owners of pedigree dogs physically resembled their dogs. Why do people buy and raise specific breeds of dogs. Is this a "thin slice" of behavior also?

In: Psychology Research Biographies and Summaries
Editors: Nancy E. Wodarth and Alexis P. Ferguson
ISBN: 978-1-61470-491-1
© 2012 Nova Science Publishers, Inc.

Chapter 116

ADOLESCENT SUBSTANCE USE DISORDER AND ATTENTION DEFICIT HYPERACTIVITY DISORDER: A LITERATURE REVIEW

*Robert Eme**
American School of Professional Psychology
Argosy University
Schaumburg Campus, IL, US

RESEARCH SUMMARY

Substance use disorder (SUD) among adolescents is a widespread, devastating public health problem, and is associated with the leading causes of death among youth under 21 (Becker & Curry, 2008). In addition, it is a major factor in delinquency with most of the $244.1 million spent by the federal government for juvenile detention and corrections, and for delinquency prevention, mentoring, and reentry programs, being spent on substance-involved youth (Califano, 2009). Despite these consequences, only 10% of adolescents with SUD receive treatment and more than 50% of those who are treated drop out or terminate with unsatisfactory progress (Becker & Curry, 2008). For example, in the largest psychosocial treatment study to date of adolescents with SUD, the Cannabis Youth Treatment Study (CYT), only 25% were in recovery at a 1-year follow up, defined as no substance use or dependence problems and living in the community (Dennis et al., 2004; Perepletichikova, Krystal, & Kaufman, 2008). This review will propose that these bleak outcomes may be due in no small measure to the failure to identify and properly treat one of the unique needs of adolescents with SUD - comorbid Attention Deficit Hyperactivity Disorder (ADHD) [Volkow, 2009]. As the review will document, an astonishing 50% of adolescents in treatment for SUD are co-morbid for ADHD and this co-morbidity is associated with an earlier onset of SUD, more severe and longer duration of SUD, more difficulty remaining in treatment, and a greater likelihood of relapse after treatment (Chan, Dennis, & Funk, 2008; Hawkins, 2009; Wilens, 2008a; Wilens et al., 2007a). Hence it is critically important that

---

* Phone: 947-691-2826; Fax 847-969-4998; Email: reme@argosy.edu.

practitioners understand the relationship between SUD and ADHD in adolescents since co-occuring disorders present serious challenges to traditional mental health and substance abuse treatments systems for adolescents (Hawkins, 2009). The purpose of this paper is to provide such an understanding with implications for treatment. It will do so by first establishing the prevalence of ADHD among adolescents in treatment for SUD. Second, it will discuss the mechanisms whereby ADHD increases the risk for SUD. Third, it will provide treatment recommendations that are informed by the prior discussion. Lastly, it should be noted that given the vastness of the literature on SUD and ADHD and given that the goal of the review is to be broadly synthetic, the paper will draw on findings of authoritative critical reviews as well as individual studies. Also, since substantial data indicate that substance abuse and substance dependence are best conceptualized as reflecting differences in substance-problem severity on a unidimensional continuum rather than distinct categories, SUD will be the nosological rubric employed to designate this conception (Martin, Chung, & Langenbucher, 2008).

Chapter 117

PERVERTED JUSTICE: A CONTENT ANALYSIS OF THE LANGUAGE USED BY OFFENDERS DETECTED ATTEMPTING TO SOLICIT CHILDREN FOR SEX

Vincent Egan[1]*, James Hoskinson[2] and David Shewan[3]

[1] Department of Psychology – Forensic Section, University of Leicester, 106 New Walk, Leicester, LE1 7EA, UK (all communications)
[2] Department of Psychology – Clinical Section, University of Leeds, Leeds, South Yorkshire, UK
[3] Deceased; Department of Psychology, Glasgow Caledonian University, Cowcaddens Road, Glasgow, G4, Scotland

RESEARCH SUMMARY

This study explored the language used by offenders soliciting sexual activities with children within Internet chat-rooms. Relational content analysis classified the linguistic content by which offenders sought to engage young persons. Eight recurrent themes encompassed the cognitions of an on-line sexual offender: 'implicit/explicit content', 'on-line solicitation', 'fixated discourse', 'use of colloquialisms', 'conscience', 'acknowledgement of illegal/immoral behaviour', 'minimising risk of detection', and 'preparing to meet offline'. The language indicated increased risk-taking behaviours of the offender, which countered the anonymity chat-rooms otherwise provide. Minimising risk of detection seemed unimportant and offenders arranged off-line meetings with little caution. Electronic anonymity may give offenders false confidence, and so encourage persons to extend on-line and virtual risk-taking into to the real world.

---

* Email: vincent.egan@le.ac.uk; Tel: (44) 0116 225 3658.

Is Developmentally Informed Therapy for Persons with ID and Criminal Personality/Offenses Relevant?

Lino Faccini*
Long Island, New York, US

Research Summary

Initially, the "Reconstructive Therapy" of Dr. Jerome Schulte, focused on the treatment of the homicidal psychotic patient. After decades of treatment applying this model with a variety of offenses, Dr. Schulte believed that it could be applied to understand and treat the "Criminal Personality", various offenses as well as treating non-clinical populations of children, adolescents and adults. The goal of therapy became one of promoting personal growth and humanness through the positive resolution of Ericksonian stages. The question remains if the successful resolution of Erickson's Psychosocial stages is relevant to the functioning of a Person with an Intellectual Disability, and Criminal Offenses? A theoretical and initial exploratory analysis suggests that the Reconstructive Therapy model can be relevant to the treatment for Persons with Intellectual Disabilities (ID) and various offenses.

---

* Lino Faccini Ph.D., Consulting Psychologist, Hfaccini@aol.com.

Chapter 119

COCAINE-DEPENDENT PATIENTS WITH ANTISOCIAL PERSONALITY DISORDER, COCAINE-DEPENDENCE AND TREATMENT OUTCOMES*

Nena Messina[†], David Farabee and Richard Rawson
UCLA Integrated Substance Abuse Programs, US

RESEARCH SUMMARY

This study compared the efficacy of two commonly used treatment approaches (cognitive–behavioral treatment and contingency management) for the treatment of cocaine dependence among methadone-maintained patients with and without antisocial personality disorder (ASPD). This disorder is strongly associated with substance abuse and recent study findings provide a strong argument against the perception that substance abusers with ASPD are unresponsive to drug treatment.

Method: Patients were randomly assigned to four study conditions including cognitive–behavioral treatment (CBT), contingency management (CM), CBT with CM, or methadone maintenance (also the control condition). The Structural Clinical Interview for Mental Disorders–IV was administered to 108 patients to assess ASPD.

Hypotheses: We hypothesized that ASPD patients in the three treatment conditions (CBT, CM, CBT + CM) would have better treatment responsivity over the 16-week course of treatment than would ASPD patients in the control condition (MM). Moreover, we hypothesized that there would be a cumulative treatment effect among ASPD patients over the course of treatment, with good performance in the CBT condition, better performance in the CM condition, and optimum performance in the CBT + CM condition. Conversely, we

---

* A version of this chapter also appears in *Advances in Psychology Research, Volume 57*, edited by Alexandra M. Columbus, published by Nova Science Publishers, Inc. It was submitted for appropriate modifications in an effort to encourage wider dissemination of research.
† Corresponding Author: Nena Messina, Ph.D., 1640 S. Sepulveda Blvd., Suite 200, Los Angeles, CA. 90025 Phone: (310) 445-0874 ext. 335; Fax: (310) 312-0559, Email: nmessina@ucla.edu, dfarabee@ucla.edu, matrixex@ucla.edu.

hypothesized that the positive treatment effect of CM would decline for the ASPD patients once the incentive was removed (i.e., during the post-treatment outcome period).

Results: A two-way analysis of variance showed that patients with ASPD were more likely to abstain from cocaine use during treatment than patients without ASPD. The strong treatment effect for ASPD patients was primarily due to the CM condition. A series of regression analyses showed that ASPD remained significantly related to CM treatment responsivity while controlling for other related factors.

Conclusion: Monetary incentives appear to reduce cocaine use among substance abusers with ASPD more than among those without ASPD. The results of the present study and other recent publications suggest that substance abusers with ASPD may be more responsive to treatment than previously believed.

Chapter 120

DELINQUENCY AND ANTISOCIAL BEHAVIOUR AMONG HIGH RISK YOUNG PEOPLE IN ADOLESCENCE*

Patrick McCrystal[†] and Kareena McAloney
Institute of Child Care Research
School of Sociology Social Policy and Social Work, UK

RESEARCH SUMMARY

This chapter presents an investigation of the patterns of offending and antisocial behaviour amongst young people from the age of 11-16 years who are categorised as high risk or vulnerable to delinquency and antisocial behaviour. The chapter will draw upon findings from the first five datasweeps of the Belfast Youth Development Study (BYDS), a longitudinal study of the onset and development of adolescent problem behaviour. Through a detailed exploration of the onset and development of delinquency and antisocial behaviour from the age of 11-16 years it will provide insights for targeting and development of appropriate interventions for school aged high risk young people who do not attend mainstream school in adolescence. The findings will form the empirical base for a discussion of the key issues around appropriate interventions and the development of conclusions in relation to young people who have received comparatively less attention in the delinquency literature but who are considered more likely to offend during adolescence.

---

* A version of this chapter also appears in *Delinquency: Causes, Reduction and Prevention*, edited by Ozan Sahin and Joseph Maier, published by Nova Science Publishers, Inc. It was submitted for appropriate modifications in an effort to encourage wider dissemination of research.
† Corresponding Author: Dr. Patrick McCrystal, Institute of Child Care Research, School of Sociology, Social policy and Social Work, Queens University Belfast 6 College Park Belfast BT7 1LP; Phone: 00442890975991; Fax: 00442890975900; Email: P.McCrystal@qub.ac.uk.

Chapter 121

GENETIC EPIDEMIOLOGY OF BORDERLINE PERSONALITY DISORDER

Marijn A. Distel[*,1], *Timothy J. Trull*[2] *and Dorret I. Boomsma*[1]

[1] Department of Biological Psychology, VU University Amsterdam, Amsterdam, The Netherlands
[2] Department of Psychological Sciences, University of Missouri-Columbia, Columbia, MO, US

RESEARCH SUMMARY

Borderline personality disorder (BPD) is a severe personality disorder characterized by impulsivity, affective instability, relationship problems and identity problems. BPD affects 1-2% of the general population, 10% of the patients in outpatient settings, 15-20% of the patients in inpatients settings and 30-60% of the patients diagnosed with personality disorders. BPD is most commonly assessed according to the diagnostic and statistical manual of mental disorders (DSM). In addition, assessment of BPD features on a quantitative or dimensional scale is increasingly used. BPD is more often diagnosed in women in clinical samples and in young individuals and is frequently co-morbid with other personality disorders and axis-I disorders.

Most studies on BPD have attempted to clarify the etiology in terms of social and environmental determinants (e.g. physical or sexual abuse). These factors are important contributors to risk, but do not explain all variation in BPD risk. Moreover, even if the association is significant, in many instances the direction of causality is unclear. Genetic factors are additional contributors to BPD risk, and there now are some large twin and family

---

[*] Address for correspondence: Marijn Distel, Department of Biological Psychology, VU University Amsterdam, Van der Boechorststraat 1, 1081 BT Amsterdam, The Netherlands. Phone: +31 20 598 8792; Fax: +31 20 598 8832; E-mail address: ma.distel@psy.vu.nl.

studies that suggest significant heritability for the disorder as well as for the quantitative assessment.

In this chapter, we first discuss the main symptoms of BPD and several assessment methods. Next, we consider the association between BPD and demographic characteristics, such as age and sex, and the co-morbidity with other disorders. After the focus on environmental covariates, we review family and twin studies into the genetics of BPD and related traits, genetic linkage and candidate gene studies of BPD. We end with a discussion of future directions in research in which we will consider multivariate studies, the discordant MZ co-twin design, the children of twins design, genome wide association studies, and genotype-environment interaction.

Chapter 122

CORRELATES AND COURSE OF RECOVERY IN PATIENTS WITH BORDERLINE PERSONALITY DISORDER – A REVIEW

Willem H. J. Martens *

W. Kahn Institute of Theoretical Psychiatry and Neuroscience, Advisor Psychiatry appointed by the European Commission (Leonardo da Vinci), and Member of the Royal College of Psychiatrists – Philosophy Interest Group, The Netherlands

RESEARCH SUMMARY

In this chapter the correlates and course of remission in patients with borderline personality disorder are studied. For this purpose the data of relevant studies were analyzed and discussed. It was found that factors like artistic talent; high intelligence; successful and positive relationships; avoidance of destructive conflicting intimacy, but also the healing impact constructive confronting relationships; remission of Axis I and II comorbidity predict recovery. In contrast, factors such as sexual abuse, trauma, parental cruelty and neglect, stigma, destructive overinvolvement of family, affective instability, recurrent suicidality and baseline psychopathology predict poor outcome. Acute symptoms such as self-mutilation, help-seeking suicide threats and attempts, as well as impulsivity seem to resolve quickly, whereas other symptoms as chronic feelings of intense anger, profound abandonment concerns, and affective instability appear to diminish more slowly.

---

* Address: Het Nateland 1, 3911XZ Rhenen (Utrecht), The Netherlands. phone: 31 (0)317 618708; email: Martens_92@hotmail.com, MartensW2000@yahoo.com.

In: Psychology Research Biographies and Summaries
Editors: Nancy E. Wodarth and Alexis P. Ferguson

ISBN: 978-1-61470-491-1
© 2012 Nova Science Publishers, Inc.

Chapter 123

NEUROPSYCHOBIOLOGY, COMORBIDITY AND DIMENSIONAL MODELS IN BORDERLINE PERSONALITY DISORDER: CRITICAL ISSUES FOR TREATMENT

Bernardo Dell'Osso[*,1], *Heather Berlin*[2], *Marta Serati*[1] *and Alfredo Carlo Altamura*[1]

[1]Department of Psychiatry, University of Milan, Fondazione IRCCS Ospedale Maggiore Policlinico, Mangiagalli e Regina Elena; Milano, Italy
[2]Department of Psychiatry, Mount Sinai School of Medicine, New York, NY, US

RESEARCH SUMMARY

Borderline Personality Disorder (BPD) affects approximately the 1-2% of the general population in the US, with an incidence up to 20% in psychiatric settings. The pathogenesis of BPD involves complex interactions between genetic, neurobiological and environmental factors, resulting in core dimensional symptoms such as emotional dysregulation, impulse dyscontrol, aggression, cognitive dysfunctions and dissociative states. BPD is often comorbid with other mental disorders such as mood disorders, anxiety disorders, psychotic spectrum disorders, other personality disorders and substance abuse/dependence. Moreover, the comorbidity between bipolar disorder, particularly type II, and BPD has been investigated in several studies, showing interesting results in terms of clinical presentation and outcome. In addition, suicidal ideation is frequently experienced by BPD subjects and almost 10% of affected patients commit suicide by adulthood. As a consequence, BPD patients are high utilizers of health care resources and the correct clinical management of this disorder represents a challenge for psychiatrists.

---

[*] Corresponding author: Dr. Bernardo Dell'Osso Department of Psychiatry, University of Milan, Fondazione IRCCS Ospedale Maggiore Policlinico, Mangiagalli e Regina Elena. Via Francesco Sforza 35, 20122, Milan.Tel.: +39 02 55035994; Fax: +39 02 50320310 Email: bernardo.dellosso@policlinico.mi.it.

Recently, neurobiological studies showed that symptoms and behaviors of BPD are partly associated with alterations in basic neurocognitive processes, involving glutamatergic, dopaminergic and serotoninergic systems. In addition, neuroimaging studies in BPD patients indicated differences in the volume and activity of specific brain regions related to emotion and impulsivity, such as the prefrontal cortex, cingulate cortex, amygdala and hippocampus.

The treatment of BPD, as reported in currently available guidelines, includes both pharmacotherapy and psychotherapy. Pharmacological treatment is generally recommended in the acute treatment of the core symptoms of BPD and in cases with Axis I comorbidity and severe impulse dyscontrol. Over the past decade, antidepressants - SSRIs in particular - have been considered the first pharmacological choice in the treatment of BPD, whereas, more recently, converging evidence indicates the efficacy of other compounds such as mood-stabilizers and atypical antipsychotics. With regard to psychotherapic interventions, long-term approaches including transference-focused psycotherapy, dialectical-behavioural psychoterapy and mentalization-based therapy seem to be particularly useful.

In light of the continuing evolution of the BPD diagnosis, of its principal clinical features and of the high incidence of comorbidity, it is very tough to draw a well defined and complete picture of the disorder and future contributions from genetic, neurobiological and neuroimaging studies are warranted.

In: Psychology Research Biographies and Summaries
Editors: Nancy E. Wodarth and Alexis P. Ferguson
ISBN: 978-1-61470-491-1
© 2012 Nova Science Publishers, Inc.

Chapter 124

NEUROBIOLOGY OF BORDERLINE PERSONALITY DISORDER: PRESENT STATE AND FUTURE DIRECTIONS

Thomas Zetzsche[1], Thomas Frodl[1], Ulrich W. Preuss[2], Doerthe Seifert[2], Hans-Jürgen Möller[1] and Eva Maria Meisenzahl[1]

[1] Department of Psychiatry and Psychotherapy,
Ludwig-Maximilians-University, Munich, Germany
[2] Department of Psychiatry and Psychotherapy, Martin-Luther-University,
Halle/Wittenberg, Germany

RESEARCH SUMMARY

Borderline Personality Disorder (BPD) is a severe and frequent psychiatric disorder with prevalence rates of 1-2% reported from community samples. Since the first inclusion of BPD in the diagnostic and statistical manual (DSM) III ongoing research provided evidence for frequent neurobiological alterations in BPD patients. In the 1980s, reductions of serotonin (5-HT) metabolites in the cerebrospinal fluid of male patients with BPD were demonstrated and thereafter numerous studies including neuroendocrine challenge experiments and electrophysiological recordings provided evidence for a 5-HT disturbance in BPD that was related to increased impulsivity in these patients. Disturbances of the hypothalamus-pituitary-adrenal (HPA) axis in BPD patients as indication for dysfunctional stress regulation were partly shown to be associated with a history of traumatization or related to comorbid major depression (MD) and posttraumatic stress disorder (PTSD). An increased rapid eye movement (REM) density in BPD was discussed as indicative of a close relationship between BPD and affective disorders or alternatively as a sign of an increased risk for development of MD in BPD patients. These findings may contribute to the explanation of the high psychiatric comorbidity of BPD, especially with affective disorders. In recent years, research focused on structural and functional brain imaging in BPD to shed light on potential biological underpinnings of the disorder related to brain function and morphology. An increased activity of the amygdala in BPD patients after presentation of aversive visual picture material was demonstrated and volume changes of brain regions especially of prefrontal and temporolimbic regions were repeatedly described in BPD. Prefrontal changes were discussed in context with increased impulsivity of BPD patients. The most frequent finding is a hippocampal volume reduction which was recently shown to be associated with severity of symptom expression in BPD, including increased lifetime aggression. Variations of amygdala volume in BPD patients were associated with comorbidity of MD and an abnormal pain processing in BPD patients was related to changes of regional brain function in BPD. Future directions should include studies for detection of genetic variations e.g. of the 5-HT system and their relationship to neurobiological alterations and clinical characteristics of BPD. Previous studies demonstrated an association between variants of 5-HT candidate genes and alterations of prefrontal and temporolimbic systems in other psychiatric disorders (anxiety, depression), and with amygdala volume changes in BPD. Longitudinal studies will be crucial to investigate whether structural or functional brain changes represent a risk factor for a more severe course of this disorder and if therapeutic interventions (psychotherapy, medication) have a positive impact on both neurobiological alterations and the clinical course of BPD.

In: Psychology Research Biographies and Summaries
Editors: Nancy E. Wodarth and Alexis P. Ferguson
ISBN: 978-1-61470-491-1
© 2012 Nova Science Publishers, Inc.

Chapter 125

PROVING THE EFFICIENCY OF MUSIC PSYCHOTHERAPY WITH BORDERLINE ADOLESCENTS BY MEANS OF A QUASI-EXPERIMENTAL DESIGN

Lony Schiltz[*]
Head of research projects at the Centre de Recherche Public-Santé, Luxembourg

RESEARCH SUMMARY

Music psychotherapy has proved to be effective with adolescents presenting different types of conduct disorders related to an underlying borderline personality organization. The recent understanding of borderline personality organization in adolescents and the methodological problems of clinical research with natural groups are summed up.

Several follow-up studies of adolescents, based on an integrated quantitative and qualitative methodology, combining psychometric test, projective tests, observational frames and rating scales, and including the utilization of a control group, have shown significant modifications in the imaginary and symbolic elaboration of aggressive drives, reducing the tendency towards auto- or hetero-aggressive acting out, towards somatization or towards the inhibition of pulsional functioning, and leading to a resumption of the blocked process of subjectivation.

The results of the studies are interpreted in reference to recent theoretical developments in the psychopathology of adolescence, based on new psychological and neuropsychological research results with dissociation and complex posttraumatic stress states. A general theory of the action of music psychotherapy is still missing. We propose a theoretical model of its impact on the blocked process of subjectivation.

---

[*] Professional address: Lony Schiltz, CRP-Santé, Luxembourg, 1A-1B,rue Thomas Edison, L-1445 Strassen , Luxembourg.
Address for correspondence: Schiltz Lony10, rue Gabriel de MarieL-2131 LuxembourgTel 00352 433668
E mail : lony.schiltz@education.lu.

Chapter 126

A DISSOCIATIVE MODEL OF BORDERLINE PERSONALITY DISORDER

Colin A. Ross
The Colin A. Ross Institute for Psychological Trauma, Richardson, Texas, US

RESARCH SUMMARY

A dissociative model of borderline personality disorder is presented. According to this model, borderline personality disorder, dissociative identity disorder, and post-traumatic stress disorder are variants of each other. All three disorders are based on a structural dissociation of the psyche, with intrusions and withdrawals of psychological content from the executive self. Borderline personality disorder is a form of dual personality without personification and elaboration of the ego states. Conversely, dissociative identity disorder is a complex, elaborated form of borderline personality. The two disorders share similar etiologies and treatments. All of the nine DSM-IV-TR diagnostic criteria for borderline personality disorder can be accounted for within this dissociative model, and the model fosters a more empathic, therapeutic counter-transference than the ones commonly provoked by the disorder. Borderline personality disorder (BPD) is classified as an Axis II personality disorder in DSM-IV-TR (American Psychiatric Association, 2000): the ninth diagnostic criterion for BPD is "transient stress-related paranoid ideation or severe dissociative symptoms" (pp. 710). However, there is no discussion of dissociation in the DSM-IV-TR text for BPD and there are no rules for when "severe dissociation" warrants a separate Axis I diagnosis of a dissociative disorder. This is a significant problem because dissociative disorders were diagnosed using a structured interview, the Dissociative Disorders Interview Schedule (Pincus, Rush, First, & McQueen, 2000; Ross, 1997) in 59% of a sample of 93 general adult psychiatric inpatients with BPD in one study (Ross, 2007). In this study, 20% of the BPD inpatients were in the dissociative taxon on a self-report measure, the Dissociative Experiences Scale (Bernstein & Putnam, 1986). This means that they reported pathological dissociation, not simply normal absorption or other experiences, according to that measure. In the same study, 41 individuals with BPD also completed the Structured Clinical Interview for DSM-IV Dissociative Disorders (Steinberg, 1995): these inpatients had elevated average total dissociation scores of 9.6 on that measure, indicating considerable dissociative symptoms. In the two other studies in the literature, dissociative disorders were readily identified among individuals with BPD using either a structured interview or a diagnostic checklist (Conklin & Westen, 2005; Sar, Kundakci, Kiziltan, Yargic, Tutkun, Bakim, Bozkurt, Keser, & Ozdemir, 2003).A number of studies reviewed by Ross (1997; 2007a) have looked at the reciprocal relationship and found that over 50% of individuals with clinical diagnoses of dissociative identity disorder meet criteria for BPD. As well, BPD and dissociative identity disorder are accompanied by similar patterns of extensive comorbidity all across Axis I and II (Ross, 2007). The extensive overlap between BPD and Axis I dissociative identity disorder can be understood in several different ways:

- Co-occurrence of separate disorders.
- One disorder is secondary to the other.
- An artifact of a mistaken diagnostic system.
- The two are variants of each other.

In this paper I will present a clinical model according to which dissociative identity disorder (DID) and BPD are variants of each other and BPD is best regarded as an Axis I dissociative disorder. My goal here is to outline the model, not to argue fully for it, or to fully reference the relevant literature.

Chapter 127

BORDERLINE SYMPTOMATOLOGY AND EMPATHIC ACCURACY

William Schweinle[1], Judith M. Flury[2] and William Ickes[2]
[1] University of South Dakota, US
[2] University of Texas at Arlington, US

RESEARCH SUMMARY

Psychotherapists and clinical psychologists have offered anecdotal accounts of a phenomenon known as "borderline empathy." These accounts suggest that people with borderline personality disorder may have an above-average ability to "read" the minds of others, including the minds of their therapists. In this essay, we examine the past and recent research findings that are relevant to the phenomenon of borderline empathy. The results of our own research using the empathic accuracy paradigm reveal that people with borderline personality are probably not better at "reading" others in terms of their general ability level. However, they can appear to be more accurate when paired with non-borderline individuals because the borderline individuals are particularly difficult to "read" themselves, thereby putting their more "readable" non-borderline interaction partners at an empathic disadvantage. In other words, borderline individuals may not be more empathic than other people; instead, they may simply be more difficult to "read" than other people are.

Chapter 128

PATTERNS OF INTERPERSONAL BEHAVIORS AND BORDERLINE PERSONALITY CHARACTERISTICS

Glenn Shean[1]* and Kimberly Ryan
Psychology Department College of William & Mary
VA, US

RESEARCH SUMMARY

Linehan (1993) identified two sub-syndromal patterns of Borderline Personality Disorder among her therapy patients. Similar patterns were identified by Leihener and colleagues (2003) in a clinically diagnosed sample of Borderline hospitalized patients. These sub-syndromes are referred to as "autonomous" and "dependent" types. This research attempted to determine if similar sub-syndromal patterns could be observed in a college student sample that evidenced high scores on a questionnaire measure of borderline symptoms. Interpersonal functioning of participants was assessed utilizing the Inventory of Interpersonal Problems (IIP). Hierarchical cluster analysis of the IIP profiles of individuals evidencing prominent borderline characteristics revealed that participants formed two groups that were consistent with previously published descriptions of autonomous and dependent sub-types. The autonomous subtype was characterized by problems associated with being overly assertive, issues related to lack of intimacy, and keeping others at a distance. The dependent subtype was characterized by submissiveness, feelings of having little influence over others, difficulty communicating one's needs, excessive obtrusiveness, and low self-confidence. These sub-typal patterns of BPD have implications for therapeutic intervention strategies.

---

* Corresponding author: Glenn Shean, Ph.D., FAX (757) 221-3896; email address: gdshea@wm.edu.

BORDERLINE PERSONALITY AND SOMATIC SYMPTOMATOLOGY

Randy A. Sansone[1]* and Lori A. Sansone[2]

[1] Departments of Psychiatry and Internal Medicine at
Wright State University School of Medicine in Dayton, Ohio US
[2] Primary Care Clinic at Wright-Patterson Air Force Base in Dayton, Ohio US

RESEARCH SUMMARY

According to the *Diagnostic and Statistical Manual of Mental Disorders, 4th edition, text revision* (DSM-IV-TR) (American Psychiatric Association, 2000), borderline personality disorder (BPD) is an Axis II phenomenon that is traditionally conceptualized and defined according to explicit *psychological* criteria. However, a proportion of these individuals evidence notable *somatic* symptomatoogy that is oftentimes excessive, exaggerated, and/or even feigned. In this chapter, we will discuss the existing research regarding the somatic symptomatology observed in BPD and provide a brief summary of our recent research findings in this fascinating area.

---

* Please direct all correspondence to: Randy A. Sansone, M.D., Sycamore Primary Care Center, 2115 Leiter Road, Miamisburg,Ohio,45342.Telephone:937-384-6850.FAX:937-384-6938.E-mail: andy.sansone@khnetwork.org.

In: Psychology Research Biographies and Summaries
Editors: Nancy E. Wodarth and Alexis P. Ferguson
ISBN: 978-1-61470-491-1
© 2012 Nova Science Publishers, Inc.

Chapter 130

BORDERLINE PERSONALITY AND SEXUAL IMPULSIVITY

Randy A. Sansone[1], and Lori A. Sansone[2]*
[1] Departments of Psychiatry and Internal Medicine at
Wright State University School of Medicine in Dayton, Ohio, US
[2] Primary Care Clinic at Wright-Patterson Air Force Base in Dayton, Ohio, US

RESEARCH SUMMARY

Borderline personality disorder (BPD) has been associated with the clinical phenomenon of sexual impulsivity both in the current Diagnostic and Statistical Manual of Mental Disorders as well as a number of historic and contemporary diagnostic interviews and self-report measures for the disorder. However, upon a careful review of the existing literature, the supporting data is relatively sparse. This literature, which consists of both case reports and empirical studies, indicates that BPD is, on many occasions, associated with sexual impulsivity—but not invariably. The association between BPD and sexual impulsivity is heightened in the presence of a history of childhood sexual abuse as well as substance abuse in adulthood. In this communication, we discuss and summarize our impressions of these findings.

---

* Please address all correspondence to: Randy A. Sansone, M.D., Sycamore Primary Care Center, 2115 Leiter Road, Miamisburg, Ohio, 45342. Telephone: 937-384-6850. FAX: 937-384-6938. E-mail: Randy.sansone@khnetwork.org.

In: Psychology Research Biographies and Summaries
Editors: Nancy E. Wodarth and Alexis P. Ferguson

ISBN: 978-1-61470-491-1
© 2012 Nova Science Publishers, Inc.

Chapter 131

AN HISTORICAL PERSPECTIVE OF BODY IMAGE AND BODY IMAGE CONCERNS AMONG MALE AND FEMALE ADOLESCENTS IN JAPAN

*Naomi Chisuwa[1] and Jennifer A. O'Dea[2],**
[1] Bachelor of Human Life Science; MSc, Australia
[2] Faculty of Education & Social Work
University of Sydney, Australia

RESEARCH SUMMARY

This review describes the body image, body image concerns and factors influencing body image disturbance amongst Japanese adolescents and compares the historical prevalence and trends with those of Westernized countries. Body image concerns are now a concerning issue in contemporary Japanese society as they also become a more global issue. Several reports from other Asian and non-Western countries including Japan have increasing rates of body image concerns. As body image concerns are related to societal norms, culture and ethnicity, their study requires an understanding of body image disturbance within different cultural contexts. Although considered less prevalent than in the West, Japan has an early history of body concerns and also eating disorders. The reported studies and trends outlined in this review suggest that, as in Western countries, the interest in and study of body image concerns and eating disorders in Japan have increased over the last three decades. The authors also report on the findings of some new qualitative interviews conducted among male and female Japanese adolescents and some of these unique findings are presented in this chapter.

---

* Author for correspondence: A/Prof Jennifer A. O'Dea; Faculty of Education & Social Work; Room 911, Building A35, NSW, 2006; Australia; Tel 61-2-93516226; Fax- 61-2-93512606; Email: j.o'dea@edfac.usyd.edu.au.

In: Psychology Research Biographies and Summaries
Editors: Nancy E. Wodarth and Alexis P. Ferguson
ISBN: 978-1-61470-491-1
© 2012 Nova Science Publishers, Inc.

Chapter 132

BODY IMAGE AMONG ABORIGINAL CHILDREN AND ADOLESCENTS IN AUSTRALIA

*Renata L. Cinelli and Jennifer A. O'Dea**
University of Sydney, Australia

RESEARCH SUMMARY

In the next decade, levels of obesity, body image concerns and dissatisfaction are expected to continue to escalate in tandem for children and adolescents, including those from diverse ethnic backgrounds (Dounchis, Hayden, & Wilfley, 2001). Holt and Ricciardelli (2008) concur that there is increasing evidence of weight and muscle concerns that include body dissatisfaction along with problem eating. This is an alarming trend because it has a vast array of health implications for young people including physical, cultural, social and mental health consequences. Young people who are overweight and obese in modern Westernized societies are often stigmatized and ostracized, and overweight adults are known to suffer various forms of discrimination (Strauss & Pollack, 2003; Latner & Stunkard, 2003). Body image concerns are associated with overall poor self concept in early adolescents, including poor physical, social and academic self concepts (O'Dea, 2006) as well as low overall self esteem (Strauss & Pollack, 2003). Further to that people with poor body image are known to be susceptible to dieting which can lead to eating disorders (Dounchis et al., 2001). The adverse outcomes of poor body image among children and adolescents suggest an urgent need for these issues to be addressed in both health and educational settings.

Owing to the plethora of studies surrounding adolescent and adult females' body image, it is known that dissatisfaction and a preoccupation with unrealistic thinness is entrenched among many women (Rierdan & Koff, 1997; Snapp, 2009). This is particularly true of Caucasian, upper class women (Rierdan & Koff, 1997; Snapp, 2009). Whilst the trends become less prominent when focusing on males, there is recent evidence from the literature

---

* Author for correspondence-A/Prof Jennifer A. O'Dea, Faculty of Education & Social Work, Room 911, Building A35, NSW, 2006, Australia, Tel 61-2-93516226, Fax- 61-2-93512606, j.o'dea@edfac.usyd.edu.au.

that societal body image pressures are also reaching men (Grammas & Schwartz, 2009), adolescents and children as young as five years old (O'Dea & Caputi, 2001).

Moreover, whilst there is a lack of data on minority populations, it has been shown that the desire for the "perfect" Westernized body may permeate traditional cultures, such as Pacific Islander populations (McCabe, Ricciardelli, Waqa, Goundar, & Fotu, 2009) and the Indigenous Aboriginal population of Australia (Ricciardelli, McCabe, Ball, & Mellor, 2004; Wang & Hoy, 2004). Further, whilst it is known that higher proportions of Indigenous Australian adolescents are overweight than their non-Indigenous counterparts, McCabe and colleagues (2005) recognise that little is known about the associated behaviours and attitudes (McCabe, Ricciardelli, Mellor, & Ball, 2005). This underrepresentation needs to be addressed in order to redress some of the health and education inequities facing the Indigenous Australian population.

It is well known that body image perceptions are influenced by a variety of sociocultural factors, including the media, family and peers (e.g. Hargreaves & Tiggemann, 2004; Nollen et al., 2006; Ricciardelli et al., 2004). It has also been identified that for African Americans, the influence on body image perceptions of parents and family is greater to that of Caucasians for whom peer influence appears to be greater (Parnell et al., 1996). Similar to the findings of Parnell and colleagues (1996), Cinelli and O'Dea (2009) found that for Indigenous Australian adolescents, the influence of parents through advice and feedback was a prominent factor in determining adolescents' body image. This could be attributable to the strong family ties and kinship of Aboriginal culture (Walker, 1993).

It is for the above reasons that the unique focus of this chapter will be on the body image of Aboriginal Australians.

Body image is defined as:

"A persons' perceptions, thoughts and feelings about his or her own body" (Grogan, 2008, p.3).

"...how people think, feel, and behave with regard to their own physical attributes" (Muth & Cash, 1997, p.1438).

"...the multifaceted psychological experience of embodiment, especially but not exclusively one's physical appearance...it encompasses one's body-related self-perceptions and self-attitudes, including thoughts, beliefs, feelings and behaviours." (Cash, 2004, p.1)

Davis and colleagues (2010) explain that body image is classically defined as the discrepancy between one's ideal and perceived body size or one's body dissatisfaction (Davis, Sbrocco, Odoms-Young, & Smith, 2010). Further, the authors explain that body image is only one component of attractiveness and that, particularly cross-culturally, ideals of attractiveness and beauty can vary and encompass many components (Davis et al., 2010).

Body image is a process that undergoes constant fluctuation throughout the lifespan and is a composite of both psychological and physiological factors (Janelli, 1993). Janelli (1993) further described body image as encompassing the surface and internal workings of the body as well as attitudes, values, and reactions to one's body.

Body dissatisfaction is defined as:

"A persons' negative thoughts and feelings about his or her own body" (Grogan, 2008, p.4).

These definitions propose that body image is a subjective concept and likely to differ between individuals. Flynn and Fitzgibbon (1998) adopt a definition similar to Grogan (2008) and define body image as feelings and thoughts people have about their bodies. Body image is frequently explained as an individual's mental picture of his or her own body, as well as his or her satisfaction with this image (Thomas, 2001). Further, body image has been postulated as an elastic and changeable concept that can be determined through new information and social experience (Grogan, 2008). In that way, body image can be damaged or enhanced through outside influences, such as peers and the media. It is for this reason that school-based education and intervention programs are of such importance in the promotion of a positive and healthy body image.

Willows (2005) explains culture to be broadly defined as values, beliefs, attitudes and practices that are accepted by members of a group or community. Rucker and Cash (1992) note that body image clearly develops in a cultural context. Thus, groups from different countries and cultures may differ in their perspectives or understandings of bodies, shapes and weight, along with what is realistic and desirable.

Further, over the decades, there has been extensive research into the influences on body image. Stanford and McCabe (2005) identify that society provides messages about how people should ideally look, and that it is both the actual and the perceived messages that influence body image. Further, these messages are not just coming from society and the media, but from family members and peers, among other sources (e.g. McCabe & Ricciardelli, 2003; Mellor, McCabe, Ricciardelli, & Merino, 2008; Mellor et al., 2009; Ricciardelli et al., 2004).

It has been speculated that adoption of Western body ideals is detrimental to body ideals of men and women due to the often unrealistic nature of these ideals (Humphry & Ricciardelli, 2004). Mussap (2009), in a study of Muslim-Australian women, found support for potential risks to body image encountered by women who adopt Western values, and the benefits in retaining heritage cultural values that promote a positive self image. Similarly, Humphry and Ricciardelli (2004) report that acculturation with Western society and the adoption of the slim ideal female body size are the primary factors that have contributed to higher levels of eating pathology among Asian women. Considering this, it could be concluded that exposure to Western society and the messages it projects can be detrimental to the health of both Western people and people from other non Western cultures.

Chapter 133

THE PSYCHOLOGY OF BODY IMAGE: UNDERSTANDING BODY IMAGE INSTABILITY AND DISTORTION

Jennifer S. Mills, Kaley Roosen and Rachel Vella-Zarb
Department of Psychology, York University, Toronto, Canada

RESEARCH SUMMARY

In this chapter we consider the psychology of body image and analyze the concepts of body image instability and body image distortion. Rather than representing a stable or static trait, we propose that body image is in constant flux, continuously shifting as a result of factors both internal and external to the individual. We review the literature supporting the view that people's perceptions of the size and/or shape of their bodies are not fixed. Drawing from published empirical studies, including research on personality, the effects of exposure to media images, social norms, and weight-related feedback, determinants of body image will be reviewed and critically examined. As a corollary to the concept of body image malleability, it is further proposed that people tend to be inaccurate when assessing what their bodies look like. Much of the research to-date on body image distortion has focused on individuals with clinical eating disorders who exhibit extreme body image distortion (e.g., anorexia nervosa). Such individuals typically believe that their bodies are much heavier than they really are. However, even individuals without clinically significant disorders are often poor at recognizing the size and shape of their own bodies. Interestingly, people tend to underestimate their weight (in lb or kg), whereas they tend to overestimate their body size. Possible reasons for this discrepancy in body image accuracy findings are discussed. In summary, people generally exhibit what we call poor 'body acuity.' There is little evidence of perceptual dysfunction underlying body image inaccuracy and distortion. However, certain perceptual influences (i.e., attentional biases) appear to exacerbate poor body acuity.

Chapter 134

MEASUREMENT OF THE PERCEPTUAL ASPECTS OF BODY IMAGE

Rick M. Gardner and Dana L. Brown
Department of Psychology, University of Colorado Denver, US

RESEARCH SUMMARY

Body image disturbance (BID) is an important aspect of several pathologies in psychology, particularly eating disorders. BID is commonly thought to include two components; a perceptual component and an attitudinal component. The perceptual component refers to how accurately individuals perceive the size of their body, also known as body size estimation or BSE. The attitudinal component refers to the thoughts and feelings one has about the size and/or shape of their body, which is also known as body dissatisfaction. While both components have been shown to play an important role in eating disorders, they are largely independent of each other. This chapter reviews the clinical relevance of measuring BSE in relation to eating disorders and provides an overview of research findings. A broad historical overview is provided that highlights the various techniques that have been developed to assess BSE including analogue scales, image marking, optical distortion methods, and figural drawing scales. Analogue scales require participants to adjust the horizontal distance of a pair of calipers or two points of light to show the width of various body parts. Image marking procedures require participants to draw their body on a vertically mounted piece of paper or to mark on the paper the width of certain body parts. Recent optical distortion methods typically employ computer software that presents the participant with an image of themselves that has been distorted in width and participants are asked to adjust the image to match both the actual and ideal size of their body. These images are typically static digital images, although photographs have occasionally been used as well. Each method is discussed along with any relevant limitations or methodological concerns. Psychophysical techniques such as the method of constant stimuli, signal detection theory, and adaptive probit estimation are described in relation to methodological concerns such as distinguishing sensory from non-sensory components of BSE. Video distortion techniques that incorporate psychophysical techniques appear to be the most precise for measuring BSE.

In: Psychology Research Biographies and Summaries
Editors: Nancy E. Wodarth and Alexis P. Ferguson

ISBN: 978-1-61470-491-1
© 2012 Nova Science Publishers, Inc.

Chapter 135

BODY IMAGE AND CANCER

Özen Önen Sertöz*
Ege University School of Medicine
Department of Psychiatry
Division of Consultation Liaison Psychiatry
Izmir-Turkey

RESEARCH SUMMARY

The diagnosis and treatment of cancer can result both physical and psychiatric morbidity. Physical and psychological changes during the course of cancer may alter an individual's body image. Alterations in body image can contribute to the psychosocial adjustment of cancer patients. Early studies investigating the role of body image among cancer patients primarily have paid attention to breast cancer patients. The ongoing studies than examined body image disturbances and factors associated with body image changes in patients with different types of cancer.

In general factors related to body image changes in cancer patients are due to: 1) cancer treatments (chemotherapy, radiation therapy, hormone therapy and surgery); 2) results of treatments such as hair loss, weight loss or weight gain, loss of an organ, scars; 3) psychological distress related to cancer diagnosis, its treatments and cancer related issues; 4) personality properties (those who place importance on their appearance are more likely to experience distress when faced with a greater self-discrepancy in their appearance; 5) gender (women are more prompt to have more concerns than men about physical appearance; and 6) age. In addition to all these factors there is literature knowledge that body image concerns can change in follow-up period of a cancer diagnosis.

In this chapter, body image disturbances in cancer patients, factors related to body image disturbances, body image disturbances in different types of cancer, impact of body image disturbances on quality of life and sexuality will be discussed. Also treatment approaches for body image disturbances in cancer patients will be reviewed in the light of the literature.

---

* E-mail: onensertoz@gmail.com.

Chapter 136

BEYOND THE MEDIA: A LOOK AT OTHER SOCIALISATION PROCESSES THAT CONTRIBUTE TO BODY IMAGE PROBLEMS AND DYSFUNCTIONAL EATING

Marion Kostanski[*]
Department Psychology and Social Sciences
Victoria University, Australia

RESEARCH SUMMARY

The activities of shopping for clothes and dressing oneself are a major component of our everyday lives. As noted by Goffman, 1990, a large portion of our social recognition and engagement centres on the preliminary assessment we make of others' presentation and external cues. Extending on this theory, it is argued that one's experience and beliefs around the act of dressing, and particularly purchasing clothes, will have a strong influence on how one feels about, and engages with, their body. Through a series of interviews and the development of a self report inventory, the current research offers an evaluation of the impact that these activities have on young women's psychosocial wellbeing and health. Outcomes of both quantitative and qualitative research indicated that over 40% of the variance in reported experiences was explained by four primary factors; social engagement, self identity processes, use of popular media such as fashion magazines, and emotional affect.

As predicted, shopping for clothes was identified as an important personal and social activity for many participants. Reliance on popular media for informed choice, updates on trends and knowing what was important was also strongly endorsed. Of significance was the prevalence of reported negative affective experiences in relation to the experience of shopping for clothes. Issues such as depressed mood, feeling frustrated, and being embarrassed to ask for assistance, were consistently reported to be a consequence of this

---

[*] Email: Marion.Kostanski@vu.edu.au.

activity for the women. "Affect" was found to significantly predict over 30% of the variance in reported body image dissatisfaction in young women.

The outcomes of this research suggest that there are practical and pragmatic steps that may alleviate some of the negative experiences. Further the outcomes of this research confirm that shopping for clothes is imbued with very powerful explicit and implicit messages that impact strongly on how we feel and perceive ourselves. The underlying dynamic of this process is a paradoxical dilemma, wherein the women are drawn to engage in a social process that incorporates both elements of pleasure and necessity and simultaneously struggle with an internalised attribution style that leaves her with a sense of being personally responsible for many of the things that go wrong. The research confirms that there are many extraneous factors that impact on and influence how women perceive and feel about their body. Research into the development of educational programmes that empower women in articulating and addressing their experiences of engaging in their world from a "non self-deficit" perspective of faulty attributions is recommended.

In: Psychology Research Biographies and Summaries
Editors: Nancy E. Wodarth and Alexis P. Ferguson
ISBN: 978-1-61470-491-1
© 2012 Nova Science Publishers, Inc.

Chapter 137

ALEXITHYMIA, BODY IMAGE AND EATING DISORDERS

Domenico De Berardis[1,2,*], *Viviana Marasco*[1], *Daniela Campanella*[1], *Nicola Serroni*[1], *Mario Caltabiano*[1], *Luigi Olivieri*[1], *Carla Ranalli*[1], *Alessandro Carano*[2], *Tiziano Acciavatti*[2], *Giuseppe Di Iorio*[2], *Marilde Cavuto*[3], *Francesco Saverio Moschetta*[1] *and Massimo Di Giannantonio*[2]

[1] NHS, Department of Mental Health, Psychiatric Service of Diagnosis and Treatment, Hospital "G. Mazzini" Teramo, Italy
[2] Department of Neurosciences and Imaging, Chair of Psychiatry, University "G. d'Annunzio" of Chieti, Italy
[3] IASM, L'Aquila, Italy

RESEARCH SUMMARY

It is widely recognized that the body dissatisfaction and an excessive concern about body weight and shape are core characteristic of Eating Disorders (EDs) and are used to determine self-worth. Recently, there was an increased interest about the body image as a multidimensional issue that involves perceptual, attitudinal and behavioral characteristics. Many researchers have focused their attention mainly to the perceptual and attitudinal aspects of body image whereas only few studies have investigated the behavioral consequences related to a negative body image. Moreover, it is known that alexithymia may play an important role in EDs: specifically alexithymics patients may show a higher psychological distress than nonalexithymics and the presence of an alexithymic trait may be related to a higher severity of EDs themselves. Some core aspects of alexithymic construct, as a difficulty in distinguishing emotional states from bodily sensations, may be more characterized in

---

* Correspondence: Domenico De Berardis, MD, PhD. NHS; Dipartimento di Salute Mentale, Servizio Psichiatrico Diagnosi e Cura, Ospedale Civile "G. Mazzini" Teramo, p.zza Italia 1, 64100 Teramo (Italy) • Tel. +39 0861429708 • Fax +39 0861429706 • E-mail: dodebera@aliceposta.it.

patients with EDs and a possible explanation might be that ED patients may appear dramatically and deeply incapable of being in touch with their inner emotive world. As consequence, these subjects may focus their attention on negative perceptual aspects of body bypassing emotional experiences. Taken together, these findings may suggest that alexithymia and body image disturbances may be strongly correlated in EDs and, therefore, the aim of this paper will be to elucidate these relationships along with the presentation of a clinical study on 64 patients with a DSM-IV diagnosis of anorexia nervosa.

Chapter 138

A META-ANALYTIC REVIEW OF SOCIOCULTURAL INFLUENCES ON MALE BODY IMAGE

Bryan T. Karazsia[1,]*** *and Kathryn Pieper*[2]
[1] Department of Psychology, The College of Wooster, Wooster, OH, US
[2] The Section of Developmental and Behavioral Sciences,
Children's Mercy Hospitals and Clinics
Kansas City, MO, US

RESEARCH SUMMARY

Male body dissatisfaction is prevalent and associated with maladaptive outcomes. Discrepancies exist in this literature concerning the importance of sociocultural influences on men's body dissatisfaction. The present meta-analysis explored the extent to which these discrepancies may be related to the way in which constructs are assessed. We hypothesized that studies that assessed muscularity as a component of sociocultural influences or men's body dissatisfaction would have larger effect sizes than studies that did not assess muscularity. Results largely supported this hypothesis; the average effect sizes of the relationship between internalization and awareness of ideal body figures and men's body image differed as a function of methodology. When muscularity was assessed, the magnitude of effect sizes was similar to those reported with female samples. These results have implications for research and interventions with males.

---

* Please address correspondence to: Bryan T. Karazsia; Department of Psychology; The College of Wooster; Wooster, OH 44691; E-mail: bkarazsia@wooster.edu; Phone: 330-263-2302; Fax: 330-263-2276.

In: Psychology Research Biographies and Summaries
Editors: Nancy E. Wodarth and Alexis P. Ferguson
ISBN: 978-1-61470-491-1
© 2012 Nova Science Publishers, Inc.

Chapter 139

TOUCH AND BODY: A ROLE FOR THE SOMATOSENSORY CORTEX IN ESTABLISHING AN EARLY FORM OF IDENTITY (REVIEW ARTICLE)

*Michael Schaefer**

Department of Neurology, Otto-von-Guericke University Magdeburg,
Magdeburg, Germany

RESEARCH SUMMARY

A major cortical representation of our body can be found in the primary somatosensory cortex (SI). While classic studies understand the body map representation in SI as fix and reflecting the physical location of peripheral stimulation in the form of the famous somatosensory homunculus, recent studies challenge this view and suggest a more complex role for SI. For example, experiments using simple visuo-tactile illusions demonstrate that SI reflects the perceived rather than the physical location of peripheral stimulation. Moreover, it has been suggested that SI represents an early concept of our body that may also include important dimensions of our self. This review reports results of recent experiments that provide support for this view. For example, SI seems to respond differentially when observed touch is attributed to the own body compared to another body (in both cases in absence of any real touch!). Further experiments on observing touch on other's body report that activity in the somatosensory cortex is closely associated with the personal trait of empathy. Hence, it is proposed that the somatosensory cortices may be involved in social perception processes and thereby establish first forms of a unique body image and a personal identity.

---

* Correspondence to: Michael Schaefer, PhD; Department of Neurology; Otto-von-Guericke University Magdeburg; 39120 Magdeburg, Germany; Tel.: +49(0) 391-6117542; Fax: +49(0) 391-6715233; Email: mischa@neuro2.med.uni-magdeburg.de.

In: Psychology Research Biographies and Summaries
Editors: Nancy E. Wodarth and Alexis P. Ferguson

ISBN: 978-1-61470-491-1
© 2012 Nova Science Publishers, Inc.

Chapter 140

NOTHING COMPARES TO YOU: THE INFLUENCE OF BODY SIZE OF MODELS IN PRINT ADVERTISING AND BODY COMPARISON PROCESSES ON WOMEN'S BODY IMAGE

Doeschka J. Anschutz[1]*, Tatjana Van Strien[b,2], Eni S. Becker[1] and Rutger C. M. E. Engels[1]

[1] Behavioural Science Institute, The Netherlands
[2] Institute for Gender Studies
Radboud University Nijmegen, The Netherlands

RESEARCH SUMMARY

Associations between body size of print advertising models, body comparison processes and body-focused anxiety were examined. Normal-weight females viewed advertisements of slim models, or the same models horizontally stretched to make them look more average sized. Participants were instructed to focus either on the positive or the negative features of the models. The results showed that when participants viewed average sized models, they felt better about their own body, regardless of body comparison instruction. Interestingly, when participants focused on negative features of the models, they also felt better about their own body, regardless of body size of the models.

---

* Corresponding author: Doeschka J. Anschutz; Behavioural Science Institute; Radboud University Nijmegen; P.O. Box 9104, 6500 HE Nijmegen, The Netherlands; Phone +31 24 3611818; Fax +31 24 3612776; E-mail: d.anschutz@pwo.ru.nl.

Chapter 141

BODY IMAGE IN PEOPLE OF AFRICAN DESCENT: A SYSTEMATIC REVIEW

D. Catherine Walker
The University at Albany, State University of New York, US

RESEARCH SUMMARY

In the United States of America, Black people are more likely to be overweight or obese and are also more likely to suffer from many of the related chronic diseases. Based on these data, it might be expected that Black men and women would suffer from greater body image dissatisfaction. However, research suggests that Black women and Black men are more satisfied with their bodies than are White women and men, respectively. Historically, research on body image has been conducted using predominantly White female samples. As a result, it is not clear whether or not the research generalizes to young males, older men and women, and men and women from different racial and ethnic backgrounds. The purpose of this chapter is to examine body image research in people of African descent. Two questions that will be addressed are whether or not body image differs in Black people compared to research that has been conducted using primarily White participants, and whether body image has different relationships to variables such as self-esteem, body mass index (BMI), and eating disorder symptoms in these two groups. In addition, possible reasons for differences (e.g., mediators and moderators) will be considered.

Chapter 142

LOW SES CHILDREN'S BMI SCORES AND THEIR PERCEIVED AND IDEAL BODY IMAGES: INTERVENTION IMPLICATIONS

Simone Pettigrew,[1] *Melanie Pescud[2] and Robert J. Donovan
[1] University of Western Australia, Perth, Australia
[2] University of Western Australia, Perth, Australia
[3] Curtin University of Technology, Perth, Australia

RESEARCH SUMMARY

BMI cut-offs were used in conjunction with the Children's Body Image Scale to provide a comparison between actual BMI and perceived and ideal body images among 90 low socioeconomic children aged seven to 10 years. A third of the sample was classified as overweight or obese, with a higher incidence among boys (38% versus 28% for girls). Two-thirds underestimated their current body size and only around 5% considered themselves overweight or obese. Just over 70% selected an underweight ideal body size. Intervention developers thus face the dual challenge of providing children and their families with the information and skills they need to prevent childhood obesity while addressing a lack of awareness of actual body weight among children that is combined with an unrealistic ideal body size preference. This task is complicated by the need to minimise weight concerns that can result in eating disorders. The results suggest the need for a family-based approach that targets parents of young children to increase awareness of healthy body sizes and lifestyle behaviours before children have become overweight, formed inaccurate weight-related beliefs, and/or become dissatisfied with their bodies.

---

* Corresponding author: Professor Simone Pettigrew; University of Western Australia; M261, 35 Stirling Highway; Crawley WA 6009; Australia; Ph: +61 8 6488 1437; Fax: +61 8 6488 1072; simone.pettigrew@uwa.edu.au.

Chapter 143

THEORETICAL AND METHODOLOGICAL CONSIDERATIONS IN ASSESSING BODY IMAGE AMONG CHILDREN AND ADOLESCENTS

Margaret Lawler and Elizabeth Nixon
School of Psychology and Children's Research Centre,
Trinity College Dublin, Ireland

RESEARCH SUMMARY

Body image dissatisfaction, a prevalent concern among children and adolescents, has been identified as a significant risk factor in the onset of eating pathology, depression and low self-esteem (Levine & Smolak, 2002; Stice & Bearman, 2001; Stice, Presnell, & Spangler, 2002). Given the negative implications of body image dissatisfaction, it is important to examine how body image is currently conceptualized and measured. This chapter proposes to explore theoretical and methodological issues underpinning the assessment of body image dissatisfaction among children and adolescents. Careful consideration of the assessment of body image dissatisfaction is further warranted in light of emerging literature which highlights important gender differences in body appearance concerns. While an ultra-thin body ideal is emphasized for females, the male appearance ideal endorses a muscular physique characterised by broad shoulders and a well developed chest. As such, girls typically demonstrate a drive for thinness, while boys endorse a drive for muscularity. Empirical findings support this position, demonstrating that girls are most satisfied with their bodies at below average levels of adiposity, with dissatisfaction increasing with increased body mass. For boys however, body dissatisfaction is reflected in a desire among some to lose weight, and a desire among others to gain weight and become more muscular (McCabe & Ricciardelli, 2004). Such gendered body image patterns have important implications for the assessment of body image dissatisfaction. Indeed, concerns have been raised that commonly used measures of body image dissatisfaction solely address one's desire to be smaller or thinner, which is a predominantly female concern. Specifically, it has been argued that the figural rating scales may produce a conceptual bias by manipulating adiposity only, therefore confounding body mass with muscularity. This may be of theoretical consequence for males who aspire to a muscular ideal. Questionnaire measures have also been criticized due to their failure to identify the direction of body discontent (desire to be bigger versus smaller), which may lead to the underestimation of body dissatisfaction among males. In light of these important gendered patterns, this chapter will review the conceptual frameworks and strengths and limitations of existing methods of assessing body dissatisfaction among children and adolescents.

Chapter 144

Issues Pertaining to Body Image Measurement in Exercise Research

Rebecca L. Bassett and Kathleen A. Martin Ginis
McMaster University, Hamilton, Ontario, Canada

Research Summary

Recent meta-analyses have established a positive relationship between exercise and body image [Hausenblas & Fallon, 2006; Reel, 2007; Campbell & Hausenblas, 2009]. However, further research is necessary to answer numerous remaining questions regarding the relationship between exercise and body image. For example, the mechanisms by which exercise interventions improve body image are not well understood. Likewise, characteristics of the most effective exercise programs for enhancing body image remain unknown. Future research should aim to understand such ambiguities regarding the exercise-body image relationship. In order to maximize the impact of future exercise research, proper measurement of body image is critical.

Several important considerations for the measurement of body image were highlighted in an article by Thompson [2004]. In the current commentary, Thompson's article is used as a framework for discussion of issues pertaining to body image measurement specifically with regard to exercise research. Five considerations are addressed: 1] Defining the specific dimension of body image being considered and measure accordingly. 2] Considering multiple measures of body image. 3] Selecting valid and reliable body image measures. 4] Considering sample characteristics. 5] Considering the appropriateness of state or trait body image measures. The commentary will serve as a useful guide for proper measurement of body image within exercise research.

Chapter 145

NEGATIVE BODY IMAGE PERCEPTION AND ASSOCIATED ATTITUDES IN FEMALES

Tamara Y. Mousa[1] and Rima H. Mashal[2]

[1] Researcher Assistant in the Department of Nutrition and Food Science,
University of Jordan. Amman, Jordan
[2] Assistant Professor of Nutrition
Department of Nutrition and Food Science,
University of Jordan, Amman, Jordan

RESEARCH SUMMARY

Negative body image perception has predisposed females, particularly adolescent and young females, to be more preoccupied with their body image than males. This has been explained by the perception of female beauty with extreme thinness. Western females are preoccupied with their body image due to social and cultural norms that emphasize on thinness, which is internalized as a symbol of success. Furthermore, beauty Western ideals have recently been found to influence body image perception of Arabic females through mass media. Negative body image perception has been indicated to contribute to body image dissatisfaction. Because females are concerned about their body image and weight, they tend to correct imperfections through engaging in negative eating attitudes and behaviors. It has also been documented that body image dissatisfaction is associated with acknowledging eating disorders, increasing the risk of exhibiting health compromising behaviors. In all, well-controlled prospective studies on negative body image perception and the factors associated with it are encouraged. Research should also attempt to develop intervention programs to improve body image of females.

---

[1] Correspondence to: Tamara Yousef Mousa, MSc. Researcher Assistant at the Department of Nutrition and Food Science, University of Jordan. Amman 11196 – Jordan, P.O. Box: 960364; Telephone/Fax number: 00962-6-5604301; E-mail: mousa_tamara@yahoo.com;
[2] E-mail: rima@ju.edu.jo.

Chapter 146

BODY IMAGE IN YOUNG AND ADULT WOMEN WITH PHYSICAL DISABILITIES

Nancy Xenakis[1] and Judith Goldberg[2]
[1] Program Coordinator
Initiative for Women with Disabilities
NYU Hospital for Joint Diseases
New York, NY, US
[2] Director
Initiative for Women with Disabilities
NYU Hospital for Joint Diseases
New York, NY, US

RESEARCH SUMMARY

Recent literature has shown that women with physical disabilities often face physical and emotional barriers to their own health and wellness. Persons with disabilities are often seen as "others" in relation to the general population. Attitudes toward people with physical disabilities are generally negative, simplistic and discriminative. Moreover, women with a physical disability must deal with Westernized gender roles and beauty ideals that are constantly imposed upon them. As a result, this group of women often has difficulty developing a healthy image of their bodies, socializing and expressing themselves, especially when compared with their able-bodied counterparts.

In particular, young women, as they reach adolescence, develop a growing awareness of just how different their bodies are when compared with their able-bodied peers. This unhealthy self concept is often prpetuated by the perceived influence of various socio cultural factors such as the media, peers and adult figures regarding thinness and body ideal. Their disabilities become imperfections. These young women must also overcome myths that they are asexual or incapable of handling sexual relationships. Physicians can also reinforce these myths by infantilizing these young women with physical disabilities well into adulthood though many have aspirations of marriage and motherhood.

People with disabilities have become increasingly able to live fulfilling lives in recent decades. This is due largely to studies that have confirmed that once barriers are addressed and minimized; women with physical disabilities lead active and productive lives and have much to contribute to society. American with Disabilities Act legislation has allowed more women with disabilities to enter the mainstream environment socially, educationally and vocationally. The involvement of professionals, programs and services assists these women to increase their self-confidence, self-competence and independence.

The Initiative for Women with Disabilities (IWD), a hospital-based center serving young and adult women with physical disabilities offers accessible gynecology, primary care, physical therapy, nutrition consultations, exercise and fitness classes, wellness and social work services and youth based programming. Its mission is to empower women to pursue a healthy lifestyle.

In: Psychology Research Biographies and Summaries
Editors: Nancy E. Wodarth and Alexis P. Ferguson
ISBN: 978-1-61470-491-1
© 2012 Nova Science Publishers, Inc.

Chapter 147

THE NON SATISFIED PATIENT IN AESTHETIC SURGERY – MEDICAL ATTITUDE

Alberto Rancati[1], Maurizio Nava[2], Marcelo Irigo[3] and Braulio Peralta[3]

[1] University of Buenos Aires, Universidad Catolica Argentina, Buenos Aires, Argentina
[2] Direttore Struttura Complessa di Oncologia Chirurgica Ricostruttiva-Chirurgia Plastica, Plastic Surgery Unit, Fondazione IRCCS Istituto Nazionale dei Tumori, Milano, Italy
[3] Universidad Catolica, Argentina, Buenos Aires, Argentina

RESEARCH SUMMARY

Usually, patients undergoing plastic surgery have only the expectation of success about the practice they will undergo, and on the same way, surgeons are prepared and technically trained to achieve better result. But what happens when things go wrong?

How can we manage this critical situation where patient receives this bad news and will probably blame the surgeon for this unexpected outcome?

Elective cosmetic surgery is an increasingly high risk area of medical professional liability, and, although some claims of negligence associated with elective plastic surgery are generated because the patient's expectations were not met, others arise from a genuine adverse outcome where results need revisions, and perhaps surgical planning was not the best.

Unfortunately sometimes this narrow limit between an adverse event and a medical error is forced to be seen as malpractice by lawyers, family patients and friends.

In: Psychology Research Biographies and Summaries
Editors: Nancy E. Wodarth and Alexis P. Ferguson
ISBN: 978-1-61470-491-1
© 2012 Nova Science Publishers, Inc.

Chapter 148

MOTIVATED BEHAVIORS: THE INTERACTION OF ATTENTION, HABITUATION AND MEMORY

John W. Wright and Roberta V. Wiediger
Departments of Psychology, Veterinary and Comparative Anatomy,
Pharmacology and Physiology, and Programs in Neuroscience and Biotechnology
Washington State University, Pullman, Washington, US

RESEARCH SUMMARY

Motivated behaviors are simultaneously fascinating and difficult to understand. Our fellow humans often exhibit behaviors that appear to have no underlying logic or reasonable explanation. This chapter attempts to identify the important contributors to motivated behaviors. We begin by defining motivation and its relationship with need states. Next the complicated processes of habituation and sensitization are discussed, followed by an analysis of selective attention. The role of memory systems in directing successful motivated behaviors is addressed along with identification of the brain structures that appear to be involved. In this regard there is much to be learned. The chapter concludes with summaries of current research findings concerning the brain angiotensin system's importance in memory consolidation and retrieval. This section includes descriptions of the impact of currently prescribed antihypertensive medications such as angiotensin converting enzyme (ACE) inhibitors and angiotensin receptor blockers (ARBs) on cognition. The overall goal of this chapter is to assist the reader to better understand and appreciate the complex issue of human motivated behaviors from the perspective of research contributions made using both human and animal subjects.

In: Psychology Research Biographies and Summaries
Editors: Nancy E. Wodarth and Alexis P. Ferguson

ISBN: 978-1-61470-491-1
© 2012 Nova Science Publishers, Inc.

Chapter 149

ATTENTION AND MOTIVATION INTERDEPENDENCE IN SELF-REGULATION. A NEUROCOGNITIVE APPROACH

M. Rosario Rueda*, Alberto Acosta and Milagros Santonja
Universidad de Granada, Spain

RESEARCH SUMMARY

Inner desires and motives often result in confrontation with what is requested by others or considered socially appropriate, and even with one's own goals. Regulating internally-generated impulses is therefore an important ability for accomplishing goals and instructions as well as complying with social norms. In Psychology, this ability has been linked to the concept of self-regulation. The term "self-regulation" refers to those processes by which people exercise control over their emotional and behavioral responses in order to accomplish their own goals and/or to adapt to the cognitive and social demands of specific situations. The type of processes implicated in such ability involve modulating the intensity, frequency and duration of verbal and motor responses, activating and/or inhibiting behaviors according to situational demands in the absence of external monitoring, delaying acting upon a desired object or goal and modulating emotional reactivity (Fonagy & Target, 2002; Thompson, 1994; Kopp, 1992). Thus, it is no surprise that the ability to self-regulate is been shown to relate to important aspects of socialization during childhood, as emotionality, delay of gratification, compliance, moral development, social competence, empathy, adjustment, and academic performance (Eisenberg et al., 2004). As a matter of fact, self-regulation is thought to be "essential for transforming the inner animal nature into a civilized human being" (Vogs & Baumeister, 2004, p. 1).

Although increased evidence shows that some regulatory operations may be carried out in an automatic, nonconscious mode (Fitzsimons & Bargh, 2004), most definitions of self-regulation place the emphasis on processes exerted by the self in a conscious and deliberate

---

* Corresponding author: M. Rosario Rueda, Dpto. Psicología Experimental, Universidad de Granada – Spain. Phone: +34 958 249609; Email: rorueda@ugr.es.

way which activation entails some effort. Within this framework, the ability to self-regulate has been linked to executive aspects of attention (Posner & Rothbart, 1998; Rueda, Posner & Rothbart, 2004). According to this view, the brain network underlying executive attention constitutes the neural basis for action monitoring and is activated in situations that involve conscious detection, inhibitory control and resolution of conflict produced by dominant but inappropriate responses.

Based on the motivational properties of emotions, other studies highlight the effect of affective variables over attentional processes. Affects appear to exert their influence either by facilitating the processing of relevant information in a substantially automatic mode (Öhman, 1997) or, in a more elaborated way, by demanding additional involvement of control processes on affective-relevant situations (Gross, 2002). In addition, motivational variables and strategies are shown to modulate aspects of self-regulation. There is evidence of the influence of promotion-approach versus prevention-avoidance styles on processes of decision making, generation of alternatives, probability estimates and evaluation of outcomes (Higgins & Spiegel, 2004).

In this chapter, we stress the contribution of control processes related to attention for emotional and behavioral regulation, placing emphasis on the specific neural systems involved in such processes. In addition, we analyze the influence of motivational and emotional variables on the functioning of attentional control in an effort to understand their interdependence for regulating behavior.

Chapter 150

THE MOTIVATIONAL FUNCTION OF EMOTIONS: A "FEELING IS FOR DOING" PERSPECTIVE

Rob M. A. Nelissen and Marcel Zeelenberg
Social and Economic Psychology, Tilburg University, The Netherlands

RESEARCH SUMMARY

In this chapter we outline a recently developed "Feeling-is-for-Doing" perspective for the influence of specific emotions on decision-making and behavior. This perspective holds that discrete emotions present functional psychological mechanism involved in orchestrating goal-directed behavior. Studies corroborating the basic premises of this perspective are presented, along with results indicating that investigating the impact of specific emotions on people's decisions is indeed illustrative of the fundamental motives underlying their behavior. The Feeling-is-for-Doing perspective is then related to and compared with other theories about emotional influences on decision-making.

Always view interactions with others through the dispassionate lens of game theory: [...] Successful game strategies are often counter-intuitive; once you accept that idea, emotions start to make a lot more sense.

The Mind Game. Hector MacDonald, 2000; p. 49

In: Psychology Research Biographies and Summaries
Editors: Nancy E. Wodarth and Alexis P. Ferguson

ISBN: 978-1-61470-491-1
© 2012 Nova Science Publishers, Inc.

Chapter 151

SOCIAL PSYCHOLOGICAL MOTIVATIONS AND FOUNDATIONS OF DIETARY PREFERENCE

Marc Stewart Wilson[*,1] *and Michael W. Allen*[†,2]
[1]Victoria University, Wellington, New Zealand
[2]Sydney University, Sydney, Australia

RESEARCH SUMMARY

This chapter represents a summary of a programme of research conducted over the past ten years focusing on the motivations, explanations, and correlates of dietary preference and behaviour. While there is a significant body of literature attesting to the psychophysiological correlates and of different dietary practices, as well as a clinical literature on pathological dietary behaviours and avoidances, there is only a relatively small body of research investigating the psychological motivations for adopting different practices. In a number of studies we have sought to locate diet into existing theories of choice and behaviour in social psychology, focusing particularly on the motivational foundation of social values, materialism, and beliefs about hierarchy and tradition. In this chapter we bring together the findings of this range of studies to try to give an overall picture of how dietary behaviour can be fitted into the broad context of social psychology. As well as discussing the role that values, materialism, and other beliefs and attitudes account for a range of dietary behaviours we have as a specific interest the foundations of the 'decision' to consume or abstain from consuming meat, and animal-derived products. As well as acting as a microcosm for broader dietary behaviour, meat abstention also represents a social 'deviant' practice in many Western cultures, as it is adopted by a minority.

---

[*] Correspondence should be addressed to Dr. Marc Wilson. Senior Lecturer, School of Psychology, PO Box 600, Victoria University of Wellington, Wellington, New Zealand, Telephone 463-5825, Fax 463-5402, Email: marc.wilson@vuw.ac.nz.
[†] Senior Lecturer, University of Sydney, Discipline of Marketing, School of Business, Economics and Business Building (H69), Sydney NSW 2006, Australia, Phone: +61 2 9351 6003, Fax: +61 2 9351 6732, Email: m.allen@econ.usyd.edu.au.

In: Psychology Research Biographies and Summaries
Editors: Nancy E. Wodarth and Alexis P. Ferguson
ISBN: 978-1-61470-491-1
© 2012 Nova Science Publishers, Inc.

Chapter 152

SELF-DETERMINATION THEORY AND THE THEORY OF PLANNED BEHAVIOR: AN INTEGRATIVE APPROACH TOWARD A MORE COMPLETE MODEL OF MOTIVATION

Martin S. Hagger[*,1] *and Nikos L. D. Chatzisarantis*[†,2]
[1]University of Nottingham, Nottingham, United Kingdom
[2]University of Plymouth, Devon, United Kingdom

RESEARCH SUMMARY

The aim of this chapter is to provide an overview of recent research that integrates two key theories of motivation: the theory of planned behavior and self-determination theory. The chapter will adopt an evidence-based approach to evaluate how the integration of these theories provides a more complete model of motivation. After an overview of the component theories, two theoretical premises for theoretical integration will be discussed: (1) self-determination theory provides a formative explanation for the origin of the antedecents of intentional behavior and (2) self-determination theory constructs operate at a generalized contextual level and reflect the origin or *locus of causality* of an action while theory of planned behavior constructs are situational and reflect expectations regarding engagement in a specific future behavior. Empirical evidence for the integration of these theories is then presented in the form of a meta-analysis of 13 published studies. The meta-analytically derived correlations corrected for sampling and measurement error will then be used as a basis for a path analysis examining the pattern of relations among the variables from the integrated theory. The implications of the integrated models for future research and interventions are discussed.

---

[*] Correspondence concerning this chapter should be addressed to Martin S. Hagger, School of Psychology, University of Nottingham, University Park, Nottingham, NG7 2RD, United Kingdom, email: martin.hagger@nottingham.ac.uk.
[†] Nikos L.D. Chatzisarantis, School of Psychology, University of Plymouth, Portland Square, Drake Circus, Plymouth, Devon, PL4 8AA, United Kingdom, email: nikos.chatzisarantis@plymouth.ac.uk.

Chapter 153

MOTIVATION AND RISK BEHAVIORS: A SELF-DETERMINATION PERSPECTIVE

Clayton Neighbors*, Melissa A. Lewis, Nicole Fossos and Joel R. Grossbard

University of Washington, WA, US

RESEARCH SUMMARY

Motivation lies at the root of many risk-related behaviors, including alcohol abuse, problem gambling, risky sex, and disordered eating behaviors. This chapter provides a review of empirical work examining risk-related behaviors from the perspective of Self-Determination Theory. Theoretical implications for incorporating self-determination in prevention and treatment of risk-related behavior are also considered.

Self-Determination Theory presents a humanistic perspective on motivation, assuming that individuals intrinsically strive to fulfill basic needs for competence, relatedness, and autonomy. In negotiating the environment, externally regulated behaviors are internalized and integrated into the self. Individual differences in motivational orientations emerge as a function of exposure to different environments with some individuals tending to operate more autonomously and others generally more oriented toward extrinsically controlling factors. A considerable volume of basic research has supported the main tenets of Self-Determination Theory and a growing body of literature has begun to explore its application to risk-related behaviors.

A large proportion of the chapter focuses on etiology, reviewing multiple connections between self-determination and risk behaviors with emphasis on social motivations and influences. Research related to alcohol abuse, problem gambling, risky sexual behavior, and disordered eating behaviors are reviewed in turn. Discussion and review of prevention and treatment implications focus primarily on correction of normative misperceptions, mandated

---

* Please send correspondence to Clayton Neighbors, University of Washington, Department of Psychiatry and Behavioral Sciences, 4225 Roosevelt Way NE, Box 354794, Seattle, WA, 98195-6099; Phone (206) 685-8704; E-mail *claytonn@u.washington.edu*. Preparation of this chapter was supported in part by National Institute on Alcohol Abuse and Alcoholism Grants R01AA014576 and T32AA07455.

treatment, and motivational interviewing. Finally, theoretical discussion is presented regarding the conceptualization of self-determination and intrinsic motivation related to potentially "addictive" healthy and unhealthy behaviors.

Chapter 154

A Motivational-Cognitive Model of Prospective Memory: The Influence of Goal Relevance

Suzanna L. Penningroth and Walter D. Scott
Department of Psychology, University of Wyoming, Laramie, Wyoming, US

Research Summary

Prospective memory is defined as memory for actions to be performed in the future, such as remembering to take a medication or remembering to mail a bill. A cognitive approach has yielded significant advances in our understanding of prospective memory processes. However, in this chapter, we argue that further insight can be gained by integrating motivational constructs. Specifically, we outline a new, goal-based motivational-cognitive model of prospective memory in which goal-related prospective memories are viewed as benefiting from both effortful and automatic processing throughout all phases of the prospective memory task. Drawing on contemporary goal frameworks, the new model views goals as knowledge structures with associative links to prospective memories. As a result of these associative connections, goal-related prospective memories are predicted (a) to be perceived as more important, (b) to benefit from greater use of mnemonic strategies, (c) to show greater accessibility in memory, (d) to show preferential allocation of attention during retrieval and performance, and (e) to benefit from automatic retrieval processes. Consequently, these processes are predicted to contribute to superior performance for goal-related prospective memories. In this chapter, we also review evidence that supports our new model. By guiding research into the motivational processes contributing to prospective memory, we hope to contribute to a more complete and ecologically valid understanding of prospective memory performance.

In: Psychology Research Biographies and Summaries
Editors: Nancy E. Wodarth and Alexis P. Ferguson

ISBN: 978-1-61470-491-1
© 2012 Nova Science Publishers, Inc.

Chapter 155

THE ROLE OF GOAL FACILITATION AND GOAL CONFLICT IN MOTIVATION

Winifred A. Gebhardt[*]
Leiden University Institute for Psychological Research
Clinical, Health and Neuropsychology
Leiden University, The Netherlands

RESEARCH SUMMARY

Psychological theories on motivation generally focus on one single attitude object, or goal, at a time. However, people always hold multiple goals simultaneously. Therefore, motivation with respect to one goal should be considered within the context of other goals that are part of the individual's personal goal system. Some goals coincide when the attainment of one goal leads to goal progress of another. Others goals may be in conflict with one another. A conflict in goals occurs when various equally desired end states are mutually exclusive, either because they draw from similar limited resources or because they are logically incompatible. Conflict in goals may lead to mixed emotions about a goal and to feelings of ambivalence. Empirical research within the field of health behavior strongly suggests that examining behavior within the context of the personal goal structure adds significantly to our understanding of behavioral change.

---

[*] Address: P.O. Box 9555, 2300 RB Leiden, The Netherlands; Gebhardt@fsw.leidenuniv.nl + 31-71 5274084 (phone); + 31-71 5274678 (fax).

Chapter 156

THE IMPLICIT NATURE OF GOAL-DIRECTED MOTIVATIONAL PURSUITS

Jay L. Wenger
HACC: Central Pennsylvania's Community College
Lancaster Campus, Pennsylvania, US

RESEARCH SUMMARY

During the past 20 years, there's been an abundance of research that has addressed the distinction between implicit and explicit cognitive processes. Implicit processes are those that can occur spontaneously and without conscious intent or awareness; explicit processes are those that occur with such intent and awareness. Recently, several of these studies have included addressing the effects of various motivational pursuits – in particular, goal-directed pursuits.

Researchers who investigate the implicit nature of goal-directed pursuits usually propose that such endeavors are represented as organized knowledge structures housed within a person's overall network of underlying associations. As a result, these structures can be activated in the same way that other concepts are activated. In other words, if appropriate cues are presented in the environment, these structures become activated; in turn, they operate toward completion, and both the activation and the operation can occur without the need for conscious awareness and/or maintenance.

As examples, consider two experiments. In one experiment, participants who were incidentally exposed to words related to the goal of achievement (e.g., succeed, attain, master), tended to perform better on a task, compared to participants who were not primed with the same words (Bargh, Gollwitzer, Lee-Chai, Barndollar, & Trotschel, 2001). In a second experiment, participants who were asked to concentrate on specific characteristics of a close friend, tended to express more willingness to help in a subsequent situation, compared to participants who were not asked to concentrate on characteristics of a friend (Fitzsimons & Bargh, 2003). In these experiments, the goals that were activated were achievement and helpfulness, respectively. In both cases, the goals apparently operated without the need for conscious awareness or maintenance.

In: Psychology Research Biographies and Summaries ISBN: 978-1-61470-491-1
Editors: Nancy E. Wodarth and Alexis P. Ferguson © 2012 Nova Science Publishers, Inc.

Chapter 157

PROCRASTINATION AND MOTIVATIONS FOR HOUSEHOLD SAFETY BEHAVIORS: AN EXPECTANCY-VALUE THEORY PERSPECTIVE

*Fuschia M. Sirois**
Department of Psychology, University of Windsor, Windsor, Canada

RESEARCH SUMMARY

Research into why individuals do or do not engage in important health behaviors is often approached from the perspective of expectancy-value theories of motivation. Such theories suggest that the motivation to engage in a behavior is regulated by the outcome expectancies for the behavior and the value of the outcome. However, the relationship of expectancies and values to stable individual differences known to affect motivation are often overlooked. In this chapter the links between procrastination, a behavioral style known to be linked to poor health behaviors, and household safety behaviors were examined using an expectancy-value theory (EVT) framework. Adults ($N = 254$) recruited from the community and the Internet completed self-report measures of procrastination, health self-efficacy, household safety behaviors, previous experiences with household accidents, and questions about the importance of keeping their homes free from potential accidents. Despite the fact that chronic procrastinators were more likely to have experienced a household accident that could have been prevented, procrastination was negatively related to the performance of household safety behaviors. Procrastination was also negatively related to health-self-efficacy and household safety value. Hierarchical regression testing the EVT variables found support for the predictive value of both outcome expectancies (self-efficacy) and value, but not their product, in explaining household safety behaviors after controlling for procrastination. Separate path analyses tested whether self-efficacy and valuing household safety mediated the relationship

---

* Correspondence concerning this article should be addressed to Fuschia M. Sirois, Ph.D. (Psychology), B.Sc. (Biochemistry/Nutrition), Department of Psychology, University of Windsor, 401 Sunset Ave., Windsor, Ontario, Canada   N9B 3P4. Tel: 1 519 253-3000, ext. 2224; Fax: 1 519 973-7021; E-mail: fsirois@uwindsor.ca.

between procrastination and household safety behaviors. Safety value and self-efficacy each partially mediated the procrastination-household safety behaviour relationship after controlling for procrastination. These findings suggest that EVT may be useful for explaining motivations for household safety behaviors in general, and may also provide insight into the lack of motivation for these behaviors demonstrated by procrastinators.

Chapter 158

STIMULUS AND INFORMATION SEEKING BEHAVIOR – A COMPARATIVE AND EVOLUTIONARY PERSPECTIVE

Wojciech Pisula[*]
Warsaw School of Social Psychology and Institute of Psychology,
Polish Academy of Sciences, Warsaw, Poland

RESEARCH SUMMARY

Organisms need information about their own organism's state, and about the surrounding in order to survive and reproduce. Even the simple organisms, such as protozoans utilize instantly available information that is provided by oncoming stimulation. The very first form of stimulus seeking – testing movements - develops in Platyhelminthes. The further evolution of stimulus seeking behavior is discussed in terms of the theory of integrative levels. The new qualities emerging at the developing levels of integration change both mechanisms of behavior, and it's form. The major steps of information seeking behavior evolution are: orienting reflex, locomotor exploration, investigatory responses, perceptual exploration, manipulatory responses, play, and cognitive curiosity. The analysis of each behavioral activity is conducted on the basis of comparative method. The cognitive activity is presented as an product of exploratory activity and play evolution. Therefore, the multi factorial nature of motivation of information seeking is finally discussed.

---

[*] Chodakowska 19/31; 03-815 Warsaw, Poland; wojciech.pisula@wp.pl.

Chapter 159

PSYCHOSOCIAL CORRELATES OF PERSONAL NORMS

K. P. H. Lemmens, R. A. C. Ruiter, I. J. T. Veldhuizen and H. P. Schaalma

Maastricht University; Sanquin Blood Bank, Southeast Region, The Netherlands

RESEARCH SUMMARY

Personal norms are the main motivator of intention to perform pro-social behaviour. They reflect the beliefs people have about what is right and what is wrong. Schwartz's norm activation model states that awareness of consequences and ascription of responsibility are related to personal norms, but it is not clear how, as the norm activation model can be interpreted as a moderator and a mediator model. In this chapter we compared both interpretations of the norm activation model and found that our data support a mediator model. This means that personal norms are influenced by awareness of consequences and ascription of responsibility. Targeting awareness of consequences and ascription of responsibility would activate personal norms which increases the behavioural intention.

In: Psychology Research Biographies and Summaries
Editors: Nancy E. Wodarth and Alexis P. Ferguson

ISBN: 978-1-61470-491-1
© 2012 Nova Science Publishers, Inc.

Chapter 160

STRATEGIES INVOLVED IN THE MOTIVATION OF INDIVIDUALS TO PURSUE TESTING TO DETERMINE THE PRESENCE OF HIV

Brad Donohue*, Courtney Irwin, John Fordham and Daniel N. Allen
Department of Psychology, University of Nevada, Las Vegas, US

RESEARCH SUMMARY

HIV has become a worldwide pandemic. Indeed, there are a number of factors that are involved in the transmission and progression of HIV to AIDS. Therefore, this chapter first identifies the various behaviors that have contributed to the risk of contracting HIV. Although HIV testing is an essential component in the detection and transmission of HIV, individuals who are most at-risk of contracting HIV often fail to pursue such testing. This is unfortunate because knowledge of one's seropositivity can assist in the management of this disease, and reduce transmission of HIV to others. This chapter will highlight scientific advances in the detection of HIV, as well as methods of motivating individuals to effectively manage this potentially fatal condition.

---

* Corresponding author. Bradley C. Donohue, Ph.D., Department of Psychology, University of Nevada Las Vegas, Box 455030, 4505 Maryland Parkway, Las Vegas, NV 89154-5030, USA. Tel.: +1.702.895.0181. FAX: +1.702.895.0195. E-mail: bradley.donohue@unlv.edu.

Chapter 161

MOTIVATIONAL INCONTINENCE: PHILOSOPHICAL VIEWS ACROSS THE GAP BETWEEN NORMATIVE BELIEFS AND ACTIONS

Suzie Ferrie
School of Biosciences, University of Sydney, Australia

RESEARCH SUMMARY

The familiar experience of a conflict between our actions and our normative beliefs was termed *akrasia* by the ancient Greeks. Philosophical theories of akrasia are helpful in illuminating situations of unwilling addiction as well as other disorders of motivation. The phenomenon of akrasia creates problems for theories of rational action, and this difficulty has meant that some philosophical approaches to akrasia have been forced to deny that akrasia really exists at all. If genuine akrasia is to be adequately characterised, it may be helpful to examine these attempts and their outcomes.

Chapter 162

COMMUNITY PSYCHOANALYSIS: DEVELOPING A MODEL OF PSYCHOANALYTICALLY-INFORMED COMMUNITY CRISIS INTERVENTION

Mark B. Borg, Jr. [*]
**Community Consulting Group, New York,
William Alanson White Institute, New York, US**

RESEARCH SUMMARY

In this chapter I define and illustrate key concepts, practices and intervention strategies from the seemingly disparate fields of community psychology and psychoanalysis (specifically, relational/interpersonal psychoanalysis). Through a number of examples from my own work as both a clinical psychoanalyst and community practitioner, I hope to illustrate how a useful intersection has been, and can be, developed to cross-pollinate and enliven the practice of community crisis intervention (as well as how such work can also be usefully applied to clinical psychoanalysis itself). I present an overview of key psychoanalytic and community psychology concepts, such as transference, countertransference, enactment, empowerment and primary prevention, and show through a number of examples how these undergird the development of a psychoanalytic approach to community crisis intervention. I will present a number of new concepts—*community character*, *point of impact*, and *project group methodology*—which I will then use in describing the development of a model of psychoanalytically-informed community crisis intervention. I will also reverse the lens and utilize the community psychoanalytic concepts to illuminate clinical work with individual patients.

---

[*] Corresponding author: Community Consulting Group, 156 Fifth Avenue, Suite 725, New York, NY 10010, TEL: (212) 978-0266, FAX: (212) 741-1697, Email: oedtrex@aol.com.

In: Psychology Research Biographies and Summaries
Editors: Nancy E. Wodarth and Alexis P. Ferguson
ISBN: 978-1-61470-491-1
© 2012 Nova Science Publishers, Inc.

Chapter 163

SOCIAL REPRESENTATIONS: THE HEART OF COMMUNITY PSYCHOLOGY[*,†]

Inari Sakki, Raul Kassea, Teemu Vauhkonen and Anna-Maija Pirttilä-Backman
University of Helsinki, Finland

RESEARCH SUMMARY

Social representations are at the heart of communal psychology for several reasons: they are people's understanding of the topical issues and their contexts, because by definition they are the everyday theories that people form of new and threatening issues. The theory of social representations acknowledges the interconnections between perception, thinking, emotions, values, norms and action. The approach is also open to a variety of data gathering and analyzing methods. All this means that it is optimally wired to deal with people's everyday experiences.

Everyday theories are formulated in day-to-day interaction, but they also have their roots in history and they get new material from the mass media. The theory introduces three processes in the formation of social representations: anchoring, objectification and naturalization. By making a distinction between the nucleus and the periphery of the representations, the theory also gives important new insights into why changes are sometimes so difficult to achieve. This also means that the theory is very useful in the promotion of change.

Results from our own studies done in Cameroon concentrating on women's roles and positions will be used to demonstrate the specific aspects of the theory and its usability.

---

[*] Some parts of this chapter have been previously presented and discussed in Pirttilä-Backman, Sakki and Kassea in Järventie, Paavonen and Lähde (Eds.) (2006) and in Kassea (2006). They are reproduced with the permission of the publishers.

[†] This study has been financially supported by Academy of Finland, grant number 47724.

In: Psychology Research Biographies and Summaries
Editors: Nancy E. Wodarth and Alexis P. Ferguson
ISBN: 978-1-61470-491-1
© 2012 Nova Science Publishers, Inc.

Chapter 164

HEALTH, SOCIAL AND EDUCATIONAL IMPACTS OF TWO FLOOD DISASTERS IN ENGLAND: PSYCHOLOGICAL PROCESSES, COMMUNITY RESPONSES AND STRATEGIES

Bob Carroll, Ian Convery, Ruth Balogh, Hazel Morbey and Gonzalo Araoz
University of Cumbria, England

RESEARCH SUMMARY

This paper will draw upon two studies by the authors. The first is a study of the health and social impacts of the floods in Carlisle, England (Carroll et al, 2006) and the second is a study of the impact on schools of the 2007 floods in Kingston Upon Hull (k/a Hull), England. The findings of the Carlisle study revealed that there was severe flooding in 1600 homes and 400 businesses and important buildings housing the City Council, utility services and the emergency services. There was severe disruption to people's lives and many suffered psychological health issues. These are examined under symptoms, stressors and coping mechanisms. The part played by community organisations and the value of the community is identified. The Hull study of the impact of the floods revealed that most of the 90 schools were affected in some way. The impact upon schools, head teachers, staff and pupils and the coping mechanisms and place of the school in the community are identified. The commitment and dedication to the task of recovery by the staff, often at personal expense, is revealed as part of identifying with the school and loyalty to the school and wider community. The importance of the school as a stable force in the community and in community resilience is shown. The psychological processes of identity, attachment, alienation, dialectics and resilience are examined in the context of both studies. Community responses by health authorities are proposed for psychological health recovery. The part played by community agencies in resilience is examined and proposals for empowerment and cooperation between community and local and national agencies.

In: Psychology Research Biographies and Summaries
Editors: Nancy E. Wodarth and Alexis P. Ferguson
ISBN: 978-1-61470-491-1
© 2012 Nova Science Publishers, Inc.

Chapter 165

How do we Teach them? Using Self-Help Support Groups to Promote Knowledge Translation

*Ann Dadich**
Centre for Industry and Innovation Studies (CInIS),
University of Western Sydney, Australia

Research Summary

Knowledge translation holds a pivotal place in the mental health care sector. For the individual consumer, it can facilitate the adoption of strategies that promote wellbeing. This in turn can alleviate clinician workload and optimise the efficient use of limited resources within a service.

Despite the associated benefits, knowledge translation remains limited in the mental health care sector. Whether a consequence of time and/or capacity, clinicians do not consistently convey to their patients information about strategies that promote wellbeing. This can have significant consequences, including poor patient outcomes; additional burden on time-poor clinicians; and the inappropriate use of under-resourced services.

Given these consequences, it is essential to identify avenues that can facilitate knowledge translation, particularly among consumers of mental health services. One such avenue is the self-help support group (SHSG).

Self-help support groups have much to offer people with mental health issues. In addition to being financially accessible, participants have been found to experience behavioural and cognitive improvements, as well as spiritual transformation. Research also demonstrates relationships between group involvement and reduced psychiatric symptoms, reduced hospitalisation rates, reduced reliance on medication and community services, and a reduction in the financial cost attributed to these services.

---

* Corresponding author: Email: A.Dadich@uws.edu.au, Telephone: +61 +2 9685 9475.

An additional benefit of SHSGs is their role in knowledge translation. This was indicated in a study exploring the group experiences of young people. The study involved 53 young people, aged 15 to 31 years, all of who had accessed a SHSG to address a mental health issue.

Among the benefits associated with SHSGs, the young people spoke of opportunities to increase their mental health literacy (Jorm, et al., 1997). Through group participation, they became relatively more aware of the signs and symptoms associated with mental illness; the treatments and services available to them; as well as strategies – or *tricks of the trade*, that help to promote and/or maintain wellbeing. As such, the young people acquired 'knowledge and beliefs about mental disorders which aid their recognition, management or prevention'.

Given their capacity to enhance mental health literacy, this chapter argues that SHSGs represent an innovative way to facilitate knowledge translation. Services wanting to communicate to patients information about treatments and therapies, might find value in working with existing groups, or supporting new ones. Included as part of a suite of strategies towards knowledge translation, SHSGs have the potential to promote patient wellbeing, and in turn, alleviate the burden placed on time-poor clinicians and under-resourced services.

Chapter 166

The Promise and Challenge of Applying Community Psychology's Praxis of Empowerment to the Burgeoning Field of Community-Based Conservation

*Daniel A. DeCaro**
Department of Psychology, Miami University, 100 Psychology Building, Oxford, OH, US

Research Summary

The United Nations (2009) lists the eradication of poverty, oppression of women, and inadequate education, health and child care – causes to which community psychology is inextricably devoted – as among the world's most pressing social issues. Using natural resource conservation as a stepping stone, conservationists have recently begun to develop community-centered methods to confront these very problems (Western & Wright, 1994). However, the movement faces many implementation challenges, ranging from a lack of guiding frameworks, research methods, and concrete interventions of empowerment to an inability to garner community support (Brockington et al., 2006; Stankey & Shindler, 2006). In this commentary, I argue that community-based conservation and the stakeholders it serves are in dire need of psychological science (Jacobson & McDuff, 1998) and a psychology of community in particular (DeCaro & Stokes, 2008). Drawing on my experience working among conservation biologists and subsistence farmers in Kenya, I discuss how community psychology is uniquely situated to make a significant positive impact simply by partnering with the burgeoning community-based conservation movement. In surveying the potential for collaboration, I point out the promising theoretical, empirical, and practical benefits of collaboration, provide concrete recommendations for collaboration, and identify key challenges such work should address. My hope is that this commentary will not only draw

---

* Corresponding author: E-mail: decaroda@muohio.edu, Phone: 513-529-2400, Fax: 513-529-2420.

attention to an important opportunity but will also provide a useful roadmap for a critical community psychology in developing nations.

Chapter 167

FAMILY PSYCHO-SOCIAL FACTORS IMPACTING PARENT'S OWN CURRENT LIFE PERCEPTION IN FAMILIES OF CHILDREN WITH LEUKEMIA DURING THEIR FIRST HOSPITALIZATION

Marta Tremolada[1], Sabrina Bonichini[1], Marta Pillon[2] and Modesto Carli[2]

[1]Department of Developmental and Social Psychology, University of Padova, Italy
[2]Department of Paediatrics, Oncology Hematology Division, University, Hospital of Padova, Italy

RESEARCH SUMMARY

Background: It has been repeatedly shown that social support seems to be a key factor in dealing with the experience of pediatric cancer diagnosis and treatment. Studies have shown that lack of perceived social support is associated with increased risk for development of post-traumatic stress symptoms. Previous research has failed to report statistically significant correlations between parental coping and the sociodemographic and illness-related variables it examined.

Aim: This study aims to explore what happens to the parent's own current life perception in relation to their child's disease factors and to family psycho-social factors in the second week after the diagnosis communication.

Method: Patients were 118 leukemic children and their families recruited at the Haematology-Oncologic Clinic of the Department of Pediatrics, University of Padova. All parents were Caucasian with a mean age of 37.39 years (SD = 6.03). Most parents had 13 years of school (50.8%); 32.2% had 8 years; 5.9% had a college education; 9.3% had a degree or diploma; and 1.7% had 5 years of school. The parents who participated were mostly mothers (N = 101) and only a few were fathers (N = 17) because the mothers were more proximal to the child during hospitalization while fathers stayed with other siblings or continued to work to maintain the family. Children's mean age was 5.89 years (SD = 4.21, range = 1 year–17 years). Most of the children had Acute Lymphoblastic Leukemia (ALL) (N = 98), while 20 had Acute Myeloid Leukemia (AML).

The families were contacted by a clinical psychologist during the first hospitalization of their children. Project aims were explained and informed consent was requested. The parents were interviewed in a separate room of the Clinic adopting Ecocultural Family Interview-Cancer (Tremolada et al., 2005) from which we derived 8 family Psycho-Social Factors (including Social Support) and the Life Stress Events. The Ladder of Life (CCSS) and SES questionnaires were compiled by parents during the child's first hospitalization.

Results: Life perception was really low at this time, even if there was a big standard deviation that underlined the variability of the parent's emotive state. A hierarchical regression model identified the Child's Diagnosis, Child's Age, Parent's Age and Social Support as factors that impacted upon the parents' Current Life Perception.

Discussion: Child's diagnosis, child's age, parent's age and social support impact upon parents' current life perceptions. In detail, parents of children with AML perceive a worse life than parents of children with ALL. The increasing age of the child is positively associated with her/his evolutionary coping strategies so to help parents in their caregiver role. For this purpose we may also discuss that older parents can have more experience to care for children and that they can be more "expert" in their parenting role in this difficult time. Finally, social support is confirmed as a valid resource to help parents coping with the child's illness, especially in this acute time.

Chapter 168

THE QUALITY OF PARTICIPATION IN THE PERCEPTION OF CITIZENS: FINDINGS FROM A QUALITATIVE STUDY

Terri Mannarini[1] *and Angela Fedi*[2]
[1]University of Salento, Italy
[2]University of Turin, Italy

RESEARCH SUMMARY

Although in the last decade top-down participatory settings (e.g., citizen juries, deliberative polls, participatory budgeting, open space technology, etc.) have increased in type and number, not many qualitative studies exploring the subjective experience of participants are available in community psychology literature. Nevertheless, given the role of public involvement in promoting virtuous development processes, investigating the motivation, expectations, beliefs and feelings of the citizens involved in public participatory settings can contribute to make them successful and attractive. This chapter explores the experience of people taking part in three consultative arenas. Twelve participants involved in three different Open Space Technology settings were interviewed. They were asked to report on their feelings, perceived cost, benefits, and outcomes, as well as to elaborate on the concept of participation, and on their relationship with politics and political institutions. The main findings can be summarized as follows: a) the issue addressed in the specific participatory setting and the presence and relevance of the institutions made individuals differently perceive and narrate their experience; b) participants were likely to underestimate the problematic facets of participation, and specifically the power issue; c) the concept of participation was tightly connected to the notion of "citizen identity"; d) commitment towards the "public" characterized the majority of participants, instead of the traditional commitment towards the "group"; d) the OST settings were likely to empower people at the individual rather than at the collective level.

Chapter 169

School as a Resilient Context for Resilient African American Youth

Anne Gregory[1] and Robert Jagers[2]
[1] Rutgers University, US
[2] University of Michigan, US

Research Summary

Jason waits outside the door of the assistant principal's office. He has been sent by his English teacher for "defiance" and "disruption." Jason is familiar with what will happen next. This is the third time he has been sent to the office. The door opens and a rushed assistant principal looks at Jason with disapproval and ushers him into her office.

In: Psychology Research Biographies and Summaries ISBN: 978-1-61470-491-1
Editors: Nancy E. Wodarth and Alexis P. Ferguson © 2012 Nova Science Publishers, Inc.

Chapter 170

MEETING THE MENTAL HEALTH AND COMMUNITY CARE NEEDS OF ASYLUM SEEKERS AND REFUGEES IN SWITZERLAND: INTEGRATING SOCIAL AND POLITICAL CONCERNS IN CLINICAL PRACTICE

Betty Goguikian Ratcliff
Faculty of Psychology and Educational Sciences,
University of Geneva and Appartenances-Genève, Switzerland.

RESEARCH SUMMARY

The phenomenon of forced migration has become one of the world's major problems. Several armed conflicts around the planet, both within and between nations, have created an increasing number of asylum seekers, refugees and displaced persons (Thiollet, 2009). Therefore, during the last two decades, the provision of appropriate health and social care for the victims of organized violence has become a major focus of concern (Ingleby, 2005).

In western countries, the idea that prevention and care should be provided to victims of organized violence is now generally accepted, as this group has proved to be « at risk » (Mollica, Caspi-Yavin, 1992; Silove, Sinnerbrink, Field, Manicavasagar, Steel, 1997). However, several specific difficulties in dealing with these culturally diverse populations have been pointed out. First of them is how to improve the access to health services; second, how to address language and communication barriers (Bolton, 2002; Jacobs, Chen, Karliner, Agger-Gupta, Mutha, 2006); third, how to train professionals to recognize and deal with the illness of people from different backgrounds and perspectives (Helman, 2005) ; fourth, how to decide what kind of care is needed and has a chance to succeed, *i.e.* the intervention level (somatic, psychological, social-administrative, communitarian) when different problems are present at the same time (Ingleby, 2005 ; Goguikian Ratcliff, in press).

Furthermore, the issue of cultural validity of the assumptions and models underlying our evaluation and therapeutic practices has stirred considerable controversy (Kleinman, Eisenberg, Good, 2006). As a matter of fact, when dealing with immigrant populations, health care services have to face a considerable level of drop-outs and/or non-compliant behaviours, which points to a poor degree of consensus and satisfaction with the help proposed (Karliner Jacobs, Chen, Mutha 2006; Bughra, 2004, Fernando, 2005). As professionals become aware of the difficulties of practising in an intercultural context, the need for more theoretical conceptualization in order to build integrative and alternative approaches is starting to come to the fore.

This chapter aims to present the experience gained during fifteen years of practice in *Appartenances*, an innovative mental health service for migrants in Switzerland. After describing the historical and political background that led to the creation of this association, we discuss the development and activities of the Geneva regional office during the last decade. Finally, we identify some « good practices » in this area and describe our intervention program, which integrates social and political issues in clinical practice.

In: Psychology Research Biographies and Summaries
Editors: Nancy E. Wodarth and Alexis P. Ferguson

ISBN: 978-1-61470-491-1
© 2012 Nova Science Publishers, Inc.

Chapter 171

AGGRESSIVE BEHAVIOR OF DRIVERS: A NEW QUESTIONNAIRE DEFINING THE DIFFERENCE BETWEEN HOSTILE AND INSTRUMENTAL BEHAVIOR WHILE DRIVING

*Lipaz Shamoa-Nir and Meni Koslowsky**
Department of Psychology, Bar-Ilan University, Israel

RESEARCH SUMMARY

As part of an investigation of commuting stress, a new tool was developed for differentiating between two types of aggressive behavior in drivers: instrumental and hostile. The questionnaires evaluate aggressive behavior by measuring the level of aggression of each behavior and categorizing the behavior as instrumental or hostile. Two studies were conducted. In the first one, participants (N=104) received a questionnaire in which items culled from each aggression domain were tested along with attributes such as gender, age, driving experience; and previous involvement in a driving incident (a road accident or traffic ticket). Analysis showed that the questionnaire's internal consistency was high for each aggression type and age comparisons for the two measures were found to be significant. In the second study, analysis of the data (N=326) enabled us to refine the operational definition of aggressive driving and to sharpen the distinction between the two types of aggression. Theoretical and practical perspectives of the instrument were discussed.

---

* Corresponding author: Phone: +972-3-5317945 Fax: +972-3-5350206, Email: koslow@mail.biu.ac.il.

In: Psychology Research Biographies and Summaries
Editors: Nancy E. Wodarth and Alexis P. Ferguson
ISBN: 978-1-61470-491-1
© 2012 Nova Science Publishers, Inc.

Chapter 172

THE RHIZOMATIC POTENTIAL IN/FOR/OF COMMUNITY PSYCHOLOGY

Mark B. Borg, Jr.[*]
Community Consulting Group, New York, US
William Alanson White Institute, New York, US

RESEARCH SUMMARY

A *rhizome* is a root-like subterranean stem, commonly horizontal in position, which tends to produce roots below and send up shoots progressively to the upper surface. The term *rhizomatic* describes an approach to/perspective on theory and research that allows for multiple, non-hierarchical entry and exit points in data representation and interpretation—as opposed to an *arborescent* conception of knowledge, which works with dualist categories and binary choices. In this chapter, the author suggests that through its emphasis on collaboration, empowerment praxis can—and does—operate as a rhizome, forming and maintaining a multitude of productive connections, at bare minimum, between community stakeholders and community practitioners. Rhizomatic functioning confronts the notion of community as a hierarchic *whole*, and puts into circulation the *sense of community* as a complex, open network of networks which create/enable the potential for multitudinous—often unthought-of, alien, and super-molecular—connections.

---

[*] Corresponding author: Community Consulting Group, 156 Fifth Avenue, Suite 725, New York, NY 10010, TEL: (212) 978-0266, FAX: (212) 741-1697, Email: oedtrex@aol.com.

In: Psychology Research Biographies and Summaries
Editors: Nancy E. Wodarth and Alexis P. Ferguson
ISBN: 978-1-61470-491-1
© 2012 Nova Science Publishers, Inc.

Chapter 173

LIMITS TO GENERAL EXPERTISE: A STUDY OF IN- AND OUT-OF-FIELD GRAPH INTERPRETATION

Wolff-Michael Roth
University of Victoria
British Columbia, Canada

RESEARCH SUMMARY

Graphs are pervasive features in professional science journals, which makes graphing one of (if not the) most important practice (and therefore skill) of professional science. Scientists generally are expected to be experts in graphing. Contrary to this expectation, recent investigations showed that scientists asked to interpret graphs from introductory-level textbooks in their own field did not at all exhibit expert-like behavior. The present study was designed to understand better the nature of graphing practices among professional scientists. I investigated the similarities and differences in scientists' interpretation of structurally identical in-field and out-of-field graphs. Seventeen physicists interpreted 3 graphs that were derived from entry-level university textbooks in ecology—for cross validation purposes, these were the same graphs used in an earlier expert-expert study—and 3 structurally identical graphs from the field of physics. My analyses reveal that the graphing expertise of physicists is limited even within their field. Their graph interpretations are highly idiosyncratic and contingent both within and across content domains. Common to the interpretive practices on in-field and out-of field graph was that scientists interpreted them according to the purposes of (a) graphing in science in general and (b) those of the graph interpretation interview session specifically. In using varying resources and in experiencing breakdowns, they exhibited considerable differences between in-field and out-of-field graph interpretations. Working on in-field graphs, they drew on general knowledge and prior experiences from their professional life, whereas in the context of out-of-field graph interpretations, scientists provided verbal equivalents for the visible, surface features of the line graphs and drew on mundane everyday life experiences to explicate them.

In: Psychology Research Biographies and Summaries
Editors: Nancy E. Wodarth and Alexis P. Ferguson
ISBN: 978-1-61470-491-1
© 2012 Nova Science Publishers, Inc.

Chapter 174

CONCEPTUAL COMBINATION: MODELS, THEORIES, AND CONTROVERSIES

Bing Ran[1,] and P. Robert Duimering[2,†]*

[1]School of Public Affairs, Pennsylvania State University at Harrisburg
Middletown, PA, US

[2]Department of Management Sciences, University of Waterloo
Waterloo, Ontario, Canada

RESEARCH SUMMARY

This paper provides a comprehensive and critical review of the major theories and models of conceptual combination, by highlighting agreements and controversies in the literature, and identifying future directions for research. The review summarizes the basic arguments of ten major models and then presents an analytical framework to compare and contrast these models along four dimensions: (1) the causal role of schemata in the model; (2) the role of cognitive harmony or consistency in the model; (3) the pragmatic orientation in the model; and (4) the explanatory scope of the model. The review identifies areas of agreement and disagreement among the various models and theories and calls for a synthesis theory to address various theoretical weaknesses and empirical gaps in the current explanations.

---

[*] Tel: +1 717 948 6057; Fax: +1 717 948 6320 Email: bingran@psu.edu.
[†] Tel: +1 519 888 4567 ext. 2831; Fax: +1 519 746 7252 Email: rduimering@uwaterloo.ca.

In: Psychology Research Biographies and Summaries
Editors: Nancy E. Wodarth and Alexis P. Ferguson
ISBN: 978-1-61470-491-1
© 2012 Nova Science Publishers, Inc.

Chapter 175

A Test of the Cognitive Theory of Obsessions: Study of Internal Structure and Validity of the Obsessive Beliefs Questionnaire in Italian Individuals

Stella Dorz[*,1,4], *Caterina Novara*[1], *Massimiliano Pastore*[2], *Ezio Sanavio*[1], *Luigi Rocco Chiri*[3] *and Claudio Sica*[3]

[1]Department of General Psychology, University of Padova, Italy
[2]Department of Developmental and Social Psychology, University of Padova, Italy
[3]Department of Psychology University of Firenze, Italy
[4]Casa di Cura Parco dei Tigli, Private Clinic (Padova), Italy

Research Summary

Background: A widely-held belief is that obsessions arise from the misinterpretation of normal intrusive thoughts (e.g., misinterpreting unwanted harm-related thoughts as a sign that one is going to act on them). This leads the person to perform compulsions such as repeated checking. Misinterpretations are said to arise from various types of beliefs (e.g., the belief that thoughts inevitably give rise to actions). In support of this theory, some studies have shown that such beliefs are correlated with obsessive-compulsive disorder (OCD). The Obsessive Beliefs Questionnaire (OBQ) is an 87-item self-report instrument developed by an international group (Obsessive Compulsive Cognitions Working Group - OCCWG) to assess cognitions thought to be relevant to the etiology and maintenance of obsessions and compulsions. The OBQ contains six scales measuring as many dysfunctional beliefs: Inflated responsibility, Overimportance of thoughts. Excessive concern about the importance of controlling one's thoughts, Overestimation of threat, Intolerance of uncertainty, and

---

[*] Stella Dorz, Dipartimento di Psicologia Generale, University of Padua, via Venezia, 8, 35131 Padova, Italy (049-8276600) or Casa di Cura Parco dei Tigli, via Monticello, 1, 35037 Teolo-Padova, Italy (fax. 049-9997549). Email: stella.dorz@unipd.it.

Perfectionism. To date, the OBQ has been mainly studied in clinical and non-clinical individuals drawn from English-speaking populations. Results showed that the questionnaire generally has a good internal consistency (Cronbach alpha coefficients equal or above .80) and an adequate test-retest reliability. However, three OBQ domains (Tolerance of uncertainty, Overestimation of threat and Perfectionism) appeared to be OCD-relevant but not OCD-specific, since they did not discriminate individuals with OCD from anxiety controls. In addition, correlations with measures of OCD symptoms, mood and worry, showed that the OBQ was as highly correlated with the non-OCD symptom measures (anxiety, depression and worry) as it was with OCD ones. Lastly, an exploratory factor analysis revealed that a three-factor solution best explained the internal structure of the questionnaire. In summary, such results raise doubts about the cognitive theory of obsessions and compulsions even though more studies are needed before the theory can be reformulated.

Aims and method: The present paper reports on the Italian validation of the OBQ: the extent to which the psychometric properties of the OBQ (and, in particular, its internal structure) are equivalent to the original one may reveal interesting clues about the structure of beliefs and their relationships with OCD symptoms. The OBQ was administered to 752 Italian undergraduate students along with the Padua Inventory (a measure of OCD symptoms), the Beck Anxiety Inventory and the Beck Depression Inventory.

Results: exploratory factor analyses did not replicate the original six-factor structure of the OBQ, nor the three-factor structure obtained by analyizing the original American sample. A confirmatory factor analysis revelead that the Italian version of the OBQ was best described by five factors and 46 items. In particular, the Italian version was characterized by the absence of the intolerance of uncertainty and overestimation of threat scales, and by the subdivision of the responsibility scale into the scales responsibility for harm and responsibility for omission. Internal consistency and temporal stability of the five scales of Italian version of the OBQ was satisfactorily; intercorrelations among the five scales were moderately high. Results from convergent and discriminant validity revealed that Perfectionism, Responsibility for harm and Control thoughts resulted good predictors of OCD symptoms, whereas Responsibility of omission and Importance of thoughts did not predict OCD symptoms at all in a regression analysis model.

Findings were discussed in terms of relevance and specificity of cognitive constructs to OCD symptoms.

In: Psychology Research Biographies and Summaries
Editors: Nancy E. Wodarth and Alexis P. Ferguson
ISBN: 978-1-61470-491-1
© 2012 Nova Science Publishers, Inc.

Chapter 176

HAPTIC ABILITIES IN INFANCY AND THEIR RELATION TO VISION: A REVIEW

Arlette Streri[1]
Université Paris Descartes, France

RESEARCH SUMMARY

The old debate concerning the primitive unity (nativist conception) or the separation (empiricist conception) of senses at birth has been revived in recent years, as difficulties in the methodology of studying perception in babies were overcome. How can babies know by touch? To answer to this question, three aspects of human infants' haptic abilities are presented in this review. How the young babies: 1. Perceive information and form a perceptual representation of objects derived from the hands alone; 2. Transfer this information to vision in an intermodal process; 3. Obtain haptic knowledge in limited exploration conditions as they do in the visual modality? Using a habituation/dishabituation procedure, experiments have revealed that infants, from birth, are able to discriminate object shapes in the manual as well as in the visual mode. These abilities are a prerequisite for understanding the relations between the haptic and the visual sensory modalities in cross-modal transfer tasks. Using an intersensory successive preference procedure, several experiments provided evidence for cross-modal recognition from touch to vision from birth. The links however are limited, partial and not reciprocal. Nevertheless, adaptations of paradigms for studying visual cognition reveal that the haptic system shares some amodal mechanisms with the visual modality. Despite various discrepancies between both modalities, conceiving the world is possible with the hands as well as the eyes soon after birth.

---

[1] Address for correspondence: Arlette Streri, "Laboratory for Psychology of Perception" UMR. 8158, centre Biomédical des Saints-Pères - 45, rue des Sts Pères 75270 Paris cedex 06 France Email: arlette.streri@parisdescartes.fr.

In: Psychology Research Biographies and Summaries
Editors: Nancy E. Wodarth and Alexis P. Ferguson

ISBN: 978-1-61470-491-1
© 2012 Nova Science Publishers, Inc.

Chapter 177

EMOTIONAL MODULATION OF SELECTIVE ATTENTION: EXPERIMENTAL EVIDENCE IN SPECIFIC PHOBIA

Marlen Figueroa[1], Sonia Rodríguez-Ruiz[*,1], José L. Mata[1,2], Walter Machado-Pinheiro[3] and Jaime Vila[1]

[1]University of Granada, Granada, Spain
[2]University of Jaén, Jaén, Spain
[3]Federal Fluminense University, Rio de Janeiro, Brazil

RESEARCH SUMMARY

Empirical research has demonstrated that emotional information is rapidly and extensively processed and that assessment of that information takes place automatically, outside of conscious awareness (Edelstein & Guillath, 2008). This processing bias presumably occurs in conditions that require the healthy or anxious individual to scan the enviroment for information (Mathews & MacLeod, 1994). So, the attention is captured by, or shifted towards, emotionally relevant stimuli. Multiple factors can explain how emotion drives attention. This chapter throws light on some of these factors.

---

[*] Departamento de Personalidad, Evaluación y Tratamiento Psicológico Facultad de Psicología Universidad de Granada Campus de la Cartuja s/n 18071, Granada (Spain) Phone: (+ 34) 958 24 37 53 (Lab) (+ 34) 958 24 62 50 (Office) Fax: (+ 34) 958 24 37 49 E-mail: srruiz@ugr.es.

In: Psychology Research Biographies and Summaries
Editors: Nancy E. Wodarth and Alexis P. Ferguson
ISBN: 978-1-61470-491-1
© 2012 Nova Science Publishers, Inc.

Chapter 178

THE MODERATING EFFECT OF SWITCHING COSTS IN CONSUMERS' RELATIONSHIP DISSOLUTION: A CROSS-CULTURAL ANALYSIS

Carmen Antón Martín[*] *and Carmen Camarero Izquierdo*[†]
Department of Business and Marketing, University of Valladolid, Spain

RESEARCH SUMMARY

The current work analyzes the impact of deficiencies in firms' policies on the customers' intent to break the relationship and the moderating role of switching costs. The work is developed in the context of car insurance services. Concretely, in this context, we differentiate two legal situations that can influence the dissolution process: the countries where consumers comply with the legal obligation to take out car insurance and the countries where consumers feel that the legislation is more permissive and fail to comply with the legal obligation. A comparison of consumers from these two contexts (Spanish and Venezuelan consumers) allows us to derive some conclusions.

---

[*] Tel: +34-983-42-34-13, Fax: +34-983-42-38-99 E-mail: anton@eco.uva.es.
[†] Tel: +34-983-42-33-32, Fax: +34-983-42-38-99. E-mail: camarero@eco.uva.es.

Chapter 179

TRIPARTITE CONCEPTS OF MIND AND BRAIN, WITH SPECIAL EMPHASIS ON THE NEUROEVOLUTIONARY POSTULATES OF CHRISTFRIED JAKOB AND PAUL MACLEAN

Lazaros C. Triarhou[*]

Economo–Koskinas Wing for Integrative and Evolutionary Neuroscience,
University of Macedonia, Thessaloniki, Greece

RESEARCH SUMMARY

The 'triune brain', conceived by Paul D. MacLean (1913–2007) in the late 1960s, has witnessed more attention and controversy than any other evolutionary model of brain and behavior in modern neuroscience. Decades earlier, in his book *Elements of Neurobiology* published in 1923 in La Plata, Argentina, neurobiologist Christfried (Christofredo) Jakob (1866–1956) had formulated a 'tripsychic' brain system, based on his deep understanding of biological and neural phylogeny. In a historical context, 1923 was also the year of publication of Sigmund Freud's *The Ego and the Id*, whereby the founder of psychoanalysis solidified his tripartite model of the mental apparatus. Tripartite systems of the human mind have been surmised since Plato and Aristotle; they continue to our era, an example being Robert J. Sternberg's triarchic theory of human intelligence. In view of the fact that both Jakob and MacLean invested a considerable part of their long and distinguished careers studying comparative, and particularly reptilian neurobiology, the present article revisits their neuroevolutionary models, underlining the convergence of their anatomical-functional propositions, in spite of a time distance of almost half a century.

---

[*] E-mail address: triarhou@uom.gr, phone +30 2310 891-387, fax +30 2310 891-388.

Chapter 180

CATEGORY-SPECIFIC SEMANTICS IN ALZHEIMER'S DEMENTIA AND NORMAL AGING?

Keith R. Laws[*,1], *Tim M. Gale*[1,2,3], *F. Javier Moreno-Martínez*[4], *Rebecca L. Adlington*[1], *Karen Irvine*[1] *and Sunil Sthanakiya*[1]

[1] School of Psychology, University of Hertfordshire, UK
[2] Department of Psychiatry, QEII Hospital, Welwyn Garden City, UK
[3] School of Computer Science, University of Hertfordshire, UK
[4] Departamento de Psicología Básica I, U.N.E.D. Madrid, Spain

RESEARCH SUMMARY

Category-specific deficits represent the archetypal illustration of domain-specific cognitive processes. These deficits describe individuals who, following certain types of neurological damage show dissociations in their ability to recognise and name exemplars from within specific domains e.g. living or nonliving things. Cases described over the past 25 years have formed a pivotal foundation for the development of models describing the structure and organisation of lexical-semantic memory. In this chapter, we review the evidence on whether category deficits in AD are consistent with the loss of isolated categorical information, an artefact of confounding psycholinguistic variables (e.g. age of acquisition, word frequency, and familiarity) or an exaggeration of some pre-existing normal cognitive difference. Finally, we present emerging evidence that female AD patients show worse semantic memory impairment than male patients. In this context, we discuss a possible role for the apolipoprotein E (APOE) ε4 allele, which is associated with a greater probability for developing AD in women and impacts more on the cognitive performance of healthy women than men.

---

[*] University of Hertfordshire College LaneHatfield, Hertfordshire AL10 9AB, UK.

In: Psychology Research Biographies and Summaries
Editors: Nancy E. Wodarth and Alexis P. Ferguson
ISBN: 978-1-61470-491-1
© 2012 Nova Science Publishers, Inc.

Chapter 181

PREVERBAL CATEGORY FORMATION
THE ROLE OF REAL-WORLD EXPERIENCE

Birgit Träuble[*], *Lysett Babocsai and Sabina Pauen*
University of Heidelberg, Germany

RESEARCH SUMMARY

Studies on categorization using the object-examination task (OET) show that infants carry out a global-to-basic level shift in their second half of their first year of life. What underlies performance in the OET still remains unclear, however. Following one view, infants in an OET activate previously acquired knowledge about real-world exemplars. This suggests that categorization performance in the OET should vary with the amount of experience infants have with real-world exemplars displayed by the experimental material. The present studies test this hypothesis, by comparing the categorization performance of infants who do not have regular contact to cats or dogs (Experiment 1) with the performance of infants who live with a cat or a dog at home (Experiment 2). Analyses based on data from $N = 80$ 9- and 11-month-old infants reveal that 11-months-olds who have experience with cats or dogs make a clear categorical distinction whereas infants without such experiences do not show any categorization response. This set of findings suggests that experience with real-world animals influences performance of infants participating in an OET providing a basic-level contrast within the animate domain.

---

[*] University of Heidelberg Hauptstrasse 47-51 D-69117 Heidelberg, Germany Tel. +49 (0)6221 54-7347 Fax +49 (0)6221 54-7326 E-mail: birgit.traeuble@psychologie.uni-heidelberg.de.

In: Psychology Research Biographies and Summaries
Editors: Nancy E. Wodarth and Alexis P. Ferguson
ISBN: 978-1-61470-491-1
© 2012 Nova Science Publishers, Inc.

Chapter 182

PERIPHERAL RESPONSES ELICITED BY MOTOR IMAGERY: A WINDOW ON CENTRAL AND PERIPHERAL NERVOUS SYSTEM RELATIONSHIPS THROUGH MOTOR COMMANDS INHIBITION

C. Collet and A. Guillot[*]
University of Lyon, Claude Bernard University, Lyon, France

RESEARCH SUMMARY

The aim of this paper was to examine the way in which motor commands addressed to the somatic and autonomic effectors are inhibited during Motor Imagery (MI). Three experiments are described, each referring to specific motor requirements. The first requested the participants to lift a weighted dumbbell with their preferential hand (flexion of the forearm), while seating in a chair. In the second task, the participants were asked to perform 3 consecutive vertical jumps on a force plate, while the third was a coincidence anticipation task requiring intercepting a table-tennis ball thrown by a robot, with the inner side of the hand. All were performed under actual vs. mental practice. In the first experiment, a subliminal muscular activity was recorded during MI, which was specific to the type of muscle contraction. In the second experiment, MI was shown to reduce postural sway amplitude in the standing position on both the anterior-posterior and the lateral axes compared to the control condition (standing motionless on the force plate). In the third experiment, the autonomic responses recorded during MI showed the same pattern that those recorded during actual movement. While performing MI, the 3 motor commands were thus shown to be affected differentially with reference to somatic and autonomic inhibition. Experiment 1 provided evidence that direct voluntary commands are not fully inhibited during MI. Although this process remained not solved, it is supposed at organising peripheral effectors during the preparation phase, as for the actual execution of the movement. The

---

[*] CRIS-EA 647 – Laboratory of Mental processes and Motor performance, 27-29 Boulevard du 11 Novembre 1918, 69622 Villeurbanne Cedex, France. christian.collet@univ-lyon1.fr – aymeric.guillot@univ-lyon1.fr.

incomplete inhibition of motor commands was confirmed by the second experiment as postural adjustments were not inhibited. Accordingly, MI may thus have a more limited effect on automatic sensori-motor processes usually associated to voluntary motor commands. This was confirmed in the third experiment in which autonomic nervous system regulations were preserved during MI. These findings should be used in MI program (in sport training or clinical rehabilitation), as incomplete inhibition may give feedback information to the central nervous systems. Further research should nevertheless investigate the processes of somatic motor commands inhibition.

Chapter 183

RATIONALITY: THE DESIRE FOR AN ABSOLUTE WITHOUT A CAUSE

Todd McElroy[1], Jacob Conrad and Dominic Mascari[2]
[1,2] Appalachian State University, Boone, North Coralina, US

The irrationality of a thing is no argument against its existence, rather a condition of it.
Friedrich Nietzsche
German philosopher (1844 - 1900)

Friedrich Nietzsche depicts us as creatures bound by an irrational determinism.

This ascription to irrational forces is commonplace and many, if not most, people adhere to this belief. Such a belief is not surprising in light of how the unconscious was, for many years, thought of as a mythical, dark place where sadistic urges and sexual perversions resided. These terrifying forces, however, were reportedly kept at bay by a surrealistic chasm that lies just between conscious realization and the dark abode of unbounded hedonistic acceptance. Not a pretty picture considering that the unconscious constitutes a large part of what it means to be human.

Taking such a position, as some do, seems troubling to those trying to further a scientific understanding of human psychology. Practically speaking, if we are bound by such a circumstantial existence then why strive for more? In other words; why should we place such effort in making better decisions when the choices that we make will inevitably be tainted by irrational concomitance with unconscious forces?

In this chapter we take a very different view, following a broad perspective that portrays predecisional thought as one of cooperation between two forces working toward a common outcome. Rather than ascribing our fate to the inescapable void of irrational fallibility, we make the case that decision choice can be better understood by approaching it as a complementary superordinate process and perhaps, at times, a contradictory process. Nevertheless, the essence of the decision process is always an interactive product of conscious and unconscious influences. We believe that furthering the understanding of this dualistic pairing will allow us to achieve a better understanding of decision processing and allow for more optimal decision making.

Why are we not rational? This question seems at first insulting and even perfunctory at times. In fact, one can just as easily posit the question: how often is it that we actually need to be rational? In a world that has built-in guides for many of our motivations and desires, it is arguable that we do not really need to spend a great deal of effort on improving and trying to understand this question. If one merely acquiesces to the forces that direct them then no further contemplation is needed. Thankfully, many people are not satisfied with relaxing in the flow of life's river.

In an attempt to address this question we make the assertion that much of the decision making operation is carried out by unconscious processing. In direct contradiction to what most people have succumbed to as *reality*, we propose that our view of the world is colored by the unconscious lens through which it is viewed. In short, we are creatures making choices to and fro but we are largely unaware of the forces that lay out direction for those choices. And because we lack perceptual awareness of this, it is probably the case that this is an *ad hominem* artifact. The most likely reason for such an arrangement is that a lack of such awareness leaves us with the security of directing ourselves, rather than being the object of direction.

Evidence of this can be found in the understanding that we rarely do things that are thoroughly thought out. If a person gives this proposal due regard they will quickly realize that, more often than not, they do things without thinking. We do not have knowledge of why we are doing a particular act or behavior. Rather we are functioning to fulfill some goal or motive that has been set in motion. This behavior is initiated and staged by a process that is unbeknownst to us. Imagine how we would function if we gave thought to our every motion?

Further, imagine if we walked around in life with a full spectrum of our world. That is to say, if we consistently walked through life with an elaborated notion of where we are and our future intentions of what we hope to achieve. How much room would be left for any other unexpected occurrences, or merely appreciating the many aspects of life that bring so much joy to the experience? No, it seems more likely that we are creatures who simply rely on feelings of direction and goals rather than thinking most acts through.

While this seems to call into question the essential assumption of autonomous human beings, we make the case that this is not an exception to humanity but rather it is the rule. Ironically, it is more likely that we are driven largely by aspects of our self that are not conscious to us; by forces which allow us to function as the human beings that we are.

In fact, one could argue that what it is to be human is best described in terms of the complimentary (or at times contradictory) interaction between the conscious and unconscious. So how can we come to better understand this process that holds such promise of insight for rational understanding? It is our proposition that a better understanding can be gained through observing the choice per se as a decision process established as a means that is derived and made within, and in light of, the larger directionality determined by the ends that we seek.

We view the "means" as largely decided by the conscious and the "end" as directed by the unconscious. People behave with regard to the means and are predestined by unconscious forces to seek achievement of the end. The direction of the unconscious impetus is by and large not something that we are privy to in our conscious deliberation. It is well known in decision making research that we often act and make decisions based upon feelings and heuristics rather than analytic thought. Based upon this understanding it is reasonable to propose that we very often act in accordance with a directive that is laid out for us by an unconscious; an unconscious that has a predictable goal that is directed to achieve a desirable end. A goal encrypted by an unconscious director. A direction not filled with trickery or pejorative ends but one that helps us along our path and clears a way for a more achievable end.

In sum, we are attempting to address the assumption that most people believe their decision making is guided by conscious thinking; evaluating prospects of a given situation and, after a thoughtful analysis, choosing the option that they most prefer. Contrary to this belief, we propose that humans are surrounded by unconscious goals and motives that are directing them toward a desired outcome. We make the proposal that the conscious nature of these actions can only be understood to the extent that it exists within a particular goal setting. In other words, the impetus for a decision choice is being directed by unconscious forces. And while we are conscious of particular behaviors and preferences directed toward a decision, we are not privy to the goal setting. Why is this important the reader might ask? The importance of this understanding lies in the fact that the goal setting can have profound influences on decisions that are based within the same parameters with only the goal differing between them. And these choice preferences are the behavioral manifestations that we point to as defining rationality.

Chapter 184

THE COGNITIVE EFFECTS OF ANXIETY ON SEXUAL AROUSAL

Philippe Kempeneers[1,2], Romain Pallincourt[2] and Sylvie Blairy[3]
[1]University of Liege, Unit of Clinical Psychology, Belgium
[2]Alexians' Psychiatric Hospital, Henri-Chapelle, Belgium
[3]University of Liege, Unit of Cognitive-Behavioural Clinical Psychology, Belgium

RESEARCH SUMMARY

Anxiety and sexual arousal have often been considered as incompatible. Since the end of the 20th Century, however, researches have impaired theories centred on the inhibitory effect of the stress and on peripheral explanations; they rather focus attention on the complexity of the relations between the two states and on cognitive mechanisms.

Now sexual arousal tends to be regarded as a complex response that requires the convergent interpretation of internal and external stimuli. Anxiety may have different effects on this process, sometimes neutral, sometimes facilitating and sometimes inhibitory.

On the one hand, anxiety can trigger a vegetative emotional reaction that may be associated to a concomitant erotic stimulation. Thus, anxiety facilitates the sexual response: this can be called a *priming effect*. This effect is regularly observed in labs, mainly among women. It likely also works in certain compulsive sexual behaviours or, more commonly, in those numerous persons that report being sexually aroused when stressed.

On the other hand, anxiety can cause a massive irruption of non erotic cues in working memory. Therefore, cognitive function available for treating erotic stimuli is diminished and sexual response is impaired. This is an effect of *cognitive interference*. A trait called *erotophobia* could be regarded as a vulnerability factor to cognitive interference. Erotophobic subjects are characterized by a trend to focus upon danger-related information when they are in a sexual situation and by a higher risk of sexual dysfunction.

Anxiety is a recognised etiological factor in the domain of sexual dysfunctions. Previous researches have reported reduced sexual responses in individual suffering from anxiety (Bodinger et al., 2002; Leiblum et al., 2007; Meana & Nunnick, 2006; Purdon & Holdaway, 2006; Rellini, 2008.) Whether this is caused by concerns regarding self-image, one's physical appearance, one's performance as a lover or the fear of getting pregnant, or fears of being abandoned or worries relating to everyday difficulties, or whether it is the result of a social phobia, a panic disorder or a history of sexual abuse, all the observations converge towards one point: anxiety and sexual stimulation are not a good match.

Among clinicians, it was widely believed, for a long time, that anxiety was an antagonistic state of sexual responses. Many authors have theorised on this issue. The most well known, Masters and Johnson (1970) described the now famous performance anxiety mechanism: worried about their sexual performance, dysfunctional patients cannot indulge in pleasure; they behave like a worried spectator, concerned about their own performance, thus managing to inhibit the sexual responses for which they are hoping and praying. This form of vicious circle was presented as the primary cause of chronic sexual dysfunction. In 1974, Kaplan pointed out that other causal factors were sometimes added to the anxiety of performance, which were more deeply rooted in the history of the subject but also related to anxiety: the fear of intimacy, for instance, the feeling of guilt associated with sexuality or the fear of being abandoned. The fact is that up until quite recently, clinicians tended to represent anxiety and sexual arousal as irreconcilable states. They were more or less explicitly inspired by the works of Wolpe (1958) on reciprocal inhibition. The principle of reciprocal inhibition postulated an incompatibility between certain neurovegetative states. Specifically, anxiety, a state where the activity of the sympathetic system predominates, was considered to be incompatible with sexual arousal, whose initiation requires parasympathetic activity. According to Wolpe (1958), anxiety and arousal states are mutually exclusive. Wolpe's theory attributes the inhibitory effect of one state upon the other to a direct physiological causality effect.

In the beginning, the theory of reciprocal inhibition was very appealing to clinicians sensitive to the almost constant presence of elements of anxiety implicit in functional problems. However, beyond the field of sexual dysfunctions, various elements caused doubt regarding such a simple and direct inhibitory relationship. First, several anecdotes evoked the possibility of sexual arousal stimulated by stress. For examples, stories of lovers who were stimulated by the fear of being caught in the act, stories of couples where sexual relations following a "good old" argument were all the more intense, or stories of rape carried out in the heat of anger. Clinical observations then became systematic. Since the work of Marshall, Laws & Barbaree (1990), we now know that certain types of criminal sexual behaviour are stimulated by stress or are the result of humiliation. It is also the case for certain cases of paraphilia and for compulsive sexual behaviour where stress is often a trigger (Bancroft & Vukadinovic, 2004; Kafka, 2007). Moreover, surveys carried out among the general population also showed that anxiety and arousal can sometimes go hand in hand. For instance, the survey published in 2003 by the Bancroft team showed that 28.3 % of the interviewed men have reported that anxiety put a strain on their sexual interests, while 20.6 % considered it to be stimulating. Twenty percent is fairly significant. It is highly unlikely that we are only dealing with marginal cases of compulsive or deviant sexuality. The survey by Lykins, Janssen and Graham carried out in 2006 on female students also showed similar results. In this survey, 10 % of the students reported to be sexually stimulated by anxiety. Clearly, anxiety is not only an antagonist of sexual functioning; it can also, and quite often, be an agonist. This rapidly led to the belief that anxiety-arousal relations were probably more complex than the reciprocal inhibition theory suggested. During the last two decades, we have gone from a theory centred on inhibition and the peripheral physiological mechanisms to a theory insisting more on the complexity of the relations between the two states and on the cognitive explicators.

Chapter 185

EXPERIENCING LONELINESS IN CHILDHOOD: CONSEQUENCES FOR PSYCHOSOCIAL ADJUSTMENT, SCHOOL ADJUSTMENT, AND ACADEMIC PERFORMANCE

Lucy R. Betts and Anna S. A. Bicknell
Division of Psychology, Nottingham Trent University,
Nottingham, United Kingdom

RESEARCH SUMMARY

Feelings of loneliness are central to the human experience, with most individuals encountering loneliness at some time (Weiss, 1974). The chapter will begin by providing a brief overview of the topic of loneliness and experiences of loneliness in adults to provide a context for children's loneliness. Next, we will discuss loneliness in childhood because experiencing loneliness during childhood has been identified as an antecedent of loneliness in adulthood (Cacioppo, Hawkley, & Berntson, 2003). Although some short- and long-term consequences of childhood loneliness have been explored, the present chapter aims to review the research evidence outlining the consequences of childhood loneliness for psychosocial adjustment. Specifically, given the importance of positive peer relationships during childhood for psychosocial adjustment, school adjustment, and academic performance (Wentzel, 1999), the chapter will discuss the research evidence that experiencing loneliness can have negative consequences for children in the context of the school environment. In particular, the chapter will explore children's experiences of loneliness with regard to peer relationships, school adjustment, and academic performance.

The chapter will then move on to discuss potential explanations of loneliness during childhood, focusing on how children's interpretations of social situations may influence their loneliness in school. Consequently, the chapter will make links between children's ability to interpret social situations, attribution styles, and loneliness. In support of this argument, the chapter will present the findings from a small-scale cross-sectional study with 135 children (66 male and 69 female) aged between 11- and 15-years old ($M = 12.62$, $SD = 1.04$) from the UK. Children completed measures of social and emotional experiences of loneliness and reported their attribution style in response to positive and negative social outcomes. The results indicate that adopting a more negative attribution style in both positive and negative circumstances was predictive of higher levels of loneliness. These results add further support to the argument that children's ability to interpret social situations influences their psychosocial adjustment assessed as loneliness.

In: Psychology Research Biographies and Summaries
Editors: Nancy E. Wodarth and Alexis P. Ferguson

ISBN: 978-1-61470-491-1
© 2012 Nova Science Publishers, Inc.

Chapter 186

AGEING AND PSYCHOLOGICAL WELL-BEING

Juan Carlos Meléndez-Moral
Department of Developmental Psychology, Faculty of Psychology,
University of Valencia, Spain

RESEARCH SUMMARY

Demographic changes in the last century have produced longer life expectancy, and therefore there is a greater proportion of elderly in the population. As a consequence of this, there has been a growing interest in the research with elderly people, especially in terms of their well-being. There is research evidence that well-being in the elderly may be understood as a two components construct: subjective well-being, that remains relatively stable during life span; and psychological well-being, that negatively changes with age, especially its dimensions of personal growth and purpose in life.

Chapter 187

LONELINESS IN SEXUAL OFFENDERS

Emily Blake and Theresa A. Gannon*
University of Kent, Kent, United Kingdom

RESEARCH SUMMARY

A great number of researchers and clinicians have observed that sexual offenders often appear to be socially isolated, experiencing few close intimate relationships and greater feelings of loneliness compared to other offenders and community controls (Bumby & Hansen, 1997; Garlick, 1991; Saunders, Awad & White, 1986; Marshall, Hudson & Robertson, 1994). These findings are consistent with the more general research on loneliness that suggests that lonelier people are more likely to have poor social skills, have difficulty in forming relationships, and hold negative or hostile opinions of other people. These findings have also prompted researchers to investigate whether the loneliness experienced by sex offenders is related to the development of sexual offending behaviour. Particular questions of importance relate to whether the loneliness experienced by sex offenders is caused by social skill deficits, which in turn contribute to sexual offending, or whether it is the direct experience of loneliness itself, in the absence of social skills deficits that facilitates sexual offending? Conversely could the sexual offending behaviour or subsequent incarceration for such acts be the cause of sexual offenders' loneliness? This chapter aims to answer these questions by describing what researchers have learnt about the loneliness of sex offenders, and what impact loneliness has on offending behaviour. First we define loneliness using information available from general psychology, then we discuss the research evidence for loneliness in sexual offenders and the theories that attempt to explain the link between loneliness and sexual offending.

---

* Corresponding author: School of Psychology, Keynes College, University of Kent, Kent, CT2 7NP, E-Mail: eab28@Kent.ac.uk, Loneliness in Sexual Offenders.

LONELINESS AND LIFE: FROM BEGINNING TO END

*Ami Rokach**
York University, Toronto Canada, and Centre for Academic Studies,
Yehuda, Israel

RESEARCH SUMMARY

Loneliness is a prevailing experience, which every person has experienced at some point in his or her life. It is a subjective experience, which is influenced by one's personality, life experience and other situational variables. The present study examined the influence of age and gender on the experience of loneliness; not on its presence or absence, but rather on its qualitative apects. Seven hundred and eleven participants from all walks of life volunteered to answer an 82-item yes/no questionnaire, reflecting on their loneliness experiences and what it meant to them. Four age groups were compared: youth (13-18 years old), young adults (19-30 years old), adults (31-58 years old) and seniors (60-80 years old). Within and between gender comparisons were also done. Results revealed that loneliness is indeed affected by one's age and gender.

---

* Corresponding author: arokach@yorku.ca, Mailing address:, 58 Trumpeldor St., Petach Tikva 49403, Israel.

Chapter 189

THE EXPERIENCE OF LONELINESS WHILE STUDYING ABROAD

Holly A. Hunley*
Loyola University Chicago, Chicago, Illinois, US

RESEARCH SUMMARY

Anecdotal evidence and previous research have indicated that experiencing some stress while traveling abroad is a rather common occurrence. Part of this stress may be explained by the experience of loneliness. Specifically, students who study abroad are removed, at least in part, from their usual social support systems, which may lead them to feel as though they lack close attachments or people on whom they can rely for support. Undergraduate students studying abroad at Loyola University's Rome Center during the 2004 fall semester (Rome Center Study I) and the 2006-2007 fall and spring semesters (Rome Center Study II) completed questionnaires, which examined aspects of loneliness, psychological distress, and functioning while abroad. In general, these studies provide evidence that loneliness is associated with adverse consequences for students who study abroad. Specifically, students experiencing more loneliness also experienced greater psychological distress and demonstrated lower levels of functioning while studying abroad. Further, having fewer friends was associated with greater loneliness and lower levels of functioning, while having lower quality friendships while studying abroad was related to greater loneliness, lower levels of functioning, and greater psychological distress, particularly depression. Finally, there was weak support that less frequent contact with friends at home was related to the experience of more loneliness. Despite the increasing numbers of students who study abroad each year, there remains a limited body of research into the psychological aspects of studying abroad. Therefore, it is important to investigate factors such as loneliness and psychological distress that may hinder students from taking full advantage of their study abroad experiences. The results of these studies should be reviewed by universities and study abroad programs and

---

* Corresponding author: Jesse Brown VA Medical Center, 820 S. Damen Avenue (Psychology #116B), Chicago, IL 60612, +1-312-569-0345, hhunley@luc.edu.

used to enhance students' experiences while studying abroad by nurturing students' social support while abroad, providing intercultural training, and offering mental health resources for students abroad.

Chapter 190

DENYING THE NEED TO BELONG: HOW SOCIAL EXCLUSION IMPAIRS HUMAN FUNCTIONING AND HOW PEOPLE CAN PROTECT AGAINST IT

Richard S. Pond*, Jr., Joseph Brey and C. Nathan DeWall
University of Kentucky, Lexington, Kentucky, US

RESEARCH SUMMARY

Humans are fundamentally social creatures. Our quality of life rests on the people we connect with, and not just because we depend on them for food, clothing, and shelter. Instead, we thrive on interpersonal contact, and because of this our psychological, and even physiological, well-being is hampered when we become socially disconnected. The current chapter focuses on what happens when people experience unfulfilled belongingness. Specifically, we review evidence about how social exclusion hampers us in ways that affect our cognitions, emotions, and behaviors. We review evidence about how people cope with the pain of exclusion. And we also discuss recent work that shows how people can be buffered from the deleterious effects of exclusion. The findings that we review demonstrate that social exclusion strikes at the core of human functioning, yet we also hope to show that the negative consequences associated with social disconnection can be effectively reduced.

---

* Corresponding author: Richard S. Pond, Jr, 0003 Kastle Hall, Department of Psychology, University of Kentucky, Lexington, KY 40506-0044 Email: ricky.pond@gmail.com.

In: Psychology Research Biographies and Summaries
Editors: Nancy E. Wodarth and Alexis P. Ferguson
ISBN: 978-1-61470-491-1
© 2012 Nova Science Publishers, Inc.

Chapter 191

SEXUAL ALIENATION: A REVIEW OF FACTORS INFLUENCING THE LONELINESS OF GAY, LESBIAN, AND BISEXUAL ADOLESCENTS

Bradley J. Bond
University of Illinois at Urbana Champaign, Illinois, US

RESEARCH SUMMARY

Adolescence is a tumultuous time of development, as transformations continually influence the emotional well-being of the American teenager. Lesbian, gay, or bisexual (LGB) teens experience loneliness with more saliency than their heterosexual peers. It is important to understand the factors influencing the loneliness of sexual minority youth given the social hindrances that they face. This commentary reviews the socialization agents known to influence feelings of loneliness among LGB adolescents. By reviewing the socialization agents in an effort to provide researchers with a concise review of important variables that need to be explored in future studies of LGB adolescents to better understand the emotional development of this population.

In: Psychology Research Biographies and Summaries
Editors: Nancy E. Wodarth and Alexis P. Ferguson
ISBN: 978-1-61470-491-1
© 2012 Nova Science Publishers, Inc.

Chapter 191

BEING LONELY IN A CROWD: POPULATION DENSITY CONTRIBUTES TO PERCEIVED LONELINESS IN CHINA

Zhenzhu Yue, Cong Feng, Xinyue Zhou and Ding-Guo Gao
Department of Psychology and Center for Socio-Cultural Studies and Mental Health, Sun Yat-Sen University, Guangzhou, China

RESEARCH SUMMARY

"A number of porcupines huddled together for warmth on a cold day in winter; but, as they began to prick one another with their quills, they were obliged to disperse"
(Schopenhauer, 1964, p. 226).

People feel lonely even they live in heavily populated areas like China, in spite of being surrounded by millions of people. Yet it is unclear why loneliness cannot be alleviated by high population density. In this article, we argue that population density not only cannot lessen the feelings of loneliness, it also has the potential to exacerbate the perceived loneliness. We propose a number of possible mechanisms. First of all, we argue that people tend to disconnect themselves from others as a protective mechanism in heavily populated areas because crowding environment can be harmful to them physiologically and psychologically. And this self-defense mechanism may have the potential to decrease social ties and contribute to the feelings of being utterly alone and cut off. Moreover, habituation of social withdrawal may be over-generalized, so that people exposed to crowded living conditions for a long period become defensive and hostile chronically (Baum & Valins, 1977, 1979). This will make people around them more vulnerable to loneliness. Finally, since loneliness is contagious, when people come into contact with large number of other people daily, the perceived loneliness will spread out rapidly. Therefore, the quantity of contact does not translate into quality of contact (LoD, 2006). Quantity of contact may also have the potential to decrease the quality of contact. The implication for heavily populated societies like China is discussed.

Chapter 193

COPING WITH GENETIC RISK: IMPOSING CONTROL ON THE UNCERTAINTY OF RISK

*Holly Etchegary**
Interdisciplinary Research Group (IDR), Halifax, Canada

RESEARCH SUMMARY

The sequencing of the human genome allows the identification of genetic variants at multiple loci that influence risks for a variety of common diseases. Several common diseases (e.g., cancer, heart disease, diabetes) have important hereditary influences, and rapid developments in genetics suggest that more and more people will be identified 'at risk.' Genetic discoveries have the potential to improve disease outcomes, but they also highlight gaps in our knowledge about patient-level factors such as how individuals respond to a threat to their health and how they cope with that threat. There have been few empirical applications of psychological theories to understand genetic testing decisions and outcomes, although there have been calls for this approach. Drawing upon interviews with individuals at risk for Huntington disease (HD), this chapter adopts a stress and coping framework to explore how people cope with genetic illness in the family. Qualitative data analyses revealed that coping strategies were dynamic and varied and could be classified as primary control coping, secondary control coping and social comparison strategies. Important distinctions were observed in coping strategies among 1) those who had undergone genetic testing and received a test result; 2) those who remained at risk; and 3) those affected with HD, along with their caregivers. Implications for clinical practice and genetics health services are discussed.

---

* Contact Information: Holly Etchegary, PhD, Research Associate, Interdisciplinary Research Group (IDR), IWK Health Centre, 5850/5980 University Ave, PO Box 9700, Halifax, NS, B3K 6R8, Phone: 902-470-7021, Fax: 902-470-8227, Email: holly.etchegary@iwk.nshealth.ca.

Chapter 194

SELF-HANDICAPPING AS AN ANTICIPATORY SELF-PROTECTION STRATEGY

Sean M. McCrea[1], Andrea L. Myers[1] and Edward R. Hirt[2]
[1]University of Konstanz, Germany
[2]Indiana University Bloomington, US

RESEARCH SUMMARY

Imagine for a moment that you face an important upcoming performance. How well did you do the last time you completed such a test? What will be required to do well this time around? Do you possess the adequate knowledge and skills? How will you feel if you fail? What will your friends and family think of you if you do not succeed? Thoughts like these involve mental simulation, the construction of mental models of past and future events. Judgments flowing from mental simulations can strongly influence how we feel and how we intend to behave in the future. In the context of academic performances, mental simulations can determine how students evaluate their past achievements, how they intend to prepare for upcoming tests, and how they expect to feel about possible performance outcomes. Although in many cases such thoughts are likely to be directed towards self-improvement and achievement, in others they may be turned towards protecting self-esteem and lead to less functional behavior. One context in which mental simulation may play a more dysfunctional role is in the execution of self-handicapping behavior.

Chapter 195

AUTOMATIC OPTIMISM
THE ROLE OF DESIRE IN JUDGMENTS ABOUT THE LIKELIHOOD OF FUTURE EVENTS

Heather C. Lench[1], Shane W. Bench[1], Sarah A. Flores[1] and Peter H. Ditto[2]
[1]Texas A&M University, US
[2]University of California, Irvine, US

RESEARCH SUMMARY

The tendency to believe that the future will be consistent with desires is perhaps the best documented bias that influences human thought. Despite decades of research on this desirability bias, very few studies have addressed what is meant by desire or how desires influence judgments about the future. The goal of this chapter is to provide a novel theoretical framework from which to understand why and when people are optimistic about the future and to report results from three studies that examined whether the desirability of future events changes how people evaluate objective probabilities about the likelihood of those events. Two studies examined the influence of desire on the use of probabilistic information in judgments about the likelihood of future life events (such as winning awards, developing cancer) and judgments about chance events (winning a game, losing a game). A third study explored whether people use probabilistic information differently when they make judgments about their own future versus the futures of others. Consistent with predictions based on a dual process framework, people judged that positive events were more likely to occur than negative events with the exact same objective probability of occurrence and they interpreted probabilistic information more loosely when they made judgments about their own futures versus the futures of others. These findings suggest that people take remarkable liberties with supposedly objective information in order to judge that their own future will be ideal.

"What a man believes upon grossly insufficient evidence is an index into his desires – desires of which he himself is often unconscious. If a man is offered a fact which goes against his instincts, he will scrutinize it closely, and unless the evidence is overwhelming, he will refuse to believe it. If, on the other hand, he is offered something which affords a reason for acting in accordance to his instincts, he will accept it even on the slightest evidence. The origin of myths is explained in this way."

-Bertrand Russell

In: Psychology Research Biographies and Summaries
Editors: Nancy E. Wodarth and Alexis P. Ferguson

ISBN: 978-1-61470-491-1
© 2012 Nova Science Publishers, Inc.

Chapter 196

SOCIAL IDENTITIES, PREJUDICES AND SYMBOLIC BOUNDARIES: CONTRIBUTIONS FROM SOCIOCULTURAL PSYCHOLOGY

Ana Flávia do Amaral Madureira
Institute of Psychology — University of Brasília, Brazil

RESEARCH SUMMARY

From the contributions of sociocultural psychology (e.g. Brunner, 1997; Cole, 1992; Rosa, 2007a, 2007b; Valsiner, 1994; Valsiner & Rosa, 2007a, 2007b; Vygotsky, 1978/1991), this paper analyzes the meaning-making processes related to the construction of social identities and prejudices. In order to analyze the affective and cultural dimensions of these meaning-making processes, the following theoretical tools will be used: (a) the conceptualization of identity processes and prejudices as boundary phenomena (Madureira, 2007a, 2007b, 2007c, 2008); (b) the general processes, specified by Ernest Boesch, of *HEIMWEH* ("homeward road": striving towards the known and the secure) and the *FERNWEH* ("road to the far away": adventure, encountering novelty and also risks) (Valsiner, 2006); (c) the Semiotic Regulatory System Model proposed by Valsiner (2003, 2005, 2007a).

It is proposed that symbolic boundaries conceptualization is a promising path to study diverse social and psychological phenomena — like the construction of social identities, prejudices and discriminatory practices — as prejudices in action (Madureira, 2008). The theoretical discussion will be illustrated with empirical examples extracted from a previous research carried out by the author (Madureira, 2007a). Presented in the conclusion are some implications for future inquiries about identity processes and prejudices as boundary phenomena.

In: Psychology Research Biographies and Summaries
Editors: Nancy E. Wodarth and Alexis P. Ferguson

ISBN: 978-1-61470-491-1
© 2012 Nova Science Publishers, Inc.

Chapter 197

WHO IS SUPPORTING EAST EUROPEAN IMMIGRANTS IN PORTUGAL? AN EXPLORATORY STUDY OF THEIR SOCIAL NETWORKS

Liliana Sousa[1] *and Madalena Alarcã*[*,2]

[1]University of Aveiro, 3810-193 Aveiro, Portugal
[2]University of Coimbra, Rua do Colégio Novo, 3000 Coimbra, Portugal

RESEARCH SUMMARY

Immigrants from East European countries constitute the most recent group of immigrants in Portugal. They show some characteristics that differentiates them from other immigrant groups in our country (Brazilian and African). All immigrants experience some common difficulties (such as, job insecurity and legalization problems) but added to this Eastern Europe immigrants also have the language difficulty.

In this context it seems relevant to get a deeper knowledge on the relational networks of East Europe immigrants, in order to plan and organize support resources which facilitate their process of integration in our country.

Therefore, this exploratory study aims at getting a better understanding of the characteristics of the social networks of these immigrants. The IARSP-R (Alarcão & Sousa, 2007) was administered to 30 East immigrants. The main findings suggest small cohesive and fragmented networks. The family, even in an immigration situation, is still the quadrant with more members, followed by friends, co-workers, professionals and neighbours. The presence of Portuguese members in the social network tends to increase the size of the network, while enhancing its fragmentation and diminishing the perception of received support. This study shows the relevance of informal social networks in the development of support to the immigrants.

---

[*] E.mail: lilianax@ua.pt

Chapter 198

WHERE FANTASY MEETS REALITY: MEDIA EXPOSURE, RELATIONSHIP BELIEFS AND STANDARDS, AND THE MODERATING EFFECT OF A CURRENT RELATIONSHIP

Bjarne M. Holmes and Kimberly R. Johnson
Heriot-Watt University, Edinburgh, UK

RESEARCH SUMMARY

Two studies investigated popular media exposure, dysfunctional beliefs about romantic relationships, ideals, and relationship satisfaction, with relationship status as a moderator. Study 1 showed positive associations between amount of television consumed and beliefs "the sexes are different" and "mindreading is expected", as well as decreased relationship satisfaction. Individuals' relationship status moderated the relationship between television consumption and standards regarding an ideal partner, with higher standards held by those not in a relationship who consumed more television. Study 2 tested associations using an experimental paradigm in which participants were exposed either to a romantic comedy manipulation or control film. Participants in relationships were more satisfied if they had viewed the manipulation film compared to those who viewed the control film. Those not in relationships were less satisfied if they had viewed the manipulation film compared to those who had viewed the control. Results are discussed within the frameworks of cultivation, social cognitive, and social comparison theories and suggestions for future work are proposed.

In: Psychology Research Biographies and Summaries
Editors: Nancy E. Wodarth and Alexis P. Ferguson
ISBN: 978-1-61470-491-1
© 2012 Nova Science Publishers, Inc.

Chapter 199

THE RELATIONSHIP BETWEEN GENDER AND DEPRESSION, SELF-ESTEEM, HOPELESSNESS, SUBMISSIVE ACTS, GUILT, SHAME AND ANGER IN ADOLESCENTS

Erol Özmen[1],*, Dilek Özmen[2], Aynur Çakmakçı Çetinkaya[2], E. Oryal Taşkın[2] and Pınar Erbay Dündar[3]

[1]Department of Psychiatry, School of Medicine, Celal Bayar University, Manisa, Turkey
[2]Department of Public Health Nursing, School of Health,
Celal Bayar University, Manisa, Turkey
[3]Department of Public Health, School of Medicine,
Celal Bayar University, Manisa, Turkey

RESEARCH SUMMARY

Literature Review and Objective: Although there were a number of research findings on gender differences in mental health problems, it is not known that it is a universal phenomenon or not. The purpose of this study was to
investigate the relationship between gender and depression, self-esteem, hopelessness, submissive acts, guilt, shame and anger in Turkish adolescents.

Methods: A cross-sectional survey of 1185 ninth-grade Turkish adolescents aged 14-19 was conducted. 708 (59.7 %) of the students were male and the mean age of students was 15.53±0.72. Hopelessness was measured by using Beck Hopelessness Scale (BHS), self-esteem was measured by using the Rosenberg Self-Esteem Scale (SES), depression was measured by using Children's Depression Inventory (CDI), guilt and shame was measured by using Guilt and Shame Scale (GSS), submissive acts was measured by using Submissive Acts Scale (SAS), anger was measured by using The State-Trait Anger Scale (STAS). Student's t-

---

* Contact Information: Erol Özmen 200 sk. No: 76 D: 3 Hatay, İZMİR, TURKEY e-mail: erolozmen@yahoo.com.

test was used to find out the relationship between gender and depression, self-esteem, hopelessness, submissive acts, guilt, shame and anger in adolescents.

Results: The findings indicate that the mean score of the SAS and BHS, anger control subscale of STAS of the boys were higher than that of the girls and the mean score of the CDI, guilt subscale of GSS, shame subscale of GSS, SES, trait anger subscale of STAS, anger-in subscale of STAS and anger-out subscale of STAS of the girls were higher than that of the boys. While there were statistically significant associations between gender and the SAS, BHS, CDI, guilt subscale of GSS, shame subscale of GSS, trait anger subscale of STAS, anger-out subscale of STAS and anger control subscale of STAS mean scores; no relationship was found between gender and the anger-in subscale of STAS and SES mean scores.

Conclusion: The results of this study point out that there are gender differences in hopelessness, depression, guilt, shame, submissive acts and anger levels but not in self-esteem levels in Turkish adolescents. The findings suggest that psychological gender differences are seen not only in individualistic societies, but also in collectivistic societies.

In: Psychology Research Biographies and Summaries
Editors: Nancy E. Wodarth and Alexis P. Ferguson
ISBN: 978-1-61470-491-1
© 2012 Nova Science Publishers, Inc.

Chapter 200

EFFECTS OF GENDER-RELATED IMAGES ON BEVERAGES INTAKE FOR YOUNG JAPANESE MEN AND WOMEN

*Kumi Hirokawa[1] and Kazuko Yamazawa[2]**

[1]Fukuyama University, Japan
[2]Tokai Gakuin University, Japan

RESEARCH SUMMARY

Advertisements of foods and beverages, particularly packaging and labeling, play an important role in consumption and taste preferences. Commercials in Japan continue to use stereotypical gender roles. In this chapter, we focused on gender associations with regard to beverages. Those associations with individuals' gender identity, including masculinity, femininity, and gender stereotyping, and beverage intake were examined. We conducted a survey on gendered images and beverage intake, and an experiment using the Implicit Association Test, to examine effects of gendered images on the perception of whether a beverage was suitable for oneself. Three hundred and sixty Japanese undergraduate university students (135 men and 225 women) participated in the survey. A questionnaire was used to obtain information about their frequency of beverage consumption, gender personality variables, and lifestyle. Gendered images for commercial messages, and beverage packaging were also collected. The results showed that coffee and isotonic beverages were seen as having masculine images. They also showed that men with high masculinity scores and low femininity scores tended to drink coffee without sugar, while women with high masculinity scores showed increased frequency of isotonic beverage consumption. On the other hand, women with high scores for femininity tended to drink less feminine-imaged beverages (i.e., tea and Japanese tea). The experiments included 20 male and 28 female Japanese undergraduate students. Priming stimuli showed no significant effect on response time.

---

* Contact Information: Please address correspondence concerning this article to Kumi Hirokawa, Department of Psychology, 1 Sanzo, Gakuen-machi, Fukuyama, Hiroshima 720-0292, Japan. Phone: +81 84 936 2112 (ext. 3426) Fax: +81 84 936 2077, Email: k-umi@umin.ac.jp.

However, participants' response time was shorter when beverages were presented with feminine images than when presented with masculine images, suggesting that feminine images tended to influence the assessment of whether a beverage was suitable for oneself. Participants with high femininity scores took time to judge whether beverages with masculine images were appropriate for themselves. It appears that gender personality may influence an individual's intake and choices for specific beverages when they are tied to gendered images.

In: Psychology Research Biographies and Summaries
Editors: Nancy E. Wodarth and Alexis P. Ferguson
ISBN: 978-1-61470-491-1
© 2012 Nova Science Publishers, Inc.

Chapter 201

OUTSIDE THE LABORATORY: THE LINGUISTIC INTERGROUP BIAS IN A NATURAL MULTIPLE-COMPARISON SETTING

Monica Rubini*,[1] Anna Rita Graziani[2] and Silvia Moscatelli[1]

[1] University of Bologna, Italy
[2] University of Modena and Reggio Emilia, Italy

RESEARCH SUMMARY

This chapter reviews the literature on the Linguistic Intergroup Bias and reports an empirical contribution in which the linguistic discrimination phenomenon is analyzed in a real life intergroup setting by adopting a multiple comparison framework. Specifically, adolescents—members of sports, religious, political and spontaneous peer-groups—freely described the ingroup and a variety of meaningful outgroups. The relationship between linguistic discrimination and perceived ingroup and outgroup entitativity was also studied. Besides highlighting a strong ingroup favouritism, the results showed that descriptions of the outgroups were not all alike: Political and religious groups were more discriminated against than informal and sports groups. Furthmore, more entitative outgroups were described in a less biased fashion. The implications of these results for the generality and pervasiveness of linguistic intergroup discrimination in real life settings are discussed.

Chapter 202

ALIENATION, INACTION, AND ENGAGEMENT IN POLITICAL DECISION-MAKING: PASSIVE WAR OPPONENTS ACTIVELY AVOID NEWS OF THE WAR AND ARE MOTIVATED TO DEROGATE PROTESTORS

Winnifred R. Louis, Fiona Kate Barlow and Deborah J. Terry
The University of Queensland, School of Psychology, QLD, Australia

RESEARCH SUMMARY

A great deal of research in social psychology has investigated the predictors of collective action or political protest, yet in reality only a tiny fraction of individuals ever attend rallies or meetings, or volunteer for particular causes. Very little research has examined the predictors of political alienation in their own right, despite findings that across Western democracies, participation in public politics is dropping and cynicism and alienation are increasingly prevalent (e.g., Putnam, 2000). In the present data, supportive national and political identities and norms were found to promote engagement and activism. Distress about the Iraq war was associated with higher intentions to engage in peace activism, and for politically active opponents of the war, war distress was associated with positive affect towards protestors. In contrast, politically alienated participants (who passively opposed the Iraq war) were more likely to intend to avoid news of the war actively, and for this group the perceived inefficacy of protest was associated with hostility towards peace activists. The study documents for the first time a form of active emotional displacement, in which the perception that political activism is futile increases alienated participants' avoidance behaviour and motivates anger at those who are playing an active role agitating for social change. The implications of this cycle of cynicism and withdrawal are discussed.

In: Psychology Research Biographies and Summaries
Editors: Nancy E. Wodarth and Alexis P. Ferguson
ISBN: 978-1-61470-491-1
© 2012 Nova Science Publishers, Inc.

Chapter 203

THE SOCIAL PSYCHOLOGY OF URBAN LEGENDS

David Main and Sandy Hobbs
University of the West of Scotland, UK

RESEARCH SUMMARY

Research on "urban legend", also known as "contemporary legend", has grown rapidly since the publication of Brunvand's *Vanishing Hitchhiker* (1981). Although the work which has been undertaken has often been interdisciplinary in character, with a few exceptions (e.g. Hobbs, 1987), psychologists did not contributed initially to the growth of this field of study. More recently, that situation has changed. Psychologists have published theoretical work (e. g. Guerin and Miyazaki, 2006) and empirical research (e. g. Heath, Bell and Sternberg, 2001) on contemporary legend. This paper reviews these psychological contributions and draws attention to a number of issues on which psychologists may throw an increasing amount of light. For instance, what is the relationship between "rumor" and "urban legend"? How best may contemporary legends be classified? What psychological and social functions do urban legends serve? In considering future developments in this field, the authors discuss the implications of the proposal by Hobbs (2005) that there are more similarities than is often realised between the transmission of rumors or legends, on the one hand, and some academic discourse on the other. If this claim is justified, then the understanding of rumour and legend may be enhanced by linking their study to research on "academic folklore" (e.g. the study of the concept of the "Hawthorne Effect" by Chiesa and Hobbs, 2008).

Chapter 204

SOCIO-CULTURAL FACTORS THAT AFFECT THE TRADITIONAL EDIRNE HOUSE

Nevnihal Erdoğan[1] and Damla Atik[2] *

[1]Kocaeli University, Faculty of Architecture and Design
Department of Architecture, İzmit/Kocaeli, Turkey
[2]Trakya University, Faculty of Engineering and Architecture
Department of Architecture, Edirne, Turkey

RESEARCH SUMMARY

Studies of cultural differences in architecture and the interrelation between culture and architecture have begun to receive attention in a major way primarily in the last twenty years. In this paper an abstract model of the relationship seen between cultural and social values and architecture are presented, and a case study of the traditional Edirne house in Turkey is provided to help exemplify and clarify the model. So with this approach, this relationship has been analyzed through the traditional Edirne house in which different ethnical and cultural groups live.

The relationship between house form and socio-cultural factors can be explained within a model. Therefore, a model is used which consists of four parts and is flexible is used. It shows the linkages between architectural artifacts selected or devised by culture, architectural values, social norms and social values. The elements depicted in the model can be probed by the systematic exploration of some questions like "What architectural artifacts are in use?" "What architectural values affected the circumscription of the choice of artifacts?"

The model is illustrated through a case study of the traditional Edirne house, focusing on how social values, such as religious beliefs and male-female relationships, the family structure, the status of the family in the society, the privacy of the family, the neighborhood, hospitality, and social values in a Turkish-Islamic tradition relate to build form in Edirne. Finally, the traditional Edirne house is used to explain an artifact of culture that is a synthesis of the subcultures of Thrace and Anatolia.

---

* Contact Information: e-mail:nevtrakya@hotmail.com and e-mail:archidam22@hotmail.com.

Chapter 205

SOCIAL REPRESENTATIONS OF RELIGION OF MALTESE UNIVERSITY STUDENTS

Mary Anne Lauri[*,1], *Josef Lauri*[†,1] *and Bart Duriez*[‡,2]
[1] University of Malta, Malta
[2] K.U. Leuven, Belgium

RESEARCH SUMMARY

Social representations is a relatively new area of research which is rapidly becoming an important tool in understanding social behavior. In this chapter we will be using this theory to understand how university students in Malta look upon religion. A self-administered questionnaire was given to a random sample of 650 students at the University of Malta, of which 421 completed the questionnaire. The questionnaire consisted of 35 questions about religious attitudes and behavior, and also included the Post-Critical Belief Scale (Duriez et al., 2005). The data were subjected to statistical analysis. The results were used to identify the different social representations which students had of religion. The implications for understanding how religious beliefs correlate with religious behavior among students in tertiary education will be discussed.

---

[*] Department of Psychology, University of Malta, Malta, mary-anne.lauri@um.edu.mt.
[†] Department of Mathematics, University of Malta, Malta, josef.lauri@um.edu.mt.
[‡] Department of Psychology, K.U.Leuven, Belgium, Bart.Duriez@psy.kuleuven.ac.be.

Chapter 206

SELF-STEREOTYPING AND SUN SIGN: FURTHER EVIDENCE THAT ASTROLOGY-RELATED BELIEFS INFLUENCE THE SELF-CONCEPT

Michael Riketta[*]
University of Tübingen, Germany

RESEARCH SUMMARY

Several previous studies found associations between astrological sun signs and self-judgments of personality. One explanation is that people incorporate attributes associated with their sun sign into the self-concept (self-stereotyping). This study tested this explanation in a sample of 146 German adults. Twelve personality descriptions were derived from the astrological literature, one for each sun sign. Participants had to rank the personality descriptions according to their similarity with the self, being uninformed about the astrological origin of the descriptions. Participants preferred the description of their own sun sign significantly over the other descriptions (mean rank 5.90). Supporting a self-stereotyping explanation and extending previous research, this effect occurred only among participants who knew at least one attribute of their sun sign, believed in astrology, or were suspicious of the study purpose. It is concluded that astrology can affect people's lives by altering their self-views.

---

[*] Contact information: Dr. Michael Riketta, University of Tübingen, Psychological Institute, Friedrichstr. 21, 72072 Tübingen, Germany. Email: michael.riketta@uni-tuebingen.de.

Chapter 207

VALUES AND FEAR OF CRIME

Silvia Russo and Michele Roccato[*]
Department of Psychology, University of Torino, Italy

RESEARCH SUMMARY

The feeling of unsafety, usually operationalised as fear of crime, is mainly studied by sociologists and criminologists, who rely upon sociological or socio-demographic variables to account for fear variations. However, some psycho-social variables may be effectively used to predict such fear. In this chapter we examined, in a psycho-social perspective, whether individual values priorities exert influence on personal fear of crime (or concrete fear) and concern about crime as a social problem (or abstract fear), performing a secondary analysis of the data gathered by the Observatory of North-West on a representative sample of the Italian population over 18 ($N = 1,667$). We tested two structural equation models, both aimed at predicting concrete and abstract fear of crime using values among our independent variables. In the first one we used Schwartz's approach to values (assessing values in terms of Openness to change vs. Conservatism and Self-enhancement vs. Self-transcendence), and in the second one we used Inglehart's approach (assessing values in terms of Materialism vs. Post-materialism). Besides individual values, we took into account four sets of independent variables: Socio-demographic characteristics, victimization experiences, political variables, and mass media exposure. Findings from previous research on fear of crime were partially confirmed. Concrete fear of crime was positively influenced by direct and indirect victimization and size of area of residence. Abstract fear of crime was positively influenced by direct victimization, and negatively influenced by education, size of area of residence, and National TV news watching. As concerns the innovative part of our research, values influenced abstract fear as well as concrete fear. When we operationalised values using Schwartz's model, both concrete and abstract fear of crime were negatively influenced by

---

[*] Silvia Russo, Department of Psychology, University of Torino, Via Verdi, 10, 10124 Torino, Italy. Telephone: ++390116702055, Fax: ++390116702061, E-mail: aivlisss@gmail.com. Michele Roccato, Department of Psychology, University of Torino, Via Verdi, 10, 10124 Torino, Italy. Telephone: ++390116702015, Fax: ++390116702061, E-mail: roccato@psych.unito.it (corresponding author).

Openness to change. When we operationalised values using Inglehart's model, Materialism exerted a positive influence on concrete fear of crime and Post-materialism exerted a negative influence on abstract fear of crime. Our two models accounted for almost the same proportion of variance of the two dependent variables, and the effects our two operationalisations of values exerted on fear were reasonably similar in magnitude. Limits and possible developments of this research are discussed.

Chapter 208

SOCIAL PHYSIQUE ANXIETY, BODY IMAGE, DISABILITY, AND PHYSICAL ACTIVITY

Jeffrey J. Martin
Wayne State University, MI, US

RESEARCH SUMMARY

The purpose of this chapter is to examine social physique anxiety (SPA), and the role of physical activity (PA) in reducing SPA in people with disabilities. SPA is the anticipation or experience of anxiety as a result of the perception that others are devaluing ones body. SPA grew out of Impression Management Theory (Leary, 1995) which suggests people try to enhance others favorable impressions of them or reduce their unfavorable appraisals. The experience of SPA is often the response to the perception that impression management efforts are failing. In this chapter important constructs (i.e., SPA) and theories (i.e., Impression Management Theory) are discussed first. Next, the rationale for why individuals with disabilities might experience heightened SPA is examined. Then, mechanisms explaining how PA can reduce SPA are explained. Empirical research on SPA and PA with people with disabilities is reviewed next. Finally, major findings are summarized and I conclude the chapter with future research directions.

Chapter 209

SOCIAL ANXIETY AND PSYCHOSIS

Erguvan Tugba Ozel-Kizil and Bora Baskak
Ankara University School of Medicine, Department of Psychiatry,
Neuropsychiatry Research Unit, Ankara, Turkey

RESEARCH SUMMARY

Contrary to the classical distinction of psychosis and neurosis, anxiety and psychosis often occur together. Social anxiety disorder (SAD) is one of the most common comorbid anxiety disorders in patients with psychoses like schizophrenia and bipolar disorder. Psychosis accompanied by SAD was also related to lower quality of life and higher rates of suicide attempts and substance/alcohol abuse. The relationship between psychosis and social anxiety may be beyond the epidemiological findings of high comorbidity, previous literature refers to both phenomenological and neurobiological associations. Patients with SAD have a mild degree of ideas of reference, at a significantly higher level than healthy controls. Moreover, social anxiety has been defined as one of the four fundamental symptoms of schizotypy, which has been conceptualized as an attenuated/latent form or phenotypic variant of schizophrenia. Social anxiety which leads to social withdrawal may also interfere with negative symptoms in schizophrenia and differentiation of these may be difficult due to similarities at symptomatic level and co-occurence of these symptoms. Besides, social anxiety and psychosis may share similar cognitive schemas; both have attributional biases with different patterns. Cognitive behavioural treatment has yielded good results in favor of both negative symptoms and social anxiety in patients with schizophrenia However, data concerning the association of social anxiety and psychosis is scarce and the differential diagnosis of social anxiety and psychosis in terms of referentiality is controversial. In this chapter, the association of psychosis and social anxiety, as well as the processes that may underlie this association will be discussed in the light of previous research.

Chapter 210

THE RELATIONSHIP BETWEEN SOCIAL ANXIETY AND DRINKING BEHAVIOUR: A REVIEW OF THE LITERATURE

*Annette Raber and Penelope A. Hasking**
School of Psychology & Psychiatry, Monash University, Melbourne, Australia

RESEARCH SUMMARY

Social anxiety and alcohol consumption are both commonly occurring disorders with potentially incapacitating consequences for sufferers. Their relationship has generated significant research in the last few decades. A major objective of such research has been to explain the high co-morbidity rates that exist between social anxiety disorder and alcohol use disorders. Despite many studies establishing co-morbidity between social anxiety and alcohol consumption, inconsistencies have appeared in research examining this connection. For example, some research has demonstrated a positive relationship between social anxiety and drinking, whilst other research has revealed a negative relationship or none at all. These discrepancies have led to studies considering the role of potentially moderating and/or mediating alcohol-related variables in the relationship between social anxiety and alcohol use. This review reports on findings with respect to three such variables, namely alcohol expectancies, self-efficacy and drinking motives. It is hoped that a better understanding of the relationship between social anxiety and alcohol use will lead to improvements in the prevention and treatment of these disorders.

Social anxiety disorder (SAD) and alcohol use disorders (AUD) commonly co-occur with potentially incapacitating consequences for those affected. Significant research has been generated in attempting to explain the high co-morbidity rates (Morris et al., 2005). Empirical studies exploring the relationship between SAD and AUD have generally fallen into four categories; genetics of the co-morbidity, neurobiology of the co-morbidity, effects of alcohol (due to its anxiolytic properties) on social anxiety, and the role of mediating and moderating cognitive variables on the relationship (Tran et al., 2008). This review reports on findings

---

* Corresponding author: Email: Penelope.Hasking@ monash.edu, Ph: + 61 3 9902 4024, Fax: + 61 3 9905 3948.

with respect to this last group of studies, and on three such variables, namely alcohol expectancies, self-efficacy and drinking motives.

Chapter 211

SOCIAL ANXIETY IS CONTAGIOUS

Anna Park, Nicole Sharp and William Ickes
University of Texas at Arlington, TX, US

RESEARCH SUMMARY

Social anxiety (or shyness) is a specific type of anxiety that occurs in social situations. Socially anxious individuals become preoccupied with their behavior in social situations and fear that it will cause them to be negatively evaluated. In the present chapter, we offer a unique perspective on this phenomenon by reviewing research findings which suggest that social anxiety may be "contagious." A number of studies have provided evidence that when a socially anxious individual interacts with a less anxious partner, the less anxious partner becomes more self-conscious and emulates many of the behaviors displayed by the more anxious individual (Garcia, Stinson, Ickes, Bissonnette & Briggs, 1991; Heery & Kring, 2007). We begin by discussing the process by which this "contagion" phenomenon occurs. We then consider the specific ways in which this contagion becomes evident: in negative, self-focused thoughts and feelings; in a more closed and defensive body posture and body orientation; and in other nonverbal behaviors such as greater fidgeting but reduced gazing, smiling, and gesturing. We conclude by offering suggestions for future research.

In: Psychology Research Biographies and Summaries
Editors: Nancy E. Wodarth and Alexis P. Ferguson
ISBN: 978-1-61470-491-1
© 2012 Nova Science Publishers, Inc.

Chapter 212

THE RELATIONSHIP BETWEEN SOCIAL PHYSIQUE ANXIETY AND EXERCISE BEHAVIOR: DOES THE FULFILLMENT OF BASIC PSYCHOLOGICAL NEEDS MATTER?

Diane E. Mack[*], Philip M. Wilson, Benjamin D. Sylvester, J. Paige Gregson, Susanna Cheung and Samuel Rimmer
Brock University, St. Catharines, Ontario, Canada

RESEARCH SUMMARY

Background: Social physique anxiety (SPA) represents one subtype of social anxiety stemming in part from the prospect or presence of negative interpersonal evaluation involving one's physique (Hart, Leary, & Rejeski, 1989). Higher levels of SPA are typically associated with lower levels of psychological and behavioral functioning (Salovey et al., 2000). Meta-analytic evidence, however, indicates that SPA is inconsistently related to exercise behavior (Mack, Wilson, Waddell, & Gasparotto, 2008). This finding has led to speculation that SPA may influence exercise behavior indirectly, through relationships with other psychological mechanisms, rather than directly (Martin Ginis & Mack, in press).

Purpose: The purpose of this study was to examine whether perceived psychological need satisfaction in exercise contexts mediates the SPA – exercise behavior relationship. Methods: A convenience sample of undergraduate students (N = 266; n_{female} = 171) completed the Social Physique Anxiety Scale (Martin, Rejeski, Leary, McAuley, & Bane, 1997), the Godin Leisure-Time Exercise Questionnaire (Godin & Shephard, 1985) and the Psychological Need Satisfaction in Exercise Scale (Wilson, Rogers, Rodgers, & Wild, 2006).

Results: A weak negative relationship between SPA - exercise behavior scores was found (r = -0.11; 95% CI = -0.23 to 0.01). Adopting a multiple mediation approach (Preacher

---

[*] Corresponding author: E-mail: dmack@brocku.ca, Behavioural Health Sciences Reseach Lab, Department of Physical Education and Kinesiology, Brock University, 500 Glenridge Ave, St. Catharines, ON, CANADA L2S 3A1, Tel: (905) 688-5550 (4360).

& Hayes, 2008), the fulfillment of the three psychological needs (i.e., autonomy, competence, and relatedness) mediated the SPA – exercise behavior relationship (point estimate = -1.99; Bias Corrected and Accelerated Confidence interval (BCa CI) = -3.25 to -0.84), with perceived competence and relatedness serving as unique mediators in this sample.

Discussion: The fulfillment of psychological needs in exercise contexts may represent one mechanism through which the SPA – exercise behavior relationship may be better understood. Overall, results suggest that people who feel that their bodies are negatively appraised within exercise contexts are less likely to sustain their behavior if they feel incompetent or socially disconnected from others. Future research may want to investigate other mediators to explain the SPA – exercise behavior relationship.

Chapter 213

Social Anxiety and Cardiovascular Reactivity: An Interpretation in Terms of Differential Effort Mobilization

Margit Gramer
Department of Psychology, Karl-Franzens Universität, Graz, Austria

Research Summary

Research on the cardiovascular effects of trait social anxiety in evaluative task conditions has mainly been guided by the assumption that cardiovascular activation is proportional to experienced anxiety (Lazarus, 1968; Rapee, 1995). Empirical findings in this field are only partly consistent with a threat interpretation, however. In several studies, substantial differences in experienced distress between high and low socially anxious individuals were not paralleled by differential cardiovascular activation (Baggett, Saab, & Carver, 1996; Edelman & Baker, 2002; Grossman, Wilhelm, Kawachi, & Sparrow, 2001; Mauss, Wilhelm, & Gross, 2003; 2004; Wilhelm, Kochar, Roth, & Gross, 2001). Some studies did observe enhanced reactivity in socially anxious individuals (Burns, 1995; Feldman, Cohen, Hamrick, & Lepore, 2004; Turner, Beidel, & Larkin, 1986) but there is also evidence of reduced cardiovascular activation compared to nonanxious individuals (Larkin, Ciano-Federoff & Hammel, 1998). In explanation of these discrepant results, some authors have suggested that cognitive processes might be more important indicators of social anxiety (Baggett et al., 1996; Mauss et al., 2003) and group differences might be obtained in *subjective perceptions* of physiological arousal rather than actual cardiovascular activity (Papageourgiou & Wells, 2002). It has not been considered, however, that cardiovascular arousal is not necessarily an indicator of distress emotions. Enhanced cardiac activity has been observed in appetitive (Gramer & Huber, 1996; Light & Obrist, 1983; Smith, Allred, & Carlson, 1989) and aversive conditions (Lovallo, Wilson, Pincomb, Edwards, Tompkins, & Brackett, 1985). Furthermore, several psychophysiological theories (Dienstbier, 1989; Obrist, 1981; Wright, 1996) relate cardiovascular activation in evaluative performance situations to effort and task engagement rather than affective arousal.

A main aim of this chapter is to outline how psychophysiological theories on performance-related cardiovascular activity may further the understanding of inconsistent cardiovascular effects of trait social anxiety. First, psychophysiological theories and their potential relationship to theoretical concepts of social anxiety are presented. In a second part, initial empirical evidence is provided and further research agenda are sketched out.

Chapter 214

WHY IS THE ANXIETY LEVEL OF JAPANESE PEOPLE HIGH? A CROSS-CULTURAL STUDY ON ANXIETY AND SYSTEM TRUST AMONG JAPAN, CHINA, AND THE UNITED STATES

Yumiko Nara
The Open University of Japan, Chiba City, Japan

RESEARCH SUMMARY

This study examined the feelings of anxiety people feel about everyday life risks, their level of trust in the social risk management system, and the relationship between anxiety and trust. Social surveys using questionnaires were carried out before and after the Sichuan Earthquake in China, and the same survey was also conducted in Japan and the U.S. The survey results showed that the respondents in Japan had the highest levels of anxiety about 19 kinds of risk; earthquakes, traffic accidents, fire, cancer, contaminated food, crime, illness and injury, decreased income, decreased assets, financial difficulties after retirement, global warming, health hazards from genetically modified food, side effects of drugs, nuclear accidents, Internet scams, leaks of personal information on the Internet, defamation on the Internet, Internet sex victimization, and computer viruses. The level of system trust was the highest for the Chinese respondents, even after the Sichuan Earthquake. These findings indicate that a high level of trust in the risk management system is related to lower levels of anxiety about everyday life risks. The higher levels of anxiety shown by the Japanese respondents apparently reflect their feeling that the risk management system is either insufficient or untrustworthy.

Chapter 215

THE COGNITIVE ETIOLOGY OF SOCIAL ANXIETY DISORDER

Iulian Iancu[*] and Damian Barenboim

Yavne Mental Health Center, Yavne and the Beer Yaakov Mental Health Center,
Beer Yaakov, affiliated with the Sackler School of Medicine,
Tel Aviv University, Tel Aviv, Israel

RESEARCH SUMMARY

Social anxiety disorder (SAD) is characterized by marked anxiety about social or performance situations in which there is a fear of embarassing oneself under scrutiny by others. It is a common disorder with early onset, significant comorbidity and functional impairment. Despite the growing understanding of the condition, information is lacking on etiology. SAD is a disorder with cognitive dysfunction in which a socially anxious individual's biased perspective–taking and expected failure to meet expectations in a situation result in the characteristic symptoms of the disorder. Research has shown that socially anxious individuals tend to interpret ambiguous stimuli or events as negative or events as negative or threatening.

The current chapter provides an overview for the cognitive understanding of SAD (the prevailing models from the nineties), together with a short review of recent studies on the subject and some tips on the effectiveness of cognitive–behavioral treatment for SAD.

---

[*] Corresponding author: E-mail: iulian1@bezeqint.net.

Chapter 217

SOCIAL ANXIETY IN THE COLLEGE STUDENT POPULATION: THE ROLE OF ANXIETY SENSITIVITY[*]

Angela Sailer and Holly Hazlett-Stevens[†]
University of Nevada, Reno, Nevada, US

RESEARCH SUMMARY

Most college students experience some degree of social anxiety on occasion. However, many suffer chronic anxiety across social situations coupled with a strong fear of negative evaluation. In addition to impaired occupational and social functioning, severe social anxiety or social phobia can carry profound consequences for college students. Social anxiety is a prominent motivation for college student drinking (Burke and Stephens, 1999). In addition to social isolation, social anxiety is associated with depressogenic cognitions, both of which leave socially anxious students at an increased risk for depression (Johnson et al., 1992). Anxiety sensitivity – fear of anxiety-related sensations due to perceived consequences of physical, mental, or social harm – might play an important role in the development of social anxiety (Hazen et al., 1995). Unlike panic disorder, in which individuals typically fear anxiety symptoms out of fear of physical harm or loss of mental control, socially anxious individuals fear perceived social consequences of others noticing their anxiety. Socially anxious college students also judge others who appear anxious more negatively than do college students without social anxiety (Purdon et al., 2001). Although panic disorder treatments target anxiety sensitivity directly with interoceptive exposure strategies, this approach is just beginning to receive attention for the treatment of social anxiety. After a brief review of the literature describing the nature of social anxiety among college students, this chapter will examine the specific role of anxiety sensitivity in its development and maintenance. Finally, results from a preliminary investigation comparing the effects of interoceptive exposure delivered in a social

---

[*] A version of this chapter was also published in *Anxiety in College Students,* edited Benjamin Ayers and Michelle Bristow published by Nova Science Publishers, Inc. It was submitted for appropriate modifications in an effort to encourage wider dissemination of research.
[†] Correspondence author: Holly Hazlett-Stevens, University of Nevada, Department of Psychology/298 Reno, NV 89557, Email: hhazlett@unr.edu.

context to social context exposure without the interoceptive component will be presented and discussed.

Chapter 217

FLUENT SPEAKERS' ADVICE FOR COMMUNICATING WITH PEOPLE WHO STUTTER: THE CONCEPT OF MUTUAL HELP AND ITS EFFECTS ON SUCCESSFUL STUTTERING MANAGEMENT

Stephanie Hughes[*,1], Rodney Gabel[#,2] and Farzan Irani[†,3]
[1] Governors State University, Monee, Illinois, US
[2] Bowling Green State University, US
[3] Texas State University – San Marcos, US

RESEARCH SUMMARY

Stuttering, a disorder of communication that disrupts the smooth, forward flow of speech, is often perceived negatively by fluent speakers. This chapter begins with a review of fluent speakers' attitudes toward stuttering and their perceptions of the effects of the disorder on the lives of people who stutter (PWS). A qualitative study is then presented which examines fluent speakers' beliefs about the ways in which PWS and fluent speakers may help each other to communicate more effectively. The results of this study suggest that while fluent speakers generally believe that they should treat PWS with patience and respect, there is some confusion regarding the ways in which these positive attitudes should manifest themselves as active behaviors. In addition, fluent speakers believe that PWS can facilitate communication by engaging in behaviors that reduce or eliminate stuttering. Many of these behaviors have been reported in the stuttering literature as adversely affecting the successful management of stuttering by PWS. The authors conclude the chapter with a discussion of how PWS may experience unintentional prejudice or discrimination from fluent speakers and how the public's perceptions may be altered to alleviate negative attitudes toward stuttering and individuals who stutter.

---

[*] Corresponding Author: Stephanie Hughes, Ph.D., CCC-SLP, Governors State University, s-hughes@govst.edu.
[#] rgabel@bgsu.edu.
[†] firani@txstate.edu.

Chapter 218

STEREOTYPES AS ATTRIBUTIONS

Mark J. Brandt and Christine Reyna
DePaulUniversity, Chicago, Illinois, US

RESEARCH SUMMARY

Why are some groups better off than others? Why are women more likely to take care of the children? How come Blacks generally achieve less educationally and economically? Stereotypes provide answers to these kinds of questions, albeit imperfectly, and help us provide meaning to the social world around us. Early stereotype researchers suggested that stereotypes help people explain and rationalize the position of groups in society (Lippman, 1922). While the influence of this observation has waxed and waned over the years, the explanatory power of stereotypes continues to be an important function of social stereotypes. The current chapter reviews research examining the role of stereotypes as explanatory and rationalization agents and the impact of stereotypes on intergroup behavior. We suggest that stereotypes serve explanatory and attributional functions at three interrelated levels of analysis: (a) individual level, wherein stereotypes are analyzed in terms of the attributional dimensions they imply (locus, stability, controllability); (b) intragroup level, in which stereotypes define and explain by combining stereotypic traits on dimensions of warmth and competence, which in turn predict unique patterns of emotions and behaviors; and (c) intergroup level, in which stereotypes explain the social order by providing compensatory or causally relevant traits in reference to other relevant groups. The resulting attributional signature of stereotypes influences attitudes and behaviors.

Chapter 219

PUBLIC ATTITUDES TOWARD CLUTTERING AND STUTTERING IN FOUR COUNTRIES**

Kenneth O. St. Louis[1],*, Yulia Filatova[2], Mehmet Coşkun[3], Seyhun Topbaş[4], Sertan Özdemir[4], Dobrinka Georgieva[5], Elise McCaffrey[6] and Reshella D. George[7]

[1] West Virginia University, Morgantown, West Virginia, US
[2] Moscow State Pedagogical University, Moscow, Russia
[3] Private Practice, Marmaris, Turkey
[4] Anadolu University, Eskisehir, Turkey
[5] SouthWest University, Blagoevgrad, Bulgaria
[6] Portland State University, Portland, Oregon, US
[7] James Madison University, Harrisonburg, Virginia, US

RESEARCH SUMMARY

Purpose. Using an adaptation of the *Experimental Edition of the Public Opinion Survey of Human Attributes* (*POSHA-E*), investigators sought to compare public attitudes toward cluttering with those toward stuttering in four country samples, each in a different language. The *POSHA-E* was developed to measure public attitudes of stuttering but was modified to provide written definitions of cluttering and stuttering. *Method*. Convenience samples of 60 to 90 adult respondents from Turkey, Bulgaria, Russia, and the USA (302 total) rated *POSHA-E* items on 1-9 scales for cluttering and stuttering after reading the definitions. *Results*. Public attitudes toward cluttering and stuttering were similar for all respondents combined, but significant differences occurred. Attitude differences from country-to-country were greater than differences for cluttering versus stuttering. *Conclusions*. Positive and negative attitudes toward cluttering appear to be similar to those toward stuttering, and a cluttering stereotype appears likely.

---

*Address correspondence to: Kenneth O. St. Louis, Ph.D., Department of Speech Pathology and Audiology, 805 Allen Hall, PO Box 6122, West Virginia University, Morgantown, WV 26506-6122, Phone: 304-293-2946, FAX: 304-293-2905, Email: kstlouis@wvu.edu.

In: Psychology Research Biographies and Summaries
Editors: Nancy E. Wodarth and Alexis P. Ferguson

ISBN: 978-1-61470-491-1
© 2012 Nova Science Publishers, Inc.

Chapter 220

THE FORMATION OF STEREOTYPES IN CHILDREN: EVIDENCE FROM AGE AND RACE STUDIES

Denise Davidson*, Vanessa R. Raschke and Sandra B. Vanegas
Loyola University, Chicago, Illinois, US

RESEARCH SUMMARY

This chapter explores the formation of stereotypes in children, particularly negative stereotypes that children hold about others. Theoretical views about stereotype formation in children are presented, and evidence from developmental studies on racism and ageism is summarized. Empirical research is also provided in an attempt to address unanswered questions about negative stereotype formation in children. Commonalities in the development of stereotypes will be drawn, with implications given about the course of stereotype development, and how children's reliance on stereotypes can be lessened.

---

*Address correspondence to Denise Davidson, Department of Psychology, Loyola University Chicago, 1032 W. Sheridan Rd., Chicago, Il. 60660. E-mail: ddavids@luc.edu.

Chapter 221

BAYESIAN RACISM: A MODERN EXPRESSION OF CONTEMPORARY PREJUDICE

Eric Luis Uhlmann[*,1] *and Victoria L. Brescoll*[2]
[1]Northwestern University, US
[2]Yale University, US

RESEARCH SUMMARY

The present chapter identifies, assesses, and examines the correlates of a previously understudied expression of contemporary prejudice— *Bayesian racism*, the belief that it is rational to discriminate against individuals based on stereotypes about their racial group. Individual differences in Bayesian racism are strongly related to intergroup prejudice and *negatively* correlated with indices of reliance on probabilities and logical thinking. Moreover, individuals who endorse Bayesian racism are unwilling to rely on base rates unfavorable to a high-status ingroup (i.e., Ivy League students). We relate the concept of Bayesian racism to existing theories of intergroup prejudice and outline future directions for research on the underpinnings of such beliefs.

---

[*] CONTACT: Eric Luis Uhlmann, Ford Motor Company Center for Global Citizenship, Kellogg School of Management, Northwestern University, Donald P. Jacobs Center, 2001 Sheridan Road, Evanston, IL 60208-2001, Tel: (203)-687-9269, E-mail: e-uhlmann@northwestern.edu.

In: Psychology Research Biographies and Summaries
Editors: Nancy E. Wodarth and Alexis P. Ferguson

ISBN: 978-1-61470-491-1
© 2012 Nova Science Publishers, Inc.

Chapter 222

STEREOTYPES ON THE BRAIN: USING EVENT-RELATED BRAIN POTENTIALS TO INVESTIGATE STEREOTYPING

Silvia Tomelleri and Luigi Castelli
Dipartimento di Psicologia dello Sviluppo e della Socializzazione,
University of Padova, Padova, Italy

RESEARCH SUMMARY

According to a social cognitive perspective, stereotypes have been defined as cognitive structures that contain the perceiver's knowledge, beliefs, and expectations about social groups (Hamilton & Trolier, 1986). Perceivers regularly rely on stereotypes to simplify the complex social environment and quickly make sense of the social world. Because of the importance and pervasiveness of stereotypes in everyday life, these phenomena have been at the top of the interests of social psychological research. Traditionally, the nature and functions of stereotypes have been primarily investigated by using self-report measures (i.e., questionnaires) and more cognitive measures (mainly based on response latencies and accuracy) in order to infer the underlying cognitive mechanisms. However, responses in computerized tasks represent the final outcome of a large number of intervening cognitive processes, and variations in the response latencies may not often be attributed to a single specific process. Recently, the emergence of neuroscience has provided social psychology with new methods that can override this limitation. In particular, the event-related brain potential (ERP) technique can provide a direct, on line, continuous measure of processing between a stimulus and a response, giving direct access to the various stages of information processing between perception and behavior (Luck, 2005).

The main goal of this chapter is to introduce readers to recent social neuroscience research that has applied the ERP approach to the study of stereotypes and to show the major advances that it has produced in relation with the existing theories. We will first provide a brief overview of the recording, theory, and interpretation of the ERPs. Then, we will review studies that have used ERPs as useful tools to further investigate various aspects related to stereotyping:a) stereotype violation and confirmation; b) the influence of stereotype activation on behavioral processes, with specific attention given to the mechanisms involved in self-regulation; c) individual and situational differences in self-regulatory processes linked to the expression of stereotypes. In the chapter we will try to highlight how the integration of different methods, theories, and levels of analysis from both neuroscience and social psychology (i.e., the social neuroscience approach) can greatly facilitate a most comprehensive understanding of different important aspects of the human social mind.

Do Managers' Perceptions Coincide with Established Stereotyping of Older Workers' Capabilities[*]

Trude Furunes[#] and Reidar J. Mykletun
University of Stavanger, Norway

Research Summary

Due to population ageing, Western societies' future economic growth may have to rely on the capacity of older workers in the labour market(Ilmainen, 2009). However, research suggests that stereotyping, age discrimination and negative manager attitudes may lead to early retirement and workforce losses(Furunes & Mykletun, 2007, 2010). Previous research indicates that there exist several stereotypes of how workers' capabilities change with age. To our knowledge this study is the first to profile managers' perceptions of age-related changes of the workforce and how these perceptions relate to both prevailing stereotypes of ageing workers and also to research outcomes describing older workers' adaption to the workplace. Whereas previous studies on stereotypes of older workers show an extensive list of negative characteristics, this study shows that managers perceive ageing as contributing to increased managerial and interpersonal skills, creative problem solving capacities, and work moral. On the negative side, age contributes to impaired learning capacities and basic functions. The findings of this study are closer to results of extensive research on older workers' capabilities and only partially in line with prevailing stereotypes of older workers. It is likely that managers working with older workers will develop conceptualisations of this part of the workforce that are closer to the characteristics demonstrated by research on actual behaviour, hence prevailing stereotypes of these workers may not be so general and persistent as argued by extant research.

---

[*] Peer reviewed by Dr. Christina Björklund, PhD, Karolinska Institute, Sweden.
[#] Correspondence address: Trude Furunes, University of Stavanger, Norway, e-mail: trude.furunes@uis.no, Phone: +47 53 81 37 62.

Chapter 224

ADS AND SPORTS: STEREOTYPICAL SCENES

Stephane Heas, D. Bodin, L. Robene and J. Blumrodt
European University of Britain, France

RESEARCH SUMMARY

Purpose: The advertisementsof sportsare far from being able to reflect the changing realities of sports or physical activities in a country such as France. The purpose is to test the proposition that the gender relationships portrayed in specific sport advertisements perpetuate traditional and sexist stereotypes, are far from egalitarian shared social representations, and far from egalitarian social and professional activities[1].

Design/Methodology/Approach: There were 700 advertisements of sports in several French magazines analyzed during a twenty-two-year period (1986-2008) constituting the support of content analysis, using specific spreadsheet software(Sphinx®). Specifically, four men's readerships magazines and four women's magazinesare strongly represented here because of their large national diffusion. There are 25 encodings used to analyze this corpus, and they distinguish the people displayed, setting of Advertisements (nature, area's sport, and undetermined places), situations of equality or domination between male/female and *vice versa*, domination between male/male, domination between female/female, and the colours used, the appearance of physical movement, skin colour, the presence of hair and hairs, etc.

Findings: In sports advertisements and which use sports, males are over-represented: 57.4% are present, *versus* 18.5% females present. Women in sports are generally in situations of inequality or subordination: face to face, males dominating the females (11.9% of all ads, 28.5% of face to face ads). On the contrary, females rarely dominate the males: these amounts to occur five times less often (2.1% of all advertisements' situations, and 5.2% of face to face ads respectively).Men in sports seem to be more dynamic individuals: males move more often than their female counterparts (50.1% *versus* 36% respectively). Especially, a man's physical movements are more frequent when several men are represented in the magazine ads. Females are represented with fewer activities, often seen as spectators of male sporting

---
[1] Research conducted with the support of ANR-08-VULN-001-PRAS-GEVU, universities of Lyon, Rennes, France.

events, and even nowadays are over-sexualised. However, on average, sports ads promote the entire female body (48.3% for women *vs* 42.7% for men):this frequency rejects the arguments of militant feminists who think that women are more often "cut" from advertisements. The male characters, strangely, are more often photographed in portrait style (9.2% for men *vs* 5.6% for women).The women are over-sexualized in the ads for sports: their breasts, legs and calves are more frequently seen in the advertisements. These body parts are over-represented more often than that of their male counterparts: 22.4% *vs* 14.2% respectively. These averages confirm stereotypes, and reinforce the previous sociological studies' results(Goffman, 1976; Wolin, 2003; Cortese, 2007; Grau et *al.*, 2007). Gender imbalance is reinforced by such adjuncts such as 1) colour utilisation, for instance, blue (31.3%) *versus* one percent for pink, 2) outdoor background which reinforces sociological link between males and outside activities, and 3) type of physical activities portrayed (traditional masculine sports in Europe like football-soccer, rugby or motorsports).

By and large, sports ads remain to be created from a classical masculine point of view rather than a gender reversal. Different shocking visuals are easier to remember by the public but are drowned in all ads of sports. On average, the advertisements of sports maintain an andrological point of view.

Research Limitations/Implications: Extensions of the present study, and future research, could increase both the breadth and depth of the investigation, and thereby contribute significantly to the wealth of knowledge pertaining to gender in advertising. During some periods of the year, advertisements can be less "gender'stereotypical". For example, in 1996 and 1997, in France there were some ads which had reversed the gender domination (Perret, 2003). In the long term, the ads of sports are always portraying the masculine point of view. Female athletes are often always devaluated.

Practical Implications: There is still some way to go before sports advertisements reflect the real world, *a fortiori* an ideal world where equality is normal, and improves gender's innovations into advertising in the future. For instance, to propose gender egalitarian ads, (without women's degradations into visuals, or through sexists or demeaning slogans- not analysed here), to reinforce advertisement agencies' social responsibility or sports enterprises' social responsibility, to boost egalitarian relations between males and females, all done by extensions between different ethnic, sexual, generational, religious, etc., groups.

Originality/Value: This study examines a widespread social phenomenon in a specific and national context upon a large corpus (seven hundred ads of sports) and not only on provoking ads, nor during a period of time with most egalitarian ads.

In: Psychology Research Biographies and Summaries
Editors: Nancy E. Wodarth and Alexis P. Ferguson
ISBN: 978-1-61470-491-1
© 2012 Nova Science Publishers, Inc.

Chapter 225

PSYCHOLOGICAL IMPLICATIONS OF STEREOTYPING AMERICAN INDIANSTHROUGH THE USE OF NATIVE-THEMED MASCOTS, NICKNAMES, AND LOGOS

Jesse A. Steinfeldt[*,1], *Paul Hagan*[1] *and M. Clint Steinfeldt*[2]

[1] Department of Educational Psychology, Indiana University, Bloomington, Indiana, US
[2] Department of Athletics, Fort Lewis College, US

RESEARCH SUMMARY

The use of American Indian culture and imagery as mascots, nicknames, and logos in sport is a common societal practice that has been met with opposition from psychological research and from those interested in social justice and advocacy. Native-themed mascots, nicknames, and logos are considered harmful to American Indian communities because they misuse cultural symbols and sacred practices (e.g., eagle feathers, drums), perpetuate stereotypes of American Indians (e.g., noble savage, bloodthirsty savage, a historic race that only exists in past-tense status), and deny American Indians control over societal definitions of themselves. Additionally, this practice creates a racially hostile educational environment, and an estimated 115 organizations (e.g., American Psychological Association, American Counseling Association, Society of Indian Psychologists, National Association for the Advancement of Colored People) have produced resolutions calling for the immediate retirement of Native-themed mascots, nicknames, and logos. Because American Indians do not have control of these images, this process of racialized mascotery allows mainstream America to stereotype, undermine, and appropriate American Indian culture while systematically teaching the ideology of White supremacy. This manuscript describes ways that these stereotypic representations affect the psychological functioning of American Indians, and how this practice is harmful to both American Indian communities and to

---

[*] Correspondence should be directed to Jesse A. Steinfeldt, Ph.D., Department of Educational Psychology, Indiana University, 201 N. Rose Avenue, Bloomington, IN, 47403; 812 856-8331 (phone); 812 856 8333 (fax); jesstein@indiana.edu.

members of the mainstream culture. In sum, this manuscript provides an overview of psychological research and theory, discusses educational interventions and legislation aimed at curtailing this practice, and provides perspectives for the reader to have a greater understanding of the hegemonic and deleterious nature of racialized mascotery.

Chapter 226

THE COMPLEX ROLE OF MOTIVATION IN STEREOTYPING AND STEREOTYPE THREAT EFFECTS

Lisa R. Grimm[*] *and Julie Milligan Hughes*
The College of New Jersey, Ewing, New Jersey, US

RESEARCH SUMMARY

We examine the role of human motivation on stereotyping. People are motivated to carve the world into comprehensible segments (i.e., engage in categorization) that allow them to predict characteristics of new things or people. Categorization is a basic cognitive process that helps us structure our mental world to represent the physical world and relies on the similarity of unknown objects or people to previously created and stored categories. Objects can be grouped based on characteristics (e.g., red objects) or relational information (e.g., student). Our ability to classify new objects or people into known categories allows us to infer unknown features or behaviors and provides us with a known set of guidelines to use during interactions. For example, knowing someone is a student may lead us to ask about the individual's current classes. With objects, imperfect classification could lead to errors in prediction and interactions. Similarly, human stereotypes develop from this fundamental motivational drive for order, but can have deleterious consequences. We discuss the development of stereotypes and their application by children and adults. Even young children spontaneously categorize individuals on the basis of gender and ethnicity, and use group membership to infer individual possession of stereotypic traits. As children get older, their awareness of stereotypes includes an awareness of collectively endorsed stereotypes (McKown & Weinstein, 2003), and children use this stereotype knowledge to make sense of their social world as well.

Furthermore, our research suggests motivation plays a critical role beyond the generation and use of stereotypic information in the classification of others. Simply, motivation explains how merely mentally representing negative stereotypic information about one's groups can

---

[*] Please address all correspondence to:Lisa R. Grimm, Department of Psychology, The College of New Jersey, P.O. Box 7718, Ewing, NJ 08628-0718, grimm@tcnj.edu.

result in performance decrements. When a negative-group stereotype is associated with a group an individual belongs to, he or she can experience a decline in performance, or a *stereotype threat effect*. For example, a woman who knows of the stereotype that "women are bad at math" will experience a decline in her performance when taking a math test. We argue that a motivational framework can account for stereotype threat effects. Negative stereotypes induce a motivational state that is associated with avoidance and vigilance, while positive stereotypes induce a motivational state associated with approach. We use this framework to explain stereotype threat effects and offer solutions for improving the performance of stereotyped groups using evidence from mathematical problem solving, learning classification rules, and motor performance, specifically golf putting.

In: Psychology Research Biographies and Summaries
Editors: Nancy E. Wodarth and Alexis P. Ferguson
ISBN: 978-1-61470-491-1
© 2012 Nova Science Publishers, Inc.

Chapter 227

AMBIVALENCE IN STEREOTYPES AND ATTITUDES: THE IMPLICATIONS OF POSSESSING POSITIVE AND NEGATIVE PERCEPTIONS

Kimberley A. Clow[1] and Rosemary Ricciardelli[2]
[1] University of Ontario Institute of Technology, Canada
[2] York University, Canada

RESEARCH SUMMARY

The content of most stereotypes are not uniformly negative. African Americans are stereotyped as loud and aggressive, but also as musical and athletic. Asian Americans are stereotyped as being cold and aloof, but also as high in intelligence. People express more respect for men than women, but more liking for women than men. Thus, rather than uniform negativity, many stereotypes appear to be ambivalent, containing both positive and negative elements simultaneously. Ambivalent sexism and the stereotype content model have emerged to explain the ambivalence that is prevalent in intergroup attitudes. This chapter will review these theories and key findings in the field, as well as present applied data investigating stereotypes of men in nursing and stigma toward the wrongly convicted to illustrate how the ambivalence of intergroup attitudes can suggest support for stigmatized groups, while at the same time discriminating against them.

In: Psychology Research Biographies and Summaries
Editors: Nancy E. Wodarth and Alexis P. Ferguson
ISBN: 978-1-61470-491-1
© 2012 Nova Science Publishers, Inc.

Chapter 228

EPILEPSY: MYTHS, STEREOTYPES AND STIGMA

Jane McCagh
Liverpool Hope University, Hope Park, Liverpool, United Kingdom

RESEARCH SUMMARY

This chapter will discuss how epilepsy has been perceived throughout history and across different cultures. The chapter will highlight how historical conceptions of epilepsy and misrepresentation in the media have perpetuated current stereotypical perceptions of the disorder. Consequently, misconceptions about epilepsy serve to propagate discrimination and stigmatoward people with the condition. The myths that surround epilepsy will be explored emphasising how misconception, discrimination and stigma affect the quality of life of people with the condition. Myths, stigma and stereotypes can result in multiple interrelated psychosocial outcomes which can impede the cohesive integration of people with epilepsy in society. The impact of these factors on important psychosocial outcomes such as self esteem, depression, anxiety, employability, opportunities for social interaction and interpersonal relationships will be discussed.The chapter will explore these outcomes highlighting how society can be effective in engendering positive attitudes towards people with epilepsy. To conclude, educational interventions aimed at people with epilepsy, their families, employers, teachers and society at large will be considered along with future research suggestions with a view to reduce the impact of stigma and improve the social functioning of people with epilepsy.

WHAT IS EPILEPSY?

Epilepsy is the most prevalent serious neurological disorder in the world (Brodie & Schachter, 2001).In the region of 50 million people have epilepsy worldwide. Eighty percent of people with epilepsy live in developing countries with little if any access to treatment

In: Psychology Research Biographies and Summaries
Editors: Nancy E. Wodarth and Alexis P. Ferguson

ISBN: 978-1-61470-491-1
© 2012 Nova Science Publishers, Inc.

Chapter 229

STEREOTYPES TOWARD FOOD AND EATING BEHAVIOR

Atsushi Kimura[1], Yuji Wada[1,*] and Takashi Oka[2]

[1] Sensory and Cognitive Food Science Laboratory,
National Food Research Institute, Tsukuba, Ibaraki, Japan
[2] Department of Psychology, NihonUniversity, Setagaya, Tokyo, Japan

RESEARCH SUMMARY

In the last few decades, several studies, mostly performed in Western countries, have started to reveal the existence of various food and eating stereotypes. Interestingly, these studies imply that many people are still influenced by unfounded nutritional beliefs and practices regardless of the growing amount of scientific knowledge on nutrition and health. The aim of this chapter is to provide a brief overview of empirical research on food-related beliefs and stereotypes.

Firstly, we illustrate that consumer food choice and evaluation are influenced by various stereotypical beliefs about food. For example, people tend to categorize foods based on subjective beliefs (e.g., high-fat/low-fat, local/imported, branded/unbranded) and those beliefs further influence a consumer's food selections and food product evaluations (for example, a belief that local food products are more expensive than imports may prevent consumers from buying local products). We also discuss the nature of magical beliefs about food and health.

Secondly, we review consumption stereotypes, which are stereotypes based on what and how much people eat. Specifically, we focus on gender-based consumption stereotypes, in which femininity and masculinity are primarily associated with specific patterns of consumption. We discuss the nature of gender-based consumption stereotypes among the younger population in relation to social appeal and/or pressure. Young women often experience social pressure based on gender-based consumption stereotypes and form

---

* Corresponding author: E-mail address yujiwd@affrc.go.jp, Fax: +81-(0)29-838-7319 Phone: +81-(0)29-838-7357.

psychological barriers against consuming masculine foods and drinks. There is fear that these stereotypical attitudes among females result in several pathological eating behaviors.

Finally, we discuss the feasibility of introducing implicit attitude measures for the study of food-related stereotypes, partly based on our recent studies.

Chapter 230

GENDER STEREOTYPES AND MENTAL ROTATION: THE ROLE OF SELF-BELIEF

Angelica Moè
Department of General Psychology – University of Padua, Italy

RESEARCH SUMMARY

A large body of evidence has shown male superiority in performance of a mental rotation task, notably the MRT proposed by Vandenberg and Kuse (1978). The difference is considerable, males scoring as much as one standard deviation higher than females. Many reasons have been put forward for this underscoring by females: biological, cultural, strategic and motivational. Males are favoured by lateral specialisation, early familiarisation with spatial tasks and toys, use of holistic strategies, and an incremental theory of spatial abilities. Recently, gender stereotyping has been considered to be one of the factors affecting test accuracy, particularly for females. As a result of widely held stereotyping, females are thought to be less able than males in spatial tasks such as mental rotation. Awareness of this stereotype can intimidate females and increase theirexpectation of performing poorly, this indeed having negative affect on performance. Research examining these male/female differences and the underlying causes is reviewed and suggestions made for channels of future research.

In: Psychology Research Biographies and Summaries
Editors: Nancy E. Wodarth and Alexis P. Ferguson
ISBN: 978-1-61470-491-1
© 2012 Nova Science Publishers, Inc.

Chapter 231

WHEN STEREOTYPES BECOME LIFE THREATENING: KNOWLEDGE AND ATTITUDES ABOUT HIV/AIDS AMONG OLDER WOMEN AND THE HEALTH CARE PROVIDERS WHO TREAT THEM

Jennifer Hillman* and Molly Beiler
The Pennsylvania State University, Berks College, Reading Pennsylvania, US

RESEARCH SUMMARY

According to the Centers for Disease Control (2005), approximately 15 percent of all new HIV/AIDS cases are among those aged 50 and older. The greatest increase in infection appears among older Black and Latino women who contract the virus through heterosexual contact. With the rapid growth of the older adult population in the next decade, it becomes critical that stereotypes regarding elderly sexuality are examined and dispelled. Older women are often subject to ageism; many health care providers fail to ask appropriate questions regarding their sexual health and remain unaware of unique age and gender specific risk factors. Stereotypes to be examined include beliefs that older women are asexual and have no need for HIV/AIDS education. Additional barriers to prevention include older women's lack of experience with condoms, culture specific factors including machismo, and stigma and discrimination toward older adults living with HIV/AIDS. This chapter will focus on knowledge and attitudes about HIV/AIDS among elderly women and health care providers, and will provide relevant clinical and public policy recommendations.

---

* Please address correspondence to: Jennifer Hillman, Penn State Berks, PO Box 7009, Reading, PA or via e-mail at JLH35@psu.edu.

Chapter 232

AN ANALYSIS OF RESPONSE TIME CHARACTERISTICS WITH STRENGTH AND REVERSIBILITY OF STEREOTYPES FOR DETERMINING OPTIMUM CONTROL POSITION ON A HORIZONTAL DISPLAY

Alan H. S. Chan*
City University of Hong Kong, China

RESEARCH SUMMARY

In this paper, the effects of few design parameters on human performancefor a common horizontal display/rotary control arrangement wereexamined. The results showed that the knob position, pointer type, and scale side and in particular the control position x scale side interaction significantly affectedhuman response time. Response time was found to decrease with increasing values of stereotype proportion and index of stereotype reversibility, andthe extents of decrease were different for the top and bottom controls. Based on the consideration of response time and stereotype characteristics, the optimum location for positioning a rotary control on a horizontal scale was found.

---

* Phone: 2788 8439; E-mail: alan.chan@cityu.edu.hk.

Chapter 233

A FRENCHMAN, AN ENGLISHMAN, AND A GERMAN…STEREOTYPES IN HUMOROUS TEXTS

Arthur Asa Berger[*]

RESEARCH SUMMARY

Stereotypes are conventionally understood to be generalizations about the behavior and characteristics of some group of people--based on race, nationality, ethnicity, religion, occupation, gender, and so on. Stereotypes can be negative, neutral, positive, or mixed. Some common stereotypes are that women are lousy drivers, Jews are cheap, Scots are thrifty, British people are snobs, and that Japanese are honest. The negative stereotype of the Japanese is that are also robotic and a bit fanatic. Stereotypes generally involve people characterizing some group on the basis of a limited experience with a relatively small number of representatives of that group. But in many cases, stereotypes are learned, from exposure to stereotypes found in the media and carried in jokes and other forms of humor.

Statistically speaking, stereotypes are overgeneralizations based on sampling errors—assuming that all members of some group are like some of the members of the group—the one that has been "sampled" either in person or carried in the media. From a semiotic perspective, stereotypes involve a process known as synecdoche, which can be defined as "a part that stands for the whole" or vice versa. Thus, the Pentagon "stands for" the United States military establishment and Uncle Sam "stands for "America." Synecdoche is a weak for of metonymy, which involves communication by association. Metonymy, along with metaphor, pervades our use of language and is often found in advertising, where associations are quick ways of providing people exposed to the advertising with reference points and information they already have that can be used to sell products and service.

Stereotypes are often used in formulaic genres that rely on stereotypes to suggest character types and personalities. These stereotypes or "stock types" enable audiences of

---

[*] 118 Peralta Avenue, Mill Valley, CA94941, US, Tel: (415) 383-2999, E-mail arthurasaberger@gmail.com.

these texts (the term used in academic jargon for works of all kinds, and in this case, riddles, jokes and other kinds of humor) to quickly come to conclusions about various characters and means that the writers of these texts do not have to spend time in these texts developing and establishing their characters. Thus, if a script writer needs a gangster, making that character an Italian, to tie in with all the news in the media about the mafia in Italy, is an understandable choice. What we are dealing with is "types" of people. Henri Bergson wrote that "every comic character is a *type*. Inversely, every resemblance to a type has something comic in it." (Quoted in Sypher, 1956.) These types often have fixations that drive their behavior, as we seen in plays such as Moliere's *The Misanthrope* and *The Miser*.

In my work on humor, I developed a typology that focuses on the techniques in humorous texts that generate everything from smiles to mirthful laughter. Most theories of humor attempt to explain why we laugh. The most important theories are Freud's notion that humor is based on unconscious or masked aggression, Aristotle's belief (and Hobbes) that humor is based on a sense of superiority, and Schopenhauer's belief that all humor is based on incongruity. There are many writers and humor theorists who support one of these three why theories. My work on humor doesn't' attempt to deal with why we laugh but what makes us laugh. I made an analysis of many forms of humor, such as jokes, theatrical comedies, and cartoons from texts in many different periods and came up with 45 different techniques that, I argue, inform all humor.

Chapter 234

A STOCHASTIC MODEL OF PROSPECTIVE MEMORY

Jack D. Arnal and James M. Lampinen
University of Arkansas, US

RESEARCH SUMMARY

Prospective memory describes the cognitive process that allows an individual to delay the completion of an intention without keeping the task at the forefront of attention. This process has been referred to as everyday memory by past researchers to emphasize how common this type of memory is, varying from the mundane (e.g., buying milk) to the atypical but critical (e.g., apprehending a suspect). The authors examine the classification and components of prospective memory, as well as describing the typical paradigm used to study this cognitive process. Additionally, the current theoretical frameworks of the prospective memory process are discussed. Specifically theories of a resource consuming monitoring process and theories of spontaneous retrieval of the delayed intention are discussed. The current mathematical model of prospective memory is examined, and advantages and disadvantages are discussed. Finally, a new mathematical model of the prospective memory processes is proposed and evaluated, drawing component from both diffusion process models and race models.

Predicting Where Fly Balls Will Land: Lack of Conscious Awareness of How We Navigate to Catch Baseballs

Dennis M. Shaffer*, Andrew B. Maynor,
April Utt and Bethany A. Briley
The Ohio State University, US
Mansfield, Department of Psychology

Research Summary

Baseball outfielders typically have difficulty articulating how they reach their destination when navigating to catch baseballs. Research has confirmed that outfielders utilize simple control heuristics to optically maintain control over the ball. The strategy of using these simple control heuristics provides ongoing guidance without indicating precise information concerning where the ball is located in space and where it will land. Despite the simplicity of these heuristics, fielders appear to remain unaware of how they accomplish the task of navigating to where the ball will eventually land. When asked how they run to catch fly balls, fielders typically report a strategy based on their conscious awareness of the location of the ball that suggests they know where the ball is located in three-dimensional space and where it will land. In the current chapter we show that observers believe that they can predict where fly balls will land after seeing only a portion of the ball's flight. In two experiments, observers greatly misestimated where baseballs will land in both video and live conditions, irrespective of their baseball experience or confidence in their abilities. These results demonstrate that observers are largely unaware of the extent of their reliance on unconscious visual-tracking control mechanisms that guide them to their destination.

---

* Correspondence concerning this article should be addressed to: Dennis M. Shaffer, The Ohio State University—Mansfield, 1680 University Drive, Mansfield, OH 44906, Telephone: (419) 755-4274, FAX: (419) 755-4367, e-mail: shaffer.247@osu.edu.

Chapter 236

Cognitive Processes in Communication between Pilots and Air Traffic Control

Alice F. Healy[1], Vivian I. Schneider[1] and Immanuel Barshi[2]

[1] University of Colorado, Boulder, US
[2] NASA Ames Research Center, US

Research Summary

We have been probing the cognitive processes underlying communication between pilots and air traffic control. To study these processes, we developed an experimental paradigm analogous to the natural flight situation, in which pilots receive navigation instructions from air traffic control, repeat them, and follow them. In the experimental task, individuals typically hear navigation instructions, repeat them aloud, and then follow them, navigating in a space displayed on a computer screen. We describe a series of studies addressing 2 sets of relevant issues. The first set is empirical and concerns parameters for optimizing the ability to comprehend and remember the instructions, considering the length and wordiness of the instructions, the modality in which the instructions are presented, and the effects of repeating the instructions on their correct execution. The second set of issues is theoretical and concerns the mental representation of both the verbal content of the instructions and their spatial implications.

In: Psychology Research Biographies and Summaries
Editors: Nancy E. Wodarth and Alexis P. Ferguson
ISBN: 978-1-61470-491-1
© 2012 Nova Science Publishers, Inc.

Chapter 237

THE EFFECT OF VISUO-SPATIAL ATTENTION ON LONG-TERM MEMORY ENCODING

Stephan Josef Stegt[1] and Cristina Massen[2]*
[1]University of Bonn, Bonn, Germany
[2]Max-Planck-Institute for Human Cognitive and Brain Sciences,
Leipzig, Germany

RESEARCH SUMMARY

Existing studies about the effects of attention on long-term memory encoding focused on the effects of 'frontal', executive attentional mechanisms and made use of paradigms of divided attention. We investigated the impact of visuo-spatial ('posterior') attention on long-term memory encoding. In four experiments, we used a standard spatial cuing paradigm and presented words either under valid or invalid cuing conditions. Performance in yes-no-recognition, cued recall and free recall was enhanced in the valid cuing-condition, whereas no effect was found for source-monitoring. The results show not only divided, but visuo-spatial attention considerably influences memory encoding, and the impact of visuo-spatial attention is different from that of divided attention.

---

* Correspondence concerning this chapter should be addressed to Stephan Stegt or Cristina Massen.

In: Psychology Research Biographies and Summaries
Editors: Nancy E. Wodarth and Alexis P. Ferguson
ISBN: 978-1-61470-491-1
© 2012 Nova Science Publishers, Inc.

Chapter 238

EXPOSURE TO AMBIGUOUS TONE SEQUENCES INDUCES SHORT-TERM PLASTICITY OF PITCH PERCEPTION

Annemarie Seither-Preisler[*,1,2], *Linda Johnson*[1], *Erich Preisler*, *Stefan Seither*[1] *and Bernd Lütkenhöner*[1]

[1] Section of Experimental Audiology, ENT Clinic,
Münster University Hospital, Münster, Germany
[2] Current address: Department of Psychology, Cognitive Science Section,
University of Graz, Graz, Austria

RESEARCH SUMMARY

The sounds of voiced speech and of many musical instruments are composed of a series of harmonics that are multiples of a low fundamental frequency (F0). Perceptually, such sounds may be classified along two major dimensions: The fundamental pitch, which corresponds to F0, and the spectral pitches of the overtones that provide the basis for the sensation of timbre. Strikingly, fundamental pitch sensations occur even when F0 is missing in the spectrum, a phenomenon termed 'virtual pitch'. We designed an Auditory Ambiguity Test (AAT) comprising 100 ambiguous tone pairs, where a rising overtone spectrum is associated with a falling missing F0, and vice versa. By letting subjects of varying musical competence classify these sequences according to the perceived pitch shift, we found that non-musicians predominantly based their decisions on spectral cues, while amateur and professional musicians predominantly based their decisions on the virtual pitch (Seither-Preisler et al., *J. Exp. Psychol.: HPP*, 33(3), 2007). This suggests that the perception of harmonic tones is either a function of congenital musical talents or of long-term musical

---

[*] Corresponding author: Annemarie Seither-Preisler, PD Dr. University of Graz, Department of Psychology, Cognitive Science Section, Universtätsplatz 2, A-8010 Graz, Austria, Email: annemarie.seither-preisler@uni-graz.at, Tel: ++43 316 380 5080, Fax: ++43 316 380 9806.

experience. We here present a follow-up study that was designed to test for learning-induced plasticity. Eleven subjects, who did not play a musical instrument at the time of the experiment, were randomly assigned to an exposure group (N=5) and a training group (N=6). Both groups were repeatedly tested with the AAT over a period of 8 weeks (1 session per week; 3 AAT presentations per session). The training group additionally received trainings between the 3 AAT presentations. There was one block of spectral training with the 'Noise Shift Test (NST)' and one block of virtual pitch training with the 'Present Fundamental Frequency Test (PFT)'. The AAT scores increased steadily over the eight weeks period, both in the exposure group (p=0.0012) and the training group (p=0.0006), regardless of the type of training. Thus, there was a general increase in the salience of virtual pitch sensations. The same effect, although weaker, was observed over the 3 subsequent AAT presentations of a session (exposure group: p=0.062; training group: p=0.01). These results suggest that short-term exposure to harmonic sounds enforces virtual pitch perception regardless of explicit training. This interpretation is in line with our previous study in which we attributed perceptual differences between musical competence groups to learning-induced long-term plasticity. The observed effects may reflect the biological relevance of a unitary fundamental pitch sensation for the analysis of complex auditory scenes.

Chapter 239

THE INTERACTION OF AUTOMATIC PROCESSES AND COGNITIVE RESOURCES IN READING: A COMPENSATORY FRAMEWORK

Jeffrey J. Walczyk[1]*, Min Wei, Peijia Zha and Diana A. Griffith-Ross*
Louisiana Tech University, US

RESEARCH SUMMARY

This article presents a theoretical account of the interaction between automatic processes and cognitive resources (attention & working memory) in reading: *Compensatory-Encoding Theory*. The theory postulates that once readers advance beyond beginning reading, neither inefficient skills, poorly written text, nor distracting reading environments need lower comprehension. The theory describes how, with advancing skill, readers more efficiently prevent automatic processes from failing and provide timely, accurate data to working memory even when automatic processes cannot. Compensatory actions include slowing reading rate, pausing, looking back in text, reading aloud, rereading, and explicit memory searching. The theory accounts for the findings of studies that have reported low correlations between the efficiency of reading subcomponent processes and comprehension as well as for why many interventions that have targeted improving comprehension by improving decoding have not been successful. Theoretical implications for reading research and cognitive science are considered. Implications of the theory for educational practice are also derived.

The proliferation of reading process models has prompted reading researchers to call for more integrative accounts encompassing a broader array of phenomena (Nist & Simpson, 2000; Winne, 1996). In this chapter, a comprehensive framework is proposed for understanding the interaction between automatic processes and cognitive resources (attention & working memory) in reading, an interplay poorly understood. To this end, a *Compensatory-Encoding Theory* is proposed, an expansion of the Compensatory-Encoding

---

[1] Address correspondence concerning this article to: Jeffrey J. Walczyk, Department of Psychology, P.O. Box 10048, Louisiana Tech University, Ruston, LA 71272. E-mail: Walczyk@latech.edu.

Model (see Walczyk, 2000). The theory features many innovations over the model. (a) A greatly expanded list of the ways in which readers support automatic processes that falter and overcome those that fail is provided. (b) A clear explanation of what compensatory processes are and how they interweave with other processes is presented. (c) For the first time, compensatory actions are mapped onto the reading problems, either hardware-based, inefficiency-based, or knowledge-based, that either avert or resolve. Moreover, compensatory actions are ranked according to their hypothesized order of use when reading problems occur. (d) Suggestions are made concerning how the use of compensatory actions improves developmentally. (e) New predictions have been added. (f) Finally, theoretical implication of the theory for reading research and cognitive science are proffered.

Chapter 240

A MOTIVATIONAL-COGNITIVE APPROACH TO PROSPECTIVE MEMORY

Suzanna L. Penningroth and Walter D. Scott
Department of Psychology, University of Wyoming, Laramie, Wyoming, US

RESEARCH SUMMARY

Prospective memory tasks are tasks that one must remember to perform in the future, such as keeping a dentist appointment or turning off the water sprinklers. A cognitive approach has yielded significant advances in our understanding of prospective memory processes. However, in this chapter, we argue that further insight can be gained by integrating motivational constructs. Specifically, we outline a new, goal-based motivational-cognitive model of prospective memory in which goal-related prospective memories are viewed as benefiting from both effortful and automatic processing throughout all phases of the prospective memory task. Drawing on contemporary goal frameworks, the new model views goals as knowledge structures with associative links to prospective memories. As a result of these associative connections, goal-related prospective memories are predicted (a) to be perceived as more important, (b) to benefit from greater use of mnemonic strategies, (c) to show greater accessibility in memory, (d) to show preferential allocation of attention during retrieval and performance, and (e) to benefit from automatic retrieval processes. Consequently, these processes are predicted to contribute to superior performance for goal-related prospective memories. In this chapter, we also review evidence that supports our new model. By guiding research into the motivational processes contributing to prospective memory, we hope to contribute to a more complete and ecologically valid understanding of prospective memory performance.

In: Psychology Research Biographies and Summaries
Editors: Nancy E. Wodarth and Alexis P. Ferguson

ISBN: 978-1-61470-491-1
© 2012 Nova Science Publishers, Inc.

Chapter 241

LABORATORY MEMORY TASKS AND AUTOBIOGRAPHICAL RECOLLECTION: COGNITIVE AND NEUROFUNCTIONAL EVIDENCE FOR DIFFERENTIAL FORMS OF EPISODIC MEMORY

Martina Piefke[*]

Physiological Psychology, Department of Psychology and Sports Sciences,
University of Bielefeld, Germany

RESEARCH SUMMARY

The classic model of episodic memory refers to both laboratory tasks requiring the conscious recall or recognition of experimental materials and autobiographical recollection of one's personal past experiences. Recent research in cognitive neuroscience, however, showed evidence that laboratory and autobiographical memory may share aspects of conscious retrieval and reference to the temporal and spatial context at the time of encoding of information, but are different from each other in some important respects. The autobiographical memory domain is characterized by self-referential information processing, subjective emotional evaluation of memories, and the accompanying autonoetic conscious awareness. In contrast, laboratory episodic memory requires the effortful search for impersonal target information and the intentional use of retrieval strategies. Subregions of the prefrontal, medial temporal, and retrosplenial cortices appear to be differentially involved in the neural processing of each type of episodic memory, thus suggesting that they are supported by anatomically and functionally overlapping, but also segregated neural circuits. The empirical data reviewed here support the view that laboratory and autobiographical episodic memory can at least in part be distinguished on the cognitive-behavioral and the neurofunctional levels. Accordingly, the review proposes an integrated view of laboratory and

---

[*] Correspondence to: Martina Piefke, Physiological Psychology, Department of Psychology and Sports Sciences, University of Bielefeld, Universitätsstr. 25, 33615 Bielefeld, Germany. Tel.: ++49-521-106-4484. Fax : ++49-521-106-6049. E-mail: martina.piefke@uni-bielefeld.de.

autobiographical forms of episodic memory which accounts for an overlap, but also emphasizes the unique features distinguishing the two memory types.

In: Psychology Research Biographies and Summaries
Editors: Nancy E. Wodarth and Alexis P. Ferguson

ISBN: 978-1-61470-491-1
© 2012 Nova Science Publishers, Inc.

Chapter 242

A Comparative Neuropsychological Approach to Cognitive Assessment in Clinical Populations

Isabelle Boutet[*,1], Cary Kogan[1] and Norton W. Milgram[2]

School of Psychology, University of Ottawa[1],
Ottawa, Ontario, Canada
Division of Life Sciences, University of Toronto at Scarborough,[2]
Scarborough, Ontario, Canada

Research Summary

Comparative neuropsychology refers to a line of research where tests originally developed to investigate cognitive processes in animals are modified for use with humans. We have used a comparative neuropsychological approach to develop a new test battery specifically for use with clinical populations. The new battery evaluates object discrimination, egocentric spatial abilities, visual and spatial working memory, and cognitive flexibility. We have investigated the usefulness of this battery in two clinical groups: in a geriatric population and in patients with Fragile-X syndrome (FXS), a genetic condition associated with mental retardation. Our results in geriatric participants indicate age differences on tasks that evaluate egocentric spatial abilities, cognitive flexibility, and object recognition. Our results with FXS patients indicate strengths in egocentric spatial abilities and visual working memories alongside weaknesses in object discrimination, cognitive flexibility, and spatial working memory. These studies illustrate the utility of comparative neuropsychology to the study of cognition in normal and clinical populations. Future directions for novel test development and translation to the clinic are discussed within the comparative framework.

---

* Corresponding author: Isabelle Boutet, PhD; School of Psychology; University of Ottawa; 125 University St.; Ottawa, Ontario; K1N 6N5; Tel: 613-562-5800 x2612; Fax ; 613-562-5150; *Email:iboutet@uottawa.ca*.

In: Psychology Research Biographies and Summaries
Editors: Nancy E. Wodarth and Alexis P. Ferguson

ISBN: 978-1-61470-491-1
© 2012 Nova Science Publishers, Inc.

Chapter 243

THE MECHANISMS OF MASKED SEMANTIC PRIMING: A STATE OF THE ART

Eva Van den Bussche[*,†] *and Bert Reynvoet*[*]
Department of Psychology, University of Leuven, Belgium

RESEARCH SUMMARY

Masked or subliminal priming has recorded a research history filled with debate and controversy. Marcel (1983) was one of the first to report that unconsciously presented words primed semantic associates. His results were looked at with great scepticism, but as the years went by, and research methodology improved, it was repeatedly shown that subliminally presented stimuli can influence the processing of subsequent stimuli. As the existence of subliminal priming effects was now no longer questioned, the debate progressed beyond existence claims and focused on whether subliminal primes can activate their semantic meaning. Dehaene et al. (1998) proposed an account that suggests that subliminal primes are processed in a series of stages, including semantic categorization. Several other accounts however have claimed the opposite, namely that subliminal information is not processed semantically. Furthermore, the conditions under which subliminal semantic priming effects can or can not be observed remains an important object of discussion that has produced numerous inconsistent research results. Therefore, the aim of the present chapter is to expose some of the mechanisms underlying subliminal semantic priming by reviewing the research results on subliminal semantic priming conducted throughout the years. Based on this review of the literature we propose a new context dependent account, able to explain many of the earlier contradictory research findings, able to reconcile the previous accounts and able to be implemented in a broader theoretical framework, such as the Global Neuronal Workspace model of Dehaene and Naccache (2001).

---

*Both authors contributed equally to this work

[†] Eva Van den Bussche Faculty of Psychology and Educational Sciences University of Leuven, Campus Kortrijk E. Sabbelaan 53, 8500 Kortrijk Belgium Phone: +32-(0)56-24 60 74 Fax: +32-(0)56-24 60 52 E-mail: Eva.Vandenbussche@kuleuven-kortrijk.be.

In: Psychology Research Biographies and Summaries
Editors: Nancy E. Wodarth and Alexis P. Ferguson
ISBN: 978-1-61470-491-1
© 2012 Nova Science Publishers, Inc.

Chapter 244

THE ROLE OF ALLELES 4 AND 2 OF THE APOE GENE AND COGNITIVE TESTS IN THE EARLY CONVERSION OF MILD COGNITIVE IMPAIRMENT TO ALZHEIMER DEMENTIA

Ana Barabash[1], Alberto Marcos[2], Inés Ancin[1], Blanca M. Vazquez[1], Pedro Gil[3], Cristina Fernández[4], Juan José López-Ibor[1] and José Antonio Cabranes[1,*]

[1] Department of Psychiatry, Madrid, Spain
[2] Department of Neurology, Madrid, Spain
[3] Department of Geriatrics, Madrid, Spain
[4] Epidemiological Unit, Hospital Clínico San Carlos, Madrid, Spain

RESEARCH SUMMARY

Late onset Alzheimer's disease (AD) is considered as a polygenic disorder resulting from the coincidence of a moderate number of genetic functional variants, located in candidate genes and others, each contributing small effects. Many studies focused mainly on identifying common risk alleles make it possible to predict the conversion from normal cognitive individual to Mild Cognitive Impairment (MCI), and from MCI to neurodegenerative dementia. We review the increasing literature about the genetics of AD under the light of our experience. We report a prospective study of apolipoprotein E (APOE) genotype in 89 patients diagnosed as MCI based on the Petersen criteria and supported by the MMSE, GDS scale and neuropsychological tests. After a median follow up of 49.6 months, 27 subjects remained with MCI and 62 subjects developed AD. This latest group was stratified again into two subgroups considering whether they converted to AD before (n=40) or after (n=22) 20

---

* Correspondence concerning this article should be addressed to Jose Antonio Cabranes, Psychiatry Department, Hospital Clínico San Carlos, C/ Martín Lagos s/n. 28040, Madrid, Spain. Tel: 0034913303808; Email: jcabranes.hcsc@madrid.salud.org.

months of evolution. In order to assess the risk associated to each genotype, a control group (n=90) matched for age and sex and without memory impairment (MMSE≥28) was included. Patients who developed AD showed significantly lower values than MCI subjects in the CAMCOG (76% sensitivity and 67% specificity), for prompt detecting the onset of AD, with a 4.65-fold times increased risk of converting to AD (p<0.001). The presence of at least one APOE 4 allele was associated with risk of developing MCI (OR: 6,04; 95%CI: 2,76–13,23; p<0,001) but did not have an effect on the predictive cumulative hazard ratio (HR: 1.2; 95%CI: 0.73-2.1; p:0.32) of developing AD. Though it did not reach a statistically significant level, the presence of at least one APOE 2 allele showed a protective effect for the risk of developing MCI (OR: 0,57; 95%CI: 0,14–2.26). No patient was homozygous for 2/2 and no patient with rapidly progressive disease carried the 2 allele either (HR: 0.4; 95%CI: 0.05-2.7; p: 0.25). Our data demonstrated a strong association of APOE 4 carrier status by itself with MCI, predicting a higher risk to suffer MCI. APOE 2 variant showed an interesting protective effect to MCI. Notwithstanding, the presence of at least an allele 4 when the patient is suffering MCI did not change the probability of progression to AD.

Chapter 245

HOW DYSLEXIC TEENAGERS COPE AT SCHOOL: COULD A NEW MEASURE BE HELPFUL IN SCREENING THOSE IN DIFFICULTY?

Neil Alexander-Passe
School of Psychology, London South Bank University, London, UK

RESEARCH SUMMARY

Dyslexics form one of the largest groups who encounter educational difficulties, especially in school with both academic and social curriculums. Such difficulties may affect their emotional well-being and result in numerous adverse coping strategies which may affect their ability to access the school curriculum.

This chapter investigates N=26 dyslexic teenagers from several perspectives: (1) Using a number of standardised measures (self-esteem, coping and depression) to assess how they cope with parents, peers and teachers; (2) Interviewing them about how they cope, looking at their strategies and reflecting on their relationships with parents, peers and teachers; (3) Analysis of the standardised measures to locate factors to explain how dyslexic teenagers cope; and (4) Investigating an experimental teenager screening measure which aims to allow parents to assess their dyslexic child's positive and negative coping strategies, as a reaction to school and their relationships with peers and teachers.

Resulting standardised measure data suggests: (1) There are significant gender differences in how males and females cope; (2) There are differences between task based coping and emotional coping amongst dyslexics; (3) Avoidance plays a part in coping strategies for all dyslexic teenagers; (4) Self-esteem rates vary according to the coping strategy chosen; and (5) Depression features in the coping of dyslexics, especially females.

Three factors were identified and named 'Trying', 'Avoiding' and 'Feeling good' from the standardised measures, using factor analysis and Pearson Correlations.

Resulting interview case studies suggest: (1) Avoidance is a key coping strategy; (2) There is apprehension about letting others know they are dyslexic; (3) Hobbies are vital for their self-esteem and motivation; (4) They excel in non-academic subjects; and (4) Their difficulties cause them stress and frustration.

Using responses from parents, the experimental parental measure was validated using correlations and factor analysis from the standardised measure. Thus parents were able to identify all three factors and a reduced N=21 parental measure was created from N=47 experimental items.

Combining all elements of the study:

(1) Dyslexic teenagers use two types of coping, described as 'Trying' and Avoiding' with an independent self-esteem scale 'Feeling good', as found by standardised measures;

(2) Parents were aware of their child's helplessness due to their dyslexia;

(3) The experimental scale was successful but needs further development with other samples;

(4) Depression and emotional coping features in the coping of dyslexics, especially females; and

(5) Findings from the two interview studies indicate that avoidance is a key coping strategy.

Overall, profiles were produced which indicate that teenagers with dyslexia suffer emotionally at school from their hidden disability and this needs to be taken into account when managing them in the classroom.

In: Psychology Research Biographies and Summaries
Editors: Nancy E. Wodarth and Alexis P. Ferguson
ISBN: 978-1-61470-491-1
© 2012 Nova Science Publishers, Inc.

Chapter 246

INTEREST AND MOTIVATION: A CULTURAL-HISTORICAL AND DISCURSIVE PSYCHOLOGICAL APPROACH

Wolff-Michael Roth and Pei-Ling Hsu
University of Victoria, Canada

RESEARCH SUMMARY

The theoretical concepts of (situational and individual) interest and motivation are of central importance to educational psychologists, because they denote phenomena that are said to mediate cognition and learning, and therefore individual development. In general, interest and motivation are approached predominantly from individualist cognitive perspectives, as entities or processes said to be embodied in the individual mental structure. The method, however, is not without its critics. Thus, the existing approaches to motivation can be seen as tools in the hands of the ruling class and therefore, psychology as a servant to the interests of this class. Whereas scholars may not agree with such analyses, the cultural-historical and sociocultural origins in the work of the Russian social and educational psychologist Lev Semenovich Vygotsky point us to other possible problems with individualist approaches to motivation and interest. According to Vygotsky, all higher mental functions have their origin in inter-human societal relations. That is, therefore, rather than studying forever-inaccessible structures of minds for the situational and individual interests a person develops and their relation to a person's motivations, a sociocultural and cultural-historical approach begins with studying societal relations generally and societal relations in which interests and motivations are (a) the topic of talk or (b) resources in the pursuit of other topics. This, then, leads us to the approach taken in discursive psychology, a relatively new discipline that already has made substantial contributions to the study of cognition generally and to the study of knowing and learning more specifically. In this chapter, we draw on an empirical study of career interests and motivations of high school biology students who were given the opportunity to participate in internship experiences in a university science laboratory. The scientists had offered these opportunities for the express purpose of increasing enrollments in the university's science faculty. Here we outline and exemplify a discursive approach to studying interest and motivation, which is an important and necessary perspective because participation in any human activity is always mediated societally, culturally, and historically. We show how interest and motivation talk is produced and the intelligibility of such talk shared as cultural resource. We suggest that a discursive approach has significant possibilities for educational psychology, because ontogenetically, we learn what interest and emotion are in and through participation with others in conversations about interests and motivations. Therefore, interest and motivation are phenomena that for any individual are brought about in social interactions and discourse situations rather than phenomena that can be theorized as having their independent origin *within* the individual human being. We conclude with recommendations for a discursive approach to the study of interest and motivation that parallels a similar approach we take to "purely cognitive issues" such as conceptions and conceptual change.

Chapter 247

Reading Fluency and Dyslexia: Innovative Developments in the Role of Associative Learning and Repetitive Exposure in Skill Acquisition

Sebastián Aravena[*] *and Jurgen Tijms*
IWAL Research, IWAL Institute for Dyslexia, Amsterdam,
The Netherlands, and EPOS, Department of Psychology,
University of Amsterdam, The Netherlands

Research Summary

In this chapter we will engage in a theoretical quest for ways to ameliorate reading fluency in dyslexics. In the first section we will provide an overview of research on dyslexia and dyslexia treatment and we will discuss the limitations of traditional interventions to ameliorate the poor reading fluency of dyslexic children.

In the second section of the chapter we will have a closer look on reading fluency, often referred to as the 'neglected' aspect of reading. We will discuss the essential role of extensive reading experience in the development of reading fluency and focus on repeated reading, the most familiar and most researched approach to fluency training.

A state of the art overview of insights from cognitive neuroscience, concerning fluent and disrupted reading, will be given in the third section of the chapter. In this light we will discuss cognitive, neurobiological and connectionist models on reading development and additionally focus on other areas of skill learning, such as chess.

In the fourth section we will amalgamate the various insights, draw several conclusions regarding fluency-oriented instructional practices, and proposed some new directions for dyslexia treatment. Additionally, we will demonstrate the unique possibilities provided by edugames, or computer-game training, for the implementation of the proposed educational

---

[*] Correspondence concerning this chapter should be addressed to Sebastián Aravena, IWAL, Amaliastraat 5, 1052 GM, Amsterdam, The Netherlands. E-mail: sebastianaravena@iwal.nl.

principles. As an example we will present an edugame, called LexyLink, which we developed in our own laboratory and which we are currently testing in our institute.

CULTURAL INFLUENCES ON THE LEARNING OF SCIENCE: AN AFRICAN PERSPECTIVE

Fred N. Keraro[*] and Mark I. O. Okere
Egerton University, Department of Curriculum, Instruction and Educational Management, Kenya

RESEARCH SUMMARY

In many developing countries in Africa, learners' cultural background seems to be one of the major factors that militate against their learning of formal science in schools. On many occasions, the stakeholders in education attribute poor performance in science to bad teaching, the difficulty and the abstractness of science. What they fail to address, however, are the circumstances of the learners, which are mainly cultural. The influence of culture on the learning of science in schools should be addressed seriously by teachers, parents and educational planners. Culture has the categories of beliefs, practices, behaviour, communication skills, values and attitudes. This chapter presents empirical studies on the influence of culture on the learning of science in primary and secondary schools in Kenya. The chapter is divided into three major sections. Section one examines the manifestations of cultural influence on the learning of primary science in schools in four cultural communities in Kenya, the Maasai and Kipsigis of the Rift Valley province, and the Abagusii and Luo of Nyanza province. Section two is about the influence of cultural beliefs in the form of metaphors concerning "heat" in form three students' explanations of everyday life experiences in Nyandarua district. Section three examines the influence of the Bukusu culture of Bungoma district, on students' conceptions of the topic "nutrition" in secondary school biology. The chapter concludes with a discussion on the challenges this poses to science education in Africa.

---

[*] P. O. Box 536 – 20115, Egerton, Kenya. E-mail fnkeraro@yahoo.com.

Chapter 249

NON-LINEAR DYNAMIC MODELING OF MICRODEVELOPMENTAL PROCESSES OF STUDENTS' CONCEPTUAL CHANGE IN SCIENCE

Li Sha[1] and Xiufeng Liu[2]

[1] Faculty of Education, Simon Fraser University, Canada
[2] Graduate School of Education;
State University of New York at Buffalo, US

RESEARCH SUMMARY

This chapter reports a study using non-linear dynamic and microdeveopmental approaches to modeling students' conceptual change in science. Cognitive processes of children's conceptual change in learning a scientific concept, i.e. magnetism, were intensively observed at an interval of minutes, and a mathematical model was then applied to fit the observed patterns. Based on the comparison between the three simulated trajectories and the three empirical trajectories, we identified a dynamic reciprocal interaction between the student's actual developmental level and the instructor-guided potential developmental level responsible for different microdevelopmental trajectories. It was also found that the dynamic interaction between the rate of cognitive growth and the difficulty of learning content explained the variability of individual students' learning trajectories. The research findings suggest that cognitive processes of conceptual change in science are a self-organizing system in which various trajectories of learning emerge through the interactions between student parameters (e.g., prior knowledge and rate of learning) and teacher parameters (e.g., instructional goals and pace of teaching).

In: Psychology Research Biographies and Summaries
Editors: Nancy E. Wodarth and Alexis P. Ferguson
ISBN: 978-1-61470-491-1
© 2012 Nova Science Publishers, Inc.

Chapter 250

PHONOLOGY, DISCREPANCY, INSTRUCTION AND DYSLEXIA: ADVERSARIES OR ALLIES?

Peter Brooks[1] and John Everatt[*,2]
[1] Private Educational Psychologist, UK
[2] University of Surrey, UK

RESEARCH SUMMARY

This chapter will consider recent debates about educational psychology assessments. Although work in the UK will form the basis of the discussion, the arguments should be seen to be relevant to educational practices around the world and the evidence covered will be multinational. The discussion focuses on issues related to literacy development and the identification of literacy learning difficulties (dyslexia) and, therefore, the chapter will review the debate on the validity and reliability of IQ-achievement discrepancy criteria as a way of identifying specific literacy learning weaknesses and alternative positions arguing for practices that adopt narrow behaviourist models in terms of their theoretical explanations and educational input. Definitions of dyslexia that encompass all word level literacy weaknesses will also be covered and evidence will be presented for phonological skills being a key component to literacy development and for the power of instructional techniques in education. The chapter will consider cognitive assessment procedures that evaluate a range of skills (literacy, phonological processing, verbal and non-verbal reasoning, semantic, vocabulary and visuo-spatial skills) possessed by the individual and the potential advantages of such procedures for the identification of appropriate intervention strategies. This background will be used to propose that progress in the provision of a range of interventions that can be used effectively with all learners requires a recognition of the complementary nature of these views and argues for research to assess the efficacy of this complementary perspective. It will also be used to argue for the need for investigations that recognise the overlap and relationships between usual development and a spectrum of learning difficulties.

---

[*] For correspondence: John Everatt; Department of Psychology, University of Surrey, Guildford, Surrey GU2 7XH, UK; E-Mail: j.everatt@surrey.ac.uk.

The focus of the chapter is an appeal for the need to combine the roles of individual differences and instructional precision in education as well as research investigating the efficacy of using these perspectives in combination.

In: Psychology Research Biographies and Summaries
Editors: Nancy E. Wodarth and Alexis P. Ferguson
ISBN: 978-1-61470-491-1
© 2012 Nova Science Publishers, Inc.

Chapter 251

DYSLEXIA AND LOSS OF THE LEARNING DIALOGUE

Neil Alexander-Passe[1] and Bob Zimmer[2]
[1] London South Bank University, London, UK
[2] The Open University, Milton Keynes, UK

RESEARCH SUMMARY

The Coping Inventory for Stressful Situations (CISS) (Endler & Parker, 1999) identifies three main behaviors in response to stress – trying hard to perform, blaming oneself or others for one's failure, and avoiding exposure altogether.

It has been shown that, amongst pupils with dyslexia, these three behaviors are associated with different genders (Alexander-Passe, 2004a, 2006, in press) and different levels of self-esteem and depression (Alexander-Passe, 2004a, 2006) – in particular:

- Trying hard to perform – mainly males, gaining academic self-esteem from teacher approval
- Avoiding exposure – mainly females, shielding overall self-esteem
- Blaming – mainly females, losing personal self-esteem and showing depression.

As it happens, these three behaviors are opposites to the three that make up the simplest possible, basic learning dialogue (Zimmer, 2001; Zimmer & Chapman, 2004; Zimmer, 2008):

- Listening receptively rather than blaming, so as to invite thinking
- Showing comprehension rather than just trying hard, so as to invite listening in return, and
- Sharing one's own thinking rather than avoiding exposure, so as to invite comprehension.

Evidence from the dyslexia literature shows that the three CISS behaviors are common amongst pupils with dyslexia, indicating that dyslexic pupils are often disengaged from the basic learning dialogue.

It was hypothesized that this non-engagement is due to teachers themselves not offering the basic learning dialogue.

Accordingly, the dyslexia literature was analyzed for reports of teachers' not offering receptive listening, or comprehension of pupils' thinking, or their own thinking in response.

Reports fitting this description were found in unfortunate abundance. In particular, teachers of dyslexic pupils were found often to impose:

- Rote teaching in place of their own thinking
- Judgmental discounting in place of receptive listening, and
- Humiliation for failure in place of comprehension.

It is concluded that learning by dyslexic pupils is at risk from teaching that does not support the basic learning dialogue.

An implication is that, for support of dyslexic pupils, care for the learning dialogue itself may be what matters most.

In: Psychology Research Biographies and Summaries
Editors: Nancy E. Wodarth and Alexis P. Ferguson
ISBN: 978-1-61470-491-1
© 2012 Nova Science Publishers, Inc.

Chapter 252

COGNITIVE LOAD THEORY AND INSTRUCTIONAL DESIGN: AN OUTLINE OF THE THEORY AND REFLECTIONS ON A NEED FOR NEW DIRECTIONS TO CATER FOR INDIVIDUAL DIFFERENCES AND MOTIVATION

Wayne Michael Leahy
Macquarie University, New South Wales, Australia

RESEARCH SUMMARY

Cognitive load theory (hereafter CLT; see Sweller, 2006; Sweller, van Merrienboer & Paas, 1998; Sweller, 1994; 1988) has been used for nearly two decades to develop innovative learning formats in instructional design. It essentially draws upon some aspects of the information processing/schema theory approach to learning. The theory maintains that it is critical to take into account the limitations of our working memory if learning is to be efficient. Using hundreds of controlled empirical studies comparing conventional instructional formats to formats guided by CLT has generated positive results. These have been critically reviewed and generally accepted in the field of educational psychology.

The use of CLT designed formats suggest there is less mental effort for the learner, a reduced training time, higher performance on test scores and transfer to similar problems, and longer duration for retention of information. The theory presents one perspective of our cognitive architecture.

Among the many CLT instructional designs used, two concern individual differences and motivation. These are:

1. The prior knowledge of the learner (termed the expertise reversal effect - see Kalyuga, Ayres, Chandler & Sweller, 2003) and
2. Mental rehearsal (termed the imagination effect – see Ginns, 2005; Leahy & Sweller, 2007; 2005; 2004).

The expertise reversal effect is an interesting and counter intuitive effect explored by CLT where learners who have some prior knowledge of the instructional material may do worse, under certain conditions, rather than better than those learners with no prior knowledge.

The second condition, mental rehearsal, is a learning strategy that has been used for many years (e.g. Sackett, 1934; 1935). It has been known variously by other terminology including "anticipative reasoning" (Dunbar, 2000) and "self-explanation" (Renkl, 1997). Since 1998, CLT has researched this approach in a series of experiments and termed it the "imagination effect". A number of motivational and cognitive issues have emerged that illustrate the conditions that make the strategy either viable or unproductive.

One of the relevant limitations of CLT is that the experiments do not cater *enough* for individual differences of the learner. Important factors within the field of individual differences such as motivation, learning styles or gender for example are not adequately taken into account.

This chapter will outline CLT, and then provide a summary of various experiments conducted within its theoretical framework. The experiments include exploration of the expertise reversal effect, the use of an imagination strategy (imagination effect) and unique work on CLT and motivation conducted by Pass, Tuovinen, van Merrienboer and Darabi (2005) and Pass and van Merrienboer (1993). From all of these studies, the chapter will identify some issues and limitations emerging concerning motivation and individual differences. New directions that may address these will be suggested.

Chapter 253

ATTITUDE TOWARDS SCHOOL, MOTIVATION, EMOTIONS AND ACADEMIC ACHIEVEMENT

Angelica Moè*, Francesca Pazzaglia, Patrizio Tressoldi and Cristina Toso

Dipartimento di Psicologia Generale – Università di Padova, Italy

RESEARCH SUMMARY

Attitude towards school is an important predictor of academic well-being (McCoach, 2002; McCoach & Siegle, 2003; Patrick, Anderman, & Ryan, 2002). Furthermore, the underlining motivational and affective components and their relationship with academic achievement are not yet well established.

The present research aimed to explore the relationship between attitude towards school including the motivation and emotions connected to the academic setting, and achievement. The general hypothesis is that the attitude towards school mediates the effects of motivational and affective aspects on academic achievement.

To test this hypothesis we adopted two methods. First, we examined the structural relationships between attitude towards school, motivations, emotions and achievement. Second, we verified the efficacy of an educational training focused on motivation and emotions (Friso, Moè & Pazzaglia, 2004) in improving the attitude towards school. Results confirmed the mediating role of the attitude towards school in shaping the relationship between affective-motivational variables and academic achievement, but also showed a direct influence of self-confidence on school achievement. Educational implications are highlighted.

---

* Correspondence to: Angelica Moè; Department of General Psychology; Via Venezia, 8; 35131 Padova, Italy; tel. ++39-049-8276689; e-mail: angelica.moe@unipd.it.

In: Psychology Research Biographies and Summaries
Editors: Nancy E. Wodarth and Alexis P. Ferguson
ISBN: 978-1-61470-491-1
© 2012 Nova Science Publishers, Inc.

Chapter 254

INDIVIDUAL DIFFERENCES IN ATTITUDE TO SCHOOL AND SOCIAL REPUTATION AMONG PEERS: IMPLICATIONS FOR BEHAVIOURAL ADJUSTMENT IN EDUCATIONAL SETTINGS

Estefanía Estévez[1] *and Nicholas Emler*[2]

[1] Universidad Miguel Hernández de Elche, Alicante, Spain
Departamento de Psicología de la Salud, Av de la Universidad,
Edificio Altamira; Alicante, Spain
[2] University of Surrey, Guildford, United Kingdom;
Faculty of Arts and Human Sciences,
Guildford, Surrey, United Kingdom

RESEARCH SUMMARY

Behavioural adjustment problems in schools are becoming matters of increasing concern among professionals of education and psychology. Although it is well-known that adolescence is a period of particular risk for involvement in antisocial activities, there are still questions to be addressed if we are to understand the *whys* behind such behaviours, and especially why this problem is present or is more serious in some adolescents than in others. There is now greater consensus among researchers regarding the role played by family in the origin and development of behavioural problems in children. Particular characteristics of the family environment, such as negative or avoidant communication between parents and children and the lack of parental support , have been highlighted in this context. However, an intrinsic feature of the adolescent period is its opening to new relations with significant others apart from parents, mainly peers and teachers, as well as to new social contexts such as the school.

In this communication we analyse the relevance of social life at school, school environment and school experience in adolescent behavioural adjustment. We particularly examine the link among social experience at school and other two factors that have caught the attention of researchers in the last two decades but that unfortunately have not been addressed in depth in the scientific literature: we are referring to attitude to formal authority and social reputation among peers. With attitude to authority we refer in the present communication to the attitude the adolescent holds towards the school as a formal institution and towards teachers as formal figures. Social reputation among peers makes reference to the social recognition on the part of others in the same classroom or school. Both factors, namely *attitude to school* and *reputation among peers* seem to be closely associated to antisocial behaviour among students and, from our point of view, both deserve more attention as well as a jointly consideration and analysis due, on the one hand, to their link and join contribution to the explanation of certain risk behaviour that occur in schools and, on the other hand, to their important implications for the design of prevention and intervention programs at the school settings.

In: Psychology Research Biographies and Summaries
Editors: Nancy E. Wodarth and Alexis P. Ferguson
ISBN: 978-1-61470-491-1
© 2012 Nova Science Publishers, Inc.

Chapter 255

DYSLEXIA AS A SYNDROME: DON'T LET 'READING DISABILITY' STEAL THE SHOW

Tim Miles
School of Psychology Univ.Bangor, Wales, UK

RESEARCH SUMMARY

This chapter proposes a 'stipulative' definition of dyslexia, in which it is emphasises that the phenomena of dyslexia constitute a syndrome. Some of the main characteristics of the syndrome are then described. They include lateness in learning to read, poor spelling, slowness in appreciating the significance of symbolic material, and other manifestations which will be described below. The condition often runs in families. It is argued that if dyslexia is defined simply as 'poor reading' or 'reading disability' there is risk that the many other manifestations of the syndrome, including the positive talents of dyslexics, will be overlooked.

In: Psychology Research Biographies and Summaries
Editors: Nancy E. Wodarth and Alexis P. Ferguson
ISBN: 978-1-61470-491-1
© 2012 Nova Science Publishers, Inc.

Chapter 256

GENDER-MOTIVATED BIAS CRIMES: EXAMINING WHY SITUATIONAL VARIABLES ARE IMPORTANT IN THE LABELING OF HATE CRIMES

H. Colleen Sinclair and Jordan T. Hertl[*]
Mississippi State University, Department of Psychology,
Social Science Research Center, Mississippi State, MS, US

RESEARCH SUMMARY

Prototype theory (Harris et al., 2004; Inman & Baron, 1996) states that people have certain expectations when it comes to perpetrators and victims of acts of discrimination. The present study applied prototype theory to examine which variables affect the application of the label "bias crime." To examine the factors that affect hate crime labeling, a scenario was developed wherein victim type, severity of assault, assault location, and victim-perpetrator relationship were systematically varied. The likelihood that the participants would perceive bias as a motive and the labeling of the scenario as a hate crime were significantly affected by the independent variables. When it came to victim type, scenarios featuring an African-American victim were more likely to be labeled as a hate crime than those targeting a non-minority woman. Other factors that resulted in an increased likelihood of the application of the hate crime label were 1) the attack was committed by a stranger (instead of an acquaintance), 2) the attack was more severe (i.e., aggravated instead of simple assault), and 3) the attack occurred following a political meeting (e.g., NAACP, NOW) instead of occurring after a college class.

---

[*] Corresponding author: E-mail: csinclair@ssrc.msstate.edu.

In: Psychology Research Biographies and Summaries
Editors: Nancy E. Wodarth and Alexis P. Ferguson

ISBN: 978-1-61470-491-1
© 2012 Nova Science Publishers, Inc.

Chapter 257

TOWARD A PSYCHOLOGICAL CONSTRUCT OF ENMITY

Christopher R. Jones[*,1] *and Chris Loersch*[2]
[1]The Ohio State University, Columbus, OH, US
[2]University of Missouri – Columbia, MS, US

RESEARCH SUMMARY

This chapter addresses a phenomenon pertinent to interpersonal hate: enmity. We first review the existing literature relevant to enemies, including a discussion of the relative neglect of this topic and the paucity of research on "the dark side of relationships." The remainder of the chapter addresses definitional, theoretical, and methodological issues in studying enmity. In particular, we provide a novel construct definition of interpersonal enmity in which an enemy is a person someone dislikes; believes is malevolent or threatening; and wishes some degree of social, psychological, or physical harm upon. The benefits of this approach over other conceptualizations are discussed, as are multiple unresolved issues in conceptualizing enmity. The remainder of the chapter discusses future directions for research on enemy relationships including different classes or types of enemies, the integration of enemies with the self, the influence of enmity on person perception, and the role of individual differences in the development of enemy relations. Finally, we argue for the need to move beyond questionnaire and interview methodologies and discuss the benefits which can be obtained by more rigorous hypothesis testing and experimental design in this research area.

---

[*] Corresponding author: Psychology Building, Ohio State University, 1835 Neil Avenue, Columbus, OH 43210-1287. E-mail: jones.2333@osu.edu.

In: Psychology Research Biographies and Summaries
Editors: Nancy E. Wodarth and Alexis P. Ferguson
ISBN: 978-1-61470-491-1
© 2012 Nova Science Publishers, Inc.

Chapter 258

HATE, REVENGE AND FORGIVENESS: A HEALTHY, EGO-STRENGTHENING ALTERNATIVE TO THE EXPERIENCE OF OFFENSE

Patrick F. Cioni
Private Practice of Counseling and Psychotherapy,
Scranton, Pennsylvania, US

RESEARCH SUMMARY

Forgiveness is a choice, a process and an internal response that involves release of negative affect including anger which, when chronic, can develop into hatred. It is not forgetting or condoning, and it does not necessarily lead to reconciliation though that is potentiated. The process of forgiveness includes 1) re-constructing cognitions about the offender and self and 2) re-imaging the offender and re-experiencing self and violator. This object transformation results in ego development since objects and object constellations are the building blocks of ego identity (Kernberg, 1984). The ego is empowered to more effectively deal with conflict and associated negative affect due to abatement of anger and decreased internal arousal. This increases the ego's ability for effective communication and conflict resolution.

Stages of forgiveness and gradated cognitions typical of each stage are identified. Each forgiveness stage includes increasingly efficacious cognitions which exemplify a process of cognitive upleveling and ego strengthening. The distinction between forgiveness and reconciliation is important. Forgiveness is an intrapersonal event or process which potentiates but does not necessitate a behavioral coming together, while reconciliation is interpersonal and involves a behavioral encounter. Reconciliation involves risk-taking behavior which can become less threatening to the individual with increasing forgiveness and growing ego strength.

Chapter 259

DO YOU HATE ME? HAVE I HURT YOU?: DEFENSES AGAINST GROWTH, SEPARATION, AND INDIVIDUATION THAT CREATE INTERPRETIVE ENACTMENTS PART ONE: FENDER BENDERS AND THE SHARED DEFENSIVE SYSTEMS OF LESS DIFFICULT PATIENTS

Robert Waska[*]

Institute for Psychoanalytic Studies,
Private Psychoanalytic Practice in San Francisco
and Marin County, CA, US

RESEARCH SUMMARY

All patients struggle with psychological conflicts regarding love, hate, and knowledge. Some patients are troubled by phantasies of causing hurt and hatred in the object as a result of their quest for separation, individuation, and personal creativity. Success, ambition, differentiation, growth, change, and personal difference are all seen as creating, injury, unhappiness, anger, hatred, and rejection in the object. Therefore, these patients create intense and rigid defensive patterns of submissive, subordinate, and passive relating to prevent these internal catastrophes. These defensive mechanisms are mobilized through projective identification and create frequent patterns of interpretive enactments and counter-transference acting out.

This paper will highlight these vexing and humbling patterns of interpretive acting out we often find ourselves in as we try to reach out to patients but barely find a foothold before they slip away or before we lose our own therapeutic balance. Case material will be used for illustration to specifically examine how the defensive avoidance of certain wishes, feelings,

---

[*] Corresponding author: E-mail: drwaska@aol.com, Telephone: 415-883-4735, P.O. Box 2769 San Anselmo, CA 94979 US.

and secret needs become part of the counter-transference and influence or pervert the interpretive process. As a result, the analyst may indeed be making helpful and accurate interpretations while also missing out on the more core aspects of the patient's in the moment phantasy and internal conflict. Theoretical and clinical material will be used to examine this phenomenon.

In: Psychology Research Biographies and Summaries
Editors: Nancy E. Wodarth and Alexis P. Ferguson
ISBN: 978-1-61470-491-1
© 2012 Nova Science Publishers, Inc.

Chapter 260

Do You Hate Me? Have I Hurt You?: Defenses against Growth, Separation, and Individuation That Create Interpretive Enactments Part Two: Pit Stops and the Shared Defensive Systems of More Difficult Patients

Robert Waska*
Institute for Psychoanalytic Studies,
Private Psychoanalytic Practice in San Francisco
and Marin County, CA, US

Research Summary

Some more disturbed patients in psychoanalytic treatment are struggling with primitive depressive anxieties and conflicts regarding separation and individuation. They feel obligated to follow what they believe their object needs, wants, or demands while at the same time feeling restricted and wanting to oppose or reject those needs for their own ambitions and choices. However, the phantasy of rejection and punishment as well as lasting harm to their object results in great conflict and a sense of entrapment. So, the patient is left with feeling they will create hate and harm if they admit their own needs, differences, accomplishments. Thus, these differentiation and individuation states are cloaked and camouflaged. While working with such patients, the analyst frequently is subject to projective identification attacks in which the patient's defenses against change, growth, separation, and individual choice become acted out in the interpretive field. Two cases are used for illustration and the need for careful counter-transference monitoring is discussed.

---

* Corresponding author: E-mail: drwaska@aol.com, Telephone: 415-883-4235, P.O. Box 2769 San Anselmo, CA 94979 US.

In: Psychology Research Biographies and Summaries
Editors: Nancy E. Wodarth and Alexis P. Ferguson
ISBN: 978-1-61470-491-1
© 2012 Nova Science Publishers, Inc.

Chapter 261

HATE AND LOVE SCRIPTS – COMMON ELEMENTS

Barbara Gawda

Department of Psychology, Maria Curie-Sklodowska University,
Lublin, Poland

RESEARCH SUMMARY

The presented research explains the common traits of affective scripts of hate and love and examines their mysterious nearness. We propose that this nearness is connected to common elements of mental representations of these feelings. The text first describes the script conceptions, the scripts theories concerning love and hate, and the theories that explain their nearness. The authors analyzed 180 stories about love and 180 stories about hate from the same group of people. These participants were of the same age, intellect, and educational level. The aspects of content and structure of scripts were compared. We concentrated on Schank and Abelson's conception of script elements: partner (positive/negative characteristics and emotions), actions (away from others/towards others), actor (positive/negative emotions), and story's type of ending (positive/negative). We used a multidimensional scaling method, Proxscal, to show the two scripts' common area.

In: Psychology Research Biographies and Summaries
Editors: Nancy E. Wodarth and Alexis P. Ferguson
ISBN: 978-1-61470-491-1
© 2012 Nova Science Publishers, Inc.

Chapter 262

HATE: NO CHOICE AGENT SIMULATIONS

*Krzysztof Kulakowski, Malgorzata J. Krawczyk
and Przemyslaw Gawroński*

RESEARCH SUMMARY

We report our recent simulations on the social processes which -- in our opinion -- lie at the bottom of hate. First simulation deals with the so-called Heider balance where initial purely random preferences split the community into two mutually hostile groups. Second simulation shows that once these groups are formed, the cooperation between them is going to fail. Third simulationprovides a numerical illustration of the process of biased learning; the model indicates that lack of objective information is a barrier to new information. Fourth simulation shows that in the presence of a strong conflict between communities hate is unavoidable.

Chapter 263

THE INFLUENCE OF PRENATAL MOTHER-CHILD ATTACHMENT ON THE ATTACHMENT AT THE AGE OF 6 MONTHS AND ITS OBJECTIVATION BY THE INTRAUTERINE FETAL ACTIVITY

Helmut Niederhofer[a,1] *and Alfons Reiter*[b]

[a]Department of Child and Adolescent Psychiatry, University of Innsbruck, Austria
[b]University of Salzburg, Austria

RESEARCH SUMMARY

This study investigates the influence of prenatal mother-child attachment on intrauterine fetal movements and postnatal attachment (0;6 years). 2 questionnaires (The Parental-Fetal Attachment Scale (Cranley, 1981) and Axis II (Thero to Three, 1994)), answered by 92 mothers (18-38 years) were used to identify the attachment category. Intrauterine fetal activity (head/arm/leg/fetal heart rate) was observed by ultrasound for 5 minutes. For statistical analyses, regression analysis (SPSS-PC+) was used.

The results show, that there might be high stability of secure and insecure-avoidant attachment. Insecure-ambivalent attachment also remains stable until the age of 6. Pre- und perinatal insecure-avoidant attachment seems to reduce the probability of later secure attachment and vice versa. In our sample, there was no significant association between attachment and intrauterine fetal movements.

---

[1] Corresponding author; Helmut Niederhofer, M.D., Ph.D., Department of Child and Adolescent Psychiatry, University of Innsbruck, Anichstrasse 35, 6020 Innsbruck, Austria.

In: Psychology Research Biographies and Summaries
Editors: Nancy E. Wodarth and Alexis P. Ferguson
ISBN: 978-1-61470-491-1
© 2012 Nova Science Publishers, Inc.

Chapter 264

MOTHER-INFANT INTERACTION IN CULTURAL CONTEXT: A STUDY OF NICARAGUAN AND ITALIAN FAMILIES

Ughetta Moscardino, Sabrina Bonichini and Cristina Valduga
Department of Developmental and Social Psychology, University of Padua, Italy

RESEARCH SUMMARY

Although a common goal for parents is to promote their children's successful development in a respective society, there is considerable cross-cultural variation in the beliefs parents hold about children, families, and themselves as parents. Previous research suggests that in traditional rural areas across the world, parents highly appreciate interrelatedness in their conceptions of relationships and competence, whereas in urban settings of Western industrialized societies, parents seem to promote independent parent–child relationships from early on. The purpose of this study is to compare conceptions of parenting and mother-infant interactions in two cultural contexts that may be expected to hold different beliefs about parent-child relationships: Nicaraguan farmer families and middle-class Italian families. Fifty-six mothers from central Nicaragua (n = 26) and northern Italy (n = 30) and their infants aged 0-14 months participated in the study. Mothers were interviewed regarding their childrearing beliefs and behaviors, and were videotaped interacting with their infants during a free play session. Maternal responses were qualitatively analyzed using a thematic approach; maternal behaviors were coded into one of the following categories: social play, object play, motor stimulation, verbal stimulation, and face-to-face interaction. Findings indicated that: 1) Nicaraguan mothers emphasized interdependence and connectedness to other people in their socialization goals, whereas Italian mothers placed greater focus on childrearing strategies consistent with a more individualistic orientation; 2) Nicaraguan mothers exhibited a higher overall frequency of behaviors related to motor stimulation and face-to-face interaction, whereas Italian mothers were more likely to engage in social play, object play, and to emit a greater overall number of verbal behaviors towards their infants during the free-play session. Our results suggest that parents' conceptions of childcare reflect culturally regulated norms and customs that are instantiated in parental behavior and contribute to the structuring of parent-child interactions from the earliest months of life, thus shaping infant and children's developmental pathways. Implications for theory on the psychology of family relationships as well as for clinical practice are discussed.

In: Psychology Research Biographies and Summaries
Editors: Nancy E. Wodarth and Alexis P. Ferguson
ISBN: 978-1-61470-491-1
© 2012 Nova Science Publishers, Inc.

Chapter 265

FUSSY MOTHERS AND FUZZY BOUNDARIES – RELATIONSHIPS IN FAMILIES WITH OVERWEIGHT CHILDREN

Laurel D. Edmunds[1]

Department of Primary Health Care, University of Oxford, Oxford, UK
iOpener Ltd, Twining House, Banbury Road, Oxford, UK

RESEARCH SUMMARY

Aim: The aim was to highlight some family relationships which enhance or hinder coping with child weight management, rather than the usual focus on the dietary and physical activity aspects of child weight management.

Methods: Parents with concerns about their children's weight volunteered to be interviewed. The interviews were semi-structured and covered the life histories of the focal child and any other relatives that interviewees deemed relevant. Standardised body shapes and photographs were used to illustrate descriptions. Analyses were thematic and iterative and used a Grounded Theory approach.

Results: Parents of 40 overweight children (48 parents in total) from the UK, took part in face-to-face interviews, mostly in their own homes. Parents reported their children's healthy dietary and physical activity behaviours, and their attempts to maintain these into adolescence. (Parents also recalled the social consequences of being in contact with teachers, health care professionals and strangers; Edmunds, 2005; 2008.) Pertinent here were the descriptions mothers gave of behaviours revealing their over-protectiveness in response to their child's lack of self-confidence, or other morbidity. They also reported the positive and negative influences of fathers and grandmothers. Two case studies are presented that illustrate some of the complexities of family relationships and how these were overcome.

Conclusion: Many child weight interventionists are concerned with diet and physical activity and may not appreciate how family relationships are affected by the presence of an overweight child. Documenting some of these relationships and their impact, may improve

---
[1] Correspondence to: Laurel D. Edmunds, PhD. Email: laureledmunds@gmail.com, www.laureledmunds.com.

the effectiveness, particularly of treatment or secondary prevention interventions within the family setting.

Chapter 266

MATERNAL SENSITIVITY AND THE CHARACTERISTICS OF CHILD-DIRECTED SPEECH

Leila Paavola[1,*], *Kaarina Kemppinen*[2] *and Sari Kunnari*[1]

[1]Faculty of Humanities/Logopedics, University of Oulu, Oulu, Finland
[2]Department of Child Psychiatry, Kuopio University
and Kuopio University Hospital, Kuopio, Finland

RESEARCH SUMMARY

This chapter begins with the discussion of the concept of sensitivity – its original definition and subsequent attempts to develop the concept further. It is suggested that one fruitful way to continue study in this field might be to examine maternal sensitivity and the characteristics of child-directed speech (CDS) together. It was hypothesized that sensitivity is reflected in many different ways in maternal behavior; rather than being a parenting dimension that exists apart from other dimensions it might permeate all interactive behavior, including language-facilitating aspects of CDS.

Research in CDS concerning its characteristics and its role in child language development is reviewed in the second part of the chapter. Investigations on maternal sensitivity and CDS per se are scarce. Our earlier research indicated that during a child's prelinguistic developmental stage general activity in communication is characteristic of highly sensitive mothers. In turn, the associations between maternal sensitivity and more specific aspects of CDS were not very clear. In particular, the lack of association between maternal sensitivity and naming was somewhat puzzling, because in the research literature the role of naming is strongly emphasized as a language facilitating element of CDS around the onset of word production. It was concluded that individual differences among children in their early abilities

---

[*] Corresponding author: Leila Paavola, Senior Lecturer, PhD, Faculty of Humanities/Logopedics, P.O.Box 1000, FI-90014 University of Oulu, Finland, Tel +358-8-553 3469, Fax +358-8-553 3383, E-mail Leila.Paavola@oulu.fi.

to participate in communicative interaction might have at least partly explained this result. Hence, the interaction sequences that include maternal naming should be examined in more detail.

The last part of the chapter before the conclusions reports the results of our recent analyses. The data comprise samples of videotaped free-play sessions of 27 Finnish-speaking mothers and their healthy 10-month-old children. From the samples of 100 first maternal utterances the numbers of naming utterances and also different words introduced in the acts were calculated. In addition, the interaction sequences in which naming occurred were analyzed in terms of a child's focus of attention; whether maternal utterance that named something followed or redirected the child's initial focus of attention. Thereafter, the relationship between the results from the naming analyses and the ratings of maternal sensitivity derived from the CARE-Index parent-child assessment method was examined. Sensitivity was associated with maternal skills in following the child's focus of attention when providing names to objects. Furthermore, in order to fine-tune the complexity of CDS to the developmental level of a prelinguistic child the mothers high on sensitivity tended to use relatively few different words in their naming utterances.

In: Psychology Research Biographies and Summaries
Editors: Nancy E. Wodarth and Alexis P. Ferguson

ISBN: 978-1-61470-491-1
© 2012 Nova Science Publishers, Inc.

Chapter 267

RECRUITMENT AND RELATIONSHIPS: RESEARCH WITH STIGMATIZED AND SOCIALLY ISOLATED MOTHERS

Nicole L. Letourneau[1], Linda A. Duffett-Leger and Catherine S. Young

University of New Brunswick, Faculty of Nursing, Fredericton, NB. Canada

RESEARCH SUMMARY

Research involving stigmatized and socially isolated populations presents a wide variety of challenges. Yet, these populations may benefit most from research. Recruitment challenges are typically exacerbated by intersecting barriers to participation. Lessons learned during the recruitment of two examplar populations (mothers with postpartum depression, and mothers of infants who have experienced intimate partner violence), highlight the importance of attention to relationships at various levels during the recruitment process and the impact these can have on the involvement of potential participants in research. Micro, mediator, and macro level barriers and enablers to research participation are explored.

---

[1] Correspondence to: Nicole L. Letourneau, PhD, RN , Professor and Canada Research Chair in Healthy Child Development, University of New Brunswick, Faculty of Nursing, PO Box 4400 Fredericton, NB Canada E3B 2A5, Tel: 506-458- 7647, Fax: 506-453-4565, E-mail: nicolel@unb.ca.

Chapter 268

SHIFTING PATTERNS OF PARENTING STYLES BETWEEN DYADIC AND FAMILY SETTINGS: THE ROLE OF MARITAL DISTRESS

Allison F. Lauretti[1] and James P. McHale[2]
[1] Children's Hospital Boston, US
[2] University of South Florida, St. Petersburg, FL, US

RESEARCH SUMMARY

This paper examines changes in how parents interact with their toddler-aged children as they move from dyadic to family contexts. Levels of parental involvement and quality of parenting behavior in the two different contexts were examined in sixty two-parent families with a 30-month-old son or daughter. An independent evaluation of marital distress was also conducted, and it was hypothesized that parents in distressed marriages would appear less competent when parenting their toddler in the presence of their partner than when parenting the child alone, while parents in less distressed marriages would show greater consistency across contexts. Results were generally in line with this prediction; mothers in distressed marriages indeed showed a steeper decline in sensitivity as they moved from the dyadic to family context than did mothers in less distressed marriages. Fathers in distressed marriages showed a more precipitous decline in their level of involvement with the toddler as they moved from dyadic to family settings than did fathers in less distressed marriages. We argue that the most thorough understanding of the child's early family environment will proceed from future investigations that assess, and compare, both dyadic and family group-level in the same study.

In: Psychology Research Biographies and Summaries
Editors: Nancy E. Wodarth and Alexis P. Ferguson
ISBN: 978-1-61470-491-1
© 2012 Nova Science Publishers, Inc.

Chapter 269

THE INTERRELATIONS OF PERCEPTIONS OF FAMILY ADAPTABILITY AND COHESION, SELF-ESTEEM AND ANXIETY/DEPRESSION IN LATE ADOLESCENCE

Rapson Gomez[1] and Suzanne McLaren
School of Behavioural and Social Sciences and Humanities,
University of Ballarat, Ballarat, Australia

RESEARCH SUMMARY

This study examined several models depicting the role of adolescent ratings of their self-esteem on the relationships of their perceptions of linear and curvilinear family cohesion and adaptability with their anxiety/depression. A total of 385 participants, aged from 18 to 20 years, completed the FACES-III, and self-rating questionnaires covering self-esteem and anxiety/depression. Results showed that self-esteem had additive and some mediating effects on the relations between the linear family measures and anxiety/depression. Self-esteem also moderated the relation between linear cohesion and anxiety/depression. The theoretical and treatment implications of these findings are discussed.

---

[1] Correspondence concerning this article should be addressed to Rapson Gomez, School of Behavioural and Social Sciences and Humanities, University of Ballarat, University Drive, Mount Helen, Ballarat, Victoria, 3353, Australia. email: r.gomez@ballarat.edu.au.

Chapter 270

Communicative Functions of Emotions in Sibling Relationships

Nazan Aksan[*,1], *H. H. Goldsmith*[2], *Marilyn J. Essex*[2]
and Deborah Lowe Vandell[3]

[1]Koc University, Istanbul, Turkey
[2]University of Wisconsin-Madison, WI, US
[3]University of California-Irvine, CA, US

Research Summary

Intrapersonal functions ascribed to emotions are varied. Arguments and evidence abound showing that individual differences in emotionality at the behavioral level of analysis, correlates at the cognitive and physiological levels of analysis not only form defining features of manifest pathology but also constitute risk factors to psychopathology. However, interpersonal functions of emotions remain under-examined, although most emotion theorists would agree that emotions carry signal value and must therefore serve communicative functions during social interactions, and despite the central role emotions play in many theoretical frameworks that seek to understand relationships. The only exception to this trend is research on marital interaction. This body work has relied on sequential analytic methods to examine the communicative functions of emotions and have linked those patters to long-term relationship outcomes such as divorce. In the current study, we applied this methodology to the verbal content and nonverbal affective tone of young children's interactions with their siblings at home in a free play context. As a first step, we asked if we could identify lawful communication chains using only children's non-affective verbal behavioral exchanges, amidst apparently random streams of transactions and conversational turns characteristic of young children's play. We then asked whether young children utilized the information in their siblings' nonverbal affective tone over and above the information contained in the verbal-behavioral channel to alter their subsequent responses in free-flowing interactions. Our

---

[*] Corresponding author: Nazan Aksan, Rumeli Feneri Yolu, Koc University, Sariyer, Istanbul 34450 Turkey, Tel: (90) 212-338-1894, naksan@ku.edu.tr.

findings supported the hypothesis that young children do utilize the emotional, affective tone of their siblings' verbal messages and that those emotional expressions play a key role in the regulation of sibling conflict.

Chapter 271

CHILDHOOD SIBLING RELATIONSHIP QUALITY AND ACHIEVEMENT OUTCOMES IN UNIVERSITY STUDENTS: MEDIATION BY PSYCHOLOGICAL DISTRESS AND PERSONAL MASTERY

Amy Kraft[1], Charles Stayton[1], Arthi Satyanarayan[2] and Linda J. Luecken[1,*]

[1] Arizona State University; Department of Psychology, Tempe, AZ, US
[2] Rice University; Department of Psychology, Houston, TX, US

RESEARCH SUMMARY

Recent research suggests that sibling relationships during childhood affect developmental trajectories well into and past adolescence. The current study hypothesized that childhood sibling relationship quality would be correlated with achievement motivation and college GPA in young adulthood. In addition, mediational models evaluated current distress and personal mastery as mediators of the relation between childhood sibling relationships and achievement-related outcomes. Data was collected through a survey administered to 392 students at a large public university (mean age = 18.9, SD=1.1; 47% female; 74% Caucasian, 8% Hispanic, 6% African American, 6% Asian, 6% other). Participants had at least one sibling and were from continuously married families or families in which the parents divorced at least two years previously. Survey measures assessed sibling relationship quality, current distress (anxiety and depressive symptoms), personal mastery, achievement motivation, and self-reported college GPA. Poor sibling relationships during childhood were significantly associated with lower achievement motivation and lower college GPA, both of which were mediated by current levels of distress. Personal mastery mediated the relation between sibling

---

[*] Corresponding author: Linda J. Luecken, Box 1104, Department of Psychology, Arizona State University, Tempe, AZ 85287, E-mail: *Linda.Luecken@asu.edu*, Phone: 480-965-6886, Fax: 480-965-8544.

relationship quality and achievement motivation. A multiple mediator model found both personal mastery and current distress to significantly mediate the relationship between sibling relationships and achievement motivation. This study highlights the considerable influence of sibling relationships on academic outcomes, and provides further insight into possible interventions for individuals experiencing poor academic achievement.

Chapter 272

LINKING CHILDREN'S PERSONAL CHARACTERISTICS, EXTERNALIZING BEHAVIOR AND RELATIONSHIPS IN FAMILY AND SOCIAL ENVIRONMENTS: SOME DEVELOPMENTAL CASCADES

I. Roskam, J. C. Meunier, M. Stievenart and G. Van De Moortele

Université Catholique de Louvain, Department of Psychology,
Louvain-la-Neuve, Belgium

RESEARCH SUMMARY

For several decades, children's externalizing (EB) has been associated in research with a variety of personal, family, and community factors. More specifically, EB has been identified as being a major risk factor inhibiting the establishment of positive relationships with parents, siblings and peers. Several previous studies conducted with hard-to-manage children indeed proposed a dynamic model describing coercive processes in parent-child relationships and concomitant dangers for social exclusion, even victimization in peer groups and between siblings. Evidence was produced demonstrating the role of both personal and environmental influences, suggesting that EB resulted from transactional and progressive networks of influence between the child and her/his social world.

Considering this progressive interplay between the child and her/his environment, the concept of developmental cascades (Masten, 2005, 2007) offers an interesting theoretical and methodological framework for the description, the explanation, and the opening to effective interventions, in this important area of science and practice. Allowing for the conceiving of models of bidirectional influences, and progressive effects, from one domain of adaptation to another, developmental cascade modeling should indeed permit a better understanding of associations between predictors and consequences of EB.

In such a topic, children of pre-school age are of particular interest since the description of cascades in early development could provide important guidelines for prevention and early intervention programs. Given what we know about the critical importance of early intervention, this augurs for close analysis and detailed appreciation of the factors and processes involved.

The present chapter intends to test linkages among the child's personal characteristics (IQ, executive functioning, personality traits), EB and relationships in family and social environments (parent-child relation, siblings relationships, social competence with peers). The conceptual model postulates strong linkages among the child's personal characteristics, EB and relationships in family and social environments. It is tested in a sample of 253 referred and non-referred preschoolers coming from the French-speaking part of Belgium. The conclusion focuses on important issues both for clinical assessment and related intervention strategies, and research about early development of difficult relationships in family and social environments.

Chapter 273

PREVENTION OF THE NEGATIVE EFFECTS OF MARITAL CONFLICT: A CHILD-ORIENTED PROGRAM

Patricia M. Mitchell, Kathleen P. McCoy, E. Mark Cummings[1], W. Brad Faircloth and Jennifer S. Cummings
University of Notre Dame, Notre Dame, IN, US

RESEARCH SUMMARY

A psycho-educational program for advancing children's coping skills and reactions to marital conflict was evaluated. Families with a child between the ages of 4 and 8 were randomly assigned to one of three groups: 1) parent program only; 2) parent and child program; or 3) self-study (control group). Parents in the parent-only and parent-child groups received the same psycho-educational program. Only children in the parent-child group received the child program which consisted of four visits in which children learned about marital conflict and family relationships; were taught about emotions and different levels of emotions; and were given tools for coping with conflict that would help them react in optimal ways for their development. Analyses suggested the promise of a child program for older children (ages 6-8) with regard to improved emotional security about marital conflict. However, consistent with other research, simply educating children about coping with marital conflict had minimal effects on outcomes associated with conflict between the parents.

---

[1] Corresponding author: Dr. E. Mark Cummings, Department of Psychology, Haggar Hall, University of Notre Dame, Notre Dame, IN 46556, phone: (574) 631-3404, fax: (574) 631-1825, Cummings.10@nd.edu.

Chapter 274

PSYCHOLOGICAL PROCESSES AFFECTING POST-DIVORCE PATERNAL FUNCTIONING

Nehami Baum
The Louis and Gabi Weisfeld School of Social Work,
Bar Ilan University, Ramat Gan, Israel

RESEARCH SUMMARY

This chapter will discuss three inter-related psychological processes that affect the paternal functioning of non-custodial divorced fathers and illustrate their operation in three examples: of a disengaged father, a father in perpetual conflict with his ex-wife, and a father who continues to meet his children's needs. The processes are: mourning the many losses of divorce, separating the spousal role and identity from one's paternal role and identity, and seeing one's ex-wife and children as distinct and separate from one another. All of these processes are essential to coping with the "absence-presence" that characterizes the father's post divorce reality: the absence of his spousal role and presence of his paternal role. This chapter will end with practical suggestions for clinicians.

Chapter 275

BIG, BUFF AND DEPENDENT: EXERCISE DEPENDENCE, MUSCLE DYSMORPHIA AND ANABOLIC STEROID USE IN BODYBUILDERS

Dave Smith[1], Bruce Hale[2], Deborah Rhea[3], Tracy Olrich[4] and Kevan Collier[5]

[1] Manchester Metropolitan University, Manchester, UK
[2] Pennsylvania State University – Berks, Reading PA, US
[3] Texas Christian University, Fort Worth, TX, US
[4] Central Michigan University, Mount Pleasant, MI, US
[5] University of Chester, Chester, UK

RESEARCH SUMMARY

Over the past thirty years a great deal of attention has been paid by psychology researchers to the psychological characteristics of athletes in many different sports. In addition, there has also been an increasing research focus on psychological issues relating to exercise activities. This has led to a great improvement in our understanding of sport and exercise psychology, but one activity that has been largely neglected despite it being both a competitive sport and a popular exercise activity is bodybuilding.

However, the existing bodybuilding research shows a number of interesting psychological issues that are prevalent in the sport. For example, researchers have investigated issues such as exercise dependence, muscle dysmorphia, and rampant drug use in bodybuilding. A common theme linking all these issues is that of addiction. Bodybuilding appears to have an addictive quality in several different ways: bodybuilders can be addicted to the actual activity of lifting weights, the social aspects of being involved in the bodybuilding scene (the so-called 'bodybuilding lifestyle'), and simply being big and muscular. In addition, even the most casual of observers will notice that the use of various muscle-enhancing drugs, such as anabolic steroids and human growth hormone, is the rule rather than the exception in the 'hardcore' bodybuilding scene. The aim of this chapter is to examine issues of addiction in bodybuilding, reviewing past research, presenting some new findings and making suggestions for future research. First, Dave Smith of Manchester Metropolitan University and Bruce Hale of The Pennsylvania State University will review and synthesise their findings on exercise dependence in bodybuilders, focusing on the psychological antecedents, correlates and consequences, and charting the development and validation of their Bodybuilding Dependence Scale. Deborah Rhea of Texas Christian University will then critically examine the extant literature on muscle dysmorphia, and present a new, empirically-validated model of this phenomenon. The remainder of the chapter will focus on anabolic steroid use by bodybuilders. Tracy Olrich of Central Michigan University will examine the current literature on motivations for, and psychological effects of, anabolic steroid use in bodybuilders. Finally, Kevan Collier of Rathbone and Dave Smith will report new findings from a UK-based qualitative study examining the psychosocial context of steroid use in recreational bodybuilders and the motives of these individuals for steroid use. Conclusions will then be drawn from these studies and recommendations made for future research on addictive behaviour in bodybuilders.

In: Psychology Research Biographies and Summaries
Editors: Nancy E. Wodarth and Alexis P. Ferguson
ISBN: 978-1-61470-491-1
© 2012 Nova Science Publishers, Inc.

Chapter 276

SEEKING SAFETY THERAPY FOR MEN: CLINICAL AND RESEARCH EXPERIENCES

Lisa M. Najavits[1], Martha Schmitz[2], Kay M. Johnson[3], Cary Smith[4], Terry North[5], Nancy Hamilton[6], Robyn Walser[7], Kevin Reeder[8], Sonya Norman[9] and Kendall Wilkins[10]

[1]Harvard Medical School/McLean Hospital, Boston MA, US
[2]San Francisco VA Medical Center, CA, US
[3]St. Luke's-Roosevelt Hospital,
Crime Victims Treatment Center, New York, NY, US
[4]Vet Centers, Readjustment Counseling Service,
Department of Veteran Affairs. Washington DC, US
[5]VA Omaha, NE, US
[6]Operation PAR, St. Petersburg, FL, US
[7]VA Palo Alto, CA, US
[8]Central Arkansas Veterans Healthcare System, AR, US
[9]VA San Diego Healthcare System and University of California,
San Diego, CA, US
[10]San Diego State University and University of California,
San Diego, CA, US

RESEARCH SUMMARY

This chapter highlights clinical and research experience on the use of Seeking Safety therapy with men clients. Seeking Safety is a present-focused, coping skills model that addresses trauma and/or substance abuse, from the start of treatment. Its major goal is to help clients increase safety in their lives. The model was designed for both genders, and all types of traumas and substances. We describe how it has been implemented in various settings with men including mental health and substance abuse programs, veterans' hospitals, correctional settings, and residential treatment. The authors represent a range of clinicians and researchers who have conducted the model with men for many years. We describe key themes, treatment strategies, and research studies on Seeking Safety with men.

In: Psychology Research Biographies and Summaries
Editors: Nancy E. Wodarth and Alexis P. Ferguson

ISBN: 978-1-61470-491-1
© 2012 Nova Science Publishers, Inc.

Chapter 277

RELATIONSHIP BETWEEN PERSONALITY SCALES OF IMPULSIVENESS AND DISCOUNTING OF MONETARY GAINS AND LOSSES IN SMOKERS AND NEVER SMOKERS

Taiki Takahashi[1,*], *Hidemi Oono*[2], *Yu Ohmura*[3],
Nozomi Kitamura[1] *and Mark Radford*[4]

[1]Department of Behavioral Science, Hokkaido University, Sapporo, Japan
[2]Department of Biological Psychiatry, Graduate School of Medicine,
Tohoku University, Sendai, Japan
[3]Department of Neuropharmacology, Hokkaido University Graduate School
of Medicine, Japan
[4]Symbiosis Group Limited, Australia

RESEARCH SUMMARY

Personality scales of impulsiveness have been associated with discounting behavior. It has also been shown that nicotine has an effect on the performance of various tasks measuring impulsivity. This study has two main objectives: (1) to determine the relationship between the impulsive personality and the degrees to which delayed and uncertain monetary gains and losses are discounted, and (2) to examine whether the relationship between the impulsive personality and the four types of discounting differ between smokers and never smokers. 31 current smokers and 32 never smokers participated in this experiment. They were required to choose between immediate and delayed monetary gains (and losses), or between guaranteed and probabilistic rewards (or losses). Following completion of this task, they completed two personality questionnaires – Barratte's Impulsiveness Scale (BIS) and the Sensation Seeking Scale (SSS). Several BIS and SSS subscales were positively correlated with the degrees of

---

* Corresponding author: Taiki Takahashi: Telephone number: +81-11-706-3057, Fax number: +81-11-706-3066, E-mail: taikitakahashi@gmail.com. Institute for Department of Behavioral Science, Hokkaido University, Sapporo, Japan.

discounting for delayed monetary gains and losses, but negatively correlated with uncertain monetary gains. Moreover, when dividing participants by smoking status, we found differences between smokers and never smokers in the correlation pattern between impulsive personality and the four types of discounting. Neuro-psychological bases of impulsive behavior, such as discounting behavior, may differ between smokers and never smokers.

In: Psychology Research Biographies and Summaries
Editors: Nancy E. Wodarth and Alexis P. Ferguson

ISBN: 978-1-61470-491-1
© 2012 Nova Science Publishers, Inc.

Chapter 278

SEXUAL ABUSE IN MEN WITH SUBSTANCE USE PROBLEMS: ASSESSMENT AND TREATMENT ISSUES

Christine M. Courbasson[1], Jim Cullen[2] and Karolina Konieczna[3]

[1]Head, Eating Disorders and Addiction Clinic
Acting Director of Training, Psychology Practicum Training Program
Centre for Addiction and Mental Health
Assistant Professor, Department of Psychiatry
University of Toronto, Canada
[2]Clinic Head/Manager Rainbow Services
Centre for Addiction and Mental Health
Assistant Professor, Factor-Inwentash Faculty of Social Work
University of Toronto, Canada
[3]Douglas Institute, Montreal, Canada

RESEARCH SUMMARY

Research suggests that a high prevalence of men with substance use problems have experienced sexual abuse at one point in their life. Men who have been sexually victimized frequently use substances to cope with unpleasant feelings resulting from the abuse, they experience many psychosocial problems and they tend to report sexual abuse much less than women. They also experience more extreme substance use than women with a history of sexual abuse. The present chapter reviews the prevalence and the significance of this problem, outlines significant gaps in the clinical and research literature, discusses the need for gender sensitive assessment approaches, and relevant treatment strategies specific to men that can enhance both substance use treatment and general functioning of these clients.

In: Psychology Research Biographies and Summaries
Editors: Nancy E. Wodarth and Alexis P. Ferguson
ISBN: 978-1-61470-491-1
© 2012 Nova Science Publishers, Inc.

Chapter 279

EXPLAINING TYPE 2 DIABETES: COMPARING PATIENTS' AND PHYSICIANS' MODELS IN MEXICO

Raminta Daniulaityte[1], Javier E. García de Alba García[2] and Ana L. Salcedo Rocha[2]

[1] Center for Interventions, Treatment and Addictions Research, Wright State Univ., School of Medicine, Dayton, OH, US
[2] Social Epidemiological and Health Services Research Unit (UISESS), Guadalajara, Mexico

RESEARCH SUMMARY

Conducted in Guadalajara, Mexico, the study focuses on patients' and physicians' beliefs about diabetes causality. The study was conducted in two stages and used cultural consensus model. First, qualitative interviews were conducted with a convenience sample of 28 Type 2 diabetes patients. On the basis of the elicited themes, 21 scenarios on diabetes causes were developed. In the second stage, a convenience sample of 46 Type 2 diabetes patients and 25 physicians working at the primary care level was recruited. Participants were asked to rate each scenario on a three-point scale. Scenario-type interviews were consensus analyzed using ANTHROPAC. Patients and physicians shared very different cultural models of diabetes causality. The patient model included emotional, environmental, some behavioral, and hereditary causes of diabetes. The physician model emphasized heredity as a single most important cause of diabetes. Differences between patient and physician views of diabetes causality may contribute to mistrust and miscommunication in medical interactions. There is a need for clinical practice that would include psychosocial stress and environmental factors in diabetes prevention and care.

Chapter 280

COGNITIVE DYSFUNCTION IN COCAINE ABUSE: EVIDENCE FOR IMPAIRMENTS IN IMPULSE CONTROL AND DECISION-MAKING

Laurie M. Rilling[*,1] *and Bryon Adinoff*[1,2]
[1]University of Texas Southwestern Medical Center, Dallas, TX, US
[2]VA North Texas Health Care System, Dallas, TX, US

RESEARCH SUMMARY

Cocaine is one of the most widely abused psychoactive substances in the United States, with an estimated 1.3 million Americans using the drug on a regular (at least monthly) basis. Even occasional cocaine use can result in serious medical complications, such as cardiac damage, vascular ischemia, respiratory failure, and persistent alterations in neural function. In this chapter, we will examine the most recent research on impulsivity and decision-making in cocaine use. First, we will present a brief overview of the cognitive processes affected by cocaine use. Next, we will review the relevant literature detailing the status of inhibitory control and decision-making in cocaine users, as well as their proposed neuroanatomical correlates. Finally, we will attempt to integrate these findings with the current view of cocaine addiction and relapse, with an emphasis on the role of impulsivity and decision-making in continued cocaine use despite the elevated risk of negative consequences.

---

[*] Correspondence: Laurie M. Rilling, Ph.D., UT Southwestern Medical Center, 5323 Harry Hines Blvd., Dallas Texas 75390-8846; Telephone: (214) 648-4646; E-mail: laurie.rilling@utsouthwestern.edu.

In: Psychology Research Biographies and Summaries
Editors: Nancy E. Wodarth and Alexis P. Ferguson
ISBN: 978-1-61470-491-1
© 2012 Nova Science Publishers, Inc.

Chapter 281

CURRENT CONTROVERSIES IN THE ASSESSMENT AND TREATMENT OF HEROIN ADDICTION

Robert J. Craig[*]
Jesse Brown VA Medical Center, Chicago, IL, US

RESEARCH SUMMARY

This paper addresses controversial topics in the assessment and treatment of heroin addiction. Included in the discussion are issues of dose and outcome, difficulties with toxicology screens, the role of co-occurring Axis I and Axis II disorders, the introduction (and extinction) of newer medications to treat heroin dependence, difficulties of measuring treatment outcome, models of heroin dependence, the role of user personality, and the question of heroin maintenance treatment.

---

[*] Address inquiries concerning this paper to rjcraig41@comcast.net.

In: Psychology Research Biographies and Summaries
Editors: Nancy E. Wodarth and Alexis P. Ferguson

ISBN: 978-1-61470-491-1
© 2012 Nova Science Publishers, Inc.

Chapter 282

NEW RESEARCH ON METHAMPHETAMINE ABUSE (GENDER DIFFERENCES IN METHAMPHETAMINE EFFECTS: REVIEW OF ANIMAL AND HUMAN STUDIES)

*Bin Liu and Dean E. Dluzen**
Department of Anatomy; Northeastern Ohio Universities
College of Medicine (NEOUCOM), OH, US

RESEARCH SUMMARY

Psychostimulants, including amphetamine, cocaine, methylenedioxy-methamphetamine, nicotine, methylphenidate and methamphetamine (MA), represent the most commonly abused drugs *[National Institute on Drug Abuse webpage: Commonly Abused Drugs; http://www.nida.nih.gov/drugpages/drugsofabuse.html]*. In recent years, experimental and clinical studies on MA have experienced resurgence, in part, due to the increased abuse of this psychostimulant and the serious medical and social problems associated with MA abuse. According to the 2004 **National Survey on Drug Use and Health**, nearly 12 million Americans have tried MA *[National Survey on Drug Use and Health - SAMHSA web site; http://oas.samhsa.gov/nsduh.htm]*.

MA use can produce neurochemical changes in abusers as shown by post-mortem (Wilson *et al.*, 1996) and neuroimaging studies (McCann *et al.*, 1998; Sekine *et al.*, 2001; Volkow *et al.*, 2001a;b). This psychostimulant is a well established neurotoxic agent producing degeneration of monoaminergic nerve terminals as well as a diverse array of actions leading to cell death and apoptosis in various brain regions (Cadet *et al.*, 2003; Davidson *et al.*, 2001; Seiden *et al.*, 1993). Depletions of neurochemicals resulting from MA have been demonstrated in non-human primates (McCann *et al.*, 1998; Villemagne *et al.*, 1998; Woolverton *et al.*, 1989) and rats (Cass, 1997; Ricaurte *et al.*, 1980; Wallace *et al.*,

---

* Correspondence: Dean Dluzen; Department of Anatomy; Northeastern Ohio Universities College of Medicine (NEOUCOM); 4209 State Route 44; Post Office Box 95; Rootstown, OH 44272-0095; TEL: 330-325-6300; FAX: 330-325-5913; E-mail: ded@neoucom.edu.

2001). In specific, MA administration produces significant dopamine (DA) and serotonin (5-HT) depletions in the striatum and nucleus accumbens (Amano *et al.*, 1996; Cass, 1997; Ricaurte *et al.*, 1980; Sabol *et al.*, 2001; Seiden and Ricaurte, 1987; Wallace *et al.*, 2001; Wilson *et al.*, 1996). The increased use and adverse effects exerted by MA indicate the need for a consideration of this psychostimulant within this review.

An important, but often neglected, characteristic of MA use and resultant effects upon behavioral and neurobiological responses are differences which exist between males and females. This represents a critical issue as it can differentially affect approximately half the population. Moreover, the significance for considering the issue of gender in neurobiological research, and, in particular, in response to MA has been emphasized (Bisagno *et al.*, 2003; Cahill, 2006). In this way, uses of, responses to, and treatments for, MA should require gender considerations. In this chapter, we summarized findings on gender differences in MA effects in animals and humans. Since the focus of this review is upon MA, we have limited our review to this specific psychostimulant, however, in certain instances data from other drugs of abuse are included. In this report the terms gender and sex will be used interchangeably, although the former is more often associated with human studies (Dluzen, 2005).

Social Norms and Areca Quid Chewing in Taiwanese Adolescents - A Preliminary Study

Shih-Ming Li[1,2,*] and Jehn-Shyun Huang[1]

[1]Department of Dentistry, National Cheng Kung University, Tainan, Taiwan
[2]Institute of Counseling Psychology, Toko University, Chia-Yi, Taiwan

Research Summary

Introduction: Social norms and personality play important roles in the initiation and maintenance of addictive behaviors. The aim of this preliminary study was to explore how social norms and personality influence areca quid chewing in adolescents. *Materials and Methods:* A total of 179 students from a junior high school in Chia-Yi city (Taiwan) participated in the study in 2003. Areca quid-chewing behavior and intention scales were used to determine attitude to, and usage of, areca quid. Social norm and conscientiousness scales were denoted as factors for perceived social environment and personality factors. *Results:* Forty of the sample (22.5%) has been areca-quid users. The mean scores for the subjective and behavioral social norms were 7.7±3.75 (range 4-20) and 11.8±3.26 (range 4-19). Statistical significance was demonstrated for the relationships between behavioral and subjective social-norm scores and intention to chew for the high-conscientiousness group (r=.27, p=.008; r=.416, p<.001), but not for the low-conscientiousness analog. *Conclusions:* The intention to chew areca quid was enhanced by the perceived social norms in highly conscientious Taiwanese adolescents.

---

* Corresponding Author: Shih-Ming Li, Address: No.51, Sec 2,University Rd, Pu-tzu City,Chia-Yi County 613 Taiwan, Institute of Counseling Psychology, Toko University, Chia-Yi, Taiwan. E-mail address: shiming@mail2000.com.tw.

Chapter 284

FOR THE HEALTH OF IT: A BRIEF VERSION OF THE SITUATIONAL HUMOR RESPONSE QUESTIONNAIRE (MARTIN & LEFCOURT, 1984)

Dave Korotkov*, Ian Fraser, Mihailo Perunovic and Marvin Claybourn
Department of Psychology, St. Thomas University
Fredericton, New Brunswick, Canada

RESEARCH SUMMARY

The two studies reported herein examined the construct validity and reliability of a brief 12-item version of the Situational Humor Response Questionnaire (SHRQ; Martin & Lefcourt, 1984). In this research, separate samples of participants were administered the SHRQ, several other humor and laughter measures, as well as scales related to daily stress, mood, and perceived physical symptomatology. The results from both studies indicate that, with few notable exceptions, the 12-item version was comparable in performance to the 21-item version. Specifically, the brief version was found to have acceptable levels of reliability and construct validity, be correlated with higher levels of extraversion, optimism, happiness, vigor, positive mood and lower levels of negative mood, and stress. Further, sex differences were absent and both measures were found to moderate the relationship between stress and physical symptoms, positive mood, as well as vigor. As predicted, high scores on the two SHRQs and stress measures were associated with greater levels of vigor, positive mood, and less physical symptomatology. The 12-item SHRQ appears to be a useful measure for those interested in a quicker assessment of this valuable humor construct.

---

* Address correspondence to: korotkov@stu.ca.

In: Psychology Research Biographies and Summaries
Editors: Nancy E. Wodarth and Alexis P. Ferguson
ISBN: 978-1-61470-491-1
© 2012 Nova Science Publishers, Inc.

Chapter 285

DEVELOPMENTS IN CULTURAL COMPETENCY RESEARCH

Georgia Michalopoulou, Pamela Falzarano, Cynthia Arfken and David Rosenberg

Wayne State University School of Medicine
Department of Psychiatry and Behavioral Neurosciences

RESEARCH SUMMARY

Racial and ethnic minority groups are known to experience poor health status and increased health risks, which are remarkably consistent across a range of illnesses and health care services, even when social determinants are controlled. These disparities occur in the context of cultural differences between physicians and patients. A considerable body of research indicates cultural barriers and biases on the part of physicians affect clinical recommendations resulting in lower quality of services and thus contributing to health disparities. The response has been an emphasis on cultural competency training for physicians. Unfortunately, that response, while needed, does not adequately address the cultural gap between physicians and patients and does not necessarily result in culturally competent care. Studies conducted with an eye towards addressing health disparities and formulating an evidence based cultural competency intervention are described in this chapter. It is suggested that cultural competency judgments may be quantified using patient rather than physician reports, and that this largely overlooked measurement strategy may enhance research within this area of inquiry. The relationship of the cultural competency construct and variables such as satisfaction with the medical encounter has been proven to be important to health care behaviors and is examined in this chapter. Finally, as a strategy to address health disparities by empowering patients, the implementation of a simple intervention which would address communication barriers between African American patients and their physicians is reviewed.

Chapter 286

THE DYNAMICS OF PAIN AND AFFECT: TOWARD A SALIENT PHENOTYPE FOR CHRONIC PAIN

Patrick H. Finan[1] and Howard Tennen[2]
[1]Department of Psychology, Arizona State University
[2]Department of Community Medicine, University of Connecticut, US

RESEARCH SUMMARY

For decades, clinical evidence has suggested that the subjective experiences of pain and emotion are intertwined. More recently, neuroimaging data have supported this notion, implicating both cortical and subcortical brain regions in overlapping regulatory roles for pain and emotion. There is a need presently to focus research efforts on the identification of salient phenotypes that more fully explicate the relation of pain and emotion, specifically in the context of chronic pain. This can be accomplished through the identification of endogenous brain mechanisms that can be translated into clinically relevant markers of vulnerability and resilience, and through the description of naturalistic processes that promote or inhibit adaptation to chronic pain. The present chapter focuses on how variability in the dynamics of the affect system and its covariation with pain processes influence both brain function and daily experience with chronic pain. Specifically, the chapter addresses the roles of both positive and negative affects during states of heightened pain and provides a rationale for why characterization of affective reactivity to pain at the levels of brain function and daily process is essential to the evolution of more highly targeted treatment strategies.

In: Psychology Research Biographies and Summaries
Editors: Nancy E. Wodarth and Alexis P. Ferguson

ISBN: 978-1-61470-491-1
© 2012 Nova Science Publishers, Inc.

Chapter 287

HYPNOSIS AS AN ADJUNCT TO COGNITIVE-BEHAVIOURAL THERAPY INTERVENTION FOR THE TREATMENT OF FIBROMYALGIA

Antoni Castel[1,2] *Rosalía Cascón*[1,3] *and Maria Rull*[1,2,3]

[1] Pain Clinic. Hospital Universitari de Tarragona Joan XXIII. Spain
[2] Multidimentional Pain Research Group. IISPV. Universitat Rovira i Virgili. Spain
[3] Universitat Rovira i Virgili. Spain

RESEARCH SUMMARY

The purpose of this study is to explore the contributing effects of hypnosis on a cognitive-behavioural therapy intervention for the treatment of chronic pain in patients with fibromyalgia.

The study is structured in four sections. Firstly, it introduces what fibromyalgia is, why it has become a current concern for health psychology and what are the more effective treatments for this syndrome. Specifically, individual and group cognitive-behavioural therapy as part of a multidisciplinary treatment are described as commonly recognised as an effective psychological treatment in fibromyalgia patients. Also, a brief review on the use of clinical hypnosis to reduce both acute and chronic pain is offered, noting that there are only few studies that focus on fibromyalgia-related pain.

Secondly, the methods and procedures of this study are specified. A sample of patients with fibromyalgia were randomly assigned to one of the two treatment conditions: 1) Cognitive-behavioural group therapy treatment; or 2) Cognitive-behavioural group therapy treatment with hypnosis. The contents of each psychological treatment program are carefully described. To assess the efficacy of the designed treatment programs, some outcome measures were taken before and after the treatment. These variables were: pain intensity, pain quality, anxiety, depression, functionality, and some sleep dimensions such as quantity, disturbance, adequacy, somnolence, and problems index.

Thirdly, the main results from this study are exposed. The analysis shows clinically significative improvements in both psychological treatment groups. However, patients who received cognitive-behavioural group therapy plus hypnosis showed greater improvement than those who received cognitive-behavioural group therapy without hypnosis.

And finally, a conclusion on the evidences described, some limitations to be considered in following studies and some recommendations on the treatment of patients with fibromyalgia are followed.

Can Technology Improve the Treatment of Chronic Insomnia? A Review of Best Practices

Norah Vincent*
Department of Clinical Health Psychology, Faculty of Medicine,
University of Manitoba, Manitoba, Canada

Research Summary

The use of technology to treat common health problems, such as chronic insomnia, is a growing trend in the health psychology field. The experience of persistent insomnia, as defined by a difficulty with falling asleep, staying asleep, and/or early morning awakening, coupled with sleep-related daytime impairment affects a large number (10%) of adults (Morin, LeBlanc, Daley, Gregoire, & Merette, 2006). Those with chronic insomnia are at an increased risk for a number of health problems (Elwood, Hack, Pickering, Hughes, & Gallacher, 2006; Crum, Storr, Chan, & Ford, 2004) and laboratory based studies show that restricting the sleep of healthy individuals to 50 to 75% of that normally obtained often produces unrecognizable impairments in vigilance and working memory (Van Dongen, Maislin, Mullington, & Dinges, 2003). The two main treatments for chronic insomnia consist of cognitive behavioral therapy and pharmacotherapy, however, consumers often express a preference for cognitive behavioral therapies (Morin, Gaulier, Barry, & Kowatch, 1992; Vincent & Lionberg, 2001). In response to this need, a variety of intervention websites and handheld microcomputer devices have been developed to provide cognitive behavioral intervention to those with this problem. Additionally, the potential use of telehealth to treat individuals with this problem will be discussed. This paper will review these new technologies and highlight the evidence base for these approaches. Additionally, considerations regarding who might most benefit from using these supports will be examined, as will receptivity to these innovations. Implications of the use of technology for the delivery of cognitive behavioral therapy services will be discussed.

---

* Phone (204) 787-3272; Fax: (204) 787-3755; Email: NVincent@exchange.hsc.mb.ca.

Chapter 289

BENEFIT FINDING PREDICTS IMPROVED EMOTIONAL HEALTH FOLLOWING CARDIAC REHABILITATION

Bruce W. Smith, Paulette J. Christopher, Laura E. Bouldin, Erin M. Tooley, Jennifer F. Bernard and J. Alexis Ortiz

University of New Mexico, US
Albuquerque, New Mexico, US

RESEARCH SUMMARY

Objective: The purpose of this study was to determine whether benefit finding was related to better emotional health in cardiac patients following cardiac rehabilitation. Benefit finding refers to the ability to find something positive or grow in response to a stressful event.

Design: Participants were cardiac patients (21% female and 22% ethnic minority) in a 12 week cardiac rehabilitation program. Benefit finding was assessed before and after the rehabilitation program. The main hypotheses were that benefit finding would predict increased positive emotion and decreased negative emotion at follow up when controlling for baseline emotion and other potential predictors of emotional health. The main outcome measures were positive and negative emotion following the rehabilitation program.

Results: Path analyses showed that benefit finding was related to more positive emotion and less negative emotion at follow-up when controlling for other predictors of emotion at follow up. In addition, positive reframing coping and income were related to more positive emotion, ethnic minority status was related to more negative emotion, and tangible social support was related to less negative emotion at follow-up.

Conclusion: Benefit finding may improve emotional health during cardiac rehabilitation. Health psychology interventions should focus on enabling cardiac patients to find more benefits in the process of coping with and recovering from heart disease.

Chapter 290

NEGOTIATING BLAME AS A FAT CHILD'S PARENT: A CASE STUDY

*Riina Kokkonen**
Department of Psychology, University of Eastern Finland
Joensuu, Finland

RESEARCH SUMMARY

In recent years, the so-called "fatness epidemic" has been subjected to critical examination by different researchers questioning the biomedical definition of fatness as a self-induced health risk and focusing on the discrimination and blame directed at fat people. Attention has also been paid to the ways fat people themselves interpret and account for their fatness in the prevailing negative atmosphere, but the viewpoints of *the parents of fat children* have received less attention. As the primary caretakers, parents are often the ones blamed for their child's weight and are easily viewed as somehow "improper" parents. It is therefore important to look at the ways these parents interpret and manage the ambient messages implying their deviance from the norms of "good" parenthood. In this chapter, my aim is to take this subject up for discussion by presenting an analysis of the interviews of two mothers whose children have been determined to be "overweight" or "obese" by health care. These interviews are part of my current study concerning the ways the parents of Finnish fifth-graders discuss their children's health and their own role and responsibilities as parents. These two interviews stood out as clear exceptions to the other interviews, for they revolved around the issues of the child's weight and the blaming of the parents. I will present a close reading of these two interviews and analyze the multiple ways the mothers discursively and rhetorically managed the blame and tried to position themselves as worthy parents.

---

* Address: Psychology, University of Eastern Finland; P.O. Box 111; FIN-80101 Joensuu, Finland; Gsm: +358-050-344 7254; E-mail: riina.kokkonen@uef.fi.

In: Psychology Research Biographies and Summaries
Editors: Nancy E. Wodarth and Alexis P. Ferguson
ISBN: 978-1-61470-491-1
© 2012 Nova Science Publishers, Inc.

Chapter 291

TRUST IN HEALTH CARE: CONCEPTUAL ISSUES AND EMPIRICAL RESEARCH

Rocio Garcia-Retamero[1,2]* *and Yasmina Okan*[1]

[1]Universidad de Granada, Spain
[2]Max Planck Institute for Human Development, Berlin, Germany

RESEARCH SUMMARY

Over the past few decades, there has been a shift from an emphasis on medical paternalism to the recognition of the importance of an informed patient. A balance may be achieved by encouraging patients and physicians to share decision making. Patients' trust in their physician has been suggested as a crucial factor influencing patients' willingness to participate in decision making. Investigating which variables influence trust in physicians and in heath care institutions, therefore, becomes more essential than ever. Our aim in this chapter is to examine the conceptual issues and empirical research regarding patients' trust in the different constituents of the health care system. First, we explain the meaning of trust and provide an overview of the instruments that have been developed to measure the concept. Second, we describe different types of trust and some of the variables that influence each of them. Third, we explain the impact of trust in health care systems and discuss the elements of trust that may be particularly important in this context. Finally, we describe several relevant results that emerge from a review of the literature on the topic and open avenues for future research. We conclude that empirical research clearly complements theory and suggests that developing a trustworthy health care system requires more than competent physicians. More importantly, it needs health workers that have the motivation and capacity for empathetic understanding of patients, as well as institutions that sustain ethical behaviors and so provide a basis for trust.

---

* Send correspondence to: Rocio Garcia-Retamero; Facultad de Psicologia, Universidad de Granada; Campus Universitario de Cartuja s/n, 18071 Granada (Spain); Tel: 0034 958 246240; Fax: 0034 958 246239; Email: rretamer@ugr.es.

In: Psychology Research Biographies and Summaries
Editors: Nancy E. Wodarth and Alexis P. Ferguson
ISBN: 978-1-61470-491-1
© 2012 Nova Science Publishers, Inc.

Chapter 292

IMPROVING THE PUBLIC HEALTH IMPACT OF INTERNET-DELIVERED INTERVENTIONS

Rik Crutzen
Maastricht University, CAPHRI, The Netherlands

RESEARCH SUMMARY

The key problem in Internet-delivered interventions is high rates of attrition: people leave the website before actually using it. The aim of this chapter is to better understand compatibility between design and user needs. Thereby we can improve the public health impact of Internet-delivered interventions targeting health risk behaviours (e.g., a sedentary lifestyle, high fat intake, and cigarette smoking) by retaining website visitors' attention through "interactional richness" and thus creating a more positive user experience. Such a positive user experience leads to increased "e-retention" (i.e., the actual use of the intervention by the target group once they access its website). Previous studies assessed and favourably evaluated the efficacy of Internet-delivered interventions without considering use data, whereas the public health impact of an intervention largely depends on the actual use of the intervention website by the target group. Furthermore, the development and application of theories regarding e-retention is timely, since no such theories currently exist. I therefore developed an integrative theoretical framework that provides a theory-driven solution for a practice-based problem with direct applications within the mushrooming field of Internet-delivered interventions.

In: Psychology Research Biographies and Summaries
Editors: Nancy E. Wodarth and Alexis P. Ferguson

ISBN: 978-1-61470-491-1
© 2012 Nova Science Publishers, Inc.

Chapter 293

LEISURE AND DEPRESSION IN MIDLIFE: A TAIWANESE NATIONAL SURVEY OF MIDDLE-AGED ADULTS

*Luo Lu**
Department of Business Administration, National Taiwan University, Taiwan

RESEARCH SUMMARY

We aimed to explore middle-aged people's subjective leisure experiences, and to further examine associations of such experiences with their depressive symptoms in a Chinese society--Taiwan. Known correlates of depression such as demographics, physical health and social support, were taken into account. Face-to-face interviews were conducted to collect data using structured questionnaires from a national representative sample of community older people ($N = 1143$, aged 45-65). Using hierarchical multiple regression, we found that (1) being female, had lower family income were demographic risk factors of depression; (2) worse physical health, lack of independent functioning in ADL, and disability were related to more depressive symptoms; (3) greater social support was related to less depressive symptoms; (4) having controlled for all the above effects of demographics, health, and social support, positive leisure experiences in terms of satisfaction and meaningfulness were independently related to fewer depressive symptoms. The benefits of meaningful leisure pursuits for successful midlife transition and prospective ageing were discussed.

---

* Correspondence concerning this article should be addressed to Prof. Luo Lu, Department of Business Administration, National Taiwan University, No.1, Sec. 4, Roosevelt Road, Taipei 106, Taiwan, ROC. Tel: +886-2-33669657. Fax: +886-2-23625379. E-mail: luolu@ntu.edu.tw.

In: Psychology Research Biographies and Summaries
Editors: Nancy E. Wodarth and Alexis P. Ferguson
ISBN: 978-1-61470-491-1
© 2012 Nova Science Publishers, Inc.

Chapter 294

FOLLOWING THE LIFE-COURSE OF AN EXPECTATION: A CASE STUDY EXAMINING THE EXCHANGE OF EXPECTATIONS IN A HOMELESS SHELTER IN NEW YORK CITY

Mark B. Borg, Jr.* and Leroy Porter

[1]Community Consulting Group, New York William Alanson White Institute, N.Y., US
[2]Community Consulting Group, New York Fisk University, Nashville, TN, US

RESEARCH SUMMARY

In this chapter, the authors present a study of expectations of clients and staff members as met and shaped by the dynamics of the New York City homeless shelter system. A case study is presented of one resident who traversed New York City's homeless shelter system over a two-year time period—a shelter for male individuals, many of whom were dually diagnosed—mentally ill chemical abusers (MICA). In the study, contemporary theories of *Reasoned Action* and its offshoot, *Planned Behavior,* are used to illustrate issues surrounding the conceptualization of *intentions* and other proximal antecedents affecting a person's expectations of life in the shelter. The authors use the constructs of *Implementation Intentions*, *Behavioral Expectation*, and *Behavioral Willingness* to measure the degree to which expectations are realized in terms of hope and of despair. The authors see this cycle of hope and despair as a dynamic—and sometimes defensive—process that continually transforms and is transformed by, bureaucratic, social and other aspects of the shelter system itself. Also considered in the study are the ways that the theories of reasoned action and planned behavior can inform and be informed by system-level dynamics viewed through the lens of community level security operations. The authors define this artifact as *Community Character*. Through an analysis of this construct the authors propose a dramatic distinction between expectations which can be seen to have a *life-course* and those that do not. The aim

---

* Corresponding author: Mark B. Borg, Jr., Ph.D. Community Consulting Group, 156 Fifth Avenue, Suite 725, New York, NY 10010, Tel: (212) 978-0266, Fax: (212) 741-1697, Email: oedtrex@aol.com.

of the study is to use contemporary behavioral health and community psychology theories and research methodologies to begin to develop a model describing the process of configuring behavioral intentions, expectations and motivation as they interact and play out in the life-cycle of an expectation.

In: Psychology Research Biographies and Summaries
Editors: Nancy E. Wodarth and Alexis P. Ferguson
ISBN: 978-1-61470-491-1
© 2012 Nova Science Publishers, Inc.

Chapter 295

EXPLORING THE BLACK BOX OF TRUST ON OUTCOMES: THE CASE OF PATIENT-PHYSICIAN ENCOUNTERS

Yin-Yang Lee and Julia L. Lin

[1] Department of Health Management, I-Shou University, Kaohsiung, Taiwan and, Department of Ophthalmology Department, YongKang Veterans Hospital, Taiwan
[2] Graduate School of Management and, College of Management, I-Shou University, Kaohsiung, Taiwan

RESEARCH SUMMARY

Trust in the patient-physician relationship has been widely discussed, but detailed conceptual analyses and empirical information are scarce in the extant literature as trust relates to patient outcomes. Based on expectancy and social exchange perspectives, this paper intends to narrow this theoretical gap by introducing four mediators: compliance, the placebo effect, patient disclosure, and physician's caring behavior. Two moderators, the Pygmalion effect and physician reputation, are also proposed to enhance trust and in turn, affect patient health. In addition to our long emphasis upon advancing diagnostic tools and pharmacological therapies, the profound implications of this paper highlight the importance of efforts in building trust both for health care providers and policymakers.

In: Psychology Research Biographies and Summaries
Editors: Nancy E. Wodarth and Alexis P. Ferguson
ISBN: 978-1-61470-491-1
© 2012 Nova Science Publishers, Inc.

Chapter 296

EXPECTATIONS IN A TIME OF SELF-DOUBT

A. Ralph Barlow and Pastor Emeritus
Beneficent Church (United Church of Christ), Providence, R.I., US

RESEARCH SUMMARY

Expectations of religion in certain areas of the globe in the contemporary era are at a crossroads. The defining crisis was the decision in the late 1940s to turn over basic control of Christian missions, dominated for too long by the West, to indigenous peoples of colonial empires.

This chapter explores the psychology of expectations within a particular historical context characterized by the tension between two conflicting drives: dominance and affirmation of indigenous leadership, or triumphalism and servanthood marked by self-doubt. That conflict is directly related to cultural, societal expectations.

The chapter begins with an autobiographical sketch of a scene in the author's sophomore year in college. It moves on to a comparison between two buildings in Providence, Rhode Island, USA, known to the author through a ministry there of 33 years. Those two scenarios attempt to place in bold relief the conflict in religion since World War II, particularly during and following the Vietnam era.

The major research data comes from the author's study of Liston Pope, late Dean of Yale Divinity School (1949-1962) and Gilbert Stark Professor of Social Ethics (1947-1973).

Pope's major contributions hinged on his insight that "indigenous" leadership in religious undertakings should take precedence over the concept of leadership from "the outside."

The broad implications of the concept of "indigenous" -- we can now appreciate -- characterized Pope's faculty appointments at Yale during the 1950s. Pope's leadership was in the vanguard of a re-definition of the role of religion in contemporary life.

The chapter's attempt to understand the conflict in Liston Pope – a paradox indeed, given his leadership -- between excessive ambition and insecurity explores a probable connection between his addiction to alcohol and his excessive longing, or expectancy.

Pope's conflict between a fierce ambition and a growing sense of insecurity, or self-doubt, was prefigured culturally in American history following the Spanish-American war, particularly in the decline of Protestantism until the early 1930s when a resurgence of liberalism asserted itself once again.

The concluding observation of the chapter is that the dynamics of indigenous leadership offer positive expectations for Christian communities throughout the world, as documented by statistics demonstrating the strength of Christian witness in global areas where those dynamics are convincingly present.

In: Psychology Research Biographies and Summaries
Editors: Nancy E. Wodarth and Alexis P. Ferguson
ISBN: 978-1-61470-491-1
© 2012 Nova Science Publishers, Inc.

Chapter 297

COPING WITH THE EXPECTATION OF SOCIAL ACCEPTANCE

C. Nathan DeWall, Richard S. Pond, Jr. and Ian Bonser
University of Kentucky, US

RESEARCH SUMMARY

U.S. culture is a seething caldron of positive expectations. College students expect to earn more money, have more friends, and gain more respect from others than ever before. What are the costs and benefits of such overly positive expectations? In this chapter, we will review experimental, correlational, and physiological research investigating the cognitive, emotional, and behavioral consequences of unmet expectations regarding social acceptance. We will demonstrate how an unmet expectation for social acceptance increases aggression and self-defeating behavior, reduces prosocial behavior and intelligent thought, and promotes a hostile cognitive bias toward people in one's social environment. We will also review evidence showing that increases in psychological traits related to expectations of social acceptance may have positive consequences for psychological well-being, but may have negative consequences for responses to social rejection. These results suggest that thwarting the expectation for social acceptance strikes at the core of human psychology, with dramatic consequences for a large variety of processes.

Chapter 298

GROUP HARDINESS: A RESPONSE TO THE STRESSES OF COMPLEX ADAPTIVE SYSTEMS

*Joshua L. Ray and Donde Ashmos Plowman**
University of Tennessee, Department of Management, Knoxville, TN, US

RESEARCH SUMMARY

Researchers are beginning to utilize a complexity framework for explaining the functioning of organizations. This framework explains organizational functioning as characterized by a far from equilibrium state that demonstrates a sensitivity to initial conditions arising from nonlinear interactions and emergent self-organization. However, researchers have yet to address the tremendous levels of stress that individuals and groups experience while working under these conditions. Psychological research has examined factors that lead to resilience as evidenced by psychological hardiness. We apply the findings of individual hardiness research to address the experience of stress by individuals in the organization. Furthermore, we extend the principles of individual hardiness to the group level by paralleling the individual hardiness components (i.e. control, commitment, and challenge) with group level constructs (i.e. enactment, organizational identification, and sensemaking). Hence, we argue that the hardiness concept at both the individual and group levels might be appropriate for addressing the stress inherent in complex adaptive systems.

---

* Corresponding Author: Phone: 865-974-1674, Fax: 865-974-2048, Email: dplowman@utk.edu.

In: Psychology Research Biographies and Summaries
Editors: Nancy E. Wodarth and Alexis P. Ferguson

ISBN: 978-1-61470-491-1
© 2012 Nova Science Publishers, Inc.

Chapter 299

THE INFLUENCE OF EXPECTATIONS ON RECOVERY, QUALITY OF LIFE, AND TREATMENT SATISFACTION IN SURGICAL PATIENTS

Maren Weiss[1]*, Michael Siassi[2], Werner Hohenberger[3] and Friedrich Lösel[1]

[1]Department of Psychology, University Erlangen-Nuremberg, Germany
[2]Bethesda Hospital Bergedorf, Hamburg, Germany
[3]Department of Surgery, University Erlangen-Nuremberg, Germany

RESEARCH SUMMARY

Recovery from surgery is not only influenced by medical facts, but also by psychological variables. Even in the 1950ies, Janis (1958) valued "work of worrying" as a crucial condition for successful recovery. Our longitudinal study is designed to describe fears and expectations before surgery, and to reveal their influence on recovery in a sample of patients undergoing colorectal surgery. We are especially interested in expectations concerning the application and removal of an artificial anus (stoma).

Methods: 79 patients undergoing major colorectal surgery were investigated before surgery as well as three months and twelve months after surgery. Patients who received a temporary stoma ($n = 35$) completed an additional follow-up three months after reversal of the stoma. At every time point, we performed a semi-structured interview that assessed (amongst other aspects of illness and well-being): Anxiety, patient's expectations, and treatment satisfaction. Additional questionnaires were used to assess quality of life, personality, and coping.

Results: Before surgery, 25% reported severe anxiety, whereas 43% expressed no fear. Anxiety predicted treatment satisfaction, but no other aspect of recovery (e.g., quality of life, duration of hospital stay). Before surgery, 44% of our patients did not expect long-term

---

* Corresponding author: Department of Psychology, University Erlangen-Nuremberg, Bismarckstr. 1, 91054 Erlangen, Germany, (0049)9131-8526218, Email: Maren.Weiss@psy.phil.uni-erlangen.de.

impairment due to surgery, and only 6% expected severe problems after surgery. Three months after surgery, 32% of the patients declared that they had expected a faster recovery. Twelve months after surgery, this percentage had increased to 41%. Expectations did not influence any aspect of recovery in our general sample. Patients waiting for stoma formation expected more problems; after surgery, they often experienced a "positive disappointment", as the stoma did not impair them as much as expected. On the other hand, patients with a temporary stoma were often disappointed after stoma removal and were less satisfied with medical treatment.

Conclusion: Stoma surgery leads to a characteristic course of expectations and disappointments. Although expectations and disappointments did not influence recovery as we had anticipated, they influenced treatment satisfaction.

In: Psychology Research Biographies and Summaries
Editors: Nancy E. Wodarth and Alexis P. Ferguson

ISBN: 978-1-61470-491-1
© 2012 Nova Science Publishers, Inc.

Chapter 300

FUTURE FROM THE PAST: THE MISTAKES OF FUTUROLOGY

A. V. Yurevich
Institute of Psychology of the Russian Academy of Sciences, Moscow, Russia

RESEARCH SUMMARY

Humankind has forever sought to extend its time perspective by linking its interest in the present with the lessons of the past and attempting to look into the future. F.L. Polak stressed that throughout history the development of civilization has been stimulated and guided by the images of the future created by the more gifted and talented members of society (Polak, 1973, p.7). One of the best known researchers of science, E.Torrance, analyzed historical episodes to demonstrate, first, that science and culture have always been spurred by vivid images of the future which exerted massive influence on them, and second, that the potential "strength" of this or that culture was proportional to the clarity and vigor of these images (Torrance, 1978). "Future shocks" eloquently described by A.Toffler (Toffler, 1970) often provided irritants for mankind whose impact was every bit as strong as the challenges of the present.

Predicting the future, once the traditional occupation of palm-readers and star-gazers, has turned into a major industry which has scientific and cultural elements (at present, though, the burgeoning popularity of star-gazers and palm-readers has prompted a movement in the opposite direction). The role of the former has been taken on by futurology and of the latter, by science fiction as well as the plots it has suggested to the media, the cinema, etc. In the 1970s studies of the future were already a rapidly developing multi-million dollar industry (Dickson, 1977, p. 4). In the US, for example, there were more than 400 independent futurological groups that used more than 150 various prognostication methodologies (ibid). By the 1970s science fiction had emerged as one of the most popular literary genres.

Many of the science fiction and futurological forecasts were set in 2000 because of the magic spell of the date separating millennia. As J. Benford noted, everybody wanted to peep behind the veil that hid the magic number 2000 (Benford, 1995, p.1). Now that we are into the 21st century there is every opportunity to look at the future-turned-present through the prism of the past, i.e. see to what extent predictions have come true.

In: Psychology Research Biographies and Summaries
Editors: Nancy E. Wodarth and Alexis P. Ferguson

ISBN: 978-1-61470-491-1
© 2012 Nova Science Publishers, Inc.

Chapter 301

A Christian Perspective on Hope, Expectancies and Therapy

Thomas V. Frederick
Hope International University Southern California, CA, US

Research Summary

This paper will explore the meaning and nature of hope from both a psychological and Christian perspective. This exploration will develop the function of the therapist as a *harbinger of hope*. Three types of literatures will be reviewed. First hope will be developed from a pastoral psychology perspective focusing on Donald Capps' contributions through the notion as pastors as agents of hope. Second, hope or expectancies will be reviewed focusing on recent research in positive psychology; namely, hope as a vitrue and optimism about the furture. Finally, The Christian therapist acts as a *harbinger of hope* by acting as both priest and prophet. The priestly role of harbingers includes encouragement and confession. By listening for God's active movement in giving life and blessing, harbingers encourage and support sufferers. Harbingers engage in supportive relationships by hearing confession – understanding the total experiences of sufferers. Finally, harbingers challenger sufferers to find their ultimacy in the in-breaking kingdom of God.

In: Psychology Research Biographies and Summaries
Editors: Nancy E. Wodarth and Alexis P. Ferguson
ISBN: 978-1-61470-491-1
© 2012 Nova Science Publishers, Inc.

Chapter 302

HUMAN ANTIDEPRESSANTS AND THE OLD SONG-AND-DANCE ROUTINES: ZEROING IN ON THE LIFE-COURSE (AND LACK THEREOF) OF EXPECTATIONS IN CLINICAL PRACTICE

Mark B. Borg, Jr.
Community Consulting Group, New York, New York, US

RESEARCH SUMMARY

I wish to follow up on the study conducted by myself and Leroy Porter (this volume) with a brief clinical vignette to assess the ways that our conceptualization of expectation—combined with an assessment of the influence of cultural factors/dynamics—might be utilized to inform clinical practice.

Through much clinical and cultural research (cf. Borg et al., 2009), as well as in my work with analytic patients, I have developed a poignant and provocative hypothesis: For generations our (U.S.) culture has been breeding—not just manufacturing—antidepressants, *Human Antidepressants*. The term Human Antidepressant (H.A.D.) denotes a dynamic pattern wherein a person has developed a particular interaction pattern—a *song-and-dance routine*—that plays out in all significant relationships, a pattern which essentially enacts a stance toward others (as well as the associated *expectation*s at play within and between self and others) in which it is the person's primary task in life to *heal* others.

It has been suggested that a child's first *job* in life is to provide a kind of *therapy* to his/her primary caregiver—usually the mother—and that the child's very survival is subjectively experienced as being contingent on how well that job is done (cf. Searles, 1975). The familial/cultural etiology of this process goes beyond the scope of this commentary; though the dynamics of H.A.D. are highly associated with our cultural/political/economic "Liberal Individualistic" (vs. community-oriented) environment, which incessantly—though unconsciously—pits individual rights against the needs of others. This, therefore, makes this a process where *expectations* (ones which do not, in our terminology, have a *life-course*) are also cultural artifacts that are developed mutually/reciprocally, are sustained by behavioral intentions that result in habitual roles/behaviors and concomitant interactions patterns, and then lead to repetitive self-defeating dynamics that affect all significant relationships.

Obviously, children are not diagnosticians; so the distinction that the child will register is simply between *happy* and *not-happy* (not-happy becomes a catch-all term for "Depression," but at the earliest stage it also includes anything from mild dysthymia to full-blown Major Depression, anxiety states, mood instabilities, and other inconsistencies in affect). The child registers any state in his/her caregiver other than "Happy" as a danger to his/her very existence. So much the worse for the child who grows up with actual depression in his/her primary caregiver, but the desperate need to ensure that the parent is "well" plays out regardless of the actual emotional state/condition of the caregiver. This, therefore, sets up *behavioral intentions* that are consistent with the role of H.A.D., and the sustains the co-occurring *expectancy values*—a process thought to precede all behaviors: decisions to act or not act that are the result of an assessment of the likelihood of specific outcomes associated with the act along with the subjective value assigned to those outcomes—associated with this role.

In: Psychology Research Biographies and Summaries
Editors: Nancy E. Wodarth and Alexis P. Ferguson
ISBN: 978-1-61470-491-1
© 2012 Nova Science Publishers, Inc.

Chapter 303

THE PSYCHOLOGY OF DENIAL IN THE POLITICAL CONTEXT: THE CASE OF TORTURE

Daryn Reicherter, Alexandra Aylward, Ami Student and Cheryl Koopman
Stanford University, Palo Alto, California, US

RESEARCH SUMMARY

The psychology of denial is examined within the political context. We use the issue of state-sanctioned torture to expand the psychological concept of denial beyond cognitive and psychoanalytic psychology to include factors drawn from social and political psychology. Historical and political perspectives are also incorporated, as are intra-psychic perspectives. The political issue of torture is an interesting focus for expanding the psychological understanding of denial because although torture is not legal in any country, it is practiced in two-thirds of the world's nations (Amnesty International, 2001). State-sanctioned torture is conducted with the implicit (if not explicit) support of each nation's government. However, no countries publicly acknowledge that their governments sanction torture, and its occurrence is often rigorously denied. This chapter focuses on three manifestations of the denial of torture: 1) denial that torture is sanctioned; 2) denial of self-serving political motivations for sanctioning torture; and 3) denial of the humanity of the victims of torture. An analysis of these manifestations suggests a complex model is needed for understanding the psychology of denial in the political context. Several components of this model are drawn from psychoanalytic and information-processing perspectives. Constructs from cognitive psychology also include schema, e.g., the enemy image, and scripts, e.g., "the ticking time bomb scenario." Additional components merit inclusion for understanding how denial operates in relation to torture, e.g., deindividuation; and social norms. Therefore, a consideration of the psychology of denial in relation to torture highlights a number of social psychological and societal factors that should be included in a model of the psychology of denial in the political context.

Chapter 304

REPRESSION: FINDING OUR WAY IN THE MAZE OF QUESTIONNAIRES

Bert Garssen[1]*
Helen Dowling Institute for Psycho-oncology, Utrecht, The Netherlands

RESEARCH SUMMARY

Repression is typically associated in literature with terms such as non-expression, emotional control, rationality, anti-emotionality, defensiveness and restraint. Whether these terms are synonymous with repression, indicate a variation, or are essentially different from repression is uncertain. We have discussed the similarities and differences between these concepts elsewhere (Garssen, 2007). In addition, a multitude of questionnaires has been developed in this field, which presents yet another problem for evaluating studies. In the present review, we critically discuss the various questionnaires used for measuring repression and related constructs, and then present our assessment on which scales are reliable and valid and which are not. The most appropriate repression measure is the Marlow Social Desirability (MC SD) scale, or the combination of the MC SD and an anxiety/distress scale. The question whether the MC SD scale alone, or the combination measure is the best repression measure remains unsettled. Future studies should apply several of the reliable and valid repression measures and study their interrelationships, as well as their relationships with several distress, personality and objective measures.

---

* Corresponding author: E-mail: bgarssen@hdi.nl, Tel.: 31-30-252-4020, Fax : 31-30-252-4022.

In: Psychology Research Biographies and Summaries
Editors: Nancy E. Wodarth and Alexis P. Ferguson
ISBN: 978-1-61470-491-1
© 2012 Nova Science Publishers, Inc.

Chapter 305

HIDDEN CURRICULUM IN EDUCATION AND THE SOCIAL PSYCHOLOGY OF DENIAL: GLOBAL MULTICULTURAL EDUCATION FOR SOCIAL TRANSFORMATION

Beth Salyers and Greg Wiggan
University of North Carolina, Charlotte, North Carolina, US

RESEARCH SUMMARY

Numerous educational studies have lauded the importance of social bonds in schools and institutional ties as being crucial to students' sense of self and to school achievement. The hidden curriculum [curriculum of exclusion] in schools however can undermine students' identity development and result in academic disengagement. It follows that self-affirmation in school plays a positive role in student engagement and in their academic success. Using postmodernism as a theoretical framework, this chapter examines the processes and implications of the contemporary hidden curriculum. The authors propose a global multicultural education as a positive school effect that helps validate students' sense of self while serving to improve school achievement. We argue that a transformative global multicultural education helps to nurture inclusion, thus reducing subsequent effects of social and cultural denial, and marginalization in schools. The implications of this chapter are important for teachers, administrators and all those interested in student success.

In: Psychology Research Biographies and Summaries
Editors: Nancy E. Wodarth and Alexis P. Ferguson
ISBN: 978-1-61470-491-1
© 2012 Nova Science Publishers, Inc.

Chapter 306

REPRESSION QUESTIONNAIRES COMPARED

Bert Garssen, Margot Remie and Marije van der Lee
Helen Dowling Institute for Psycho-Oncology, Rubenslaan,
Utrecht, the Netherlands

RESEARCH SUMMARY

Literature on repression is abundant with terms such as repression, non-expression of negative emotions, emotional control, rationality, type C response style and defensiveness. However, it is uncertain whether these terms are synonymous with repression, denote a variation, or are essentially different from repression. In addition, a multitude of questionnaires has been developed in this field, which presents yet another problem for evaluating studies.

Elsewhere we have discussed overlap of and differences between the various repression-related concepts (Garssen, 2007a) and critically reviewed eleven repression-related questionnaires (Garssen, 2009). The present study compares various repression questionnaires in two groups of women with breast cancer (N = 102 and 145). A secondary factor analysis yielded two factors, which were labelled: repression and anxious defensiveness. The relevance of this finding for future studies is that only scales belonging to the repression cluster are valid measures for measuring repression. The Marlowe Crowne Social Desirability scale is recommended as the most adequate repression measure.

In: Psychology Research Biographies and Summaries
Editors: Nancy E. Wodarth and Alexis P. Ferguson

ISBN: 978-1-61470-491-1
© 2012 Nova Science Publishers, Inc.

Chapter 307

WHERE ARE ALL THE BLACK MALE STUDENTS? AFRICAN AMERICANS' SCHOOL ACHIEVEMENT, THE SOCIAL PSYCHOLOGY OF DENIAL, AND ARTS EDUCATION AS A MEDIATING INFLUENCE

Calvin W. Walton and Greg Wiggan
University of North Carolina, Charlotte, North Carolina, US

RESEARCH SUMMARY

Research has indicated that African Americans are often displaced in schools and males in particular, are denied access to quality academic programs and are tracked into vocational training, and some are even forced out of schools. Since the establishment of the Individuals with Disabilities Education Act (IDEA) of 1975, there has been growing interest in understanding the relationship between African American male students and special education assessment. In this research we explore the impact that the historic denial of educational equality and culturally responsive pedagogy has had on the disproportionately high placement of African American males in special education programs for the mentally disabled, and behaviorally and emotionally challenged. Our research reveals three primary catalysts for special education placement of African American male students: 1) persistent patterns of discrimination, 2) biases in assessments, and 3) social differences in students' behaviors and learning styles. The findings further reveal that the integration of culturally responsive and reflective arts education into teacher pedagogy and curriculum helps to mediate school disengagement, and addresses the multiple intelligences and learning styles of African Americans. This research has important implications for teacher education programs, as it increases awareness and provides strategies and techniques for arts integration that may lead to higher levels of cognitive development and academic achievement in African Americans and the broader student population.

In: Psychology Research Biographies and Summaries
Editors: Nancy E. Wodarth and Alexis P. Ferguson
ISBN: 978-1-61470-491-1
© 2012 Nova Science Publishers, Inc.

Chapter 308

HIGH DENIAL AND MODERATE ACCEPTANCE LED TO SUCCESS AND REDUCED GUILT

Marilyn Lanza[1]* and Scott Prunier[2,3],†
[1]Edith Nourse Rogers Memorial Veterans Hospital, MA, US
[2]YMCA, 6 Henry Clay Drive; Merrimack, NH, US
[3]TOP Fitness Strength and Conditioning, NH, US

RESEARCH SUMMARY

From the first moment of consciousness in the intensive care unit when I did not recognize my husband or son to today, when I sit writing in my office, this journey continues to take me further than any of the doctors predicted and only my husband envisioned. Through redefinition of denial and acceptance has come continued success and reduced guilt. I, through denial, was able to focus on the positive aspects and reduce the negatives such as guilt, remorse, blame and preoccupation with shame, self-reproach and contrition.

---

* Corresponding authors: 781-687-2388 (Phone), 978-687-3337 (Fax), E-mail: *Marilyn.Lanza@va.gov*.
† 603-883-7444 (Phone), 603-386-6213 (Fax), E-mail: *scott@gotopfitness.com* This work is supported by the Edith Nourse Rogers Memorial Veterans Hospital.

In: Psychology Research Biographies and Summaries
Editors: Nancy E. Wodarth and Alexis P. Ferguson
ISBN: 978-1-61470-491-1
© 2012 Nova Science Publishers, Inc.

Chapter 309

THE CONDITIONAL ADJUSTMENT HYPOTHESIS: TWO WAYS OF DEALING WITH DISSONANCE

Tor G. Jakobsen
Trondheim Business School, Jonsvannsveien, Trondheim, Norway

RESEARCH SUMMARY

Political science has been described as a borrowing discipline. Social psychological theories are often used to explain public opinion, yet Festinger's theory of cognitive dissonance has received only limited attention in this branch of political science. In short, this argument outlines how to solve a psychological state of discomfort when one experiences inconsistency of having conflicting thoughts. I argue that Festinger's work can be helpful in explaining why some people agree with the dominating views in their countries, while others disagree. This paper is an elaboration of the theoretical arguments outlining the conditional adjustment hypothesis, a hypothesis which argues that confidence in institutions will indicate how disposed a person is to adjust to or react against the economic policies of his regime. In addition, I provide an overview over the use of Festinger's theory in political science. Derived from Festinger's work, the conditional adjustment hypothesis is thoroughly explained in this paper. My contention is that it can help us better to understand public opinion.

In: Psychology Research Biographies and Summaries
Editors: Nancy E. Wodarth and Alexis P. Ferguson
ISBN: 978-1-61470-491-1
© 2012 Nova Science Publishers, Inc.

Chapter 310

EXPLORING THE USEFULNESS OF "DENIAL" AS A CONCEPT FOR UNDERSTANDING CHRONIC ILLNESS AND DISABILITY

Sally Lindsay*
Bloorview Research Institute, Bloorview Kids Rehab, and Dalla Lana School of Public Health, University of Toronto, Toronto, Ontario, Canada

RESEARCH SUMMARY

Being diagnosed with a chronic illness or disability requires ongoing adjustment in order to adapt and cope successfully (Green-Hernandez et al. 2001; Lindsay 2008; 2009a; Paterson 2001). There is little doubt that coming to terms with such a diagnosis can be particularly difficult. Thus, shock and disbelief are often followed by a period of denial in which patients attempt to overcome the disruption to their lives (Bury 1982; Green-Hernandez et al. 2001). Denial can involve many different cognitive strategies including avoiding thinking about something, contradicting it, or focusing on alternative explanations (Kirmayer and Looper 2006). It is often an initial response that is used to fend off anxiety when encountering a life-altering event or threatening situation (Freud 1961; Joachim and Acron 2000; Martz et al. 2005; Rapley 1998; Treharne et al. 2004). Some researchers argue that denial can be a useful coping mechanism early on in the illness experience (Freud 1961; Kubler-Ross 1969); however, prolonged denial can cause strong, negative pathological connotations and hinder a successful adaptation (Fernando 2001; Seligman 2000; Telford et al. 2006).

Patient characteristics often influence how and the extent to which denial is experienced. For example, there is some evidence to support that patterns of denial vary by gender (Ketterer et al 2004), age (Treharne et al. 2004) and ethno-cultural status (Halstead et al. 1993; Roy et al. 2005; Njoku et al. 2005). Denial of emotional distress tends to be more common among men than women and may also contribute to a lack of clinician recognition and help seeking (Ketterer et al. 2004). In terms of ethno-cultural differences, Njoku et al.

---
* Corresponding author: Email: slindsay@bloorview.ca.

(2005) found that Latinos and African Americans used denial significantly more often than European Americans. Furthermore, differences in denial have also been found by length of time since diagnosis and age. In particular, patients who have been recently diagnosed tend to have greater denial than patients who have had their illness for longer (Treharne et al. 2004). Similarly, younger patients also report having greater difficulties coming to terms with their illness than older patients (Lindsay 2008; 2009b; Treharne et al. 2004).

Examining the construct of "denial" of disability/chronic illness can further develop our understanding of the structure of adaptation to loss of body integrity (Livneh et al 2006). Psychoanalytic and grief theories can be drawn upon to inform current understandings about what constitutes a "normal" adjustment following loss or trauma (Bowlby 1980; Glick et al. 1974; Telford et al. 2006). For example, Livneh (1991) identified over forty interrelated stage models, all of which identify "denial" as an early phase of adjustment. Such models continue to have a strong presence in today's understandings about the grief process and adaptation to illness (Holmes 1972; Schuchter and Zisook 1993).

Evidence suggests that disengagement types of coping (e.g., denial, avoidance) are linked to lower levels of adaptation to a chronic condition (Martz et al. 2005), lower quality of life (Klein et al. 2007) greater anxiety, depression, externalized hostility (Livneh et al. 1999), delayed treatment seeking and poor adherence to treatment regimens (Grace et al. 2004; Katz et al. 2002; Shore 2001), poor psychological adjustment and poor physical health (Bechtold et al 2003; Jones 2003).

In: Psychology Research Biographies and Summaries
Editors: Nancy E. Wodarth and Alexis P. Ferguson
ISBN: 978-1-61470-491-1
© 2012 Nova Science Publishers, Inc.

Chapter 311

CHILD AND ADOLESCENT PERSONALITY DEVELOPMENT AND ASSESSMENT: A DEVELOPMENTAL PSYCHOPATHOLOGY APPROACH

Tina D. Du Rocher Schudlich, Ryan C. Erps, Britnee Davenport and Alyssa Hertel
Western Washington University, Bellingham, Washington, US

RESEARCH SUMMARY

This review approaches child and adolescent personality assessment from a developmental psychopathology perspective. Essential to understanding personality assessment in children is understanding how individual personality development occurs in children and adolescents. An overview of emotional and personality development will be presented, including discussion of temperament, emotional expression and understanding, and emotion regulation and coping. Temperament and personality are discussed and differentiated. Relational influences on personality development such as parent-child relationships, marital relationships, family processes, and sibling relations are considered. Preliminary results from our new study on the bi-directional effects of marital relations and infant emotionality are highlighted. Multi-method procedures, including observational data assessing parents' conflict behaviors and emotions and infants' emotional and behavioral regulation in the context of parents' conflict are presented. The role of infants' temperament in these relations is considered. Extra-familial influences on personality, such as culture and religion are also presented. Finally, normal and abnormal personality development and assessment in children and adolescents are discussed from a developmental psychopathology approach, which emphasizes that both the assessment and development of personality in children are fluid processes to be considered over time, rather than static constructs observed at a single point in time. Borderline personality disorder is used as an example to describe how the developmental psychopathology approach can elucidate understanding of the abnormal development of personality over time. Recommendations for assessment approaches are made based on these overviews, including a discussion of specific methods' strengths and weaknesses. An objective, multi-method, multi-source, multi-setting approach for assessment is offered. Age-specific approaches to assessment and age-related issues to consider in assessment are integrated into the recommendations. Future directions for research are discussed.

In: Psychology Research Biographies and Summaries
Editors: Nancy E. Wodarth and Alexis P. Ferguson
ISBN: 978-1-61470-491-1
© 2012 Nova Science Publishers, Inc.

Chapter 312

INTEGRATING EVIDENCE-BASED TREATMENT INTO AN ATTACHMENT GUIDED CURRICULUM IN A THERAPEUTIC PRESCHOOL: INITIAL FINDINGS

Karen Stubenbort, Veronica Trybalski and Krista Zaccagni*
Family Resources of Pennsylvania
Pittsburgh, PA, US

RESEARCH SUMMARY

Child maltreatment is associated with detrimental developmental effects. In view of the fact that child maltreatment typically occurs within the context of a caretaking relationship, attachment-guided treatments have been found effective in addressing developmental problems in abused children. This chapter describes the dissemination of a trauma-focused cognitive behavioral treatment model (TF-CBT) into a Theraplay-guided therapeutic preschool for maltreated children. At the end of the study all of the children in the program displayed significant developmental gains. The study did not support the expectation that children receiving the integrated treatment model would show greater gain. There was a small difference in outcome, particularly the adaptive domain. Although the differences were not significant, the authors believe they are in accordance with theoretically guided expectations. These results are discussed as are both the Theraplay-guided and TF-CBT models.

---

* Corresponding author: Karen Stubenbort, Ph.D. Family Resources of PA. 141 S. Highland Avenue, Pittsburgh, PA 15206. Phone: 724.355.5075, Kstubenbort@zoominternet.net.

In: Psychology Research Biographies and Summaries
Editors: Nancy E. Wodarth and Alexis P. Ferguson
ISBN: 978-1-61470-491-1
© 2012 Nova Science Publishers, Inc.

Chapter 313

ASSESSING INDIVIDUALS FOR TEAM WORTHINESS": INVESTIGATING THE INTERSECTION OF THE BIG FIVE PERSONALITY FACTORS, ORGANIZATIONAL CITIZENSHIP BEHAVIOR AND TEAMWORK APTITUDE

Janet L. Kottke and Shinko Kimura
California State University, San Bernardino, California, US

RESEARCH SUMMARY

Teams and teamwork have become very popular areas of organizational strategy, but selecting competent employees for teamwork remains difficult to do, let alone do well. This chapter addresses the requisites we consider important for the team "worthiness" of an individual. These fundamental team "worthiness" elements are factors of the Big Five Personality model, organizational citizenship behavior (OCB) contextualized as dispositions, and cognitive aptitude specific to teamwork. We review briefly the history of each of these constructs, illustrate assessments of the constructs, and then describe an original research study in which the unique and shared variance of these constructs was examined with confirmatory factor analysis. The results indicated the Big Five personality and organizational citizenship behavior constructs were comparably related to the teamwork aptitude construct. The most surprising result was the strong relationship of the sportsmanship variable to the Big Five construct. This result supports our conjecture that organizational citizenship represents a lower level factor of personality.

Chapter 314

PERSONALITY TRAITS AND DAILY MOODS

Cristina Ottaviani[a], David Shapiro[b], Iris Goldstein[b] and Valerie Gofman[b]*

[a]Department of Psychology, University of Bologna, Italy
[b]Department of Psychiatry, University of California, Los Angeles, US

RESEARCH SUMMARY

Previous research has shown that personality traits and emotional states are associated with variations in blood pressure. The major aim of this chapter is to examine the relationship between personality traits and diary reports of moods on a work and an off-work day. Secondary aims are to compare mood reports in men and women as a function of the day of recording. A healthy sample of 110 women and 110 men rated their moods in a diary three times an hour on a work and a nonwork day. Personality scales were administered. Significant effects of mood intensity were obtained for work vs. off days and in interaction with scores on personality tests of anxiety, anger out, cynical hostility, and depression. Given the health significance of emotion in mental and physical health, these findings in healthy individuals suggest that personality traits may affect the regulation of blood pressure via their effects on emotional responses to daily life events and thereby serve as risk factors for hypertension.

---

* Department of Psychiatry, 760 Westwood Plaza, Los Angeles, CA 90095, US. e-mail: dshapiro@ucla.edu.

In: Psychology Research Biographies and Summaries
Editors: Nancy E. Wodarth and Alexis P. Ferguson

ISBN: 978-1-61470-491-1
© 2012 Nova Science Publishers, Inc.

Chapter 315

WEIGHT? WAIT! IMPORTANCE WEIGHTING OF SATISFACTION SCORES IN QUALITY OF LIFE ASSESSMENT

*Chia-huei Wu**
Department of Psychology
National Taiwan University, Taiwan

RESEARCH SUMMARY

Importance weighting is a common practice in Quality of Life (QOL) research. The basic idea is that items for specific life domains contained in a QOL measurement have different importance for different individuals; therefore, in capturing participants' perceptions, feelings, or evaluations in these domains, information on domain importance should be incorporated into the scoring procedure and reflected in the final score. Accordingly, importance weighting is proposed to serve this purpose, and the common procedure is to weight the satisfaction score by the importance score for each domain. This idea is so common that many instruments adopted this weighting procedure in their scoring system without examining its necessity and appropriateness. To date, there is extensive evidence to draw the conclusion of the (in)appropriateness of using importance weighting of satisfaction scores. Hence, the purpose of this article is to provide a systematic review of the literature on the issue of importance weighting. In the following sections, I first introduce the notion of importance weighting. Then, the empirical utility of importance weighting is reviewed to see if importance weighting contributes to predicting criterion variables. In the third section, the literature on the appropriateness of importance weighting based on a psychological perspective is reviewed. Finally, a conclusion on importance weighting and the implications for QOL are provided.

---

* Send correspondence to: Chia-huei Wu; 4F, No.147, Sec. 1, Xinguang Rd., Wenshan District, Taipei City 116, Taiwan (R.O.C.); TEL: 886-2-86614712.
Email: b88207071@ntu.edu.tw

Chapter 316

A Psycho-Social Approach to Meanings and Functions of Trait Labels

Astrid Mignon[1,*] and Patrick Mollaret[2]
[1] Université de Lille 3, France
[2] Université de Reims, France

Research Summary

In daily life, adjectives as "sympathetic" "aggressive" are used to speak about people. But what do we mean when we say that Mary is sympathetic? What kind of knowledge do we communicate about Mary? This chapter aims at analyzing the different meanings of those adjectives within trait psychology and social psychology frameworks. In trait psychology, they are called "personality traits" and are defined as "generalized and personalized determining tendencies - consistent and stable modes of an individual's adjustment to his environment" (Allport & Odbert, 1936, p. 26). Sympathetic is considered as a descriptive psychological property of Mary. This definition is convenient in personality assessment tradition, because it enables the measure of individual differences based on correlational design. Nevertheless, this definition of traits is subordinate to the study of personality and individual differences and does not enable to analyse the meaning and the function of traits-labels. In social psychology, two complementary perspectives share the idea that trait labels are polysemous entities and that their meaning is directly linked to their social function. The perspective of the theory of traits as generalized affordances (Beauvois & Dubois, 2000) enables to distinguish evaluative knowledge- how others act toward targets who possess these traits (behavioral affordances)-, from descriptive knowledge- how targets who possess theses traits act (descriptive behavior)-, deemed to be of limited importance in trait common usage. Sympathetic is used to communicate the social value of Mary, her social affordance which guides my own behavior towards Mary (I invite Mary to my birthday) rather than her psychological property. The other perspective stipulates that traits refer to both the descriptive

---

[*] Please address correspondence to: Astrid Mignon, E-mail address: astrid.mignon@univ-lille3.fr; Phone: 03 20 41 69 55; U.F.R. de Psychologie, Université de Lille 3, B.P. 06149, 59653 Villeneuve d'Ascq Cedex, France.

behaviors and the descriptive states (Mollaret & Mignon, 2007). Sympathetic is also a descriptive knowledge of Mary's states Mary's state (e.g. Mary feels happy). This description implying a state verb directs a perception of Mary as acted by the situation (Brown and Fish, 1983). We will report new research, based on experimental design, showing that person perception depends on the function of personality traits which is determined by social practices. Implications of different meanings of traits, both for individual differences and also for other kind of judgments (e.g. judgment of responsibility) will be presented.

In: Psychology Research Biographies and Summaries
Editors: Nancy E. Wodarth and Alexis P. Ferguson
ISBN: 978-1-61470-491-1
© 2012 Nova Science Publishers, Inc.

Chapter 317

COMPARING THE PSYCHOMETRIC PROPERTIES OF THE COMMON ITEMS IN THE SHORT AND ABBREVIATED VERSIONS OF THE JUNIOR EYSENCK PERSONALITY QUESTIONNAIRES: A MEAN AND COVARIANCE STRUCTURES ANALYSIS APPROACH

Rapson Gomez[*,1] *and Andre Gomez*[2]

[1]School of Psychology, University of Tasmania, Australia
John W. Fisher, School of Education, University of Ballarat, Victoria, Australia
[2]School of Psychology, Deakin University, Melbourne, Australia

RESEARCH SUMMARY

This study used the mean and covariance structures analysis approach to examine if there is measurement and construct invariance across the common items of the abbreviated (JEPQRA) and short (JEPQRS) versions of the Junior Eysenck Personality Questionnaire Revised (JEPQR). Participants were adolescents, between 15 and 17 years of age. One group of 439 participants completed the JEPQRA, while another groups of 466 participants completed the JEPQRS. The findings showed equivalency for factor structure, loadings, variances, covariances, and mean scores. Most of the item intercepts and error variances were also invariant. The implications of these results for the development of shorter questionnaires from their longer counterparts are discussed in relation to the JEPQR, and for questionnaires in general.

---

[*] Corresponding Author: Rapson Gomez, School of Psychology, University of Tasmania, Private Bag 30 Hobart, Tasmania, Australia 7001. Electronic mail may be sent to Rapson.Gomez@utas.edu.au.

In: Psychology Research Biographies and Summaries
Editors: Nancy E. Wodarth and Alexis P. Ferguson
ISBN: 978-1-61470-491-1
© 2012 Nova Science Publishers, Inc.

Chapter 318

SUCCESSFUL PSYCHOPATHY: UNRESOLVED ISSUES AND FUTURE DIRECTIONS

Kristin Landfield, Meredith Jones and Scott Lilienfeld
Department of Psychology, Emory University, Atlanta, Georgia, US

RESEARCH SUMMARY

In 1982, at age 16, Barry Minkow started ZZZZ Best (pronounced "Zee Best") carpet cleaning company in his parents' garage. Minkow soon franchised ZZZZ Best into a chain, and by age 20, he was the boy wonder of Wall Street and CEO of a $300 million company. Then Los Angeles mayor Tom Bradley declared the day ZZZZ Best went public "Barry Minkow Day." Minkow was a media darling and appeared on the Oprah Winfrey show as a model young entrepreneur. A whiz at generating capital, he borrowed money from a usurious lender and obtained $2000 from his grandmother. He gradually convinced more and more investors to buy into ZZZZ Best, offering promises of large dividends. Eventually, Minkow branched into an insurance restoration business that claimed to restore buildings from fire and water damage in excess of $50 million (Akst, 1990).

Minkow's company, however, wasn't quite what it appeared to be. In fact, it never operated as a profitable business. Indeed, the insurance restoration business performed no restorations and was little more than a paper trail. By age 22, Barry had been convicted of 57 counts of fraud and sentenced to serve 25 years in federal prison. He had forged $13,000 worth of money orders from a liquor store. He also stole and sold his grandmother's jewelry, staged break-ins at ZZZZ Best's offices, and amassed illegal credit card charges. Moneys from the companies investors were being used to launder narcotics….the list goes on.

According to his biographer Daniel Akst (1990), Minkow used quick-talking and confidence tricks to dupe thousands of people. Barry was charming and engaging, spontaneous and fearless, and ambitious and egotistical. According to Akst (1990), "Barry amazed everybody right up until the end. Some of his lieutenants have felt remorse, or shame, or the need to rationalize. Barry's personality, by contrast, appears seamlessly, coherently false, free of guilt or worry over what he has done. Even at the end, his insincerity was utter" (p. 266). At his sentencing, Judge Dickran Tevrizian told, Minkow, "You're dangerous because you have this gift of gab, this ability to communicate," adding, "You don't have a conscience." Remarkably, after serving a number of years in prison, Minkow emerged several years ago as a successful evangelical minister.

In many respects, Barry Minkow embodies many or most of the features of the still controversial construct of successful psychopathy. Psychopathy, traditionally regarded as a largely or entirely unsuccessful disorder, is increasingly coming to be recognized as a condition sometimes associated with successful, perhaps even above average, functioning (Lilienfeld, 1994; Lykken, 1995). Indeed, over the past decade, research on successful psychopathy has increased markedly in quality and quantity. Nevertheless, this intriguing body of literature raises at least as many questions as answers.

Chapter 319

Score Reliability in Personality Research

Matt Vassar, Denna L. Wheeler and Jody A. Worley

Research Summary

Score reliability is a central feature of measurement. Both researchers and practitioners are under ethical obligation to ensure that any assessment devise utilized have strong psychometric qualities. This is true when the instrument is needed to conduct research or used to derive therapeutic goals. However, a simple knowledge of the reliability coefficient is not sufficient. A true understanding of reliability theory is necessary to fulfill this obligation. Helms, Henze, Sass, and Mifsud (2006) rightly note the reliability data are often treated as "mystical forces that supercede validity rather than as data that should be analyzed and interpreted in a manner analogous to validity data" (p. 631). Hence, the primary ambition of this chapter is to inform the reader of reliability theories and estimation procedures, including the assumptions underlying such estimates, and provide researchers and practitioners with accessible information for the interpretation and reporting of reliability data. Before this goal may be pursued, however, it is necessary to briefly mention the theoretical nature of personality measurement.

Personality measurement is a reflection of personality theory. Specifically, there are two major theoretical models of personality measurement. One is appropriate for the types of psychometric analyses discussed in this chapter; the other is not. Researchers must examine the theoretical basis for personality measurement and not blindly follow a given set of procedures. The two models have been given various names. Hershberger (1999) used the terms *taxonomic* and *dimensional* to describe these models of personality. Speaking in broader terms, but reflecting the same theoretical foundation, Bollen and Lennox (1991) used the terms *causal indicators* and *effect indicators*, and more recently, Edwards and Bagozzi (2000) used the terms *formative* and *reflective* constructs.

The fundamental difference between the two models is found in the question: *Does a response reflect the construct or define the construct?* The taxonomic (a.k.a. formative) model posits that a person possesses a particular trait when he/she endorses one or more indicators of the trait. The dichotomously scored MMPI is an example of this theoretical model. For example, the following brief stems from the MMPI Somatization scale, *No ear ringing, Bothered by acid stomach, Skin doesn't break out,* all measure some form of physical complaint but are not necessarily related to each other. One would not expect substantial inter-item correlations on a formative scale. A taxonomic scale is simply a composite of individual items with higher levels of endorsement reflecting a higher trait level. Traditional psychometric analysis including coefficient alpha estimation is not appropriate for taxonomic measures and should not be interpreted.

By contrast, the dimensional (a.k.a. reflective) model posits that a person's level on a trait is reflected in his/her response to items. The items reflect more or less extreme positions on the trait but all items reflect a single trait and, therefore, significant inter-item correlations are expected. Classical test theory (CTT), reliability analysis, and factor analysis all assume the use of reflective measurement and treat measures as functions of latent variables and error. The measurement issues discussed in this chapter assume the use of a dimensional measure of personality.

In any testing, measurement or assessment context there is a desire to have consistency and accuracy among test scores. A frequently used method for evaluating a measurement device is the degree of reliability among the scores obtained. The term, reliability, is used in different ways to refer either to the stability of scores over time, the equivalence of scores across alternative measures or forms of a measurement instrument, or the internal consistency of scores produced by the items included on a particular instrument administered in a single setting. The higher the degree of reliability among scores, the more confident we can be that similar scores would be obtained if the same instrument or inventory was administered to the same individuals in the future, all else being equal. In addition to thinking about reliability as the consistency of scores within or between measures, or across time, reliability can also be interpreted as the extent to which the scores reflect measurement error.

The differences observed between scores produced from a particular measurement scale that are attributable to anything other than real differences in aspects of the trait being measured are termed *measurement error*. Measurement error may originate from a variety of sources in the process of measurement. Some of the sources may be systematic and occur with repeated administrations of the scale. Other sources of error may be random or unsystematic and therefore occur in unpredictable ways across repeated measurements. For example, measurement error results when the obtained scores are related to an associated attribute. That is, the observed scores include measurement error if the scores are related to something other than the trait being measured. Measurement error may also result from temporary conditions in the setting or environment in which the scores were acquired. Likewise, if scores are influenced by the process of administering the instrument, such as how the instructions were explained or the time allowed for completion, measurement error is observed in the reduction of the observed reliability of scores.

Chapter 320

RESTYLING PERSONALITY ASSESSMENTS

Willem K. B. Hofstee[*]
The Heymans Institute, University of Groningen, Netherlands

RESEARCH SUMMARY

Personality is a matter of assessment, not an objective natural science; at least for the near future, that alternative is not in sight. Consequently, students of personality might as well try to optimize their assessment methods as such. One obstacle to optimal personality assessment is reliance on self-report, and the subjective definition of personality that it implies. To enhance the reliability and validity of assessments, knowledgeable others should be enlisted to report on the characteristic behavior of the target person. This intersubjective approach to personality appears to have consequences for the content of personality questionnaires: A shift from experiential to behavioral item content is appropriate. Another obstacle to faithful assessment is the reliance on relative scales in reporting about personality. The implied model, based on classical applied statistics, ignores the bipolar nature (e.g., introverted vs. extraverted) of personality assessments; its range of application is limited to approaches in which individuals are compared with one another. I explore the consequences of an alternative psychometric-statistical model based on proportional scores on a bipolar scale. Its side-effect is to challenge current ideas about personality structure.

---

[*] Grote Kruisstraat 1-2; 9712 TS Groningen, Netherlands; tel. +31 50 3636366; w.k.b.hofstee@rug.nl.

Chapter 321

THEORY AND PRACTICE IN THE USE AND INTERPRETATION OF LIKERT-TYPE SCALES WITHIN A CROSS-CULTURAL CONTEXT

*Boaz Shulruf**
University of Auckland, New Zealand

RESEARCH SUMMARY

This Chapter introduces theoretical and empirical comprehensive models that combine three well-established theories and relate to the underlying cultural contexts of individuals completing Likert-type questionnaires. The theoretical model incorporates the stages of responding to Likert-type questionnaires, the effects of response sets and cross cultural effects measured by collectivist and individualist attributes. This theoretical model, named the ImpExp, is empirically tested by measuring the effects of a range of response biases (social desirability, extreme/mid point response set, 'don't know' response, acquiescence, and context) and collectivist and individualist attributes. This results in a second model, the Collectivist-Individualist Model of Response Bias (CIMReB), which suggests an explanation for the way in which collectivist and individualist attributes affect how people respond to Likert-type questionnaires. The CIMReB relates to the five stages of the cognitive process of responding to questions and partially supports the ImpExp model.

These two models together provide a comprehensive framework for the design and implementation of psychological scales within cross cultural contexts. The main findings indicate that collectivist and individualist attributes interact with other response sets and mostly affect the magnitude of the answers (i.e. the extent to which extreme responses are used). The actual content of the answers is affected to a lesser extent. Some examples are provided to demonstrate the usefulness of the models in interpreting answers to Likert-type questionnaires within cross cultural and cross national environment. The Chapter concludes

---

* For correspondence please contact: Dr. Boaz Shulruf; Faculty of Education; The University of Auckland, Private Bag 92019; Auckland, New Zealand; Tel: +64 9 3737599 ext 89463; b.shulruf@auckland.ac.nz.

with some practical recommendations relating to the design and analysis of such questionnaires.

In: Psychology Research Biographies and Summaries
Editors: Nancy E. Wodarth and Alexis P. Ferguson
ISBN: 978-1-61470-491-1
© 2012 Nova Science Publishers, Inc.

Chapter 321

CONSTRUCT AND RESPONSE BIAS CORRELATES IN SUMMATED SCALE DEFINITIONS OF PERSONALITY TRAITS

John T. Kulas[1] *and Alicia A. Stachowski*[2]

[1] Saint Cloud State University, Saint Cloud, Minnesota, US
[2] George Mason University, Fairfax, Virginia, US

RESEARCH SUMMARY

Graphic rating scales are frequently used in the collection of self-report data. Although the specification of these response scales is common, they have been identified as being particularly susceptible to several response biases – most notably acquiescence, central tendency, and extremity. The possibility that these response styles may be more or less prominent in individuals of different *trait* standing has been acknowledged, but has resulted in conflicting conclusions and recommendations. The current chapter posits that response biases are particularly problematic in the assessment of personality, because they may be characterized as sources of true construct variance (i.e., extreme option endorsement or avoidance, central tendency, and yeah/nay-saying are facet dimensions of some FFM constructs). Unfortunately, the source of true construct variance is scattered across different traits. This is problematic for establishing trait orthogonality – if "other" construct variance is introduced into FFM measurement because of response bias, scale correlations would be expected not solely because of construct association, but also because of measurement method/response bias shared across trait specifications. We used a large archival dataset to estimate relationships between FFM trait (and subfacet) standing and response styles along a 5-point graphic rating scale (ranging from response options of Very Inaccurate to Very Accurate). In addition to identifying personological content associated with acquiescence and extremity, implications of this investigation: 1) point toward some of the observed FFM trait correlations potentially being attributable to response style confounds, and 2) suggest adjective checklists or forced-choice formats may be preferable to graphic rating scale specification in personality assessment.

Chapter 323

ACADEMIC AND EVERYDAY PROCRASTINATION AND THEIR RELATION TO THE FIVE-FACTOR MODEL

Gidi Rubenstein

RESEARCH SUMMARY

Procrastination is a complex psychological behavior that affects everyone to some degree or another. This study examined academic procrastination (AP) and procrastination in everyday life (EP) and their relations to the Five-Factor Model (FFM) of personality among 267 male and female Israeli students, who filled in a demographic questionnaire, the shortened version of Costa and McCrae's (1992) NEO-FFI, Milgram, Srolof, and Rosenbaum's (1988) everyday life procrastination scale, and Toubiana and Milgram's (1992) academic procrastination scale. The two types of procrastination were strongly and positively associated with one another, AP was positively related to neuroticism (N) and extraversion (E) and negatively related to conscientiousness (C); and EP was also positively related to N but not to E and negatively related to C. Stepwise regression analyses indicated that when EP is the dependent variable, only AP, A, and E are included in the regression equation, whereas when AP is the independent variable, EP and all the FFM variables are included in the equation. Men scored significantly higher than women on AP but not on EP. In light of these findings, we discuss a personality typology of procrastinators, based on the FFM.

Chapter 324

PERSONALITY AND ATTITUDE TOWARD DREAMS

Barbara Szmigielska and Małgorzata Hołda
Jagiellonian University, Kraków, Poland

RESEARCH SUMMARY

Dream research focuses mainly on the formal characteristics of dreams (e.g., mood, realism, coloring, dream recall frequency) and dream content but little research has been conducted to date on the functional aspects of dreams. Dreams have always been the focus of human enquiry and have always played a significant part in human life. Every society has developed its own theories of dreams. Therefore, the functional aspects of dreams such as affective response to dreams and dreaming (liking/disliking, fear, curiosity etc.), subjectively perceived role of dreams, private concepts of dreams and dreaming, or different kinds of behavior influenced by dreams (trying to interpret one's own dreams, believing they have special meaning, behaving according to the clues offered by the dream, sharing dreams with other people, etc.) all seem to be equally important in the investigation of dreams. In studies on the functional aspects of dreams, the term *attitude toward dreams* is commonly used. No clear definition of attitude toward dreams has been provided, however. Furthermore, different studies take different components of attitude into account — some measure only the affective response to dreams, others also consider beliefs about dreams or the influence of dreams on waking life. Because of this ambiguity, the present authors propose their own definition of attitude toward dreams based on the classical, three-component definition of attitude. Some of the previous research has shown that attitude toward dreams correlates substantially with personality traits, particularly with the openness to experience factor of the Five Factor model of personality. Some results also suggest a relationship between attitude toward dreams and neuroticism. The present study was designed to explore the relationship between attitude toward dreams and the Big Five personality factors. The sample consisted of 108 participants aged 19-33, 62 women and 46 men. Attitude toward dreams was measured with a 56-item self-report scale (Attitude toward Dreams Scale – ADS) specifically developed for the present study and psychometrically verified. Participants also completed the Polish version of the NEO-PI-R.

In: Psychology Research Biographies and Summaries
Editors: Nancy E. Wodarth and Alexis P. Ferguson
ISBN: 978-1-61470-491-1
© 2012 Nova Science Publishers, Inc.

Chapter 325

SOCIAL DOMINANCE ORIENTATION, AMBIVALENT SEXISM, AND ABORTION: EXPLAINING PRO-CHOICE AND PRO-LIFE ATTITUDES

Danny Osborne[1] and Paul G. Davies[2]
[1]University of California, Los Angeles, California, US
[2]University of British Columbia, Okanagan, British Columbia

RESEARCH SUMMARY

Abortion continues to be one of the most hotly debated issues in American politics. Despite its prominence in the public discourse, little social psychological work has been done to understand the ideological bases of individuals' attitudes toward abortion. The current chapter seeks to address this oversight by using social dominance theory (Sidanius and Pratto, 1999) and the theory of ambivalent sexism (Glick and Fiske, 1996) to explain attitudes toward abortion. Specifically, we argue that individuals with a preference for group-based hierarchy – a variable referred to as social dominance orientation (SDO) – use beliefs about gender roles in order to justify their attitudes toward abortion. We tested this hypothesis by having 242 participants complete the SDO scale (Pratto, Sidanius, Stallworth, and Malle, 1994) and the Ambivalent Sexism Inventory (ASI; Glick and Fiske, 1996) – a measure that divides gender role attitudes into two components: 1) hostile sexism (HS) and 2) benevolent sexism (BS). After controlling for religiosity and previous abortion experience, multiple regression analyses indicated that SDO was significantly associated with attitudes toward both elective abortion (e.g., the woman wants an abortion, regardless of the reason) and traumatic abortion (e.g., the woman is pregnant as a result of rape or incest). The relationships between SDO and attitudes toward the two types of abortion were, however, mediated by the ASI. Specifically, HS and BS mediated the relationship between SDO and opposition to elective abortion, while only BS mediated the relationship between SDO and opposition to traumatic abortion. The implications of these findings are discussed within the context of intergroup relations.

Chapter 326

FACTOR STRUCTURE, SEX EFFECTS AND DIFFERENTIAL ITEM FUNCTIONING OF THE JUNIOR EYSENCK PERSONALITY QUESTIONNAIRE REVISED - ABBREVIATED: A MULTIPLE-INDICATORS MULTIPLE-CAUSES APPROACH

Rapson Gomez[*,1] *and Andre Gomez*[2]
[1]School of Psychology, University of Tasmania, Australia
[2]School of Psychology, Deakin University, Australia

RESEARCH SUMMARY

The Junior Eysenck Personality Questionnaire Revised-Abbreviated (JEPQR-A) provides scales for measuring extraversion, neuroticism, psychoticism, and lie. This study used the multiple-indicators multiple-causes model procedure, with robust estimation, to examine simultaneously the factor structure of the JEPQR-A, the differential item functioning (DIF) of the JEPQR-A items as a function of sex, and the effects of sex on the JEPQR-A factors, controlling for DIF. Male ($N=218$) and female ($N=220$) adolescent participants, between 15 and 17 years of age completed the JEPQR-A. The results provided support for the 4-factor structure of the JEPQR-A. Although an extraversion item and a psychoticism item showed DIF, their magnitudes were small. Controlling for DIF, females scored higher than males for the extraversion and neuroticism factors, while males scored higher for the psychoticism factor.

---

[*] Corresponding Author: Rapson Gomez, School of Psychology, University of Tasmania, Private Bag 30 Hobart, Tasmania, Australia 7001. Electronic mail may be sent to Rapson.Gomez@utas.edu.au.

In: Psychology Research Biographies and Summaries
Editors: Nancy E. Wodarth and Alexis P. Ferguson
ISBN: 978-1-61470-491-1
© 2012 Nova Science Publishers, Inc.

Chapter 327

ONLINE COLLABORATIVE LEARNING: THE CHALLENGE OF CHANGE

Baruch Offir[1,]*, Ingrid Barth[2,†] and Orit Zeichner[‡]
Distance Learning Laboratory
School of Education
Bar-Ilan University, Israel

RESEARCH SUMMARY

Desktop videoconferencing and project-based online collaborative learning can create new directions in higher education. However, the transition from the "safe space" of a conventional classroom course to a new learning environment often represents a major change for both faculty and students. Faculty need to know what kind of support can help students cope with the challenges of an unfamiliar learning environment in order to make this transition less difficult. In this paper we describe how we create conditions for an effective online collaborative learning environment within the framework of a course module. During the course, the students acquire judgment and decision making abilities for integrating technological systems into their field of expertise. We discuss the difficulties of evaluating outcomes in learning environments that are essentially different from conventional university courses. We conclude by sharing the lessons learned and identify critical factors that helped our students move from the familiar "chalk and talk" model to the relatively uncharted territory of project-based online collaborative learning and show that provision of "safe places" represents one of the most important contributions of online collaborative learning environments.

---

* Prof.. Baruch Offir (corresponding author) Head, Distance Learning Laboratory. School of Education; Bar-Ilan University; Ramat-Gan 52900; Israel; Tel: +972-3-5318447; Fax: +972-3-5353319; Offir-e@inter.net.il; Offirb@mail.biu.ac.il.
† Dr. Ingrid Barth - ingbarth@zahav.net.il.
‡ Dr. Orit Zeichner - zeichno@mail.biu.ac.il.

Chapter 328

THE INFLUENCE OF PERSONALITY AND SYMPTOMS SEVERITY ON FUNCTIONING IN PATIENTS WITH SCHIZOPHRENIA

Ana Fresan[1]*, María García-Anaya[1], Rogelio Apiquian[2] and Humberto Nicolini[2]

[1] Clinical Research Division,
National Institute of Psychiatry Ramón de la Fuente,
Mexico City, Mexico
[2] Carracci Medical Group, Mexico City, Mexico

RESEARCH SUMMARY

Introduction: Patients with schizophrenia exhibit a broad range of cognitive, emotional and behavioral symptoms that affect their psychosocial functioning. Research findings that link symptom dimensions to functioning in schizophrenia are inconsistent. This suggests that other variables may contribute to patients' functioning. It has been documented that personality differences are detectable among patients with schizophrenia and are stable after illness onset. Thus, personality seems to be a particularly promising form of individual difference that may be related to functioning in schizophrenia.

Objective: To determine the influence of personality features and symptom severity in the level of functioning of patients with schizophrenia.

Method: One-hundred patients with schizophrenia were recruited. Diagnoses were based on the SCID-I. Symptom severity was assessed with the Scales for the Assessment of Positive and Negative Symptoms (SAPS and SANS) while personality was assessed using the Temperament and Character Inventory (TCI). The Global Assessment of Functioning (GAF) was employed to estimate global psychosocial functioning. Sample was divided in groups, based in a cutoff point of 60 of the GAF score, forming groups of high and low functioning.

---

* Correspondence: Ana Fresán, PsyD, PhD; Clinical Research Division. National Institute of Psychiatry Ramón de la Fuente. Calz. México-Xochimilco No 101. Tlalpan, Mexico City, 14370, MEXICO. Tel: (5255) 56 55 28 11 ext 204; Fax: (5255) 55 13 37 22; E-mail: fresan@imp.edu.mx.

Results: More than half of the patients were classified in the low functioning group (61%). Significant differences were found between groups in terms of symptom severity and temperament and character dimensions. The temperament dimension "Persistence" and the character dimension "Self-directedness" were significant predictors of low functioning as well as the negative symptom "Apathy."

Conclusions: Motivation and goal directed behaviors are important factors that promote an adequate functioning in patients with schizophrenia. Patients with a combination of low "Persistence" and low "Self-directedness" might be an especially vulnerable group for which efforts should be made to provide supportive and reinforcing treatment interventions.

Circumventing Self-Reflection When Measuring Emotions: The Implicit Positive and Negative Affect Test (IPANAT)

Markus Quirin[*], *Miguel Kazén*[†] *and Julius Kuhl*[‡]

University of Osnabrueck, Institute of Psychology, Osnabrück, Germany

Research Summary

This paper presents a recently developed method for the indirect assessment of emotional traits and states, the Implicit Positive and Negative Affect Test (IPANAT). In the IPANAT individuals make judgments about the degree to which artificial words sound like mood adjectives (e.g., happy or helpless). It is proposed that cognitive representations of emotions as being dominant in individuals with high sensitivity to these emotions instantaneously bring the judgments into their line. Recent findings are summarized that speak for appropriate reliability and validity of the IPANAT. As a paper-pencil test, the IPANAT is easy in application and takes no longer than 2 minutes. These properties may render this measure attractive for both basic and applied psychology.

---

[*] mquirin@uos.de.
[†] mikazen@uos.de.
[‡] j.kuhl@gmx.net.

Chapter 330

STRUCTURED MMPI-2 CLIENT FEEDBACK IN THE IDENTIFICATION OF POTENTIAL SUPPLEMENTAL TARGETS OF CHANGE

Alan R. King and Joseph C. Miller*
University of North Dakota,
Grand Forks, North Dakota, US

RESEARCH SUMMARY

Contemporary structured psychotherapies are often designed for manualized, short-term (usually 12-16 sessions) delivery with observable and focused targets of therapeutic change. The time-limited nature of many contemporary psychotherapies limits therapists to a focus on a small number of treatment targets and objectives. The role of traditional psychometric testing in structured therapies has been difficult to discern from the literature. Reliance on broad trait based symptom inventories has been largely replaced by functional applied behavior analysis with an emphasis on observables. An additional shortcoming of traditional psychometric evaluation has been the absence of a systematic approach to identifying treatment targets from findings and providing clients digestible feedback about their results. The present article explores some of these theoretical and pragmatic limitations in the use of broad symptom inventories such as the Minnesota Multiphasic Personality Inventory (MMPI-2) in the course of assessment for short-term structured interventions. A method described previously in the literature (McCray & King, 2003) for providing systematic test feedback and identifying supplemental treatment goals was modified in this chapter for use with the MMPI-2. While unreasonable to expect full remission of broader maladaptive response tendencies through short term interventions, the recognition and partial attenuation of disruptive behavioral, attitudinal and emotional reactions to stressors could prove exceedingly

---

* Correspondence should be sent to Alan R. King, Psychology Department, University of North Dakota, P.O. Box 8380, Grand Forks, ND 58202-8380, alan_king@und.nodak.edu.

helpful in a subset of clinical cases. Randomized controlled trials of structured therapies with and without reliance on traditional testing would provide a new and interesting line of research with potential promise for enhancing the efficacy and effectiveness of treatment.

In: Psychology Research Biographies and Summaries
Editors: Nancy E. Wodarth and Alexis P. Ferguson

ISBN: 978-1-61470-491-1
© 2012 Nova Science Publishers, Inc.

Chapter 331

BEYOND THE TRAITS OF THE FIVE FACTOR MODEL: USING DEVIANT PERSONALITY TRAITS TO PREDICT DEVIANT BEHAVIOR IN ORGANIZATIONS

James M. LeBreton[*] *and Jane Wu*[†]

Purdue University; Department of Psychological Sciences;
West Lafayette, IN, US

RESEARCH SUMMARY

Although the five factor model (FFM) has served as an important catalyst for personality-related organizational research, we agree with the suggestions of previous researchers that personality research should expand beyond this basic framework (Block, 1995; Lee & Ashton, 2004). This is especially true for researchers seeking to understand and predict counterproductive or deviant behaviors. The basic thesis of this commentary is that optimal, dispositionally-based prediction of counterproductive organizational criteria will be achieved when researchers begin assessing counterproductive personality traits. In short, we believe prediction may be enhanced by increasing the nomological convergence between our predictor and criterion spaces.

Although a number of aberrant personality traits may be relevant to predicting counterproductive and deviant behaviors, we briefly introduce three of the most promising traits labeled by some as the "Dark Triad" (Paulhus & Williams, 2002): Machiavellianism, narcissism, and psychopathy. Below we 1) define each of these traits, 2) describe how they are related to (but not redundant with) the global traits comprising the FFM, and 3) illustrate how these constructs may be mapped into the nomological space of organizational criteria (especially counterproductive and deviant work behaviors).

---

[*] lebreton@psych.purdue.edu.
[†] jwu@psych.purdue.edu.

ON THE TEST-RETEST RELIABILITY OF THE AUTOBIOGRAPHICAL MEMORY TEST

Filip Raes[1,*], *J. Mark G. Williams*[2] *and Dirk Hermans*[1]

[1] Department of Psychology, University of Leuven, Belgium
[2] Department of Psychiatry, University of Oxford, UK

RESEARCH SUMMARY

The Autobiographical Memory Test (AMT; Williams & Broadbent, 1986) is frequently used by researchers to assess specificity of memory retrieval. This test asks respondents to describe a specific autobiographical memory in response to cue words. In contrast to the AMT's frequent use, however, little is known about its reliability. The present paper examined the test-retest reliability of the AMT. In five studies, undergraduates completed the Autobiographical Memory Test (AMT; Williams & Broadbent, 1986) twice, with mean time interval between test an retest varying over studies from 1 to 5 months. Each time, an alternate AMT was used at retesting. In a sixth study, depressed patients completed the AMT twice: once at admission to a hospital, and again 3 months later. Results document relatively satifactory test-retest reliability of the AMT in assessing people's level of memory specificity.

---

* Correspondence concerning this article should be addressed to Filip Raes, Department of Psychology, University of Leuven, Tiensestraat 102, B-3000 Leuven, Belgium. Electronic mail may be sent to filip.raes@psy.kuleuven.be.

Trait Anger, Anger Expression, and Themes of Anger Incidents in Contemporary Undergraduate Students

Sandra P. Thomas
University of Tennessee, Knoxville
Knoxville, Tennessee, US

Research Summary

Guided by Trait-State Anger Theory (Spielberger et al., 1983), trait anger, anger expression, and written narratives of anger incidents were examined in 305 undergraduate students. Fischer et al.'s (2004) coding scheme was used to assess reasons for anger, the relational context of the incident, methods of expressing anger, and outcomes. The chief provocateur for all students was a non-romantic intimate, but important differences were observed when comparing 3 subgroups: (1) students scoring high on angry temperament, (2) those scoring high on angry reaction, and (3) those scoring low on the entire trait anger scale. Interventions for dysfunctional anger are proposed.

Chapter 334

SOCIAL ANXIETY IN THE COLLEGE STUDENT POPULATION: THE ROLE OF ANXIETY SENSITIVITY

Angela Sailer and Holly Hazlett-Stevens*
University of Nevada, Reno
Nevada, US

RESEARCH SUMMARY

Most college students experience some degree of social anxiety on occasion. However, many suffer chronic anxiety across social situations coupled with a strong fear of negative evaluation. In addition to impaired occupational and social functioning, severe social anxiety or social phobia can carry profound consequences for college students. Social anxiety is a prominent motivation for college student drinking (Burke and Stephens, 1999). In addition to social isolation, social anxiety is associated with depressogenic cognitions, both of which leave socially anxious students at an increased risk for depression (Johnson et al., 1992). Anxiety sensitivity – fear of anxiety-related sensations due to perceived consequences of physical, mental, or social harm – might play an important role in the development of social anxiety (Hazen et al., 1995). Unlike panic disorder, in which individuals typically fear anxiety symptoms out of fear of physical harm or loss of mental control, socially anxious individuals fear perceived social consequences of others noticing their anxiety. Socially anxious college students also judge others who appear anxious more negatively than do college students without social anxiety (Purdon et al., 2001). Although panic disorder treatments target anxiety sensitivity directly with interoceptive exposure strategies, this approach is just beginning to receive attention for the treatment of social anxiety. After a brief review of the literature describing the nature of social anxiety among college students, this chapter will examine the specific role of anxiety sensitivity in its development and maintenance. Finally, results from a preliminary investigation comparing the effects of interoceptive exposure delivered in a social

---

* Correspondence concerning this article should be addressed to Holly Hazlett-Stevens, University of Nevada, Department of Psychology/298 Reno, NV 89557, or the author can be reached via email at: hhazlett@unr.edu.

context to social context exposure without the interoceptive component will be presented and discussed.

Chapter 335

COPING, MENTAL HEALTH STATUS, AND CURRENT LIFE REGRET IN COLLEGE WOMEN WHO DIFFER IN THEIR LIFETIME PREGNANCY STATUS: A RESILIENCE PERSPECTIVE*

Jennifer Langhinrichsen-Rohling[†], Theresa Rehm, Michelle Breland and Alexis Inabinet
University of South Alabama, Mobile, Alabama US

RESEARCH SUMMARY

This study examined the current mental health status, coping strategies, and perceived life regret of three types of female college students ($n = 277$): those who had never been pregnant (67.9%, $n = 188$); those who became pregnant at or before age 18 who were a priori considered to be resilient (14.8%, $n = 41$); and those who had experienced a pregnancy after age 18 (17.3%, $n = 48$). Data were collected at a diverse urban public university in the Southeast. This university has a significant number of commuter and non-traditional students. Results indicated that college women who had experienced an adult pregnancy reported significantly fewer maladaptive coping strategies than never-pregnant college women and those who had experienced a teenage pregnancy. Surprisingly, both groups of ever pregnant college women expressed significantly more life regret than never pregnant college women. Among the college women who had experienced a teenage pregnancy, two groups were delineated: those who were "thriving" versus those who were "at-risk" with regards to their current symptoms of depression, hostility, and hopelessness. Women in the "at-risk" group

---
* This project was supported by Grant No. 2001-SI-FX-0006 awarded by the Office of Juvenile Justice and Delinquency Prevention, Office of Justice Programs, U.S. Department of Justice. Points of view or opinions in this document are those of the author and do not necessarily represent the official position or policies of the U.S. Department of Justice.
† Correspondence concerning this article should be addressed to Jennifer Langhinrichsen-Rohling, 385 Life Sciences Building, Psychology Department, University of South Alabama, Mobile, AL., 36688-0002, or the author can be reached via email at jlr@usouthal.edu.

were significantly *less* likely to be simultaneously parenting and attending college than those in the "thriving" group. One potential implication is that identifying and intervening with these potentially at-risk college women may help improve retention rates and student morale at universities with a diverse student body.

In: Psychology Research Biographies and Summaries
Editors: Nancy E. Wodarth and Alexis P. Ferguson
ISBN: 978-1-61470-491-1
© 2012 Nova Science Publishers, Inc.

Chapter 336

SEXUAL BEHAVIORAL DETERMINANTS AND RISK PERCEPTION RELATED TO HIV AMONG COLLEGE STUDENTS

Su-I Hou[1,*] *and Joseph M. Wisenbaker*[2]

[1]Department of Health Promotion Behavior,
College of Public Health,
The University of Georgia, US

[2]Department of Education Psychology
and Instructional Technology,
The University of Georgia, US

RESEARCH SUMMARY

Young adults such as college students are known to engage in frequent and unprotected sexual activities, the primary route for HIV transmission, yet their risk perception towards HIV infections have been low. This study aimed to examine the extent to which HIV risk perception among college students may be explained by behavioral factors (number of partners and condom use by type of sexual activity, and partner's risk) and selected background variables (sexually transmitted infections history, sexual orientation, age, and gender). A web-survey was administered in a major university in the Southeastern U.S. (N=440). Study information with survey website address and login password were disseminated through flyers, colored mini-handouts, classroom announcements, student newspaper advertisements, and several e-mail listserv student organizations. Informed consent was obtained as part of the login process. The innovation of the study is to assess a comprehensive array of sexual behaviors and their relationships on risk perceptions via the Internet. Bivariate analyses were used to first examine the relationships between individual behavioral or background variables and students' perceived HIV risk. Multiple logistic

---

[*] Requests for reprints should be addressed to: Su-I Hou, DrPH, RN, CHES; Department of Health Promotion and Behavior, College of Public Health, The University of Georgia, 309 Ramsey Center, 300 River Road, Athens, GA 30602. Phone: 706-542-8206; Fax: 706-542-4956. Email: shou@uga.edu.

regressions were then performed to investigate how well the various behavioral determinants and background variables together distinguished between students with higher or lower perceived risk of HIV infection. Data showed that, after considering all the variables together, number of partners for oral (OR=1.293), vaginal (OR=1.255), and anal (OR=1.846) sex were the three variables which revealed significant predictions to perceived risk. Results support the use of the Intent in obtaining sensitive behavioral information and suggest that public health messages addressing multiple partners in conjunction with type of sexual activity can be important in influencing HIV risk perception among college students.

In: Psychology Research Biographies and Summaries
Editors: Nancy E. Wodarth and Alexis P. Ferguson
ISBN: 978-1-61470-491-1
© 2012 Nova Science Publishers, Inc.

Chapter 337

THE IMPACT OF A LECTURE SERIES ON ALCOHOL AND TOBACCO USE IN PHARMACY STUDENTS

Arjun P. Dutta,[*] Bisrat Hailemeskel,[†] Monika N. Daftary[‡] and Anthony Wutoh[Π]

Howard University, College of Pharmacy, Nursing and Allied Health Sciences, School of Pharmacy, Washington, DC, US

RESEARCH SUMMARY

Studies related to alcohol and drug use in healthcare students, namely nursing, pharmacy, and medicine suggest that drug and alcohol abuse continues to be a growing problem among health profession students. A review of the more recent literature involving pharmacy students, has noted higher levels of alcohol and drug use when compared to the undergraduate student population. Interestingly, the use and/or abuse of tobacco have largely been overlooked in studies involving substance abuse in pharmacy students. This study documented the current alcohol and tobacco use in pharmacy students and conducted a lecture series on the use and abuse of alcohol and tobacco. The lecture series was successful in increasing the awareness of the use and potential abuse of alcohol in the students. Attitudinal changes in students following the lecture series were also assessed.

---

[*] Office: 503-352-7281; Fax: 202-806-4478; Email: adutta@pacificu.edu; The author is currently the Assistant Dean for Academic Affairs at Pacific University, School of Pharamcy, Forest Grove, OR.
[†] Office: 202-806-4210; Email: bhailemeskel@howard.edu.
[‡] Office: 202-806-4206; Email: mdaftary@howard.edu.
[Π] Office: 202-806-4209; Email: awutoh@howard.edu.

Chapter 338

THE GOULD VERSUS HECKHAUSEN AND SCHULZ DEBATE IN THE LIGHT OF CONTROL PROCESSES AMONG CHINESE STUDENTS

Wan-chi Wong[1],*, Yin Li[2] and Ji-liang Shen[3]
[1]Chinese University of Hong Kong, China
[2]Peking University, China
[3]Beijing Normal University, China

RESEARCH SUMMARY

In response to the Gould versus Heckhausen and Schulz debate (1999) on the claim to universality of the life-span theory of control, the present study aims to examine the theoretical formulation of Heckhausen and Schulz in the context of contemporary China, with specific reference to the control processes applied by Chinese students in their academic pursuits. A new instrument, the OPS-Scales in the Domain of Academic Achievement (OPSAA), was constructed and examined in the pilot study. The main part of the research program consists of three studies. Study One and Study Two respectively investigated the control processes endorsed by Chinese students in the pre-deadline and post-deadline situations relating to two important public examinations, namely the University Entrance Examination and the Test of English as a Foreign Language (TOEFL). Study Three examined the application of control strategies among junior and senior high school students in a less critical situation (i.e., before an internal school examination). The results of the studies lend support to the thesis about the primacy of primary control. As predicted, the Chinese students made extensive use of selective primary control, selective secondary control, and compensatory primary control in the urgent pre-deadline situation. The control strategies applied in the post-deadline situation continued to be characterized by primary control striving in both the success and the failure conditions. Such primary control striving also

---

* Correspondence concerning this article should be addressed to Wan-chi Wong, Department of Educational Psychology, Chinese University of Hong Kong, Shatin, NT, Hong Kong, China. E-mail: wanchiwong@cuhk.edu.hk.

demonstrated its adaptive value by significantly correlating to the positive affect subscale of the Positive and Negative Affect Schedule (PANAS). On the other hand, the endorsement of compensatory secondary control in the failure condition did not show its adaptive value. In integrating the results of Study One, Study Two and Study Three, differences were found across the compared age groups. The ascending slope in the application of compensatory secondary control was confirmed among the subjects who ranged from pre-adolescents through adolescents to young adults. For further development of the research program, it is suggested that Lakatos's idea of sophisticated falsification would be worth considering. Attempts are made to define the "hard core" of the research program, and to propose new auxiliary hypotheses on the basis of the present study. Several lines for future research are also discussed.

Chapter 339

WRITING YOUR WAY TO HEALTH? THE EFFECTS OF DISCLOSURE OF PAST STRESSFUL EVENTS IN GERMAN STUDENTS

Lisette Morris, Annedore Linkemann and Birgit Kröner-Herwig*
Clinical Psychology and Psychotherapy
University of Göttingen, Germany

RESEARCH SUMMARY

In 1986 Pennebaker and Beall published their renowned study on the long-term beneficial health effects of disclosing traumatic events in 4 brief sequential writing sessions. Their results have been confirmed in various studies, but conflicting results have also been reported. The intent of our study was to replicate the experiments from Pennebaker and Beall (1986), Pennebaker et al. (1988), and Greenberg and Stone (1992) using a German student sample. Additionally, essay variables that point to the emotional processing of events (e.g., depth of self-exploration, number of negative/positive emotions, intensity of emotional expression) were examined as potential mechanisms of action. Trait measures of personality which could moderate the personal consequences of disclosure (alexithymia, self-concealment, worrying, social support) were also assessed. In a second study the experimental condition (disclosure) was varied by implementing "coping" vs. "helping" instructions as variations of the original condition. Under the coping condition participants were asked to elaborate on what they used to do, continue to do, or could do in the future to better cope with the event. Under the helping condition participants were asked to imagine themselves in the role of a adviser and elaborate on what they would recommend to persons also dealing with the trauma in order to better cope with the event. The expected beneficial effects of disclosure on long-term health (e.g., physician visits, physical symptoms, affectivity) could not be corroborated in either the first or the second study. None of the examined essay variables of emotional processing and only a single personality variable was able to explain significant variance in the health-related

---

* Prof. Dr. B. Kroener-Herwig; Georg-Elias-Mueller-Institut für Psychologie; Dep. Clinical Psychology and Psychotherapy; Gosslerstr. 14; D - 37073 Goettingen; Email: bkroene@uni-goettingen.de.

outcome variables influence. Nevertheless, substantial reductions in posttraumatic stress symptoms (e.g., intrusions, avoidance, arousal), were found in both experiments. These improvements were significantly related to essay variables of emotional expression and self-exploration and were particularly pronounced under the activation of a prosocial motivation (helping condition).

Repeated, albeit brief, expressive writing about personally upsetting or traumatic events resulted in an immediate increase in negative mood but did not lead to long-term positive health consequences in a German student sample. It did, however, promote better processing of stressful or traumatic events, as evidenced by reductions in posttraumatic stress symptoms. The instruction to formulate recommendations for persons dealing with the same trauma seems more helpful than standard disclosure or focusing on one's own past, present, and future coping endeavours. Overall, expressive writing seems to be a successful method of improving trauma processing. Determining the appropriate setting (e.g., self-help vs. therapeutic context) for disclore can be seen as an objective of future research.

In: Psychology Research Biographies and Summaries
Editors: Nancy E. Wodarth and Alexis P. Ferguson
ISBN: 978-1-61470-491-1
© 2012 Nova Science Publishers, Inc.

Chapter 340

TEST ANXIETY AND ITS CONSEQUENCES ON ACADEMIC PERFORMANCE AMONG UNIVERSITY STUDENTS

Mohd Ariff Bin Kassim[1,*], *Siti Rosmaini Bt. Mohd Hanafi*[1,†] *and Dawson R. Hancock*[2,‡]

[1] Universiti Tenaga Nasional; Pahang, Malaysia;
[2] University of North Carolina at Charlotte; Charlotte, North Carolina, US

RESEARCH SUMMARY

Some educators have failed to acknowledge the prevalence of test anxiety and its effect on academic performance among university students. This study addresses this issue at the university level using data collected through the Revised Test Anxiety (RTA) instrument and Sarason's four-factor model as a basis for measuring test anxiety. The study also investigates the effect of demographic factors on test anxiety. Findings reveal that test anxiety is significantly and negatively related to academic performance. Reasons for these findings are addressed.

---

[*] ariff@kms.uniten.edu.my; Telephone – 012-6097503.
[†] rosmaini@kms.uniten.edu.my; Telephone – 09-4552043.
[‡] Address for Correspondence: Dawson R. Hancock, Ph.D. University of North Carolina at Charlotte; 9201 University City Boulevard; Charlotte, North Carolina, U.S.A. 28223; Electronic Mail – *DHancock@ uncc.edu*; Telephone – (704)687-8863.

In: Psychology Research Biographies and Summaries
Editors: Nancy E. Wodarth and Alexis P. Ferguson

ISBN: 978-1-61470-491-1
© 2012 Nova Science Publishers, Inc.

Chapter 341

THE PREVALENCE OF DEPRESSION AMONG FEMALE UNIVERSITY STUDENTS AND RELATED FACTORS

Fernando L. Vázquez[*,1], *Ángela Torres*[2], *María López*[1], *Vanessa Blanco*[1] *and Patricia Otero*[1]

[1] Faculty of Psychology, University of Santiago de Compostela, Spain
[2] Faculty of Medicine, University of Santiago de Compostela, Spain

RESEARCH SUMMARY

In many countries, university students now constitute a significant proportion of their age group. As in the general population, depression is relatively frequent in this group, and affects women more than men. In the study described here we evaluated the prevalence of depression, depressive symptoms and associated factors among 365 young women sampled randomly, with stratification by year and discipline, from among the 18,180 female students attending a Spanish university (65.9% of its total student roll). The prevalence of current major depressive episode was 10.4% (95% CI 7.5-14.0%). Among students with current depression, the commonest symptoms were depressed mood (86.5%) and alteration of sleep (78.9%). Some 52.6% of depressed students had suffered one or more previous depressive episodes ($M = 1.2$; $SD = 1.5$), and 13.2% had attempted suicide, but the existence of previous depressive episodes did not increase the risk of a current episode. Increased risk was associated with recent problems, which multiplied the odds of depression by 2.31 (95% CI 1.26-4.26), and with smoking in the past month, which multiplied the odds of depression by 2.01 (95% CI 1.09-3.89), but not with the use of alcohol, cannabis or cocaine in the past month. Nor was there any significant association between depression and declared social class, monthly family income, university course level, geographical background (urban or rural), persons lived with during term time (family, friends, etc.), whether all the previous year's exams had been passed, sports activity, or academic discipline.

---

[*] Corresponding author. Universidad de Santiago de Compostela, Facultad de Psicología, Departamento de Psicología Clínica y Psicobiología, Campus Universitario Sur, 15782 Santiago de Compostela, Galicia, Spain. E-mail: pcfer@usc.es.

In: Psychology Research Biographies and Summaries
Editors: Nancy E. Wodarth and Alexis P. Ferguson
ISBN: 978-1-61470-491-1
© 2012 Nova Science Publishers, Inc.

Chapter 342

RELATIONSHIPS BETWEEN MOOD, COPING AND STRESS SYMPTOMS AMONG STUDENTS WHO WORK IN SCHOOLS

Dafna Kariv[1,*] *and Tali Heiman*[2,†]

[1] School of Business Administration,
The College of Management, Israel
[2] Department of Education and Psychology,
The Open University of Israel, Israel

RESEARCH SUMMARY

The study examined the mood states of 229 men and women who are simultaneously full-time students and school staff when coping with their dual-demanding stressful environments. A causal model was developed to demonstrate that the dual-demanding stressors that the respondents faced affected their moods; these moods are pre-behavioral factors that affected their coping strategies. Results of multilevel analyses indicated that men and women differ in the magnitude of their experienced moods, but both genders experience vigorous moods as a prime emotional reaction to the dual-demanding environment. Moods were found to affect both male and female coping strategies, in all categories except social support. The genders differed in the coping strategies adopted, except for task-oriented strategies. In addition, the analyses revealed gender differences in expressing angry and depressed moods, where females reported experiencing higher levels. These results reinforce our assumption that coping with dual-demanding environments, especially by individuals who are employed in stressful occupations, reflects not only a gender-based tendency but also the mood states that derive from the stressors. Results revealed that men and women manifest identical patterns in coping with dual-demanding stressors, and that these patterns are related to their moods. Thus, coping strategies seem to depend on context rather than on gender.

---

[*] E-mail address: dafiran@nonstop.net.il. Address: Yizhak Rabin Boulevard, Rishon Le Zion, Israel.
[†] E-mail address: talihe@openu.ac.il. Address: 108 Ravutski Street., Ranana, 43107, Israel.

Chapter 343

EXAMINING ANGER EXPRESSION REACTIONS AND ANGER CONTROL BEHAVIORS OF TURKISH STUDENTS

*Ibrahim Kisac**
Gazi University, Ankara, Turkey

RESEARCH SUMMARY

The aim of this research is to examine anger expression reactions and anger control behaviors with respect to gender and education levels of the students when they are angry.

Subjects were recruited from Gazi University, Abidinpasa High School and Aksaray Anatolian Hotel and Tourism Vocational High School and consist of 466 students. Inventory was prepared by the researcher to collect data about demographic qualities and anger behaviors of the students. Data were analyzed by frequency, percent and chi-square techniques.

Results indicated that when the students get angry, they "sulk or make sour face"(77%), "try to think that everybody does not have to behave as they want"(76%) and "think that they can handle with the situation which made them angry" (75%). According to gender variable, male students significantly "say nasty things to the others", but "try to be more intelligent and indulgent", "to be more coolheaded", "more think that not being able to control anger is a weakness" and "more think that they will not let others make them angry" than female students. On the other hand, it was found that female students more "sulk or make sour face", "feel helpless, feel cry" and "say sarcastic words to the person who made them angry" than male students when they are angry. According to educational status, it was determined that while female high school students significantly "yell or scream more", "argue with the person who made them angry" and "say nasty things to the others" more than female university students, female university students "express their anger in a more suitable way", "try to see pozitif sides of the case", "try to convince themselves not to be angered" more and "think that

---

* Gazi University, Vocational Education Faculty, Department of Educational Sciences, 06500 Besevler – Ankara / Turkey, kisac@gazi.edu.tr.

everybody does not have to behave as they want" when they feel angry. It was seen that while male high school students "make fun of the person who made them angry" more, male university students "do nothing at all, quite; suppress their their anger" more, "sulk or make sour face" and "withdraw from the people".

Chapter 344

CORONARY PRESSURE MEASUREMENT IN DECISION MAKING FOR EQUIVOCAL LEFT MAIN CORONARY ARTERY DISEASE

Kohichiro Iwasaki
Department of Cardiology, Okayama Central Hospital, Okayama, Japan

RESEARCH SUMMARY

It is often difficult for equivocal left main coronary artery (LMCA) disease to make decision about coronary artery bypass surgery (CABG). We investigated the usefulness of coronary pressure measurement for decision making for CABG to equivocal LMCA disease. We measured coronary pressure in 16 patients with equivocal LMCA disease. Fractional flow reserve (FFR) was calculated at the maximal hyperemia from the simultaneously recorded aortic (Pa) and distal coronary pressure (Pd) by the ratio of Pd/Pa. If FFR of LMCA was <0.75 we selected CABG and if it was ≥0.75 we selected medical therapy. We followed these patients for 26.5±10.8 (13-39) months. Eight patients underwent medical therapy (medical group) and eight patients underwent CABG (surgical group). The FFR of LMCA was 0.91±0.01 in medical group and 0.61±0.03 in surgical group (p<0.0001). There were no significant differences in reference vessel diameter (3.63±0.71 vs 3.31±0.86mm), minimal lumen diameter (1.84±0.26 vs 1.69±0.45mm), percent diameter stenosis (48.4±7.8 vs 48.9±9.0%) between the medical and surgical groups. During follow up no patient in medical group had cardiac event and two patients in surgical group hospitalized for congestive heart failure. In conclusion coronary pressure measurement for equivocal left main coronary artery disease is clinically useful to make decision about CABG.

Chapter 345

ANTITERRORIST EMERGENCY VENTILATION: SYSTEM, STRATEGY AND DECISION-MAKING

Xianting Li[1]*, Hao Cai[1,2] and Lina Zhao[1]

[1]Department of Building Science, School of Architecture,
Tsinghua University, Beijing, China
[2]Engineering Institution of Engineering Corps, PLA
University of Science and Technology, Nanjing, China

RESEARCH SUMMARY

There are two kinds of antiterrorist emergency ventilation system. One is to defend indoor environment against chemical and biological agent (CBA) attacks. The other is to supply calmative gas to incapacitate terrorists when they hold hostages in public buildings. What kind of system and ventilation strategy can be used for antiterrorism, and how to make decision are introduced in the chapter. There are six sections in the chapter.

How the emergency ventilation systems work is introduced in the first section.

The second section is on the theory of contaminant dispersion and identification of contaminant source. For the theory of contaminant dispersion, both computational fluid dynamics (CFD) method and analytical formula of contaminant distribution are introduced. For the theory of contaminant source identification, an algorithm to identify the position and intensity of contaminant source with limited number of sensors is proposed and demonstrated for its effectiveness.

The third section is on the evacuation model and evaluation of exposure risk. Both cellular automata (CA) model and spatial-grid evacuation model (SGEM) are introduced for modeling evacuation process. The relative exposure risk index, EFCS, and absolute exposure risk index, PIR, are introduced to evaluate the exposure risk of contaminant.

Both the second section and third section are the fundamental of emergency ventilation. Based on section 2 and 3, the ventilation strategy and decision-making are introduced for

---

* Corresponding author: Xianting Li, Department of Building Science, School of Architecture, Tsinghua University, Beijing, 100084, P.R. China. Tel: +86-10-62785860; Fax: +86-10-62773461; E-mail: xtingli@tsinghua.edu.cn.

emergency ventilation against contaminant suddenly released in public building in section 4 and for emergency ventilation to rescue hostages held by terrorists in section 5, respectively.

In: Psychology Research Biographies and Summaries
Editors: Nancy E. Wodarth and Alexis P. Ferguson

ISBN: 978-1-61470-491-1
© 2012 Nova Science Publishers, Inc.

Chapter 346

DECISION-MAKING IN A STRUCTURED CONNECTIONIST AGENT ARCHITECTURE

Carter Wendelken[1] and Lokendra Shastri[2]

[1] Helen Wills Neuroscience Institute, UC-Berkeley, Berkeley, CA, US
[2] International Computer Science Institute, Berkeley, CA, US

RESEARCH SUMMARY

To understand the mapping between networks of neurons and the mental constructs that underlie complex cognition and behavior is a central problem for the field of neurocomputing. The structured connectionist approach tackles this problem directly by investigating the relation between connectionist circuits and cognitive operations. One structured connectionist model, SHRUTI, has demonstrated how a system of simple, neuron-like elements can encode a large body of relational causal knowledge and provide a basis for rapid inference. The SHRUTI model explored the use of spreading activation across structured representations and temporal synchrony variable binding within a connectionist network. This article will describe the transformation of the SHRUTI model into a decision-making agent architecture. Key contributions of this effort include the development of a connectionist encoding of goals and utility and of connectionist mechanisms for cognitive control that support goal-oriented behavior. Specific connectionist circuits encode long-term goals or drives, associate value with possible events, and propagate utility from effects to possible causes. Together, these mechanisms support reactive planning and simple goal-driven decision-making. However, successful operation in more complex decision scenarios, such as those involving conflicting subgoals, requires top-down control mechanisms. Several such control mechanisms are described; it is then shown that each can be implemented via some combination of a small set of control primitives. Each of these control primitives -- including monitoring, filtering, selection, maintenance, organization, and manipulation – is implemented as a simple connectionist circuit.

In: Psychology Research Biographies and Summaries
Editors: Nancy E. Wodarth and Alexis P. Ferguson

ISBN: 978-1-61470-491-1
© 2012 Nova Science Publishers, Inc.

Chapter 347

COGNITIVE DYSFUNCTION IN COCAINE ABUSE: EVIDENCE FOR IMPAIRMENTS IN IMPULSE CONTROL AND DECISION-MAKING

Laurie M. Rilling[*,1] *and Bryon Adinoff*[1,2]

[1] University of Texas Southwestern Medical Center, Dallas, TX, US
[2] VA North Texas Health Care System, Dallas, TX, US

RESEARCH SUMMARY

Cocaine is one of the most widely abused psychoactive substances in the United States, with an estimated 1.3 million Americans using the drug on a regular (at least monthly) basis. Even occasional cocaine use can result in serious medical complications, such as cardiac damage, vascular ischemia, respiratory failure, and persistent alterations in neural function. In this chapter, we will examine the most recent research on impulsivity and decision-making in cocaine use. First, we will present a brief overview of the cognitive processes affected by cocaine use. Next, we will review the relevant literature detailing the status of inhibitory control and decision-making in cocaine users, as well as their proposed neuroanatomical correlates. Finally, we will attempt to integrate these findings with the current view of cocaine addiction and relapse, with an emphasis on the role of impulsivity and decision-making in continued cocaine use despite the elevated risk of negative consequences.

---

[*] Correspondence: Laurie M. Rilling, Ph.D., UT Southwestern Medical Center, 5323 Harry Hines Blvd., Dallas Texas 75390-8846; Telephone: (214) 648-4646; E-mail: laurie.rilling@utsouthwestern.edu.

In: Psychology Research Biographies and Summaries
Editors: Nancy E. Wodarth and Alexis P. Ferguson
ISBN: 978-1-61470-491-1
© 2012 Nova Science Publishers, Inc.

Chapter 348

EXPERT SYSTEMS, GIS, AND SPATIAL DECISION MAKING: CURRENT PRACTICES AND NEW TRENDS

Khalid Eldrandaly*

Assistant Professor of Computer Information Systems
Interim Head of Information Systems and Technology Department
College of Computers and Informatics
Zagazig University, Egypt

RESEARCH SUMMARY

Spatial decision making is a routine activity that is common to individuals and to organizations. Spatial decision making problems are multi-facetted challenges. Not only do they often involve numerous technical requirements, but they may also contain economical, social, environmental and political dimensions that could have conflicting objectives. Solving these complex problems requires an integrative use of information, domain specific knowledge and effective means of communication. Although geographic information systems (GIS) and expert systems (ES) have played important roles in solving spatial decision problems, each of these tools has its own limitations in dealing with such problems. For instance, GIS is a great tool for handling physical suitability analysis. However, it has limited capabilities of incorporating the decision maker's preferences, experiences, intuitions, and judgments into the problem-solving process. Expert Systems, which is capable of addressing heuristic analysis, lacks the capabilities of handling spatial data/knowledge that are crucial to spatial analysis. The need for improvement of the performance of these tools in solving highly complex spatial decision-making problems has promoted the integration of GIS and ES. Numerous mechanisms enabling interoperability between GIS and ES have appeared over the years. Examples range from primitive solutions such as simple, loose coupling to much more sophisticated approaches, such as COM technology and Ontology. In this study, both primitive and advanced techniques for integrating GIS and ES are discussed.

---

*Khalid Eldrandaly: khalid_eldrandaly@yahoo.com.

In: Psychology Research Biographies and Summaries
Editors: Nancy E. Wodarth and Alexis P. Ferguson

ISBN: 978-1-61470-491-1
© 2012 Nova Science Publishers, Inc.

Chapter 349

DEVELOPMENT OF RESPONSE INHIBITION AND DECISION-MAKING ACROSS CHILDHOOD: A COGNITIVE NEUROSCIENCE PERSPECTIVE

Wery P. M. van den Wildenberg* and Eveline A. Crone
Department of Psychology, Universiteit van Amsterdam, the Netherlands
Laboratory of Neurobiology and Cognition,
CNRS and Université de Provence, Marseille, France
Center for Mind and Brain, University of California, Davis, CA, US

RESEARCH SUMMARY

Recent advances within the field of neuroimaging and psychophysiological recording techniques have enabled the identification of key brain regions that contribute to developmental changes in cognitive control and decision-making. This chapter will focus on two influential paradigms in the field of experimental cognitive neuroscience that have contributed to our understanding of the nature of the increasing ability in children to control their own thoughts and actions as they grow older. The first section reviews the current cognitive developmental theories of behavioral inhibition. Response inhibition comes into play when prepotent, overlearned, or ongoing responses have to be suppressed in favor of executing an alternative response and is generally considered an important element of cognitive control and flexibility. These theories are supported by neuroimaging studies that identify the lateral prefrontal cortex as being relevant in tasks that require the on-line manipulation of information and the suppression of responses. The second part of this chapter provides an account of the development of cognitive processes involved in decision-making. Decision-making is required for a variety of behavior and often involves the consideration of multiple alternatives and reasoning about distant future consequences. According to the somatic-marker theory, the possible outcomes of a choice are mediated by emotions that are accompanied by anticipatory somatic activity. The theory underlying emotional self-

---

* Correspondence can be addressed to the first author at the Department of Psychology, Universiteit van Amsterdam, Roetersstraat 15, 1018 WB, Amsterdam, the Netherlands (e-mail: *wery@dds.nl*).

regulation assigns an important role to the ventromedial prefrontal cortex. Finally, the examination of developmental changes in cognitive control functions from the perspective of cognitive neuroscience has also led to better characterizations of behavioral deficits found in disordered child populations.

ENABLING PREGNANT WOMEN TO PARTICIPATE IN INFORMED DECISION-MAKING REGARDING THEIR LABOUR ANALGESIA

Camille Raynes-Greenow[1], Christine Roberts[1] and Natasha Nassar[2]

[1] The Kolling Institute of Medical Research
Northern Clinical School, The University of Sydney, Australia
[2] The Telethon Institute for Child Health Research
Centre for Child Health Research,
The University of Western Australia, Australia

RESEARCH SUMMARY

The pain of labour is a central part of women's experience of childbirth. Many factors are considered influential in determining women's experience of and her satisfaction with childbirth. Women's expectations of the duration and level of pain suffered, quality of her care-giver support, and involvement in labour decision making are the most commonly reported factors.

Significantly, there have been more clinical trials of pharmacological pain relief during labour and childbirth than of any other intervention in the perinatal field however to what degree this evidence is available or discussed with pregnant women before labour is unclear.

In: Psychology Research Biographies and Summaries
Editors: Nancy E. Wodarth and Alexis P. Ferguson

ISBN: 978-1-61470-491-1
© 2012 Nova Science Publishers, Inc.

Chapter 351

ADOLESCENT DECISION-MAKING ABOUT SUBSTANCE USE: A VIDEO-BASED ASSESSMENT

Kristen G. Anderson[1], and Sara J. Parent[2]*

[1]University of California, San Diego, Departments of Psychology & Psychiatry CA, US
[2]University of California, San Diego, Department of Psychology CA, US

RESEARCH SUMMARY

Adolescence is a period characterized by rapid cognitive and social change. As youth move through adolescence, they are faced with a myriad of decisions regarding risky behavior, including substance involvement. Given the importance of the social sphere for teens, these decisions are often influenced by peers. There is a growing body of research into the processes underlying adolescent decision-making regarding alcohol and drug use. However, few process-oriented assessment approaches have been developed to understand how youth make these decisions in the moment. This chapter briefly reviews the literature on adolescent decision-making regarding alcohol and drugs, presents a social-information processing model for adolescent substance use, and describes the development of a novel video-based approach to assessing adolescent decision-making. This assessment integrates methods traditionally used in the educational setting as well as those developed for clinical populations of youth. Preliminary data from the development phase of the assessment will be presented. The implications for adolescent research in risk taking, substance involvement and intervention with youth will be discussed.

---

* Correspondence to: Kristen G. Anderson, Ph.D., Reed College, Department of Psychology, 3203 S.E. Woodstock Avenue, Portland, Oregon 97202, Kristen.Anderson@reed.edu.

In: Psychology Research Biographies and Summaries ISBN: 978-1-61470-491-1
Editors: Nancy E. Wodarth and Alexis P. Ferguson © 2012 Nova Science Publishers, Inc.

Chapter 352

INTERPROFESSIONAL DECISION MAKING IN ELDERLY CARE: MORALITY, CRITERIA AND HELP ALLOCATION

Pirjo Nikander
Department of Sociology and Social Psychology,
University of Tampere, Finland

RESEARCH SUMMARY

Talk and interaction between health and social care professionals form one central arena where statutory decisions concerning the care of elderly people are made. Cooperative work between members of different professional groups in meetings, or in teams is also a practical arena where various agreed upon policies and principles of elderly care are turned into practice through talk. In this chapter, I analyze interprofessional meetings as a practical site for decision making over service and help allocation to elderly people and their carers. I attempt to lay out for view some characteristics of professional deliberation and decision making. Discursive analysis of professional-professional interaction and talk is seen here as a powerful means of studying help allocation, and the unfolding of institutional criteria and morality.

The interdisciplinary field of discourse studies has in recent years produced an ample supply of work on institutional and lay caring relations. The existing literature already provides information on the construction of elderly identities (Paoletti 1998; see also Nikander 2002), on the discursive construction of frailty (Taylor 1992), of caring relations and the professionals' role as part of the care arrangements (e.g. Grainger 1993), on intergenerational relations (e.g. Cicirelli 1993), and on professional construction of client or patient cases (e.g. Nikander 2003, 2005).

Empirical research on professional or institutional discourses in elderly care falls roughly into three distinctive areas of interest (c.f. Linell 1998). Perhaps most prominently, research has focused on professional – lay discourse i.e., on encounters involving the co-presence of doctors and elderly patients (e.g. Coupland and Coupland 1998, 1999), elderly mental patients and attorneys (Holstein 1990), or for instance district nurses and patients (Leppänen 1998). A second area of research gives discourse *within* specific professional groups centre focus. Analysis of nurses' actions within a medical unit may for instance tease out specifics of how this professional group constitutes patient classes or patient types as part of their own everyday ordering work (Latimer 1997). Third, discursive analysis on care and caring relations has also been concerned with interprofessional discourse, i.e., encounters, cooperation and joint decision-making *between* individuals from different professional groups. Research in this area varies from managerial interests (e.g. Dockrell and Wilson 1995) to a focus on professional roles and narratives (Housley 2003), and joint professional categorization work (e.g. Nikander 2003, 2005). It is this area of research that this chapter also hopes to contribute to.

In terms of its methodological stance, the current chapter draws on prior work on discourse analysis, categorization in institutional settings as well as work that analyses categorization in talk more broadly (e.g. Antaki and Widdicombe 1998; Baker 1997; Boden 1994; Hester and Eglin 1993; Housley 2003; Nikander 2000, 2002). It provides numerous illustrations and detailed analyses of professional care allocation. Doing this, the chapter hopefully shows how the criteria and morality of decision making are jointly constructed in interaction, and how the responsibilities of professionals as well as the rights and responsibilities of elderly clients and of their carers are discursively carved and talked into being in institutional meeting talk. Special focus in the chapter will be given to the ways in which professionals use *imageries and ideals concerning the caring relationship and the life course* as part of their descriptive work.

In the remaining sections of this chapter I will first introduce the data and the institutional setting in which they were collected. Following this, I will then move to the analysis of two elderly client cases and provide several data excerpts on both. To conclude, I will briefly discuss possible benefits and practical implications of discursive analyses of professional argumentation.

ANALYSING THE EFFECTS OF MORTALITY SALIENCE ON PREJUDICE AND DECISION-TAKING

Agustin Echebarria- Echabe* and Francisco J. Valencia Gárate
Department of Social Psychology. Psychology faculty,
The University of the Basque Country, Spain

RESEARCH SUMMARY

Recently (Echebarria & Fernandez, 2006) we carried out a quasi-experimental study on the effects of the terrorist attacks against the railways in Madrid and found that these attacks provoked a generalized prejudice directed not only against groups regarded as the responsible of the attacks but also against other non-related group (Jews). A generalized displacement toward more conservative values and political options was also found. Here we present two follow-up experimental studies designed to analyse the socio-psychological processes that might underlie these changes. The first study manipulated, through pictures, the salience of death- related thoughts without involving any personal or group based threat. The generalized increment of prejudices and group bias are reproduced but only at an implicit level. The second study proved that mortality salience affects how social dilemmas are approached. Participants assigned to the mortality salient condition approached a health related dilemma in terms of losses, independently of how it was experimentally framed. In contrast, control participants shifted their choices in function of the experimental manipulation. We discuss the implications of these results in terms of understanding the effects of terrorism from the Terror Management Theory.

---

* E-mail: pspeteta@ss.ehu.es.

Chapter 354

BURNOUT AND COMPASSION FATIGUE: THE CASE OF PROFESSIONAL NURSES IN PRIMARY HEALTH CARE FACILITIES IN THE FREE STATE PROVINCE, SOUTH AFRICA

Michelle Engelbrecht[1], Henriëtte van den Berg[2] and Coen Bester[3]

[1]Centre for Health Systems Research & Development,
University of the Free State, South Africa
[2]Department of Psychology, University of the Free State, South Africa
[3]Department of Industrial Psychology, University of the Free State, South Africa

RESEARCH SUMMARY

The skills, effort and commitment of staff play a crucial role in determining the quality of services rendered by health care institutions. In South Africa, nurses form the backbone of the primary health care (PHC) system. Therefore, their well-being is of paramount importance in the effective provisioning of health services and programme implementation. However, South African public health services are seriously crippled by severe staff shortages due to a flight of skills from the public to the private sector and to other countries. Furthermore, the growing demands made by the HIV/AIDS epidemic on health human resources are unabatedly escalating. This research aimed to determine levels of burnout, compassion satisfaction/fatigue and job satisfaction among professional nurses working in PHC facilities in the Free State Province, South Africa. The study also examined the influence of personal and work-related factors on burnout experienced by professional nurses. A group of 543 professional nurses in the Free State public health sector — all professional nurses servicing the antiretroviral treatment (ART) programme (n=182) and approximately 30% of professional nurses working in PHC facilities (n=361) — participated in the study. The study employed a combination of quantitative and qualitative approaches. Two open-ended questions identified factors that contributed to job satisfaction and dissatisfaction. Demographic information and a compilation of standardised instruments (Maslach Burnout Inventory; Professional Quality of Life Scale; Interpersonal Conflict at Work Scale;

Organizational Constraints Scale; and Quantitative Workload Scale) constituted the quantitative section. An extremely high response rate (97%) was achieved. High levels of burnout and compassion fatigue were identified. Results indicated that the majority of respondents frequently experienced emotional depletion, reduced capacity for emotional control and negative feelings, such as anxiety, depression, irritability and anger. Respondents also experienced a very high workload, with professional nurses working in facilities not rendering ART services reporting significantly higher levels of workload than their counterparts working in ART rendering facilities. Workload and work-related constraints consistently explained most of the variance in the indices of burnout and compassion fatigue. Forty percent of respondents noted the main source of their job satisfaction as the opportunity to help relieve patients' suffering. To a large extent, the research found that the well-being of professional nurses was significantly affected by chronic work overload and occupational stress. Recommendations focused on the development of an intervention comprising strategies directed at both the work environment and the individual worker.

In: Psychology Research Biographies and Summaries
Editors: Nancy E. Wodarth and Alexis P. Ferguson

ISBN: 978-1-61470-491-1
© 2012 Nova Science Publishers, Inc.

Chapter 355

BURNOUT AND THE ANTITHESIS OF BURNOUT: DEVELOPING POSITIVE INTERVENTIONS FOR THE WELL-BEING OF CHINESE TEACHERS IN HONG KONG

David W. Chan[*]
The Chinese University of Hong Kong

RESEARCH SUMMARY

The evolution of the conceptualization of burnout and the three components of burnout (emotional exhaustion, depersonalization, and reduced personal accomplishment) were first briefly reviewed with a focus on the studies of teacher burnout in Hong Kong, leading to the introduction of the notion of the antithesis of teacher burnout. Teacher burnout and its antithesis were then discussed in the context of positive psychology with reference to the three orientations to happiness (the pleasant life, the meaningful life, and the engaged life) and the twenty-four character strengths that could be subsumed under six virtues or strength domains in the hierarchy of strengths. Strength-based interventions and more broadly positive interventions were introduced as effective interventions to promote the antithesis of burnout. Among the effective positive intervention exercises, gratitude interventions were more closely examined and discussed in the context of the conceptualization and assessment of gratitude. Despite that scant research attention has been accorded to the conceptualization and applications of gratitude in both Western and Chinese societies, it is maintained that gratitude interventions are well-suited for helping Chinese teachers combat burnout and cope with the experience of burnout, considering that gratitude has always been valued in Chinese culture and represents a prized attitude and an aspired way of life.

---

[*] Correspondence concerning this article should be addressed to David W. Chan, Department of Educational Psychology, the Chinese University of Hong Kong, Shatin, NT, Hong Kong. E-mail: davidchan@cuhk.edu.hk.

REDUCING BURNOUT THROUGH SUPPORT IN THE WORKPLACE AND THE FAMILY DOMAIN

Lieke L. ten Brummelhuis
Department of Social and Behavioral Sciences, Utrecht University, The Netherlands

RESEARCH SUMMARY

The ever-increasing numbers of employees suffering from burnout provides good reason to investigate support measures that are effective in reducing this syndrome. In this contribution, I compare different types of support based on the source (work or family) and the resource provided (emotional or instrumental) in order to determine which reduces feelings of burnout best. Based on a sample of 473 employees at 24 organizations, the study showed that family support reduced feelings of burnout somewhat more than work support, and that emotional support played an important role in diminishing burnout, unlike instrumental support. Several interaction effects of support on the relationship between demands and burnout were found. Emotional work support (e.g. supervisor support) attenuated the harmful effect of working hours on burnout. Finally, emotional work support and having a good relationship with their partner reduced burnout more among male employees than among female employees. Based on these findings, I conclude that emotional support in both the workplace and the family domain is most effective at reducing burnout.

In: Psychology Research Biographies and Summaries
Editors: Nancy E. Wodarth and Alexis P. Ferguson

ISBN: 978-1-61470-491-1
© 2012 Nova Science Publishers, Inc.

Chapter 357

THE ROLE OF PERSONALITY AND COPING STYLE IN BURNOUT DEVELOPMENT: A STUDY ON NEED FOR RECOVERY FROM WORK

Marc van Veldhoven and Geertje van Daalen[*]
Tilburg University, The Netherlands

RESEARCH SUMMARY

This chapter presents an explorative study that investigates the importance of personality characteristics and coping styles in the development of burnout at work. Need for recovery is an indicator of failing recovery and correlates high with feelings of emotional exhaustion (Veldhoven, 2008), which are assumed to be at the core of the burnout syndrome (Cordes and Dougherty, 1993). It is an early indicator of burnout development. Need for recovery is measured two times with a two-year interval in a sample of 101 workers in a health care institution. Two types of multiple regression equations are compared: the first predicting time2 need for recovery while controlling for time1 need for recovery, and the second predicting the average need for recovery across time1 and time2. Age, gender and work demands serve as control variables in both types of analysis. The results show that inability to withdraw from work, negative affectivity and lack of palliative coping style are significant predictors of both time2 need for recovery and the average need for recovery across time1 and time2, illustrating the importance of personality characteristics and (to a lesser degree) coping styles in recovery processes. Subtle differences exist between the two types of analysis. Conceptual and methodological issues that follow from this study are discussed. Research results of this study point at factors that can be targets for individual stress management in employees who report (early signals of) burnout.

---

[*] Address corresponding author: Dr. G. van Daalen, OSA Institute for Labour Studies, Tilburg University, P.O. Box 90153, NL-5000 LE Tilburg, The Netherlands. Phone: +31 13 4668070. Fax: +31 13 4663349. E-mail: G.vanDaalen@uvt.nl.

Chapter 358

WHOSE EXHAUSTION IS GREATER THAN WHOSE? BURNOUT IN COLORECTAL SURGEONS, VASCULAR SURGEONS AND COLORECTAL NURSE SPECIALISTS WORKING IN THE NATIONAL HEALTH SERVICE

A. Sharma[1]*, L. G. Walker[2] and J. R. T. Monson[3]

[1] Academic Surgical Unit, University of Hull, England
[2] Oncology Health Centre and Institute of Rehabilitation, University of Hull, England
[3] University of Rochester Medical Center, Rochester, NY, US

RESEARCH SUMMARY

INTRODUCTION: It has been suggested that changes to the organisation of the National Health Service (NHS), and changes in clinical practice, are associated with increased burnout in health care professionals. It has also been suggested that dealing with patients who have cancer is particularly demanding. Coping strategies used in response to work-related stress are also deemed to be of importance in determining who will suffer from burnout. The aim of this study was to compare burnout, coping strategies, retirement intentions and job satisfaction in two groups of surgeons with varying cancer workload, and a group of surgeons and nurses working in the same specialty. METHODS: A list of all consultant colorectal surgeons (CRS), colorectal clinical nurse specialists (CNS), and vascular surgeons (VS) working in the NHS was obtained from the respective societies. Participants were sent a questionnaire booklet consisting of standardised questionnaires (Maslach Burnout Inventory, Coping Questionnaire) and various *ad hoc* questions to obtain information about demographics, cancer workload and job satisfaction. Independent predictors of clinically significant burnout were identified using logistic regression. RESULTS: 455 CRS, 398VS and 326 CNS were sent booklets. The response rate was CRS -55.6%, VS- 62.3% and CNS -

---

* Mr A Sharma, Academic SpR in Surgery, Academic Surgical Unit, University of Hull, Castle Hill Hospital, Cottingham, Hull, HU16 5JQ, UK, Email A.Sharma@hull.ac.uk, Telephone (+44) 1482 623225, Facsimile (+44) 1482 623274.

54.3%. (1) CRS and VS- 49% of colorectal surgery was cancer-related compared to 7.5% of vascular surgery (p=0.001). 32% of all respondents had high burnout. There were no significant between-group differences in personal accomplishment or emotional exhaustion, although vascular surgeons had higher depersonalization (p=0.04). Multivariate analyses showed that job dissatisfaction independently predicted all aspects of burnout, whereas being married or cohabiting reduced the risk. High depersonalisation was more common in younger surgeons. Positive coping strategies including spending time with the family, relaxing, exercising, mixing with friends were predictive of lower levels of burnout.(2) CRS and CNS- Compared to CNS, CRS had significantly higher levels of depersonalisation (17.4% vs 7.4%) and lower personal accomplishment (26.6% vs 14.2%). Seventy-seven percent of CRS, and 63.4% of CNS, stated their intention to retire before the statutory retirement age. Dissatisfaction with work, intention to retire early, intention to retire as soon as affordable, and self-perceived poor training in communication and management skills were also significantly associated with high burnout in both groups. Positive coping strategies predicted lower levels of burnout in these two groups as well.CONCLUSION: We found high levels of burnout in this national cohort of CRS, VS and CNS. Burnout was unrelated to cancer workload. CNS's had less burnout than CRS and this may be related to their different working practices, responsibilities, and management structure. Positive coping strategies were associated with lower levels of burnout, and training in coping methods may reduce burnout. In view of the high levels of burnout, there is an urgent need to improve working conditions in the NHS.

Chapter 359

THE ROLE OF ACHIEVEMENT AND SOCIAL STRATEGIES AND OF WORK-LIFE AREAS IN JOB BURNOUT

Hely Innanen[*], *Aino Juvakka and Katariina Salmela-Aro*
University of Jyväskylä, Finland

RESEARCH SUMMARY

The aim of this chapter is to examine the extent to which work-life related factors (workload, control, reward, community, fairness and values) and psychological characteristics (achievement and social strategies) simultaneously contribute to job burnout. Coping was operationalized as cognitive and behavioural efforts to handle external or internal demands that could exceed individual's resources. The participants were employees in four organizations: an information technology company, a hospital, a university, and a large service organization ($N = 1746$). The employees filled in the Strategy and Attribution (SAQ), Areas of Work-life Survey (AWLS) and Maslach Burnout Inventory (MBI) questionnaires. The results showed that the both work-life related factors and the strategy factors were related to the dimensions of job burnout: exhaustion, cynicism, and professional efficacy. Workload was the most significantly related to exhaustion, value conflicts to cynicism, and both control and reward to professional efficacy. The results showed further that scarcity of optimistic strategies was the most significantly related to exhaustion, avoidance and social pessimism to cynicism, and optimistic achievement strategies to professional efficacy. Finally, the results revealed that the work-life related factors were more strongly related than the strategy factors to the three dimensions of job burnout. However, the strategies acted as mediators in the relation between some of the work-life related factors and burnout.

---

[*] Hely Innanen, Aino Juvakka, and Katariina Salmela-Aro, Department of Psychology, University of Jyväskylä. For any correspondence, contact: Hely Innanen, The University of Jyväskylä, P.O. Box 35, 40014 Jyväskylä, Finland; e-mail:hely.innanen@jyu.fi.

Secondary Traumatization - Just Another Form of Burnout?

Judith Daniels
University of Bielefeld, Germany

Research Summary

During the past several years there has been a growing interest in the negative effects that therapy may have on therapists. Of special interest is a phenomenon called secondary traumatization, which can arise while working with traumatized clients. It comprises a set of typical trauma-related symptoms that appear in trauma survivors with posttraumatic stress disorder including hyperarousal (sleeping disturbances, edginess, and concentration problems), avoidance (avoiding reminders of the trauma as well as intense emotions) and intrusions (overwhelming recollections of the traumatic incident in the form of intrusive memories or nightmares). Over the course of the last several years, the construct of secondary traumatization (also named vicarious traumatization and compassion fatigue) has been gaining more and more empirical support. Recently published studies have investigated symptoms of posttraumatic stress disorder in populations as diverse as counselors, nurses, social workers and trauma therapists working with victims and criminal offenders. The authors have emphasized different aspects of the phenomenon, including or excluding changes in belief systems and symptoms referring to workplace behavior. Therefore, there is an ongoing discussion whether the construct should be construed as a form of burnout or a distinct, work-related phenomenon. This chapter will give an overview of current research in the field and discuss empirical and theoretical evidence concerning the differentiation of both constructs. A new instrument for the assessment of secondary traumatization will be introduced at the end of this chapter.

Chapter 361

EMOTIONAL OPENNESS AS A PROTECTIVE FACTOR AGAINST BURNOUT

Philippe A. Genoud and Michaël Reicherts*
University of Fribourg, Departement of Psychology, Fribourg, Switzerland

RESEARCH SUMMARY

A number of studies on burnout consider this syndrome to be an emotional resource deficit amongst individuals who are confronted with extreme demands. From a more general perspective, researchers have also examined the role of emotions and emotion processing ('emotional intelligence', 'emotion work' etc.) in protecting against burnout. The recent development of the model "Emotional openness" (Reicherts, 2007), with a multidimensional structure of affect processing (as represented by the individual), opens new perspectives on the relationship between emotion processing and burnout.This chapter will elaborate upon the relationship between the five dimensions of emotional openness and the three components of burnout, defined by Maslach & Jackson (1981) as emotional exhaustion, depersonalization and reduced personal accomplishment. Regression analyses based on a sample of 232 nurses and other health-care personnel (*e.g.* dieticians or physical therapists) show that emotional openness significantly predicts burnout. More specifically, Cognitive-conceptual representations of emotions, Communication and Regulation of emotions and the Perception of internal and external bodily indicators of emotions have differentiated associations with the components of burnout. The implications of these findings on the articulation of these two concepts not only allow a better understanding of emotion processing and its impact on the aetiology and persistence of the burnout syndrome, but could also be useful in the creation of intervention and prevention programs.

---

* philippe.genoud@unifr.ch.

In: Psychology Research Biographies and Summaries
Editors: Nancy E. Wodarth and Alexis P. Ferguson
ISBN: 978-1-61470-491-1
© 2012 Nova Science Publishers, Inc.

Chapter 362

INFLUENCE OF EMOTIONAL LABOR IN DEMANDING CLASSROOM SITUATIONS ON HEALTH AND WELL-BEING OF TEACHERS

Anja Philipp* and Heinz Schüpbach[+]
University of Freiburg, Department for Work- and Organizational Psychology, Freiburg, Germany

RESEARCH SUMMARY

A considerable number of teachers suffer from burnout. The way teachers cope with demands in their profession, especially with emotional demands in the classroom is an important factor influencing their health and well-being. This contribution focuses on the emotional labor of teachers facing interruptions in class and the consequences for health and well-being associated with the different strategies of emotional labor. Furthermore, a situation-specific perspective is taken and a first indication for a situation-specific use of the emotional labor strategies is presented.

---

* philipp@psychologie.uni-freiburg.de.
+ heinz.schuepbach@psychologie.uni-freiburg.de.

In: Psychology Research Biographies and Summaries
Editors: Nancy E. Wodarth and Alexis P. Ferguson
ISBN: 978-1-61470-491-1
© 2012 Nova Science Publishers, Inc.

Chapter 363

THE INFLUENCE OF SOCIAL COMPETENCE ON OCCUPATIONAL STRESS OF NURSING HOME STAFF CARING FOR DEMENTIA PATIENTS

J. Haberstroh[1], J. Franzmann[1,2], K. Krause[1,2] and J. Pantel[1]

[1]JWG-UniversityFrankfurt, Germany
[2]Technical University of Darmstadt, Germany

RESEARCH SUMMARY

Two thirds of nursing home residents in Germany suffer from dementia. Due to this fact, the study focuses particularly on problems associated with dementia care. These problems are major reasons for occupational stress in nursing home staff, a group at high risk for burnout syndrome. The study to be described will analyze the influence of social competence on occupational stress of nursing home staff caring for dementia patients. Thus, a theoretical model is designed and evaluated. The model is based on theories and empirical research on occupational stress in general and on specific theories and empirical research on occupational stress in nursing home staff. Furthermore, an intervention program is introduced that aims at increasing the social competence of professional caregivers who care for residents suffering from dementia. This program seeks to reduce the professional burden and occupational stress of caregivers while helping to increase the quality of life of residents suffering from dementia. The model designed provided the basis for the development of a training program. This program was implemented and evaluated in two controlled training studies using multiple control group designs and process measurement. Fifty-three nursing home professionals participated in the first study, being in daily contact with residents suffering from dementia; 33 nursing home professionals took part in the second study. Regarding both studies, the contents of the training programs focused on problems and strategies in communicating with dementia patients or colleagues, respectively. The evaluation of the training sessions confirms effects for all relevant variables. The "social competence" of caregivers increased and their "occupational stress" decreased while the "quality of life of residents suffering from dementia" increased. Furthermore, the results of multivariate time series analyses show that positive effects concerning the variables "occupational stress" and "quality of life" can be attributed to the increased "social competence" of the caregivers. Therefore, it can be concluded that training nursing home professionals in social competence is a method to indirectly reduce their work stress and support dementia patients. The results of this study underline the influence of social competence on occupational stress of nursing home staff and quality of life of residents suffering from dementia. It can be implied that the training program developed is an effective option to improve the situation of dementia care in nursing homes. To make the intervention widely applicable, it is important to develop efficient methods to multiply the contents of the skills training. In addition, the consolidated findings of this study should be used to extend theoretical research on social competence in dementia care in connection with occupational stress of nursing home staff.

In: Psychology Research Biographies and Summaries
Editors: Nancy E. Wodarth and Alexis P. Ferguson
ISBN: 978-1-61470-491-1
© 2012 Nova Science Publishers, Inc.

Chapter 364

FAMILY VIOLENCE THERAPISTS: PERSONAL AND SOCIAL RESOURCES, ROLE COMPETENCE, SECONDARY TRAUMATIZATION, AND BURNOUT

*Anat Ben-Porat and Haya Itzhaky**
Bar-Ilan University, Ramat-Gan, Israel

RESEARCH SUMMARY

The study examined the relationship between personal resources (self-esteem and mastery), social resources (social, colleague, and managerial support) and perceived role competence on the one hand, and secondary traumatization and burnout on the other among family violence therapists. The research population consisted of 143 social workers employed at family violence prevention centers and at battered women's shelters in Israel. The findings revealed that self-esteem, mastery, social support, and colleague support correlated negatively and significantly with secondary traumatization and the burnout. The findings further revealed that knowledge/ problem solving ability and influence, which are components of role competence, correlated negatively and significantly with secondary traumatization and burnout. Finally, managerial support did not correlate significantly with secondary traumatization and burnout. A high intercorrelation was found between secondary traumatization and burnout.

---

* Correspondence concerning this article should be addressed to: Haya Itzhaky, Ph.D., Full Professor and former Director of the School of Social Work, Bar-Ilan University, Ramat Gan 52900, Israel. Electronic mail may be sent to: itzhah@mail.biu.ac.il.

Chapter 365

RELATIONSHIP BETWEEN DESIRE FOR CONTROL AND JOB CONTROL AND THEIR EFFECTS ON JOB BURNOUT IN HEALTH-CARE PERSONNEL

Marcel Lourel[1]*, Farida Mouda[1], Maude Paltrier[2]
and Sandra Chevaleyre[1]

[1]Department of Psychology, University of Rouen, France
[2]Department of Psychology, University of Amiens, France

RESEARCH SUMMARY

There are many definitions of control. Here, we begin by defining the various kinds of control (locus/perceived control, job control, desire for control). Then we present the aim of the present study dealing with the effects of two variables on burnout (Maslach & Jackson, 1981, 1986): job control based on Karasek's (1979) job demand/control model, and desire for control, a concept first proposed in the theoretical model by Burger et al. (1992; Burger & Cooper, 1979). We investigated the desire for control (DC), job control (JC), and burnout in 108 health-care workers (mean age 41.14, sd 10.08). Desire for control was measured on the Burger and Cooper scale; the Karasek subscale was used to assess job control; burnout was rated on the Maslach and Jackson scale. The results of analyses of variance showed that high DC and low JC affected emotional exhaustion and depersonalization; low JC affected personal accomplishment. In conclusion, the difference between DC and JC, and their implications for medical staff and health-care organizations are discussed.

---

* Dr. Marcel Lourel, Department of Psychology, Laboratory Psy-NCA, Rue Lavoisier ; 76821 Mont Saint Aignan, France, E-mail: marcel.lourel@univ-rouen.fr .

In: Psychology Research Biographies and Summaries
Editors: Nancy E. Wodarth and Alexis P. Ferguson
ISBN: 978-1-61470-491-1
© 2012 Nova Science Publishers, Inc.

Chapter 366

DIMENSIONS OF TEACHER BURNOUT AND RELATIONS WITH PERCEIVED SCHOOL CONTEXT

Einar M. Skaalvik and Sidsel Skaalvik
Department of Education, Norwegian University of Science and Technology
Trondheim, Norway

RESEARCH SUMMARY

In this study the authors analyzed relations between teachers' perception of the school context and teacher burnout. Participants were 2249 teachers from 113 elementary schools and middle schools in five regions of Norway. Teacher burnout was measured with a modified version of the Maslach Burnout Inventory – Educators Survey measuring three dimensions of burnout: Emotional Exhaustion, Depersonalization, and Reduced Personal Accomplishment. A Perceived School Context Inventory measuring six dimensions of the school context was developed for the purpose of this study. The dimensions were: Discipline Problems, Time Pressure, Relation to Parents, Supervisory Support, Teacher Autonomy, and Collective Culture. SEM-analysis revealed that all six school context variables were predictive of teacher burnout, but the dimensions of burnout were differently predicted by the school context variables. Time pressure was the far strongest predictor of emotional exhaustion whereas relation to parents was the strongest predictor of depersonalization and reduced personal accomplishment.

Chapter 367

HOSPITAL PHARMACISTS' JOB STRESSES: MANAGERIAL RECOMMENDATION FOR PROFESSIONAL WORK HEALTH

Blossom Yen-Ju Lin[1]*, Ying-Chen Yeh[2] and Wen-Hung Lin[3]

[1]Institute of Health Service Administration, China Medical University,
Taichung, ROC, Taiwan
[2]Respiratory Therapy Division, Taichung Veterans General Hospital,
Taichung, Taiwan, ROC, Taiwan
[3]Taichung Hospital, Department of Health, Executive Yuan,
Taichung, Taiwan, ROC, Taiwan

RESEARCH SUMMARY

Pharmacist behavior studies are rare in the healthcare industry. Most of the identified researches reviewed in this study were conducted more than ten years ago. Few studies have led to hospital executives to lack concern over quality of occupational life of hospital pharmacists. This study aims to delineate the possible stress sources of hospital pharmacists and to understand how the demographics of hospital pharmacists are related to these possible stress sources. 247 hospital pharmacists responded to, by mail, the 44-item structured questionnaire covering six dimensions of stress in pharmacies: dispensing, work climates, consultation, management, hospital rules for the pharmacy, and healthcare industry environments. What was discovered is that the top-10 stress burdens applied to the areas of dispensing (accuracy, peer support, speed, and physical demands), pharmacy management (job complexity, academic publication requirements, and high labor turnover rate), and hospital rules (high frequency of changing drug brands, taking part in hospital activities, and equity of salary and fringe benefits). Further, hospital pharmacists' personal backgrounds, including gender, education, work experience, and their hospital accreditation status, were

---

* Corresponding author: Lin, Blossom Yen-Ju, Ph.D. Associate Professor, Institute of Health Service Administration, China Medical University, 91 Hsueh Shih Rd., Taichung, 404, Taiwan, ROC, Phone: 886-4-22053366 (Ext. 6308), Fax: 886-4-22076923, E-Mail: yenju1115@hotmail.com.

related to their job stress. Confronted with the aforementioned stressors, pharmacists need to appraise their significance and consider what resources and process designs could be used to help them cope with such stressors. The identified stress sources included in this developed survey could be applied in future research to gauge and recognize the effects of such stress on hospital pharmacists' work outcomes, including job satisfaction, quitting intentions, and personal health status. Finally, the managerial implications would be discussed further for the work health in pharmacist professionals.

Chapter 368

`MALE DEPRESSION´ IN MALE ADOLESCENTS: A GERMAN COMMUNITY STUDY

A. M. Möller-Leimkühler[*], J. Heller and N. C. Paulus
Department of Psychiatry, Ludwig Maximilians University of Munich, Germany

RESEARCH SUMMARY

Young males may hide their depressive symptoms including burnout by externalizing behaviour not considered in common depression inventories. This has been called 'male depression´. Although there is a large amount of clinical evidence, scientific evidence is still lacking. The present chapter refers to a study which has aimed at further validating the concept of male depression. A community sample of male adolescents aged 18 (n=1004) was asked to complete the WHO-5 Well-being Index (Bech 1998) and the Gotland Scale of Male Depression (Rutz 1999). Principal component analysis with promax rotation was calculated to analyze the dimensional structure of the Gotland Scale symptoms. Cluster center analyses were used to classify the sample according to the symptoms´ characteristics. General well-being was rather reduced, and 22% of the respondents were seen to be at risk of male depression. There was no evidence for the hypothesis that young males tend to mask their depressive symptoms with distress symptoms. Depressive and male distress symptoms appeared to be mixed in a dominant factor, while male distress symptoms constitute an additional minor factor. A cluster of 38% of those at risk for depression could be identified who reported significantly elevated male distress symptoms. Irritability turned out to be the single item of the Gotland Scale with the highest item-total correlation. Male distress symptoms should be considered when diagnosing depression in men. Further research is needed with respect to comorbidity and differential diagnoses, which should also include bipolar depression.

---

[*] Corresponding author: Priv.Doz. Dr.rer.soc. Anne Maria Möller-Leimkühler, Department of Psychiatry, Ludwig-Maximilians-University of Munich, Nußbaumstr. 7, D-80336 Munich, Germany, Tel: 0049 89 5160 5785, Fax: 0049 89 5160 5522, e-mail: Anne-Maria.Moeller-Leimkuehler@med.uni-muenchen.de.

In: Psychology Research Biographies and Summaries
Editors: Nancy E. Wodarth and Alexis P. Ferguson

ISBN: 978-1-61470-491-1
© 2012 Nova Science Publishers, Inc.

Chapter 369

PSYCHOLOGICAL ASPECTS OF BURNOUT AMONG STAFFS IN LONG-TERM CARE HOMES

Jin Narumoto[*]
Department of Psychiatry, Graduate School of Medical Science,
Kyoto Prefectural University of Medicine, Japan

RESEARCH SUMMARY

Aging society is now a worldwide problem. As the society becomes aged, need for long-term care homes for older adults increases rapidly. However, the staffs working in these homes have been reported to be extremely vulnerable to burnout compared to other professions because of the inherent characteristics of their work including lack of appreciation from the residents and recognition as a professional. Since burnout is related to their intention to continue their work and a quality of care, it is critical to investigate how to prevent them from burnout to maintain stable and sufficient stuffing, and a high quality of care. Among factors related to the burnout, psychological aspects of the staffs are focused in this chapter. Psychological factors including personality and coping style are known to affect perceived distress of environmental factors and are important in light of developing effective intervention. The author reviewed results and ideas from investigations of psychological predictors of the burnout among the staffs in long-term care homes and made some recommendations to prevent the burnout and suggestions for future research.

---

[*] Department of Psychiatry, Graduate School of Medical Science, Kyoto Prefectural University of Medicine, 465 Kajii-cho, Kawaramachi-Hirokoji, Kamigyo-ku, Kyoto 602-8566, Japan Tel.: +81-75-2515612; Fax: +81-75-2515839; E-mail: jnaru@koto.kpu-m.ac.jp.

Burnout Among French High-School Students

Sandra Zakari[1], Vera Walburg[2] and Henri Chabrol[1]
[1]Unité de Recherche Interdisciplinaire, Centre d'Etudes et de Recherche en Psychopathologie (CERPP), Université de Toulouse II – Le Mirail, France
[2]Université Paris XI, Villejuif, France

Research Summary

Several previous studies explored the burnout symptoms among working population. But little research is done concerning burnout in a high-school students population. That is why the aim of the two researches presented in this paper is to investigate this area. The first study explored burnout risk factors and the second study analyses the relationships between burnout and coping strategies and academic motivation.

Study 1: 252 high school students from sixth-form classes participated in this study by completing questionnaires measuring burnout, academic stress, depression and suicidal ideas. The results indicate that 47.6% had high burnout scores. Burnout seems to be essentially determined by school-related events, such as academic stress. Besides, burnout is strongly linked to depression but did not have a direct impact on suicidal ideas.

Study 2: 445 high-school students were involved in this survey; they completed a burnout and an academic motivation scale so as the Brief-Cope Inventory. The results show a strong positive relationship between a high burnout score and emotional coping, whereas active coping is linked to low burnout scores. In addition, a high burnout score predicts a low academic motivation. It can be inferred that signs of burnout occur among French high-school students similarly to those among adults in professional situations. Likewise, burnout at this age tends to have a negative impact on academic motivation and mental health.

In: Psychology Research Biographies and Summaries
Editors: Nancy E. Wodarth and Alexis P. Ferguson

ISBN: 978-1-61470-491-1
© 2012 Nova Science Publishers, Inc.

Chapter 371

THE CONTRIBUTION OF PERSONALITY TO POSITIVE PSYCHOLOGY

Ashley B. Love and Mark D. Holder[*]
University of British Columbia, Okanagan, Kelowna B.C., Canada

RESEARCH SUMMARY

Traditionally, psychology has adopted the medical model and focused on the diagnoses and treatments of illness and dysfunction. Recently, there has been a renewed interest in positive psychology, which emphasizes personal strengths and how they contribute to subjective well-being including happiness and life satisfaction. Personality theory and assessment have played important roles in positive psychology. One of the most consistent findings is that personality traits are among the strongest predictors of happiness and life satisfaction. For example, extraversion is an important positive correlate of happiness while neuroticism is an important negative correlate. The link between happiness and personality is so strong that researchers have argued that happiness can be viewed as a type of stable extraversion. The assessment of personality in positive psychology research has additional important roles. Assessing personality can provide insights into individual differences in the efficacy of programs designed to promote subjective well-being. Additionally, personality differences play a role in which strategies a person chooses to enhance their well-being and whether these strategies are effective. Furthermore, assessing personality allows researchers to estimate the predictive strength of different factors (e.g., spirituality and friendship quality) over and above the variance accounted for by personality traits. Researchers can then determine if the measurement of other factors is important, or if it is sufficient to focus on personality. Future research in positive psychology would benefit from a continued consideration of the role of personality. This consideration should include studying personality at the facet level (current work focuses largely at the broader trait level) and an examination of the subjective well-being of people with personality disorders. Individuals

---

[*] University of British Columbia, Okanagan, 3333 University Way, Kelowna B.C., Canada V1V 1V7, Email: mark.holder@ubc.ca, Phone: 250 807-8728.

with personality disorders account for a relatively high percentage of prison populations and, even if they are not incarcerated, they may be involved in other antisocial, high risk behaviours (e.g., extramarital affairs or excessive gambling). Unfortunately, individuals with personality disorders have proven resistant to treatment, often due to their lack of desire to adhere to a treatment plan. Examining the relation between personality disorders and subjective well-being may lead to the development of effective treatments by taking into account what contributes to the well-being of these individuals, increasing their motivation to comply with a course of treatment.

Chapter 372

STUDY OF MALE BODY IMAGE AND FACTORS IN THE DEVELOPMENT OF EATING DISORDERS IN FRATERNITY AND NON-FRATERNITY MALES

Kylee K. Ferris and F. Richard Ferraro[*]
University of North Dakota, Grand Forks, ND, US

RESEARCH SUMMARY

Issues of body image and eating disorders are more prevalent in women. However, there is a growing incidence of these issues in males. Unfortunately, even though men are suffering from body dissatisfaction and eating disorders, there have not been many studies conducted on these topics with men. Therefore, there may be men who are not being diagnosed because the risks factors for men are not as defined as they are for females. The purpose of this study is to investigate male risk factors. More specifically, this study is designed to determine if being a member of a fraternity during the individual's undergraduate career is a risk factor for body dissatisfaction, perfectionism and eating disorders. This specific dimension was chosen because there have been studies done to show that a female's participation in a sorority may place them at greater risk for developing an eating disorder and experiencing body dissatisfaction. In order to examine male attitudes, six measures were used in a survey and administered to both 97 undergraduate males in a fraternity and those who are not, at the University of North Dakota. Results indicated non-fraternity males had a higher drive for thinness and degree of perfectionism on the Eating Disorder Inventory-3 than fraternity males, indicating they are more at risk for developing an eating disorder. Fraternity males were more likely to report regular exercise compared to non-fraternity males. Non-fraternity males showed that they are at greater risk for experiencing obligatory exercise. This study

---

[*] Address all correspondence to :F. Richard Ferraro, Ph.D., Professor of Psychology, Chester Fritz Distinguished Professor, Director, General/Experimental Ph.D. Program, Fellow, National Academy of Neuropsychology, Dept. Psychology - University of North Dakota, Corwin-Larimore Rm. 215, 319 Harvard Street Stop 8380, Grand Forks, ND 58202-8380, 701-777-2414 (O), 701-777-3454 (FAX), f.ferraro@und.nodak.edu.

extends the literature on male eating disorders and the risk factors which apply to males. Further research is needed to understand other risk factors.

Efficacy at Fulfilling the Need for Closure: The Construct and Its Measurement

Yoram Bar-Tal[1] and Małgorzata Kossowska[2]
[1]Tel Aviv University, Israel
[2]Jagiellonian University, Poland

Research Summary

Since the introduction of the conceptualization and the scale of "The Need for Cognitive Closure" (NFC) by Kruglanski and Webster, it has generated a lot of research (for review see: Kruglanski, 1996; Webster & Kruglanski, 1994). According to Kruglanski, NFC predisposes individuals to freeze their epistemic process and thus to achieve greater certainty in their inferences. NFC has been found to foster the use of a large variety of cognitive and motivational biases. One of the basic assumptions behind the NFC is that epistemic freezing is the easier default option and that all people are capable of achieving cognitive closure if only the appropriate cognitive structure is available to them. Thus, NFC (and other similar concepts) has a relatively unique status in psychology as a source of motivation, in that it is assumed that cognitive closuring behavior can appear regardless of perceived or actual ability to carry it through. We however, maintain that the use of epistemic freezing depends not only on the person's needs but also upon his/her perceived ability to perform the freezing. In this chapter we introduce a new construct: the "Efficacy at Fulfilling the Need for Closure (EFNC). EFNC is defined as the extent to which individuals perceive themselves capable of using information processing methods which are consistent with their level of NFC. Thus, we maintain that EFNC moderates the effect of NFC on cognitive closure behavior. We also present three studies in which we describe the creation and validation of a scale to measure the new concept. Study 1 describes the scale's item generation and factor structure. Study 2 investigates the EFNC construct validity. Study 3 examines the EFNC scale's predictive validity. The results of the three studies demonstrate that the EFNC Scale measures a unitary construct, achieves good psychometric properties, correlates only with constructs representing ability to use a preferred epistemic process, and does not correlate with constructs representing epistemic motivation (NFC). Finally, the EFNC shows good predictive validity in that it moderates the effect of NFC on epistemic freezing.

Chapter 374

NARCISSISTIC AND BORDERLINE PERSONALITY TRAITS: THEIR RELATIONSHIP WITH CHILDHOOD ABUSE EXPERIENCES IN A STUDENT POPULATION IN JAPAN

Hiromi Igarashi, Chieko Hasui, Masayo Uji, Masahiro Shono, Toshiaki Nagata, Zi Chen and Toshinori Kitamura
Kumamoto University Graduate School of Medical Sciences, Kumamoto, Japan

RESEARCH SUMMARY

While the association between childhood adversity and borderline or narcissistic personality disorders was reported frequently, these two personality traits have rarely been studied in their links with early life abusive experiences at the same time. In a university student population (N = 368), the concepts of narcissistic personality trait (measured by the Narcissistic Personality Inventory) and borderline personality trait (measured by the Inventory of Personality Organization: IPO) were studied regarding their independence and their relationship with childhood abuse experiences (measured by the Child Abuse and Trauma Scale: CATS). These two personality concepts were found to be discrete, but Identity Diffusion (IPO subscale) and Desire for Admiration (IPO subscale) shared a covariance. Among the childhood abuse types, Neglect and Emotional Abuse, Sexual Maltreatment, and Authoritarianism contributed to borderline personality whereas low Authoritarianism contributed to narcissistic personality. Punishment and scolding did not contribute to borderline or narcissistic personality. Because punishment and scolding (physical abuse) shared substantial covariance with the other types of abuse types, the oft-reported link between physical abuse and adolescent development of personality disorder may be spurious.

In: Psychology Research Biographies and Summaries
Editors: Nancy E. Wodarth and Alexis P. Ferguson
ISBN: 978-1-61470-491-1
© 2012 Nova Science Publishers, Inc.

Chapter 375

THE IMAGINARY COMPANION EXPERIENCE IN ADULTS: ASSET, DISORDER OR PERSONALITY FEATURE?

Lino Faccini[*]
Long Island, New York, US

RESEARCH SUMMARY

Clinical and Forensic cases are reviewed regarding how an examiner should conceptualize the adult experience of having Imaginary Companions (IC). Some clinical and forensic research indicates that there is an overlap between adult IC and Dissociative experiences/disorders. However, other forensic case studies, a phenomenological perspective and expert opinion also indicates that the adult IC experience can occur in other clinical disorders, with personality disorders, and as the sole feature of one's clinical presentation. Also, research has identified that adult ICs can be linked to acts of violence, sex offending and self-harm. The diagnostic dilemma of how to conceptualize and diagnose these cases is most pertinent when ICs are involved and blamed for the commission of violent and criminal acts. Since the creation and dismissing of Adult ICs is a conscious and voluntary experience, the legal plea of Not Guilty by Reason of (Insanity) Mental Disease or Defect is not appropriate. Several different diagnostic possibilities are presented, consistent with DSM IV-TR. The Fantasy Prone Personality is also presented as another diagnostic classification possibility but with no current counterpart in the DSM IV-TR. The current gap in our knowledge in how to diagnose the presentation of ICs in adults, especially when they are involved in the commission of criminal acts should prompt more dialogue between clinicians, forensic examiners and researchers to develop a new diagnostic nomenclature.

---

[*] Lino Faccini[*] Ph.D., Consulting Psychologist, Long Island, New York, Hfaccini@aol.com.

In: Psychology Research Biographies and Summaries
Editors: Nancy E. Wodarth and Alexis P. Ferguson
ISBN: 978-1-61470-491-1
© 2012 Nova Science Publishers, Inc.

Chapter 376

How "To Be or Not To Be": The Answer is in Identity

Lino Faccini[*]
Long Island, New York, US

RESEARCH SUMMARY

According to the Merriam-Webster dictionary, "Identity" is defined as "the sameness of essential or generic character in different instances". Essentially, how a person views oneself, is different from his personality, namely the totality of the characteristics that make up that person. The importance of identity change in treatmenthas been identified for well over 40 years, however it continues to be limited in its application to clinical disorders or populations. The nature and importance of identity change will be highlighted, and the recommendation made that it be expanded to treat different offending patterns, and even dysfunctional patterns of "normal" individuals.

---

[*] Lino Faccini Ph.D, Consulting Psychologist, Long Island, New York, Hfaccini@aol.com.

In: Psychology Research Biographies and Summaries
Editors: Nancy E. Wodarth and Alexis P. Ferguson

ISBN: 978-1-61470-491-1
© 2012 Nova Science Publishers, Inc.

Chapter 377

IS DEVELOPMENTALLY INFORMED THERAPY FOR PERSONS WITH ID AND CRIMINAL PERSONALITY/OFFENSES RELEVANT?

Lino Faccini[*]
Long Island, New York, US

RESEARCH SUMMARY

Initially, the "Reconstructive Therapy" of Dr. Jerome Schulte, focused on the treatment of the homicidal psychotic patient. After decades of treatment applying this model with a variety of offenses, Dr. Schulte believed that it could be applied to understand and treat the "Criminal Personality", various offenses as well as treating non-clinical populations of children, adolescents and adults. The goal of therapy became one of promoting personal growth and humanness through the positive resolution of Ericksonian stages. The question remains if the successful resolution of Erickson's Psychosocial stages is relevant to the functioning of a Person with an Intellectual Disability, and Criminal Offenses? A theoretical and initial exploratory analysis suggests that the Reconstructive Therapy model can be relevant to the treatment for Persons with Intellectual Disabilities (ID) and various offenses.

---

[*] Lino Faccini Ph.D., Consulting Psychologist, Hfaccini@aol.com.

In: Psychology Research Biographies and Summaries
Editors: Nancy E. Wodarth and Alexis P. Ferguson
ISBN: 978-1-61470-491-1
© 2012 Nova Science Publishers, Inc.

Chapter 378

AGGREGATING PERSONALITY CONSTRUCTS TO SECOND-ORDER CATEGORIES FOR ACQUIRING INSIGHTS TO A FIELD OF FRAGMENTATION: THE CASE OF ENTREPRENEURSHIP RESEARCH

Joakim Wincent[*,1] *and Daniel Örtqvist*[†,2]

[1] Luleå University of Technology, Umeå School of Business, Luleå, Sweden
[2] Luleå University of Technology, Luleå, Sweden

RESEARCH SUMMARY

As markers of habitual patterns of behavior, thought, and emotion, personality constructs constitute important pieces for academic research across multiple domains (Kassin, 2003). The list of different traits is almost unlimited and despite that this literature is well received, this stream can be characterized as a rather fragmented domain of research. Moreover, despite the fact that much of the research shows promise, it is notable that some constructs, although often making sense and seeming reasonable to use, have difficulties at times reporting empirical results. In some extreme cases related to some very specific domains of scholarly study, the relevance of personality has even been questioned.

---

[*] Dr. Joakim Wincent, Luleå University of Technology, Umeå School of Business, joakim.wincent@ltu.se; joakim.wincent@usbe.umu.se.
[†] Dr. Daniel Örtqvist, Luleå University of Technology, daniel.ortqvist@ltu.se.

In: Psychology Research Biographies and Summaries
Editors: Nancy E. Wodarth and Alexis P. Ferguson

ISBN: 978-1-61470-491-1
© 2012 Nova Science Publishers, Inc.

Chapter 379

PERSONALITY TRAITS AND LAY CONCEPTIONS OF INTELLIGENCE[*]

Tomas Chamorro-Premuzic[†], Georgia Dissou, Adrian Furnham and Amber Bales
Department of Psychology, Goldsmiths, University of London, UK

RESEARCH SUMMARY

This study examined the relationship between lay conceptions of intelligence, personality traits, and subjectively-assessed intelligence (SAI). 160 (118 females) British and American University students completed the NEO-FFI and a 109 item lay conceptions of intelligence inventory. In addition, they estimated their scores on a number of different abilities (e.g., vocabulary, mathematical, verbal skills). Principal Components Analyses identified three major dimensions underlying people's conceptions of the nature of intelligence, which were labelled *academic IQ*, *social awareness* and *social intelligence*. All personality dimensions were significantly and positively correlated with social awareness, and negatively with academic IQ. Social intelligence was significantly correlated with Extraversion, Openness, and Agreeableness (all positively), whilst academic IQ was significantly correlated with Extraversion, Openness, Agreeableness and Conscientiousness (all negatively). Results are discussed in terms of the theoretical conceptualization of the relationship of established personality traits with both lay conceptions and self-assessed intelligence.

---

[*] A version of this chapter was also published in Advances in Psychology Research, Volume 60, edited by Alexandra M. Columbus published by Nova Science Publishers, Inc. It was submitted for appropriate modifications in an effort to encourage wider dissemination of research.

[†] Correspondence concerning this paper should be addressed to Tomas Chamorro-Premuzic, Department of Psychology, University of Bath, BATH, BA2 7AY, UK. E-mail: t.chamorro-premuzic@bath.ac.uk.

In: Psychology Research Biographies and Summaries
Editors: Nancy E. Wodarth and Alexis P. Ferguson

ISBN: 978-1-61470-491-1
© 2012 Nova Science Publishers, Inc.

Chapter 380

PERSONALITY TRAITS AND DAILY MOODS[*]

Cristina Ottaviani[1], David Shapiro[2,†], Iris Goldstein[2] and Valerie Gofman[2]

[1]Department of Psychology, University of Bologna, Italy
[2]Department of Psychiatry, University of California, Los Angeles, US

RESEARCH SUMMARY

Previous research has shown that personality traits and emotional states are associated with variations in blood pressure. The major aim of this chapter was to examine the relationship between personality traits and diary reports of moods on a work and an off work day. Secondary aims were to compare mood reports in men and women as a function of the day of recording. A healthy sample of 110 women and 110 men rated their moods in a diary three times an hour on a work and a nonwork day. Personality scales were administered. Significant effects of mood intensity were obtained for work vs. off day and in interaction with scores on personality tests of anxiety, anger out, cynical hostility, and depression. Given the health significance of emotion in mental and physical health, these findings in healthy individuals suggest that personality traits may affect the regulation of blood pressure via their effects on emotional responses to daily life events and thereby serve as risk factors for hypertension.

---

[*] A version of this chapter was also published in Advances in Psychology Research, Volume 66, edited by Alexandra M. Columbus published by Nova Science Publishers, Inc. It was submitted for appropriate modifications in an effort to encourage wider dissemination of research.
[†] Corresponding author: David Shapiro, Department of Psychiatry, 760 Westwood Plaza, Los Angeles, CA 90095, USA, e-mail: dshapiro@ucla.edu.

Chapter 381

ADDICTION: FRONTAL PERSONALITY CHANGE BUT NOT PERSONALITY DISORDER COMORBIDITY IMPLICATIONS FOR TREATMENT OF ADDICTIVE DISORDERS

Eduardo J. Pedrero-Pérez[1], *Ana López-Durán*[2]
and Alvaro Olivar-Arroyo[3]

[1] Instituto de Adicciones, Ayuntamiento de Madrid, Madrid, Spain
[2] Universidad de Santiago de Compostela, Spain
[3] Consejería de Educación. Comunidad de Madrid, Spain

RESEARCH SUMMARY

A high prevalence of co-occurrence among addictive disorders and personality disorders has been documented. Studies have usually found between a 50 and 75 percent of addicted individuals with Axis II concurrent diagnosis. However, such diagnoses often do not take account of several changes related to the course of addiction that affect functioning of the frontal lobe and, consequently, the overall programming of behaviour. Simple diagnosis based on the ICD or DSM classifications, without regard to etiological factors, is just a still photograph reflecting a fractal of a long development process altered by addiction. Impairment of frontal cortical function due to direct effects of the substance or to mediators as stress factors, are the basis of most of the symptoms justifying the diagnosis of personality disorders. Miller's proposals on stable and induced-by-stress disorders, as well as new findings on executive dysfunction linked to addiction must be taken into consideration. Personality disorders, so understood, should be treated differently from the present, including cognitive stimulation techniques and attending to stress and coping, preventing symptomatic prescribing of drugs with dubious benefits and multiple side effects. New neurological and neuropsychological perspectives of addiction do not support concepts such as comorbidity as a priority intervention guide.

In: Psychology Research Biographies and Summaries ISBN: 978-1-61470-491-1
Editors: Nancy E. Wodarth and Alexis P. Ferguson © 2012 Nova Science Publishers, Inc.

Chapter 382

CIRCADIAN PREFERENCE AND PERSONALITY: A MINIREVIEW

Lorenzo Tonetti[*]
Department of Psychology, University of Bologna, Bologna, Italy

RESEARCH SUMMARY

The aim of this chapter is to update the status of the art of the relationship between morningness-eveningness preference and personality. To this end, keeping in mind the wide number of personality models available in literature, this chapter discusses three of them: 1) Eysenck's model; 2) Big Five model; 3) Cloninger's model. On the basis of main data reported in papers, it is suggested that future studies should focus on the Cloninger's psychobiological model of personality because it takes into account both biological (temperament dimensions) and socio-cultural (character dimensions) aspects, being thus useful to address their respective importance linking circadian rhythms with personality characteristics. To this aim, cross-cultural comparisons are specifically needed. Implications of this chapter in several applied areas are also discussed.

---

[*] Corresponding author: Department of Psychology, Viale Berti Pichat 5, 40127 Bologna – Italy, Phone: +39-051-2091877, Fax: +39-051-243086, Email: lorenzo.tonetti2@unibo.it.

In: Psychology Research Biographies and Summaries
Editors: Nancy E. Wodarth and Alexis P. Ferguson

ISBN: 978-1-61470-491-1
© 2012 Nova Science Publishers, Inc.

Chapter 383

THE IMAGINARY COMPANION EXPERIENCE IN ADULTS: ASSET, DISORDER OR PERSONALITY FEATURE?

Lino Faccini
Consulting Psychologist, Long Island, NY, US

RESEARCH SUMMARY

Clinical and Forensic cases are reviewed regarding how an examiner should conceptualize the adult experience of having Imaginary Companions (IC). Some clinical and forensic research indicates that there is an overlap between adult IC and Dissociative experiences/disorders. However, other forensic case studies, a phenomenological perspective and expert opinion also indicate that the adult IC experience can occur in other clinical disorders, with personality disorders, and as the sole feature of one's clinical presentation. Also, research has identified that adult ICs can be linked to acts of violence, sex offending and self-harm. The diagnostic dilemma of how to conceptualize and diagnose these cases is most pertinent when ICs are involved and blamed for the commission of violent and criminal acts. Since the creation and dismissing of Adult ICs is a conscious and voluntary experience, the legal plea of Not Guilty by Reason of (Insanity) Mental Disease or Defect is not appropriate. Several different diagnostic possibilities are presented, consistent with DSM IV-TR. The Fantasy Prone Personality is also presented as another diagnostic classification possibility but with no current counterpart in the DSM IV-TR. The current gap in our knowledge in how to diagnose the presentation of ICs in adults, especially when they are involved in the commission of criminal acts should prompt more dialogue between clinicians, forensic examiners and researchers to develop a new diagnostic nomenclature.

The creation of Imaginary Companions (IC) that persist into adulthood can influence one's adult functioning and lead to clinical disorders and even forensic consequences. Currently, there exists a gap in our diagnostic nomenclature in how to regard, and diagnose the existence of ICs in the forensic evaluation. Cases were reviewed from the clinical and forensic literature regarding how to conceptualize the adult IC experience. A number of studies suggest an over-lap between the adult IC experience and dissociative and other clinical disorders. However, other studies, a phenomenological perspective and expert opinion describes them as different phenomena. Cases involving IC involvement and acts of violence will also be presented, and the difficulties of how to diagnose these cases is highlighted and suggestions are offered, including the Fantasy Prone Personality (Disorder). Although the Fantasy-Prone Personality is not regarded as a valid diagnostic category according to DSM IV-TR, the focus of this article is to highlight the current ambiguity in how to regard the adult IC phenomena, the personality type who continues to possess one into adulthood, and to suggest the Fantasy Prone Personality as one possible diagnostic alternative as well as other diagnostic options.

Chapter 384

SCHIZOTYPAL PERSONALITY TRAITS: AUDITORY HALLUCINATION-LIKE EXPERIENCES AND ATYPICAL HEMISPHERIC LATERALIZATION

Tomohisa Asai[*], Eriko Sugimori and YoshihikoTanno
Department of Cognitive and Behavioral Science,
Graduate School of Arts and Sciences, The University of Tokyo, Japan

RESEARCH SUMMARY

Individual differences in schizotypal personality traits (schizotypy), which might be the predisposition to schizophrenia, have commonly been explored as a means of examining the nature and structure of schizophrenia symptoms. Research on schizotypal personality in the general population may provide a particular opportunity to study the biological and cognitive markers of vulnerability to schizophrenia without the confounding effects of long-term hospitalization, medication, and severe psychotic symptoms (Raine & Lencz, 1995).

A systematic review of general-population surveys indicated that the experiences associated with schizophrenia and related categories, such as paranoid delusional thinking and auditory hallucinations, are observed in an attenuated form in 5–8% of healthy people (Os et al., 2009). These attenuated expressions could be regarded as the behavioral marker of an underlying risk for schizophrenia and related disorders, just as high blood pressure indicates high susceptibility for cardiovascular disease in a dose–response fashion (Os & Kapur, 2009).

Auditory hallucination (AH) refers to the perception that one's own inner speech originates outside the self. Patients with AH make external misattributions of the source of perceived speech. Recent studies have suggested that auditory hallucinations in patients with schizophrenia might occur in the right hemisphere, where they might produce irregular and unpredicted inner speech, which their auditory and sensory feedback processing system does not attribute to themselves.

---

[*] Corresponding author: Department of Cognitive and Behavioral Science, Graduate School of Arts and Sciences, University of Tokyo, 3-8-1 Komaba, Meguro-ku, Tokyo 153-8902, JAPAN. Tel: +81-3-5454-6259 Fax: +81-3-5454-6979 as@beck.c.u-tokyo.ac.jp.

In the present study, general participants judged self–other attribution in speech subjectively in response to on-line auditory feedback presented through their right, left, and both ears. People with high auditory-hallucination-like experiences made external misattributions more frequently under the right- and left-ear only conditions compared with the both-ears condition. We interpreted this result as suggesting that people with a high degree of proneness to AH might have disorders in both the right and left hemispheric language-related areas: speech perception deficit in the left hemisphere and prediction violation in speech processing in the right hemisphere.

A perspective that situates schizophrenia on a continuum with general personality variations implies that this disorder constitutes a potential risk for everyone and, thus, helps to promote understanding and correct misunderstandings that contribute to prejudice.

GENETICS OF PERSONALITITY DISORDERS

Gonzalo Haro[1], Ernesto Tarragón[2], César Mateu[3], Ana Benito[3] and Cecilio Álamo[5]

[1]Patología Dual Grave. Hospital Provincial de Castellón. Comunidad Valenciana, España
[2]Departamento de Psicobiología. Universidad Jaume I de Castellón, España
[3]Grupo TXP de Investigación. Comunidad Valenciana, España
[4]Catedrático de Farmacología. Comunidad de Madrid, España

RESEARCH SUMMARY

Talking about addiction genetics and its most common comorbid disorders, Personality Disorders (PD), one of the concepts that first should be clarified is the importance of the studies logic chronology on psychiatric genetics. Thus, it should be noted that for molecular genetic techniques to be justified in any study, a substantial role of genetics in the etiology of this disorder has to be demonstrated first by epidemiological data. Genetic epidemiological studies which here is referred to are mainly three: family, twin and adoption studies. So, if these studies do not raise doubts about whether or not one disorder is inherited, it is better to focus on the environmental causes and drop molecular studies determined to "grab" some related gene. Once the genetic implication has been demonstrated in some disorder's etiology, it is time to mathematical and molecular genetic studies. By means of these studies, detecting which gene or combination of genes causes the disorder is a matter of try. This is not easy, though, considering that only 2% of the 3 billion base pairs of DNA are genes.

Once in the field of molecular genetics, difficulties manifest. The first genes isolated and characterized are either Mendelian or monogenic characters, hereditary diseases or somatic malignancies mostly, in which there is a major gene involved. The Mendelian scheme fulfills the "one gene / one disease" rule. Thus, one single-locus mutations cause one specific disease, e.g. sickle cell anemia, cystic fibrosis, phenylketonuria and Huntington's disease. Non-Mendelian characters either depend on a small number of loci (oligogenic characters) or gene plots (polygenes), with each of them showing a small effect with an environmental factor varied contribution. All these possibilities are included within the term multifactorial character.

However, unlike one might suspect, monogenic characters are not exempt of complexity. Many of them either have "reduced penetrance", meaning that not all individuals with the conferring disease genotype develop it; "variable expression", meaning that there is a huge variability on disease's severity; or "pleiotropy", when the gene has more than a single appreciable effect on the body. On the other hand, different genes may promote a single phenotype in different families. In this case is called "genetic" or "locus heterogeneity". Even more, different mutations in the same gene can cause distinguishable clinical diseases. Hence, there is an enormous genetic complexity, even through simple Mendelian characters, which are only governed by one gene. This suggests that there is a few purely Mendelian biological characters, and that may be extend to purely polygenic also.

Studies on the role of genetic factors in biopsychosocial diseases in humans have to confront many problems. Among them, the polygenic and multifactorial nature of inheritance stands out by itself, so that multiple genes and environmental factors interact in each subject in very different ways and degrees.

In: Psychology Research Biographies and Summaries ISBN: 978-1-61470-491-1
Editors: Nancy E. Wodarth and Alexis P. Ferguson © 2012 Nova Science Publishers, Inc.

Chapter 386

STRUCTURAL AND FUNCTIONAL NEUROIMAGING STUDIES OF THE ANXIETY-RELATED PERSONALITY TRAIT: IMPLICATIONS FOR THE NEUROBIOLOGICAL BASIS OF HUMAN ANXIOUS PERSONALITY

Yuko Hakamata[1,2] *and Toshiya Inada*[3]*
[1]Department of Clinical Psychology, The University of Tokyo,
Graduate School of Education, Tokyo, Japan
[2]The Japan Society for the Promotion of Science, Tokyo, Japan
[3]Seiwa Hospital, Institute of Neuropsychiatry, Tokyo, Japan

RESEARCH SUMMARY

Personality is a specific pattern of individual behavioral, emotional, and thought processesthatremain relatively stable throughout life. The pattern that is characterized by ready elicitation and maintenance of a high anxiety level is referred to as the "anxious personality". Although many researchers have proposed theoretical models of the anxious personality trait, the most influential have been "Neuroticism (vs. Emotional Stability)" developed by Eysenck (1967), the "Behavioral Inhibition System" developed byGray (1972), "Neuroticism" developed by Costa and McCrae(1985), and "Harm Avoidance" developed by Cloninger (1986).

Research on personality can be originally traced back to the "personality trait theory", which attempted to account for human personality as several measurable "traits" (Allport 1936, Cattell 1943, Fiske 1949). Such studies have been based on factorial analysis in which many adjectival termswere adopted to describe individual behavioral, emotional, or thoughtcharacteristics,and converged into several fundamental components (i.e. traits). Although researchers in this field have not reached a consensus on the number of such personality traits, they have commonly found that one of themis closely related to an

---

* Corresponding author: Vice President, Seiwa Hospital, Institute of Neuropsychiatry, Benten-cho 91, Shinjuku-ku, Tokyo 162-0851, Japan, Tel+81-3-3260-9171, Fax+81-3-3235-0961, E mailhan91010@rio.odn.ne.jp.

increased level of anxiety. In an attempt to settle this lingering controversy over the number of traits by proposing that human personality consists of five basic ones, mostly derivedfrom systematic factorial analysis, Costa and McCrae (1985)adopted the term "Neuroticism" for that related to anxiety. They considered that individuals with a high Neuroticism (N) score tend to exhibit worry, nervousness, emotionality, insecurity, inadequacy, or hypochondria.[1]

The original adoption of N can be seen in "Neuroticism (vs. Emotional Stability)" proposed by Eysenck (1967). Showing considerable similarity to N, this Neuroticism is associated with anxiety, depression, tension, feelingsof guilt, low self-esteem, lack of autonomy, moodiness, hypochondria, and obsession. However, Eysenck's theory was of distinct importance in the history of personality research because it specificallymentioned the biological basis of personality, whereas most traditional studies based on factorial analysis had made every endeavor to derive a minimum number of traitscapable of describing human personality.[2] As with the anxiety-related personality trait, he explained that individual differences in Neuroticism are based on activation thresholds in the sympathetic nervous system or visceral brain, which is also referred to as the limbic system, including the amygdala, hippocampus, septum, and hypothalamus(Eysenck, 1990).

Subsequent to Eysenck's model (Eysenck, 1967), Gray (1976, 1981) attempted to integrate it into his two basic theoretical dimensions: the "Behavioral Inhibition System" and the "Behavioral Activation System". As Eysenck assumed that an individual with high Neuroticism accompanied by strong Introversion would be much more likely to manifest anxiety symptoms(Eysenck 1969), he simply clarified that such an individual would have a highly sensitive or reactive Behavioral Inhibition System (BIS) (Gray 1981). The BIS is a system activated by warnings of punishment or non-reward, novel stimuli, and innate fear stimuli as inputs, thereby triggering behavioral inhibition, increased arousal, and increased attention as outputs. This means that strong susceptibilityto the BIS is associated with increased anxiety. In addition, he assumed the BIS to have a biological basis in the septo-hippocampal system, pointing out the similarity between the behavioral effects of hippocampal lesions and those of anxiolytic drugs. However, instead of this system, the amygdala is now considered to play a central role in the BIS (Gray and McNaughton, 2000), since its critical involvement in both fear and anxiety has become widely recognized(LeDoux 1994).

In contrast to the ideas of Eysenck and Gray, whose workcreated a rough map of the biological basis of an anxiety-related personality, Cloninger tried to determine the neurophysiological properties responsible for it. Based on various findings from studies in the fields of neuroscience, genetics, and biochemistry, he advocated that an anxiety-related temperament[3], "Harm Avoidance", is basically regulated by the serotonin neurotransmitters that are richly distributed in the hypothalamus, basal ganglia, and raphe nuclei(Cloninger

---

[1] Additionally, this trait is composed of 6 sub-facets: Anxiety, Hostility, Depression, Self-consciousness, Impulsiveness, and Vulnerability.

[2] In Eysenck's model, human personality is assumed to consist of 3 dimensions: "Neuroticism (vs Emotional Stability)", "Extraversion (vs Introversion)", and "Psychoticism". In 1967, he proposed that behavioral differences between individuals with high extraversion (extraverts) and individuals with high introversion (introverts) occur from innate drive to compensate for overactive and underactive reticulo-thalamo-cortical pathways (Eysenck, 1967).

[3] The term "temperament" has been historically defined as an individual difference particularly in emotional responses associated with physiological reactivity such as occurs in the autonomic or endocrine system and is assumed to have some neurobiological basis (Strelau, 1995).

1986).Harm Avoidance (HA) is a tendency characterized by behavioral inhibition such as pessimistic worry in anticipation of future problems, passive avoidance behavior such as fear of uncertainty and shyness of strangers, and rapid fatigability(Cloninger, Svrakic and Przybeck 1993). This theoretical hypothesis was supported by a subsequent genetic study by Lesch, Heils and Riederer (1996),which found that HA is significantly associated with the serotonin-related gene polymorphism regulating expression of the serotonin transporter gene (5HTTLPR), thus accelerating further investigation of the biological correlates of HA. HA, N developed by Costa and McCrae (1985), Neuroticism developed by Eysenck (1967), and BIS developed by Gray (1976) are similar to one another, and all reflect individual differences in the behavioral inhibition associated with increased anxiety (Morgan 2006). Because of these similarities, scientists have frequently used these anxiety-related personality traits in an attempt to elucidate the biological basis of anxious personality. To date, a significant relationship between an anxiety-related personality trait and specific genetic variation (i.e. 5HTTLPR) has been repeatedly confirmed(Munafò et al. 2009, Sen, Burmeister and Ghosh 2004, Schinka, Busch and Robichaux-Keene 2004, Munafò, Clark and Flint 2005).

Despite the accumulation of findings pertaining to genetic correlates, the neural basis of an anxiety-related personality trait (i.e. brain regions and circuits) has not been extensively investigated. Although several neuroimaging studies have so far examined relationshipsbetween the anxiety-related personality trait and brain structures or activities, no study has attempted to integrate the findings in a meaningful way.Since the anxiety-related personality trait has become widely recognized as one of the representative predisposing factors for mood and anxiety disorders (Clark, Watson and Mineka 1994), an understanding of its neurobiological basis is very much needed for clarifying the etiology of mood and anxiety disorders and for establishing better methods of intervention or prevention.

In this chapter, to derive a picture of the neurobiological basis of the anxious personality, we will first take a detailed look at the findings of structural and functional neuroimaging studies of the anxiety-related personality trait in healthy individuals. With regard to functional neuroimaging modalities such as positron emission tomography (PET) and functional magnetic resonance imaging (fMRI), we specifically focus on studies that have examined brain activitiesin a resting state, as such activities have been examined relatively extensively. We then attempt to identify brain regions and possible neural networks considered to play an important role in the anxiety-related personality trait, not only by summarizing the above-mentioned findings but also by referring to fMRI studies during the processing of cognitive or emotional tasks. Lastly, we discuss the functional aspectsthat may contribute to anxious personality via such brain regions or networks.

In: Psychology Research Biographies and Summaries ISBN: 978-1-61470-491-1
Editors: Nancy E. Wodarth and Alexis P. Ferguson © 2012 Nova Science Publishers, Inc.

Chapter 387

TOO MUCH OF A GOOD THING?: OPTIMISTIC OR PESSIMISTIC PERSONALITY TRAITS

Francine Conway and Laura Kelly
Adelphi University, Derner Institute of AdvancedPsychological Studies,
Garden City, NY, US

RESEARCH SUMMARY

The 'mind-body connection' has become a new buzz phrase that has served a variety of purposes including validating the practice of clinical psychology amongst the medical professionals.The results from a myriad of studies within this century have provided empirical evidence for the relations between the mind and body.Central to this connection are personality differences in one's world view, specifically optimistic versus pessimistic dispositions.Featured prominently in this body of literature is the beneficial role of optimism in physical health outcomes.More careful examination of the relations between optimism and health has begun to differentiate between the benefits associated with physical health and those circumscribed to psychological health.Researchers have made several additional distinctions regarding research on optimism: some studies have elaborated on whether the relations between optimism and health are linear or curvilinear and others have highlighted the differences between optimism and pessimism.

Since personality differences account for the variation of emotional experiences from one person to the next, it shapes how one regulates their emotional experiences which in turn influence health (Brickman, Coates, & Janoff-Bulman, 1978). Emotion regulation, as defined by Gross (1998) is the process by which people influence the emotions they have and how they experience and express these emotions. These processes can be automatic or controlled and conscious or unconscious (Gross, 1998).These emotion processes are largely influenced by individual differences in personality. Personality differences in dispositional factors such as optimism have attracted the interest of researchers as well as lay persons.The culture is littered with the pursuit of happiness and ways of training oneself to adopt a more optimistic view of life.Spurring the discussion has been the synchronicity between optimism and the very human condition to desire pleasurable emotional experiences and perhaps equally strongly shun painful ones. This chapter examines the optimism discourse occurring in the spheres of both empirical research and popular culture. We introduce a different perspective on the matter that is influenced by a parallel discourse which has not yet become a part of the lexicon of optimism although the evidence already exists, that of balance achieved through mindfulness.

Chapter 388

ILLNESS RECOGNITION AND BELIEFS ABOUT TREATMENT FOR SCHIZOPHRENIA IN A COMMUNITY SAMPLE OF MEXICO CITY: DIFFERENCES ACCORDING TO PERSONALITY TRAITS

Ana Fresán[1], and Rebeca Robles-García[2]*

[1]Subdirección de Investigaciones Clínicas. Instituto Nacional de Psiquiatría Ramón de la Fuente, Mexico City, Mexico

[2]Dirección de Investigaciones Epidemiológicas y Sociales. Instituto Nacional de Psiquiatría Ramón de la Fuente, Mexico City, Mexico

RESEARCH SUMMARY

Previous studies have detected different variables influencing the attitude towards individuals with schizophrenia. It has been considered that individual's knowledge about schizophrenia has an important role in shaping attitudes about people diagnosed with the disorder, and that a lack of knowledge may increase prejudice and discrimination of these individuals. However, additional factors related to particular characteristics of the *perceiver*, such as personality traits, may have a direct influence in the recognition of schizophrenia as a mental disease and the subsequent attitudes related to the disorder.

Objective: To assess temperament and character features, based on Cloninger's biosocial model of personality, relating people's recognition and beliefs about schizophrenia. We also examined personality differences according to the subjects' belief about the most adequate treatment for symptoms.

Method: A case vignette describing a patient with paranoid schizophrenia was used to assess subjects' recognition of the disorder and their belief about treatment options.

---

* Corresponding author: Subdirección de Investigaciones Clínicas. Instituto Nacional de Psiquiatría Ramón de la Fuente, Mexico City, Mexico., Calz. México-Xochimilco No 101. Tlalpan, Mexico City, 14370, MEXICO., Tel: (5255) 41 60 50 69, Fax: (5255) 55 13 37 22, E-mail: a_fresan@yahoo.com.mx; fresan@imp.edu.mx.

Personality traits were assessed using the Temperament and Character Inventory-Revised (TCI-R). A total of 203 subjects who recognized symptoms as part of a mental disorder and 203 age-gender-and educational level-matched subjects who didn't recognize mental illness were included.

Results: A greater number of subjects recognizing mental illness considered psychiatric intervention – the use of medication and hospitalization – as the adequate treatment for the symptoms described in the vignette. Also, they exhibited higher scores in the temperament dimension "Persistence". When personality traits were compared in terms of the belief about the most adequate treatment, subjects who considered non-psychiatric, non-restrictive interventions – such as talking – had higher "Reward Dependence" and "Cooperativeness" scores independently of their status in the recognition of mental illness.

Conclusions: Our results support the notion that individual differences may have a direct influence in the recognition and management of mental disorders, in particular schizophrenia, among the general population. Although additional studies are required, these results may have important implications for anti-stigma campaigns for schizophrenia, as it is possible that part of the knowledge, attitudes and behaviors related to stigmatization are deeply rooted in the subject's personality and may require an additional or different management in these campaigns.

Chapter 389

PERSONALITY TRAITS: REFLECTIONS IN THE BRAIN

Feryal Cam Celikel
Associate Professor of Psychiatry
Gaziosmanpasa University School of Medicine, Tokat, Turkey

RESEARCH SUMMARY

New research suggests that the structure of human brain predicts core qualities of the individual's personality. One specific model of personality, developed by Cloninger, was based upon an association of specific personality traits to an underlying neurobiology. This seven-factor model consists of four dimensions of temperament (harm avoidance, novelty seeking, reward dependence, persistence) and three dimensions of character (self-directedness, cooperativeness, self-transcendence). Each dimension represents a specific stimulus-response sensitivity, the particular modes of behavior that resulted, and the specific neurotransmitters involved. Four dimensions of temperament are thought to be genetically independent traits and are moderately inheritable and stable throughout life. Novelty seeking is thought to be derived by the behavioral activation system. Harm avoidance is related to the behavioral inhibition system. It reflects the tendency of an individual to inhibit or interrupt behaviors. Reward dependence refers to the individual's tendency to respond intensely to signals of reward, and it involves maintaining or continuing behaviors that have been previously associated with reinforcement. Persistence is the individual's ability to generate and maintain arousal and motivation internally, in the absence of immediate external reward. It reflects perseverance in behavior despite frustration, fatigue, and lack of reward. In this model, neurotransmitters were hypothesized to be associated with behavioral manifestations: dopamine for novelty seeking (behavioral activation), serotonin for harm avoidance (behavioral inhibition), and noradrenaline for reward dependence (behavioral maintenance). Character reflects individual differences in self-concepts about goals and values in relation to experience. It is predominantly determined by socialization. Temperament provokes perception and emotion, character regulates the cognitive processes. Thus, character leads to the development of a mature self-concept. The three dimensions of character develop over the course of time, and influence personal and social effectiveness into adulthood. Self-directedness expresses individual's competence toward autonomy, reliability, and maturity. Cooperativeness is related to social skills, such as support, collaboration, and partnership. Self-transcendence refers to identification with a unity of all things in the world and it reflects a tendency toward spirituality and idealism. Findings suggest that an association exists between personality dimensions, neurotransmitters' function and regional brain metabolism. As morphometric studies have stated, regional variance in the neuronal volume of specific brain structures seem to underpin the observed range of individual differences in personality traits. In this chapter, I will particularly focus on recent work at the molecular genetic and functional imaging level with respect to specific personality traits.

In: Psychology Research Biographies and Summaries
Editors: Nancy E. Wodarth and Alexis P. Ferguson
ISBN: 978-1-61470-491-1
© 2012 Nova Science Publishers, Inc.

Chapter 390

THE CAREGIVERS OF PERSONS WITH ALZHEIMER'S DISEASE: THE IMPACT OF PERSONALITY TRAITS ON OWN STRESS PERCEPTION AND IN EVALUATING COGNITIVE AND FUNCTIONAL IMPAIRMENT OF THEIR RELATIVES

Marco Vista, Lucia Picchi[*] and Monica Mazzoni

Alzheimer Diagnostic Unit, Section of Neurology, Campo di Marte Hospital, Lucca, Italy;
*Section of Neurology, Versilia Hospital, Lido di Camaiore, Italy

RESEARCH SUMMARY

Alzheimer's disease (AD) is a degenerative pathology of the brain, causing dementia. Caregivers of persons with AD (ADcg) have to cope with cognitive impairment, behavioral symptoms and incompetence in daily living and they experience heavy burden. Besides, ADcg are the most important referent for physicians in reporting information about patients with AD (ADp), because ADp show lack of awareness of their changes. The aims of our research were to examine the relationship between specific personality traits of ADcg and perceived stress; moreover, to highlight the caregivers' capacity to be "objective" in evaluating functional abilities of ADp. In the first study, 118 ADcg were assessed using Caregiver Burden Inventory (CBI) and 16 Personality Factors- C form questionnaires (16PF-C). In the second study, 40 ADp and their caregivers were assessed in order to measure awareness using the Deficit Identification Questionnaire (DIQ); ADcg were also administered 16PF-C. Data from the first sample show that Reasoning (B), Emotional Stability (C) and Rule-Consciousness (G) were more strongly associated with caregiver burden; each indicator seems to be significant, to a different extent, for objective, developmental, physical, social and emotional burden. Caregivers characterized by emotional unstability, unable to stand

---
[*] Corresponding author: Marco Vista, MD, m.vista@usl2.toscana.it.

frustration, high self-demanding and with difficulty in self abstracting from concrete problem solving are going to perceive higher distress in caregiving ADp. In the second research, 26 of 40 ADp showed unawareness of their deficits, while 11 ADp were enough aware of their difficulties and only 3 ADp overvalued their impairment: the majority of ADp were unaware of their cognitive impairment and functional deficits in activities of daily living and overestimated their abilities compared to ADcg perception. ADcg DIQ correlated with four 16PF-C factors: Dominance (E), Liveliness (F), Social Boldness (H) and Privateness (N). This indicate an influence of personality on ADcg judgment: in fact, traits of personality such as being deeply involved in evaluating cognitive impairment and functional deficits, ability to perceive problems in daily living, especially for those aspects that could make them feel inadequate in social situations and that engage them emotionally, could influence ADcg judgment about their relatives. In conclusion, focusing on specific personality traits, which are predictive of caregivers' burden, might be helpful in planning psychological approach aimed to improve caregivers' quality of life. In order to evaluate functional abilities of ADp, even detailed scales of awareness provided by ADcg seem not to be objective means to assess ADp functional state, because they are influenced by ADcg personality.

Chapter 391

COMMUNICATING EMPATHIES IN INTERPERSONAL RELATIONSHIPS

Grace Anderson[*] *and Howard Giles*
Department of Communication
University of California, Santa Barbara, California 93106, US

RESEARCH SUMMARY

Empathy is a concept that has been widely researched across the social sciences and, more importantly, is commonly used outside of academe as a method "to open-up the channel of communication with the other" (Wikipedia, 2006). Although commonly employed colloquially, empathy is challenging to define explicitly and, hence, we shall need to begin this chapter with some conceptual wood-clearing. Prior definitions reflect the specific contexts in which empathy was measured and studied. For instance, a study measuring empathy as a response to media defines empathy differently than a study that examines empathy as an interpersonal communication construct – and these definitions are not mutually exclusive or disparate. Instead, different definitions are a result of the various dimensions of empathy that researchers choose to highlight as a function of the particular empirical study's focus. For this reason, many individuals may find empathy easier to enact than to describe its meaning in words.

This chapter will examine the major definitional variations of empathy that have developed in research on interpersonal relationships, comparing and contrasting their implications. For instance, one major difference is whether empathy is a stable trait or a changing state; this definitional difference can lead to very different methods of research. We seek to accomplish a more global definition of empathy by discussing the distinct ways in which it has been examined in the past, such as in terms of communicative competence, personal distress, and nonverbal expressions, and incorporating the many dimensions of empathy into a unified source of reference for future research. In so doing, we will discuss

---

[*] Contact: Grace L. Anderson. Department of Communication, University of California, Santa Barbara, Santa Barbara, CA 93106-4020, USA. gracea@umail.ucsb.edu; Fax: 805-893-7102.

how one individual may feel and express empathy and how that empathy may or may not be perceived as such by its recipients. The psychological origins of empathy will be identified and questions regarding motives underlying empathy will be raised, including whether it can be used as a form of impression management during social interactions.

Empathy has been recognized as an important component of health communication. Research has shown that an empathic person holds more positive attitudes towards healthy behaviors regarding smoking and alcohol consumption (Kalliopuska, 1992). Moreover, an effective health campaign will evoke empathy among its target audience because it evokes greater cognitive and affective processing of the campaign message (Campbell & Babrow, 2004). Empathic communication with people with disabilities (particularly those inflicted by cancer) will be a continuous example used to help us understand the multidimensional implications of empathic communication. Empathy can ease tensions that may occur during this form of interaction and suggestions of appropriate empathic communication will be offered. Finally, a new communication model of the *process* of empathy will be introduced.

Chapter 392

INTERPERSONAL REPRESENTATIONS: THEIR STRUCTURE, CONTENT, AND NATURE

Shanhong Luo[*]
Department of Psychology, University of North Carolina at Wilmington,
North Carolina, US

RESEARCH SUMMARY

How people represent their interpersonal relationships based on past experiences has great impact on their subsequent interactions with others. This chapter reviews previous theories and presents new propositions regarding three important aspects of interpersonal representations (IRs)—their structure, content, and nature. Specifically, the structure of IRs can be viewed as a three-level hierarchical organization, with *general representations* at the highest level, *domain-specific* representations at the midlevel, and *relationship-specific* representations at the lowest level. The content of IRs can be divided into three distinct yet interrelated components: *self representations*, *other representations*, and *relationship representations*. With regard to the nature, IRs can be conceptualized as consisting of *accurate perceptions*, *systematic biases*, and *random errors*.

---

[*] Correspondence should be sent to Shanhong Luo, Department of Psychology, Social Behavioral Science Building, University of North Carolina at Wilmington, Wilmington, NC, 28403. Email: luos@uncw.edu.

In: Psychology Research Biographies and Summaries
Editors: Nancy E. Wodarth and Alexis P. Ferguson
ISBN: 978-1-61470-491-1
© 2012 Nova Science Publishers, Inc.

Chapter 393

GENERALIZED ANXIETY DISORDER AND INTERPERSONAL RELATIONSHIPS: THE CASE FOR A SYSTEMIC INTERVENTION

Danielle Black,[1] Amanda Uliaszek,[2] Alison Lewis[2] and Richard Zinbarg[1]
[1]The Family Institute at Northwestern University, Evanston, Illinois, US
[2]Northwestern University, Evanston, Illinois, US

RESEARCH SUMMARY

Generalized anxiety disorder (GAD), one of the more common anxiety disorders, is associated with significant impairment in occupational, interpersonal and family functioning. There is growing consensus that we need to improve the effectiveness of our treatments for GAD given that even the most positive findings suggest that only 50% of patients treated with cognitive-behavior therapy (CBT) and/or medications experience what might be considered to be a cure. Whereas established treatments for GAD are individual modalities, there is evidence from several lines of research suggesting current treatments for that systemic therapy has promise to augment the effectiveness of therapy for GAD. These lines of research include (a) evidence that elevated marital dissatisfaction is associated with GAD; (b) evidence that marital and family problems are associated with other anxiety disorders including panic disorder with agoraphobia and obsessive compulsive disorder and are associated with poor outcome in the treatment of these other anxiety disorders; (c) evidence that marital and family problems are associated with major depression - another psychiatric condition closely related to GAD – and poor outcome in the treatment of major depression; (d) preliminary evidence that marital functioning and interpersonal problems predict outcome in the treatment of GAD; and (e) evidence that at least some forms of couples therapy are effective treatments for major depression and panic disorder with agoraphobia.

In: Psychology Research Biographies and Summaries
Editors: Nancy E. Wodarth and Alexis P. Ferguson
ISBN: 978-1-61470-491-1
© 2012 Nova Science Publishers, Inc.

Chapter 394

ANOTHER KIND OF "INTERPERSONAL" RELATIONSHIP: HUMANS, COMPANION ANIMALS, AND ATTACHMENT THEORY

Jeffrey D. Green[1], Maureen A. Mathews[1] and Craig A. Foster[2]
[1]Virginia Commonwealth University, US
[2]United States Air Force Academy, US

RESEARCH SUMMARY

Human-companion animal relationships provide a important but largely unexplored component of the human experience. Research examining these interspecies relationships may elucidate the depth and meaning of these relationships as well as provide unique insights into the fundamental nature of human psychology. Human-animal relationships offer a distinctive testing ground because pet choice is unilateral, whereas human friendships and romantic partner choices are mutual, and individuals may have reduced fear of rejection or evaluation from a pet than from a human relationship partner. We review and apply to human-pet relationships key elements of attachment theory, including caregiving, exploration, the malleability of attachment styles, and the role of attachment anxiety and avoidance in choosing relationship partners. We also discuss potential future research directions using relationships theories in companion animal contexts.

In: Psychology Research Biographies and Summaries
Editors: Nancy E. Wodarth and Alexis P. Ferguson

ISBN: 978-1-61470-491-1
© 2012 Nova Science Publishers, Inc.

Chapter 395

THE ROLE OF OXYTOCIN IN THE PATHOPHYSIOLOGY OF ATTACHMENT

Marazziti Donatella[1,*], Catena Dell'Osso Mari[2], Consoli Giorgio[1] and Baroni Stefano[1]

[1] Dipartimento di Psichiatria, Neurobiologia,
Farmacologia e Biotecnologie,
University of Pisa, Italy

[2] Dipartimento di Psicologia,
University of Florence, Italy

RESEARCH SUMMARY

Oxytocin is a nonapeptide synthesized in the paraventricular and supraoptic nuclei of the hypothalamus. Although OT-like substances are present in all vertebrates, oxytocin has been identified only in mammals where it seems to be fundamental in the onset of typical mammalian behaviors, including labour and lactation. In the present chapter, the physiological role of oxytocin in the regulation of different functions and behaviors will be addressed: several data, mainly coming from animal models, have highlighted the role of this neuropeptide in the formation of caregiver-infant attachment, pair-bonding and, more generally, in linking social signals with cognition, behaviours and reward. In addition, recent evidences have demonstrated alterations of oxytocin system in several human neuropsychiatric disorders, leading to the hypothesis of a possible involvement of oxytocin in the onset of mental disorders. In this frame, the psychopathological implication of the disregulation of the oxytocin system and the possible use of oxytocin or its analogues and/or antagonists in the treatment of psychiatric disorders will be discussed.

---

[*] Author to whom correspondence and reprint requests should be sent: Dr. Donatella Marazziti. Dipartimento di Psichiatria, Neurobiologia, Farmacologia e Biotecnologie, University of Pisa, via Roma, 67, I-56100 Pisa, Italy; Telephone: +39 050 835412; Fax: +39 050 21581; E-mail address: dmarazzi@psico.med.unipi.it.

Chapter 396

IDENTITY EXPLORATION AND COMMITMENT ASSOCIATIONS WITH GENDER DIFFERENCES IN EMERGING ADULTS' ROMANTIC RELATIONSHIP INTIMACY

H. Durell Johnson[*], Kristen A. Loff, George Bell, Evelyn Brady, Erin A. Grogan, Elizabeth Yale, Robert J. Foley and Trishia A. Pilosi
Pennsylvania State University, Pennsylvania, US

RESEARCH SUMMARY

Emerging adulthood is considered a time when intimacy becomes an integral aspect of romantic relationships, and Arnett (2000) argues intimacy in emerging adults' romantic relationships results from identity explorations. Previous research, however, suggests emerging adults' romantic intimacy is associated not only with identity exploration, but also with identity commitments and gender. In an attempt to examine the theorized relationships among identity exploration, identity commitment, gender, and perceived romantic intimacy, the current study examined identity and romantic intimacy responses from a sample of 271 emerging adults (183 females, mean age = 19.22 years; and 88 males (mean age = 19.29 years). Findings indicated 1) both identity exploration and commitment predict emerging adults' romantic relationship intimacy, 2) gender differences in romantic relationships differ according to emerging adults' identity status, and 3) identity status differences in romantic relationship intimacy differs for emerging adult males and females. The current study's test of Arnett's (2000) hypothesis regarding identity exploration and romantic relationship intimacy development did not fully support his theorized association. Rather, findings suggest differences in emerging adults' romantic intimacy are associated with their gender and

---

[*] Correspondence concerning this article should be addressed to H. Durell Johnson, Human Development and Family Studies, Pennsylvania State University, 120 Ridge View Drive, Dunmore, PA 18512-1699, Phone: 570-963-2672, Fax: 570-963-2535, E-mail: hdj2@psu.edu.

identity commitments as well as identity exploration. As a result, Arnett's (2000) proposal that identity exploration during emerging adulthood is a necessary precursor for intimate romantic relationships may not completely describe the association between identity and intimacy that emerges during this period, and this association may be more complex than originally theorized. Results are discussed in terms of understanding the moderating association of gender on identity exploration and commitment differences in emerging adults' reports of romantic relationship intimacy.

Chapter 397

DEVELOPMENT OF AN INTERVIEW FOR ASSESSING RELATIONSHIP QUALITY: PRELIMINARY SUPPORT FOR RELIABILITY, CONVERGENT AND DIVERGENT VALIDITY, AND INCREMENTAL UTILITY

Erika Lawrence[1], Robin A. Barry[1], Rebecca L. Brock[1], Amie Langer[1], Eunyoe Ro[1], Mali Bunde[2], Emily Fazio[3], Lorin Mulryan[4], Sara Hunt[5], Lisa Madsen[6] and Sandra Dzankovic[7]

[1] University of Iowa, Iowa City, Iowa, US
[2] CIGNA Behavioral Health Care, Minnesota, US
[3] University of Denver, Denver, Colorado, US
[4] University of Loyola, Chicago, Illinois, US
[5] Utah State University, Logan, Utah, US
[6] Emory University, Atlanta, Georgia, US
[7] Des Moines University, Des Moines, Iowa, US

RESEARCH SUMAMRY

Historically, relationship satisfaction and adjustment have been the target outcome variables for almost all couple research and therapies. In contrast, far less attention have been paid to the assessment of relationship quality. In the first section of our paper, we review the long-standing debate regarding – and clarify the distinctions among – relationship adjustment, satisfaction, and quality. We also discuss the need for an empirically-supported, psychometrically strong measure of relationship quality. In the second section, we present the Relationship Quality Interview (RQI), a semi-structured, behaviorally anchored, individual interview that yields objectively coded ratings from the interviews. It was designed to assess relationship quality across five dimensions: (a) trust, closeness, and emotional intimacy; (b) inter-partner support; (c) quality of the sexual relationship; (c) respect, power, and control;

and (e) communication and conflict management. In the third section, we provide preliminary evidence of the reliability and validity of the interview. Across two samples, the RQI demonstrated strong reliability (internal consistency, inter-rater agreement, agreement across interviewers based on two members of the same couple, correlations among the scales) convergent validity (correlations between RQI scales and self-report questionnaires assessing similar relationship dimensions), and divergent validity (correlations between RQI scales and behavioral observations of related constructs, global measures of marital satisfaction, and individual difference measures of related constructs). We conclude with a brief discussion of broader clinical issues relevant to couple assessment and prevention efforts.

Chapter 398

ASSESSING RELATIONSHIP QUALITY: DEVELOPMENT OF AN INTERVIEW AND IMPLICATIONS FOR COUPLE ASSESSMENT AND INTERVENTION

Erika Lawrence[1], Rebecca L. Brock[1], Robin A. Barry[1], Amie Langer[1] and Mali Bunde[2]

[1] University of Iowa, Iowa City, Iowa, US
[2] CIGNA Health Solutions, Eden Prairie, Minnesota, US

RESEARCH SUMMARY

Historically, relationship satisfaction and adjustment have been the target outcome variables for almost all couple research and therapies. In contrast, far less attention has been paid to the assessment of relationship quality. In the first section of our paper, we review the long-standing debate regarding -- and clarify the distinctions among -- relationship adjustment, satisfaction, and quality. We also discuss the need for an empirically-supported, psychometrically strong measure of relationship quality. In the second section, we discuss the multidimensional nature of relationship quality, and review prior research relevant to each dimension. We also introduce the Relationship Quality Interview (RQI), a semi-structured, behaviorally anchored, individual interview that yields objectively coded ratings. The RQI was designed to assess relationship quality across five dimensions: (a) trust, closeness, and emotional intimacy; (b) inter-partner support; (c) quality of the sexual relationship; (c) respect, power, and control; and (e) communication and conflict management. In the third section, we provide preliminary evidence of the reliability and validity of the interview. Across samples of dating and married couples, we examined reliability, convergent and divergent validity, and incremental validity of the RQI. In the fourth section, we discuss broader clinical issues relevant to couple assessment and intervention efforts.

In: Psychology Research Biographies and Summaries
Editors: Nancy E. Wodarth and Alexis P. Ferguson
ISBN: 978-1-61470-491-1
© 2012 Nova Science Publishers, Inc.

Chapter 399

THE TENDENCY TO FORGIVE IN PREMARITAL COUPLES: RECIPROCATING THE PARTNER OR REPRODUCING PARENTAL DISPOSITIONS?

F. Giorgia Paleari[1], Silvia Donato[2], Raffaella Iafrate[2] and Camillo Regalia[2]

[1] University of Bergamo, Italy
[2] Catholic University of Milan, Italy

RESEARCH SUMMARY

Although the tendency to forgive the partner has been shown to enhance personal and relational well-being, little is known about how this tendency originates. One possibility is that the tendency to forgive the partner develops as a function of the forgiveness exchanges people experience within their romantic relationships, thereby leading them to become more and more similar to the partner in their proneness to forgive. Another possible explanation is that social experiences people were exposed to within their own family of origin has led them to gradually internalize parental models and to become more and more similar to their parents in their willingness to forgive. These associations may be particularly evident during emerging adulthood, when engaged couples have to balance their family heritage and the forming of their new couple.

The present work aimed at providing initial evidence in support of these hypotheses by investigating in a sample of premarital couples (N=165) and their parents the extent to which young adults' tendency to forgive the partner was similar to the partner's tendency to forgive them as well as to their mothers' and fathers' tendency to forgive one another. Dyads were the units of analysis and stereotype accuracy was controlled. Results indicate that young adults' disposition to forgive the partner is similar to that of their partner and of their parents. Gender moderated these associations, as females were more similar to their parents than were males in their disposition to forgive.

The findings are consistent with the idea that premarital couples, even though strongly involved in defining their own couple identity, are nonetheless affected by the forgiveness models to which they are exposed within their family of origin.

In: Psychology Research Biographies and Summaries
Editors: Nancy E. Wodarth and Alexis P. Ferguson

ISBN: 978-1-61470-491-1
© 2012 Nova Science Publishers, Inc.

Chapter 400

IS THE SEROTONERGIC SYSTEM ALTERED IN ROMANTIC LOVE? A LITERATURE REVIEW AND RESEARCH SUGGESTIONS

Sandra J. E. Langeslag[*]

Erasmus Affective Neuroscience Lab, Institute of Psychology,
Erasmus University Rotterdam, The Netherlands

RESEARCH SUMMARY

Infatuated individuals think about their beloved a lot. The notions that these frequent thoughts resemble the obsessions of obsessive-compulsive disorder (OCD) patients and that those patients benefit from serotonin reuptake inhibitors (SSRIs), have led to the hypothesis that romantic love is associated with reduced central serotonin levels. In this chapter, the literature on this topic is reviewed and suggestions for future research are made. Previous studies have shown that romantic love is associated with lower blood serotonin levels and with lower serotonin transporter densities, the latter of which has also been observed in OCD patients. Further, SSRIs have been found to decrease feelings of romantic love and the serotonin 2 receptor gene has been associated with the love trait 'mania', which is a possessive and dependent form of love. Given that serotonin 2 receptors in the prefrontal cortex have also been implicated in impulsive aggression, this suggests that stalking behavior may be associated with these receptors. In short, the serotonergic system appears to be altered in romantic love indeed. Future research is needed to identify what parts of the serotonergic system, such as which serotonergic projections, brain areas, transmission stages and receptor types, are affected in romantic love and in what way they are altered. Furthermore, challenging the serotonergic system would be useful in determining the causal relationship between central serotonin levels and feelings of romantic love. In addition, future research

---

[*] Corresponding author: S. Langeslag. Institute of Psychology, Woudestein, T12-45, P.O. Box 1738, NL-3000 DR Rotterdam, The Netherlands. Email address: langeslag@fsw.eur.nl; Tel: +31 (0)10 408 2663; Fax: +31 (0)10 408 9009.

should specifically investigate the different aspects of romantic love, such as state, trait, requited and unrequited love and its development in time.

In: Psychology Research Biographies and Summaries
Editors: Nancy E. Wodarth and Alexis P. Ferguson
ISBN: 978-1-61470-491-1
© 2012 Nova Science Publishers, Inc.

Chapter 401

UPDATE ON PHEROMONE RESEARCH

Donatella Marazziti[*]*, Irene Masala, Stefano Baroni,
Michela Picchetti, Antonello Veltri and Mario Catena Dell'Osso*
Dipartimento di Psichiatria, Neurobiologia, Farmacologia e Biotecnologie,
University of Pisa, Pisa, Italy

RESEARCH SUMMARY

Pheromones are volatile compounds secreted into the environment (in sweat, urine) by one individual of a species and perceived by another individual of the same species, in which they trigger a behavioral response or physiological change. Besides insects, pheromones have been described in several invertebrate and vertebrate animals; moreover, they have been shown to modulate mating preferences, timing of weaning, learning ability to distinguish poisoning from not-poisoning food, social recognition and level of stress.

Several studies suggest that pheromones might play an important role also in mammals, as it has been demonstrated that they can use chemical signals for mate attraction, territorial marking, dominance and probably other functions yet to be identified, amongst which, perhaps, some social behaviors.

In humans, several studies have indicated that pheromones may influence reproductive endocrinology and have a positive effect on mood. Menstrual synchrony amongst women sharing the same environment is a long-recognized phenomenon related to pheromones produced in the armpits; these substances are not perceived as having any particolar odour, but nonetheless can influence the lenght of the mestrual cycle through the interference with different hormones. The aim of the present paper is to review the latest data on pheromones with a specific focus on humans and future developments.

---

[*] Author to whom correspondence and reprint requests should be sent: Dr. Donatella Marazziti. Dipartimento di Psichiatria, Neurobiologia, Farmacologia e Biotecnologie, University of Pisa, via Roma, 67, 56100 Pisa, Italy. Telephone: +39 050 835412; Fax: +39 050 21581; E-mail address: dmarazzi@psico.med.unipi.it.

NORMAL AND OBSESSIONAL JEALOUSY: AN ITALIAN STUDY

Donatella Marazziti[*], Marina Carlini, Francesca Golia, Stefano Baroni, Giorgio Consoli and Mario Catena Dell'Osso
Dipartimento di Psichiatria, Neurobiologia, Farmacologia e Biotecnologie, University of Pisa, Italy

RESEARCH SUMMARY

Background: Jealousy is a complex emotion spanning from normality to pathology. The present study aimed to define the boundaries between normal and obsessional jealousy by utilizing a specific self-report questionnaire.

Methods: The so-called "Questionnaire of Affective Relationships (QAR)" was administered to 400 university students of both sexes, as well as to 14 outpatients affected by obsessive-compulsive disorder (OCD). The total scores and the responses to each of the 30 items were analyzed and compared.

Results: Two hundred and forty-five (approximately 61 %) of the questionnaires given to the students were returned. Statistical analyses revealed that the OCD patients had higher total scores than the healthy students. Moreover, we were able to identify an intermediate group of subjects, consisting of 10 % of the total, who exhibited thoughts of jealousy regarding their partner, but to a lesser degree than the OCD patients. These were labeled as "healthy jealous subjects" because no other psychopathological trait could be observed. In addition, significant intergroup differences in single items were observed.

Conclusion: The present study showed that in our population of university students, 10 % of the subjects, although normal, had excessive jealous thoughts regarding their partner. In fact, we could clearly distinguish these subjects from the OCD patients and from the healthy

---

[*] Author to whom correspondence and reprint request are to be sent: Dr. Donatella Marazziti. Dipartimento di Psichiatria, Neurobiologia, Farmacologia e Biotecnologie, University of Pisa, via Roma, 67, I-56100 Pisa, Italy. Telephone: +39 050 835412; Fax: +39 050 21581. E-mail address: dmarazzi@psico.med.unipi.it.

subjects with no jealousy concerns by means of the specific questionnaire developed by us. Probably, they represent a subgroup of jealous, albeit normal, subjects.

Chapter 403

JEALOUSY, SEROTONIN AND SUBTHRESHOLD PSYCHOPATHOLOGY

Donatella Marazziti[*], *Francesca Golia, Marina Carlini, Stefano Baroni, Irene Masala, Mario Catena Dell'Osso and Giorgio Consoli*

Dipartimento di Psichiatria, Neurobiologia, Farmacologia e Biotecnologie,
University of Pisa, Italy

RESEARCH SUMMARY

Background: Different studies have suggested that some neurotransmitters may play a role in the expression of jealousy. In our study, we utilized the specific binding of ^{3}H-paroxetine (^{3}H-Par) as a peripheral tool to explore the serotonergic system in platelets of healthy subjects with and without jealousy concerns.

Methods: Twenty-one subjects with thoughts of jealousy and 21 subjects without jealousy concerns, as revealed by their score at a specific questionnaire ("Questionnaire of Affective Relationships", QAR), were included in our study. Subjects in the first group were administered a battery of self-report instruments designed to detect the presence of subthreshold psychopathology. The binding of ^{3}H-Par was carried according to a standardized protocol.

Results: The results showed a reduced density of ^{3}H-Par binding in the "jealous" subjects, as compared with the "non-jealous" subjects. In addition, most of the subjects of the first group had one or moresubthreshold psychopathological conditions.

Conclusion: We concluded that jealousy may be considered an expression of subtle forms of psychopathology, and may provoke an alteration of the serotonergic system, as reflected by the lower density of the platelet serotonin transporter.

---

[*] Author to whom correspondence and reprint request are to be sent: Dr. Donatella Marazziti. Dipartimento di Psichiatria, Neurobiologia, Farmacologia e Biotecnologie, University of Pisa, via Roma, 67, I-56100 Pisa, Italy. Telephone: +39 050 835412; Fax: +39 050 21581. E-mail address: dmarazzi@psico.med.unipi.it.

ADVANCES IN DYADIC AND SOCIAL NETWORK ANALYSES FOR LONGITUDINAL DATA: DEVELOPMENTAL IMPLICATIONS AND APPLICATIONS

William J. Burk[1], Danielle Popp[2] and Brett Laursen[2]

[1]Leiden University, The Netherlands
[2]Florida Atlantic University, Boca Raton, Florida, US

RESEARCH SUMMARY

Interdependence, a central feature of close relationships, presents contemporary scholars with theoretical and statistical challenges. Dyadic and social network analytic techniques have recently been formulated that offer several advantages over previous statistical methods by accounting for various forms of interdependence for longitudinal data collected from both relationship partners. We describe two of these methods: the Actor-Partner Interdependence Model (APIM: Kenny, Kashy, & Cook, 2006) and actor-based models of network-behavioral dynamics (Snijders, Steglich, & Schweinberger, 2007). The APIM partitions variance into estimates of behavioral stability of both dyad members (actor effects), and interpersonal influence (partner effects), while adjusting for initial behavioral similarity between partners. The actor-based models describe dyadic relationships as embedded within a multitude of interconnected dyadic relationships (i.e., social networks). These dynamic models utilize computer simulations to partition variance into parameters that ascribe similarity based on network, dyadic and individual behavioral attributes. To illustrate the applicability of both methods, we describe empirical examples from our recent work using these models techniques.

In: Psychology Research Biographies and Summaries
Editors: Nancy E. Wodarth and Alexis P. Ferguson
ISBN: 978-1-61470-491-1
© 2012 Nova Science Publishers, Inc.

Chapter 405

MOTHER-INFANT INTERACTION IN CULTURAL CONTEXT: A STUDY OF NICARAGUAN AND ITALIAN FAMILIES

Ughetta Moscardino, Sabrina Bonichini and Cristina Valduga
Department of Developmental and Social Psychology,
University of Padua, Italy

RESEARCH SUMMARY

Although a common goal for parents is to promote their children's successful development in a respective society, there is considerable cross-cultural variation in the beliefs parents hold about children, families, and themselves as parents. Previous research suggests that in traditional rural areas across the world, parents highly appreciate interrelatedness in their conceptions of relationships and competence, whereas in urban settings of Western industrialized societies, parents seem to promote independent parent–child relationships from early on. The main purpose of this study is to compare conceptions of parenting and mother-infant interactions in two cultural contexts that may be expected to hold different beliefs about parent-child relationships: Nicaraguan farmer families and middle-class Italian families. Fifty-six mothers from central Nicaragua (n = 26) and northern Italy (n = 30) and their infants aged 0-14 months participated in the study. Mothers were interviewed regarding their childrearing beliefs and behaviors, and were videotaped interacting with their infants during a free play session. Maternal responses were qualitatively analyzed using a thematic approach; maternal behaviors were coded into one of the following categories: social play, object play, motor stimulation, verbal stimulation, and face-to-face interaction. Findings indicated that: 1) Nicaraguan mothers emphasized interdependence and connectedness to other people in their socialization goals, whereas Italian mothers placed greater focus on childrearing strategies consistent with a more individualistic orientation; 2) Nicaraguan mothers exhibited a higher overall frequency of behaviors related to motor stimulation and face-to-face interaction, whereas Italian mothers were more likely to engage in social play, object play, and to emit a greater overall number of verbal behaviors towards their infants during the free-play session. Our results suggest that parents' conceptions of childcare reflect culturally regulated norms and customs that are instantiated in parental behavior and contribute to the structuring of parent-child interactions from the earliest months of life, thus shaping developmental pathways of infants and children. Implications for theory on the psychology of relationships as well as for clinical practice are discussed.

"IT'S SATURDAY…I'M GOING OUT WITH MY FRIENDS": SPENDING TIME TOGETHER IN ADOLESCENT STORIES

Emanuela Rabaglietti and Silvia Ciairano[1]
Department of Psychology, University of Torino, Italy

RESEARCH SUMMARY

During adolescence, peer relationships and friendships are relevant contexts for cognitive and social development [Bukowski, Newcomb and Hartup, 1996] and for future adult adjustment [Hartup and Stevens, 1999]. We also know that people, and particularly adolescents, by way of narration and autobiographic construction, can define and attribute meaning to their self and their relationships with others. Bruner and colleagues [Amsterdam and Bruner, 2000; Bruner, 2002] pointed out that individuals construct stories to attribute meaning and order to daily life events. By narrating one's own story it is possible to organise episodic memory, to shape the recollection of events, and to build reality [Smorti and Pagnucci, 2003]. Specifically in friendship relationships, narrative autobiographic experiences represent specific interpretative modalities used by adolescents to give meaning to the self and the others within these relationships.

In this study, which is based on adolescent narrations, we explored adolescent leisure-time behaviour in the company of friends, specifically on Saturday afternoons. We were also interested in identifying the self markers [Bruner, 1986; 1997], by which adolescents perceive themselves and others, and attribute meaning to their own experiences. Finally, we would like to investigate the relationship between the Self markers and some indicators of well-being (e.g. positive self-perception and expectations of success), social self-efficacy, adulthood (e.g. value of autonomy), and discomfort (e.g. feelings and sense of alienation).

Participants included thirty adolescents (11 girls and 19 boys) aged 14 to 20 years (M= 15.8; D.S.= 1.4) attending two different types of high school (43% lyceum, 57% technical and

---

[1] emanuela.rabaglietti@unito.it.

vocational) in the northwest of Italy. The adolescents were asked to write a essay on the subject: "It's Saturday...I'm going out with my friends".

We analysed the essays using thematic analysis of content as well as Bruner's [1986; 1997] system of self markers. The following profiles summarise our findings. Most of the adolescents go out on Saturday and they have fun, talk, share convivial activities and sometimes also illegal activities (particularly boys) with their friends. Adolescents use frequently especially the Self markers of Agency (97%), Commitment (87%), Coherence (80%) and Social references (83%). Girls use the subjective aspects of Self markers, such as Qualia and Evaluation on the bases of expectations, more frequently than boys. Older adolescents use Agency and Resources more frequently than younger adolescents. Finally, Resources and Evaluation are related to positive self-perception and Social references is linked to Social self efficacy. This study has some limitations, such as the limited number of participants and the specificity of the essay, which make it impossible to generalise these findings to adolescent social life. Nevertheless, the findings can contribute to a better understanding of the meaning that peers and friends assume in adolescence.

In: Psychology Research Biographies and Summaries
Editors: Nancy E. Wodarth and Alexis P. Ferguson
ISBN: 978-1-61470-491-1
© 2012 Nova Science Publishers, Inc.

Chapter 407

PREVENTION OF THE NEGATIVE EFFECTS OF MARITAL CONFLICT: A CHILD-ORIENTED PROGRAM

Patricia M. Mitchell, Kathleen P. McCoy, E. Mark Cummings[*],
W. Brad Faircloth and Jennifer S. Cummings
University of Notre Dame, South Bend, Indiana, US

RESEARCH SUMMARY

A psycho-educational program for advancing children's coping skills and reactions to marital conflict was evaluated. Families with a child between the ages of 4 and 8 were randomly assigned to one of three groups: 1) parent program only; 2) parent and child program; or 3) self-study (control group). Parents in the parent-only and parent-child groups received the same psycho-educational program. Only children in the parent-child group received the child program which consisted of four visits in which children learned about marital conflict and family relationships; were taught about emotions and different levels of emotions; and were given tools for coping with conflict that would help them react in optimal ways for their development. Analyses suggested the promise of a child program for older children (ages 6-8) with regard to improved emotional security about marital conflict. However, consistent with other research, simply educating children about coping with marital conflict had minimal effects on outcomes associated with conflict between the parents.

---

[*] Correspondence should be addressed to Dr. E. Mark Cummings, Department of Psychology, Haggar Hall, University of Notre Dame, Notre Dame, IN 46556, phone: (574) 631-3404, fax: (574) 631-1825, Cummings.10@nd.edu.

Chapter 408

MOTHER-INFANT BONDS: THE EFFECTS OF MATERNAL DEPRESSION ON THE MATERNAL-CHILD RELATIONSHIP

Deana B. Davalos, Alana M. Campbell and Amanda L. Pala
Colorado State University, Colorado, US

RESEARCH SUMMARY

The mother infant bond has long been recognized as being crucial in multiple areas of infant development. The value that is placed on this relationship is recognized across the world and across groups of varying socioeconomic status. The multitudes of variables that are thought to be influenced by the mother infant relationship are impressive, even staggering. Research suggests that, depending on the level of bonding or lack thereof, infants may suffer outcomes as severe as irreversible neuropsychological deficits or development of long-standing psychopathology. However, others have argued that the effects are likely much more subtle, but certainly still important. During the last two decades there has been an increase in research focusing on the effects of maternal depression on the mother infant bond. Research in this field has apparently developed out of; a recognition of a relatively higher prevalence of postpartum maternal depression than once believed and recurring observations of differences in mother/infant relationships or infant behavior associated with maternal postpartum depression. The infant behaviors that have been implicated as resulting from this theoretically compromised mother infant relationship have included slight, transient effects on sociability and affective sharing to results suggesting significant increases in irritability, cognitive delays, behavioral problems, and difficulties with attachment, among others. Longitudinal data suggest that while some problems appear to resolve relatively quickly, there are some characteristics that endure long after infancy. Specifically, some researchers have argued that children and even adolescents who experienced problems bonding with their depressed mothers are at significantly greater risk of experiencing a variety of psychological symptoms, including depression, anxiety, and problems with addiction. Again, this view is controversial and others in the field link these increased risks to other factors such as low socioeconomic status or marital discord. While there appears to be consensus among most researchers in recognizing that there are likely effects of postpartum depression on mother infant bonding that affect early development, there is little consensus regarding the specific details of these effects. In our review, we will systematically analyze research focusing on the effects of postpartum depression on the mother infant bond and those variables that are believed to be affected from potential difficulties in this bond.

In: Psychology Research Biographies and Summaries ISBN: 978-1-61470-491-1
Editors: Nancy E. Wodarth and Alexis P. Ferguson © 2012 Nova Science Publishers, Inc.

Chapter 409

SOCIAL NETWORKS AND PSYCHOSOCIAL FUNCTIONING AMONG CHILDREN AND ADOLESCENTS COPING WITH SICKLE CELL DISEASE: AN OVERVIEW OF BARRIERS, CONSIDERATIONS, AND BEST PRACTICES

Rebecca H. Foster,[1] HaNa Kim,[1] Robbie Casper,[2] Alma Morgan,[2] Wanda Brice[2] and Marilyn Stern[1,2]
[1]Department of Psychology, Virginia Commonwealth University, US
[2]Department of Pediatrics, Virginia Commonwealth University
Richmond, Virginia, US

RESEARCH SUMMARY

Over 70,000 individuals in the United States are diagnosed with sickle cell disease, yet relatively little attention has been paid to this group when compared to those diagnosed with other chronic illnesses such as asthma, cystic fibrosis, diabetes, or cancer. Like most major chronic illnesses, sickle cell disease influences familial and social relationships in numerous and ever-changing ways. Advances in sickle cell disease treatments and improved survival rates have resulted in dramatic shifts in relationship networks and psychosocial adaption for each child diagnosed. Several primary areas of concern have been identified for children and families facing sickle cell disease such as disruptions to educational and socialization processes, sudden changes in medical conditions including the persistent threat of pain crises, existential anxieties about death, the wide range of emotions that are often present in managing with the various stages of the disease and treatment, the overarching developmental trajectory of the child, and coping with having a serious illness or caring for a child with a serious illness. Literature has cited and research continues to find evidence of challenges faced by these children and adolescents including ways in which family functioning, social acceptance by peers, interactions with siblings, parenting style used in the home, and daily anxieties and pressures can play integrated roles in shaping life-long relationships and overall quality of life. Because sickle cell disease predominantly affects minority groups within the United States, families and medical professionals also must consider the cultural needs of each patient in order to promote best practices for treatment and the development of sustained, healthy relationships. While these noted challenges tend to be constant foci for all concerned with caring for and working to develop optimal relationships among individuals diagnosed with sickle cell disease, many individuals and families coping with a sickle cell disease diagnosis seem to function quite well when adaptive coping and supportive networks are present and persistent. This chapter will investigate how the many relationships that exist within the social context of a child's world are impacted by sickle cell disease. An overview will be provided examining dynamics between parents, the children diagnosed with sickle cell disease, and their peers and siblings in terms of the challenges faced and the relationship strengths displayed. Cultural influences and means of improving life-long relationships will be explored. Lastly, currently implemented interventions promoting positive relationships will be discussed as well as future directions for research and intervention studies.

In: Psychology Research Biographies and Summaries ISBN: 978-1-61470-491-1
Editors: Nancy E. Wodarth and Alexis P. Ferguson © 2012 Nova Science Publishers, Inc.

Chapter 410

PARENTING AND CHILDREN'S INVOLVEMENT IN BULLYING AT SCHOOL

Ken Rigby
University of South Australia, Australia

RESEARCH SUMMARY

Research into bullying amomg children has suggested that parents can play an important role in reducing the risk of their children becoming involved in bully/victim problems at achool .and can take steps to enable their children to cope more effectively (Smith and Myron-Wilson, 1998; Stelios, 2008; Rigby 2008). At the same time, it should be acknowledged that parental influence is limited by such factors as their child's genetic endowment (Ball et al., 2008) peer pressure at school and unpredictable life events. (Harris, 1998).

What parents can do to reduce the risk or impact of bullying on children can be considered under these headings:

1) Early childhood parenting
2) Parenting style with older children
3) Parents promoting skills that are helpful in reducing the risk of
4) Parents assisting children who are being bullied at school
5) Parents providing emotional and social support when children are bullied

Chapter 411

NEUROBIOLOGY OF SOCIAL BONDING

Donatella Marazziti[*], Alessandro Del Debbio, Isabella Roncaglia, Carolina Bianchi and Liliana Dell'Osso
Dipartimento di Psichiatria, Neurobiologia, Farmacologia e Biotecnologie,
University of Pisa, Pisa, Italy

RESEARCH SUMMARY

Social bonding development is fundamental for several animals, particularly for humans who are the most immature at birth, for its relevant impact upon survival and reproduction. Several neural and endocrine factors, most of which are still largely unknown, may modulate reproductive behaviors, mother-infant attachment and adult-adult bonding. Consequently, we aimed to review the neurobiological correlates of attachment in both animals and humans. MEDLINE and Pub-Med (1970-2008) databases were searched for English language articles using the keywords *attachment, neuropeptides, neurotrophins, pair bonding, social behavior*. We reviewed papers that addressed the following aspects of attachment neurobiology: 1) Infant-mother attachment; 2) Mother-infant attachment; 3) Adult-adult pair bonding formation; 4) Human bonding. Oxytocin and vasopressin, two neurohypophyseal peptides, are known to be involved in the attachment process. Oxytocin is supposed to facilitate a rapid conditioned association to maternal odor cues, while linking environmental cues to the infant's memory of the mother. While oxytocin plays a role in the onset of maternal behavior in rats, vasopressin seems to influence paternal behavior in praire voles. Parental behavior development requires also gonadal steroids action. In adults, oxytocin and vasopressin may contribute to pair bonding process by modulating the neuroendocrine response, behaviors and emotions associated to preference formation and pair bonding. Recently, even neurotrophins have been suggested to play a role in social bonding. In conclusion, although the neurobiological basis of social attachment is mainly based on animal data, preliminary findings suggest that the same mechanisms may occur also in humans and would involve

---

[*] Corresponding author: Donatella Marazziti, MD; Dipartimento di Psichiatria, Neurobiologia, Farmacologia e Biotecnologie, University of Pisa, Via Roma 67, 56100 Pisa, Italy. Tel:+39 050 835412; Fax:+39 050 21581; E-mail: dmarazzi@psico.med.unipi.it.

multi-sensory processing, complex motor responses and cognitive functions, such as attention, memory, recognition and motivation. The few data available in humans are intriguing and seem to open even more exciting perspectives to the treatment of a broad range of neuropsychiatric disorders.

Chapter 412

COOPERATIVE AND NON-COOPERATIVE BEHAVIOR IN PAIRS OF CHILDREN: THE RECIPROCAL EFFECTS OF SOCIAL INTERACTION IN THE ONGOING CONSTRUCTION OF A PLAY SEQUENCE

Emanuela Rabaglietti, Fabrizia Giannotta and Silvia Ciairano[*]
Department of Psychology, University of Torino, Italy

RESEARCH SUMMARY

We know that some social interactions begin and end cooperatively, while others start aggressively and end up even more so.

We also know that in some social interactions one of the partners might initially behave either cooperatively or competitively and aggressively towards the other partner, who may respond with the opposite type of behavior. However, over time, as the relationship evolves, behavioral patterns may change as each partner adapts to the behavior of the other.

We think that as social interactions evolve over time, it is possible to identify two phases: first, a reciprocal exploration phase, and second, an adjustment phase. Investigating very short term social interaction sequences of about ten minutes, we concluded that these two phases last about five minutes each.

The present study investigates the relationships between cooperative and non-cooperative or competitive behavior in pairs of children in the ongoing process of interaction during a ten-minute play sequence. To reach our goal, we first divided the time of the play sequence (10') in two phases and looked at the differences between the first and second phase (5' each). Second, we divided the pairs of children in three groups: i) initially high in cooperation; ii) initially high in competition; iii) initially high in both. Third, we looked at the outcomes using both linear and logistic regression analyses. We hypothesised that: a) initially prevalent cooperative behavior is more likely to end in cooperation; b) initially prevalent competitive behavior is more likely to end in competition; c) initially mixed social interactions (both

---
[*] ciairano@psych.unito.it.

cooperative and competitive) are more likely to end in abandonment of the interaction and doing nothing.

Our sample is composed of 125 pairs of children. 69% (N=86) of the pairs were composed of same-sex children, while the remaining 31% (N=39) were mixed. The individuals within each pair were the same age. 35% of the pairs (N =44) were eight years old, 38% (N =48) were ten years old, and 27% (N=33) were twelve years old. We observed the cooperative and competitive behavior of both the partners. The task was to finish a puzzle in ten minutes.

Our findings confirmed only our first two hypotheses. We found that initially mixed situations were also more likely to end in cooperation. These findings underline the importance of intervention programs aimed at promoting social and cooperative skills in children to avoid starting negative social cycles or patterns.

Chapter 413

SOCIAL RELATIONSHIPS AND PHYSICAL HEALTH: ARE WE BETTER OR WORSE OFF BECAUSE OF OUR RELATIONSHIPS?

Julianne Holt-Lunstad and Briahna Bushman
Department of Psychology, Brigham Young University, Provo, Utah 84602, US

ABSTRACT

When asked, "What is necessary for your happiness?" or "What is it that makes your life meaningful?" most people mention before anything else-- satisfying close relationships with family, friends, or romantic partners (Berscheid, 1985). Relationships with others form a pervasive role in our everyday lives and are generally regarded as emotionally satisfying. Although it may not be surprising that social relationships are associated psychological benefits, there is also evidence to suggest that these relationships have beneficial effects on physical health and/or the lack of meaningful relationships may be detrimental (Berkman, 1995; Cohen, 1988; House, Landis, & Umberson, 1988). In fact, reviews of the literature indicate that a lack of meaningful relationships is associated with increased risk for morbidity and mortality from a variety of causes (Berkman, 1995; House, Landis, & Umberson, 1988). Importantly, both the quantity and quality of social relationship can affect health and mortality. Overall, research suggests that having more and better quality relationships is associated with beneficial effects on health, while fewer and negative relationships are associated with detrimental effects on health (see Uchino, 2006 for a review). Therefore, a complete understanding of health-related consequences of social relationships requires simultaneous consideration of both the negative and the positive aspects of social experience.

In this chapter, the health consequences of social relationships will be examined. This chapter will proceed by first, reviewing definitions of social support; second, a brief review of the substantial body of evidence that has linked social relationships with health benefits will be provided; third, the chapter will also include a brief review of the evidence showing the negative side of relationships (e.g., negativity and conflict within relationships is associated with negative health outcomes); and finally, the bulk of the chapter will focus on a relatively newer line of research that examines relationships that are characterized by both positive and negative aspects (ambivalent relationships).

Because research has examined the positive and negative aspects of relationships separately, less is known about relationships that are not entirely positive or negative-but a mix of both negative and positive feelings. The remainder of this chapter will (1) define ambivalent relationships and provide theoretical and empirical justification for examination of ambivalent relationships; (2) summarize evidence linking ambivalent relationships to both mental and physical health outcomes; (3) provide evidence regarding maintenance of ambivalent relationships; and (4) propose future research. Thus, this chapter will summarize empirical research on the health impact of social relationships characterized by mixed-feelings (ambivalence). This data on ambivalent relationships will be presented in the context of the larger literature on social relationships and physical health and highlight the need for new directions in social relationships research.

In: Psychology Research Biographies and Summaries
Editors: Nancy E. Wodarth and Alexis P. Ferguson

ISBN: 978-1-61470-491-1
© 2012 Nova Science Publishers, Inc.

Chapter 414

LIVING IN DISCREPANT WORLDS: EXPLORING THE CULTURAL CONTEXT OF SEXUALITY AMONG TURKISH AND MOROCCAN MALE ADOLESCENTS

Barbara C. Schouten[*] *and Chana van der Velden*[1]
Department of Communication, the Amsterdam School of Communications Research, University of Amsterdam, The Netherlands

RESEARCH SUMMARY

A high percentage of Turkish and Moroccan male adolescents in the Netherlands is sexually active. At the same time, they frequently engage in risky sexual behavior, which makes them vulnerable to HIV/STDs infection. To be able to design culturally appropriate health promoting interventions, more knowledge about the factors that influence their sexual behavior is needed. Therefore, this paper reports on a qualitative study that aims to increase our understanding of the influences on Turkish and Moroccan adolescent male sexuality within a broader interest in HIV/STD prevention. Seven focus groups with 29 Moroccan and 20 Turkish boys, aged between 14 and 18 years, were conducted. Analysis of the data highlighted several factors that may hinder condom use, such as lack of knowledge, lack of perceived risk, peer norms, lack of parent-adolescent communication about sexuality, and lack of self-efficacy toward buying condoms. Results also show some significant differences between the Turkish and Moroccan adolescents. Turkish adolescents are more conservative toward sexuality, they stick more strongly to cultural traditions and they have less knowledge about HIV/STDs than Moroccan adolescents. Moroccan adolescents experiment more frequently with sex. Therefore, they may be at higher risk of getting infected with HIV/STDs. The findings of our study provide a fertile starting point for designing culturally appropriate and effective health education programs in the field of safe sex promotion for ethnic minority adolescents.

---

[*] Corresponding address: B.C. Schouten. Department of Communication, The Amsterdam School of Communications Research (ASCoR), University of Amsterdam, Kloveniersburgwal 48, 1012 CX Amsterdam, The Netherlands. Phone: +31 (0)20 5253879; Fax: +31 (0)20 525 3861; e-mail: b.c.schouten@uva.nl.

In: Psychology Research Biographies and Summaries
Editors: Nancy E. Wodarth and Alexis P. Ferguson
ISBN: 978-1-61470-491-1
© 2012 Nova Science Publishers, Inc.

Chapter 415

HIV/AIDS PREVENTION ON MEXICAN ADOLESCENTS: THE SYNTHESIS OF TWO THEORIES CONSIDERING THE INTERPERSONAL, INDIVIDUAL, AND PSYCHOLOGICAL INFLUENCES

Raquel A. Benavides-Torres[1], Georgina M. Núñez Rocha[2], Esther C. Gallegos Cabriales[1], Claude Bonazzo[3], Yolanda Flores-Peña[1], Francisco R. Guzmán Facudo[1] and Karla Selene López García[1]

[1]Universidad Autónoma de Nuevo León; Nuevo León, México
[2]Instituto Mexicano del Seguro Social; Nuevo León, México
[3]University of Texas at Austin; Texas, US

RESEARCH SUMMARY

In Mexico, HIV/AIDS is a complex public health issue that carries significant psychosocial, socio-political, and economic repercussions. Adolescence is a period of development that not only encompasses physical and social changes, but also psychological. Adolescents engaging in unprotected sexual activities during this stage of development are at risk of contracting HIV infections. This paper posits that the Theory of Planned behavior has shown to be helpful in guiding research in HIV/AIDS prevention, but remains limited in the inclusion of ecological influences. Hence, this limitation is addressed using the Ecodevelopmental Theory. Therefore, this paper aims to develop a model based on the Theory of Planned Behavior and the Ecodevelopmental Theory that will explain HIV/AIDS prevention within the context of Mexican adolescents using concepts from both theories and the empirical evidence available. Three types of influences were identified during the process of theory synthesis: a) Interpersonal influences from the microsystem were parent communication about sex and peer influences; b) Individual influences included HIV/AIDS knowledge, gender (female), and age; and c) psychosocial influences consisted of perceived behavioral control for sexual health behaviors, subjective norms (gender roles), positive HIV attitudes, and sexual intentions. Results provide insight into the complex dynamics of the synthesis of the two aforementioned theories with respect to HIV/AIDS prevention. Communication about sex is positively related to sexual health behaviors for HIV/AIDS prevention, being female, and knowledge about HIV/AIDS. Peer influence is negatively correlated with sexual behaviors for HIV/AIDS prevention. It is unclear the relationship of HIV/AIDS knowledge and sexual behaviors and being female. Gender (female) is positively correlated with sexual behaviors and perceived behavioral control, but its relationship is unclear with subjective norms. Age is positively correlated with subjective norms, but negatively correlated with sexual health behaviors. Perceived behavioral control and positive attitudes are positively correlated to intentions and sexual health behaviors. In the case of subjective norms, it was positively correlated with intentions, but not with sexual behaviors. Finally, high intentions to use condoms influence sexual health behaviors. The final model allows for a better understanding of the connections among concepts related to sexual health behaviors in HIV/AIDS prevention. Future research is recommended regarding the unknown associations between gender, knowledge, subjective norms, and attitudes for future implementation of preventions programs against this fatal disease in the Mexican Adolescents.

In: Psychology Research Biographies and Summaries
Editors: Nancy E. Wodarth and Alexis P. Ferguson

ISBN: 978-1-61470-491-1
© 2012 Nova Science Publishers, Inc.

Chapter 416

ADOLESCENTS WITH CANCER: ADJUSTMENT AND SUPPORTIVE CARE NEEDS

Luisa M. Massimo
Department of Pediatric Hematology and Oncology
G. Gaslini Scientific Children's Hospital, Genoa, Italy

RESEARCH SUMMARY

Adolescence is a difficult in-between age, even in good health, and any kind of illness can alter this situation. Living with a high risk disease for several years during adolescence requires the activation of psychological defense mechanisms, cognitive functions, perception, acceptance, memory, communication, judgment, and emotions, which taken together mean good coping. The successful evolution of the coping process ultimately leads to good quality of life and adaptation. Over the last few years, physicians and clinical psychologists have endeavored to provide a good psychosocial status to their patients, especially those with cancer and those undergoing painful and distressing treatments.

At our institution we chose to use the "narrative" approach with our sick adolescents, since it would appear to be the most suitable in individual encounters. There is often the need to overcome an important barrier through a friendly approach. Narrative medicine, more than others, lends itself to the intimate knowledge of the person being examined. Listening and talking through a patient/doctor alliance are the first steps towards true psychological healing. Over the last few years we have chosen this sort of dialogue with our adolescent patients, since they turn to us both seeking the physicians who know them well and a space where they can talk openly. The narrative approach requires time, willingness and an appropriate setting. In addition, the supportive care needs of these youngsters with cancer are often brought up in these encounters and this suggests the extent to which these needs may remain unmet. The dialogue that takes place following the "narrative" approach allows us to obtain detailed personal information and insight into the values and abilities of each subject. Undoubtedly, some psychosocial disorders can be prevented. Nowadays, pediatricians, supported by psychologists and other specialists, can create an alliance with the parents and the sick adolescents in order to adequately face pitfalls that may become the source of disorders in their physical, cognitive, emotional and behavioral development, and especially with regards to post-traumatic stress. Four different situations of adolescents who were either suffering from or who were cured of cancer are reported in detail in this chapter, including information concerning their need for understanding, discrepancy in appearance and insight, crisis in quality of life and the identity process.

In: Psychology Research Biographies and Summaries ISBN: 978-1-61470-491-1
Editors: Nancy E. Wodarth and Alexis P. Ferguson © 2012 Nova Science Publishers, Inc.

Chapter 417

THE QUALITY OF CARING RELATIONSHIPS

Tineke A. Abma[*], Barth Oeseburg, Guy A. M. Widdershoven and Marian Verkerk
University of Maastricht, The Netherlands

RESEARCH SUMMARY

In healthcare, relationships between patients or disabled persons and professionals are at least co-constitutive for the quality of care. Many patients complain about the contacts and communication with caregivers and other professionals. From a care-ethical perspective a good patient-professional relationship requires a process of negotiation and shared understanding about mutual normative expectations. Mismatches between these expectations will lead to misunderstandings or conflicts. If caregivers listen to the narratives of identity of patients, and engage in a deliberative dialogue, they will better be able to attune their care to the needs of patients. We will illustrate this with the stories of three women with Multiple Sclerosis. Their narratives of identity differ from the narratives that caregivers and others use to understand and identify them. Since identities give rise to normative expectations in all three cases there is a conflict between what the women expect of their caregivers and vice-versa. These stories show that the quality of care, defined as doing the right thing, at the right time, in the right way, for the right person, is dependent on the quality of caring relationships.

---

[*] Correspondence Address: Dr. Tineke A. Abma. University of Maastricht, Health, Ethics and Society/School for Public Health and Primary Care, PO box 616, 6200 MD Maastricht. Tel: 043-3881132; Email:T.abma@ZW.UNIMAAS.nl.

Chapter 418

AN ATTACHMENT-BASED PATHWAYS MODEL DEPICTING THE PSYCHOLOGY OF THERAPEUTIC RELATIONSHIPS

Geoff Goodman[*]
Long Island University, Brookville, New York, US

RESEARCH SUMMARY

Throughout the history of psychotherapy, clinical theoreticians have evoked various metaphors to depict the therapist-patient relationship. With the advent of attachment theory and other advances in developmental psychology in the 1950s and 1960s, a new therapeutic metaphor was born: the caregiver-infant attachment relationship. This metaphor has yielded a number of insights into the process of psychotherapy and the nature of the interactions in which the therapist and patient engage. The first objective of this article is to illuminate both the advantages and disadvantages of using this metaphor to depict the psychology of therapeutic relationships. One distinction between this metaphor and the therapeutic relationship is the state of development of mental structures in the infant versus the patient. Whereas the caregiver is behaving in response to the infant's emotional cues not contextualized by an interactional history of expectations to guide these cues, the patient enters into a therapeutic relationship with a complex and intricate interactional history of expectations. This asynchrony between the caregiver-infant attachment relationship and the therapist-patient relationship requires the therapist to behave in sometimes noncomplementary ways to challenge and interpret these transferential patterns rather than simply responding to emotional cues, as a caregiver would do. These interactional expectations, typically organized around definable patterns of behavior in the therapeutic relationship, are "often neither conscious and verbalizable nor repressed in the dynamic sense" (Lyons-Ruth, 1999, p. 589), and thus pose challenges to traditional psychotherapy

---

[*] Correspondence concerning this article should be addressed to Geoff Goodman, Ph.D., Clinical Psychology Doctoral Program, Long Island University, 720 Northern Blvd., Brookville, NY 11548 (516-299-4277 (O), 516-299-2738 (F), ggoodman@liu.edu).

models that rely exclusively on symbolization to produce therapeutic change. This new understanding of therapeutic change forces therapists to focus more intensively on their own attitudes and behaviors vis-à-vis the patient as the quintessential instruments of change. Various aspects of the therapeutic relationship, in addition to verbalized interpretations of repressed conflict, have thus come under increased scrutiny. I present an attachment-based pathways model for understanding the interrelations among three relationship-based concepts used in contemporary psychotherapies: working alliance, patient attachment and therapist caregiving, and transference and countertransference. Thus, the second objective of this article is to sensitize therapists and psychotherapy process researchers to the structure and functioning of these interrelated concepts to increase therapeutic effectiveness.

Chapter 419

A STUDY OF THE RELATIONSHIP BETWEEN SELF-CONSCIOUS AFFECTS, COPING STYLES, AND DEPRESSIVE REACTION AFTER A NEGATIVE LIFE EVENT

Masayo Uji[*,1], *Toshinori Kitamura*[1] *and Toshiaki Nagata*[2]
[1]Department of Clinical Behavioural Sciences,
Kumamoto University Graduate School of Medical Sciences, Japan
[2]Kyushu University of Nursing and Social Welfare, Japan

RESEARCH SUMMARY

This study aimed to explore how the affects that result from conflictive social interpersonal relationships influence mental health, as well as to investigate how specific coping styles mediate between these affects and mental health.

The Test of Self-Conscious Affect-3 (TOSCA-3, Tangney, Dearing, Wagner, & Gramzow, 2000) assesses six self-conscious affects, namely guilt-proneness, shame-proneness, externalization, detachment, alpha pride, and beta pride. In this study, we selected for analysis the four affects that originated from negative evaluations of the presented scenarios (guilt-proneness, shame-proneness, externalization, and detachment). We used the Coping Inventory for Stressful Situations (CISS, Endler, and Parker, 1990) for estimating coping style, specifically task-oriented coping, emotion-oriented coping, and avoidance-oriented coping.

A structural equation model that makes it possible to explore the causal relationship between self-conscious affects, coping styles, and mental health, was chosen as a statistical technique. Among the 394 Japanese university students who agreed to participate in this study, 298 experienced moderate to severe stressful negative life events during the four-

---

[*] E-mail ujimasayo@excite.co.jp; Telephone +81-(0)96-373-5183; Fax + 81-(0)96-373-5181. Address: Department of Clinical Behavioural Sciences, Kumamoto University Graduate School of Medical Sciences, 1-1-1 Honjo, Kumamoto, Japan 860-8556.

month study. Of those 298 respondents, 268 completed every item of the TOSCA-3, the CISS, and the Self-rating Depressive Scale (SDS, Zung, 1965). These 268 were subjected to a structural equation model.

Among the four affect categories which occur under stressful situations, only shame-proneness directly contributed to a depressive reaction, whereas the other three (guilt-proneness, externalization, and detachment) did not. Individuals with shame-proneness tended towards an emotional-oriented coping style, but this inhibited task-oriented coping. Guilt-proneness induced task-oriented coping and avoidance-oriented coping. Externalization induced task-oriented coping and emotion-oriented coping. Detachment gave rise only to avoidance-oriented coping. Interestingly, among the three coping styles, only task-oriented coping induced a depressive reaction, whereas emotion-oriented coping and avoidance-oriented coping did not.

We discuss these results primarily from the psychological perspective but also look briefly at how they might be applied to a clinical setting within psychiatry.

In: Psychology Research Biographies and Summaries
Editors: Nancy E. Wodarth and Alexis P. Ferguson

ISBN: 978-1-61470-491-1
© 2012 Nova Science Publishers, Inc.

Chapter 420

THE NEUROPSYCHOLOGY OF PASSIONATE LOVE

Elaine Hatfield and Richard L. Rapson
University of Hawaii, US

RESEARCH SUMMARY

Throughout history, artists, poets, and writers have been interested in the nature of passionate love, sexual desire, and sexual behavior. In the 1960s, social psychologists and sexologists began the systematic investigation of these complex phenomena (see Berscheid & Hatfield, 1969; Hatfield & Rapson, 1993; Hatfield & Rapson, 2005, for a review of this research). Yet, only recently have neuroscientists and biochemists begun to explore these complex phenomena.

In this entry, we will review what these distinguished theorists and researchers have learned about these processes.

Chapter 421

WOMEN, SUBSTANCE USE AND POST-TRAUMATIC STRESS DISORDER

Christine M. Courbasson[1] and Irina Schelkanova[2]

[1]Concurrent Disorders Service, Centre for Addiction and Mental Health, Department of Psychiatry, University of Toronto, Canada
[2]University of Toronto, Canada

RESEARCH SUMMARY

The high rate of substance use, a significant problem among women who have experienced trauma and violence, underscores the need for a closer look at methodological gaps and treatment efficacies, which can influence the rate of successful recoveries. Post-traumatic stress disorder (PTSD) consists of a number of serious symptoms one can experience after being exposed to threat of death or serious injury. The consequential response involves intense fear, helplessness, re-experience of the traumatic event, avoidance of stimuli associated with the trauma, or persistent anxiety. Up to 80% of women seeking substance abuse treatment report lifetime histories of sexual and/or physical assault, and many of these women have symptoms of PTSD. Women with comorbid PTSD and substance use disorders (SUD) are poorly served in substance use treatment. They have reduced treatment retention rates and outcomes, and treatment is further complicated when other mental health difficulties related to PTSD are present. Yet, there is a lack of literature about effective ways to address PTSD in substance use treatment. The chapter undertakes a critical overview of the recent literature on women with comorbid PTSD and substance abuse, outlines methodological problems in the clinical research and presents ways to bridge gaps in research. This chapter also presents new strategies to maximize treatment effectiveness of PTSD, substance use and possible concurrent disorders.

SELF-NARRATIVE AND THE CONSTRUCTION OF IDENTITY IN ASIAN AMERICAN YOUNG ADULTS

Qi Wang*, Jessie Bee Kim Koh, Yan-Xiang Amber Liang, Yexin Jessica Li and Sean Lindsey
Cornell University, US

RESEARCH SUMMARY

The present study examined identity construction in Asian Americans across important domains of life experience. One hundred and six (81 females, 25 males) Asian American young adults participated and each wrote an in-depth "self-analysis." Based on Kağıtçıbaşı's (2005) autonomous-related self framework, content analysis was performed on these self-narratives within five distinct thematic domains: personal, family and important others, achievement, gender and sexuality, and ethnicity. Autonomy (as opposed to heteronomy) and relatedness (as opposed to separateness) were frequent themes across these domains and showed different manifestations between domains. The findings are discussed in light of the narrative construction of an autonomous and yet socially connected self that entails personal, social, and ethnic concerns.

---

* Correspondence concerning this article should be addressed to Qi Wang at the Department of Human Development, Cornell University, Martha Van Rensselaer Hall, Ithaca, NY 14853-4401. Electronic mail may be sent to qw23@cornell.edu. Tel: 607-255-9376. Fax: 607-255-9856.

In: Psychology Research Biographies and Summaries ISBN: 978-1-61470-491-1
Editors: Nancy E. Wodarth and Alexis P. Ferguson © 2012 Nova Science Publishers, Inc.

Chapter 423

SEXUAL ABUSE IN MEN WITH SUBSTANCE USE PROBLEMS: ASSESSMENT AND TREATMENT ISSUES

Christine M. Courbasson[1], Jim Cullen[2]
and Karolina Konieczna
[1]University of Toronto, Canada
[2]Ethical Culture Fieldston Schoo, New York, US

RESEARCH SUMMARY

Research suggests that a high prevalence of men with substance use problems have experienced sexual abuse at one point in their life. Men who have been sexually victimized frequently use substances to cope with unpleasant feelings resulting from the abuse, they experience many psychosocial problems and they tend to report sexual abuse much less than women. They also experience more extreme substance use than women with a history of sexual abuse. The present chapter reviews the prevalence and the significance of this problem, outlines significant gaps in the clinical and research literature, discusses the need for gender sensitive assessment approaches, and relevant treatment strategies specific to men that can enhance both substance use treatment and general functioning of these clients.

Chapter 424

CONSTRUCT AND CRITERION VALIDITY OF AN OBJECTIVE MEASURE OF RESPONDENTS' SUBJECTIVELY ACCEPTED LEVEL OF RISK IN ROAD TRAFFIC

Andreas Hergovich[*,1], *Martin E. Arendasy*[2], *Markus Sommer*[2] *and Bettina Bognar*[3]

University of Vienna, Ausria
[1]Social Psychology Research Group,
Dept. of Psychology, Differential
[2]Personality Research Group
[3]Fa. Dr. G. Schuhfried, Mödling

RESEARCH SUMMARY

The present article outlines a theory-based approach to the construction and psychometric evaluation of more behavioural based measures of willingness to take risks in road traffic. Based on the risk homeostasis theory (Wilde, 1994) several traffic situations varying on the degree of objective danger where filmed. Respondents were asked to indicate at which point the action that is contingent to the described situation will become too dangerous for them to carry out. Latencies at the item level were obtained. The first study deals with the dimensionality of this newly developed measure which is referred to as the Vienna Risk Taking Test Traffic. The second study investigates the generalizability of these results to a sample of professional driver applicants. The third study locates the newly developed measure within the context of the Giant Three model of personality. Confirmatory factor analyses indicated that the Vienna Risk Taking Test Traffic loads on the Giant Three factor 'Adventurousness', thereby confirming the construct validity of the behavioural based measures of willingness to take risks. Two additional studies investigate the criterion validity

---

[*] Correspondence address: Prof. Dr. Andreas Hergovich, Universität Wien, Fakultät für Psychologie, Liebiggasse 5, 1010 Wien, Austria. e-mail: andreas.hergovich@univie.ac.at.

of the newly constructed measure using accident rates as well as respondents' performance in a standardized driving test as criterion measure. Despite the wealth of literature supporting the predictive validity of personality-related and ability-related determents of fitness to drive these two kinds of predictor variables have previously been studied in isolation. In order to overcome this methodological shortcoming the incremental validity of the Vienna Risk Taking Test over and above a rather comprehensive set of ability and personality tests was investigated. In line with theoretical considerations the newly developed objective personality test contributed incrementally to the prediction of respondents' performance in a standardized driving test as well as to the prediction of their accident rates. The theoretical implications of the results presented in this article are discussed in the light of current theoretical model on fitness to drive.

In: Psychology Research Biographies and Summaries
Editors: Nancy E. Wodarth and Alexis P. Ferguson
ISBN: 978-1-61470-491-1
© 2012 Nova Science Publishers, Inc.

Chapter 425

THE PSYCHOLOGICAL DISTURBANCES OF WAR-TRAUMATIZED ADOLESCENTS IN RURAL AND URBAN AREAS OF BOSNIA AND HERZEGOVINA AND IT'S CORRELATION WITH POVERTY AND HOPELESSNESS

Mevludin Hasanović[*,1], *Edin Haračić*[2], *Šemsa Ahmetspahić*[2], *Sanja Kurtović*[2] *and Hajrudin Haračić*[3]

[1]Department of Psychiatry, Tuzla University Clinical Center, Tuzla, Bosnia and Herzegovina
[2]School of Philosophy, University of Tuzla, Tuzla, Bosnia and Herzegovina
[3]Primary Health Care Center "Dom zdravlja" Teočak, Teočak, Bosnia and Herzegovina, Hasanović et al:
Rural and Urban Adolescents of Postwar Bosnia and Herzegovina

RESEARCH SUMMARY

The study examined the psychological health of war-traumatized adolescents in rural and urban areas of Bosnia and determined it's correlation with poverty and hopelessness. The study was carried out in Teočak and Tuzla, Bosnia and Herzegovina, in March 2007. PTSD prevalence was significantly higher amongst rural than urban adolescents. Depression was present with no statistical difference between the rural and urban groups. All adolescents reported high hopelessness scores with again no difference between groups. Prevalence of PTSD was positively correlated with the prevalence of depression. Life in poor material conditions worsened psychological war consequences and academic achievement. Academic

---

[*] Correspondence to: Mevludin Hasanović, Department of Psychiatry, Tuzla University Clinical Center, Trnovac bb, 75 000 Tuzla, Bosnia and Herzegovina, *hameaz@bih.net.ba*.

achievements were negatively associated with age, severity of PTSD, depression, suicidal thoughts, hopelessness and with the mean number of trauma experiences.

In: Psychology Research Biographies and Summaries
Editors: Nancy E. Wodarth and Alexis P. Ferguson
ISBN: 978-1-61470-491-1
© 2012 Nova Science Publishers, Inc.

Chapter 426

WHAT THE SPIRITUAL AND RELIGIOUS TRADITIONS OFFER PSYCHOLOGISTS

Thomas G. Plante[*]
Santa Clara University, US

RESEARCH SUMMARY

There has been a remarkable amount of popular and professional interest in the relationship between spirituality, religion, psychology, and health in recent years. Contemporary interest in spirituality and religion is popular among not only the general population but also among many psychology professionals as well. While most people believe in God and consider themselves to be spiritual, religious, or both, most psychologists do not and have no training in religion and spirituality. Psychologists can learn much from the spiritual and religious traditions that offer principles and tools that are productive to use even if one does not share the same religious or spiritual interests. The purpose of this brief commentary is to offer thirteen spiritual and religious tools common among all of the major religious and spiritual traditions that can be utilized by contemporary professional psychologists in clinical practice and elsewhere in their professional work to enhance their already high quality professional services that they provide. In addition to the thirteen tools, relevant ethical issues are briefly discussed as well.

---

[*] Thomas G. Plante, Ph.D., ABPP is professor of psychology at Santa Clara University, adjunct clinical associate professor of psychiatry and behavioral sciences at Stanford University School of Medicine, and in private practice in Menlo Park, California. He has authored a dozen books including, *Using Spiritual and Religious Tools in Psychotherapy*. Address correspondence to Thomas G. Plante, Psychology Department, Alumni Science Hall, Room 203, Santa Clara University, Santa Clara, CA. 95053-0333; Email: tplante@scu.edu; Telephone: 408-554-4471.

Chapter 427

AN ATTACHMENT-BASED PATHWAYS MODEL DEPICTING THE PSYCHOLOGY OF THERAPEUTIC RELATIONSHIPS

*Geoff Goodman**
Long Island University, US

RESEARCH SUMMARY

Throughout the history of psychotherapy, clinical theoreticians have evoked various metaphors to depict the therapist-patient relationship. With the advent of attachment theory and other advances in developmental psychology in the 1950s and 1960s, a new therapeutic metaphor was born: the caregiver-infant attachment relationship. This metaphor has yielded a number of insights into the process of psychotherapy and the nature of the interactions in which the therapist and patient engage. The first objective of this article is to illuminate both the advantages and disadvantages of using this metaphor to depict the psychology of therapeutic relationships. One distinction between this metaphor and the therapeutic relationship is the state of development of mental structures in the infant versus the patient. Whereas the caregiver is behaving in response to the infant's emotional cues not contextualized by an interactional history of expectations to guide these cues, the patient enters into a therapeutic relationship with a complex and intricate interactional history of expectations. This asynchrony between the caregiver-infant attachment relationship and the therapist-patient relationship requires the therapist to behave in sometimes noncomplementary ways to challenge and interpret these transferential patterns rather than simply responding to emotional cues, as a caregiver would do. These interactional expectations, typically organized around definable patterns of behavior in the therapeutic relationship, are "often neither conscious and verbalizable nor repressed in the dynamic sense" (Lyons-Ruth, 1999, p. 589), and thus pose challenges to traditional psychotherapy

---

* Correspondence concerning this article should be addressed to Geoff Goodman, Ph.D., Clinical Psychology Doctoral Program, Long Island University, 720 Northern Blvd., Brookville, NY 11548 (516-299-4277 (O), 516-299-2738 (F), ggoodman@liu.edu).

models that rely exclusively on symbolization to produce therapeutic change. This new understanding of therapeutic change forces therapists to focus more intensively on their own attitudes and behaviors vis-à-vis the patient as the quintessential instruments of change. Various aspects of the therapeutic relationship, in addition to verbalized interpretations of repressed conflict, have thus come under increased scrutiny. I present an attachment-based pathways model for understanding the interrelations among three relationship-based concepts used in contemporary psychotherapies: working alliance, patient attachment and therapist caregiving, and transference and countertransference. Thus, the second objective of this article is to sensitize therapists and psychotherapy process researchers to the structure and functioning of these interrelated concepts to increase therapeutic effectiveness.

Chapter 428

MODALITIES OF EMOTION REGULATION FOLLOWING NEGATIVE LIFE EVENTS IN ADULTHOOD AND OLD AGE

Olimpia Matarazzo[*]

Department of Psychology – Second University of Naples, Italy

RESEARCH SUMMARY

This study assessed the extent and efficacy of three regulatory modalities of the emotions elicited by negative life events: rumination, distraction and social sharing. Despite the wide literature existing on this subject, to my knowledge this is the first study comparing these regulatory modalities in order to estimate their use and effectiveness as a function of the negative event significance and of participants' gender and age group (adults *versus* the elderly).

400 persons (200 female, 200 male) participated in this study: 200 adults (30-59); 200 old people (60-89). They were randomly assigned to two research conditions: very significant vs. not-so-significant negative life events.

Participants were asked to describe either a very important negative life event or a not very important one and assess on 7-point scales when the event occurred, its appraisal, perceived importance and impact upon their beliefs, emotional intensity, the extent of rumination, distraction and social sharing, along with their relative frequency and duration, and their effectiveness to re-establish cognitive equilibrium and modulate the negative emotional burden; finally, participants' recovery from the event was assessed.

Quantitative data were first reduced by performing principal components analyses and then submitted to mediational regression analyses to evaluate the incidence of event relevance

---

[*] This research was supported by the Italian Ministry for University and Scientific Research: Grant FIRB RBAU017KNF_002 to Olimpia Matarazzo.
This article is part of a larger research on the use and effectiveness of rumination, distraction and social sharing following negative life events carried out from adolescence to old age by means of qualitative and quantitative assessments. Only the section of the study concerning the quantitative assessment in adults and the elderly is described here.

on the three regulatory modalities through mediator variables (which refer to the perceived cognitive and emotional event impact), controlling for gender and age group. Finally, multiple regression analysis was performed to assess the effectiveness of rumination, distraction and social sharing in recovering from the event.

In brief, results showed that significant events produced a higher cognitive and emotional impact than not-so-significant ones. Such impact, in turn, elicited a greater use of rumination and social sharing, a more consistent sense of pervasiveness of rumination and paradoxical effect of distraction.

Recovery from the event was positively predicted by its temporal distance and by the perceived effectiveness of rumination, whereas it was negatively predicted by the use and extent of rumination, perceived event importance and event impact upon one's beliefs. Females were more affected by the event impact and resorted to rumination and social sharing more than males. The event impact upon the two age groups was moderated by its relevance; besides, adults and the elderly differed regarding the use and the perceived effectiveness of the three regulatory modalities. The theoretical implications of these results are discussed.

In: Psychology Research Biographies and Summaries
Editors: Nancy E. Wodarth and Alexis P. Ferguson

ISBN: 978-1-61470-491-1
© 2012 Nova Science Publishers, Inc.

Chapter 429

AN ASSESSMENT OF AN INSTRUMENT WITH WHICH TO CONDUCT INTERNAL AUDITS

Mohd Ariff Bin Kasim[*], Siti Rosmaini Bt Mohd Hanafi, Asmah Abdul Aziz and Dawson R. Hancock

RESEARCH SUMMARY

As a result of the financial demise of several international corporations in recent years, the need for competent internal audits has received significant attention. Although most corporations conduct internal audits, their effectiveness has often been suspect and many of the existing instruments with which to measure internal audit effectiveness have severe limitations. Development of the new instrument to quantitatively measure the effectiveness of internal audit functions is clearly needed. This study uses the Internal Audit Professional Practice Framework to examine the validity and reliability of a new instrument with which to conduct internal audits. The results suggest that the instrument is highly reliable and conforms to the standards established by the Institute of Internal Auditors -- the professional organization governing the internal auditing profession.

---

[*] This research was funded by Universiti Tenaga Nasional (UNITEN) Research Fund (J510050048). The instrument is available upon request. All correspondence should be addressed to ariff@uniten.edu.my.

Chapter 430

RECRUITMENT AND RELATIONSHIPS: RESEARCH WITH STIGMATIZED AND SOCIALLY ISOLATED MOTHERS

Nicole L. Letourneau[1,2]*, *Linda A. Duffett-Leger*[2] *and Katherine Young*[2]
[1]Canada Research Chair in Healthy Child Development, Canada
[2]University of New Brunswick, Faculty of Nursing, Canada

RESEARCH SUMMARY

While our most vulnerable citizens are in greatest need of health and support intervention, they are often the most difficult to recruit in to studies. As such the evidence base necessary for optimal care is often lacking. Perhaps the most difficult to recruit participants are those affected by stigmatizing and socially isolating conditions or circumstances such as depression or family violence. Depressed adults are especially likely to refuse invitations to participate in research, thus posing a great risk to overlooking or underestimating important treatment-relevant correlates of depression [1]. Further, failing to recruit appropriately for studies of family violence may ultimately reinforce societal avoidance and stigmatization of abuse, ultimately harming abuse survivors [2].

Extensive literature addresses participant recruitment for different study designs including drug trials [3, 4], interventions [5-7], surveys [8-10], and qualitative studies [11-13]. The recruitment literature also refers to populations affected by chronic physical or mental illnesses [1, 14-16], homelessness [16], poverty [7], domestic abuse [8, 16] drug abuse [16, 17], sexually transmitted diseases including HIV [16, 18] or advanced age [19, 20]. Attempts to address recruitment challenges have also been described for work with vulnerable families [7, 21] and women, often focusing on reducing costs and increasing rewards for individual participation [9, 10]. Vulnerable families are often difficult to involve in research

---

* PO Box 4400 Fredericton, NB Canada E3B 2A5; Tel: 506-458- 7647; Fax: 506-453-4565; E-mail: nicolel@unb.ca.

due challenges of locating and gaining access to the sample and the burden of study participation in already stressed families [22].

In spite of this apparently extensive literature, very little is known about the micro- (individual), mediating- (gatekeeper), and macro- (systemic or society) level barriers and enablers to recruiting stigmatized, socially isolated mothers into observational or intervention studies focusing on conditions of family violence or postpartum depression. This paper draws upon experiences recruiting mothers for such studies in the Child Health Intervention and Longitudinal Development (CHILD) Studies Program at the University of New Brunswick, Canada.

Chapter 431

A Study of the Relationship between Self-Conscious Affects, Coping Styles, and Depressive Reaction after a Negative Life Event

Masayo Uji[1,*], *Toshinori Kitamura*[1] *and Toshiaki Nagata*[2]
[1]Department of Clinical Behavioural Sciences,
Kumamoto University Graduate School of Medical Sciences, Japan
[2]Kyushu University of Nursing and Social Welfare, Japan

Research Summary

This study aimed to explore how the affects that result from conflictive social interpersonal relationships influence mental health, as well as to investigate how specific coping styles mediate between these affects and mental health.

The Test of Self-Conscious Affect-3 (TOSCA-3, Tangney, Dearing, Wagner, and Gramzow, 2000) assesses six self-conscious affects, namely guilt-proneness, shame-proneness, externalization, detachment, alpha pride, and beta pride. In this study, we selected for analysis the four affects that originated from negative evaluations of the presented scenarios (guilt-proneness, shame-proneness, externalization, and detachment). We used the Coping Inventory for Stressful Situations (CISS, Endler, and Parker, 1990) for estimating coping style, specifically task-oriented coping, emotion-oriented coping, and avoidance-oriented coping.

A structural equation model that makes it possible to explore the causal relationship between self-conscious affects, coping styles, and mental health, was chosen as a statistical technique. Among the 394 Japanese university students who agreed to participate in this study, 298 experienced moderate to severe stressful negative life events during the four-

---

[*] Address Department of Clinical Behavioural Sciences, Kumamoto University Graduate School of Medical Sciences, 1-1-1 Honjo, Kumamoto, JAPAN 860-8556; FAX + 81-(0)96-373-5181; Telephone +81-(0)96-373-5183; E-mail ujimasayo@excite.co.jp.

month study. Of those 298 respondents, 268 completed every item of the TOSCA-3, the CISS, and the Self-rating Depressive Scale (SDS, Zung, 1965). These 268 were subjected to a structural equation model.

Among the four affect categories which occur under stressful situations, only shame-proneness directly contributed to a depressive reaction, whereas the other three (guilt-proneness, externalization, and detachment) did not. Individuals with shame-proneness tended towards an emotional-oriented coping style, but this inhibited task-oriented coping. Guilt-proneness induced task-oriented coping and avoidance-oriented coping. Externalization induced task-oriented coping and emotion-oriented coping. Detachment gave rise only to avoidance-oriented coping. Interestingly, among the three coping styles, only task-oriented coping induced a depressive reaction, whereas emotion-oriented coping and avoidance-oriented coping did not.

We discuss these results primarily from the psychological perspective but also look briefly at how they might be applied to a clinical setting within psychiatry.

In: Psychology Research Biographies and Summaries ISBN: 978-1-61470-491-1
Editors: Nancy E. Wodarth and Alexis P. Ferguson © 2012 Nova Science Publishers, Inc.

Chapter 432

THE WORKPLACE AFFECTIVE COMMITMENT MULTIDIMENSIONAL QUESTIONNAIRE: FACTOR STRUCTURE AND MEASUREMENT INVARIANCE

Alexandre J. S. Morin[*,1], *Isabelle Madore*[1], *Julien Morizot*[2], *Jean-Sébastien Boudrias*[2] *and Michel Tremblay*[3]

[1]University of Sherbrooke, Quebec, Canada
[2]University of Montreal, Quebec, Canada
[3]HEC Montreal, Quebec, Canada

RESEARCH SUMMARY

Employees could be affectively committed towards at least eight work-related targets: organization, career, co-workers, supervisor, tasks, profession, customers, and work. The WACMQ (Workplace Affective Commitment Multidimensional Questionnaire) was recently developed to assess these targets. This study used confirmatory factor analyses (CFAs) to test alternative factor structures, relying on a sample of 404 Canadian workers. The measurement invariance of the model across gender and linguistic groups was also examined. CFAs generally supported a 7-factor structure over the original 8-factor model, showing that two targets (profession and tasks) rather formed a single factor (occupation). Finally, CFAs supported the measurement invariance of the WACMQ across gender and language versions. In addition to this substantive purpose, this study was also designed as a methodological illustration of Millsap and Tein's (2004) procedure for the evaluation of the measurement invariance of CFA models for ordered-categorical items, as supplemented by Cheung and Rensvold's (1999) recommendations for the post-hoc probing of non-invariant factor models.

---

[*] Requests for reprints should be addressed to Alexandre J.S. Morin, University of Sherbrooke, Department of Psychology, 2500 boulevard de l'Université, Sherbrooke, QC, Canada, J1K 2R1, e-mail: alexandre.morin@usherbrooke.ca.

In: Psychology Research Biographies and Summaries
Editors: Nancy E. Wodarth and Alexis P. Ferguson
ISBN: 978-1-61470-491-1
© 2012 Nova Science Publishers, Inc.

Chapter 433

IS CARING FOR THE ELDERLY A HEALTH RISK? A QUALITATIVE STUDY ON WORK EXPERIENCE, COPING AND HEALTH BEHAVIOURS OF NURSES

Brigitte Jenull[1,], Ingrid Salem[1] and Eva Brunner[2]*
[1]Department of Psychology
Alps-Adria-University Klagenfurt,
Universitaetsstrasse 65-67, 9020 Klagenfurt, Austria
[2]Carinthia University of Applied Sciences,
Hauptplatz 12, 9560 Feldkirchen, Austria

RESEARCH SUMMARY

Caring for elderly and disabled people poses a challenge not only for society but for each person working in this domain. This study addresses individual work experiences, coping strategies and health behaviour of nurses in the elderly care.

Interviews (N = 52) were conducted and analyzed using qualitative content analysis (Elo and Kyngäs, 2008; Patton, 2002). The reliability of the developed category system was evaluated by providing interrater agreement which led to a very good result.

The interviews showed that daily routine in nursing homes was often made difficult by institutional standards and hampered by negative experiences with the residents. In addition to perceiving the hostile, egoistic and uncooperative behaviour of the residents as a burden, more than half emphasised time pressure and staff shortage as stressful. Positive working experiences were related to contacts with residents and their relatives who expressed gratefulness and appreciation but those experiences were outnumbered by unpleasant incidents. The most commonly mentioned coping strategies were taking exercises and seeking for social support. These strategies seemed to help reduce stress during leisure time. Coping with hassle during the working hours is mainly realized by communication with colleagues. On the other hand, delimitation which is defined as distancing oneself from the residents and

---

[*] E-mail: brigitte.jenull@uni-klu.ac.at

work in general, plays an important role. About one third of the interview partners could only handle wearisome demands by taking (physical) revenge on the residents or sneering at them.

Health-risk behaviours such as smoking, unbalanced diet and high levels of drug use were frequently reported and multiple risk behaviour was observed. Eighty percent of the interviewed nurses were smokers and more than half of them reported the use of drugs in order to overcome working hours. Body mass index was between 19 and 41, most respondents were at least slightly overweight.

Work conditions in nursing homes seemed to lead to self-neglect and health-risk behaviour on the part of nurses and had negative impact on the interaction with the residents. Due to demographical changes in our society and the prospective increasing demand for nursing and health professionals, nursing homes should become a healthy workplace by focusing on workplace health promotion.

Chapter 434

PSYCHOLINGUISTIC CHALLENGES IN PROCESSING ARABIC LANGUAGE

Raphiq Ibrahim
Learning Disabilities Department, University of Haifa,
Haifa, Israel

RESEARCH SUMMARY

The 2006 PISA (Program for International Student Assessment) report of worldwide scholastic achievements, showed that about 50% of Israeli Arabic students were found to exhibit the lowest reading achievement scores in the PISA tests (level 1 and below) as compared to the other participating groups. Also, the MEITZAV national testing program in Israel (2001-2002) showed achievement gap in language skills (reading and reading comprehension) between Arab students and Jewish students in the school systems. This gap was larger than those found in the other areas tested (mathematics; science and technology; and English). The aim of this chapter is to explore the cognitive basis of these difficulties, specifically the diglossic situation in Arabic. Furthermore, the chapter discusses the unique features of Arabic language that might contribute to the inhibition and slowness of reading acquisition and might even hinder the acquisition of basic academic skills. Finally, a model with comprehensive basis (cognitive and neurocognitive) will be built in order to explain the complex linguistic situation of beginning Arabic learners.

Chapter 435

THE CONTEXT OF DOMESTIC VIOLENCE: SOCIAL AND CONTEXTUAL FACTORS ASSOCIATED WITH PARTNER VIOLENCE AGAINST WOMEN

Enrique Gracia[*]
University of Valencia, Spain

RESEARCH SUMMARY

Available data indicates a high prevalence of partner violence against women in our societies. The World Health Organization in its "World Report on Violence and Health" offers a summary of 48 population-based surveys from around the world in which between 10% to 69% of women reported being physically assaulted by an intimate partner at some point in their lives (World Health Organization, 2002). Different surveys in western countries estimate that about one in four women experience intimate partner violence at some point in their lives (American Medical Association, 1994; Bachman, 1994; Bachman and Saltzman, 1995; Browne, 1993; Council of Europe, 2002; Klein, Campbell, Soler, and Ghez, 1997; Straus and Gelles, 1986). For example, an analysis of 10 prevalence studies of partner violence against women in European countries also concluded that about 25% of women suffered domestic violence during their lifetime, and between 6% to 10% of women suffered violence in a given year (Council of Europe, 2002).

Despite the high prevalence of partner violence against women, however, many instances of partner violence against women are never reported to legal authorities (APA Presidential Task Force on Violence and the Family, 1996; Bachman, 1994; Bachman and Saltzman, 1995; Heise, Ellsberg and Gottemoeller, 1999; Straus and Gelles, 1986). The "Report of the American Psychological Association Presidential Task Force on Violence and the Family"

This research was supported by Grants from the Ministry of Education and Science (SEJ2006-08666), and the Ministry of Work and Social Affairs (MUJER2007-PI-090) of Spain.

[*] Correspondence concerning this article should be addressed to Enrique Gracia, Departamento de Psicología Social, Facultad de Psicología, Universitat de València, Avda. Blasco Ibáñez 21, 46010 Valencia (Spain). E-mail: enrique.gracia@uv.es.

(1996) concluded that all indications are that family violence and abuse are significantly under-reported at all levels of society, and estimates that female victims of domestic violence are 6 times less likely to report the crime to law enforcement officials than female victims of stranger violence (Bachman, 1994; Bachman y Saltzman, 1995). For example, in a national crime survey sponsored by the Bureau of Justice Statistics, when an injury was inflicted upon a woman by her intimate partner, she reported the violence to the police only 55% of the time and she was even less likely to report the violence when she did not sustain injury (Bachman and Saltzman, 1995).

In a Canadian study the percentage of spouse violence against women not reported to the police was 60% (Bunge and Locke, 2000). Other data sources provide even lower rates of reported incidents of partner violence against women. For example, the Florida Governor's Task Force on Domestic and Sexual Violence (1997) estimated that only about one-seventh of all domestic assaults come to the attention of the police. Also, Kaufman-Kantor and Straus (1990), after examining a nationally representative sample found that 93% of domestic assaults were not reported to the police. In Europe, a Spanish study confirmed also that many instances of partner violence against women are seldom reported to the authorities, representing only between 4% and 11% of the total estimated cases. For example, 70% of women victims of fatal partner violence never reported any past incidents to the authorities (Instituto de la Mujer, 2008).

The fact that most of the cases of partner violence against women are not reported to authorities is one side of the problem of domestic violence that has received little attention by scholars and researchers in this field. This side of the problem is usually represented by a metaphor: The iceberg of domestic violence (see Gracia, 2004). That is, reported cases of domestic violence against women represent only a very small part of the victims when compared with prevalence data. In this metaphor, reported cases of partner violence against women (usually the most severe end of violence) represent only the tip of the iceberg. Most cases are submerged, have no official existence, and are invisible to protective services. But, are they also invisible to society, to the social context surrounding the victims?

Available data suggest that many cases of partner violence against women not reported to the authorities are known within the social circle of the victim (e.g., relatives, neighbors, friends, co-workers, acquaintances). For example, in the USA, the Lieberman Survey found that almost 30% of the respondents reported that they knew a woman who was currently a victim of physical abuse (Klein et al., 1997). Also, in a survey with a representative sample of 15 countries of the European Union (European Commission, 1999; Gracia and Herrero, 2006a), 36% of male and 45% of female respondents knew a victim of partner violence against women in their social circle of work, studies, family, neighborhood or friends. Also, in this survey, respondents knew someone who had subjected a woman to some form of domestic violence in the same places.

Data indicates that although many cases of partner violence against women are officially invisible (not reported to the legal authorities), they are, in many instances, socially visible. It is important, therefore, to understand not only why women do not leave a violent relationship, or why they do not report it to the police (Bachman, 1994; Dobash and Dobash, 1979; Shrader and Sagot, 2000; see Rhodes, 1998, for a review), but also is important to understand public responses to incidents of partner violence against women. This has been, however, a rather neglected area of scholarly attention in the field of partner violence against women. In the next sections of this chapter we will review research examining public perceptions, attitudes and responses to partner violence against women, as well as social and contextual factors influencing this perceptions, attitudes and responses. The idea that lies behind this analysis is that these factors play an important role in shaping the social environment in which partner violence against women takes place, which, in turn, may foster or reduce levels of partner violence against women in our societies.

Chapter 436

EXTRAVERSION AND SUICIDAL BEHAVIOR

*David Lester**
The Richard Stockton College of New Jersey, US

RESEARCH SUMMARY

There has been a great deal of research on the relationship between suicidality and extraversion/introversion, but no systematic review of this research has yet appeared. The present paper reviews this body of research in order to see if there are any consistent trends and then suggests future directions for research into this issue.

---

* E-mail: David.Lester@stockton.edu.

Chapter 437

ALCOHOL RELATED EXPERIENCES –
THE GOOD, THE BAD AND THE UGLY

Karin Helmersson Bergmark[*]
Sociology, Dept of Sociology and Addiction Research Group
Stockholm University, Sweden

RESEARCH SUMMARY

When asked about how they feel about alcohol and drinking, Swedes have tended to display negative and ambivalent attitudes. For this study reports of alcohol related experiences were used for the study of an eventual new emerging drinking culture. The aim was to analyse frequency distributions and patterns for explanatory variables, for different groups of alcohol related experiences.

As drinking levels have increased in Sweden during the last decades, on the one hand we expected to find an increase of reports of alcohol related experiences. On the other hand, we could well expect less such experiences in a time when alcohol and drinking tends to be put into an every-day practise.

Experiences from the good sides of drinking were more often reported, compared to the bad sides. A factor analysis resulted in four dimensions measuring aspects of pleasure (1), bad sides of drinking (2), ugly sides of drinking (3) and one on sexuality/aggression (4). Logistic regression analyses were used to see if these dimensions have unique characteristics that could be revealed with predictor variables. No clear such patterns were, however, found, even though some results indicate the upsurge of more pleasure-driven drinking styles.

---

[*] Contact address: Stockholm University, dept of Sociology, S-10691 Stockholm, Sweden karin.bergmark@sociology.su.se.

Chapter 438

PHYSIOLOGICAL ASSESSMENT OF FORGIVENESS, GRUDGES, AND REVENGE: THEORIES, RESEARCH METHODS, AND IMPLICATIONS

Everett L. Worthington[*] and Goli Sotoohi
Virginia Commonwealth University, US

RESEARCH SUMMARY

Forgiveness is a prosocial intrapersonal response to a transgression experienced in interpersonal context. Theorizing about forgiveness makes a myriad of distinctions, differentiating between decisions to forgive and emotional experience, and among emotions, motivations, cognition, and behavioral intensions. Research to date has not considered the conceptual advances in understanding forgiveness. Research has linked unforgiveness with poor health outcomes, but relatively little attention has been given to the physiological mechanisms that mediate the forgiveness-health connection. In the present chapter, we locate 19 empirical articles seeking to explicate the physiological processes involved in forgiving. We review the articles within an emphasis on theory. We seek to apply stress-and-coping, self-control, and broaden-and-build theories to uncovering potential questions that researchers could use to make a research agenda. Not surprisingly, in this burgeoning new field of study—forgiveness studies—more and more sophisticated research is needed.

---

[*] E-mal: eworth@vcu.edu.

Chapter 439

APPLICATION OF LCA TO A COMPARISON OF THE GLOBAL WARMING POTENTIAL OF INDUSTRIAL AND ARTISANAL FISHING IN THE STATE OF RIO DE JANEIRO (BRAZIL)

D. P. Souza[*], K. R. A. Nunes, R. Valle, A. M. Carneiro and F. M. Mendonça
UFRJ (Federal University of Rio de Janeiro) – COPPE – Industrial Engineering Program, Brazil

RESEARCH SUMMARY

One of the main environmental impacts caused by fisheries is the emission of gases from the fuels used for the vessels. These gases contribute to global warming. The aim of the this chapter is to use LCA (Life Cycle Assessment) to compare the global warming potential of artisanal and industrial fishing off the northern coast of Rio de Janeiro state (municipalities of Arraial do Cabo and Cabo Frio, respectively). For this analysis, one ton of common sea bream was adopted as the functional unit. The artisanal fishing data were obtained from interviews with local fishermen, while the industrial fishing data were collected from an industrial fishery. The study made use of the Umberto™ software package. The result of this comparison showed that industrial fishing has a greater impact on global warming than artisanal fishing.

---

[*] C.P. 68.507, CEP 21.945-970 Rio de Janeiro - RJ - Brazil - Fax + 55 21 2562 7848; UFSJ (Federal University of São João del Rey) – Praça Frei Orlando, 170; São João del Rey – MG - Brazil – CEP. 36307 352.

In: Psychology Research Biographies and Summaries
Editors: Nancy E. Wodarth and Alexis P. Ferguson

ISBN: 978-1-61470-491-1
© 2012 Nova Science Publishers, Inc.

Chapter 440

THE EFFECT OF SEXUALLY EXPLICIT RAP MUSIC ON SEXUAL ATTITUDES, NORMS, AND BEHAVIORS

Lucrezia M. Alcorn and Anthony F. Lemieux
Purchase College, State University of New York, US

RESEARCH SUMMARY

In this chapter, we review the recent literature on music and social influence, with a particular emphasis on the influence of music on sexual attitudes and behaviors. We also present an experimental study that provided an empirical investigation of the relationships between sexually explicit rap music and sexual attitudes, perceived norms, and behaviors. Results indicated no significant short-term effects of rap music on the expression of sexual attitudes or perception of norms. However, we found marginal support for sexually explicit rap in priming condom-related sexual behavior.

Chapter 441

TREATMENTS FOR CYSTIC FIBROSIS: THE ROLE OF ADHERENCE, IMPORTANCE AND BURDEN

Lynn B. Myers[*]
Department of Psychology, School of Social Sciences
Brunel University, UK

RESEARCH SUMMARY

Introduction. Cystic fibrosis (CF) is the most frequent lethal genetic disease of childhood. Nowadays due to improvements in treatment most people with CF can lead fairly normal lives. To achieve this people with CF need daily treatment consisting of various medications, chest physical therapy and pancreatic enzymes as well as paying attention to dietary needs. There has been a gradual but significant improvement in the life expectancy of CF patients due to advances in the efficacy of treatment. So what was considered a disease of childhood has now also become a chronic condition of adulthood. The current study investigated factors associated with treatments in adults with CF.

Method. Participants were 563 adults with CF recruited from the UK's Cystic Fibrosis Trust mailing list. Patients rated adherence to each treatment and reported any other treatments e.g. complementary therapies. Other measures included importance of each treatment, burden of each treatments and demographic information.

Results. The mean number of current treatments was high (10.49). Adherence varied with different behaviors, with the highest adherence for enzymes, insulin and antibiotics and lowest for physical therapy, exercise, overnight feeding and dietary supplements. Statistical analyses were correlations and Analysis of Variance. Adherence was correlated with importance and burden for the majority of treatments, meaning high adherence was related to high importance and low burden. Treatments varied in importance, with insulin and

---

[*] Address for correspondence: Professor Lynn B. Myers. Centre for the Study of Health & Well-Being, Department of Psychology, School of Social Sciences, Brunel University. Uxbridge, Middlesex, UB8 3PH. UK. Email lynn.myers@brunel.ac.uk.

antibiotics rated the highest and dietary treatments the lowest. For burden, treatments which are administered by injection or are time consuming were rated the highest e.g. insulin, nebulized medications, with easily administered treatments rated the lowest e.g. oral steroids, enzymes. For most treatments importance and burden were positively correlated, meaning that the more important the treatment the least troublesome it was rated. Nearly a quarter reported using some form of complimentary therapy with more females reporting such use. However, over 50% said that CF never or only occasionally interfered with their enjoyment of life. There were few gender differences, but some age differences.

Conclusion .Results from this study provide an insight into treatments for adults with CF, indicating a complex picture of adherence and indicate that adherence, importance and burden are usually related.

THE RELATIONSHIP BETWEEN ADOLESCENTS' MUSIC VIDEO VIEWING AND RISKY DRIVING: A TWO WAVE PANEL SURVEY

Kathleen Beullens[*], Keith Roe and Jan Van den Bulck

Leuven School for Mass Communication Research,
Katholieke Universiteit Leuven,
Leuven, Belgium

RESEARCH SUMMARY

Purpose: Music video viewing is a very popular pastime among adolescents. The public criticism of music videos has encouraged researchers to examine the effects of music video exposure. Although an association between music video exposure and several health risk behaviors (e.g. drinking) has been found, the relationship between music video viewing and risky driving has remained largely unexamined. In this study the relationship between adolescents' music video viewing and risky driving such as driving after consuming alcohol and joy riding is explored.

Methods: Participants were 354 adolescent males and females who participated in a panel study (2-year interval). Respondents were 17 or 18 years old during the first wave of data collection and did not have their driver's license yet. They completed a questionnaire on music video viewing, sensation seeking, aggression, attitudes towards joy riding and driving after the consumption of alcohol, and the intention to perform these behaviors in the future. Two years later the respondents had obtained their driver's license and were questioned on their actual risky driving behavior. The relationships between these constructs were analyzed using structural equation models.

Results: The results indicate that music video viewing is indirectly associated with joy riding and driving after the consumption of alcohol through the attitudes towards these

---

[*] Corresponding author: Kathleen Beullens, e-mail: Kathleen.Beullens@soc.kuleuven.be; Tel: +32(0)16.32.32.19// +32(0)16.32.32.20 Fax: +32(0)16.32.33.12.

behaviors and the intention to perform these behaviors in the future. More music video viewing resulted in a more positive attitude towards risky driving, even after controlling for sensation seeking and aggression. These attitudes are positively related to the intention to perform these reckless behaviors in the future and these intentions are, in turn, a good predictor of the actual risky driving behavior two years later.

Conclusions: The results indicate that music video viewing during adolescence is an important and significant predictor of risky driving two years later.

In: Psychology Research Biographies and Summaries ISBN: 978-1-61470-491-1
Editors: Nancy E. Wodarth and Alexis P. Ferguson © 2012 Nova Science Publishers, Inc.

Chapter 443

INDIVIDUALS WITH EATING DISORDERS AND STRESS

Christine Courbasson[1] and Jenany Jeyarajan[2]*

[1] Eating Disorders and Addiction Clinic, Concurrent Disorders Service
Psychology Practicum Training Program,
Centre for Addiction and Mental Health,
Department of Psychiatry, University of Toronto
Toronto, Ontario, Canada
[2] University of Toronto, Canada

RESEARCH SUMMARY

Individuals with eating disorders experience a high degree of stress. The combination of not having learned adaptive coping strategies and being exposed to challenging situations can render people vulnerable to experiencing stress and developing mental health problems. Some people may turn to problematic coping strategies such as dissociation, substance abuse, and problematic eating [Hansel, and Wittrock, 1997]. There is a high prevalence of traumatic histories and problematic coping skills to manage stressful situations in individuals with eating disorders.

This manuscript will review the literature on stress and coping in individuals with eating disorders. Binge eating, purging, and food restriction will be discussed in the context of self-regulatory process. Issues related to comorbidities will be addressed, and promising stress control strategies will be discussed.

The role of CBT, reflective activity, and mindfulness in regulatory process, stress reduction, and control will be discussed [Luck, Waller, Meyer, Ussher, and Lacey, 2005].

---

* E-mail: sneha3@hotmail.com.

In: Psychology Research Biographies and Summaries
Editors: Nancy E. Wodarth and Alexis P. Ferguson
ISBN: 978-1-61470-491-1
© 2012 Nova Science Publishers, Inc.

Chapter 444

EXTRAVERSION AND THE AUTONOMIC NERVOUS SYSTEM: AN ALTERNATIVE TO EYSENCK'S THEORY

David Lester[*]
The Richard Stockton College of New Jersey, US

Othello: Give me your hand. This hand is moist, my lady.
Desdemona: It hath felt no age nor known no sorrow.
Othello: This argues fruitfulness and liberal heart.
       Hot, hot, and moist. This hand of yours requires
       A sequester from liberty, fasting, and prayer.
       Much castigation, exercise devout;
       For here's a young and sweating devil here
       That commonly rebels.

Shakespeare's *Othello*, Act 3, Scene iv

RESEARCH SUMMARY

An hypothesis is proposed that balance in the autonomic nervous system is the physiological basis for extraversion-introversion, with extraverts as S-types and introverts as P-types.

---

[*] E-mail: David.Lester@stockton.edu.

In: Psychology Research Biographies and Summaries ISBN: 978-1-61470-491-1
Editors: Nancy E. Wodarth and Alexis P. Ferguson © 2012 Nova Science Publishers, Inc.

Chapter 445

EXTRAVERSION AND INTERVIEWING FOR EMPLOYMENT

Joshua Fogel and Mayer Schneider*
Department of Economics, Brooklyn College, Brooklyn, NY, US

RESEARCH SUMMARY

The personality trait of extraversion is often used as a factor for understanding and predicting successful job applicants. This article reviews the empirical research from scholarly journals on what is known about extraversion and job interviews. The search terms of "(extraversion) AND (employment or job) AND (interview)" were searched in the databases of Medline, PsycINFO, CINAHL, and Business Source Premier from the year of 1998 to 2008. The article reviews 21 articles. Almost all of the reviewed articles indicate that extraversion is associated with positive outcomes for employment interviews, promotion interviews, and also better job performance. Individuals that evaluate applicants for new jobs or consider current employees for promotion should assess extraversion as part of this initial hiring or promotion process.

---

[*] Correspondence: Joshua Fogel, Ph.D. Brooklyn College of the City University of New York, Department of Economics, 218A 2900 Bedford Avenue, Brooklyn, NY 11210, USA. Phone: (718) 951-3857. Fax: (718) 951-4867. e-mail: joshua.fogel@gmail.com.

Chapter 446

THE INFLUENCE OF GENDER STEREOTYPES ON CAUSAL ATTRIBUTIONS ABOUT SUCCESSFUL LEADERSHIP

R. Garcia-Retamero[*,1,2], S. M. Müller[1] and E. López-Zafra[3]

[1]University of Granada, Spain
[2]Max Planck Institute for Human Development, Berlin, Germany
[3]University of Jaén, Spain

RESEARCH SUMMARY

Although women in western societies are entering leadership positions to a greater extent than ever before, the "think male–think manager" paradigm (Schein, 1973) still seems to be influential. This paper analyzes people's predictions about the successful performance of a female or a male candidate for a leadership position. Specifically, the influence of the participant's sex, and nationality, as well as the organizational context of the employee's corporation were analyzed in a series of studies. Participants in the studies were all given a description of a large corporation in which a female or male employee was proposed for promotion to a leading managerial position. Results can be interpreted in line with the Role Congruity Theory (Eagly and Karau, 2002) stating that there is still an existent gender gap in the attribution of successful leadership performance.

---

[*] Correspondence to: Rocio Garcia-Retamero, Departamento de Psicología Experimental, Facultad de Psicología, Universidad de Granada, Campus Universitario de Cartuja s/n, 18071 Granada, Spain. E-mail: rretamer@ugr.es; Tel: +34 958 246240; Fax: +34 958 246239.

Chapter 447

ATHLETE PERFORMANCE, COPING AND ANXIETY: CLINICAL ISSUES FOR THE CONSULTANT

Thomas W. Miller[*]
University of Connecticut, US

RESEARCH SUMMARY

Performance, coping and anxiety are critical ingredients for the consultant in working with athletes at all levels. Consultation in sport requires competency and specificity. The greater the specificity of the service in terms of offering information and training that will assure athletes can adapt to both the known and unknown factors that will operate to pose threats to their career should be the primary goal(Miller, Ogilvie,. Branch, 2008). In consultation with agents or coaches, appealing to individual athletes who could benefit from any aspect of sports consultation requires each having an empirical basis to the consultation services. New recruits whether to a college or pro team will confront a number of issues within the purview of the sports consultant when signing a contract. As a consultant, it is essential to emphasize to agents and others within college or professional organizations why it is imperative that an extensive psychometric study be utilized for the benefit of both athlete and coaching staff. Individual assessment helps to diagnose potential problems and will be instructive for the organization in understanding enhancing the individual's probability of making and completing effectively in the athletic arena.

---

[*] Requests for reprints are sent to: Thomas Miller, Ph.D., ABPP Professor and Senior Research Scientist, Department of Psychology and Center for Health Intervention and Prevention, University of Connecticut, Storrs Connecticut 06268; E-mail: tom.miller@uconn.edu.

In: Psychology Research Biographies and Summaries
Editors: Nancy E. Wodarth and Alexis P. Ferguson
ISBN: 978-1-61470-491-1
© 2012 Nova Science Publishers, Inc.

Chapter 448

CULTURAL FACTORS INFLUENCING OLIVE OIL PURCHASE BEHAVIOUR: EMPIRICAL ANALYSIS USING SCANNER DATA

Juan Carlos Gázquez-Abad[1]*, Francisco J. Martínez-López[2] and Juan Antonio Mondéjar-Jiménez[3]

[1]Department of Management and Business Administration.
Faculty of Business and Economics. University of Almería, Almería, Spain
[2]Department of Marketing. Business Faculty. University of Granada, Spain, Campus Universitario de Cartuja, Granada, Spain
[3]Social Sciences Faculty (Cuenca).
University of Castilla-La Mancha. Avda. de los Alfares, Cuenca, Spain

RESEARCH SUMMARY

Olive oil is an important component in the food system in most European markets. Moreover, its consumption is gaining interest among consumers, particularly in northern Europe, the US and Canada. As a consequence of this increasing consumption it is fundamental to analyze the main factors influencing consumers' olive-oil choices for both brands and retailers to be able to compete more efficiently and satisfy consumer needs more closely. In this respect, factors such as culture or habits affect many aspects of consumer behavior such as the structure of consumption, individual decision-making and communication about the product. In a socio-cultural context like the olive-oil Spanish market, in which brand awareness is strong and the use of the product is very high, these factors are even more important. In order to do so, several Multinomial Logit Models (MNL) using olive oil scanner choice data are estimated. The results appear to support the idea that there exists a traditional strong preference towards national brands present in the market for many years confirming the main role of culture in olive-oil purchase behaviour.

---

* Corresponding author: E-mail: jcgazque@ual.es.

Chapter 449

FAMILY STRESS AND PSYCHOLOGICAL ADJUSTMENT AMONG WELFARE AND NON WELFARE IMMIGRANTS

Gila Markovizky[1], Doron Hadas[*,1] *and Miri Sarid[2]*

[1]Tel Hai Academic College, Israel
[2]Western Galilee Collage, Israel

RESEARCH SUMMARY

The present study explored the psychological adaptation of immigrants to Israel, while comparing between two populations – immigrants treated by the Department of Social Services welfare system, and immigrants non treated by the welfare system.

Research findings show that the psychological adaptation of immigrants is predicted by the resources in the immigrant's possession, indicating that the psychological adaptation of population with special difficulties, such as – the elderly, single mothers, psychiatric patients etc., is more problematic (Ross et al. 1990, Cohen and Wills, 1985). These findings were refuted by the current study, according to which, unexpectedly immigrants treated by the welfare system reported higher satisfaction from their integration in Israel, from their process of Alyia and from their life condition in Israel, compared to non-welfare immigrants)

It was found that married subjects reported more familial and economic difficulties, compared to non-married, and also related these difficulties more to negative psychological responses. , The present research' findings point to differences between the studied groups regarding the experience of the immigration crisis, apparently the stresses of immigration act differently according to 'the experienced level of balance' former to immigration. Finally, the present study has practical implications, by which an absorbing state should differentiate its treatment and policy of immigration, according to immigrants' position prior to immigration. Moreover, the 'resilience' hypothesis which is apparently supported by the present study, should be further examined empirically.

---

[*] Address for correspondence: Dr. Hadas Doron, 127 Nahal Keret St. Yokneam Moshava, 20600 Israel. e-mail: hadasdoron@012.net.il.

THE EFFECTS OF POSTPARTUM DEPRESSION ON THE MOTHER-INFANT RELATIONSHIP AND CHILD DEVELOPMENT

Deana B. Davalos[*], Alana M. Campbell and Amanda L. Pala*
Colorado State University, US

RESEARCH SUMMARY

During the last two decades there has been an increase in research focusing on the effects of maternal depression on the mother infant bond. Research in this field has apparently developed out of; a recognition of a relatively higher prevalence of postpartum maternal depression than once believed and recurring observations of differences in mother/infant relationships or infant behavior associated with maternal postpartum depression.

The infant behaviors that have been implicated as resulting from this theoretically compromised mother infant relationship have included slight, transient effects on sociability and affective sharing to results suggesting significant increases in irritability, cognitive delays, behavioral problems, and difficulties with attachment, among others. Longitudinal data suggest that while some problems appear to resolve relatively quickly, there are some characteristics that endure long after infancy. Specifically, some researchers have argued that children and even adolescents who experienced problems bonding with their depressed mothers are at significantly greater risk of experiencing a variety of psychological symptoms, including depression, anxiety, and problems with addiction. Again, this view is controversial and others in the field link these increased risks to other factors such as low socioeconomic status or marital discord. While there appears to be consensus among most researchers in recognizing that there are likely effects of postpartum depression on mother infant bonding

---

[*] Deana.Davalos@UCHSC.edu.

that affect early development, there is little consensus regarding the specific details of these effects.

In our review, we will systematically analyze research focusing on the effects of postpartum depression on the mother infant bond and those variables that are believed to be affected from potential difficulties in this bond.

In: Psychology Research Biographies and Summaries
Editors: Nancy E. Wodarth and Alexis P. Ferguson
ISBN: 978-1-61470-491-1
© 2012 Nova Science Publishers, Inc.

Chapter 451

TREATING A CLINICAL SAMPLE OF HIGHLY GIFTED UNDERACHIEVERS WITH MUSIC THERAPY AN EXPLORATORY STUDY

Lony Schiltz-Ludwig[*]
Fondation François-Elisabeth, Luxembourg

ABSTRACT

Published literature as well as personal observation show that gifted adolescents suffering from severe intellectual inhibition may generally not be helped by pedagogical means alone. This special syndrome results from a deep disturbance of the affective and drive functioning and may be treated by psychodynamic music therapy in individual sessions, combined with psycho-pedagogical applications of music in group sessions. Data drawn from an exploratory study, based on a mixed research methodology, combined a psychometric scale, a projective test and an observational frame for the therapeutic sessions and showed changes induced in the cognitive, emotional and conduct variables by music therapy treatment. We compared two clinical subgroups of students treated by the above described psychotherapeutic approach (N = 20, N = 23) to a control group (N = 43) of students who had only pedagogical measures.

Case material helps to illustrate the psychotherapeutic process.

The discussion stresses the opportunity to offer music psychotherapy to gifted underachievers as a means of tertiary prevention.

---

[*] Schiltz Lony, Ph.D. psychologist, music therapist, doctor in clinical psychology, HDR. Head of Laboratory in Clinical Psychology, Health Psychology and Arts therapies, Fondation François-Elisabeth, Luxembourg Head of studies of the postgraduate curriculum in arts therapies (DESS en Art thérapie, Université du Luxembourg) *Professional address*: Fondation François-Elisabeth, Luxembourg. Hôpital Kirchberg. 9, rue Edward Steichen. L-2540 Luxembourg. e-mail: lony.schiltz@education.lu *Mailing address* : 10, rue Gabriel de Marie. L-2131 Luxembourg. Tel 00352 433668.

In: Psychology Research Biographies and Summaries
Editors: Nancy E. Wodarth and Alexis P. Ferguson
ISBN: 978-1-61470-491-1
© 2012 Nova Science Publishers, Inc.

Chapter 452

Marital Patterns and Psychological Adjustment among Immigrants from Ethiopia and FSU

Gila Markovitzky and Hadas Doron[*]
Tel-Hai Academic College, Israel

Research Summary

The research examines the contribution of marital patterns (role division, decision making, and marital quality) to the psychological adjustment (psychological well-being, emotional state, and satisfaction) of new immigrants in Israel, according to country of origin and gender. Self reported questionnaires were filled by 236 new immigrants: 112 from the FSU and 124 from Ethiopia, who came to Israel between 1990 and 2001. The findings indicate that the most important predictor of adjustment was country of origin: immigrants from Ethiopia displayed a higher level of psychological adjustment relative to those from the CIS.

Among women and men from Ethiopia, level of egalitarianism in role division and decision-making was found to correlate significantly with psychological responses. In comparison, the immigrants from the FSU reported more equality in the family, but this was not correlated with psychological adjustment. Of all the subgroups, the Ethiopian women demonstrated the highest level of adjustment.

---

[*] Address for correspondence: Dr. Hadas Doron, 127 Nahal Keret St. Yokneam Hamoshava. 20600 Israel. e-mail: hadasdoron@012.net.il.

In: Psychology Research Biographies and Summaries
Editors: Nancy E. Wodarth and Alexis P. Ferguson
ISBN: 978-1-61470-491-1
© 2012 Nova Science Publishers, Inc.

Chapter 453

FAMILY STRESS AND PSYCHOLOGICAL ADJUSTMENT AMONG WELFARE AND NON WELFARE IMMIGRANTS

Gila Markovizky[1], Hadas Doron[1,] and Miri Sarid[2]*
[1]Tel Hai Academic College, Israel
[2]Western Galilee College, Israel

RESEARCH SUMMARY

The present study explored the psychological adaptation of immigrants to Israel, while comparing between two populations – immigrants treated by the Department of Social Services welfare system, and immigrants non treated by the welfare system.

Research findings show that the psychological adaptation of immigrants is predicted by the resources in the immigrant's possession, indicating that the psychological adaptation of population with special difficulties, such as – the elderly, single mothers, psychiatric patients etc., is more problematic (Ross et al. 1990, Cohen and Wills, 1985). These findings were refuted by the current study, according to which, unexpectedly immigrants treated by the welfare system reported higher satisfaction from their integration in Israel, from their process of Alyia and from their life condition in Israel, compared to non-welfare immigrants).

It was found that married subjects reported more familial and economic difficulties, compared to non-married, and also related these difficulties more to negative psychological responses. , The present research' findings point to differences between the studied groups regarding the experience of the immigration crisis, apparently the stresses of immigration act differently according to 'the experienced level of balance' former to immigration. Finally, the present study has practical implications, by which an absorbing state should differentiate its treatment and policy of immigration, according to immigrants' position prior to immigration. Moreover, the 'resilience' hypothesis which is apparently supported by the present study, should be further examined empirically.

---

[*] Address for correspondence: Dr. Hadas Doron. 127 Nahal Keret St. Yokneam Moshava. 20600 Israel. e-mail: hadasdoron@012.net.il.

Chapter 454

MEMORY FOR OBJECT LOCATION: ENCODING STRATEGIES IN CHILDREN

Annalisa Lucidi[1], Clelia Rossi-Arnaud[2], Laura Pieroni[2] and Vincenzo Cestari[1,3]

[1]Faculty of Educational Science, LUMSA University, Rome, Italy
[2]Department of Psychology, Università di Roma "La Sapienza"
[3]Ist. Neuroscienze, C.N.R. Rome, Italy

RESEARCH SUMMARY

A number of studies (Cestari et al., 2007; Postma and De Haan, 1996) suggest that two separate spatial processes may be involved in short-term object location memory. First, one needs to remember the precise position occupied in a given space (positional encoding per se), then one has to decide which object was at which position (object-to-position assignment). The aim of the present study was to investigate the way children of different ages code for object locations referring to the theoretical framework of working memory (Baddeley, 1986, 2000; Baddeley and Hitch, 1974). In particular, the main questions addressed in this chapter were: a) when children have to remember the location of objects do they recode visual material verbally? b) Is this process age-dependent? A modified version of Postma and De Haan's (1996) object location task was used and three relocation conditions were examined. In the first condition, subjects had to remember spatial positions in a two-dimensional matrix. In the second task, object-location associations were examined and previously occupied positions were signalled so that children only had to remember object-to-position assignment (i.e., "what was where") while in the third condition, the "combined" condition, children had to perform both positional reconstruction and object-to-position assignment. In order to examine which encoding strategy children aged 5 and 11 years spontaneously use in temporary memory for object location, we interfered with the activity of the phonological loop and the visuo-spatial sketch pad adopting a dual task methodology. In the second experiment, to further investigate the object-to-location binding, the visual and verbal characteristics of the stimuli used in the test were manipulated and children of the same two age groups were tested. Our results show that children of age 11, like adults, use mainly a phonological recoding for pictorial stimuli while younger children show a "mixed strategy" based both on visual and phonological information.

Chapter 455

PREVALENCE OF POST TRAUMATIC STRESS AND EMOTIONAL AND BEHAVIORAL PROBLEMS AMONG ISRAELI ADOLESCENTS EXPOSED TO ONGOING TERRORISM

Orna Braun-Lewensohn[*,1,2], *Smadar Celestin-Westreich*[1], *Leon-Patrice Celestin*[3], *Dominique Verté*[4] *and Ingrid Ponjaert-Kristoffersen*[1]

[1]Department of Developmental and Lifespan Psychology,
Vrije Universiteit Brussels, Belgium
[2]Department of Interdisciplinary Studies, Conflict Management and Conflict Resolution Program, Ben Gurion University, Beer-Sheva, Israel
[3]Department of Child and Adolescent Psychiatry,
Hospital of Poissy-Saint-Germain-en-Laye, France
[4]Department of Educational Sciences,
Vrije Universiteit Brussels, Belgium

RESEARCH SUMMARY

Given that to date relatively little research has been carried out into the effects of ongoing terrorist attacks with the emphasis on adolescents in urban areas, this study set out to investigate a wide range of self-reported emotional and behavioral outcomes among adolescents facing ongoing terrorism in both urban and rural locations in Israel.

913 adolescents aged twelve to eighteen years from four different locations in Israel who were exposed in different ways to terrorist attacks over a period of three years against the backdrop of ongoing terror are investigated to identify the prevalence of Post Traumatic

---

[*] Correspondence: Orna Braun-Lewensohn, Department of Interdisciplinary Studies, Ben-Gurion University of the Negev, P.O.B. 653, Beer-Sheva 84105, Israel. Email: ornabl@bgu.ac.il. Phone: 97286428413 Fax: 97286472837.

Stress (PTS) and related mental health problems by self-report measures, including Achenbach's Youth Self-Report, the Brief Symptoms Inventory and a specially designed questionnaire covering Post Traumatic Stress and exposure to terror data.

Around 90% of the adolescents experience mild to severe PTS, one fifth reported borderline or clinical emotional and behavioral problems, and one third reported mental health difficulties. Students from different locations revealed different levels of PTS and other psychological problems. Analysis according to level of exposure revealed that it was not always those whose exposure was the most objectively severe who exhibited the most symptoms.

Future research should highlight the unique characteristics of ongoing exposure to terrorism, such as the cumulative effects of exposure and risk of exposure, in order to shed light on their contribution to mental health outcomes.

In: Psychology Research Biographies and Summaries
Editors: Nancy E. Wodarth and Alexis P. Ferguson

ISBN: 978-1-61470-491-1
© 2012 Nova Science Publishers, Inc.

Chapter 456

EXTENDING THE STRESSOR-STRAIN PERSPECTIVE: A REVIEW AND ELABORATION OF THE POSSIBILITY TO REVERSE CAUSALITY IN ROLE STRESS MODELS

Daniel Örtqvist and Joakim Wincent*
Luleå University of Technology, Luleå, Sweden

RESEARCH SUMMARY

Although the current state of role stress research has to a large extent determined significant consequences, we highlight that the field do not acknowledge the complexity of role relationships, especially occasions of reverse causality.

In opening a dialogue, we discuss the possibility to an extension of the stressor-strain paradigm, that is the dominant perspective in role stress research, from explaining linear causal chains of detrimental consequences of role stress to instead researching reversed causality relationships with alternatives theories. Although we concur with previous findings, we elaborate upon the fact that what have long been indicated as important consequences of role stress may also be antecedents to role stress.

This paper examines theoretical implications of questioning causality, review typical causal role stress models and outline some method implications for using a cross-lagged design for researching reversed causality of the current role stress consequences.

---

[*] E-mail: daniel.ortqvist@ltu.se; joakim.wincent@ltu.se.

Chapter 457

ROLE STRESS IN FLEXIBLE AND CREATIVE ROLES: SOME SUGGESTIONS ON HOW TO IDENTIFY POSITIVE CONSEQUENCES

Joakim Wincent[*] *and Daniel Örtqvist*
Luleå University of Technology, Luleå, Sweden

RESEARCH SUMMARY

In this paper we illustrate that much of the traditional role stress research has related to quite static roles in role taking systems where effects of role stress typically have been viewed as detrimental (i.e., the stressor-strain perspective). We suggest a brighter picture in that role stress can have positive consequences when roles are constructed to have enough flexibility, freedom and creativity to allow for pertinent coping alternatives. In relation to this perspective, we present three approaches for examining the nature of stress and for evaluating whether role stress can have positive consequences given certain role characteristics.

---

[*] E-mail: joakim.wincent@ltu.se; daniel.ortqvist@ltu.se.

Chapter 458

THE ROLE OF CONTEXTUAL CUES AND LOGICAL TRAINING IN DIFFERENTIATING CONDITIONAL FROM BICONDITIONAL STATEMENTS IN INFERENCE TASK

Olimpia Matarazzo and Ivana Baldassarre
Department of Psychology,
Second University of Naples, Italy

RESEARCH SUMMARY

In two studies we examined the role of contextual cues and logical training in differentiating conditional from biconditional statements (i.e. the statements of the form "if p then q" from the statements of the form "if and only if p then q") in deductive inference task (i.e. establishing which conclusions necessarily follow from syllogisms whose major premise is formed by a conditional clause). We assume that the well-documented tendency to interpret conditionals as biconditionals is due not only to pragmatic factors, such as a large amount of literature posits, but also to cognitive factors: it is much easier to understand a symmetrical (biconditional) relation between two states of affairs rather than an asymmetrical (conditional) one. We expected that this tendency would be inhibited not only by the presence of contextual cues - as alternative antecedents (e.g. c, m, r) showing that the consequent (q) can be implied by other states of affairs besides the one (p) presented in conditional clause - but also by a "logical" training, that is, by elucidating the formal difference between conditionals and biconditionals. On the contrary, we expected that the statement content (abstract vs. thematic) did not affect the interpretation of conditionals as biconditionals. In the first study, three hundred twenty participants performed in counterbalanced order a conditional and a biconditional inference task introduced by a very short scenario. The experimental conditions varied in function of the following variables: discrimination between conditionals and biconditionals (embedded in the scenarios vs. inferred by participants after reading the scenarios), information facilitating the appropriate interpretation of the statements (present vs. absent), content (abstract vs. thematic). The results revealed that (1) biconditional syllogisms were easily solved in any experimental conditions; (2) conditionals generated a large amount of patterns of inferences, among which the most frequent was the biconditional one when facilitating information (i.e. alternative antecedents) was absent; on the contrary, when this information was presented, the conditional pattern of inferences was the most frequent one and the biconditional one decreased dramatically. In the second study, two hundred participants performed a conditional and a biconditional task introduced merely by the respective statements. The manipulated variables were: logical training (present vs. absent) and content (abstract vs. thematic). The results were analogous to those of the first study. On the whole, these experiments corroborate the idea that (1) biconditional interpretation of conditional statements - reconstructed from the participants' patterns of inferences – is due both to cognitive and pragmatic factors and that (2) reasoners are able to rectify this misinterpretation both in presence of contextual cues and of logical training. The theoretical implications of these results are discussed.

In: Psychology Research Biographies and Summaries
Editors: Nancy E. Wodarth and Alexis P. Ferguson
ISBN: 978-1-61470-491-1
© 2012 Nova Science Publishers, Inc.

Chapter 459

A THEORETICAL REVIEW OF PSYCHOSOCIAL STRESS AND HEALTH

Yin Paradies[*]
Centre for Health and Society,
University of Melbourne and Menzies School of
Health Research, Charles Darwin University, Australia

RESEARCH SUMMARY

Background: Psychosocial stress is one of the most ubiquitous concepts in public health. In the 21st century alone, over 350,000 articles have been indexed in PubMed under the keyword *stress*, with this research accompanied by a profusion of conceptual approaches.

Aims: This paper adds some clarity to this diverse field by reviewing the variety of concepts used in the study of psychosocial stress and health.

Method: A search of the electronic databases identified key articles providing coverage of the range of conceptual approaches to psychosocial stress.

Results: Stress is conceptualised as a stimulus or response. Approaches to studying stressors, the stress process, stress sequelae and the distribution of stressors in society are considered along with emerging directions in the study of stress.

Conclusions: There is a need to psychosocial conceptualise stress clearly in terms of the models adopted, the types of stressors considered, the contextual factors relevant to the stress process, and the aetiological importance of stress sequelae.

Declaration of interest: This work was supported by an Australian National Health and Medical Research Council (NHMRC) Training Scholarship for Indigenous Health Research (#193321), an NHMRC Population Health Capacity-Building Grant (#236235) and a Cooperative Research Centre for Aboriginal Health scholarship.

---

[*] Postal address: Centre for Health and Society, School of Population Health, 207 Bouverie St, University of Melbourne, Victoria 3010 Australia. PH: 61 3 8344 0659; Fax: 61 3 8344 0824; E-mail: yinp@unimelb.edu.au.

Chapter 460

EMPATHY: REFLEXIONS ON A CONCEPT

C. Boulanger[*,1] and C. Lançon[2]

[1]Lançon Unit, SHU de psychiatrie, Hôpital Sainte-Marguerite, Marseille, France
[2]Psychiatry Dept, SHU de psychiatrie, Hôpital Sainte-Marguerite, Marseille, France

RESEARCH SUMMARY

Under the influence of Scottish philosophy the concept of empathy changed, it is still shaky and still defined by many currents of thought. It is different from sympathy (emotional contagion). Empathy is the capacity to put oneself in another person's position to understand its feelings or to imagine its mental representation. So empathy shows itself in different phenomena such as projection, identification and altruism.

Husserl, in phenomenology, regards empathy as the decisive phenomenon from which inter-subjectivity emerges to elaborate a common world. Indeed, he renewed the comprehension of empathy and anticipated the development of neurosciences. Depraz, following Varela, shows primacy granted to others is embodied in the personal practice of compassion.

---

[*] E-mail Address: christophe.boulanger@mail.ap-hm.fr.

In: Psychology Research Biographies and Summaries
Editors: Nancy E. Wodarth and Alexis P. Ferguson
ISBN: 978-1-61470-491-1
© 2012 Nova Science Publishers, Inc.

Chapter 461

ORGANIZATIONAL SAFETY CLIMATE: IMPACT OF GENDER ON PERCEPTION OF WORKPLACE SAFETY

Seth Ayim Gyekye[1*] *and Simo Salminen*[2]

[1]Department of Psychology, Buckinghamshire New University,
High Wycombe Campus, UK

[2]Finnish Institute of Occupational Health, Occupational Safety Team,
Helsinki, Finland

RESEARCH SUMMARY

The study examined the influence of gender on the perception of workplace safety by comparing the safety perceptions of male and female Ghanaian industrial workers on Hayes et al.'s 50-item Work Safety Scale (WSS): a scale that effectively captures dimensions identified by safety experts as influencing perceptions of workplace safety. In addition, it examined the role of gender in (i) compliance with safety management policies, and (ii) accident frequency. The number of participants was 320, of which 65% were male, and 38% were single. T – test was used to test for differences of statistical significance. As anticipated, gender differences were apparent on all variables: female workers had favorable perceptions of workplace safety more often than their male counterparts. They were more compliant with safety management procedures, and had a lower accident involvement rate. Marital status changes were incorporated in further analyses to assess the impact of the presence of a spouse on the gender effect. Differences on all eight variables were not of statistical significance. From a practical perspective, exploring the impact of demographical factors such as gender, on safety perception and accident frequency provides useful information for organizations and management on the need for special safety programs for particular groups, based on their demography.

---

* Corresponding author: Department of Psychology, Buckinghamshire New University, Queen Alexandra Road, High Wycombe, BUCKS HP11 2JZ, UK Tel. 01494 22141 5076; 07810266901, Email: gas.gyekye@bucks.ac.uk; sgyekye@welho.com.

In: Psychology Research Biographies and Summaries
Editors: Nancy E. Wodarth and Alexis P. Ferguson

ISBN: 978-1-61470-491-1
© 2012 Nova Science Publishers, Inc.

Chapter 462

HIS, HER AND THEIR PERCEPTIONS OF FAMILY LIFE: A COMPARATIVE ANALYSIS OF FATHERS, MOTHERS, AND ADOLESCENTS

*Liat Kulik**[*]

School of Social Work, Bar Ilan University, Ramat Gan, Israel

RESEARCH SUMMARY

The goal of the study was to examine the extent of congruence in the perceptions of parents and their adolescent offspring with regard to the following dimensions of family life: the structural dimension (marital power relations, represented by division of household tasks and equality in decision-making); interpersonal relations (cohesion versus conflict); cognitive (perceived family coherence); and parenting (perceived parenting style of mothers and fathers). The sample comprised 399 Israeli participants from 133 families: mothers (n=133), fathers (n=133), and adolescent offspring (n=133 – 60 boys and 73 girls). The main research question was whether congruence in perceptions of family life is determined by family roles (parents versus offspring), or whether it is determined by gender (like-sex versus opposite-sex parent-child dyads). For most of the family life dimensions, congruence in perceptions of family members was determined more by family role than by gender.

---

[*] Corresponding author: School of Social Work Bar Ilan University, Ramat Gan, ISRAEL, Fax (School of Social Work): 972-3-5347228, email: kulikl@mail.biu.ac.il.

In: Psychology Research Biographies and Summaries
Editors: Nancy E. Wodarth and Alexis P. Ferguson
ISBN: 978-1-61470-491-1
© 2012 Nova Science Publishers, Inc.

Chapter 463

CASE-BASED REASONING: A THEORY FOR LEARNING THROUGH PROBLEM-SOLVING

Michael Gr. Voskoglou[*]
Graduate Technological Educational Institute (T. E. I.) School
of Technological Applications, Patras, Greece

RESEARCH SUMMARY

The paper reviews the Case-Based Reasoning (CBR) approach, which over the last few years has grown from a rather specific and isolated research area into a field of widespread interest both from academic and commercial stand, and has been developed to a theory of problem-solving and learning for computers and people.

More explicitly, following an introduction with the basic concepts and a brief historical background of CBR, we focus on the steps of the CBR process, the several types of the CBR methods, the applications of CBR to a wide range of domains and on the development trends of methods, applications and research for CBR. Finally, in our conclusion's section, we underline the differences between CBR and the classical rule-induction algorithms, we refer to the existing criticism for CBR methods and, summarizing the paper, we derive our final conclusion about the CBR approach.

---

[*] Email: voskoglou@teipat.gr.

In: Psychology Research Biographies and Summaries
Editors: Nancy E. Wodarth and Alexis P. Ferguson

ISBN: 978-1-61470-491-1
© 2012 Nova Science Publishers, Inc.

Chapter 464

EXTRAVERSION AND PERCEIVED ENERGY: DIRECT AND INDIRECT IMPACTS ON STRESS AND HEALTH

Dave Korotkov[*]

Department of Psychology, St. Thomas University,
Fredericton, New Brunswick, Canada

RESEARCH SUMMARY

This research examined the direct, moderating, and mediating roles of extraversion in relation to perceived energy, daily stress, and health status. It was hypothesized that, (1) extraversion is a construct distinct from perceived energy, (2) extraversion would moderate the stress and health relationship with introverts self-reporting more symptoms of ill-health under high stress levels, (3) extraverts who report high levels of perceived energy would also report experiencing higher levels of positive health, (4) individuals with high levels of self-reported energy, under high levels of stress, would experience fewer health problems, (5) state energy would mediate the extraversion and stress to health status relationship, and (6) state energy would mediate the relationship between extraversion and stress. To test the hypotheses, questionnaire data was collected from 543 university students. The results from several multivariate analyses provided partial support for the hypotheses. In particular, extraversion was found to be related to, but distinct from the state construct of perceived energy. It was also found that individuals who reported high levels of energy and stress, also experienced fewer symptoms of ill-health. Contrary to prediction, it was found that extraverts, under high levels of daily stress, reported more health concerns. It is speculated that this may be more a function of the analysis procedure as opposed to a theoretical corollary.

---

[*] Corresponding author: korotkov@stu.ca Phone: 506 – 460 – 0376.

Chapter 465

JOB SATISFACTION AND ORGANISATIONAL COMMITMENT: THE EFFECT OF GENDER

Norazah Mohd Suki[1] *and Norbayah Mohd Suki*[*]

[1]Labuan School of International Business & Finance,
Universiti Malaysia Sabah, Malaysia
[2]Labuan School of Informatics Science,
Universiti Malaysia Sabah, Malaysia

RESEARCH SUMMARY

The purpose of this paper is to examine the effect of gender on employees' perception of job satisfaction and organisational commitment. Gender plays an important role in creating individual attitudes pertaining to the workplace and in interpreting the meaning of these attitudes. Survey data was gathered from 112 employees in Labuan. Regression results showed that both male and female employees in Labuan have the same level of perception of job satisfaction and organisational commitment. Implications and recommendations were also discussed.

---

[*] Email: azahsuki@yahoo.com.

The Impact of Emotional Intelligence on Nursing: An Overview

José María Augusto Landa and Esther López-Zafra[*]
Department of Social Psychology University of Jaén, Spain

Research Summary

In this paper we focus on the role that Emotional Intelligence has on nursing. We pay attention to both students and professionals and the role emotional intelligence has on emotional self-concept and burnout. Our studies with nursing students yield positive relations between the Clarity and Emotional Repair components of Perceived Emotional Intelligence and all scales of the self-concept scale. On the other hand, nursing professionals that have clear feelings about their emotions and situations that occur, and are capable of dealing with those emotions, have lower levels of stress in their work. Also, those nurses who show a high ability to curtail their negative emotional states and prolong positive emotional states show higher levels of overall health than those individuals who have trouble regulating their emotions.

Our results imply that the emotional and cognitive dimensions have to be taken into account in future training programs for nursing professionals and students.

---

[*] Email: elopez@ujaen.es.

Chapter 467

The Role of Dispositional Optimism in Health Related Quality of Life Among Health Care Professionals with Musculoskeletal Pain

George N. Lyrakos[1] and Georgia Kostopanagiotou[2]*
[1] 2nd Dep. of Anesthesiology- Pain Unit, School of Medicine,
University of Athens, Attikon Hospital, Greece
[2] 2nd Department of Anesthesiology, School of Medicine,
University of Athens, Attikon Hospital, Greece

Research Summary

Throughout the world, the musculoskeletal disorders are a leading cause of chronic disease morbidity, and the chronic musculoskeletal pain affects many millions of people. Moreover chronic musculoskeletal pain impacts negatively on physical health in several ways. This chapter is an exploration of the relationship between optimism, quality of life and pain among health care professionals suffering from chronic musculoskeletal pain. Unlike studies, which have typically focused on the impact of pain in health related quality of life, the current study focused on how dispositional optimism influences patients' health-related quality of life and pain intensity. 54 men and 218 women with a mean age of 37,7 (SD 8,3) took part in the study. Participants completed a battery of questionnaires including a measure of optimism (GrLOT-R), two health related quality of life measurements (SF 12 and Euro5D) and a VAS pain meter. Bivariate analysis showed that optimism had a significant negative correlation with pain intensity. Results with the use of Principal component analysis indicated that dispositional optimism was a significant predictor for mental composite score (MCS12) explaining the 35% of the MCS12 variance.

---

[*] Corresponding author: George Lyrakos, MSc, PhDc. School of Medicine, University of Athens, Attikon University Hospital, Rimini 1 Xaidari, Athens Greece. Tel: 0030210-5832371. Fax: 0030210-5326413. email. geolyr@hotmail.com.

In: Psychology Research Biographies and Summaries
Editors: Nancy E. Wodarth and Alexis P. Ferguson
ISBN: 978-1-61470-491-1
© 2012 Nova Science Publishers, Inc.

Chapter 468

METHOD FOR DEVELOPING A SCALE TO EVALUATE MATERNAL PSYCHOLOGICAL STATUS WITH REGARD TO CHILDREN'S ORAL CARE

*Naoki Kakudate**

Division of Disease Control & Molecular Epidemiology, Department of Oral Growth & Development, Health Sciences University of Hokkaido, Hokkaido, Japan

RESEARCH SUMMARY

Several methods of developing scales to evaluate human psychological status have been determined. To develop such scales, their reliability and validity must be examined. In this review, we first describe the typical methods for developing general psychological scales; reliability factors, consistency, and stability are discussed, and validity factors, including content validity, criterion-related validity, and construct validity are explored. We then demonstrate the clinical and research applications of psychological scales with confirmed reliability and validity. The authors have developed psychological scales to evaluate the psychological state and behavior of patients with a particular focus on self-efficacy theory in dental clinical practice. Here, we describe a self-efficacy scale for oral care among mothers for their children and proved its effectiveness in predicting the number of decayed teeth and frequency of mothers' brushing for their children. These methods may also be applied to other psychological theories.

---

* Corresponding author: Naoki Kakudate, D.D.S., Ph.D., M.P.H. Division of Disease Control & Molecular Epidemiology, Department of Oral Growth & Development, Health Sciences University of Hokkaido, 1757 Kanazawa, Ishikari-Tobetsu, Hokkaido, Japan, 061-0293, Tel: +81-133-23-2551, Fax: +81-133-23-1404 E-mail: nkakudate@gmail.com.

Chapter 469

MODERATING EFFECT OF CONCERN FOR FACE ON HELP SEEKING INTENTION WHO EXPERIENCED INTIMATE PARTNER VIOLENCE DURING PREGNANCY: A RETROSPECTIVE CROSS-SECTIONAL STUDY

Ying Lau[*]
School of Health Sciences, Macao Polytechnic Institute

RESEARCH SUMMARY

Objective(s): (1) To examine concern for face and different forms of Intimate Partner Violence (IPV) on formal or informal help-seeking intention; and (2) To examine the moderating effect of concern for face on formal or informal help-seeking intention among different groups of pregnant women who suffer from IPV.

Design: A retrospective cross-sectional comparative quantitative study at a university-affiliated regional hospital among 1,200 Hong Kong Chinese pregnant women.

Measurements: The Protective and Acquisitive Face Orientation (PAFO) scale (Short Form) and the modified Cohen's Willingness to Seek Help scale were used to measure concern for face and help-seeking intention. The different forms of IPV were investigated by using the Revised Conflict Tactics Scale (CTS-2).

Results: The results of hierarchical regression models found that women with "Psychological Aggression" significantly negatively associate with formal help intention after adjusting for socio-demographic variables. Women with one subscale of Protective Face Concern: "Keep a low profile to avoid attention (KLP)" was found to negatively associate with formal and informal help-seeking intention after adjustment ($p < 0.05$). The moderating effects of "Physical Assault" and KLP on informal help-seeking intention were found.

---

[*] Corrsponding author: 5/F Centro Hotline Building, No. 335-341, Alameda Dr. Carlos D' Assumpcao, Macau, Telephone: 853 3998615 (Office phone) 853 66144064 (Mobile phone) Fax: 853 28753159 E-mail address: ylau@ipm.edu.mo.

Conclusion: IPV and concern for face have an inhibitive effect on the intention to seek help. Implications and limitations are also discussed.

In: Psychology Research Biographies and Summaries
Editors: Nancy E. Wodarth and Alexis P. Ferguson
ISBN: 978-1-61470-491-1
© 2012 Nova Science Publishers, Inc.

Chapter 470

CORRELATES OF ANTENATAL DEPRESSIVE SYMPTOMATOLOGY AMONG CHINESE WOMEN: A LONGITUDINAL STUDY

Ying Lau[*]

School of Health Sciences, Macao Polytechnic Institute, China

RESEARCH SUMMARY

A total of 2,178 women were recruited at six regional public hospitals in Hong Kong to participate in an explorative study with a two-wave, prospective, longitudinal design. The study investigated the predictors of perinatal depressive symptoms among Hong Kong Chinese women. The women were identified as depressive using the Edinburgh Postnatal Depression Scale (EPDS). Marital conflict was evaluated using the Dyadic Adjustment Scale (DAC) and parents-in-law conflict were evaluated using the Stryker Adjustment Checklist (SAC). The Interpersonal Support Evaluation List (ISEL) was used to measure the functional aspects of perceived availability of social support. The correlates of antenatal depressive symptoms were explored in their demo-socioeconomic, obstetric, and Chinese familial relational aspects. Multiple linear regression analysis revealed that earlier antenatal depressive symptoms (B = 0.572 – 0.594, β = 0.574 – 0.594, $p < 0.001$), marital conflict (B = 0.009, β = 0.036, $p < 0.05$), father-in-law conflict (B = 0.090, β = 0.073, $p < 0.01$), mother-in-law conflict (B = 0.079; β = 0.072, $p < 0.01$), and perceived availability of social support (B = -0.029 - -0.033, β = -0.106 - -0.114, $p < 0.001$) related to antenatal depressive symptomatology during the third trimester. These results provide important preventive information for antenatal depressive symptomatology among the Hong Kong population. The implications and limitations of these findings and directions for future research are suggested.

---

[*] Corresponding author: 5/F Centro Hotline Building, No. 335-341, Alameda Dr. Carlos D' Assumpcao, Macau Telephone: 853 3998615 (Office phone) 853 66144064 (Mobile phone) Fax: 853 28753159 E-mail address: ylau@ipm.edu.mo.

Chapter 471

NEW MODEL FOR BILINGUAL MINDS IN SOCIOLINGUISTIC VARIATION SITUATIONS: INTERACTING SOCIAL AND LINGUISTIC CONSTRAINTS

Rania Habib[*]

Dept. of Languages, Literatures, and Linguistics. Syracuse University, NY, US

RESEARCH SUMMARY

I present a new model for bilingual minds in sociolinguistic variation situations, proposing and incorporating a set of social constraints into Optimality Theory and the Gradual Learning Algorithm. Incorporating social constraints with linguistic constrains is essential to provide explanation of the grammar differences among speakers belonging to the same or different social groups. The naturally occurring speech of fifty-two migrant rural speakers of Colloquial Arabic to the city of Hims in Syria comprises the data set. The intra- and inter-speaker variation in the use of [q] and [ʔ] is used to demonstrate the working mechanism of the model that gives a mental representation of what occurs in a varying speaker's mind in a certain sociolinguistic setting. The shift to the use of the urban prestigious form, [ʔ], in the city indicates that social constraints are variable and setting-relative. The difference in the ranking values of social constraints among speakers influence the speakers' variable percentages of [q] and [ʔ]. Manipulating the output percentages from which speakers learn gives the specific sociolinguistic grammar of each speaker or group of speakers and their output percentages that match real life occurrences. Consequently, the model reflects on the social networks of speakers because the degree of input of a form affects the degree of acquisition of that form. Among the many advantages of this new model is giving expectation on what the speech of a speaker will sound like if certain social constraints are involved. Most importantly, this model unifies the linguistic and social aspects of language in one theoretical framework.

---

[*] Email: rhabib@syr.edu.

In: Psychology Research Biographies and Summaries
Editors: Nancy E. Wodarth and Alexis P. Ferguson
ISBN: 978-1-61470-491-1
© 2012 Nova Science Publishers, Inc.

Chapter 472

I Wouldn't Really Call it News: Audience Consumption of Physical Activity Research in the News Media

Guy Faulkner[1]*, Vanessa Richichi[1], Stephannie C. Roy[2] and Sara-Jane Finlay[2]

[1]Faculty of Physical Education and Health,
University of Toronto, Toronto, ON, Canada
[2]Office of the Vice President and Provost,
University of Toronto, Toronto, ON, Canada

Research Summary

For most people the reality of science is what they read in the press yet little attention is paid to how people use the research that they see in the media. This study examined how audiences consume news messages about physical activity research. Fourteen focus groups were held across Canada. Overall, participants interpreted news about physical activity research as sensationalized, lacking novelty, and being negative in tone. Researchers and practitioners should recognise the limitations of the media for directly influencing behaviour change. However, getting audiences to talk about what they see and hear in the news about physical activity research may be an important outcome of dissemination in maintaining physical activity on public and policy agendas.

---

* Corresponding author: Faculty of Physical Education and Health, University of Toronto, 55 Harbord Street, Toronto, ON, M5S 2W6 CANADA. Tel: 416-978-1855. Fax: 416-971-2118. Email: guy.faulkner@utoronto.ca.

Chapter 473

An Ecological Interpretation of Teacher and Teaching Schemas as Cognitively Constructed by Candidates in Training

Calliope Haritos[*]
Hunter College School of Education, NY, US

Research Summary

The present study examined the cognitive journey of teacher candidates as evidenced by their cognitively constructed schemas of the teacher role and the challenges of teaching at two developmental junctures; prior and subsequent to their first education course, which incorporated forty hours of observation/fieldwork.

Notably, both the semantic nature and endurance of teacher and teaching schemas have been sources of debate throughout the teacher development literature.

Findings of the present research, which included multiple, varied, complex, and overlapping cognitive pathways with respect to perceived teaching challenges and teacher portrait characterizations, paved with realism and idealism, respectively, are interpreted via an ecological perspective. Such a perspective denotes a cognitive map of understanding that identifies the developmental origins and foundations of candidates' constructed pathways, namely, prior socialization experience and the dynamics of changing individual and contextual variables in this regard.

The ability of candidates to stay on course, with respect to the fortitude of their initial teacher and teaching schemas, is also examined in light of its impact on post- fieldwork schemas and developmental considerations are also discussed with respect to the overall impact of such cognitively constructed routes on probable future schemas and/or behavior in the classroom.

---

[*] E-mail: charitos@hunter.cuny.edu.

In: Psychology Research Biographies and Summaries
Editors: Nancy E. Wodarth and Alexis P. Ferguson
ISBN: 978-1-61470-491-1
© 2012 Nova Science Publishers, Inc.

Chapter 474

ANALYSIS OF THE GENETICS OF BEHAVIOUR USING ANIMAL MODELS

M. Murphy*[1], Y. M. Wilson[1], A. J. Lawrence[2], T. C. Brodnicki[3] and M. C. Jawahar[1]

[1]Department of Anatomy and Cell Biology, Australia
[2]Howard Florey Institute, University of Melbourne, Melbourne, Australia
[3]The Walter and Eliza Hall Institute of Medical Research, Australia

RESEARCH SUMMARY

Many aspects of human and animal behaviours have a strong genetic contribution. Twin studies have demonstrated that up to 50% of the variation in our behaviour can be attributed to genetic factors. Individual variation in different behaviours is also found across animal populations. For this reason, animal models are increasingly being used to look for genes underlying these naturally occurring variations in behaviour. Currently there are a number of different genetic approaches using animal models which are being employed to identify these genes including conventional breeding crosses, analysis of heterogeneous stock populations, mutagenesis and the use of congenic strains. In this review we will discuss these different approaches and their advantages and disadvantages for gene identification. We will then review the growing number of studies which have used congenic strains of animals and their progress in the identification of genes responsible for different behaviours. These include behaviours associated with fear, stress and anxiety, hyperactivity, aggression, learning and memory impairments, and addiction.

---

* E-mail: m.murphy@unimelb.edu.au

In: Psychology Research Biographies and Summaries
Editors: Nancy E. Wodarth and Alexis P. Ferguson
ISBN: 978-1-61470-491-1
© 2012 Nova Science Publishers, Inc.

Chapter 475

SYMBOLIC PERSUASION AND THE SOCIAL POLITICS OF EVERYDAY LIFE

Hugh M. Lewis[*]
Principal Training Specialist, TRADOC Culture Center, US

RESEARCH SUMMARY

Social persuasion is evaluated from a human systems framework based upon the anthropological construction of human reality, focusing on the processes of social structuration [Giddens 1986: 62], anthropological culturation, psychological motivation and transformation, and the behavioral consequences of symbolic persuasion in everyday life. Persuasion is used in predictable ways in the manipulation of status-role identity vis-à-vis significant reference others, for the achievement of a constructed sense of empowerment in the world that is culturally defined and socially expressed in terms of implicit social hierarchies and selective networking patterns of interaction [Cialdini, 2001; Lewis 2005]. Persuasion constitutes the basis of the process of transculturation, the transmission of culture by *Homo symbolon*, empirically available to observation in terms of the patterns of sharing and reciprocity upon all levels of social relationship and in terms of the the behavorial and psychological response patterning intrinsic to these relationships. The basis of human persuasion is the symbolic structure of human apperceptive awareness of the world and the structured patterns of behavioral response that are the consequence of human symbolic cognition and symbolization (e.g. human intelligence). Symbolic persuasion plays a central role in the social politics of everyday life upon fundamental levels of human communication involving expressive language and paralinguistic patterns of behavioral communication, and in patterns marking social identity and status differentials intuitively implicit to the contexts of its articulation in everyday social settings. In such a manner, social identities are constructed and managed upon a daily basis, and relational hierarchies involving differential access to opportunities, authority, social dependence and resources are developed and evolve over time. Anyone seeking to successfully compete in any institutional context within any ethno-cultural or contemporary poly-cultural setting would do well to gain a basic linguistic

---
[*] E-mail: hlewis28@juno.com.

and transcultural competence in this form of persuasive symbolic social communication. These skills are acquired progressively from a very early age, extended through play and fantasy behavior, and growing sophistication is tied to symbolic differentiation of personality that is itself strongly subject to differentials of class and social stratification as well as alternate patterns of primary and secondary socialization. Basic discrepancies of ego-identity between primary and secondary contexts (i.e. primary family and extended community settings) result in distorted or delayed development of effective persuasiveness as a symbolic-behavioral mechanism of social mediation. Hyper-suggestibility, neurosis, psychosis and behavioral disorders of various kinds indicate a peculiar susceptibility to persuasion, and likewise an inability to become socially persuasive in the control and management of one's ego-identity in the world.

In: Psychology Research Biographies and Summaries
Editors: Nancy E. Wodarth and Alexis P. Ferguson
ISBN: 978-1-61470-491-1
© 2012 Nova Science Publishers, Inc.

Chapter 476

REFLECTIONS ON THE PAST AND EXPLORATIONS OF THE FUTURE: UNDERSTANDING FOOD CONSUMPTION IN ROMANTIC RELATIONSHIPS

Jennifer Bonds-Raacke[*]
University of North Carolina at Pembroke, US

RESEARCH SUMMARY

Before romantic relationships are even formed, individuals make decisions about eating out. Although this is a common everyday decision, it is also complex in nature requiring one to consider many factors such as time, money, and healthy food choices (Langholtz, Ball, Sopchak, and Auble, 1997). Past research has identified many factors that increase the likelihood of dining out. These include a desire to avoid cooking, economic reasons for those living alone (Morris, Schneider, and Macey, 1995), and shortage of time to prepare meals at home (Lazar and Smallwood, 1977).

When individuals form couples in romantic relationships, decisions involving food consumption continue to occur daily. However routine this occurrence is, it is nevertheless a critical component of romantic relationships beginning during the courtship stage and extending later into marriage (Sobal, Bove, and Rauschenbach, 2002; Rappoport, 2003). Typically, in the early stage of a relationship, individuals merge independent food systems to create a joint food system (Bove, Sobal, and Rauschenbach, 2002). This transition is crucial as it relates to marital conflict and daily interactions (Doumas, Margolin, and John 2003).

Research has identified numerous strategies that couples employ when making decisions about eating out. Genre and familiarity of the restaurant are two important attributes that are related to the decision strategy employed (Bonds-Raacke, 2006). This line of research has also discovered that the stage of the relationship, dating versus married, is important in many ways. For example, the stage of the relationship influences the number and type of strategies

---

[*] E-mail: jennifer.raacke@uncp.edu.

utilized and who in the couple is more influential in making the decisions (Bonds-Raacke, 2008).

This commentary will elaborate on the topics presented above (i.e., the social experience of eating and decision-making strategies of couples when eating out). Additionally, current research endeavors will be presented on romantic relationships in relation to satisfaction, eating regulation, and behavioral habits of eating out. Although past and current research has greatly advanced the understanding of the importance of eating in romantic relationships, this line of research is not without limitations and specific challenges that need to be discussed. One facet that remains virtually untapped is investigating how couples make decisions regarding the decision to eat at fast food restaurants. This commentary will conclude by exploring why researchers should focus on decisions of couples related to the fast food industry.

Chapter 477

AGGRESSIVE BEHAVIOR OF DRIVERS: A NEW QUESTIONNAIRE DEFINING THE DIFFERENCE BETWEEN HOSTILE AND INSTRUMENTAL BEHAVIOR WHILE DRIVING

Lipaz Shamoa-Nir[*] *and Meni Koslowsky*[†]
Department of Psychology
Bar-Ilan University, Israel

RESEARCH SUMMARY

As part of an investigation of commuting stress, a new tool was developed for differentiating between two types of aggressive behavior in drivers: instrumental and hostile. The questionnaires evaluate aggressive behavior by measuring the level of aggression of each behavior and categorizing the behavior as instrumental or hostile.

Two studies were conducted. In the first one, participants (N=104) received a questionnaire in which items culled from each aggression domain were tested along with attributes such as gender, age, driving experience; and previous involvement in a driving incident (a road accident or traffic ticket). Analysis showed that the questionnaire's internal consistency was high for each aggression type and age comparisons for the two measures were found to be significant. In the second study, analysis of the data (N=326) enabled us to refine the operational definition of aggressive driving and to sharpen the distinction between instrumental the two types of aggression. Theoretical and practical perspectives of the instrument were discussed.

---

[*] This paper is based on the first author's dissertation.
[†] Email: koslow@mail.biu.ac.il; koslowme@yahoo.com; Phone: +972-3-5317945 ; Fax: +972-3-5350206.

In: Psychology Research Biographies and Summaries ISBN: 978-1-61470-491-1
Editors: Nancy E. Wodarth and Alexis P. Ferguson © 2012 Nova Science Publishers, Inc.

Chapter 478

RELIGIOSITY AND YOUTH DESTRUCTIVE BEHAVIORS: A META-ANALYSIS

Jerf W. K. Yeung, Howard Chi-ho Cheng, Freeman K. H. Chan and Yuk-chung Chan*

Department of Applied Social Sciences
The Hong Kong Polytechnic University, China

RESEARCH SUMMARY

With note to increasing regularity of youth destructive behaviors and against the background of controversial empirical results in the relationship between religiosity and these youth behaviors, the current meta-analysis, based on 31 studies from 1995 to 2007, found a modest overall effect size ($Z_r = -.170$) between the relationship. When dichotomizing youth destructive behaviors into those with self-oriented nature and interpersonal-oriented nature respectively, a larger average effect size for the later was observed. However, there was a lack of evidence for significant diversions between effect sizes of behavioral outcomes when considered a difference whether measured by public religiosity or private religiosity, and single-items religious measures or multifaceted religious measures.

Impactions of the current findings and that for the future research are briefly discussed.

---

* Corresponding Author: Departmetn of Applied Social Sciences, The Hong Kong Polytechnic University, Hung Hom, Hong Kong; Telephone: (852) 34003874; Fax: (852) 27736558; ssjerf@yahoo.com.hk.

In: Psychology Research Biographies and Summaries
Editors: Nancy E. Wodarth and Alexis P. Ferguson

ISBN: 978-1-61470-491-1
© 2012 Nova Science Publishers, Inc.

Chapter 479

MMPI-2 CORRELATES OF PTSD AMONG GULF WAR COMBAT VETERANS

Shenell D. Evans[1], Samuel T. Gontkovsky[*,2] *and William R. Leber[3]*

[1]Jackson State University, US
[2]Center for Neuroscience and Neurological Recovery
Methodist Rehabilitation Center,
Jackson, Mississippi, US
[3]Department of Veterans Affairs Medical Center
Oklahoma City, Oklahoma, US

RESEARCH SUMMARY

This study examined the MMPI-2 clinical presentation of a sample of 80 Gulf War veterans seen in an outpatient clinic who were divided into PTSD or non-PTSD groups. Results indicated that MMPI-2 profiles differed significantly, with the PTSD group scoring higher on each of the clinical scales, with the exception of scale 5. The groups were best differentiated by effect size differences among scales F, K, 2, 7, 8, and PK. The PTSD group yielded a mean 8-1 MMPI-2 code type, whereas the non-PTSD group yielded a mean 1-3 MMPI-2 code type. The findings are generally consistent with the previous literature examining the clinical presentation of Gulf veterans.

---

[*] E-mail: sgontkovsky@hotmail.com.

In: Psychology Research Biographies and Summaries
Editors: Nancy E. Wodarth and Alexis P. Ferguson
ISBN: 978-1-61470-491-1
© 2012 Nova Science Publishers, Inc.

Chapter 480

COGNITIVE ISSUES IN IDIOPATHIC EPILEPSY

Sherifa A. Hamed[*]
Department of Neurology and Psychiatry,
Assiut University Hospital,
Assiut, Egypt

RESEARCH SUMMARY

Epilepsy is a common medical problem. Several studies suggest that idiopathic generalized or focal epilepsies can adversely affect mental development, cognition and behavior. Epileptic patients may experience reduced intelligence, attention, problems in memory, language and frontal executive functions. The exact mechanisms of epilepsy-related cognitive dysfunction are poorly understood. Cognitive deficits with epilepsy may be transient, persistent or progressive. Transient disruption of cognitive encoding processes may occur with paroxysmal focal or generalized epileptic discharges while epileptogenesis-related neuronal plasticity, reorganization, sprouting and impairment of cellular metabolism are fundamental determinants for progressive cognitive deterioration. Also antiepileptic drugs (AEDs) have differential, reversible and sometimes cumulative cognitive adverse consequences. AEDs not only reduce neuronal irritability but also may impair neuronal excitability, neurotransmitter release, enzymes and factors critical for information processing and memory. The present article serves as an overview of recent studies in cognition in adult and children patients with epilepsy. In this review, we will also discuss the known adverse mechanisms of epilepsy and AEDs on cognition.

---

[*] Corresponding author: MBBch., MSc., M.D. Consultant Neurologist, Associate Professor, Department of Neurology and Psychiatry, Assiut University Hospital, Assiut, Egypt. P.O.Box 71516. Telephone: +2 088 2371820. Fax : +2 088 2333327. +2 088 2332278; E-mail: hamed_sherifa@yahoo.com Former address:Research Center For Genetic Medicine, Children's National Medical Center, Washington DC (111 Michigan Avenue, NW, Washington, DC 20010 Main: 202-884-5000).

In: Psychology Research Biographies and Summaries ISBN: 978-1-61470-491-1
Editors: Nancy E. Wodarth and Alexis P. Ferguson © 2012 Nova Science Publishers, Inc.

Chapter 481

CULTURAL VARIATION IN NIGHTMARE: A CONTENT ANALYSIS

Kuang-ming Wu[*] *and Ruth Chu-lien Chao*
University of Denver, US

RESEARCH SUMMARY

Understanding nightmare is now a defining aspect in psychology and cultural studies with increasing centrality in research and practice, for two reasons: (a) nightmare is part of universal human experiences; (b) nightmare serves as a catalyst to appreciate cultural variations in human universal experience. Unfortunately, very few analyses of nightmare in different cultures (e.g., Western vs. Asians) have been undertaken; we remain ignorant of how people in different cultures differently perceive nightmare. Thus this study purposes to examine how people in different cultures understand nightmare by interviewing 250 US people and 250 Taiwanese. Finally, two greatest daytime nightmares—days slipping, death coming—are pondered on and resolved in unspeakable human joy.

---

[*] Contact information: Kuang-ming Wu, Ph.D. Department of Philosophy. University of Denver. 2455 S. Williams St.. Denver, CO 80210. E-mail: kmwu2002@yahoo.com. Tel: 573-529-9265.

In: Psychology Research Biographies and Summaries
Editors: Nancy E. Wodarth and Alexis P. Ferguson
ISBN: 978-1-61470-491-1
© 2012 Nova Science Publishers, Inc.

Chapter 482

HEALTH-RELATED INTERNET DISCUSSION GROUPS AS A SOURCE OF SOCIAL SUPPORT

Craig D. Murray[*], *Rachel van Schaick and Jezz Fox*
School of Health and Medicine
Lancaster University,
Lancaster, United Kingdom

RESEARCH SUMMARY

The majority of the social support literature overlooks the increasing use of internet discussion groups (IDGs) by people for health-related purposes. The aims of the study were to: investigate which health-related groups of people benefit the most from social support provided by IDGs; investigate the levels and types of social support gained from such IDGs; and to add to the current debate of whether the use of the internet increases, decreases or supplements social interactions. An online questionnaire measuring levels of perceived social support from both IDGs and conventional sources was advertised to IDGs for three health-related issues: 'extreme' behaviours (self-harm and eating disorders); chronic debilitating illnesses (multiple sclerosis and rheumatoid arthritis); chronic illnesses requiring self-management (asthma and diabetes). IDGs were found to provide high levels of social support, particularly emotional support, advice and guidance, to all of the three groups investigated. IDGs were found to be most beneficial to the extreme behaviours group, who were found to perceive more social support to come from IDGs than from family or friends. The findings of the study suggest the use of IDGs can supplement or increase social interactions. Implications of the findings are discussed.

---

[*] "Murray, Craig" c.murray@lancaster.ac.uk.

Chapter 483

METAPHORICAL SENTENCE PROCESSING AND TOPIC ABSTRACTNESS

*Xu Xu** and Lisa Paulson*
Pennsylvania State University, Harrisburg,
Pennsylvania, US

RESEARCH SUMMARY

The topic terms of metaphorical sentences are often abstract concepts. Two studies examined the effect of topic abstractness on the interpretive process of metaphorical sentences. With a self-report measurement approach, Study 1 found that participants assessed more comprehension time for metaphorical sentences with abstract topics than those with concrete topics. With an online measurement approach, Study 2 showed that it took more time to activate the metaphorical meaning of sentences with abstract topics than those with concrete topics. The studies also took into consideration such factors as aptness, familiarity, vehicle conventionality and syntactic form (metaphor vs. simile), which have been shown relevant to the comprehension process of metaphorical sentences. An effect of syntactic form on comprehension time was found with the self-report measure, but not with the online measure.

---

* Send correspondence to: Xu Xu, School of Behavioral Sciences and Education. Pennsylvania State University, Harrisburg, Middletown, PA 17057, Phone: 01-717-948-6035. Fax: 01-71.

Chapter 484

STRUCTURING THOUGHT: FOUR UNIQUE METHODS AND THE CHALLENGE OF SYNTHESIS

Michael J. Hogan[*,1] and Zachary Stein[2]

[1]School of Psychology, NUI, Galway, Ireland

[2]Harvard University Graduate School of Education, US

RESEARCH SUMMARY

A fundamental thinking skill is the ability to see the structure of thought. Awareness of the structure of thought begins with an intuitive description of the elements and relations that constitute a decision-making process and a description of the relationship between the structure and function of thought. Regardless of how one judges the quality of everyday decisions in light of the goals being pursued, it is useful, as a first step, to construct a structural map of everyday decision-making processes. This allows for objective analysis of everyday decisions and it enhances structural awareness in those who map the thinking process and in those who read the maps. The same applies to scientific thinking. Scientists advocate a particular position in the academic field and explicit mapping of their arguments enhances structural awareness, critical comparison and evaluation, and communication in the field. Overall, the mapping of decision making is a worthwhile goal, a skill that is becoming increasingly prominent and even necessary as part of expert decision making in many fields of applied science. This chapter presents a case for the cultivation of graphicacy skills in this context. We describe four thought mapping techniques that offer considerable power and potential to elucidate and enhance thinking and decision making abilities. We suggest that technological advances may allow us to merge various different though mapping techniques and further enhance an interdependent set of graphicacy skills that may help to support decision making and adaptive action in context.

---

[*] Hogan, Michael: michael.hogan@nuigalway.ie.